Workshop Manual

PORSCHE 911 G 2.7-3.0-3.2 Litre 1973-1989

A Floyd CLYMER Publication by:
www.VelocePress.com
Copyright 2020 Veloce Enterprises

INTRODUCTION

Welcome to the world of digital publishing ~ the book you now hold in your hand, was printed using the latest state of the art digital technology. The advent of print-on-demand has forever changed the publishing process, never has information been so accessible and it is our hope that this book serves your informational needs for years to come. If this is your first exposure to digital publishing, we hope that you are pleased with the results. Many more titles of interest to the classic automobile and motorcycle enthusiast, collector and restorer are available via our website at www.VelocePress.com. We hope that you find this title as interesting as we do.

NOTE FROM THE PUBLISHER

The information presented is true and complete to the best of our knowledge. All recommendations are made without any guarantees on the part of the author or the publisher, who also disclaim all liability incurred with the use of this information.

TRADEMARKS

We recognize that some words, model names and designations, for example, mentioned herein are the property of the trademark holder. We use them for identification purposes only. This is not an official publication.

INFORMATION ON THE USE OF THIS PUBLICATION

This manual is an invaluable resource for those interested in performing their own maintenance. However, in today's information age we are constantly subject to changes in common practice, new technology, availability of improved materials and increased awareness of chemical toxicity. As such, it is advised that the user consult with an experienced professional prior to undertaking any procedure described herein. While every care has been taken to ensure correctness of information, it is obviously not possible to guarantee complete freedom from errors or omissions or to accept liability arising from such errors or omissions. Therefore, any individual that uses the information contained within, or elects to perform or participate in do-it-yourself repairs or modifications acknowledges that there is a risk factor involved and that the publisher or its associates cannot be held responsible for personal injury or property damage resulting from the use of the information or the outcome of such procedures.

WARNING!

One final word of advice, this publication is intended to be used as a reference guide, and when in doubt the reader should consult with a qualified technician.

TABLE OF CONTENTS

Chapter 1 - Engine (pg 5)

1. Description
2. Maintenance
3. Removing and refitting the engine
4. The rocker gear and camshafts
5. The chain tensioner
6. Valve timing
7. Removing and refitting the cylinder heads
8. Servicing the cylinder heads
9. The flywheel
10. The cylinders and pistons
11. The crankcase and crankshaft
12. Servicing crankshaft and connecting rods
13. The intermediate shaft
14. Engine reassembly
15. Recommissioning an overhauled engine
16. The lubrication system
17. Supplemental Information
18. Fault diagnosis

Chapter 2 - Fuel System (pg 29)

1. Description
2. Maintenance
3. Air cleaner and preheater
4. Fuel filter
5. Fuel pump
6. Controls
7. Bosch fuel injection pump system (FIP)
8. Bosch continuous injection system (CIS)
9. Digital Motor Electronics injection system (DME)
10. Fault diagnosis FIP & CIS

Chapter 3 - Ignition System (pg 49)

1. Description
2. Maintenance
3. Ignition faults
4. Distributor
5. Capacitive discharge system (CDS)
6. Ignition timing
7. Breakerless ignition 1978-83 Models (CDI)
8. Digital Motor Electronics ignition system (DME)
9. Sparking plugs and HT leads

Chapter 4 - Cooling, Heating & Exhaust Emission Control (pg 61)

1. The cooling system
2. The heating system
3. Exhaust emission control
4. Vapour emission control
5. Supplemental information 1976-1983
6. Supplemental information 1978 onwards
7. Fault diagnosis

Chapter 5 - Clutch (pg 75)

1. Description
2. Maintenance
3. The control cable
4. Removing and refitting the clutch
5. Servicing the clutch components
6. Modified clutch components 1977 onwards
7. Fault diagnosis

Chapter 6 - Manual Transmission (pg 83)

1. Description
2. Maintenance
3. Removing and installing the transmission
4. Dismantling the transmission
5. Servicing the gearbox shafts
6. The differential gearing
7. Gear and backlash settings
8. The front cover and intermediate plate
9. The oil pump
10. Reassembling the transmission
11. Gearchange linkage
12. Fault diagnosis

Chapter 7 - Sportomatic (pg 101)

1. Description
2. Maintenance
3. Removing and installing the transmission
4. Separating and refitting the transmission
5. Servicing the control valve and sensor
6. Servicing the gear lever and microswitch
7. Servicing the torque converter and clutch
8. Servicing the clutch controls
9. Overhauling the transmission
10. The torque converter pump
11. Fault diagnosis

Chapter 8 - Rear Axle & Suspension (pg 115)

1. Description
2. Maintenance
3. Dampers
4. Drive shafts
5. Removing and refitting a control arm
6. Servicing a control arm
7. Removing, refitting and adjusting torsion bar
8. Radius arms
9. Anti-roll bar
10. Wheel alignment
11. Height adjustment
12. Fault diagnosis

TABLE OF CONTENTS

Chapter 9 - Front Suspension (pg 121)

1. Description
2. Maintenance
3. Suspension struts
4. Hubs
5. Control arms
6. Crossmember
7. Torsion bars
8. Anti-roll bar
9. Suspension height
10. Wheel alignment
11. Fault diagnosis

Chapter 10 - Steering (pg 129)

1. Description
2. Maintenance
3. The steering wheel
4. The steering column
5. The intermediate shaft and couplings
6. The steering linkage
7. The steering gearbox
8. Fault diagnosis

Chapter 11 - Brakes (pg 135)

1. Description
2. Maintenance
3. Brake pad renewal
4. Front brakes
5. Rear brakes
6. The master hydraulic cylinder
7. Bleeding the hydraulic system
8. The handbrake
9. Servo unit
10. Fault diagnosis

Chapter 12 - Electrical (pg 147)

1. Description
2. The battery
3. Fuses and relays
4. The starter motor
5. The alternator
6. The alternator regulator
7. Headlights
8. Safety belt warning system
9. Flasher unit
10. Windscreen wiper and washer
11. Horns
12. Instruments
13. Steering column switches
14. Automatic speed control
15. Clutch pedal switch
16. Automatic heater control
17. Automatic antenna
18. Alarm
19. Fault diagnosis

Chapter 13 - Body (pg 161)

1. Bodywork finish
2. Engine and luggage compartment lids
3. Doors, locks, fittings and glass
4. Sliding and folding roofs
5. Windscreen and backlight glass
6. Bumpers
7. Front wings
8. Air conditioning
9. Targa door window adjustment
10. Reflective rear panel
11. Electric cross arm window controls

Chapter 14 - Technical Data (pg 169)

1. Specifications 2.7 litre vehicles
2. Specifications 3.0 and 3.2 litre vehicles
3. General specifications - all models
4. Wiring diagrams

INTRODUCTION

Evolution of the 1973-1989 Porsche 911 G Series

Please note that as most of the 'new' models were introduced prior to the end of the previous year there is often confusion in dating a particular model to a specific year. For example, the "G Series 911" was introduced in the fall of 1973 as a 1974 model.

1971-1973: The early 2.4 Litre cars are included in this timeline due to the fact that some models destined for the U.S.A., Australia, Japan and Canada were fitted with Bosch mechanical fuel injection (MFI) in place of carburetors in order to bring them into compliance with emission requirements. Coincidental with the introduction of the 1973 G Series, Bosch K-Jetronic fuel injection became standard equipment and the earlier 911T and 911E model designations were replaced by the 911, 911S, and Carrera.

With acknowledgement to the official Porsche website

1973: A best-seller goes into production: Ten years after its premiere, the engineers at Porsche gave the 911 its first thorough makeover. The "G model" was produced from 1973 to 1989, longer than any other 911 generation. It featured prominent bellows bumpers, an innovation designed to meet the latest crash test standards in the United States. Occupant protection was further improved by three-point safety belts as standard equipment, as well as integrated headrests. One of the most important milestones in the 911 saga was the 1974 unveiling of the first Porsche 911 Turbo with a three-litre 260 hp engine and enormous rear spoiler. With its unique blend of luxury and performance, the Turbo became synonymous with the Porsche mystique. The next performance jump came in 1977 with the 911 Turbo 3.3 equipped with charge-air cooler. At 300 hp it was the best in its class. In 1983, the naturally aspirated 911 Carrera superseded the SC; with a 3.2 litre 231 hp engine, it became a favorite collectors' item. From 1982, lovers of fresh air could also order the 911 as a Cabriolet. The 911 Carrera Speedster, launched in 1989, was evocative of previous legendary Porsche vehicles.

1974-1977: Porsche 911 & 911S: For model year 1974, the body design of the Porsche 911 was comprehensively redesigned for the first time. In addition to a Coupé and a Targa version, a Cabriolet was also available as of model year 1983. The most striking feature of this 911 generation is the raised bumper design with black plastic bellows. Between the tail lights of the G models there is a red panel and a Porsche logo that is red or black, depending on the model year. The rear number plate is flanked by two large rubber buffers with integrated number plate lighting. The raised bumpers with bellows of the G models were the result of more stringent approval regulations in the USA. With the introduction of these regulations, bumpers had to be able to absorb impacts as a result of hitting a fixed obstacle at speeds of up to 5 mph (8 km/h) without damage to the body. To meet this requirement, vehicles for the US market had the bumpers connected to the body using hydraulic impact absorbers. For models not intended for the US market, more cost-effective impact pipes were installed instead of these hydraulic impact absorbers. These had to be replaced after a rear-end collision. However, the impact absorbers could be ordered as optional equipment. **Engines:** The standard 911 model had a flat-six engine with a displacement of 2.7 litres. This initially developed 150 hp and 165 hp as of model year 1976. The engine of the 911 S delivered an output of 175 hp.

1974-1977: Porsche 911 Carrera: The displacement of the 911 Carrera engine was increased several times during the production period of the G series and the power output varied. **Engines:** Model Years 1974-75 - Displacement: 2.7 litres, power: 210 hp
Model Years 1975-77 - Displacement: 3.0 litres, power: 200 hp.

1978-1983: Porsche 911 SC: In model year 1978, the 911 model range was reduced to two models. The 911 SC (Super Carrera) took the place of the 911 and Carrera models. As of model year 1984, the SC version was again replaced by the 911 Carrera. **Engines:** The 911 SC was powered by a 3.0-litre flat engine, the output of which was increased slightly over the years.
Model Years 1978-79 - 3.0 litres, 180 hp
Model Years 1980 - 3.0 litres, 188 hp
Model Years 1981-83 - 3.0 litres, 204 hp

1982: The Cabriolet is introduced.

1984-1989: The 911SC is superseded by the 911Carrera along with the introduction of a new 3.2-liter flat-six 231 hp equipped with the more modern Motronic fuel injection system in place of the Bosch's K-Jetronic unit. No Carrera models were produced from model years 1978 to 1983. **Engines:** Model Years 1984-89 - Displacement: 3.2 litres, power: 207 hp – 231 hp.

1989: The 911 Carrera Speedster is introduced and production of the 911 G Series comes to an end with 198,414 vehicles produced.

CHAPTER 1 - ENGINE

1. Description
2. Maintenance
3. Removing and refitting the engine
4. The rocker gear and camshafts
5. The chain tensioner
6. Valve timing
7. Removing and refitting the cylinder heads
8. Servicing the cylinder heads
9. The flywheel
10. The cylinders and pistons
11. The crankcase and crankshaft
12. Servicing crankshaft and connecting rods
13. The intermediate shaft
14. Engine reassembly
15. Recommissioning an overhauled engine
16. The lubrication system
17. Supplemental Information
18. Fault diagnosis

Supplemental Information

In its previous format, this manual covered the 2.4, 2.7 and 3.0 litre models through the 1978 model year. However, additional updates for the earlier models plus information for the 3.2 litre models through 1989 that was not available at the time the original manual was published is either merged within the appropriate chapter or included as a supplement to that chapter in this revised publication. However, where there are no differences between the earlier and later models, no additional data is included. Consequently, regardless of model year or engine size, if a separate supplement is provided the reader is encouraged to review that supplement in conjunction with the information or data within the chapter.

1 Description

The vehicles covered by this manual are fitted with a rear mounted engine of 2.7 litre (2687cc actual). 3.0 litre (2994cc actual) and 3.2 litre (3125cc actual) capacity.

The design features of these engines are identical although they are dimensionally different in relevant respects. They are air-cooled four-stroke, six cylinder engines with the cylinders arranged horizontally in two banks of three. Bore and stroke dimensions, compression ratios and other technical information for all engines are included in the **Technical Data** section of the **Appendix.**

FIGS 1 and **2** show partial transverse and longitudinal cross-sections through an engine. Note that **FIG 1** includes components of the continuous injection system (CIS) and that **FIG 2** relates to the fuel injection pump (FIP) model.

The six throw crankshaft runs in seven shell-type plain bearings which are carried in a two-piece vertically split crankcase and a single sleeve-type plain bearing at the rear. It will be evident that the two banks of cylinders are staggered. Axial movement of the crankshaft is controlled at the forward main bearing. The connecting rod plain big-end bearings are shell-type and are retained by caps which are attached to the rods by bolts and nuts. The small-end bearings are bush-type.

The intermediate shaft is driven at half crankshaft speed by helical gearing at the rear end of the crankshaft. The two coaxial oil pumps are driven from the forward end of the intermediate shaft. A sprocket wheel on each side of the helical gear provides a chain drive for each of the overhead camshafts. Each chain is tensioned by a hydraulically loaded jockey pulley and is controlled by three guide ramps. A skew gear rearwards of the crankshaft helical gear drives the ignition distributor. The flywheel or, in the case of semi-automatic transmission models, the torque converter drive plate is mounted on the forward end of the crankshaft. The clutch, in the case of manual transmission models, operates on the forward face of the flywheel. The transmission bellhousing, final drive and gearbox casing is directly attached to the forward face of the engine crankcase and the combined engine and transmission must be removed as a unit from the vehicle and subsequently separated when either the engine, clutch or transmission is to be overhauled.

The individual cylinder barrels may be of cast iron or of composite structure with a bore sleeve of cast iron and aluminium cooling fins. Each barrel carries a separate cylinder head but the camshaft/rocker gear housings each span a bank of cylinders. Cooling air from the belt driven blower at the rear of the engine is ducted over the cylinder barrels and heads and, after passing through heat exchangers associated with the exhaust system, is available to warm the interior of the vehicle. Pistons are of aluminium alloy. The gudgeon pins are retained by circlips and have a slight interference fit in their piston bores. Pistons are fitted with two compression rings and one oil control ring.

Exhaust and inlet valves of each bank of cylinders are operated via rockers by a camshaft and provision is made for the adjustment of the clearance between the valve stem tips and their rockers. Valve seats and valve guides are inserts in the aluminium heads. Each valve is provided with two valve springs. Inlet valves are solid; exhaust valves have hollow stems which are filled with sodium to improve cooling. The camshafts are handed to each bank of cylinders and differ between engine types. In the case of fuel injection pump models, the injection pump is driven by a toothed belt from the lefthand camshaft.

The engine has a 'dry' sump and the lubrication oil is contained in a separate tank. The forward of the two coaxial pumps draws oil from the tank and feeds it under pressure to the crankshaft, intermediate shaft and camshafts. Drain oil is scavenged from the bottom of the crankcase by the second larger capacity pump via a gauze strainer and intake tube and returned to the tank. Pressure oil when hot is passed through a cooler which is bypassed when the oil is cold. The main cooler is closely associated with the engine. A secondary cooler is located at the forward end of the vehicle. The lubrication system is fully covered in **Section 16**.

With engines of four capacities, a range of different compression ratios, variations which are related both to performance and to year by year modification standards, it is most important that, when new parts are required, **they are identical with those originally fitted or that alternative parts are only those nominated by the spares supplier as** being suitable for the specific engine to which they are to be fitted.

Emission control systems and features are included in **Chapter 4**.

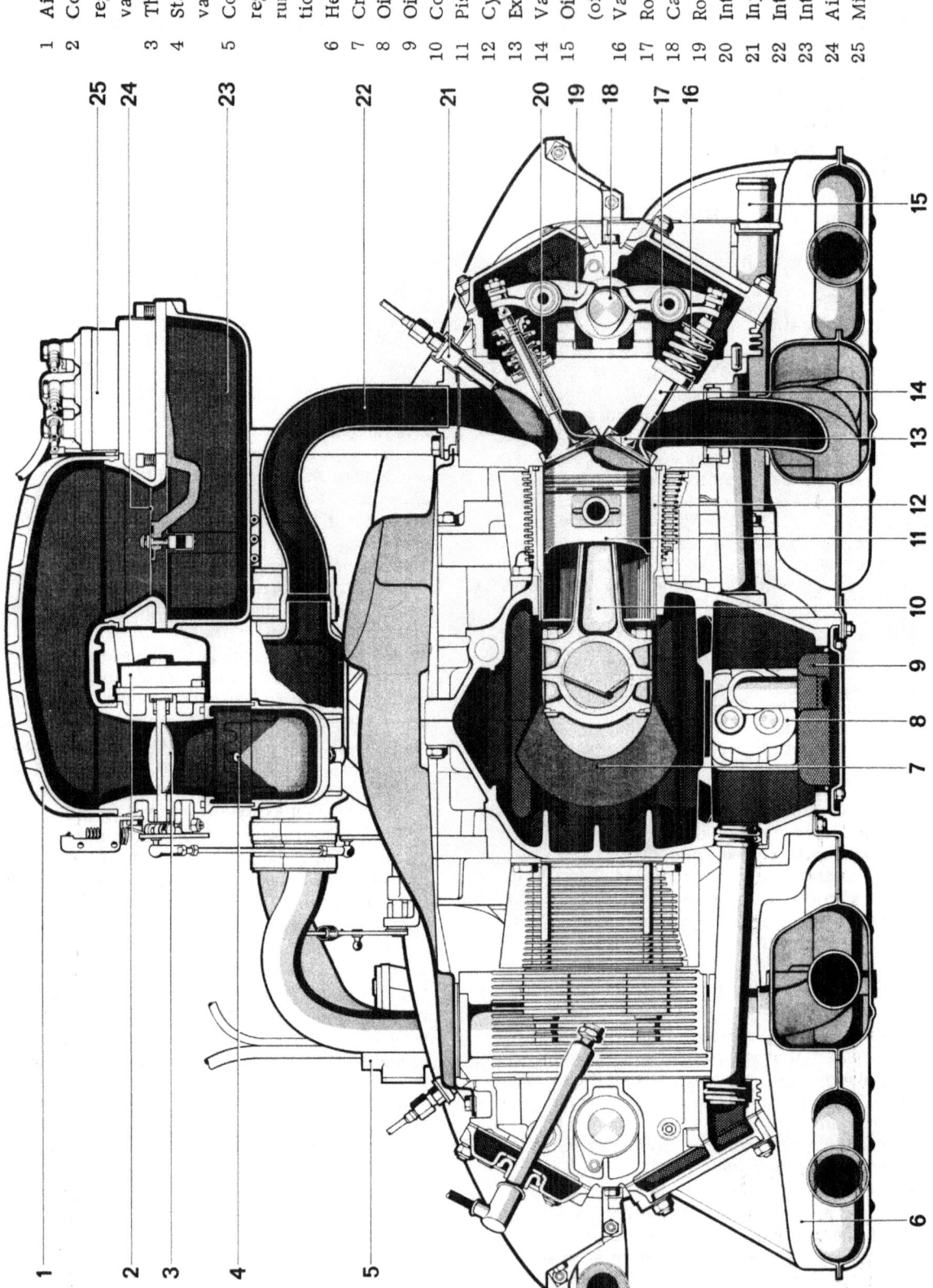

FIG 1 Transverse cross-section through engine (CIS model)

1. Air duct
2. Control pressure regulator (throttle valve position)
3. Throttle valve
4. Start (enrichment) valve
5. Control pressure regulator (warm running compensation)
6. Heat exchanger
7. Crankshaft
8. Oil pump
9. Oil screen
10. Connecting rod
11. Piston
12. Cylinder
13. Exhaust valve
14. Valve guide
15. Oil hose connection (oil tank – oil pump)
16. Valve spring
17. Rocker arm shaft
18. Camshaft
19. Rocker arm
20. Intake valve
21. Injection valve
22. Intake pipe
23. Intake housing
24. Air sensor plate
25. Mixture control unit

1 Air filter housing
2 Air inlet tube
3 Fuel injection lines
4 Oil pressure sensor
5 Crankcase
6 Oil pump
7 Pressure side (to lubrication points)
8 Suction side (to oil tank)
9 Connecting shaft
10 Oil screen
11 Oil drain plug (magnetic)
12 Crankshaft
13 Connecting rod
14 Sprocket gear
15 Intermediate shaft
16 Heat exchanger
17 Exhaust muffler
18 Distributor drive gear
19 Belt pulley
20 V-belt
21 AC generator
22 Upper air shroud
23 Coverplate

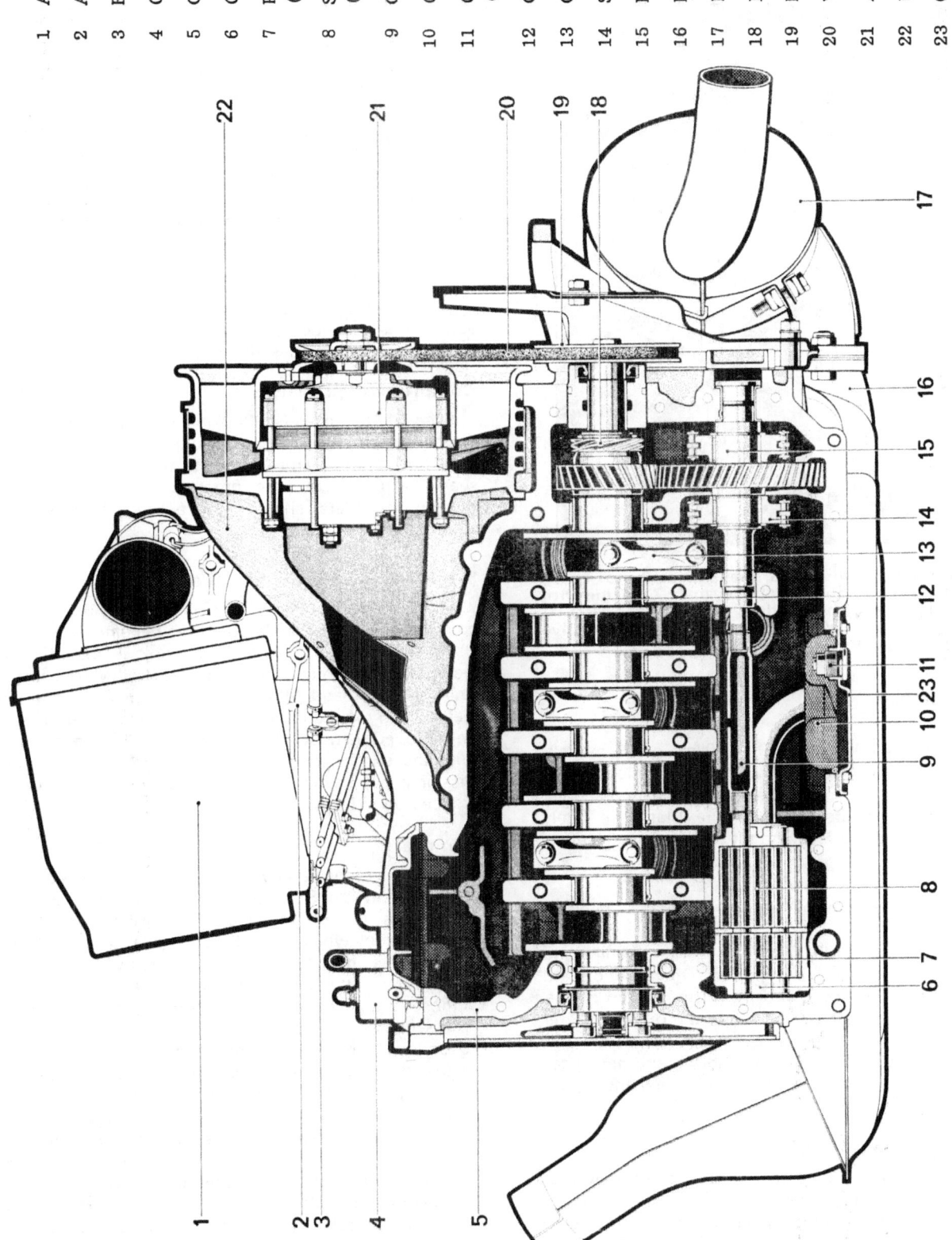

FIG 2 Longitudinal cross-section through engine (FIP model)

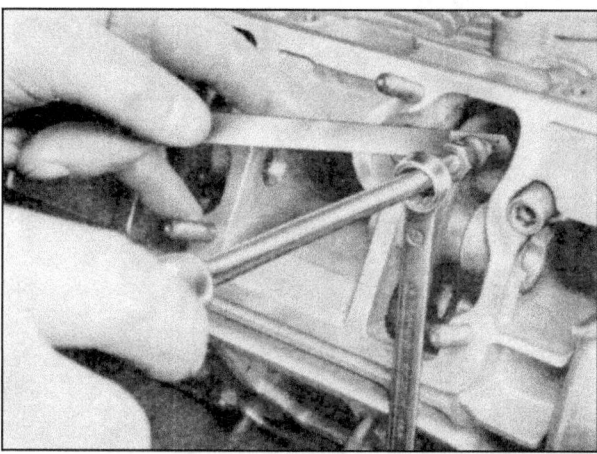

FIG 3 Adjusting valve clearances. Distributor rotor pointing to notch on body and pulley mark Z1 in line with crankcase joint with both valves closed, gives TDC on No 1 cylinder (top view). Using feeler gauge to set valve clearance (bottom view)

2 Maintenance

General:

At least every 6000 miles (10,000km) on all models, visually check over the engine and its lubrication system for oil leaks. Do not omit to check the ancillary oil cooler at the front righthand wing. Ensure that it is firmly mounted and that the feed and return pipes are secure.

Engine oil:

Maintain the level in the oil tank within the specified range at all times.

Every 12,000 miles (20,000km) on 2.7 litre, 3.0 litre and 3.2 litre models, renew the engine oil. Drain and discard the old oil from the tank and from the bottom of the crankcase. Do this after a run while the oil is hot. The procedures are included in **Section 16**. Refill the system with SAE 30 oil of a reputable brand and, after running the engine, check the level in the tank and top up if necessary.

Oil filter and gauze strainer:

At the same time as the engine oil is being renewed, renew the disposable oil filter canister and clean the gauze strainer in the bottom of the crankcase. These procedures are included in **Section 16**.

Valve clearances:

Every 12,000 miles (20,000km) on all models, check and, if necessary, adjust the valve clearances with the engine cold.

Remove the rocker gear covers and turn the engine until the piston of No 1 cylinder (rearmost lefthand) is at TDC of its firing stroke. Both valves will be closed and the Z1 TDC mark will be aligned with the crankcase mark as shown in the upper part of **FIG 3**.

Using a 0.1mm (0.004in) feeler gauge, a screwdriver and a ring spanner as shown in the lower part of **FIG 3**, adjust both the inlet and the exhaust valve clearances ensuring that the feeler gauge is located immediately above the valve stem tip. Hold the adjuster with the screwdriver when retightening the locknut and recheck the clearance before proceeding.

Turn the crankshaft through 120° to the next TDC mark and deal with the clearances of the valves of No 6 cylinder. Continue, following the firing order, to cylinder Nos 2, 4, 3 and 5.

Rocker arm shafts:

At the same time as the valve clearances are being adjusted as described earlier, check the tightness of the rocker arm shafts as described in **Section 4**.

Compression pressures:

Every 12,000 miles (20,000km), have the compression pressure of each cylinder measured as a check on the condition of the piston rings and the valves with their seats. The difference in the compression pressure between the six cylinders should not exceed 1.5kg/sq cm (21lb/sq in).

3 Removing and refitting the engine

The engine and transmission are removed as a complete unit by lowering it out from beneath the vehicle. Using a trolley jack beneath the unit is the officially recommended removal method. If a trolley jack is not available, overhead lifting gear may be used but this method will require the lid of the engine compartment to be removed as described in **Chapter 13, Section 2**. With the engine/transmission unit removed, the transmission may be separated from the engine and work may proceed on either or both.

Removal:

1 Disconnect the battery earth lead(s). Drain the oil tank as described in **Section 16**. Chock the front wheels. Raise the rear of the vehicle and position it on stands at a height which will allow removal of the engine/transmission unit downwards and rearwards.
2 Disconnect the hoses from the oil tank. Disconnect the hoses from the air cleaner. Remove the air cleaner assembly.
3 Uncouple the cables from the starter motor and from the alternator. Identify and disconnect all electrical wiring which bridges the body and engine (ignition, instrument transmitters, CIS wiring on relevant models, etc). Similarly deal with those which bridge the body and transmission (reversing light, Sportomatic transmission cables on relevant models, etc).
4 Uncouple the throttle linkage and, if relevant, the choke control. Disconnect the fuel feed pipe(s) as relevant to the type of fuel system fitted.

5 In the case of manual transmission models, uncouple the clutch cable at the release lever, and in transmission types 915/40/45 remove the release lever to clear the new exhaust pipe system. Mark the lever so that it can be installed in exactly the same position. In the case of Sportomatic transmission models, disconnect the pipelines.
6 Uncouple the hot air ducts from the heat exchangers. Uncouple the drive shafts from the transmission as described in **Chapter 8, Section 4**. Uncouple the gearchange linkage from the transmission as described in **Chapter 6, Section 11**.
7 Using either a trolley jack or overhead lifting gear, just take the weight of the engine/transmission unit. Refer to **FIG 4** and release the engine rear supports and the transmission support from the body mountings.
8 Check that all pipes, wiring and controls which bridged the engine/transmission unit and the body have been removed or disconnected before lowering the unit and withdrawing it from beneath the vehicle.
9 Separate the transmission from the engine as described in **Chapter 6, Section 3** or **Chapter 7, Section 4**.
10 Refer to **Chapter 2** and remove the fuel system components. Refer to **Chapter 4** and remove the cooling fan, cooling deflectors and covers, the exhaust system, heater ducts and, from relevant models, the emission control air injection equipment. Refer to **Chapter 12** and dismount the alternator and starter motor.

Refitment:

Reverse the removal sequence when refitting the engine/transmission unit.

4 The rocker gear and camshafts

Each camshaft is driven by a separate duplex chain from separate sprocket wheels on the intermediate shaft. Each chain is provided with three guide ramps and is tensioned by a hydraulically loaded jockey pulley. The arrangement is shown on **FIG 5**. The camshaft sprocket wheels are dowelled to camshaft flanges and vernier dowel holes in these components allow precise adjustment of the valve timing. Camshafts are specific to an engine type and are handed to lefthand and righthand cylinder banks. If a replacement camshaft is required, **ensure that the correct component is obtained.**

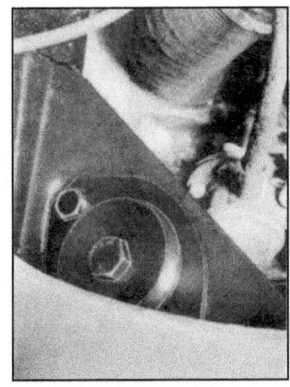

FIG 4 Righthand and lefthand engine mountings at rear (top view). Transmission support from below (lower view)

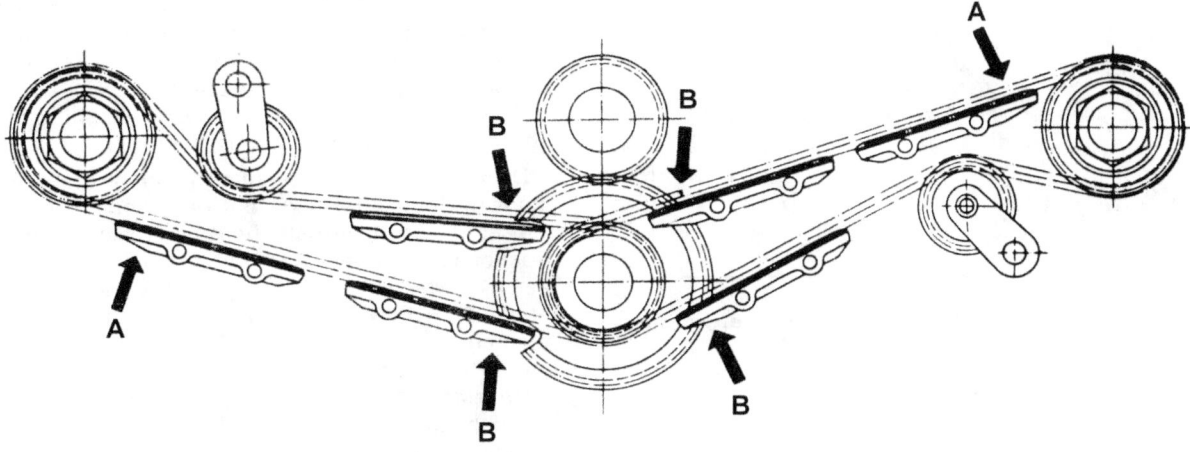

FIG 5 Positions of camshaft drive chain guide ramps

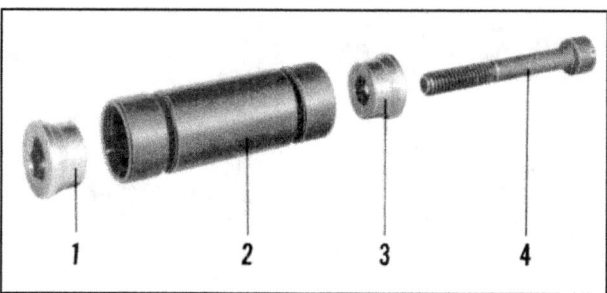

FIG 6 Components of rocker shaft. Cones expand ends to secure shaft in housing

Key to Fig 6

1 Cone nut   2 Rocker shaft   3 Cone bush   4 Allen bolt

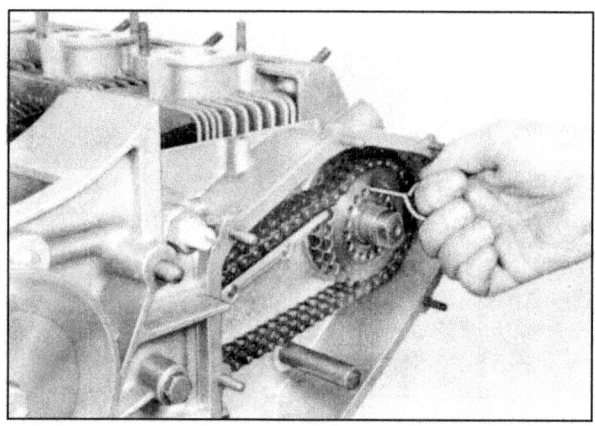

FIG 7 Withdrawing dowel which aligns vernier hole in camshaft sprocket with that in flange

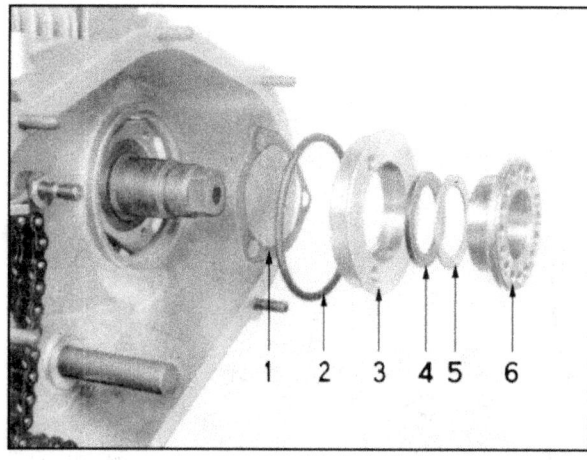

FIG 8 Sealing ring 3 and thrust washer 4 determine the end float of camshaft

Key to Fig 8

1 Paper gasket   4 Thrust washer
2 O-ring   5 Spacer
3 Sealing ring   6 Camshaft sprocket flange

Camshaft and camshaft housing removal:

1 Remove all sparking plugs. Remove the rocker covers from the relevant bank of cylinders. Mark the rockers so that they may be refitted to their original positions.

2 Refer to **FIG 6**. From each rocker shaft remove the socket-headed screw 4, push out the shaft 2, collect cones 1 and 3 and lift out the rocker. Rocker removal should be carried out with the relevant valves closed.

3 Remove the hose from between the crankcase and the chain housing cover. Remove the chain housing cover. In the case of fuel injection pump models, engines fitted with emission control air injection equipment and Sportomatic transmission models, refer to **Chapter 2, Section 8, Chapter 4, Section 3** and **Chapter 7, Section 10** when the lefthand camshaft is being dealt with.

4 Refer to **Section 5** and remove the chain tensioner and jockey pulley. Remove the nut securing the camshaft sprocket wheel (the official tools are P202 and P203). Withdraw the dowel pin from the sprocket wheel as shown in **FIG 7**. The official tool is P212.

5 Remove the outer guide ramp **A** in **FIG 5** by lifting the spring retainers with a screwdriver or wire hook. Refer to **FIG 8**. Withdraw the sprocket flange 6. Remove the drive key. Withdraw the thrust washer 4 and the spacer 5.

6 Remove the three retaining screws and push out the sealing ring 3, the 'O' ring 2 and the gasket 1. Withdraw the camshaft rearwards.

7 Remove the housing retaining nuts (hexagon) and three socket-headed nuts. Dismount the camshaft housing. Clean off all components and check them as described later.

Camshaft and camshaft housing refitment:

This is the reverse of the removal sequence except that, additionally, the camshaft timing procedure which is described in **Section 6** must be carried out. Use a new 'O' ring and gasket. Apply Tereson Atmosit or an equivalent jointing compound on relevant faces. Torque tighten the camshaft sprocket retaining nut to 10kgm (72 lb ft). Ensure that the rocker shafts are centrally disposed in their carrier bores by proceeding as follows. Insert a very thin feeler between the rocker and the housing and locate the rocker shaft so that the feeler drops into the groove in the shaft. Push the shaft until the feeler is trapped between the groove and the housing. Withdraw the feeler and push the shaft along by approximately 1.5mm (0.06in). Each groove will now be recessed into the housing bores by the same amount. Torque tighten screws 4 in **FIG 6** to 1.8kgm (13lb ft). Set the valve clearances as described in **Section 2**.

Chain housing removal and fitment:

Dismount the engine rear mounting bracket after removing four nuts. Carry out operations 1 to 6 of the camshaft and camshaft housing removal procedure described earlier. Detach the chain housing after removing the nuts which retain it to the crankcase. Chain guide ramps **B** in **FIG 5** are removed by lifting the spring retainers as shown in **FIG 9** and removing the stud bolts. The procedure for renewing the chains is included in **Section 13**.

Refitment is the reverse of the removal sequence. Use Tereson Atmosit or an equivalent jointing compound on the housing to crankcase face.

Component inspection:

Discard 'O' rings and gaskets 1 and 2 in **FIG 8**. Clean off old jointing compound. Check that the camshaft and the camshaft housing oilways are clear by blowing through with compressed air and oil. Slight scuffing of camshaft cams may be judiciously cleaned up by stoning but more severe wear will dictate the fitment of a new shaft. Rocker contact areas may be similarly treated. Check the adjusters for wear. Worn guide ramps should be renewed.

5 The chain tensioner

Removal:

Remove the relevant chain housing cover as described in **Section 4**. In the case of a lefthand tensioner, use a block of hardwood between the crankcase and the jockey sprocket wheel to jam the wheel against the chain. In the case of a righthand tensioner, use wire round the sprocket arm and a cover stud to take the load off the tensioner plunger pin. Remove the retaining nut and withdraw the tensioner noting that the plunger is under spring load. The jockey pulley assembly (note that they are handed) may now be removed if necessary.

Fitment:

Fit the jockey pulley assembly if it was removed and constrain it against the chain. If the **original tensioner** is being refitted, bleed the unit as described later and compress the assembly slowly in a vice fitted with soft jaws (a quick compression may damage the 'O' rings). Constrain the plunger in this depressed condition (the official tool is P214). Fit the tensioner and its retaining nut. Remove both constraints. If a **new tensioner** is being installed, leave the clamp 18 in **FIG 10** in position, slide the unit onto the sprocket wheel carrier shaft to a point where half the plunger pin is engaged with the arm of the tensioner. At this point turn lockring 17 until the temporary clamp 18 can be removed. Push the tensioner fully into position and fit the retaining nut.

Dismantling a tensioner:

1 Remove the tensioner as described earlier. Hold the assembly in a vice fitted with soft jaws. Refer to **FIG 10**. Hold the spring retainer down and, using a small screwdriver, extract the locking ring 17. Remove retainer 16 and spring 15.

2 Use pliers to withdraw piston 12 and, while holding plunger 10, extract lockring 11 with a small screwdriver. Discard 'O' rings 13 and 14.

3 Slowly release the plunger and withdraw it. If the intermediate piece 8 sticks inside the plunger, free it by tapping the plunger on a piece of wood.

4 Withdraw the intermediate piece and 'O' ring if it did not come away with the plunger. Discard the 'O' ring. Remove ball 7, ball retainer 6, spring 5 and guide 4. Remove bleed screw 3 and washer 2.

5 Clean and oil the bore of the housing and all internal parts. Check the action of piston 12 in the housing bore by positioning it on plunger 10 and sliding the assembly into the housing. It should move freely without drag. High spots may be eased by careful stoning.

6 At mid-1970 a modified intermediate piece and 'O' ring 9 was introduced and, if these new parts are available from the spares supplier, they may be fitted.

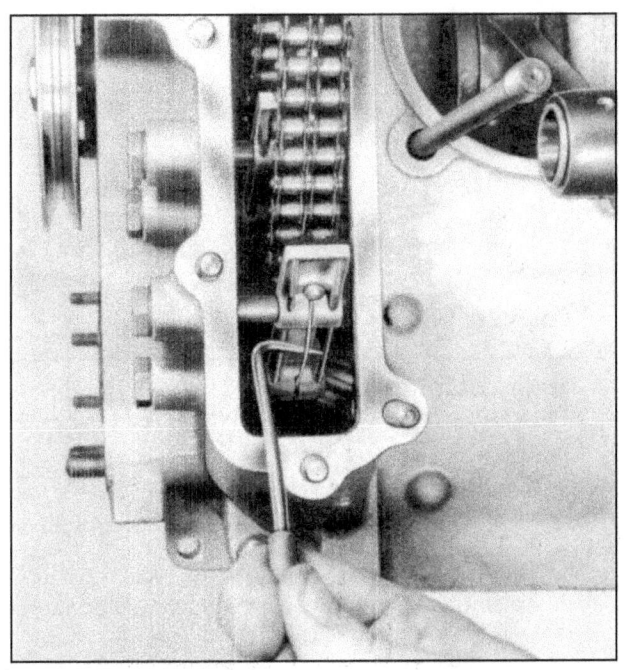

FIG 9 Lifting spring on chain guide ramp out of groove in mounting stud

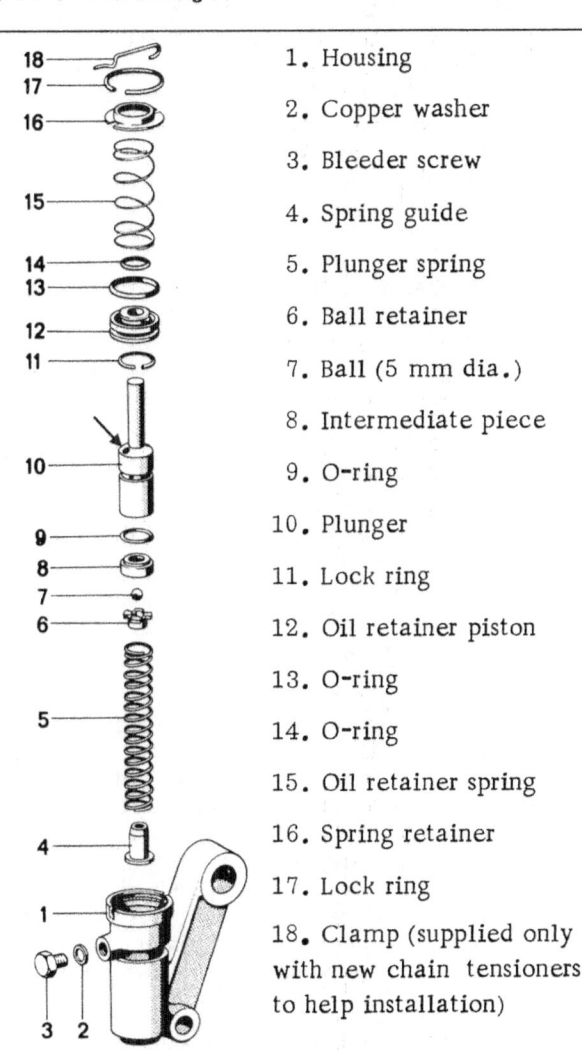

1. Housing
2. Copper washer
3. Bleeder screw
4. Spring guide
5. Plunger spring
6. Ball retainer
7. Ball (5 mm dia.)
8. Intermediate piece
9. O-ring
10. Plunger
11. Lock ring
12. Oil retainer piston
13. O-ring
14. O-ring
15. Oil retainer spring
16. Spring retainer
17. Lock ring
18. Clamp (supplied only with new chain tensioners to help installation)

FIG 10 Components of chain tensioner

FIG 11 Secure the assembly in a vice as shown, preparatory to bleeding the system

Reassembling a tensioner:

Assemble with all internal parts wetted with SAE 30 oil. Proceed as follows:

1 Fit a new 'O' ring to the intermediate piece and insert the assembly into the plunger with the ball and ball retainer. Fit the bleed screw and its washer.
2 Fill the housing with SAE 30 oil. Insert the spring into the plunger, position the guide 4, insert this assembly into the oil filled housing and secure it by fitting lockring 11.
3 Bleed the tensioner as follows. Depress ball 7 with bent wire inserted through the hole in the plunger which is arrowed in **FIG 10**. Press the plunger up and down keeping the unit filled with oil. Continue until air bubbles cease to emerge.
4 Hold the unit in a vice as shown in **FIG 11**. Fill the upper part of the housing with SAE 30 oil, fit 'O' rings 13 and 14 to piston 12 and position it over the plunger. Do not depress the piston at this stage.
5 Place the special gauge ring P214V over the plunger pin so that it rests on top of the piston. Simultaneously, open the bleed screw and depress the gauge ring until it firmly contacts the top of the housing. As soon as contact is made, tighten the bleed screw.
6 Fit the spring 15, the retainer 16 and secure with lockring 17. Check the operation of the tensioner by holding it vertically in a vice and resting a weight of 5.5kg (12lb) squarely on the plunger pin. The plunger should not yield by more than 10mm (0.40in) during a period of 5 to 10 minutes.

6 Valve timing

Timing of the camshafts in relation to the crankshaft is carried out in two stages. Stage 1, preliminary, timing may be carried out before the rockers have been assembled to the camshaft housing. If, however, the rockers have been installed, **it is imperative to note that all operations of turning the crankshaft and camshafts with the drive disconnected are undertaken with great care.** Unless the pistons and valves are correctly timed there is a possibility that they will make contact when the top of each stroke is reached. If the slightest resistance to turning is noticed, stop at once, back off a little and reset the relative positions of camshafts and crankshaft.

State 1 valve timing:

1 Refer to **FIG 12** and turn crankshaft so that pulley mark Z1 lines up with crankcase joint.
2 Camshafts are marked on the end with a punch. Turn these marks until they are vertically above camshaft centres (see outer arrows in illustration), taking the precautions mentioned at the start of this section.
3 One hole in each camshaft sprocket will line up with one in the sprocket flange. Insert the dowel (see **FIG 7**). Fit spring washer and tighten nut to 10kgm (72lb ft).

Stage 2 valve timing:

The accuracy of the preliminary timing is checked and, if necessary, adjusted as follows. The inlet valve rockers of at least Nos 1 and 4 (the rearmost cylinders of each bank) cylinders must be fitted before carrying out this procedure.

1 Set the valve clearances of Nos 1 and 4 inlet valves to 0.10mm (0.004in) as described in **Section 2**.
2 Set up a dial gauge as shown top left in **FIG 13**. The plunger must rest on the valve spring collar and be in line with the valve stem. Arrange for the plunger to extend a further 10mm (0.40in) as the valve opens. Zero the gauge.
3 Use a screwdriver to press the tensioner sprocket firmly against the chain, as shown, and block the tensioner in that position. Turn crankshaft through a complete turn so that No 1 cylinder is now at TDC on the inlet stroke and the inlet valve should have started to open. Read the dial gauge. This will be the amount of inlet valve lift at TDC and figures for the different engine types are listed in the **Technical Data** section of the **Appendix**.
4 If the lift shown by the dial gauge differs from the figure quoted for the relevant engine type, adjust the timing as follows. Remove the camshaft sprocket nut and spring washer, withdraw the dowel and check that the crankshaft pulley mark is aligned with the crankcase joint.
5 Turn the camshaft with special tool P202 as shown in **FIG 13**. Do this until the dial gauge shows the desired adjustment value specified.
6 Find the holes in sprocket and flange which line up and insert dowel. Fit washer and nut and tighten to correct torque.
7 Turn crankshaft two complete turns and check gauge reading. Readjust if necessary.

Repeat the procedure on cylinder No 4 to set the timing of the other camshaft, making sure the tensioner sprocket is firmly pressed into the chain. When adjustment is completed, remove blocks used to maintain position of tensioners. Note in **FIG 13** that a screwdriver is being used to press the tensioner into the chain to take up all backlash.

7 Removing and refitting the cylinder heads

With the engine/transmission unit removed from the car as described in **Section 3** (the transmission need not be separated from the engine unless it also is to be worked on), a bank of three heads complete with their camshaft housing may be removed as an assembly or,

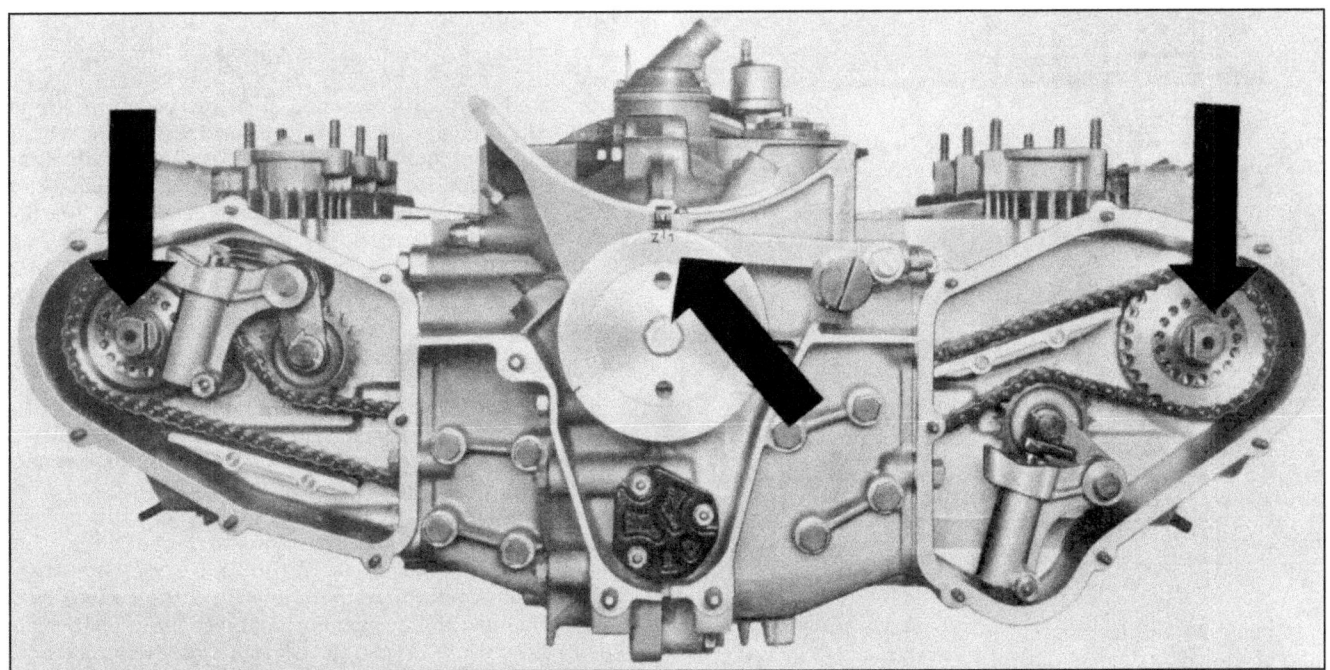

FIG 12 Checking valve timing. Outer arrows point to camshaft markings, central arrow to pulley mark Z1 aligned with crankcase joint

after removing the camshaft housing, an individual cylinder head may be removed. The procedures are as follows.

Removing a bank of cylinder heads:

Refer to **Section 4** and carry out operations 1 to 6 of the camshaft housing removal procedure. Remove the socket-headed nuts which retain the cylinder heads and lift off the camshaft housing and the cylinder heads as a unit.

Removing an individual cylinder head:

Remove the camshaft housing as described in **Section 4**. Remove the socket-headed nuts which retain the relevant cylinder head. Lift off the cylinder head.

Refitment:

Refitment is the reverse of the removal sequence in each case. Use new cylinder head gaskets and torque tighten the socket-headed retaining nuts to 3.0 to 3.3 kgm (21 to 24lb ft). Set the valve timing as described in **Section 6**.

8 Servicing the cylinder heads

Remove the cylinder heads as described in **Section 7** and separate them from the camshaft housings. if they were removed in banks of three. Keep each head identified to the cylinder from which it was removed.

Decarbonising:

Decarbonise the combustion chambers and valve heads before removing the valves. Decarbonising at this stage protects the valve seats. Use a scraper and wire brush and avoid the use of sharply pointed tools which could damage the surfaces. Be careful not to damage the joint faces. Use a tap to clear carbon from the sparking plug threads.

Valve removal:

Use a block of hardwood profiled to an approximate shape of the combustion chamber and a suitable spring compressing tool to remove the valve springs. Remove any burrs from the cotter grooves in the valve stems before pushing the valves out. Identify the valves, springs and seats to their locations and also any shims **B** in **FIG 14** which may be fitted under the valve spring seats.

Heads:

Clean the joint faces and, using a straightedge and a feeler gauge, check the head/cylinder faces and the head/camshaft housing faces for distortion. Distortion must not exceed 0.15 mm (0.006in). Excessively distorted heads cannot be salvaged and must be replaced by new components.

FIG 13 Valve timing check. Dial gauge records inlet valve lift while camshaft is turned with tool P202

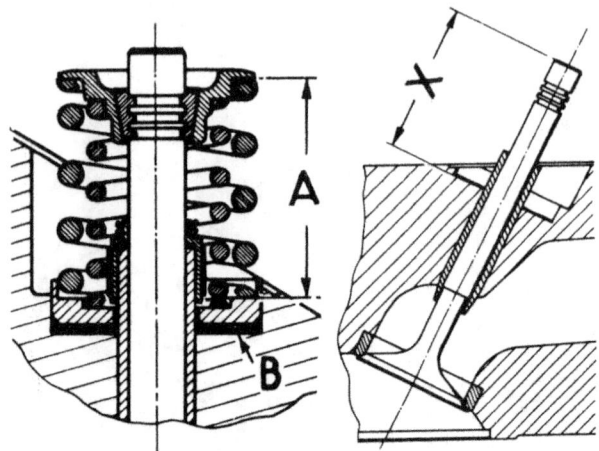

FIG 14 Installed length of outer valve spring at A, adjustment shims at B (lefthand view). Check X for length of valve stem projecting above spring seat (righthand view)

Check the tightness and the condition of valve seats and guides. The desired diametrical clearance between an inlet valve stem and its guide is 0.03 to 0.05mm (0.001 to 0.002in) with a wear limit of 0.15mm (0.006in) and that between an exhaust valve stem and its guide is 0.05 to 0.075mm (0.002 to 0.003in) with a wear limit of 0.20mm (0.008in). If the wear limit is exceeded and if the fitment of new valves alone will not result in acceptable clearances, new valve guides or new heads will be required. Similarly, if the valve seats are excessively worn, pitted or burned and will not clean up, new seats or renewal of the heads will be dictated.

Removal of unserviceable valve guides and seats and fitment and machining of new parts requires experience and facilities which will not normally be within the scope of an owner. If, however, skills and facilities are available, the procedures are as follows.

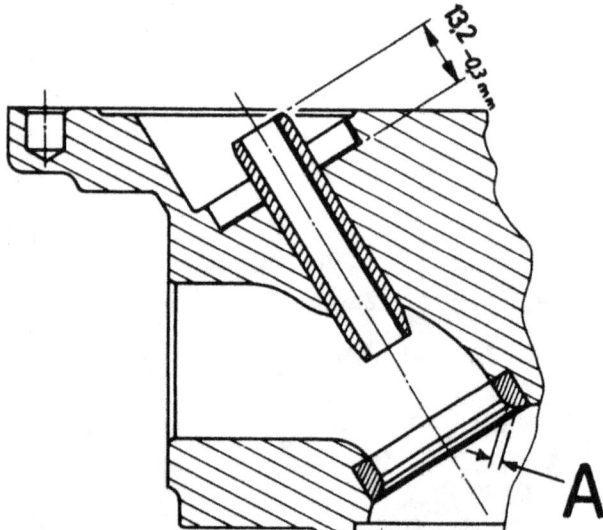

FIG 15 Correct position of valve guide with respect to valve spring seat in head. Width of valve seat is indicated at A

Valve guide replacement:

Drill through the old guide with an 11mm (0.433in) twist drill. Heat the head to 200°C (390°F) and, using a shouldered drift, drive out the shell of the old guide in the direction of the camshaft housing face. Spare guides are oversize and must be machined to give an interference fit with the head location of 0.03 to 0.06mm (0.0012 to 0.0024in). Cool the prepared guide in a deep freezer. Heat the head as before. Apply tallow to the guide as a lubricant and drive it in from the camshaft housing face side to the position shown in FIG 15. Ream the bore of the guide to 9.000 + 0.015mm (0.3543 + 0.006in).

Valve seat replacement:

Machine away the old seat until it is loose and can be knocked out without damaging the seat location. Measure the location bore very accurately. Machine the spare seat insert to give an interference fit of 0.14 to 0.18mm (0.0055 to 0.0071in) in the case of an inlet valve or 0.16 to 0.20mm (0.0063 to 0.0079in) in the case of an exhaust valve. Heat the head to 200°C (390°F). Cool the seats in a deep freezer and drive them in with a shouldered drift. Allow the head to cool slowly. Stabilise by reheating the head to the same temperature. Hold this temperature for two hours and again allow it to cool slowly. Machine the new seats ready for the valves to be lapped-in. The valve seat width A in FIG 15 should be 1.25 ± 0.10mm (0.050 ± 0.004in) for an inlet valve and 1.55 ± 0.10mm (0.060 ± 0.004in) for an exhaust valve.

Valves:

Exhaust valves have hollow stems which, to assist cooling, are filled with sodium.

Valves with excessively worn or bent stems must be rejected. Valves with seats which are excessively worn, pitted or burned cannot be salvaged although some judicious machining of the seat faces is permissible. The valve seat angle is 45°.

Lap valves to their head seats with grinding paste. Lap until the valve and the valve seats have a smooth continuous matt grey appearance over the full width of the seat areas. Wash off all traces of lapping paste, dry thoroughly, hold the valve in position and, using petrol, check for leakage into the cylinder head port. Refer to FIG 14 and check dimension X. This should be 47.50 ± 0.60mm (1.870 ± 0.024in) with a wear limit of 0.5mm (0.020in). If this limit is exceeded new valve seats should be fitted.

Valve springs:

If one spring of a pair is defective, renew both. With both spring seats fitted to a pair of springs and a load of 20kg (44lb) applied, the overall length should be 42.0 to 42.5mm (1.653 to 1.673in) but, on used springs, a variation of 5% is acceptable. Obtain new springs if the loaded dimension is less than this limit.

Reassembly:

Apply a smear of oil to the valve stems. Use new stem seals. The close-coiled ends of the outer springs must be fitted towards the cylinder head spring seats. Ensure that the collets are correctly seated. Refer to FIG 14 and measure dimension A. Using shims at B, adjust A in each case to bring it within the dimension quoted in the following tabulation for the inlet or exhaust valve of the relevant engine capacity and type.

Engine type	Inlet valve	Exhaust valve
2.7 litre	35.0 ± 0.3mm 1.378 ± 0.012in	35.5 ± 0.3mm 1.398 ± 0.012in
2.7 litre Carrera	35.5 ± 0.3mm 1.398 ± 0.012in	34.5 ± 0.3mm 1.358 ± 0.012in
3.0 litre	34.5 ± 0.3mm 1.358 ± 0.012in	As inlet
3.2 litre	34.2 + 0.3mm 1.347 + 0.012in	As inlet

9 The flywheel

Removal and refitment:

Remove the clutch as described in **Chapter 5, Section 4**. Block the flywheel from turning, refer to **FIG 16** and, using a long-handled wrench, remove the socket-headed bolts 2. Collect the spacing washer 5 and dismount the flywheel.

Refitment is the reverse of this sequence. Torque tighten bolts 2 to 15kgm (108lb ft) and apply about 2cc of graphite or molybdenum-disulphide grease into the pilot bearing 4. Refitment of the clutch assembly is covered in **Chapter 5, Section 4**.

Servicing the flywheel:

Slight damage to the starter ring gear teeth or to the forward face on which the clutch operates may be corrected by salvage machining. This work should be entrusted to a Porsche agent who can not only carry out the salvage work but can also rebalance the flywheel.

Renew a flywheel which is seriously damaged, worn or defective. Note that since flywheels and crankshafts are balanced as separate items during manufacture, no problem arises if a new flywheel has to be matched to an existing crankshaft.

The pilot bearing may be renewed by pressing it out and fitting a new one.

10 The cylinders and pistons

Cylinder removal:

Identify the cylinders and detach the air deflector plates before pulling them gently off their pistons. Ensure that neither the pistons nor the connecting rods are allowed to drop against the crankcase. Discard the joint gaskets. To preclude entry into the crankcase of dirt, etc. use lint-free rag round the connecting rods and pistons to blank off the crankcase apertures.

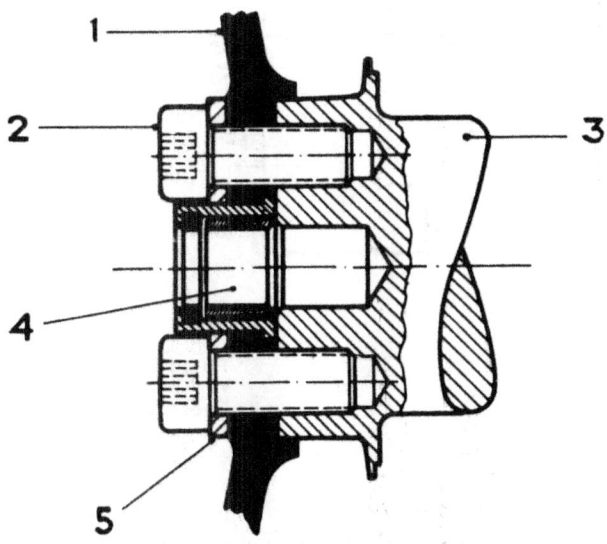

FIG 16 How flywheel is secured. Bush 4 supports rear end of gearbox input shaft

Key to Fig 16
1 Flywheel
2 Socket-head screws
3 Crankshaft
4 Bush and seal
5 Spacing washer

Cylinder fitment:

Using clean engine oil, lightly oil the pistons, rings and cylinder bores. Stagger the ring gaps evenly. Clean the crankcase and cylinder faces and fit a new gasket to the base of each. Compress the piston rings with a suitable clamp and slide the cylinders into place. Check that the holding-down studs are not fouling the cooling fins. Refit the air deflector plates.

Piston removal:

Identify each piston to its cylinder and mark which way round each is fitted in relation to the front (flywheel) end of the engine. To preclude entry of circlips, dirt, etc. into the crankcase, ensure that the lint-free rag fitted earlier is blanking off the crankcase apertures. Using a thin screwdriver at the slots provided, prise off the gudgeon pin circlips.

Gugeon pins have an interference fit in the piston bores and a piston must be heated before its gudgeon pin can be pushed out. The official tool is an electric piston heater P1a. If access to this piece of equipment cannot be arranged, hot water must be used to raise the temperature of the pistons to a minimum of 80°C (176°F). With a piston heated, the gudgeon pin can be pushed out and the piston separated from the connecting rod.

Piston fitment:

Piston fitment requires the reverse of the removal procedure and each piston must be heated to allow fitment of its gudgeon pin. Use new gudgeon pin circlips and ensure that they are correctly seated in their grooves.

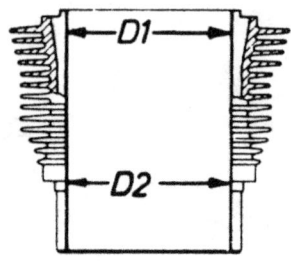
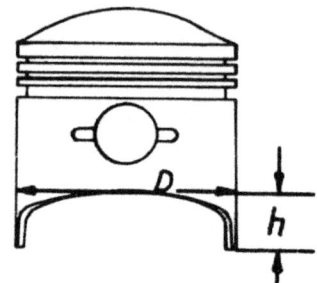

FIG 17 Checking points of cylinders and pistons

Key to Fig 17 D1 To determine cylinder wear
D2 To determine cylinder ovality and wear

Cylinder inspection:

Refer to **FIG 17**. Measure the cylinder bores up to 1974 models 2 to 3mm (0.08 to 0.12in) below the point reached by the top piston ring **D1** and at the crankcase face level **D2**. Measure round the bore at several positions so that a picture of wear and ovality can be built up. The wear limit at **D1** is 0.10mm (0.004in) and ovality should not exceed 0.04mm (0.0016in).

On 1975 and subsequent models the measuring point **D1** for wear and ovality is 30mm (1.2in) below the top edge of the cylinder and maximum wear is 0.08mm (0.0032in) more than the new size specifications. Ovality must not exceed 0.04mm (0.0016in).

Cylinder/piston clearance:

The desired diametrical clearance between the pistons and cylinder bores differs for different engines and for gudgeon pin bore, and renewal depends on the cylinder to piston clearance.

Oversize pistons are not available for the 2.7, 3.0 and 3.2 litre engines. This means that cylinders which are worn, scored, scuffed, or over the acceptable ovality tolerance must be replaced.

Piston inspection:

Refer to **FIG 17**. Measure piston diameters up to 1974 models at **h**. This position differs for different makes of piston and for different pistons and is given in the following tabulation. The wear limit is 0.10mm (0.004in).

Engine capacity and type	'h' and make of piston	
	Mahle	Schmidt
2.7 litre Carrera and S	6mm (0.24in)	—
2.7 litre S	6mm (0.24in)*	18mm (0.71in)*
*'LS' type pistons		

On 1975 and subsequent models the measuring point **h** is raised to a point level with the lower edge of the gudgeon pin bore, and renewal depends on the cylinder to piston clearance. (See chart below).

Engine capacity and type	Cylinder/piston clearance Mahle	Schmidt
2.7 litre Carrera and S	0.025 to 0.045mm (0.0010/0.0018in)	—
2.7 litre S	0.028 to 0.052mm* (0.0011/0.0020in)	0.035 to 0.060mm* (0.0014/0.0024in)
3.0 litre from Engine No 6660446 or 6669091	0.043 to 0.067mm 0.023 to 0.044mm	(0.0017 to 0.0026in) (0.0009 to 0.0017in)
3.2 litre	0.025 to 0.042mm (0.0010/0.0017in)	
		*'LS' type pistons

Serviceability of cylinders and pistons:

From the measurements of the cylinder bores and piston diameters, the ovalities and actual cylinder/piston clearances can be calculated and related to the limits and desired clearances quoted earlier and their serviceability assessed. Renew pistons and cylinders if clearance exceeds 0.15mm (0.006in).

Standard cylinders and pistons are available in either three or four grades but only in complete matching sets. For the 2.7 and early 3.0 litre engines standard sizes are available in three grades for the later 3.0 and 3.2 engines four grades are available.

Information regarding the different grades and sizes can be found in the supplement at the end of this chapter or in the **Technical Data** section of the **Appendix**.

Where relevant, the possibility of exchange replacing or reconditioning cylinders to suit oversize pistons should be considered. Consultation with the Porsche spares supplier will be essential as the diameter to which unserviceable cylinders should be reworked will not only depend upon the minimum degree of salvage required or exchanged replacements available but may also be dependent upon the oversize pistons to suit the specific engine being in stock. The new pistons must be of **exactly the same type** and make as those being replaced and the engine set must be within a weight variation of 6 to 8gr (0.21 to 0.28oz). If spare pistons of the original make are not available, it will be necessary (where relevant) to fit a **complete engine set** of the alternative make.

There are two cylinder height tolerances for new cylinders and two height tolerances for reconditioned cylinders. The cylinders fitted to one bank must be of the same height tolerance. The height tolerance code is marked on the skirt of each cylinder and the spares supplier will advise on this point.

Gudgeon pins:

Gudgeon pins at low temperatures must have an interference fit in the piston bores. Two tolerances (colour coded white and black) are available. The desired clearance of the gudgeon pin with the connecting rod small-end bush is 0.020 to 0.039mm (0.0008 to 0.0015in) with a wear limit of 0.050mm (0.0020in).

Piston rings:

Each piston is fitted with two compression rings and one oil control ring. They must be fitted with 'TOP' towards the piston crown. Certain types of oil control rings are unmarked and, being symmetrical, may be fitted either way up.

Ring gaps, measured by feeler gauge with the rings squarely in the bores of their cylinders, should be up to 1974 models generally 0.30 to 0.45mm (0.012 to 0.018in) with a wear limit of 1.0mm (0.04in). Note, however, that the rings for 'LS' type pistons should have gaps of 0.20 to 0.40mm (0.008 to 0.016in) for the top ring, 0.15 to 0.35mm (0.006 to 0.014in) for the second ring and 0.40 to 1.40mm (0.016 to 0.055in) for the oil control ring. The recommended wear limit for the compression rings is 1.0mm (0.04in) and 2.0mm (0.08in) for the oil control ring.

The gaps on 1975 and subsequent models are 0.1 to 0.2mm (0.004 to 0.008in) for compression rings with a wear limit of 0.8mm (0.032in) measured at position **D2** (see **FIG 17**), and 0.15 to 0.30mm (0.006 to 0.012in)

FIG 18 Oil pumps and intermediate drive shaft. Arrows point to pump fixings

for oil control rings with a wear limit of 1.0mm (0.039in). Where the 3-piece 'LS' ring is fitted the limits are as noted previously.

Groove side clearances up to 1974 models should be 0.075 to 0.11mm (0.003 to 0.004in) for a top ring, 0.06 to 0.072mm (0.0023 to 0.0028in) for a second ring and 0.025 to 0.052mm (0.001 to 0.002in) for an oil control ring. The wear limit in each case is 0.20mm (0.008in).

The side clearance on 1975 and subsequent models is 0.070 to 0.102mm (0.0028 to 0.0040in) for the top ring, 0.040 to 0.072mm (0.0016 to 0.0028in) for the second ring and 0.020 to 0.052mm (0.0008 to 0.002in) for the oil control ring with a wear limit on compression rings of 0.2mm (0.008in) and 0.1mm (0.004in) for oil control rings.

Ensure that, when new rings are being obtained, they are the correct type and size for the specific standard or oversize pistons to which they are to be fitted. The spares supplier will advise on this point.

11 The crankcase and crankshaft

Separating the crankcase halves:

With the cylinders, pistons, flywheel, distributor drive, V-belt pulley, etc. removed, refer to **Section 16** and remove the oil strainer, relief and safety valves, oil and breather pipe connections, thermostat and oil pressure transmitter. Remove the cover at the rear of the intermediate shaft. Remove the camshaft drive chain ramps as described in **Section 4**.

Remove the nuts securing the crankcase halves including two cap nuts which are located inside the oil cooler mounting flange. Remove the through bolts. Remove the single nut inside the lefthand chain housing aperture. Position the assembly with the righthand side downwards and lift off the lefthand half crankcase.

Crankshaft, oil pump and intermediate shaft removal:

With the lefthand half crankcase removed as described earlier, the crankshaft assembly can be lifted out. Identify all shell bearings if they are to be refitted. Remove the three nuts arrowed in **FIG 18** and lift out the oil pump and intermediate shaft. Remove the camshaft drive chains by disengaging them from the intermediate shaft sprocket wheels.

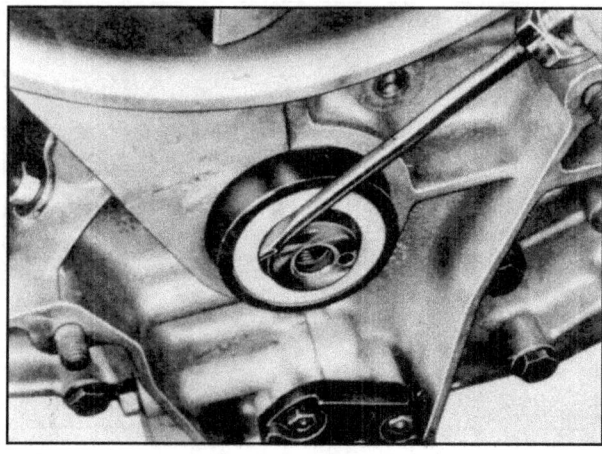

Removing oil seal from No. 8 bearing

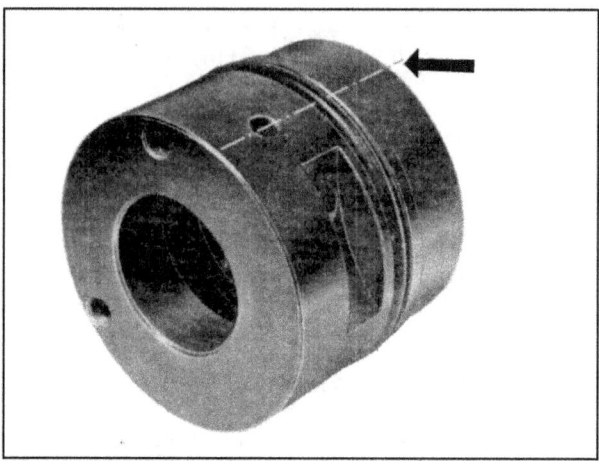

FIG 19 Marking position of dowel hole on face of bearing housing to ensure correct location (bottom).

Cleaning and inspection:

Clean old compound from the joint faces and check he faces for flatness, freedom from burrs, etc. Check that all oil passages are clear and clean by blowing through with compressed air and oil. Check that, on engines produced from December, 1970, the oil spray jets for piston cooling are operative. The jets open at 3 to 4kg/sq cm (42 to 56lb/sq in).

The work necessary to renew the crankcase bearings will be dictated by whether the original crankshaft is serviceable, whether the original crankshaft main bearing journals have had to be reground or whether an exchange replacement crankshaft is being fitted. Whichever course is adopted, the crankcase must match and it may be that an exchange replacement will be required. Note that the crankcase halves must be bolted together for measurement of the main bearing bores. The standard bore for the bearings is 62.000 to 62.019mm (2.4409 to 2.4417in). To allow oversize bearing shells to be accommodated bores may be opened out to 62.269 to 62.250mm (2.4515 to 2.4508in). The forward intermediate shaft bearing bore should be 29.800 to 29.821mm (1.173 to 1.174in) and the rear bore 24.000 to 24.021mm (0.945 to 0.946in).

Reassembly:

With the crankshaft assembly and intermediate shaft serviced as described in **Sections 12** and **13**, follow the dismantling sequence in reverse. Assemble with all internal parts adequately wetted with clean engine oil. Ensure that all bearing shell and oil feed holes coincide. Use new sealing rings on all oil passages. Use new 'O' rings and crankshaft oil seals. Apply jointing compound sparingly to the faces but keep it away from the bearings, annular grooves, etc. Torque tighten through bolts and studs evenly and gradually to 3.5kgm (25lb ft) and all nuts to 2.2 to 2.5kgm (16 to 18lb ft).

Renewing oil seal at No. 8 bearing:

Refer to the upper view in **FIG 19**. To renew the seal without dismantling the engine remove the pulley and push a small screwdriver carefully under the lip of the seal and lever out the seal. Take care not to mark the sealing surface of the crankshaft.

Coat a new seal with oil and refit it, using tool No. P.216. This is a steel cup which presses the ring into place by the action of a nut on a bolt which is screwed into the crankshaft.

Renewing front end oil seal:

This may be carried out without splitting the crankcase. Remove the flywheel as described in **Section 9**. Displace the seal from its recess with a chisel and prise it out taking care not to damage the sealing surface of the crankshaft. Lightly radius the outer corner of the recess. Remove all swarf. Lightly coat the outer surface of the new seal with jointing compound and press it into place using tool P215. It must finish flush with the crankcase. Apply oil to the sealing lip.

12 Servicing the crankshaft and connecting rods

Connecting rod removal:

Remove the crankshaft assembly as described in **Section 11**. Check that the rods and caps are identified to each other. Remove and **discard** the cap retaining bolts. Dismount the connecting rods. Inspect the rods as described later.

Connecting rod fitment:

Inject oil through the crankshaft oilways before fitting the connecting rods with the bearing shells thoroughly wetted with oil. Ensure that the shells are correctly located and that the caps are fitted the right way round and to their correct rods. Use new bolts and torque tighten the nuts to 5kgm (36lb ft). When correctly fitted the rods should swing down under their own weight.

Removing the drive gears:

Remove the circlip and, using a suitable puller, draw off the distributor drive gear, the spacer and the helical gear in one operation. Remove the spring washer and the drive key.

Fitting the drive gears:

Fit the spring washer and drive key. Heat the helical gear to 150°C (300°F) in an oil bath and, with the shoulder forwards, fit it fully onto the shaft. Fit the spacer. Heat the distributor drive gear to 100°C (212°F) and fit it onto the shaft. When cool, check that the gears are tight. Fit a new circlip.

Crankshaft inspection:

If a bearing failure has occurred, the oilways in the crankshaft, crankcase, etc must be very thoroughly cleaned and flushed. After cleaning, have the shaft magnaflux tested for cracks. A crankshaft which is cracked cannot be salvaged.

Bearings are numbered 1 to 8 from the front (the axial control bearing is No 1). After cleaning, support the shaft in V-blocks at bearings 1 and 7 and check that the eccentricity at bearings 4 and 8 does not exceed 0.04mm (0.0022in) total DTI reading. Main bearing journals 1 to 7 and all crankpin bearing clearances are best checked by using Plastigage. **Note** that No 8 bearing clearance must be checked by measurement of the diameters. The desired clearance at journals 1 to 7 and also at the crankpins is 0.030 to 0.088mm (0.0010 to 0.0034in) and, at No 8 journal, 0.048 to 0.104mm (0.002 to 0.004in). Crankshaft axial clearance controlled at No 1 main bearing should be 0.100 to 0.200mm (0.004 to 0.008in).

A crankshaft with excessive wear of the journal or crankpins may be salvaged by regrinding followed by surface rehardening. This work is outside the scope of an owner and must be undertaken by a Porsche agent. Alternatively, an exchange replacement crankshaft may be fitted. Bearing shells are available to suit three stages of regrinding.

Connecting rod inspection:

A dismantled connecting rod is shown in **FIG 20**. The desired big-end clearance has been quoted earlier. If the small-end bore to gudgeon pin clearance (see **Section 10**) exceeds the wear limit of 0.05mm (0.002in), a new small-end bush may be shrunk into the rod. An interference of 0.020 to 0.055mm (0.0008 to 0.0022in) on diameter is required. The bore should be finished reamed to 22.033 to 22.020mm (0.8674 to 0.8669in).

A bent or twisted connecting rod cannot be salvaged. The weight of a replacement rod must be within 9gr (0.32oz) of the other rods in the engine set. Used cap retaining bolts must be discarded and new bolts fitted on reassembly.

13 The intermediate shaft

Removal and fitment:

The procedure for the removal of the intermediate shaft requires the crankcase to be split and is included in **Section 11**. Following the lifting out of the intermediate shaft, the camshaft drive chains may be removed.

With the intermediate shaft inspected and serviced as described later, refer to **Section 11** for the refitment procedure. The camshaft drive chains must be fitted to both sprocket wheels before positioning the intermediate shaft into the righthand half crankcase. If the freedom of rotation of the shaft and oil pumps seems restricted, reposition the connecting shaft splines in relation to the pumps and intermediate shaft and finally mark the optimum relative position.

Gear backlash:

Backlash between the crankshaft and intermediate shaft helical gears should desirably be 0.018 to 0.050mm (0.0005 to 0.0020in). Backlash cannot be adjusted and, if excessive, can only be corrected by the fitment of a new crankshaft gear and/or a new intermediate shaft assembly.

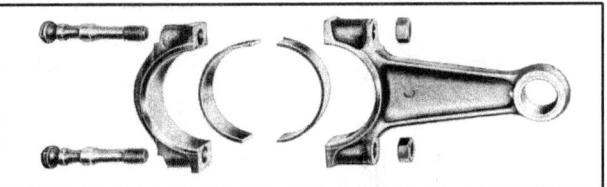

FIG 20 Connecting rod dismantled, showing bearing shells

Note that the intermediate shaft gear is finally machined during manufacture after fitment to the shaft and cannot be renewed separately. **Do not attempt to separate the gear from the shaft.**

Bearing clearances:

The desired bearing clearance at both bearings is 0.020 to 0.054mm (0.0008 to 0.0020in) with a recommended wear limit of 0.100mm (0.0040in). Bearing clearances are best checked by using Plastigage and it will be found convenient to measure these clearances at the same time as the crankshaft main bearing clearances are being checked.

Shaft bore cleaning:

A shaft which has been in service for any considerable mileage should have its bore cleaned of sludge, etc. Remove the blanking plug from the rear end of the shaft by drilling, tapping and fitting a suitable bolt to allow the plug to be pulled out. Clean the bore of the shaft and press in a new blanking plug. Check that the oilways are clear.

Axial clearance:

The desired axial float of the intermediate shaft is 0.08 to 0.12mm (0.003 to 0.005in). This is controlled by the flanged rear bearing shells and should it be excessive will require the fitment of new shells.

Sprocket wheel alignment:

Alignment of the intermediate shaft sprocket wheels with the camshaft sprocket wheels is checked and adjusted if necessary during engine reassembly. The procedure is included in **Section 14**.

14 Engine reassembly:

Assembly instructions are given in the text of each relevant section. These are largely the dismantling procedures in reverse but, as this may not always be so, the point should be checked against the text. It is then simply a matter of tackling the work in the correct sequence, of applying normal automobile engineering practice, fitting only Porsche replacement parts, using new seals, 'O' rings and gaskets and ensuring that joints are well made as it may not easily be possible to rectify an oil leak which is not discovered until the assembly and installation of the engine has been completed.

If the engine has been completely dismantled, the assembly sequence will commence with the fitment of the crankshaft and connecting rod assembly and the intermediate shaft to the crankcase halves and the assembly sequence will be the reverse of that taken during dismantling. If the engine was only partially dismantled, reverse the sequence which was then followed. Assemble

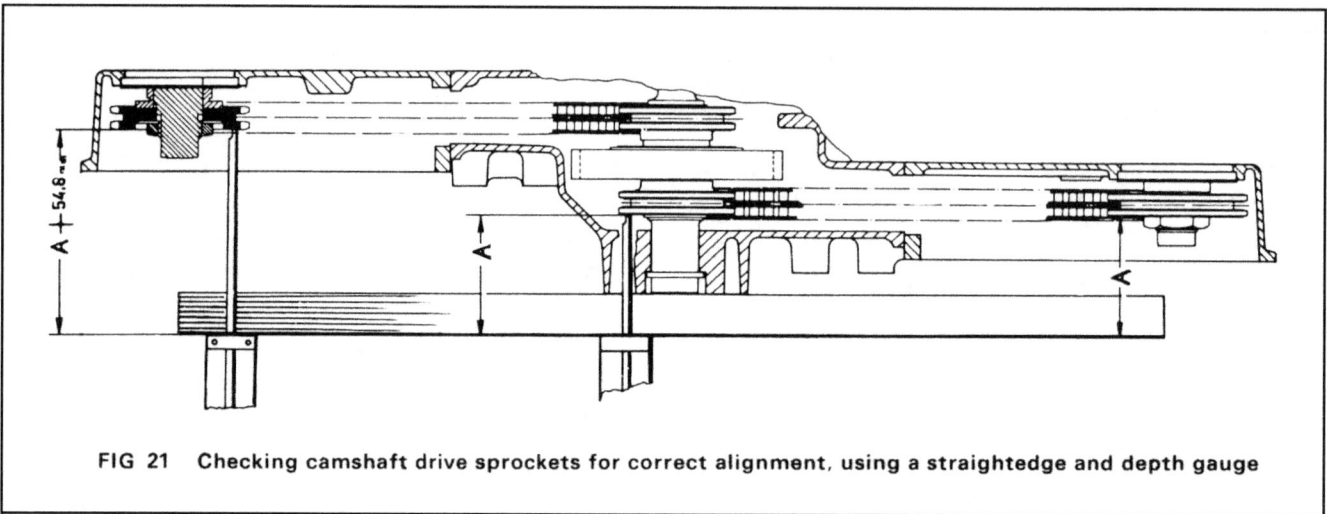

FIG 21 Checking camshaft drive sprockets for correct alignment, using a straightedge and depth gauge

working parts wetted with clean engine oil and use jointing compound where applicable. Refer to sectional texts for torque tightening figures. At each stage of assembly check, where relevant, the free rotation of the component or assembly.

To avoid the possibility of valves and pistons fouling each other, do not fit the rockers until the stage 1 valve timing procedure (see **Section 6**) has been carried out. At this point check and, if necessary, adjust the alignment of the camshaft sprocket wheels with the intermediate shaft sprocket wheels. The procedure is as follows:

1 Refer to **FIG 21** and, using a straightedge across the crankcase face and a depth gauge, measure **A** at the intermediate shaft forward sprocket wheel and at the righthand camshaft sprocket wheel. Any difference must not exceed 0.25mm (0.010in).
2 Check the corresponding dimensions for the intermediate shaft inner sprocket wheel and the lefthand camshaft sprocket wheel noting that the offset is 54.8mm (2.1575in).
3 Adjustment is made by adding or removing spacers 5 in **FIG 8** at each camshaft sprocket wheel. Stage 2 of the valve timing procedure may now be carried out.

To preclude oil draining from the old type chain tensioners, it is preferable not to invert the engine once the tensioners have been installed and it will consequently be appropriate to mount the heat exchangers, etc. before fitting the tensioners. Tensioners with self-contained oil reservoirs are not affected.

Fit the distributor and time the ignition as described in **Chapter 3, Sections 4** and **6** noting that final adjustment to the timing must be made stroboscopically after installation of the engine. Fuel system adjustments are also made on recommissioning the installed engine.

15 Recommissioning an overhauled engine

On completion of the installation of the overhauled engine and transmission into the vehicle, fill the oil tank and the transmission with the correct approved oils. Tension the cooling fan drive belt and also, if relevant, the emission control air pump drive belt. Check over to ensure that all pipes, leads and controls are reconnected and that no tools or other items have been left behind.

So that the engine may be turned without starting it, unclip the distributor cap and tape it to one side. Use the starter motor to turn the engine for some revolutions to prime the pressure oil pump. Refit the distributor cap and start the engine. Repeat the priming process if there is not an immediate rise in oil pressure. Once oil pressure has been established, check that the charging circuit is operative and that the 'no-charge' warning light goes out when a fast idling speed is reached.

Run the engine at about 2000rev/min until the oil temperature rises to about 60°C. Check that all joints and oil and fuel pipe connections are free of leaks. At idling speed, check the level in the oil tank and top up as necessary. Run the engine up to normal operating temperature and check that the oil pressure is within the range of 78 to 100lb/sq in at 5000rev/min at 80°C. Check the ignition timing stroboscopically, adjust the fuel system as described in the relevant section of **Chapter 2**. Check, where relevant, the operation of the emission control as described in **Chapter 4**.

After operating the vehicle for about 100 miles (160km), recheck for oil leaks, re-tension the drive belt(s), re-tighten the rocker shaft bolts and adjust the valve clearances. If the overhaul was extensive (new bearings, pistons, cylinders, etc.), treat the engine as if it was new and, after careful running-in, clean the oil strainer and renew the oil filter and the engine oil after 600 miles (1000km) from overhaul.

16 The lubrication system

The lubrication system is shown diagrammatically in **FIG 22**. Oil is drawn from the tank 9 by the pressure pump 3. Pressure oil is delivered via the main thermostat 5 either direct to the engine lubrication system when the oil is cold or through the main cooler 8 when the oil is hot. The bearings of the crankshaft, intermediate shaft and camshaft are pressure fed and, on later models, jets in the crankcase spray oil onto the undersides of the pistons.

The scavenge pump 2 draws drain oil (aerated) through the strainer 1 and returns it to the oil tank via a fullflow filter 12 and an auxiliary thermostat if the oil is relatively cold or via an auxiliary cooler if the oil is hot. Neither the auxiliary thermostat nor the auxiliary cooler are shown in **FIG 22**, but will be found in **FIGS 23** and **24**.

The main cooler is a matrix type. The auxiliary cooler is a coiled pipe unit.

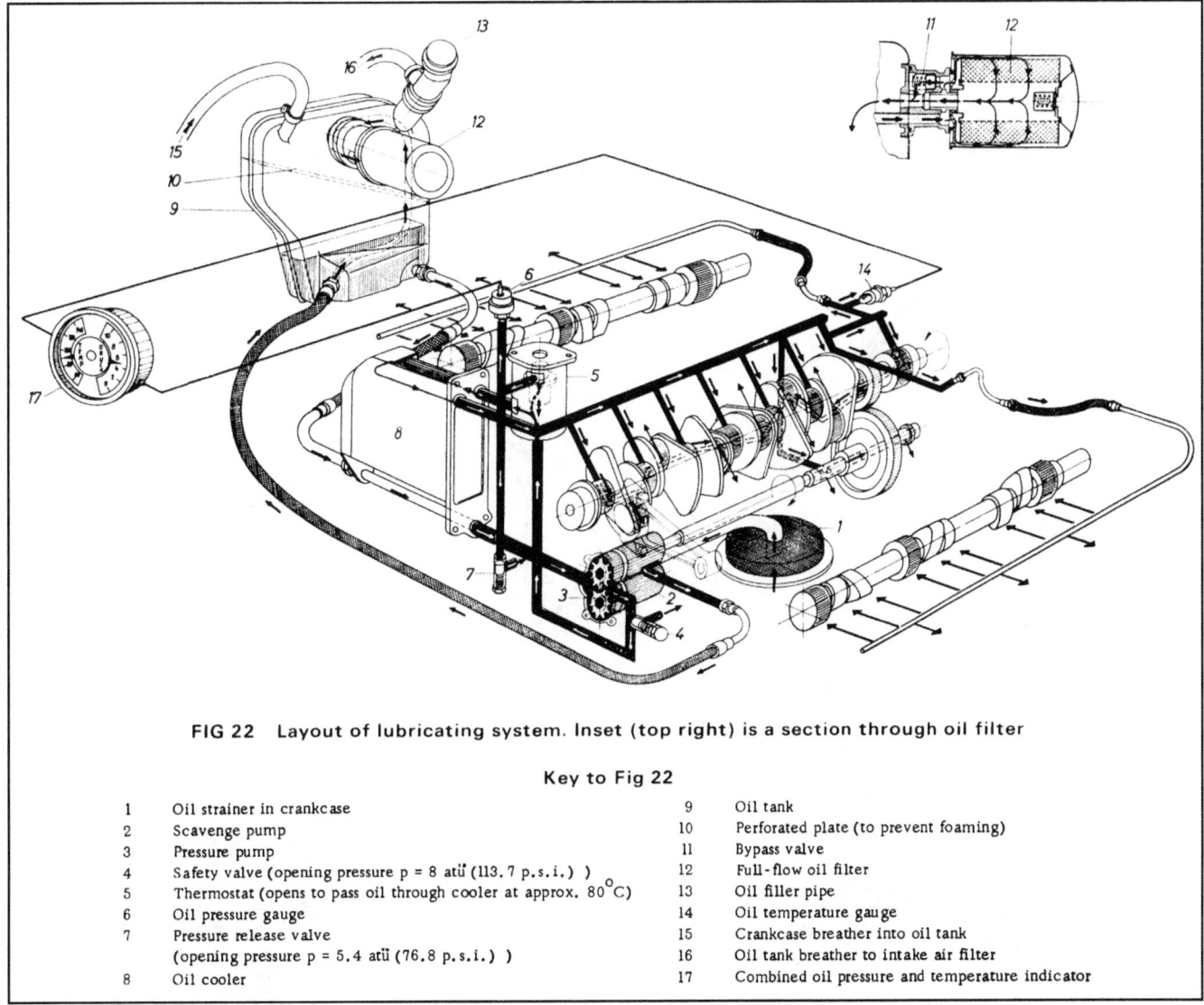

FIG 22 Layout of lubricating system. Inset (top right) is a section through oil filter

Key to Fig 22

1	Oil strainer in crankcase	9	Oil tank
2	Scavenge pump	10	Perforated plate (to prevent foaming)
3	Pressure pump	11	Bypass valve
4	Safety valve (opening pressure p = 8 atü (113.7 p.s.i.))	12	Full-flow oil filter
5	Thermostat (opens to pass oil through cooler at approx. 80°C)	13	Oil filler pipe
6	Oil pressure gauge	14	Oil temperature gauge
7	Pressure release valve (opening pressure p = 5.4 atü (76.8 p.s.i.))	15	Crankcase breather into oil tank
		16	Oil tank breather to intake air filter
8	Oil cooler	17	Combined oil pressure and temperature indicator

Gauze strainer removal and fitment:

Refer to **FIG 2**. Remove the magnetic plug 11 and drain off the residual oil from the base of the crankcase. Remove the nuts and washers which retain the coverplate 23 and strainer 10 to the crankcase halves and withdraw the assembly. Separate the two gaskets from the strainer and coverplate. Clean the strainer in petrol. Clean metallic particles from the drain plug.

Fitment is the reverse of this sequence. Use new gaskets. Do not distort the coverplate by overtightening the retaining nuts.

Renewing the oil filter:

The canister type disposable filter is screwed to a housing on the oil tank. The filter cannot be cleaned. To renew, unscrew and discard the old canister and fit a new one. Ensure that the faces of both the canister and the housing are clean and that the sealing ring is in good condition and correctly positioned.

Draining the oil tank:

With the engine oil hot after a run, jack up and remove the righthand rear road wheel. To preclude the possibility of oil contaminating the brake pads or linings, protect the wheel hub assembly with plastic or equivalent sheeting.

Position a container of adequate capacity before removing the drain plug from the bottom of the tank. Allow the old oil to drain off completely before refitting the drain plug.

Initially pour 8 litres (14 pints) of approved oil into the tank, run the engine and top up as necessary.

Oil pumps:

The gear type pressure and scavenge oil pumps are a single assembly and are shown in cross-section in **FIG 2**. To accommodate the considerable degree of aeration of the scavenged drain oil, the scavenge pump is approximately of twice the capacity of the pressure pump. The pumps are driven at half crankshaft speed by the intermediate shaft through a splined connecting shaft. No procedures are prescribed for the overhaul or repair of the oil pumps by an owner and, if either becomes unserviceable, the unit must be removed and a new or exchange replacement assembly installed.

Access to the pump assembly requires the crankcase to be split. The procedure for the removal and fitment of the pumps is included in **Section 11**. When refitting the pumps, use new joint seals and ensure that they are correctly seated.

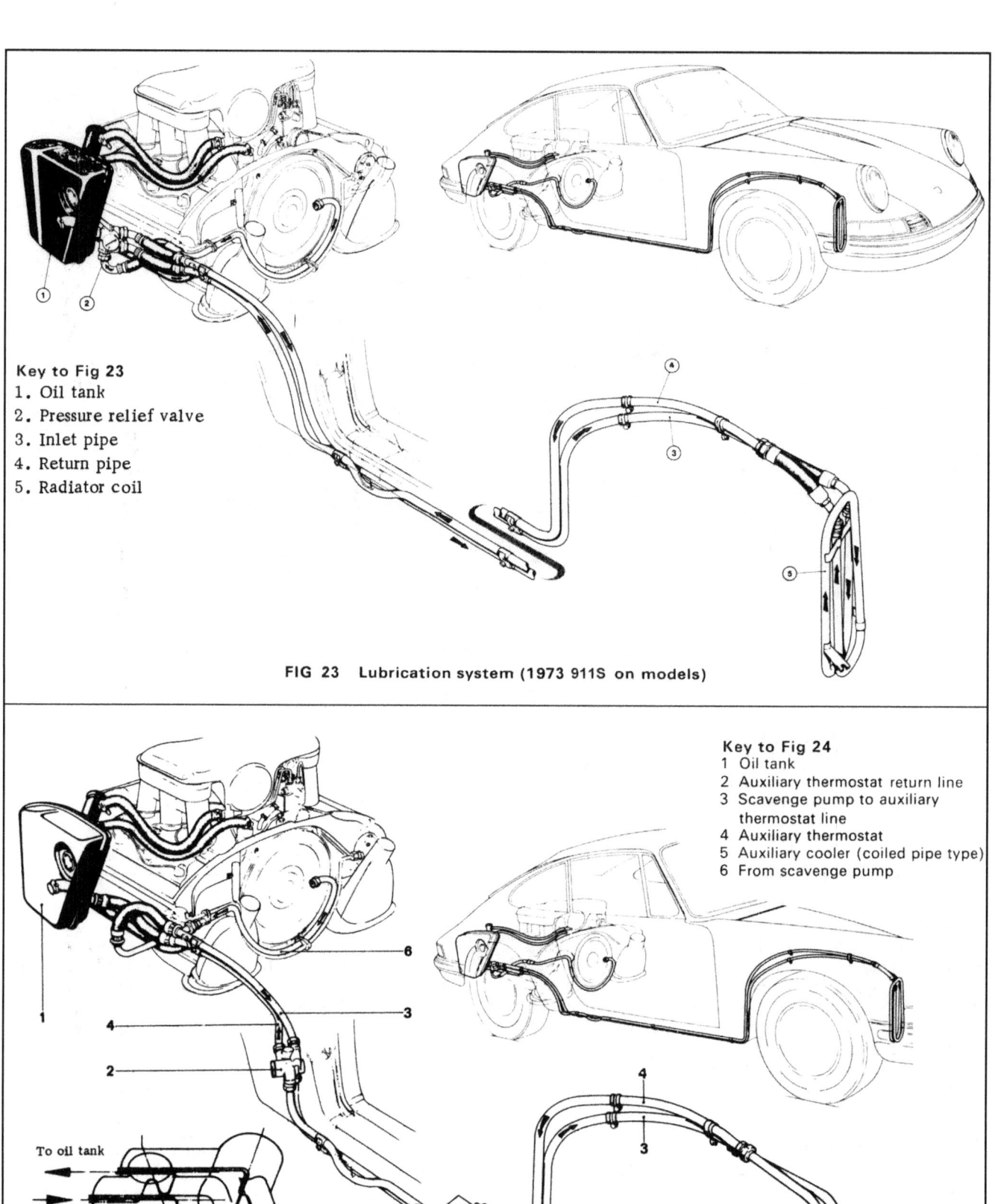

Key to Fig 23
1. Oil tank
2. Pressure relief valve
3. Inlet pipe
4. Return pipe
5. Radiator coil

FIG 23　Lubrication system (1973 911S on models)

Key to Fig 24
1 Oil tank
2 Auxiliary thermostat return line
3 Scavenge pump to auxiliary thermostat line
4 Auxiliary thermostat
5 Auxiliary cooler (coiled pipe type)
6 From scavenge pump

FIG 24　Lubrication system (1974 on models)

Relief and safety valves:

These valves are located in the crankcase and are shown arrowed **R** and **S** in **FIG 25**. The relief valve opens at approximately 5.5kg/sq cm (78lb/sq in) and allows excess pressure oil to pass to the crankcase. Should the oil pressure be excessive with the relief valve fully open or should the relief valve become inoperative, the safety valve opens and prevents excessive pressure being applied to the main cooler, oil pipes, etc.

Access to each valve and valve spring requires removal of the relevant plug **R** or **S**. Do not get the valves or springs mixed. The valve bores and the surface of the piston valves must be unscuffed and unscored.

Oil pressure transmitter:

The transmitter is located adjacent to the main thermostat and may be removed by unscrewing after disconnecting the electrical lead. A defective transmitter must be replaced by a new unit.

Main thermostat:

The main thermostat is in the pressure feed circuit. It opens at 83°C (182°F) to allow hot oil to flow through the main cooler before delivery to the engine. A defective thermostat must be replaced by a new unit.

To remove the thermostat, disconnect the lead to the oil pressure transmitter, disconnect the hose from the breather outlet, remove two retaining nuts and withdraw the thermostat.

On refitment use new 'O' rings. The offset holes in the flange preclude incorrect fitment.

Auxiliary thermostat:

The function of the auxiliary thermostat is to open the scavenge oil return line to the auxiliary cooler when the return oil temperature rises above 83°C (182°F). Incorrect operation of the thermostat will be indicated by excessively high tank oil temperature and 'coldness' of the auxiliary cooler. If the thermostat becomes defective, fit a new replacement unit.

The position of the auxiliary thermostat differs with different models but may be located by tracing the relevant scavenge oil lines.

Main oil cooler:

The main oil cooler 8 in **FIG 22** is mounted on the crankcase and may be dismounted with the engine installed in the vehicle. Access requires removal of the upper, the front and the righthand coverplates. Hold the

FIG 25 Locations of relief and safety valves

Key to Fig 25 **R** Relief valve **S** Safety valve

pipe connection hexagon when releasing the inlet pipe. Remove the upper and lower retaining nuts and lift out the cooler. Discard the seals fitted between the cooler and the crankcase.

Fitment is the reverse of this sequence. Use new seals and ensure that they are correctly seated. Hold the connection hexagon when reconnecting the inlet pipe.

Auxiliary oil cooler:

The auxiliary oil cooler is located at the front righthand wing of the vehicle as indicated in **FIGS 23** and **24**.

The auxiliary oil cooler is of coiled pipe construction. Should it be necessary to dismount the cooler, hold the connection hexagons when releasing the feed and return pipes. On refitment, ensure that the connections are adequately tightened.

NOTES

17 Supplemental information

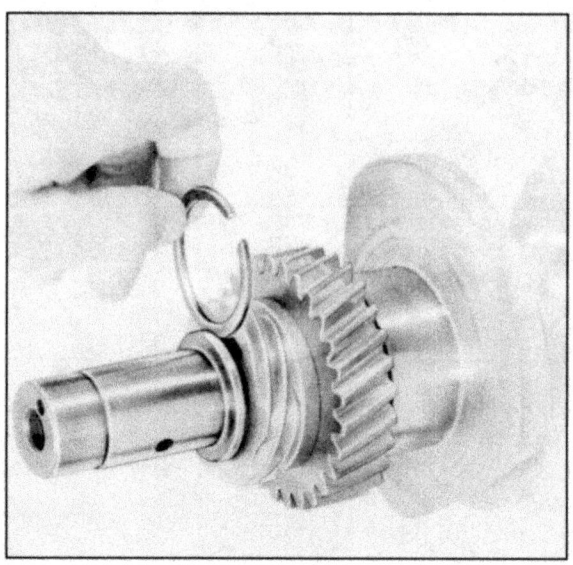

Fig. 1 Secure the distributor drive gear with a clip of the correct thickness

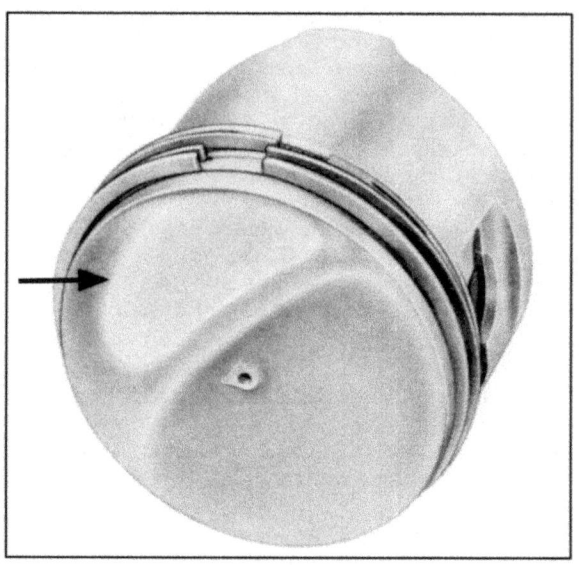

Fig. 2 Flat spot (arrow) on piston must face the inlet valve

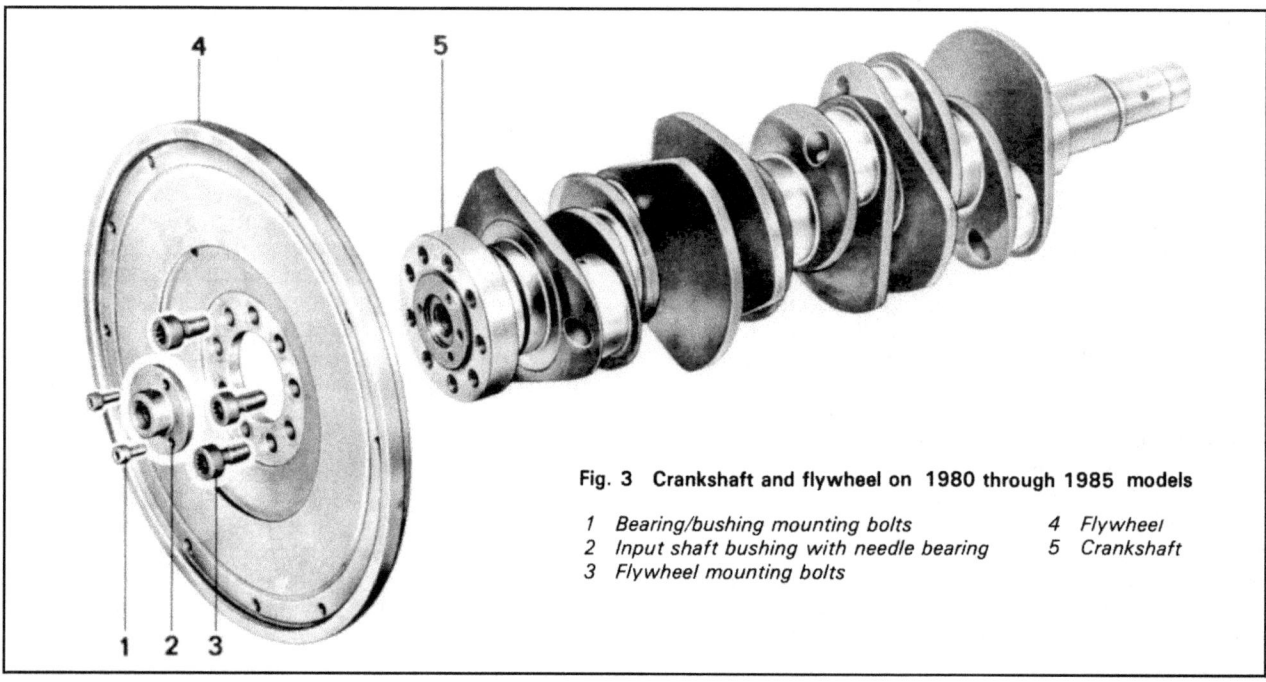

Fig. 3 Crankshaft and flywheel on 1980 through 1985 models

1 Bearing/bushing mounting bolts
2 Input shaft bushing with needle bearing
3 Flywheel mounting bolts
4 Flywheel
5 Crankshaft

Crankshaft (Figs 1 - 3 - 4)

1 Beginning in 1978 the crankshaft drive is modified from those used previously. The ignition distributor rotates counterclockwise, requiring a reverse-cut drive gear on the crankshaft.
2 The distributor drive gears for 1978 and later models are embossed with a Porsche emblem where the early model gears have a VW emblem.

Flywheel modifications 1980-1987 (Fig 3)

3 After fitting the flywheel to the crankshaft on 1980 and later models, attach the input shaft pilot bearing/bushing.
4 Apply thread sealing compound to the bearing/bushing mounting bolts and tighten them.

Pistons (Fig 2)

5 When fitting pistons on vehicles with CIS injection, be sure the flat spot on the top of the piston faces upward (toward the inlet valve).

Drivebelt modifications 1980-1987

6 The larger fan, from the 911 Turbo, is standard on all 911 SC engines used in 1980 and later models. A special drivebelt must be used on these models.
7 This drivebelt must be adjusted tighter than belts on earlier models.
8 Adjust the belt to between 0.39 and 0.59 in (10 and 15 mm) of deflection between the two pulleys, then remove one of the shims from between the pulley sections.

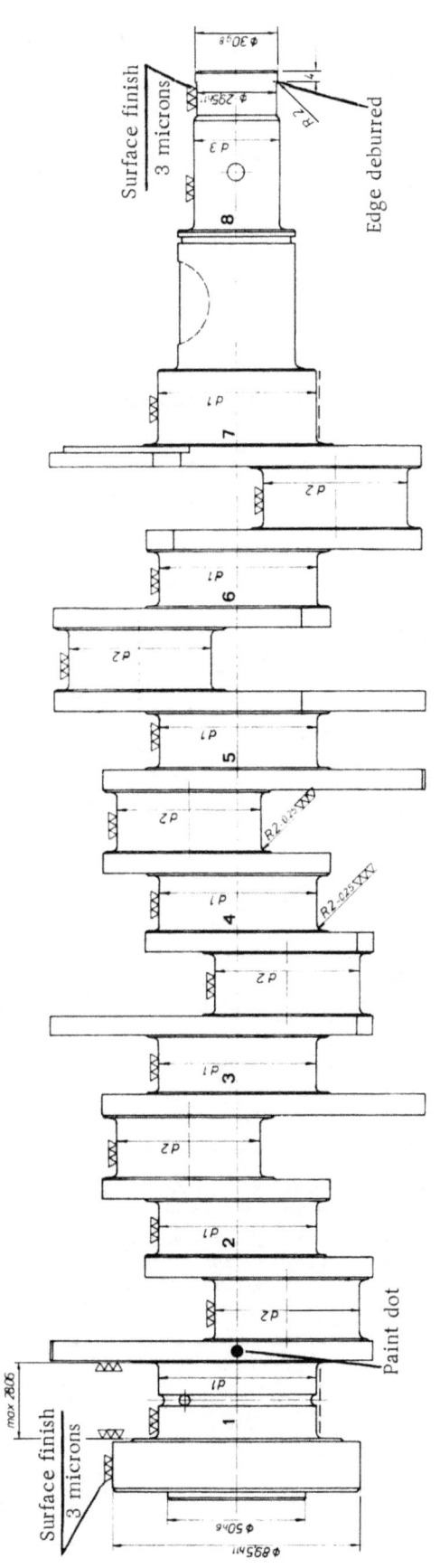

Fig. 4 Crankshaft regrinding details (1978 through 1985)

Size	Crankcase dia. Bearings 1-8	All main Bearings d1	Conrod Bearings d2	Main Bearing d 3 of Crankshaft Bearing 8	Collar dia. d4	Seat for Control Gear dia. d5	Take-up dia. d6	Guide Bearing Width A
Standard	2.561 to 2.5617 in (65.000 to 65.019 mm)	2.3629 to 2.3636 in (59.971 to 59.990 mm)	2.0871 to 2.0878 in (52.971 to 52.990 mm)	1.2206 to 1.2211 in (30.980 to 30.993 mm)	3.5373 to 3.546 in (89.780 to 90.000)	1.6549 to 1.6553 in (42.002 to 42.013 mm)	1.1804 to 1.1817 in (29.960 to 29.993)	1.103 to 1.1056 in (28.000 to 28.060)
Oversize	2.5709 to 2.5716 in (65.250 to 65.269 mm)							
-0.25		2.3530 to 2.3538 in (59.721 to 59.740 mm)	2.0772 to 2.0780 in (52.721 to 52.740 mm)	1.2108 to 1.2113 in (30.730 to 30.743)				
-0.50		2.3432 to 2.3439 in (59.471 to 59.490 mm)	2.0674 to 2.0681 in (52.471 to 52.490 mm)	1.2009 to 1.2014 in (30.480 to 30.493 mm)	3.5176 to 3.5263 in (89.280 to 89.500 mm)		1.1572 to 1.1623 in (29.370 to 29.500 mm)	
-0.75		2.333 to 2.3341 in (59.221 to 59.240 mm)	2.0575 to 2.0583 in (52.221 to 52.240 mm)	1.1911 to 1.1916 in (30.230 to 30.243 mm)				
-1.00		2.3235 to 2.3242 in (58.971 to 58.990 mm)	2.0477 to 2.0484 in (51.971 to 51.990 mm)	1.1812 to 1.1817 in (29.980 to 29.993 mm)				

Grind crankshaft oil seal surfaces only when deeply scored. Grind to dimensions of 29,5 mm and 89.5 mm respectively. Otherwise polish out to 3 microns.

After grinding, chamfer oil holes to 0,5 mm radius. Break all sharp edges to 0.2 - 0,5 mm radius. Maximum radial runout measured at bearings 1 and 7 is 0,04 mm.

Tenifer treat crankshaft after grinding. Magnaflux to check for cracks.

Do not straighten main bearing journals 3 and 5 after Tenifer treatment. All other main bearing journals can be straightened by applying pressure to the bearing journal webs.

Undersize color codes

1st undersize	blue paint dot
2nd undersize	green paint dot
3rd undersize	yellow paint dot
4th undersize	white paint dot

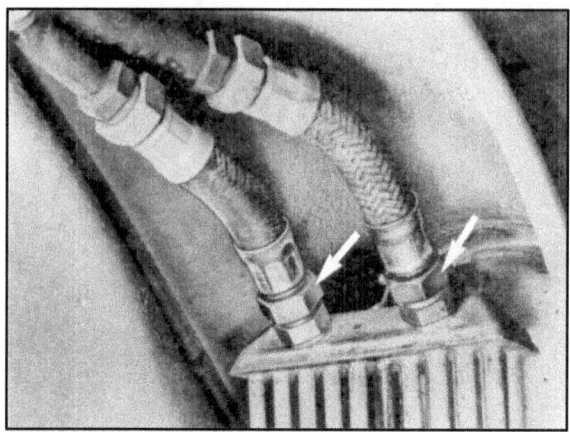

Fig. 5 Loosen the oil lines (arrows) at the cooler

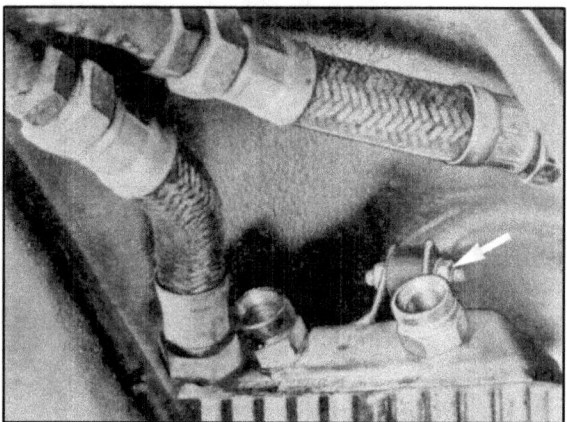

Fig. 6 Remove the nut (arrow) from the upper mount

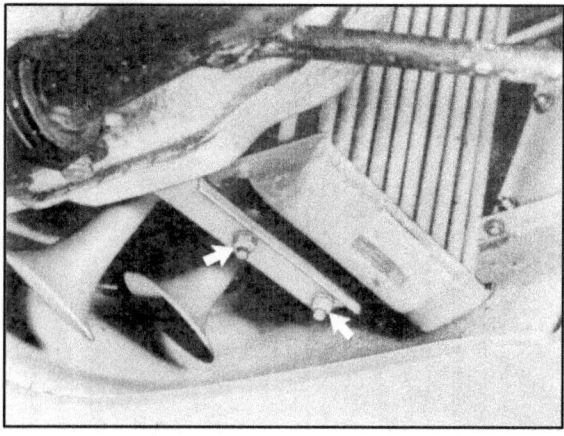

Fig. 7 Remove the lower oil cooler mounting nuts (arrows)

Oil cooler 1980-1987 (Figs 5 - 6 - 7)

9   1980 and later models have an oil cooler at the front of the vehicle.
10   Remove the front wheel from the right side of the vehicle.
11   Place an oil drain pan under the oil cooler and disconnect the oil lines. Use two wrenches, one as a counter-hold.
12   Remove the nut from the outside of the upper rubber mount.
13   Remove the two lower mounting nuts and lift the oil cooler out of position.
14   Installation is the reverse of removal.
15   Coat the threads of the oil lines with a high-temperature molybdenum disulfide grease. Be sure to use a wrench as a counter-hold at the oil cooler when attaching the oil lines.
16   Run the engine up to operating temperature and check the oil cooler for leaks.

Oil pressure release & safety valve modifications (Fig 8)

17   Later models may use a 3.39 ih (86 mm) spring in place of the 2.75 in (70 mm) spring. If the longer spring is used, a spring guide must be fitted to the spring on the end opposite the piston pressure relief valve.

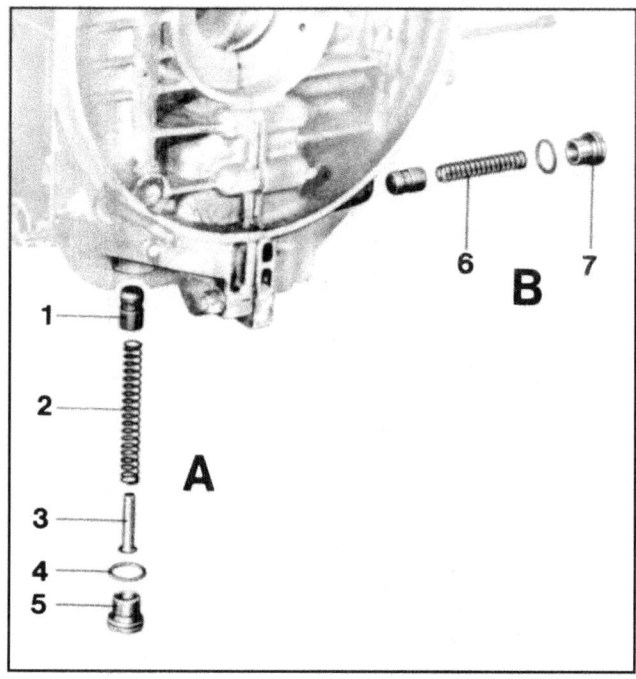

Fig. 8 Oil pressure relief (A) and safety valve (B) components from 1978 models

1 Pressure relief valve piston
2 Spring (86 mm long)
3 Spring guide
4 Gasket
5 Grooved plug
6 Safety valve spring
7 Grooved safety valve plug

NOTES

18 Fault diagnosis

(a) Engine will not start

1 Ignition system defective electrically
2 Ignition system defective mechanically
3 Dirty, pitted or incorrectly set contact breaker points
4 Ignition wires loose, insulation faulty
5 Water on sparking plug leads
6 Battery discharged, corrosion of terminals
7 Faulty or jammed starter
8 Sparking plug leads wrongly connected
9 Vapour lock in fuel pipes
10 Defective fuel pump
11 Starting fuel enrichment excessive or insufficient
12 Fuel system filter, injectors or carburetter jet(s) blocked
13 Leaking valves
14 Sticking valves
15 Valve timing incorrect
16 Ignition timing incorrect
17 Engine flooded with fuel

(b) Engine stalls after starting

1 Check 1, 2, 3, 4, 5, 10, 11, 12, 13 and 14 in (a)
2 Sparking plugs defective or gaps incorrect
3 Retarded ignition
4 Mixture too weak
5 Water in fuel system
6 Fuel tank vent blocked
7 Incorrect valve clearances

(c) Engine idles badly

1 Check 2 and 7 in (b)
2 Air leaks at manifold joints
3 Idling adjustment wrongly set
4 Over-rich mixture
5 Worn piston rings
6 Worn valve stems or guides
7 Weak exhaust valve springs

(d) Engine misfires

1 Check 1, 2, 3, 4, 5, 8, 10, 12, 13, 14, 15 and 16 in (a); 2, 3, 4 and 7 in (b)
2 Weak or broken valve springs

(e) Engine overheats

1 Weak mixture, ignition over-advanced
2 Fan belt slipping
3 Defective oil thermostat
4 Oil cooler internally blocked or externally choked with dirt
5 Loss of cooling air through badly fitted covers

(f) Low compression

1 Check 13 and 14 in (a); 6 and 7 in (c); and 2 in (d)
2 Worn piston ring grooves
3 Scored or worn cylinder bores

(g) Engine lacks power

1 Check 3, 10, 12, 13, 14, 15 and 16 in (a); 2, 3, 4 and 7 in (b); 6 and 7 in (c); and 2 in (d). Also check (e) and (f)
2 Leaking joints and gaskets
3 Fouled sparking plugs
4 Automatic ignition advance not working
5 Exhaust system blocked

(h) Burnt valves or seats

1 Check 13 and 14 in (a); 7 in (b); and 2 in (d). Check (e)
2 Excessive carbon in head

(j) Sticking valves

1 Check 2 in (d)
2 Bent or scored valve stems, defective guides
3 Defective stem seals
4 Incorrect valve clearance

(k) Excessive cylinder wear

1 Check 11 in (a); and check (e)
2 Dirty or insufficient oil. Wrong grade
3 Piston rings wrongly gapped, gummed or broken
4 Bent connecting rods
5 Dirt under cylinder mounting flanges

(l) Excessive oil consumption

1 Check 6 and 7 in (c); check (k); and 3 in (j)
2 Ring gaps too wide
3 Oil control rings ineffective
4 Scored cylinders
5 Defective scavenge oil pump
6 External oil leaks
7 Incorrect grade of oil

(m) Crankshaft or connecting rod bearing failure

1 Check 2 and 4 in (k)
2 Blocked oilways
3 Bent or worn crankshaft
4 Bearing shells wrongly fitted
5 Worn pressure oil pump, defective lubricating system
6 Loose bearings or connecting rod caps

(n) High fuel consumption

1 Car in poor mechanical condition
2 Bad driving habits, excessive acceleration in low gears
3 Incorrect ignition or fuel system adjustments
4 Flooding float chamber (carburetter models, fuel leakage)
5 Incorrect jet sizes (carburetter models)
6 Carburetter accelerating pump wrongly adjusted

(o) Engine vibration

1 Mounting failures
2 Loose alternator mounting
3 Fan out of balance
4 Clutch and flywheel unbalanced
5 Misfiring due to mixture, ignition or mechanical faults

NOTES

CHAPTER 2 - FUEL SYSTEM

1. Description
2. Maintenance
3. Air cleaner and preheater
4. Fuel filter
5. Fuel pump
6. Controls
7. Bosch fuel injection pump system (FIP)
8. Bosch continuous injection system (CIS)
9. Digital Motor Electronics injection system (DME)
10. Fault diagnosis FIP & CIS

Supplemental Information

In this chapter the supplemental information for the CIS fuel injection system has been incorporated within the original text. Data relating to the DME fuel injection system has been added as a separate section.

1 Description

The fuel tank is installed at the front of the vehicle below the luggage compartment floor. It is provided with a drain plug. The electrically actuated tank contents gauge is operated from a transmitter unit fitted to the fuel tank. Fuel is transferred from the tank to the engine fuel system by an electrically operated pump. The tank to engine fuel line arrangement is not identical on all models and, on relevant vehicle types, incorporates emission control equipment which is covered in **Chapter 4, Section 4**.

The vehicles covered by this manual are fitted with one of the following quite distinctly different fuel systems.

Fuel injection pump (FIP) models:

In this system a Bosch mechanical fuel injection pump delivers an individually metered quantity of fuel to each cylinder as each inlet valve is due to open. The injection pump receives fuel under pressure from the electrically operated supply pump. The injection pump itself is driven by a toothed flexible belt from the lefthand camshaft and is timed to the engine. The inlet port of each cylinder is provided with a fuel injector and cold starting enrichment is provided separately. Adjustment and servicing procedures are included in **Section 7**.

Continuous fuel injection (CIS) models:

In this system fuel is continuously sprayed into the inlet ports at a metered rate of flow. The engine shown in **Chapter 1, FIG 1** is fitted with this continuous fuel injection system and this illustration identifies the location of certain of the regulators, control units and injection valves which comprise this system. Cold starting enrichment is actuated electrically. Adjustments and servicing procedures are included in **Section 8**.

Digital Motor Electronics fuel injection (DME) models:

1984-1987 models are equipped with a 100% electronic engine control system. The fuel and ignition systems are integrated and the ability to diagnose and repair is limited to a few basic checks and component replacement. Should a problem occur that cannot be rectified by the data provided, the vehicle should be taken to an authorized Porsche dealer.

Intake air:

On all models, intake air is filtered. On certain models the intake air is preheated within a thermostatically controlled range of temperature.

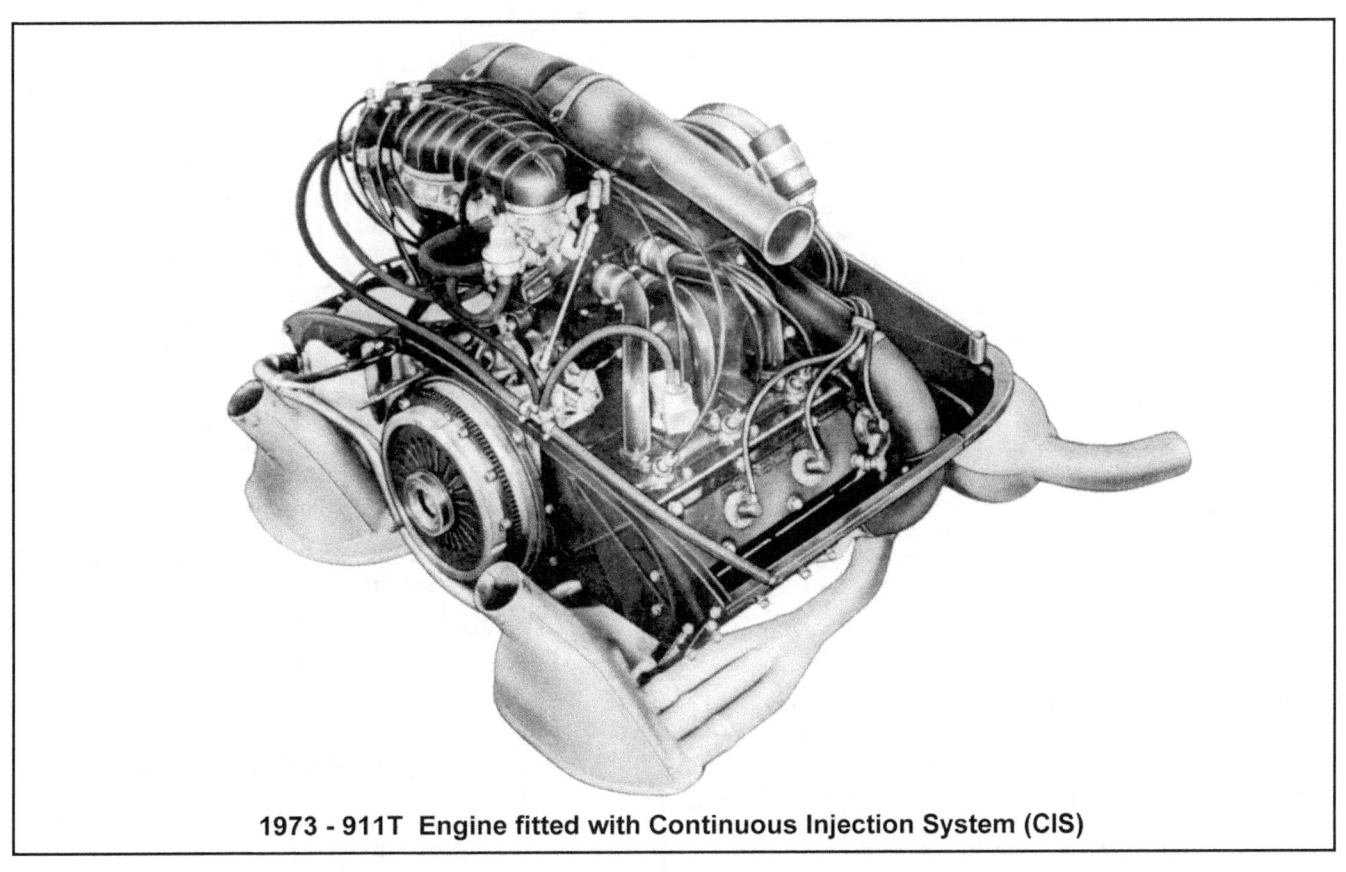

1973 - 911T Engine fitted with Continuous Injection System (CIS)

2 Maintenance

General:

At least every 12,000 miles (20,000km), check over the fuel system pipelines to ensure that all pipes and joints are tight and sound. Lightly lubricate the control pivots and ball joints and, if necessary, adjust the hand throttle control as described in **Section 6**.

Air cleaner:

Every 6000 to 12,000 miles (10,000 to 20,000km) depending upon how dusty the terrain in which the vehicle is operating may be, clean or renew the air filter element as described in **Section 3**.

Fuel filter:

If fitted, renew the in-line fuel filter every 12,000 miles (20,000km). Refer, if necessary, to **Section 4**.

FIP and CIS models:

Refer to **Section 7** or **8** for idling speed, CO content adjustments, drive belt tensioning and other procedures.

3 Air cleaner and preheater

Air cleaner element:

Access to the element is achieved by releasing the spring clips or the flexible straps and removing the cover from the canister. In the case of a dry type element, lift out the element and dislodge the accumulated dust by tapping lightly and blowing off with compressed air. Renew the element after two or three cleanings or if it is torn or damaged in any way. In the case of an oil wetted type element, wash off the contaminated oil film in petrol, dry thoroughly and re-wet the element with clean engine oil. Allow excess oil to drain off. In both cases, clean the interior of the canister before refitting the element and the canister cover.

Air preheater:

The preheater unit which controls the temperature of the intake air thermostatically is not fitted to all models. A cross-section through the unit is shown in **FIG 1**. Air flap 1 is controlled by the throttle linkage. Air flap 2 is controlled by the thermostat 3 which begins to close the hot air flap at 45°C (112°F) and opens the air bypass duct which it closes in the hot air position. At 50°C (122°F) the hot air flap should be fully closed. The throttle control linked air flap 1 starts to open at a throttle valve position of approximately 20° and is fully open at full throttle.

Adjustment of air flap 1, if necessary, is carried out with the throttle valve in the idling speed position. Release the locknut, adjust the lever actuating roller tappet so that the roller just touches the cam on the throttle valve lever and retighten the locknut.

No procedures are prescribed for the repair or renewal of the thermostat by an owner and, should the unit be defective, a complete new or exchange replacement preheater assembly should be fitted.

4 Fuel filter

FIP and CIS models:

If necessary, refer to **Sections 7** or **8** for the location of the in-line filter. A disposable-type filter cannot be cleaned and must be replaced by a new unit. Ensure that the new filter is fitted the correct way round. In the case of filters which have renewable elements, ensure that the correct new element is obtained.

5 Fuel pump

FIP and CIS models:

From 1971 onwards the fuel pump is located in the engine compartment. FIP equipped models have two fuel lines connected between the tank and the pump. These are the fuel supply (suction, marked **S**) and the pressure relief (marked **R**) line. The third pump connection is the fuel delivery line to the engine fuel system. Pumps fitted to CIS models have two connections only, the suction and the delivery.

No procedures are prescribed for the repair or overhaul of a fuel pump by an owner and, if a pump should be defective, it must be removed and a new or an exchange replacement pump fitted. Since pumps are not identical on all models, ensure that the replacement pump obtained is the same type as that removed.

Removal and fitment:

Disconnect the battery earth leads. Identify and disconnect the leads from the pump. Remove the mounting retaining nuts up to 1975 models and withdraw the pump and its mounting bracket (see **FIG 2**). Loosen the clamp which retains the pump to the bracket and remove the bracket. Uncouple the pipes from the pump and blank off the pipes and pump connections to preclude loss of fuel and/or ingress of dirt.

On 1976 models, remove the guard, unscrew the retaining clip and pull the pump downwards. Pinch the intake hose with a clamp to prevent flow when disconnected. Disconnect the electrical leads. Remove the hollow bolt from the delivery hose and collect draining fluid. Loosen the intake hose clip and remove the hose and pump.

Fitment is the reverse of this sequence. Coat the pump electrical terminals with lithium grease to suppress corrosion. Ensure that the rubber boot is correctly fitted.

On 1976 models note the following points:

The hollow bolt must be fitted with new sealing washers, the thicker washer between the banjo coupling and the pump body, and the thinner washer under the head of the bolt. Torque tighten the hollow bolt to 1.6 to 2.3kgm (11.5 to 16.5lb ft).

Position the pump with the top terminal inclined backwards about 35° and secure with the clip. Finally, check that the pipe connections are tight and free from leaks.

6 Controls

Hand throttle control:

When the hand throttle control is fully 'open', the engine speed should be between 3500 and 3800rev/min with the engine at full operational temperature. Adjustment, if required, is made at the nipple arrowed **A** in **FIG 3**. Access requires the cover to be lifted. Ensure that in the 'off' position the hand throttle does not affect the idling speed.

The procedure for dismantling the control is included in **Chapter 11, Section 8**. On reassembly, reset the pivotal friction of the lever by tightening nut **B** until a load of 6kg (13lb) applied at the clevis pin hole and at right angles to the below-floor lever is required to move the lever in its pivot.

Foot control:

Keep the pivots lightly lubricated and ensure that in the released position the control does not influence the idling speed. An adjustable stop is provided to limit the fully depressed position of the foot pedal.

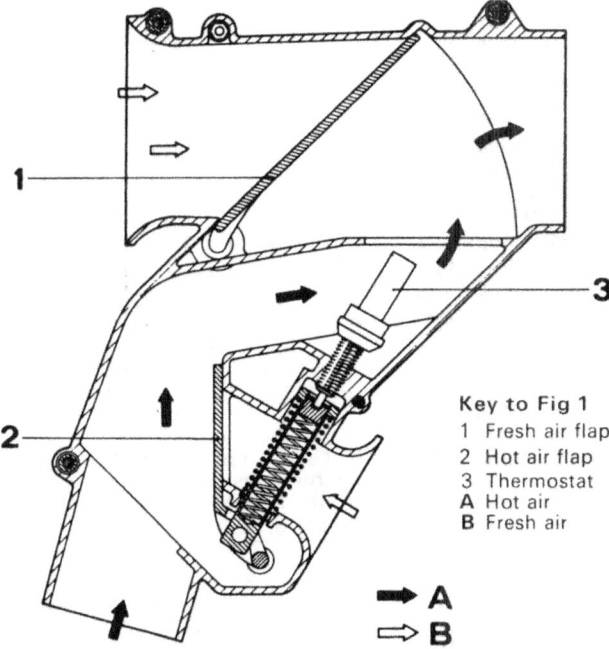

FIG 1 Cross-section through air pre-heater

Key to Fig 1
1 Fresh air flap
2 Hot air flap
3 Thermostat
A Hot air
B Fresh air

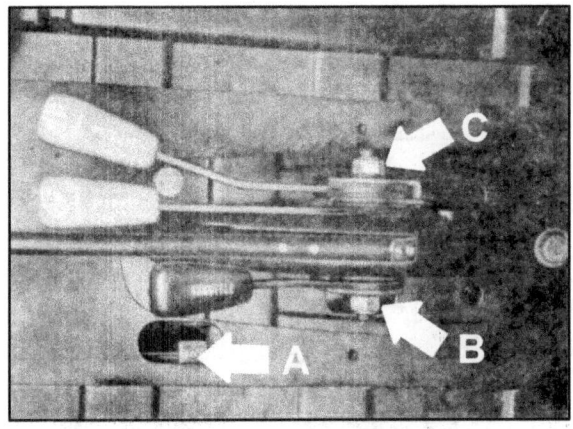

FIG 3 Hand controls

Key to Fig 3
A Hand throttle control adjuster
B Friction adjustment nut (hand throttle)
C Friction adjustment nut (heater controls)

7 Bosch fuel injection (FIP)

The layout of the mechanical fuel injection pump system is shown diagrammatically in **FIG 4**. An electrically operated pump draws fuel from the tank and delivers it to a filter. Filtered fuel passes to the engine driven injection pump. Excess fuel from the electric pump and from the injection pump is returned to the tank. A metered quantity of fuel is delivered every other engine revolution to an injection nozzle at each inlet port.

Key to Fig 4

1 Fuel pump (supply)
2 Fuel tank
3 Fuel filter
4 Cold start enrichment solenoid
5 Injection valve
6 Injection line
7 Injection pump
8 Cold start enrichment hose

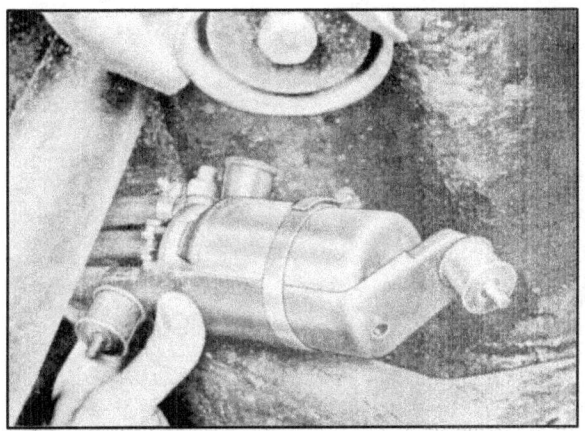

FIG 2 Pump and mounting bracket

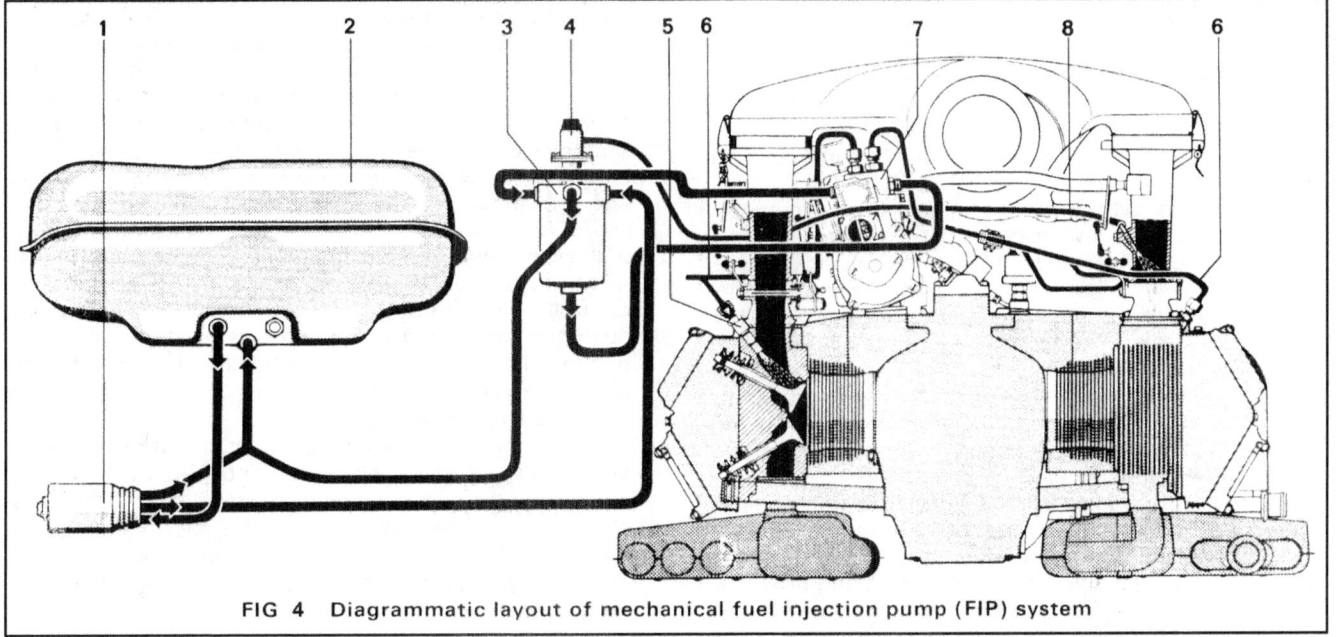

FIG 4 Diagrammatic layout of mechanical fuel injection pump (FIP) system

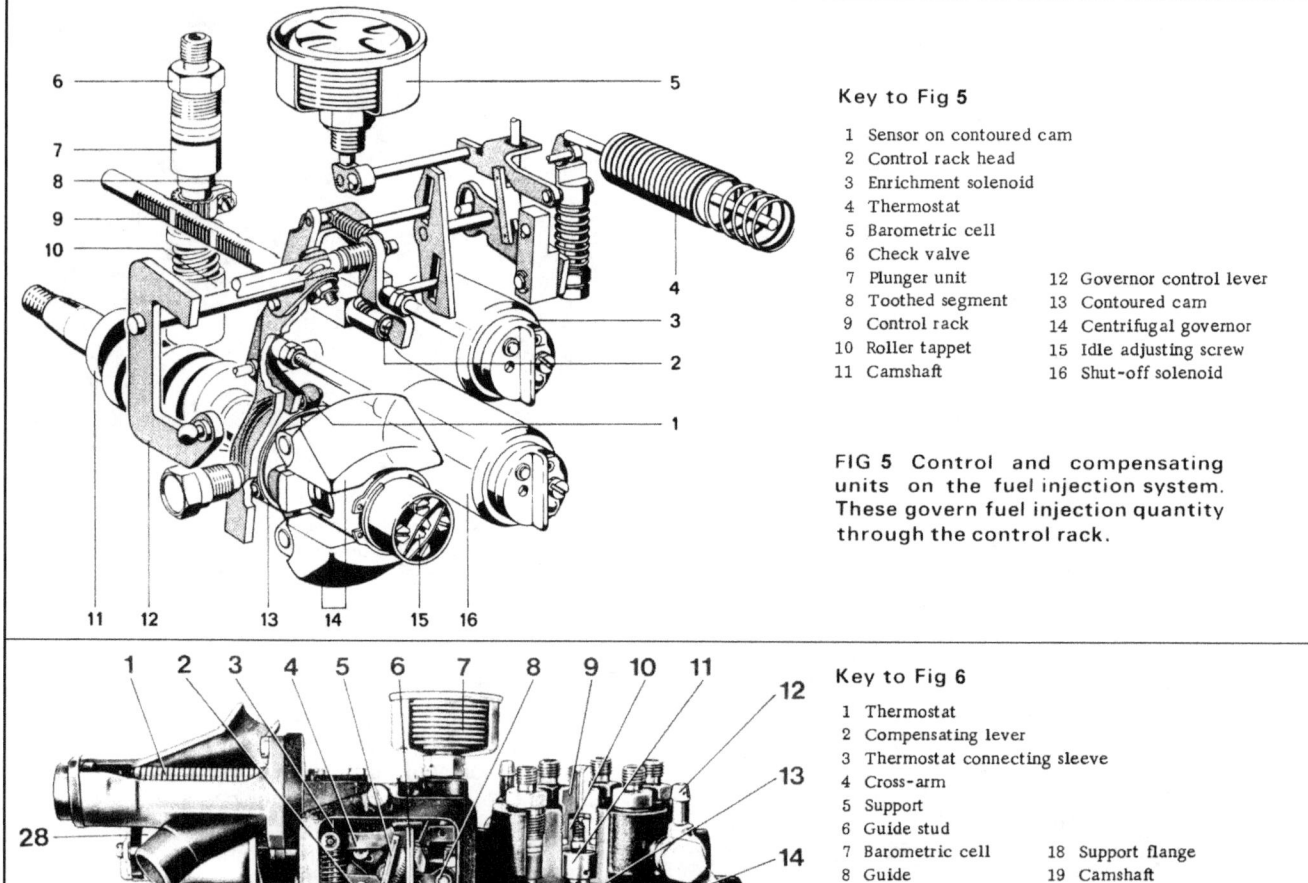

Key to Fig 5

1. Sensor on contoured cam
2. Control rack head
3. Enrichment solenoid
4. Thermostat
5. Barometric cell
6. Check valve
7. Plunger unit
8. Toothed segment
9. Control rack
10. Roller tappet
11. Camshaft
12. Governor control lever
13. Contoured cam
14. Centrifugal governor
15. Idle adjusting screw
16. Shut-off solenoid

FIG 5 Control and compensating units on the fuel injection system. These govern fuel injection quantity through the control rack.

Key to Fig 6

1. Thermostat
2. Compensating lever
3. Thermostat connecting sleeve
4. Cross-arm
5. Support
6. Guide stud
7. Barometric cell
8. Guide
9. Injector line fitting
10. Check valve
11. Plunger unit
12. Fuel inlet
13. Toothed segment
14. Plunger spring
15. Engine oil return
16. Engine oil inlet
17. Pump drive wheel
18. Support flange
19. Camshaft
20. Roller tappet
21. Contoured cam spring
22. Contoured cam
23. Sensor
24. Centrifugal governor weight
25. Idle speed adjustment
26. Shut-off solenoid
27. Access to control rack head
28. Enrichment solenoid

FIG 6 Cutaway view of fuel injection pump

Injection pump:

This is illustrated in **FIG 6**. The compensating parts shown in **FIG 5** may also be seen in this view, together with the pump camshaft 19, the roller tappets 20, the injection plungers 11 and toothed segments 13 which engage with the rack to control the volume of fuel injected.

There are six cylinders and plungers 11, the plungers being reciprocated by roller tappets operated by the camshaft. The plungers may be turned by the rack, and as they are provided with cut-off lands, timing of fuel inlet duration to the pumping cylinder is obtained. The plunger land acts as an inlet valve in conjunction with a port in the side of the cylinder. Fuel is forced from the pump cylinders into pipelines connected to the injectors in the engine cylinder heads. At a pressure of 220 to 265 lb/sq in, check valves in the injector nozzles open and fuel is sprayed onto the opening inlet valves.

Since no procedures are prescribed for the repair or overhaul of the injector pump by an owner, details of its components and construction are not applicable to this manual but it is relevant to refer to **FIG 4** and note that the datum of the fuel control rack is barometrically corrected for atmospheric pressure. Injector pump delivery pressure is of the order of 17kg/sq cm (240lb/sq in). The injector nozzles have check valves but do not have any metering function. The injector pump is driven at half engine speed from the forward end of the lefthand camshaft by a toothed belt. It is timed to the crankshaft so that each fuel injection is delivered just as the inlet valve is about to open. The timing datum of the control rack is set to suit the length of the delivery pipes (they are all of the same length) and corrected for engine speed by the governor shown in **FIG 4**. The shut-off solenoid is controlled by a throttle valve actuated microswitch and an engine speed transducer and cuts off injection during overrun. The injector pump is lubricated from the engine lubrication system with which it is connected by an oil feed and a return pipeline.

Cold starting enrichment is automatic and is provided via a solenoid valve which is controlled by time-limit and temperature-limit switches so that cold starting enrichment through separate nozzles is provided over a two-second period or for longer at lower temperatures. The cold starting thermostat responds to engine cooling air temperature.

Idling speed adjustment:

The following procedure assumes that the valve clearances are correctly set (see **Chapter 1, Section 2**), that the ignition system and sparking plugs are in good order, that the ignition timing is correct and has been stroboscopically checked and that the engine has been run up to normal operating temperature.

1 Close the hand throttle. Refer to **FIG 7** which shows one of the six adjustable air screws. Adjust these screws by small and equal amounts (clockwise to reduce idling speed and vice versa) until the engine is running at 850 to 950rev/min.
2 Run the engine at 1600 to 2000rev/min and, using synchrometer P235 (or equivalent), readjust the air screws as necessary to give substantially equal air flow to each cylinder. Recheck the idling speed.
3 Check and adjust, if necessary, the idling fuel mixture as described later. This may affect the idling speed; if it does, repeat operation 2.
4 Repeat operations 2 and 3 until the idling speed and the CO content of the exhaust gases are simultaneously within the stated limits.

Idling mixture adjustment:

Exhaust gas content measurement equipment is required. The adjustment procedure differs slightly between earlier and later models which have an access hole in the cooling air upper shroud. The spring loaded adjuster is shown in **FIG 8**. In the case of later models, use tool P230c as shown in **FIG 9**.

Adjustment is carried out with the engine stationary.

Earlier models:

With the idling speed set as described earlier, check the exhaust gas CO content. This should be within the range of 2.5 to 5.5% over an air intake temperature range of 15°C (60°F) to 40°C (104°F) proportionately. If outside this range, fit tool P230b to the adjuster, push the adjuster inwards until it engages and, turning clockwise to enrich the mixture or vice versa, make the relevant adjustment. Do not adjust by more than one notch before restarting the engine and rechecking the CO content at idling speed. If adjustment by three notches in either direction does not bring the CO content within limits, have the basic range of the injector pump reset by a Porsche agent.

Later models:

Check that the CO content at idling speed is within the following limits:

Operation in the USA	2.0 to 3.0%
Operation in Europe	2.5 to 3.5%
Carrera 2.7 litre models	2.0 to 3.0%

Turn the adjuster clockwise to enrich the mixture and vice versa. Do not adjust by more than one notch before rechecking the CO content at idling speed. If adjustment by three notches in either direction does not bring the CO content within limits, have the basic range of the injector pump reset by a Porsche agent.

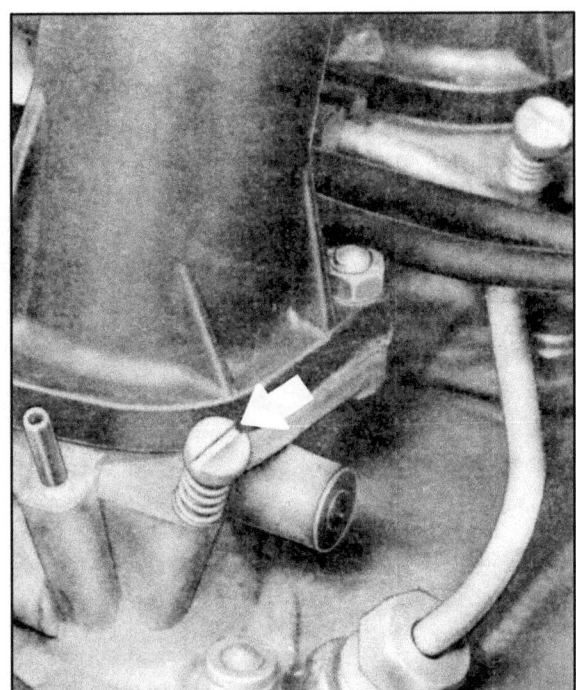

FIG 7   One of the six adjustable air screws is arrowed

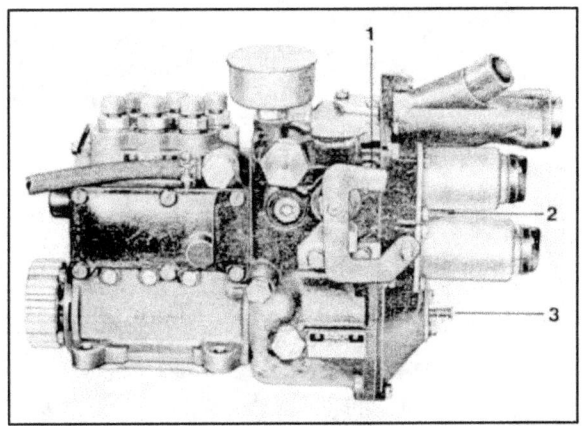

FIG 8   Fuel injection pump mixture adjustment points
1 8mm bolt   2 Allen screw (access to control rack head)
3 Idle speed mixture adjuster

FIG 9   Adjusting the idle speed mixture (later models)

FIG 10   Microswitch adjustment
Key to Fig 10   A Locknut   B Adjuster screw

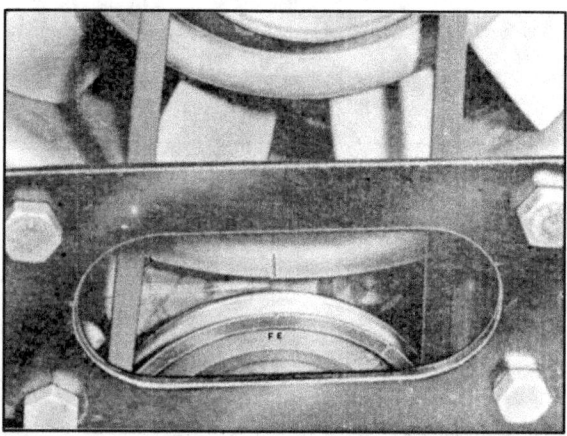

FIG 11   The F-E mark on the crankshaft pulley

FIG 12   The F-E mark on the injection pump pulley (viewed by using a mirror)

Microswitch adjustment:

Adjustment is necessary if the throttle valve linkage or the injector pump linkage has been disturbed.

1 Refer to **FIG 10** and loosen locknut A. Back off the adjuster screw B until there is a small gap between the microswitch plunger and the adjuster screw.
2 Slowly turn the adjuster screw clockwise from this position until the microswitch just closes (listen for the click sound).
3 Turn the adjuster screw clockwise by a further $\frac{1}{4}$ turn. Retighten the locknut.

Removing the injector pump:

1 Disconnect the earth straps from both batteries. Remove the air cleaner. Turn the crankshaft to bring the piston of No 1 cylinder (lefthand rear) to the TDC of its exhaust stroke. Continue turning in the direction of engine rotation to bring the crankshaft pulley F-E mark into alignment with the notch on the cooling fan casing as shown in **FIG 11**.
2 Identify and disconnect the wiring from the microswitch, the enrichment and the cut-off solenoids. Uncouple the thermostat warm air hose.
3 Disconnect the six injection pipelines, the fuel inlet and return lines, the oil feed and return lines and the linkage between the guide shaft and the governor. Using special tool P120b, remove the pump retaining nuts.
4 Push the toothed belt off the pump wheel and, unless the engine is being dismantled, secure it so that it does not disengage from the camshaft wheel. Taking care not to handle the pump by the barometric cell, lift out the pump.

Refitting the injector pump:

1 Lay the pump on its side and pour 300cc ($\frac{1}{2}$ pint) of clean engine oil into the oil return pipe orifice (top hole).
2 Set the pump to its F-E mark (when the pump is in position this may be checked by mirror as shown in **FIG 12**). Then set the crankshaft as described in operation 1 of the pump removal sequence and as shown in **FIG 11**.
3 Install the pump and fit the retaining nuts loosely. Fit the toothed belt. Push the pump sideways using tool P234b until the belt is tensioned correctly (6 to 8mm (0.25 to 0.33in) deflection at the centre of the belt under thumb pressure). Tighten the retaining nuts fully.
4 Refit the fuel and oil lines. Reconnect the wiring to the solenoids and the microswitch. Refit the warm air hose to the thermostat housing.

8 Bosch fuel injection (CIS) 1973-1975

The layout of the continuous injection system is shown in **Chapter 1, FIG 1** and in **FIG 13**. An electrically driven pump draws fuel from the tank and delivers it via an accumulator and filter to the fuel mixture control/distributor unit from which metered fuel (depending upon the control pressure) is piped to the injection valves. An injection valve is positioned adjacent to the inlet valve of each cylinder. Excess fuel is returned to the tank. Cold starting enrichment is provided by a supplementary injection of fuel into the intake manifold.

The accelerator pedal is coupled to the throttle valve and the continuous injection fuel supply is controlled by the throttled rate of air flow which lifts the sensor plate accordingly. The sensor plate lever is pivoted and counterbalanced and in contact with the control plunger of the mixture control/distributor unit. It finds a position in which the forces from the air flow, the controlled fuel pressure acting on the plunger and the counterweight are in balance. At this position the fuel flow is correct for the throttled rate of air and the engine load condition.

During initial running after starting, enrichment is provided for a limited period. This is controlled by the warm running compensation pressure regulator in which either the gradual warming up (electrically) of a bi-metal control gradually reduces the control pressure and cuts out the enrichment, or by an intake manifold depression controlled valve which operates similarly. Excess fuel is then returned to the tank. The throttle actuated pressure regulator operates similarly but controls the pressure of the fuel in relation to the throttle opening. Excess fuel is returned to the tank. The auxiliary air device opens at high manifold depression (overrun conditions) and, by admitting additional air, maintains a combustible mixture and prevents excessively high levels of CO content in the exhaust gases.

The function of the fuel accumulator is to accommodate the initial pressure surge when the pump starts up and so prevents the mixture control/distributor unit control plunger from being loaded before control pressure has built up. It also serves as a reservoir to maintain adequate pressure for a short time when the engine is switched off and so prevents vapour locks in a warm engine.

Since specialised experience and equipment are needed for diagnostic investigation of malfunctioning, the procedures prescribed for action by owners are limited. No procedures are prescribed for the repair or overhaul of defective CIS units by an owner and units which have been diagnosed as defective by a Porsche agent should be removed and replaced by new or exchange replacement units. Where relevant, removal and fitment procedures are described later.

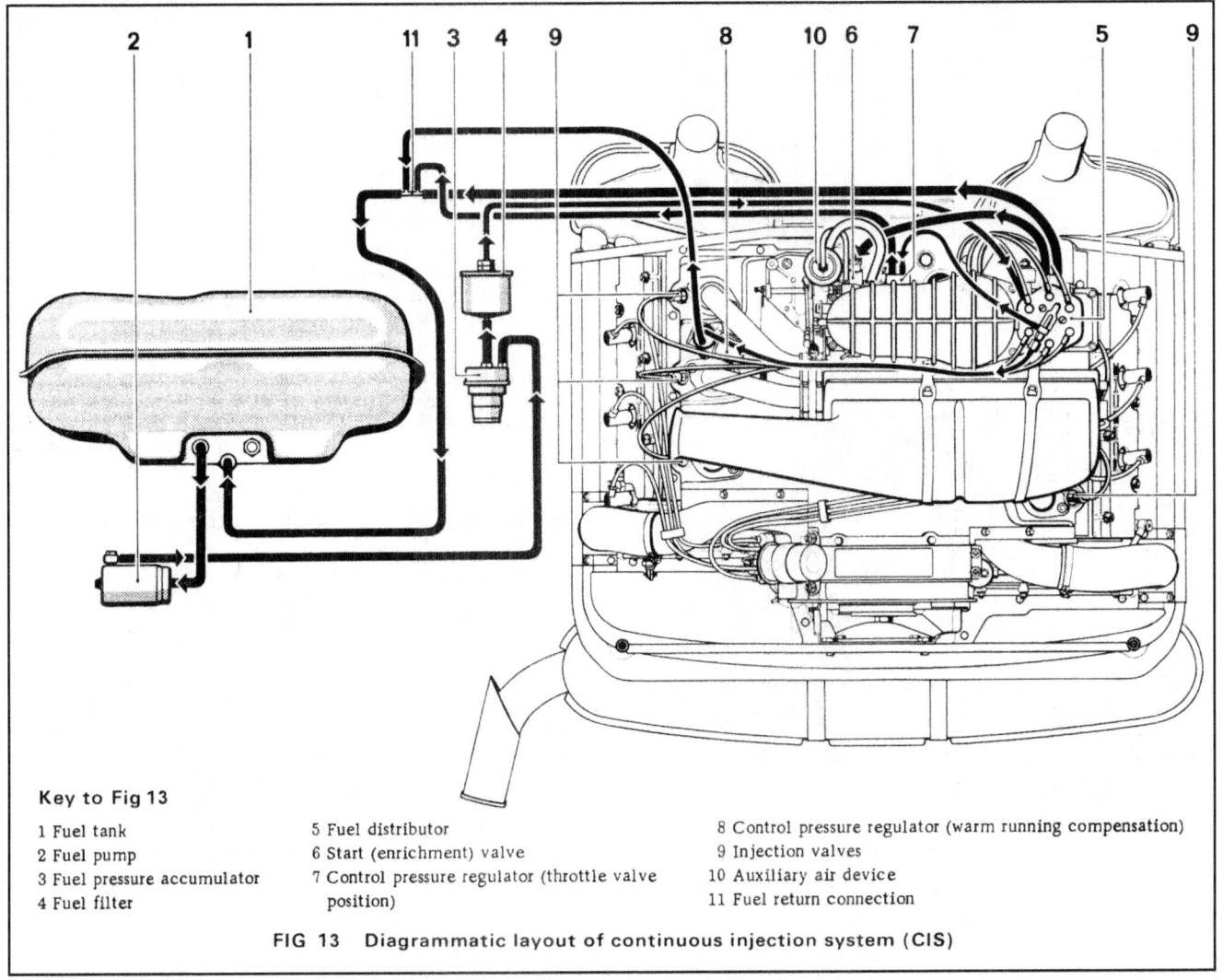

Key to Fig 13

1 Fuel tank
2 Fuel pump
3 Fuel pressure accumulator
4 Fuel filter
5 Fuel distributor
6 Start (enrichment) valve
7 Control pressure regulator (throttle valve position)
8 Control pressure regulator (warm running compensation)
9 Injection valves
10 Auxiliary air device
11 Fuel return connection

FIG 13 Diagrammatic layout of continuous injection system (CIS)

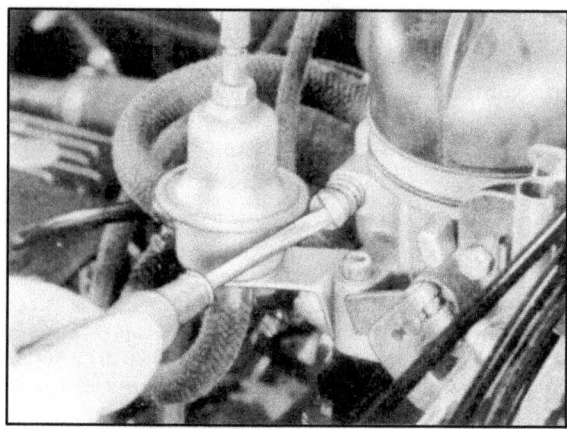

FIG 14 Adjusting the air bypass screw

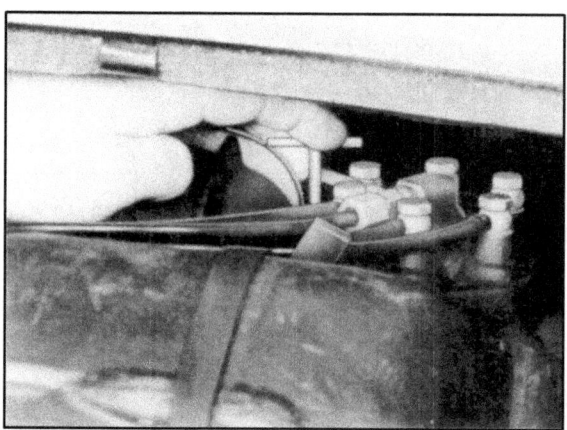

FIG 15 Adjusting the idling speed fuel mixture

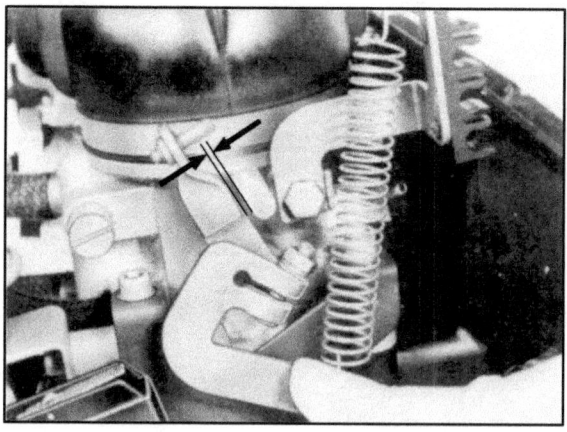

FIG 16 Full power throttle position

Adjusting idling speed and fuel mixture:

1 Run the engine up to normal operating temperature. Close the hand throttle fully and switch off the engine. Remove the filter element from the air cleaner. Connect in the exhaust gas CO content tester.
2 If an emission control air injection system is fitted, uncouple the air delivery hose at the air pump and blank off the open end of the hose.
3 Start up the engine and refer to **FIG 14**. By turning the air bypass screw as shown in the illustration, adjust the idling speed to between 850 and 950 rev/min in the case of manual transmission models or to between 900 and 1000rev/min the case of Sportomatic transmission models. If difficulty is experienced in setting the idling speed, check for a defective auxiliary air device as described later.
4 Refer to **FIG 15** and, after withdrawing the blanking off plug, insert fuel mixture adjusting tool P377 as shown. Turning the tool clockwise will enrichen the mixture and vice versa.
5 Without exerting downwards pressure upon the adjusting tool (this will cause the engine to stall), turn the tool in the relevant direction by extremely small amounts until the exhaust gas CO content is within the limits quoted in operation 6.
6 If more than $\frac{1}{2}$ turn of the adjuster in either direction is required, consult a Porsche agent as a malfunction should be suspected. The adjusted CO content of the exhaust gases should be within the following limits for the relevant model:

1973 (2.4 litre models)	1.5 to 2.0%
1974 (2.7 litre models)	1.5 to 2.0%
1975 USA models	1.7 to 2.2%
California	1.5 to 2.0%
European models	2.0 to 2.5%
1976 USA models (air pump disconnected)	2.0 to 4.0%
European models	1.0 to 1.5%
1977 European models	1.0 to 1.5%
USA models, California and high altitude States with air pump disconnected	1.5 to 3.0%

7 Repeat operations 3 and 5 until the idling speed and exhaust gas CO content are both within the ranges specified. Disconnect the CO tester, reassemble the air cleaner and, if relevant, refit the hose to the air pump.

Adjustment of full power throttle position:

When the accelerator pedal is fully depressed, the throttle linkage must be so adjusted that there is a minimum clearance of 1.0mm (0.04in) at the position which is indicated in **FIG 16**.

Microswitch adjustment:

On relevant models refer to **FIG 17**. Identify and disconnect both wires from the microswitch. Connect a battery and buzzer or battery and test light to the microswitch connections so that when the switch is closed the buzzer will sound or the test light will come on. Position a 2mm (0.08in) feeler gauge between the idle stop and the throttle valve lever as shown in the illustration.

Turn the adjuster screw as shown until the buzzer or the test light is off. Turn the adjuster back just to the on position of the switch. Remove the feeler gauge and close the throttle valve. Check that there is still at least 0.5mm (0.02in) clearance in this position. Check that with the hand throttle fully open, the microswitch is in the on position. Disconnect the test wiring and reconnect the operational wiring.

Auxiliary air device:

With the engine at normal operating temperature, note the idling rev/min. Stop the engine and remove the air cleaner element. Refer to **FIG 18** and disconnect the hose (see arrow) leading to the auxiliary air device at the throttle valve. Tightly seal off both the connection and the hose. Refit the air cleaner element and cover. Recheck the idling speed. If the idling speed has changed, the auxiliary air device is leaking and a new unit should be fitted.

Bleeding the fuel lines:

The system must be bled (prior to attempting to start the engine) whenever a fuel line or a component of the fuel system has been reconnected. Proceed as follows.

Remove the air cleaner element. Switch on the ignition so that the fuel pump runs. Refer to **FIG 19**. Press the air sensor lever upwards briefly so that the fuel lines are filled and the injection valves are heard to spray fuel.

Refit the air cleaner element and cover.

Sensor lever free movement:

If sluggish movement of the sensor lever is suspected, carry out the following check. Remove the air cleaner element and, with the ignition switched **off**, raise the lever by hand as indicated in **FIG 19**. An even resistance should be felt through the full range of movement and, on removing the pressure, the lever should drop without resistance (leaving the correctly sluggish control plunger to follow).

Sensor plate/venturi position:

Depressurise the system by spilling fuel from the pressure lines at the accumulator and at the connection arrowed A in **FIG 19**. The upper edge of the sensor plate should now be flush with the bottom of the venturi upper taper or, at most, 0.5mm (0.020in) below this point. The flexible stop may be adjusted by carefully bending the wire bow arrowed B in **FIG 19**. From April 1976 production this wire bow has been replaced by an adjusting screw.

Mixture control removal and fitment:

The mixture control/distributor unit is 25 in **FIG 1 Chapter 1** and 5 in **FIG 13**. Disconnect the fuel lines from the unit. Remove the six Allen type retaining bolts and lift off the unit and its gasket. Take care that the control plunger does not slide out.

When refitting, use a new gasket and finally bleed the system.

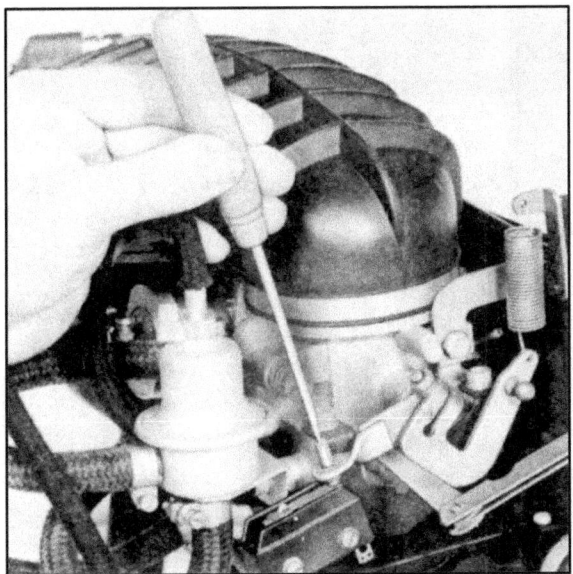

FIG 17   Microswitch adjustment

FIG 18   The auxiliary air device

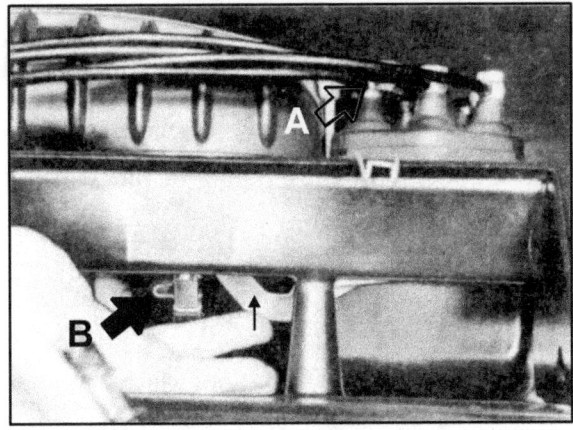

FIG 19   Bleeding the system and checking the sensor lever movement   Key to Fig 19

A Fuel feed to mixture control/distributor unit   **B** Wire bow

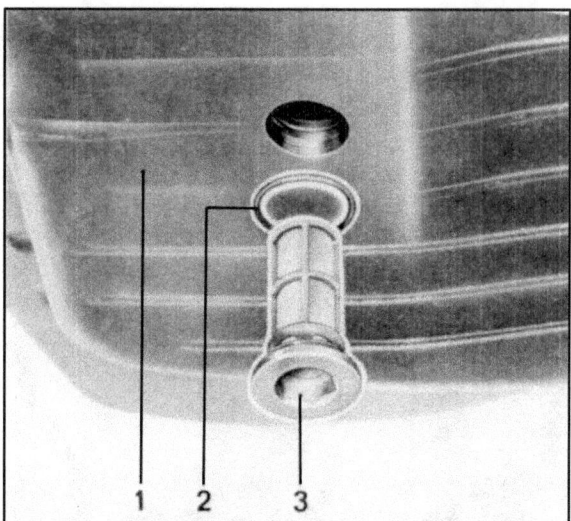

FIG 20 Fuel tank filter (CIS models)

Key to Fig 20   1 Fuel tank   2 Gasket   3 Filter plug

FIG 21 Fuel accumulator. Connections are arrowed

Throttle control pressure regulator removal and fitment:

This regulator is 2 in **FIG 1 Chapter 1** and 7 in **FIG 13**. Disconnect the fuel lines. Remove the Allen type bolts and withdraw the throttle valve housing and regulator. Remove the two Allen-type bolts and separate the regulator from the throttle housing.

Refitting is the reverse of this sequence. Ensure that the housing 'O' ring is correctly positioned. Bleed the system and have the control pressure checked and adjusted by a Porsche agent.

Warm running compensating pressure regulator removal and fitment:

Electrically controlled unit:

This regulator is 5 in **FIG 1 Chapter 1** and 8 in **FIG 13**. Disconnect the earth strap from both batteries. Identify and disconnect the wiring from the regulator. Uncouple the fuel lines. Remove the Allen-type retaining bolts. Dismount the unit.

Vacuum controlled unit:

Disconnect the battery and the warm air intake connection. Release fuel pressure by loosening the central connection at the mixture control unit, soak up escaping fuel with rag, and retighten the connection. Remove the air pump and filter. Remove left and right heater hoses, undo the heater blower clip and swing the blower upwards. Disconnect all connections to the regulator, unscrew the Allen screws and lift off the regulator.

Ensure the bottom of the regulator and holding plate are clean on refitment to ensure proper ventilation and torque tighten the hollow banjo bolt to 1.1kgm (8lb ft).

On completion of refitment, bleed the system.

Cold start enrichment valve removal and fitment:

This valve is 4 in **FIG 1 Chapter 1** and 6 in **FIG 13**. Disconnect the earth strap from both batteries. Dismount the auxiliary air device (10 in **FIG 13**. Before disconnecting, identify the disposition of the connector. Remove the Allen-type retaining bolts, withdraw the valve and uncouple the fuel line.

On refitment ensure that the 'O' ring is correctly seated and that the electrical connector is the correct way round. Bleed the system.

Fuel filter removal and fitment:

The filter is retained by an encircling clamp which, on refitment, must not be overtightened or the filter body may be deformed.

Fuel tank filter plug:

This unit is shown in **FIG 20**. The frequency of cleaning this filter will depend upon the standards of cleanliness of the fuel supplies in the country in which the vehicle is operating. On refitment of the filter plug use a new gasket 2 and torque tighten the plug to 0.8 to 0.9kgm (5.8 to 6.5lb ft).

Pressure accumulator removal and fitment:

This unit is shown in **FIG 21**. It is retained by an encircling clamp and is fitted between the pump and the in-line filter. To dismount, loosen the mounting clamp, withdraw the unit and uncouple the fuel pipes.

On completion of refitment, bleed the system.

Injection valve removal and fitment:

Uncouple the line from the injection valve and fit tool P384. Pull out the valve. Check that the rubber bushing is in good order.

To refit, push in the valve and make sure that the rubber bushing is seated below the bulge in the support sleeve. Refit the pipeline and bleed the system.

Plastic fuel lines:

To remove an unserviceable plastic fuel line, use a soldering iron, heat the fuel line in the connector area and pull off the hose.

Use tool P385 to fit new plastic hose to a connector allowing the push-on section to protrude from the tool. Push the **dry and unlubricated** hose onto the connector.

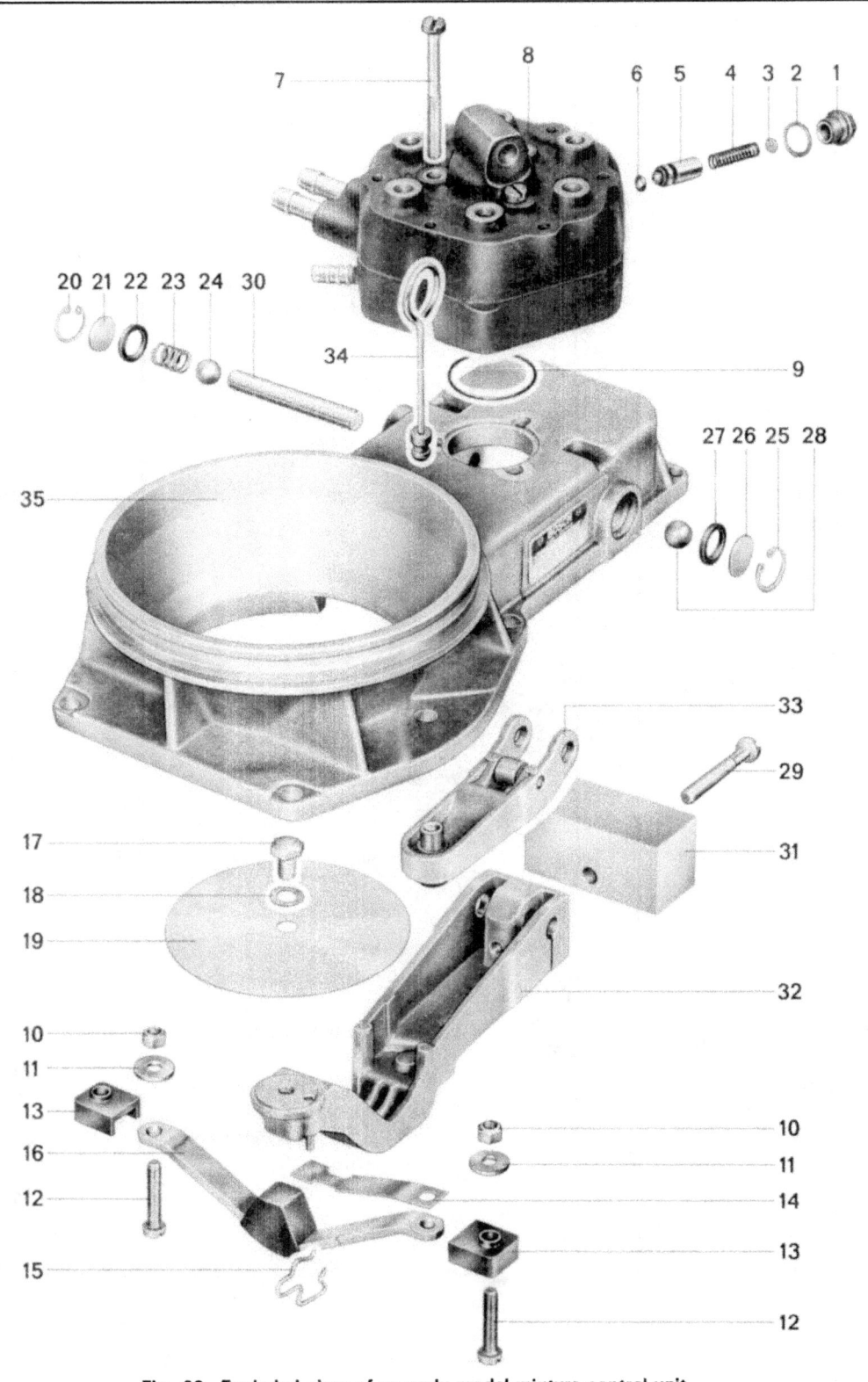

Fig. 22 Exploded view of an early model mixture control unit

1 Plug	10 Nut	19 Sensor plate	28 Ball
2 Seal A 10 x 13.51	11 Washer	20 Circlip	29 Capscrew
3 Shim	12 Capscrew	21 Cover	30 Pin
4 Spring	13 Insulator	22 Seal	31 Counterweight
5 Piston	14 Spring	23 Spring	32 Operating lever
6 Seal	15 Clip	24 Ball	33 Follower
7 Capscrew M 5 x 50	16 Stop	25 Circlip	34 Plug
8 Fuel distributor	17 Hex head screw	26 Cover	35 Air flow sensor housing
9 Seal	18 Washer	27 Seal	

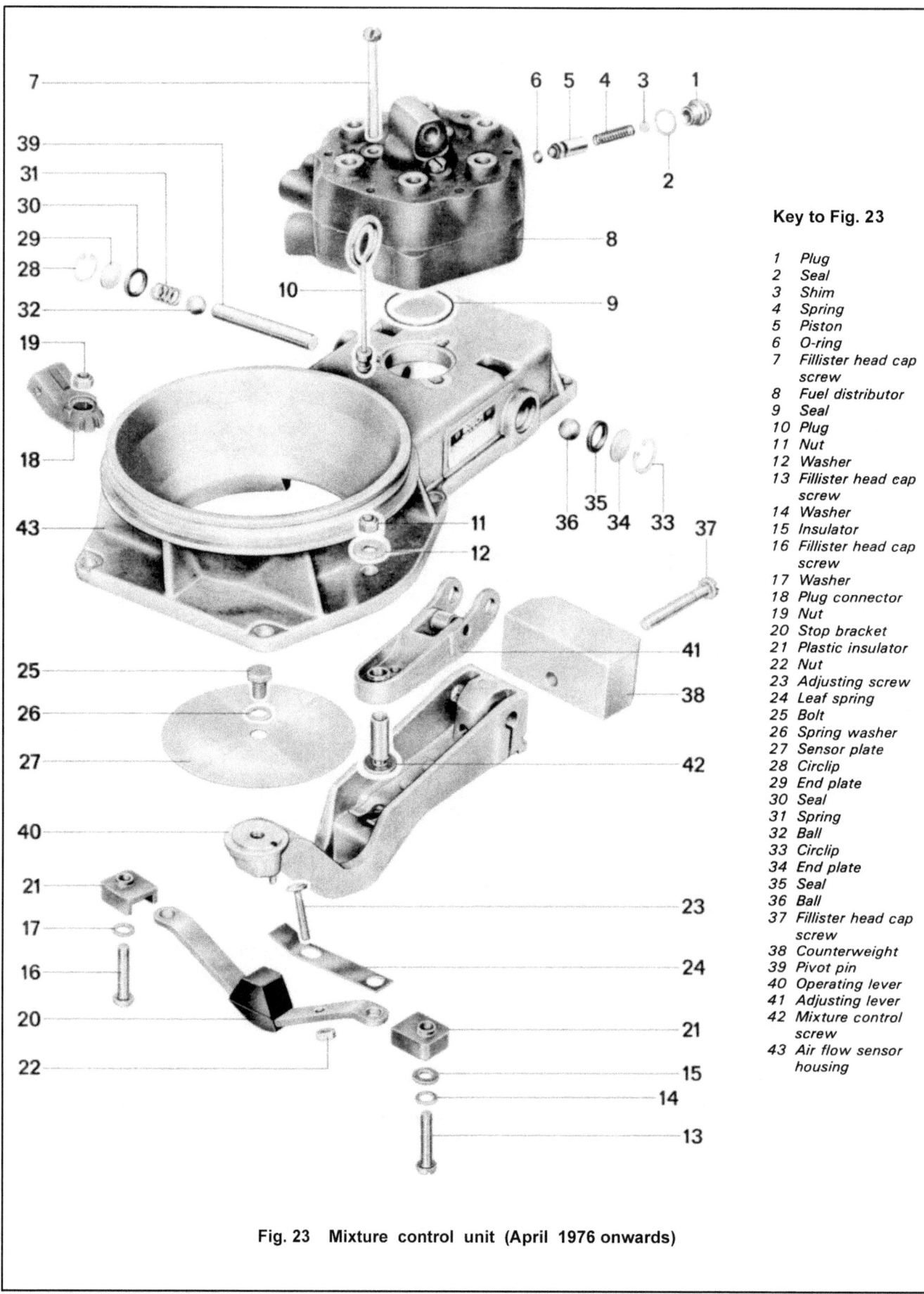

Fig. 23 Mixture control unit (April 1976 onwards)

Key to Fig. 23

1 Plug
2 Seal
3 Shim
4 Spring
5 Piston
6 O-ring
7 Fillister head cap screw
8 Fuel distributor
9 Seal
10 Plug
11 Nut
12 Washer
13 Fillister head cap screw
14 Washer
15 Insulator
16 Fillister head cap screw
17 Washer
18 Plug connector
19 Nut
20 Stop bracket
21 Plastic insulator
22 Nut
23 Adjusting screw
24 Leaf spring
25 Bolt
26 Spring washer
27 Sensor plate
28 Circlip
29 End plate
30 Seal
31 Spring
32 Ball
33 Circlip
34 End plate
35 Seal
36 Ball
37 Fillister head cap screw
38 Counterweight
39 Pivot pin
40 Operating lever
41 Adjusting lever
42 Mixture control screw
43 Air flow sensor housing

Bosch fuel injection (CIS) 1976-1983 models

Mixture control unit (Figs. 22 and 23)

Remove and replace :

1 Disconnect the negative lead from the battery.

2 Loosen and remove the banjo bolts on the fuel distributor and set them aside. Make careful notes on the location of each banjo fitting.

3 Remove the control pressure line which enters at the center of the fuel distributor.

4 Remove the fuel feed line and the fuel return line by loosening and removing the banjo bolts and banjo fittings on the sides of the fuel distributor.

5 Catch the escaping fuel in a container and wipe up all spilled gasoline.

6 Detach the plug on the air flow sensor housing (if equipped).

7 Remove the socket head screws and lift out the mixture control unit.

8 Installation is the reverse of the removal procedure with the following points which must be observed.

9 All banjo fittings must be rebuilt using new seals (soft metal washers).

10 The mating surface between the mixture control unit and the air flow sensor housing requires a new O-ring.

11 The joint between the air flow sensor housing and the air box requires a new gasket.

12 Torque the socket head screw to 7 ft-lb (1.0 m-kg).

13 Torque the banjo bolt on the fuel feed line to 7 ft-lb (1.0 m-kg).

14 Torque the banjo bolt on the fuel return line to 7 ft-lb 1.0 m-kg).

15 Torque the adapter for the control pressure line to 11 ft-lb (1.5 m-kg).

16 Torque the banjo bolts on the fuel control to injector lines to 7 ft-lb (1.0 m-kg).

Overhaul (Refer to Figs. 22 and 23) :

1 The mixture control unit consists of the fuel distributor and the air flow sensor unit.

2 Place the 'bend' of the operating lever in the protected jaws of a vise, with the venturi end of the air flow sensor housing at the top and facing you.

3 Remove the sensor plate and its mounting bolt.

4 Open the jaws of the vise slightly and place the air flow sensor housing on top of the jaws with the operating lever hanging between the vise jaws.

5 Remove the screws which hold the fuel distributor to the air flow sensor housing.

6 Take the fuel distributor in your hand and invert the entire mixture control unit. Remove the fuel distributor by twisting gently to break the seal between it and the air flow sensor housing. These pieces must remain inverted until the two units have been separated to prevent the control piston from falling out. If the control piston is dropped it must be replaced with a new one.

7 Lift out the control piston and set aside. (Fig. 24)
Remove the air flow sensor housing O-ring and dispose of it. It must be replaced with a new one. (Fig. 25)

8 Remove the plug from the adjusting screw (idle screw) access hole in the air flow sensor housing.
Refer to **Figs. 22, 23 & 26** - With the air flow sensor housing placed on a bench, operating lever up and the venturi facing away from you, loosen the lock nut on the left-hand end of the stop bracket.

9 Remove the self locking nut and plain washer. Use a new self-locking nut when rebuilding.

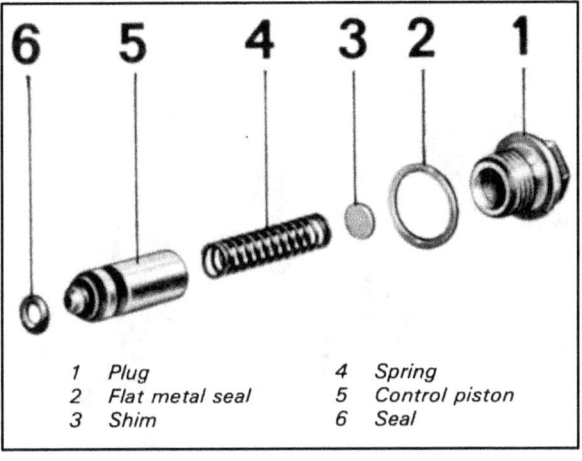

1 Plug
2 Flat metal seal
3 Shim
4 Spring
5 Control piston
6 Seal

Fig. 24 Control piston components

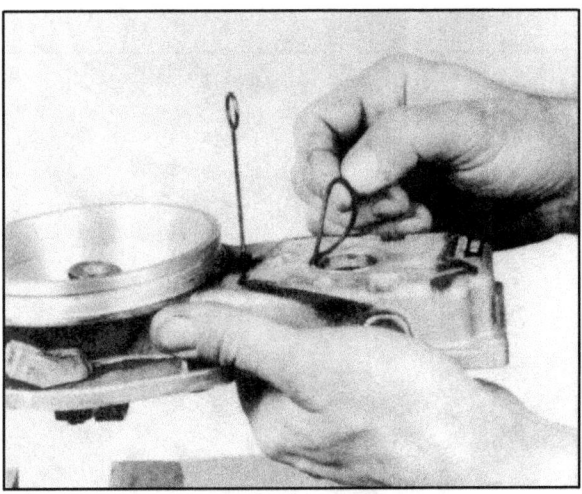

Fig. 25 Removing the old O-ring from the air flow sensor unit

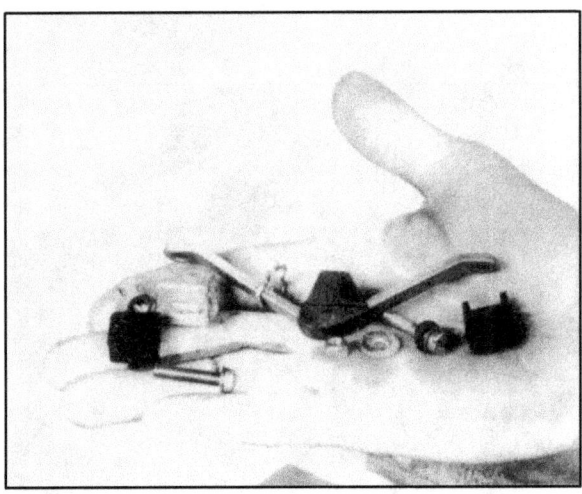

Fig. 26 Components of the stop bracket which must be removed

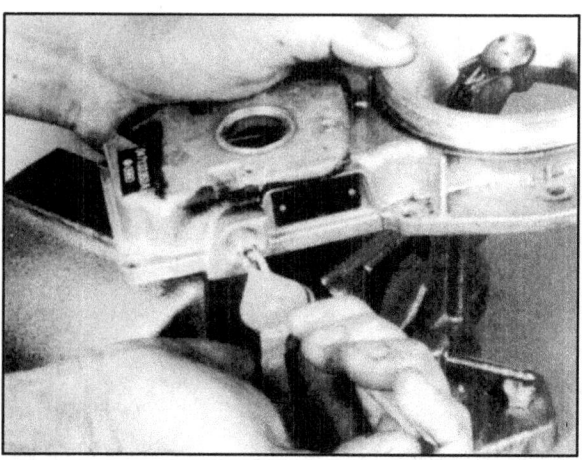

Fig. 27 Removing the circlip on the pivot shaft boss

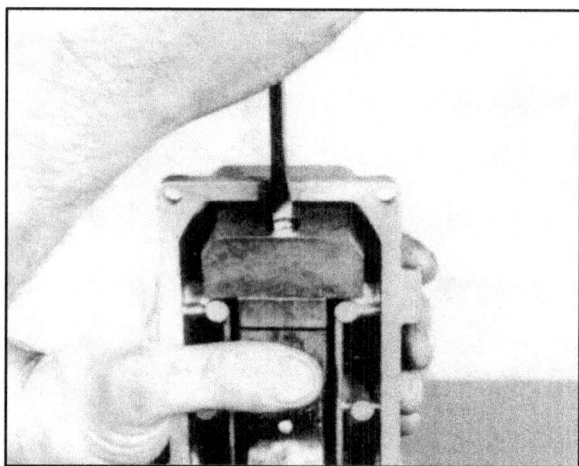

Fig. 28 Removing the counterweight bolt from the operating lever

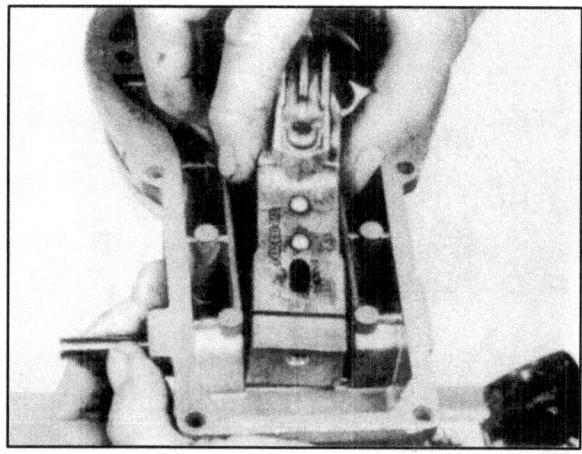

Fig. 29 Lift out the operating lever pivot shaft

10 From the bottom side of the air flow sensor housing (the side which is now facing you), remove the bolt, plain washer, insulator plate, and the insulator block. There is a protective sleeve which fits into the bore of the insulator block. This should be removed if it does not come out with either the insulator block or bolt.

11 Remove the nut and plain washer or nut and plain washer connector from the right-side bolt.

12 From the bottom, remove the bolt, plain washer, and sleeve.

13 Remove the stop bracket, leaf spring, and clip (some models use an adjusting screw in place of the clip) then remove the insulator block.

14 With the air flow sensor housing still laid on its top and the air flow sensor venturi facing away from you, remove the clip from the round boss at the right side of the casting. Carefully extract the clip as the plug it holds down is spring loaded (Fig. 27)

15 Remove the flat end plug, seal, and ball from the right side.

16 Remove the clip from the left side boss and remove the flat end plug, seal, spring and ball.

17 Press the operating lever down at the venturi end to gain access to the screw on the end of the counterweight. Remove the screw and counterweight, then gently press out the shaft on which the operating lever rides. (Figs. 28 and 29)

18 If the operating lever pivot shaft cannot easily be pressed from the air flow sensor housing, turn the adjusting screw on the pivot lever two turns clockwise, then four turns counter-clockwise if the tension on the pivot is not eliminated by the latter action. Turning the pivot screw in this manner will determine which way relieves the tension on the pivot shaft.

19 Holding the operating lever with the threaded boss at the end away from you, turn the adjusting screw clockwise until the two levers can be separated. (Figs. 30 and 31)

20 Inspect the pivot shaft for gouging and radial marking.

21 Inspect the air flow sensor housing venturi for roundness and make sure there are no nicks, gouges, or any other damage to the interior surface of the venturi.

22 Inspect the pivot arm for proper play in the needle bearing, the condition of the bearing needles, and the condition of the adjusting screws' socket and threads. Replace parts as necessary.

23 Inspect the air flow sensor plate for warpage and make sure that the central hole is round. Check carefully around the central bolt hole for evidence of overtightening (grooves around the central hole and 'wavy' appearance of the metal.

24 Assembly of the mixture control unit is the reverse of the strip down with the following items to be observed:

25 The circlips on the ends of the pivot arm must be installed with the sharp-edged side facing outward. This is for both circlips, one on each side, ahead of the end plates.

26 Torque the screw on the counterweight to 4 ft-lb (0.5 m-kg).

27 Torque the screws which hold the stop bracket to the air flow sensor housing to 4 ft-lb (0.5 m-kg).

28 When the air flow sensor plate is installed and located properly in the venturi of the air flow sensor housing (see section on **Positioning air flow sensor plate**). torque the center bolt to 4 ft-lb (0.5 m-kg). (Fig. 32)

29 The joint between the fuel distributor and the air flow sensor housing requires a new O-ring seal. Do not re-use the old one.

30 The screws holding the fuel distributor to the air flow sensor housing must be torqued to 3 ft-lb (0.35 m-kg).

31 Further reassembly instructions are found in the previous **Mixture control unit** section.

Fuel distributor inspection and assembly :

1 The following procedures can only be performed when the fuel distributor has been removed from the air flow sensor housing. Disconnecting all fuel lines and removing the fuel distributor from the vehicle is also necessary.

2 Screw all banjo bolts into their proper holes and wipe down all surfaces of the fuel distributor. Make sure that the control piston has been removed and set aside. Do not drop the control piston; if it has been dropped, it must be replaced with a new one.

3 Remove all of the banjo bolts and clean them separately to further assure that no dirt enters the fuel distributor.

4 Remove the plug from the boss alongside the fuel return and remove the flat metal seal, shim, and spring.

5 Remove the control piston from this hole by tapping the open hole gently on the palm of your hand. If this fails to dislodge the piston, a tapered wooden dowel should be used to remove it. The tapered dowel should be of a soft wood so it may be forced in for a snug fit without damaging the bore of the hole.

6 Remove the O-ring from the end of the piston with a fingernail. Do not use any metal objects for this purpose. (Fig. 24)

7 Further disassembly of the fuel distributor should not be attempted. Porsche dealers do not have any of the proper internal parts available to them, nor do they have the training or tools to assist you in work beyond this point. If, after disassembly, cleaning and testing, the fuel distributor is still found to be giving unacceptable performance, it must be replaced with a new one.

8 Inspect the bore of the fuel distributor which houses the pressure regulating piston for scoring and scratching.

9 Inspect the rubbing surfaces of the piston for signs of excessive wear, scratching, and scoring. Replace if necessary.

10 With fingernails only, install a new O-ring on the tapered part of the piston. Be careful not to damage the piston. (Fig. 24)

11 Install the spring on the piston, lubricate the O-ring with a light coating of gasoline and install the piston in the bore.

12 Place the shim in the 'cup' of the plug.

13 Install a new metal seal on the plug. Do not re-use the old one.

14 Install the plug in the fuel distributor body and torque to 9 to 11 ft-lb (1.3 to 1.5 m-kg).

15 Check the pressure of the system when the fuel distributor is reinstalled. The pressure may be raised by adding shims between the spring and thick shim.

Preliminary mixture control adjustment:

1 With the mixture control unit installed, after replacement of the operating lever, the fuel lines must be bled. Disconnect the injectors and place them in an appropriate container. Press on the sensor plate many times by hand. Remove the plug, (see **Figs. 22** or **23**) and turn the mixture control screw, using the proper tool, one or two turns in the counter-clockwise direction.

2 Turn the ignition on and remove the plugs from the safety switch on the fuel pump relay or the air flow sensor.

3 Screw the mixture adjustment screw in the clockwise direction until the injectors just barely eject fuel.

4 Turn the screw counter-clockwise one-half turn.

5 Install the injectors.

6 Adjustments to the fuel injection system require the use of expensive equipment not readily available to the home mechanic. It is therefore recommended that these fine adjustments be carried out by a Porsche dealer or competent repair shop.

Positioning air flow sensor plate:

1 Depressurize the system by slowly loosening the pressure line connection at the pressure regulator. Place a rag over the line to catch any fuel that may spill.

2 Check that the upper edge of the sensor plate is flush with the base of the taper. The plate should be no lower than 0.0197 in (0.5 mm) below the base of the taper. See **Fig. 32**.

3 If an adjustment is required, an adjusting screw is installed on the stop bracket through the leaf spring on models produced after April of 1976. Previous models can be adjusted by bending a wire clip (**Fig. 19**) securing the leaf spring to the stop bracket.

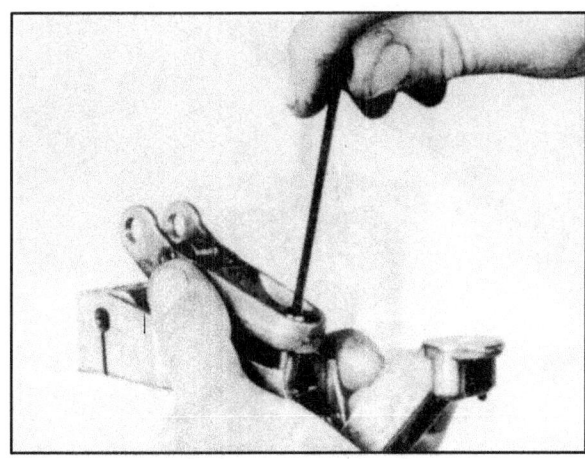

Fig. 30 Loosening the adjusting screw

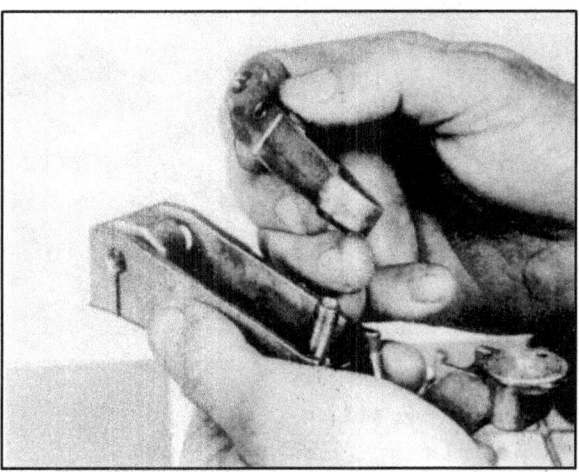

Fig. 31 Separating the pivot lever from the operating lever

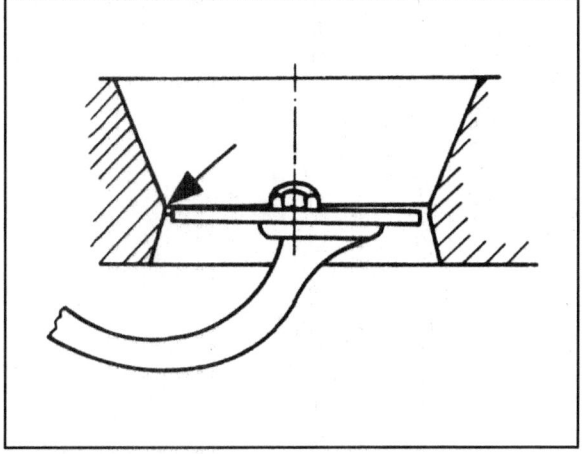

Fig. 32 Position the upper edge of the sensor plate flush with the base of the taper (arrow)

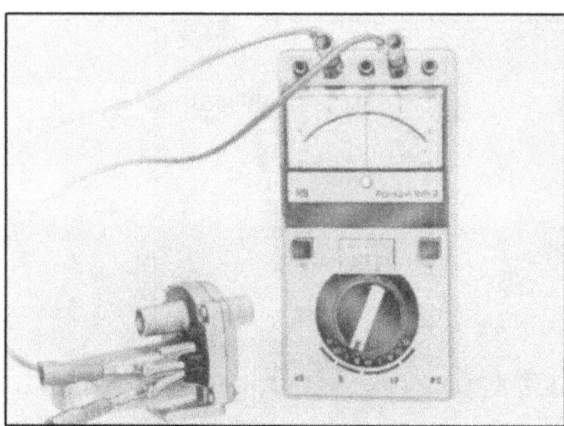

Fig. 33 Test the auxiliary air regulator with an ohmmeter

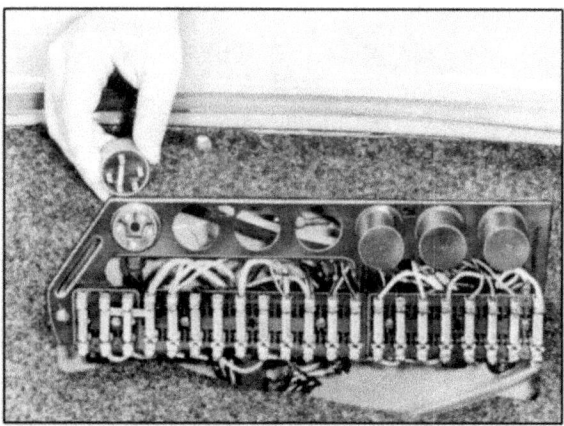

Fig. 34 Fusebox and relay panel in the luggage compartment

Fuel pump remove and replace :

1 Disconnect the negative cable from the battery.
2 Remove the guard.
3 Slightly pull the fuel pump down after loosening the strap.
4 Pinch the intake fuel hose shut and remove the pressure fuel hose banjo bolt.
5 Separate the electrical connections from the fuel pump.
6 Disconnect the intake fuel hose from the fuel pump connection loosening the hose clamp.
7 Lift away the fuel pump.
8 Installation is the reverse order of removal but make sure to install new seals on the banjo bolt of the pressure hose. The thick seal goes between the coupling and the pump body and the thin seal goes between the coupling and the head of the banjo bolt.
9 Connect the electrical leads to the correct terminals of the fuel pump. Pull the rubber cover over the electrical connections and position the pump so the upper terminal faces the rear about 35°.
10 Tighten the strap securely.
11 Connect the intake hose and remove the pinch clamp. Check the connections for leaks.
12 Install the guard and reconnect the battery negative lead.

Automatic choke :

1 If the engine speed does not increase at cold engine temperatures or the engine speed remains high when the engine is warmed up, either the auxiliary air valve or the auxiliary air regulator are defective.
2 Remove the top control line from the auxiliary air valve and plug it.
3 Start the engine. If the problem is fixed, replace the auxiliary air valve as described in **Chapter 4** (Emission Controls). If there is no change, the auxiliary air valve is good.
4 With the engine cold, if the engine speed remains slow the auxiliary air regualtor is bad.
5 Warm up the engine and disconnect a hose from the auxiliary air regulator and plug both openings.
6 If the speed drops, the auxiliary air regulator is defective. If the speed is too high, the auxiliary air valve is defective.
7 Remove the auxiliary air regulator as described in **Chapter 4** (Emission Controls), and connect an ohmmeter to both terminals. The ohmmeter should register approximately 33 ohms. **(Fig. 33)**
8 Test the auxiliary air regulator's power supply. Remove the rearmost relay (relay with the red cover) from the fuse box in the luggage compartment **Fig. 34**.
9 Attach a jumper wire between terminals 87a and 30 (refer to wiring diagram) and turn the ignition on.
10 Check for continuity at both auxiliary air regulator terminals, which the plugs have been pulled from, with a test lamp.

NOTES

9 Digital Motor Electronics (DME) fuel injection system 1984 onwards

Fuel filter replacement:

1 Disconnect the negative battery cable.
2 Locate the fuel filter. It is in the engine compartment on the left side, next to the ignition coil. (Fig. 35)
3 Using two flare nut wrenches of the correct size, detach the fuel lines, not forgetting to rap a rag around the fitting to catch escaping fuel.
4 After both fuel lines have been removed, loosen the clamp and take off the fuel filter.
5 Install the new filter. Note the direction of flow (arrow facing in the correct direction) before inserting the filter in the clamp.
6 Tighten the retaining clamp and reinstall the fuel lines on the filter.
7 Reconnect the negative battery cable.
8 Start the engine and check fuel lines as well as fuel filter for leaks.

Air filter replacement:

1 Disconnect the cover retainers and take off the housing cover with filter cartridge.
2 Remove the filter cartridge and clean the inside of filter housing with a lint free cloth.
3 Install the new filter cartridge with the arrow on the housing cover pointing to the arrow on the filter cartridge (plates in horizontal position). The filter cartridge is also marked with the word TOP. (Fig. 36)

Idle speed adjustment:

1 Run engine to operating temperature (oil temperature approximately 90°C).
2 Connect a tachometer following the manufacturer's instructions.
3 Check the idle speed.
4 If correction is necessary you must first stop the function of the idle volumetric control.
5 Locate the test socket on the engine central electric board in the engine compartment on the left side (Fig. 37).
6 Bridge test jacks B and C with a jumper wire. This stops the function of the idle volumetric control.
7 To adjust the idle speed turn the control screw (bypass) on the throttle housing until the specified speed is reached (Fig. 38).
8 Remove the jumper wire from the test jack.
9 Recheck adjustments, correcting if necessary.

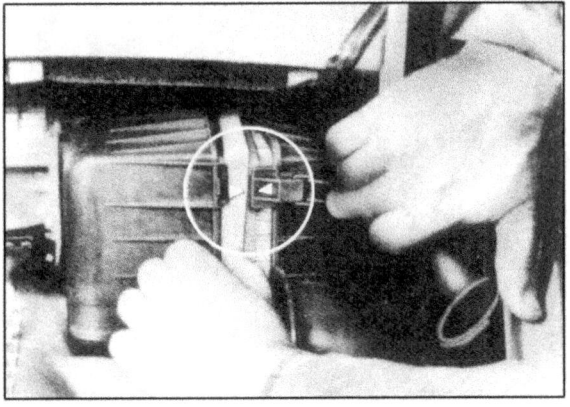

Fig. 36 When reinstalling the air filter make sure the aligning arrows are facing each other

Fig. 37 The test jack is located in the fender wall next to the ignition coil

Fig. 35 Fuel filter hose connections and hold down bolt

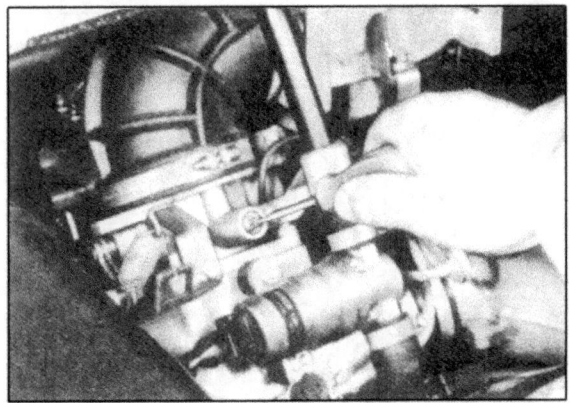

Fig. 38 The idle adjusting screw is located in the side of the throttle housing

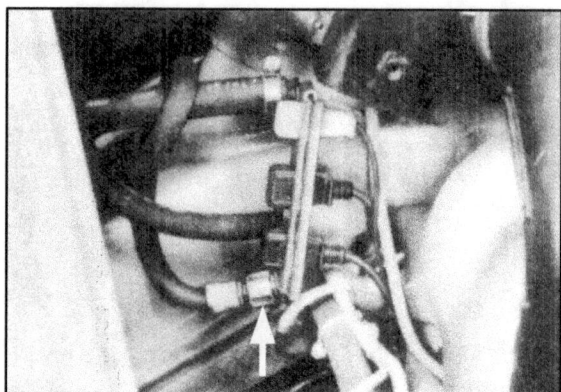

Fig. 39 Location of the fuel return hose (arrow)

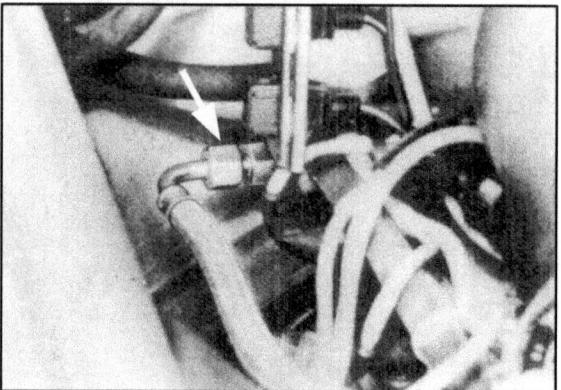

Fig. 40 With the test hose connected to the fuel return connection (arrow) the pump can be tested

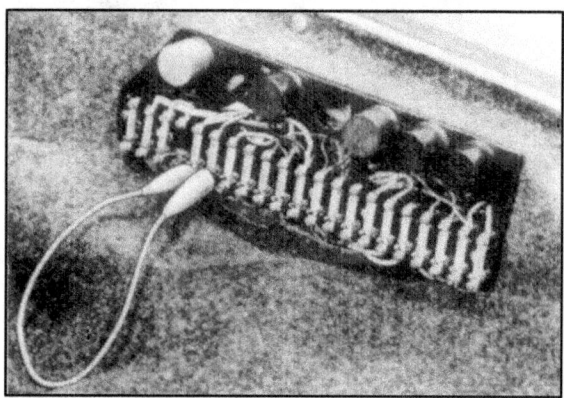

Fig. 41 Using a jumper wire bridge terminals 16 (fuel pump) and 17 (terminal 30) at the fuse block

Fig. 42 When removing the test cap (arrow) watch for the sealing ball inside

Fuel pump

Checking fuel pump delivery rate:

Note: *This test requires the use of a specially made hose, consisting of 1.5 meter low pressure fuel line with an NW6 elbow hose nipple and 14 X 1.5M connection threads. Also required is a measuring glass of at least 850 cc capacity.*

1 Unscrew fuel return hose on branch, (Fig. 39) not forgetting to counterhold the fitting with another wrench. Use a rag around the fitting to catch any escaping fuel.

2 Connect the test hose to the fuel branch. (Fig. 40)

3 Hold the end of the test hose in the measuring glass.

4 At the fuse box, bridge fuses 16 (fuel pump) and 17 (terminal 30) on inlet side of fuse box with a piece of wire. The fuel pump should now run. (Fig. 41)

5 Let the fuel run into the measuring glass for 30 seconds, then disconnect the jumper wire.

6 The fuel pump should deliver at least 850 cc in 30 seconds.

7 If the fuel amount is insufficient, check for a clogged fuel filter or clogged or kinked fuel lines. If no apparent reason can be found the fuel pump may be defective.

Checking fuel pressure:

Note: *In order to preform this test a fuel pressure gauge of at least 40 psi will be needed with a compression fitting with M 14 X 1.5 connection threads.*

1 Unscrew and remove the capped nut on the test connection of fuel distribution line, using a rag wrapped around the nut to catch escaping fuel. **Note:** *Use caution so as not to allow fuel to contact hot engine or electric sparks. Make sure the sealing ball does not fall out when removing the capped nut.* (Fig. 42)

2 Connect the pressure gauge to the test connection. (Fig. 43)

3 Using a piece of wire with two alligator clips attached to the ends, bridge fuses 16 (fuel pump) and 17 (terminal 30) on the inlet side of fuse box. The fuel pump should run. (Fig. 41)

4 The pressure reading should be within specification.

5 If the fuel pressure is low, check all the hoses and fittings for leaks or blockage. If no apparent reason can be found for the low pressure the fuel pump may be defective.

6 After the test is complete remove the gauge, not forgetting to use a rag to catch the fuel, and reinstall the test cap and sealing ball.

Fig. 43 Fuel pressure gauge installed on the test connection

Checking fuel lines and intake hoses :

1 Starting at the fuel filter, inspect all fuel lines and fuel fittings for leaks. (Fig. 44)
2 Check the tightness of all coupling nuts and hose clamps in the fuel and air systems. (Fig. 45)

Fault diagnosis :

DME fuel injection is part of a total electronic engine management system and troubleshooting requires the use of a digital code reader. The DME control unit has the ability to store fault codes relating to both the fuel injection and ignition systems. Any detected faults cause the Check Engine light to illuminate and the appropriate fault codes will be identified and stored for at least 50 engine starts. However, if the positive battery cable or the DME control unit connector is disconnected, the fault code memory will be erased.

The Check Engine light illuminates as a self test whenever the ignition switch is in the on position. After the engine starts, the throttle valve closes, and the Check Engine light should go out. This indicates that there are no fault codes stored in the DME control unit.

Major system failures will cause the Check Engine light to illuminate and remain on until the fault is remedied. In this condition the vehicle will still run but drivability will be poor.

Intermittent failures may also cause the Check Engine light to illuminate or flash and the light may go out if the intermittent fault goes away. However, the corresponding fault code will still be stored in the DME control unit.

Fig. 44 Check all indicated hoses and connections (arrows) for loosness and fuel leaks

Fig. 45 Check all indicated hoses and clamps (arrows) for loosness and air leaks

NOTES

10 Fault diagnosis

It is assumed that the sparking plugs are in good order and that the valve clearances, ignition system and timing, idling speed, etc. are all correctly adjusted and that electrical power is available to all relevant units. Check these basic requirements before consulting the fault diagnosis lists.

Lists (a) to (d) apply to **all models**; (e) to (i) are only relevant to **FIP models** and lists (j) to (n) are applicable to **CIS models** only.

All models:

(a) Insufficient fuel delivered

1 Tank air vent restricted
2 Fuel feed pipe blocked
3 Air leak in feed to fuel pump
4 Fuel filter(s) dirty
5 Fuel pump defective
6 Fuel vapourising in pipeline due to heat

(b) No fuel delivery

1 Check all items in (a)
2 Fuel feed pipe ruptured or disconnected
3 Defective fuel gauge or transmitter (tank empty)
4 Punctured fuel tank (tank empty)

(c) Excessive fuel consumption

1 Leaks at fuel line connections
2 Dirty air cleaner element
3 Excessively high engine temperature
4 Idling speed too high
5 Cold start enrichment not cutting out
6 Brakes binding
7 Tyres under-inflated
8 Vehicle overloaded

(d) Idling speed too high

1 Incorrect adjustment
2 Throttle control sticking
3 Hand throttle incorrectly set
4 Incorrect mixture adjustment
5 Worn throttle valve(s)
6 Worn throttle valve spindle bush(es)
7 Air leaks at manifold joints

FIP models ONLY:

(e) Difficult starting

1 Enrichment solenoid defective
2 Defective relay
3 Thermoswitch defective
4 Control rod setting incorrect

(f) Rough idling

1 Check 1, 4, 5, 6 and 7 in (d)
2 Restricted warm air flow to thermostat
3 Thermostat defective
4 Injection valve(s) defective
5 Compression varies between cylinders

(g) Excessive fuel consumption

1 Check (c); 2 and 3 in (f)
2 Injection pump basic setting incorrect
3 Defective injection pump
4 Linkage incorrectly set

(h) Poor acceleration transition, backfiring

1 Check 2, 3 and 4 in (g)
2 Check synchronisation of throttles

(i) Backfiring on overrun

1 Check 2 in (h)
2 Microswitch requires adjustment
3 Engine speed transducer defective

CIS models ONLY:

(j) Difficult starting

1 Incorrect control pressure
2 Defective cold start enrichment valve
3 Microswitch inoperative
4 Sensor plate datum setting incorrect
5 System requires bleeding

(k) Rough idling

1 Check 1, 4, 5, 6 and 7 in (d); 2 and 3 in (j)
2 Auxiliary air device defective
3 Warm running compensation pressure regulator defective
4 Injection valve(s) defective
5 Excessive difference in injection valve opening pressures
6 Compression varies between cylinders

(l) Excessive fuel consumption

1 Check (c); 2 and 3 in (j); 3 in (k)
2 Mixture control/distributor unit plunger tight
3 Sensor plate lever pivot tight or seized
4 Defective throttle valve control pressure regulator
5 Basic adjustment too rich

(m) Poor performance, backfiring

1 Check 2, 3 and 4 in (l)
2 Check for air leaks after sensor plate venturi position
3 Basic adjustment too weak

(n) Engine 'diesels'

1 Check 3 in (j); 2 and 3 in (l)

CHAPTER 3 - IGNITION

1 Description
2 Maintenance
3 Ignition faults
4 Distributor
5 Capacitive discharge system (CDS)
6 Ignition timing
7 Breakerless ignition 1978-83 Models (CDI)
8 Digital Motor Electronics ignition system (DME)
9 Sparking plugs and HT leads

1 Description

The distributor is driven by 2:1 skew gearing from the rear of the crankshaft (see **Chapter 1, FIG 2**, item 18). HT to the distributor is provided by a capacitive discharge system (CDS) which replaces the ignition coil of the conventional earlier system. CDS provides higher voltage for starting with negligible voltage drop at high speeds and greatly reduced wear of the distributor contact breaker points.

The components of the system are shown in **FIG 1** and a schematic wiring diagram in **FIG 2**. The housing of the CDS unit is made from light alloy, cast with cooling fins to help dissipate heat generated by the system. The voltage transformer looks very similar to a conventional coil, but the resistance, voltage gain ratio and inductivity differ completely and the transformer is designed and constructed to match the electrical characteristics of the CDS unit.

Refer to **FIG 2**. When the ignition is switched on the DC converter 5 increases the battery voltage from 12 volts to 450 volts and charges the storage capacitor 7 through periodic impulses at a frequency of approximately 3000 Hz, which produces a high pitched whistle in the DC converter. When the contact breaker points 3 open the igniter trigger unit 8 releases an impulse to the thyristor base 9 which becomes conductive. The storage capacitor then discharges through the thyristor and the voltage transformer 10, causing a high voltage surge on the secondary side that is carried through the distributor and thence to the sparking plugs. With this system the voltage rise at the sparking plug occurs much faster and current losses, that occur with most conventional systems, are virtually eliminated.

Distributors are not identical for all models and may be of either Marelli or Bosch manufacture. A centrifugally actuated switch is built into all distributors and this automatically limits the maximum engine rev/min which can be attained. All distributors incorporate centrifugal automatic advance/retard of the ignition timing while later models also incorporate automatic vacuum advance/retard in addition.

The firing order on all models is 1, 6, 2, 4, 3, 5.

2 Maintenance

Distributor contact breaker points:

Every 12,000 miles (20,000km), remove the rotor arm, apply a smear of grease to the surface of the cams, check and adjust, if necessary, the contact breaker points to a gap of 0.37 to 0.43mm (0.015 to 0.017in). Check the ignition timing stroboscopically as described in **Section 6**. Adjust if necessary.

The rotor arm on earlier Marelli distributors (not provided with vacuum advance/retard) is retained by two screws (see **FIG 3**) and, on later units (with vacuum advance/retard), by the single screw arrowed in **FIG 4**.

Adjustment of the contact breaker points using a screwdriver and feeler gauges is shown in **FIG 5** for the Marelli distributor and in **FIG 6** for the Bosch distributor.

FIG 1   Components of Capacitive Discharge System
1 CDS unit   2 Ignition voltage transformer   3 RPM sensor

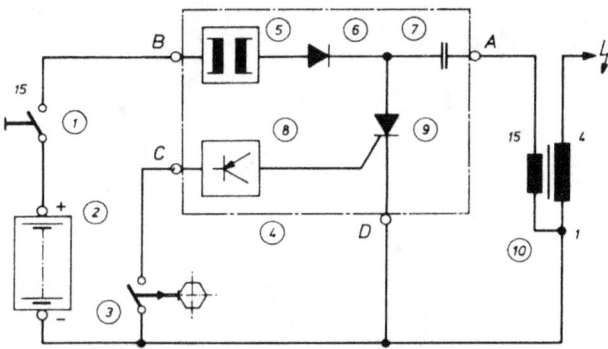

FIG 2   Schematic wiring diagram of CD system

1 Ignition switch
2 Battery
3 Breaker points
4 CDS unit
5 DC converter (amplifier)
6 Rectifier
7 Storage capacitor
8 Ignition trigger unit
9 Thyristor (load-sensitive switch)
10 Ignition voltage transformer

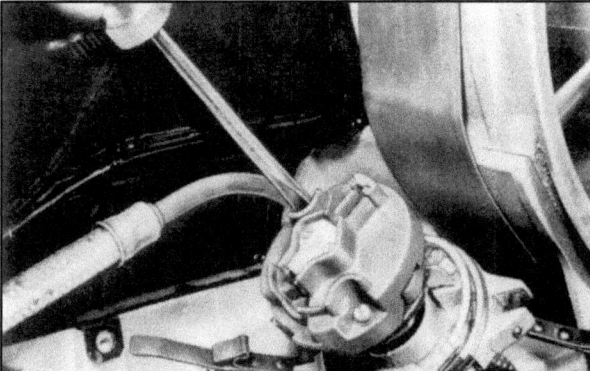

FIG 3   Earlier type Marelli distributor. Removing the rotor arm

FIG 4 Later type Marelli distributor with the rotor arm retaining screw arrowed

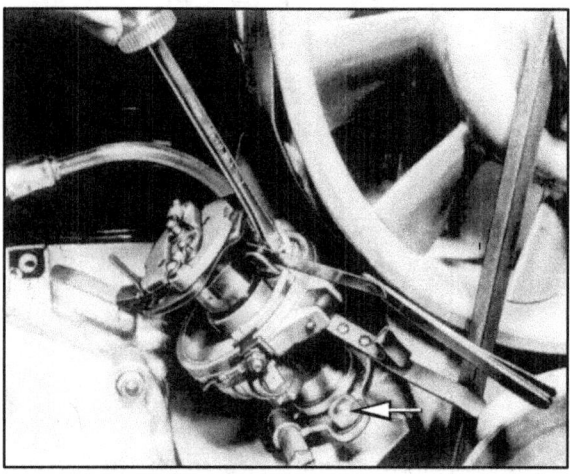

FIG 5 Adjusting earlier type Marelli distributor points gap. The distributor retaining nut is arrowed

FIG 6 Adjusting earlier type Bosch distributor points gap. Loosening fixing screw (left) and checking gap with feelers (right)

Distributor cap and contact breaker:

At regular intervals, remove the cap and clean it thoroughly. The inside surfaces must be clean and dry. Check central brush by pressing it in. It should spring out again. Slight erosion of the brass terminals is normal.

If dirty, clean the contact points with fuel on a cloth. Slight corrosion may be rectified with a fine file, but the mating surfaces must be quite flat and must meet squarely. The best cure for contact breaker troubles is to fit a new set, as described in **Section 4**.

Sparking plugs and HT leads:

Clean the plugs and reset the gaps every 6000 miles (10,000km). The procedure is described in **Section 7**. Depending upon the type of sparking plug in use and upon how hard the vehicle is driven, the fitment of a new set of plugs every 12,000 miles (20,000km) may be desirable.

Keep the HT leads clean and dry at all times and, if new leads are required, ensure that the instructions in **Section 7** regarding their lengths are followed.

3 Ignition faults

If the engine runs unevenly, set the hand throttle to give an engine speed of about 1000rev/min and disconnect and reconnect each HT cable from its sparking plug in turn. Doing this to a plug which is firing properly will accentuate the uneven running but it will make no difference if the plug is not firing. Locate the faulty plug and, taking care not to touch any metal part of the lead while the engine is running, remove the insulator. With the engine running, hold this lead so that the conductor is about 3mm (0.12in) away from the cylinder head. A strong, regular spark will confirm that the fault lies with the sparking plug which should be cleaned or renewed. If, on the other hand, there is no spark, suspect the cable or its connection at the distributor cap.

If the spark is weak and irregular, check the condition of the HT cable and, if it is perished or cracked, renew it. If no improvement results, check the distributor cap. It must be clean and dry. Check that good contact is being made between the centre carbon brush and the rotor arm and that there is no 'tracking' which will show as a thin black line between the electrodes or to a metal part in contact with the cap. 'Tracking' cannot be rectified except by fitting a new cap.

If the contact breaker points are serviceable and the gap is correctly set but there is no spark, use a 0 to 20 range voltmeter and check that there is voltage throughout the LT circuit with the ignition switched on. Trace and correct any faulty cable, loose connection or defective ignition switch.

If the LT circuit is in order but the trouble persists, refer to **Section 5**.

4 Distributor

A Marelli or a Bosch distributor may be fitted. All distributors have centrifugal automatic advance/retard and a centrifugally actuated maximum engine speed limiting switch. Distributors fitted to later models also incorporate vacuum automatic advance/retard. The advance/retard characteristics and the maximum engine cut-off speed are not identical for all models and a new or exchange replacement distributor must be of the same type as that originally fitted.

Fitting new points:

FIGS 3 and **5** show the earlier Marelli (without the vacuum advance/retard) distributor. To fit a new set of points, it is necessary to remove the distributor as described later. Remove the rotor. Remove the points complete with the stationary plate.

FIG 6 relates to the earlier Bosch (without the vacuum advance/retard) distributor. To renew the points, remove the cap and rotor, loosen the terminal assembly nut, remove the moving arm pivot lockring and lift off the arm. Remove the retaining screw and lift out the fixed contact plate.

Fit the new points and set the gap. Refit a Marelli unit as described later. In both cases, check and adjust the timing stroboscopically as described in **Section 6**.

FIGS 7 and **8** relate to later (with the vacuum advance/retard) Marelli and Bosch distributors respectively. Remove the cap, rotor and dust cover. Disconnect the wire from the contact breaker, remove the arrowed screws and lift out the points assembly.

Fit the new points, set the gap and check and adjust the timing stroboscopically as described in **Section 6**.

Distributor removal and fitment:

Refer to **FIG 9**. To provide a datum, set the crankshaft pulley Z1 mark as shown at TDC arrow with No 1 piston at TDC of its compression stroke (both valves closed). Remove the cap, wiring and vacuum pipe (if fitted) from the distributor.

Remove the retaining nut arrowed in **FIG 5** from earlier units but **do not disturb the long clamp bolt**. Mark the position of the slotted bracket in relation to the crankcase on later units before removing the retaining nut arrowed in **FIG 7**. In all cases, note the orientation of the rotor arm before withdrawing the distributor from its location.

Refitment of the original distributor is the reverse of the removal sequence. Use a new seal. Set the rotor to the noted position. Align a later type unit to the mark made before removal. Fit the retaining nut and check and adjust the timing stroboscopically as described in **Section 6**.

If a new distributor is being fitted, set the pulley to the datum as described earlier. On earlier units (without vacuum advance/retard), set the rotor arm so that it points in the direction of the rear edge of the blower while inserting the neck of the distributor into the crankcase. The arm will move as the gears engage. Slacken the long bolt on the split clamp plate and turn the distributor to the left until the contact breaker just opens. The tip of the rotor arm should then be vertically over a notch on the rim of the distributor body. This position is shown in **FIG 10**. Check the timing stroboscopically as described in **Section 6**.

In the case of later type distributors (with vacuum advance/retard), proceed similarly but leave the retaining nut (see **FIG 7**) loose and rotate the body in the elongated slot until the points just open. Tighten the retaining nut. Check and adjust the timing stroboscopically as described in **Section 6**.

Distributor repair or overhaul:

No procedures are prescribed for the repair or overhaul of a distributor by an owner. A suspect distributor should be passed to a Porsche agent for investigation.

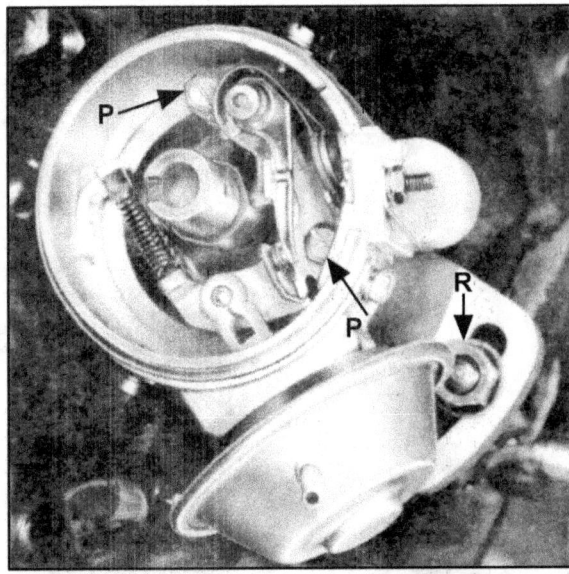

FIG 7   Later type Marelli distributor

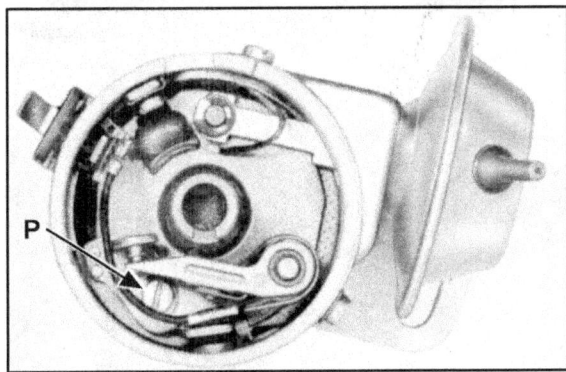

FIG 8   Later type Bosch distributor
P Points retaining screws   R Distributor retaining nut

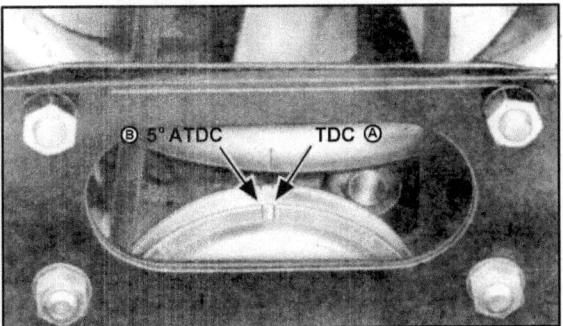

FIG 9   Crankshaft pulley timing marks

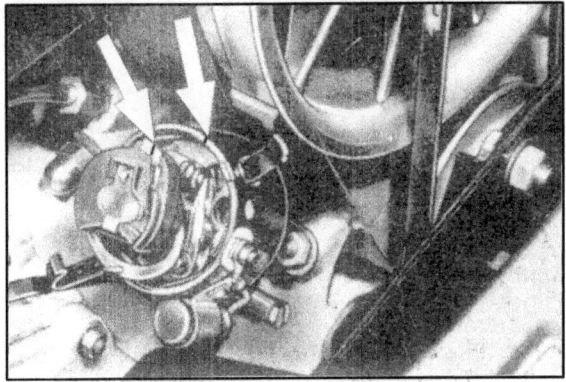

FIG 10   Distributor timing marks

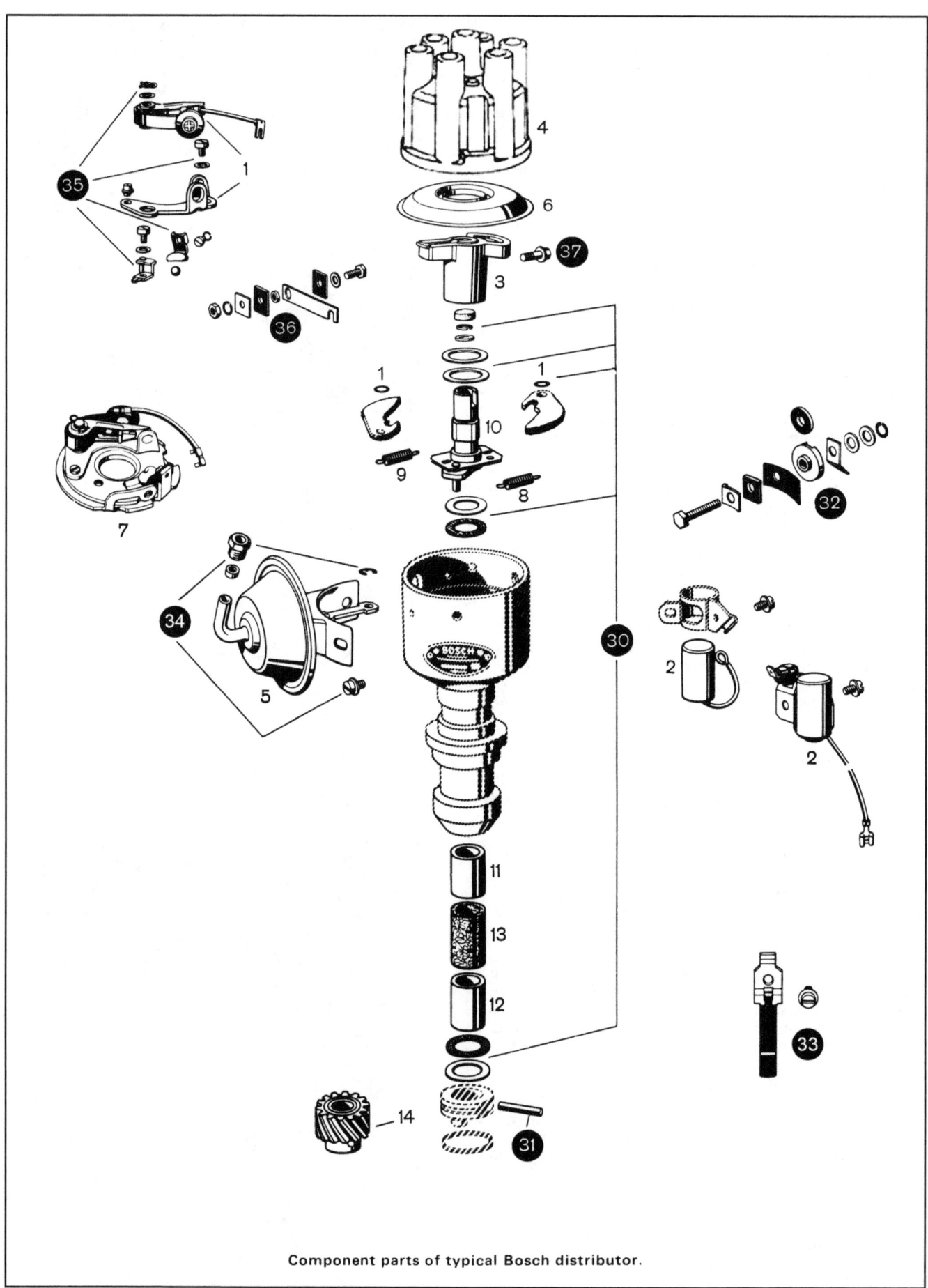

Component parts of typical Bosch distributor.

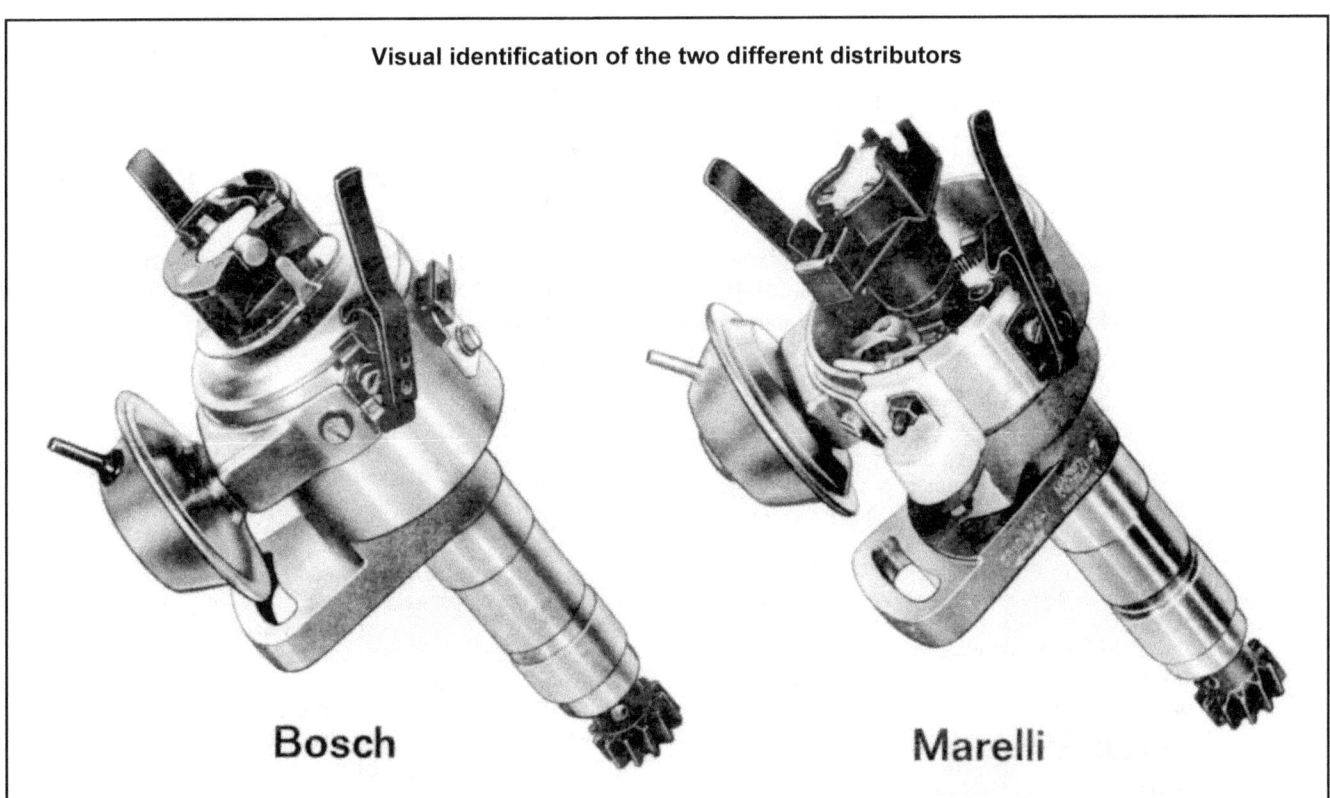
Visual identification of the two different distributors

Bosch Marelli

5 Capacitive discharge system (CDS)

Precautions:

To ensure personal safety and to prevent damage to the CDS unit, the following rules should be observed when performing tests.

(a) Do not attach instruments or components such as a suppressor, test light or stroboscopic timing light to terminal 15, it carries 460 volts.

(b) The ignition voltage transformer cannot be replaced with a conventional induction coil and neither can it be wired or tested as a coil.

(c) Do not stop the engine by placing a jump wire or any other conductor between terminal 15 and earth.

(d) Disconnect the battery earth straps when working on a CDS unit.

(e) Ensure the ignition is switched off before connecting or disconnecting wires and always make sure the dust cover is properly installed on terminal 15.

(f) If a battery is being recharged in situ, the supply and earth straps must be disconnected.

(g) Do not use a battery boost quick charger to start the engine.

(h) Ensure the battery is properly connected, i.e. positive to positive and negative to negative.

(i) Do not touch the leads of the voltage transformer shortly after its removal, there still may be a charge between terminal 'A' and earth which cannot be released by grounding. Do not touch the leads when operating the CDS unit on a test bench or in the car without the transformer; in such cases where the storage capacitor is defective due to an inter-terminal short.

Checking the system in the vehicle:

1 First check the breaker points and all electrical connections.

2 Switch on the ignition. The CDS unit should make a whistling sound; if not, remove the connection from the CDS unit and connect a voltmeter between terminal 'B' (centre terminal of connector) and earth. With the ignition switched on it should read at least 11 volts. It is possible for this reading to be recorded and there is still no whistling sound when the connector is re-plugged in. In these instances and where there is no reading, the CDS unit must be renewed.

3 If the whistle is audible, check terminal 4 for high voltage by disconnecting the HT lead from the voltage transformer and connecting a spark monitor, adjusted to a 10mm (0.40in) spark gap. Crank the engine with the starter and if there is no spark, or if it occurs only infrequently, complete checks 4 and 5.

4 Remove all connections from the transformer. With an ohmmeter measure the resistance in the primary coil between terminals 1 and 15. It should be between 0.4 and 0.6 ohms. Measure the resistance in the secondary coil between terminals 1 and 4; the value should be between 650 and 790 ohms.

5 Check the CDS unit current draw. Connect an ammeter into wire 15, at the coupling from the ignition switch. Disconnect the distributor terminal 1 wire to prevent an incorrect reading. The current draw should be between 1.0 and 1.9amps. If not, renew the CDS unit. Voltage at the unit between terminal 'B' and earth must be at least 11 volts, this can be measured by connecting an additional voltmeter between the ammeter input (+ terminal) and earth. After completing the test, reconnect the distributor terminal 1 wire.

6 The rev/min sensor can be checked only with an ohmmeter. The measured resistance between terminals 'A' and 'B' must be within a range of 170 to 210 ohms and between terminals 'A' and 'C' 200 to 300 ohms.

6 Ignition timing

Static timing with a test lamp:

If, on refitting the distributor as described in **Section 4**, the engine will not start because the ignition timing has been 'lost'; retime the ignition as follows:

1 Set the crankshaft pulley to the datum described in **Section 4**. Remove the distributor cap and the wiring from the distributor body. Check that the points gap is correctly set.
2 Connect a separate battery/test lamp across the contact breaker points so that the light is on when the points are closed and off when the points are open. In the case of earlier distributors, loosen the long bolt on the split clamp. On later units, loosen the retaining nut arrowed **R** in **FIG 7**.
3 With the rotor arm pointing towards the position which is occupied by the No 1 cylinder cap segment when the cap is fitted, turn the distributor body clockwise until the test lamp comes on.
4 Slowly turn the distributor body anticlockwise and stop immediately the test light goes out. Tighten the split clamp bolt or, on later units, the retaining nut.
5 Disconnect the test lamp, reconnect the distributor wiring and fit the cap. Check the timing under a stroboscopic light and adjust as necessary.

Dynamic timing with a stroboscopic light:

Follow the manufacturer's instructions and connect up a stroboscopic light triggered to No 1 cylinder so that it illuminates the crankshaft pulley (the area shown in **FIG 9**). Run the engine up to normal operating temperature and switch on the stroboscopic light.

With the vacuum line connected (later models), run the engine at 850 to 950rev/min and, after slightly loosening the clamp bolt or, on later models, the nut arrowed in **FIG 7**, turn the distributor body until the arrow (**A** or **B**) specified in **Technical Data** for the relevant model appears to align with the stationary datum mark. Tighten the clamp bolt or the retaining nut.

Disconnect the vacuum line (later models) and run the engine up to 6000rev/min. If necessary, readjust the distributor to within the timing range quoted in **Technical Data** for the relevant model. If the adjustment required is more than two or three degrees, some slight malfunctioning of the advance/retard mechanism(s) is indicated and it may be considered desirable to have the distributor investigated by a Porsche agent.

7 Breakerless ignition 1978-83 models (CDI)

1 All models produced from 1978 through 1983 are equipped with a breakerless capacitor discharge ignition (CDI).
2 Beginning with the 1978 models all distributors rotate in an anticlockwise direction. These distributors can not be exchanged with distributors made for use in earlier models. (FIG 11)
3 European models have a mechanical speed control which cuts out the ignition when the engine reaches 6800 ±200 rpm.
4 North American vehicles use an electronic speed relay which cuts off the fuel pump at 6850 ±150 rpm.
5 North American models, beginning in 1980, have a distributor with a double vacuum unit for advance and retard control.

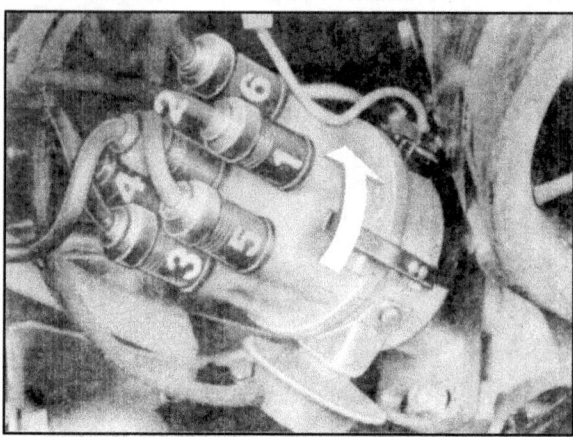

FIG 11 Anticlockwise distributor 1978 onwards

8 Digital Motor Electronics ignition system (DME)

1984 through 1987 model vehicles are equipped with a 100% electronic engine control system. The fuel and ignition system are no longer considered two separate systems. Because of the equipment and knowledge required to diagnose and repair this system, work for the home mechanic is limited to a few basic checks and component replacement. If a problem should occur that cannot be diagnosed by the checks provided, the vehicle should be taken to a qualified service technician.

Precautions when working on the ignition system

1 Always turn off the ignition or disconnect the battery negative cable when working on the ignition system. Such jobs include the following:
 a) Connecting engine testing equipment (timing light, dwell angle/speed tester, ignition oscilloscope, etc.).
 b) Replacement of ignition system parts (spark plugs, ignition coil, distributor, ignition cables, etc.).
2 Never start engine without a firmly connected battery.
3 Mixing up power supply connections, e.g. wrong connection of the battery, could lead to destruction of the control units.
4 Never disconnect the battery while engine is running.
5 Never use a boost battery charger to start the engine. Only use a second 12V battery for outside starting help.
6 Disconnect the battery from the car network before boost charging.
7 Only measure resistance values after turning off the ignition or disconnecting the battery.
8 Pull off both control unit plugs before checking the compression.
9 Never replace the specified ignition coil with a different ignition coil.
10 Never connect a shielded capacitor on ignition coil terminals 1 and 15.
11 Ignition coil terminal 1 must not be used for ground connection when installing a burglar alarm system (ignition coil would be destroyed with the "ignition on").
12 Never connect battery positive (+) or test lamp to ignition coil terminal 1.
13 Never disconnect the ignition lead between the ignition coil terminal 4 and high voltage distributor terminal 4 while the engine is running.
14 To avoid destruction of the ignition control unit, the secondary side of the ignition system must be shielded with at least 4 k-ohms, whereby the original distributor rotor with a 1 k-ohm shielded resistor must be installed.

Adjusting the ignition timing

1 Run the engine until normal operating temperatures are reached. Oil temperature should be 180 to 190°F (80 to 90°C).
2 Connect a hand held tachometer according to the manufacturer's instructions. The car's tachometer is run from the ignition control unit and may not give as exact a reading.
3 Leave the hoses connected to the vacuum advance unit on the distributor unless otherwise stated in the Specifications.
4 Make sure that the ignition is turned off, then install a timing light according to the manufacturer's instructions.
5 Start the engine and check the idle speed on the hand held tachometer. If the idle speed is not within the idle speed specified for your model, refer to Chapter 2 for adjustment instructions.
6 Aim the beam of the timing light at the crankshaft pulley where it passes the mark on the blower housing. Note: Due to the high RPM's required, the following 'full advance' timing checks should only be performed by a qualified technican or repair shop.

1977 911S – North America (except California)

1 On 1977 911S North American models except California, the vacuum hose to the distributor should be plugged before setting the timing to specifications.
2 If the timing mark does not appear in the beam of the strobe light as a steady image, loosen the nut on the distributor hold down plate and turn the distributor back and forth until a steady image is seen.
3 Tighten the nut securely and recheck the timing.

1978, 1979 – North American models

1 1978 and 1979 North American models should have the vacuum hose attached when setting the timing.
2 After the timing is set, disconnect the vacuum hose and check the advance of the timing. When the engine is run at 6000 rpm the timing should advance to 26° ±2° BTDC.

1978 to 1980 – European models

1 1978 through 1980 European models should have the vacuum hose disconnected while setting the timing. The advance test should have the number 1 cylinder firing at 24° to 31° BTDC at 6000 rpm.
2 If the advance is not operating properly, remove the distributor and have it examined by a Porsche dealer.

1980 – North American models

1 On 1980 North American models set the idle speed with the vacuum hoses disconnected from the ignition distributor. Set the ignition timing to specifications. Connect the vacuum lines and reset the idle speed.
2 Disconnect the vacuum hoses to test the centrifugal advance. Check the timing at 3000 rpm to be 15 to 20° BTDC or 19 to 25° BTDC at 6000 rpm.
3 Connect the blue vacuum line to the retard terminal and test the timing to be 3 to 7° ATDC at idle.
4 Connect the blue line to the advance terminal. The timing at idle should be 8 to 12° BTDC.
5 If the advance or retard tests don't give the proper results, remove the distributor and have it inspected by a Porsche dealer.
6 Connect the vacuum hoses to their proper positions and set the idle.

1981 through 1983 models

1 Set the idle speed and ignition timing to specifications for 1981 through 1983 models with the vacuum hose disconnected.
2 Test the timing for 25° BTDC at 4000 rpm and adjust it if necessary. Be sure the timing does not exceed 25° BTDC at 6000 rpm while the vacuum hose is disconnected.
3 Connect the vacuum hose and check the timing at 4000 rpm to be 28 to 32° BTDC.

1984 through 1987 models

1 The ignition timing on later models is controlled by an on board computer and no adjustment is necessary.

Checking the DME ignition system

Due to the complexity of the DME ignition system, testing by the home mechanic is limited to checking all the ground connections for tightness and a visual inspection of all the plug connectors to make sure they are secure and corrosion free. These checks are shown in the following illustrations. If the problem still exists after performing these checks the vehicle should be taken to a qualified technician.

Fig. 12 location of DME components

1 Ignition coil
2 Distributor
3 Pressure regulator
4 Pressure damper
5 Air flow sensor
6 Throttle switch
7 Idle positioner
8 Fuel injectors
9 Fuel pressure test connection
10 TDC sensor test connection

Out of view component locations

DME control unit, DME relay and Altitude correction box (underneath drivers seat)

Speed sensor/reference mark sensor (accessible from below, to the left of the flywheel)

Engine temperature sensor II (accessible from below, on cylinder head at cylinder No. 3)

TDC sensor (accessible from the engine compartment, above the flywheel)

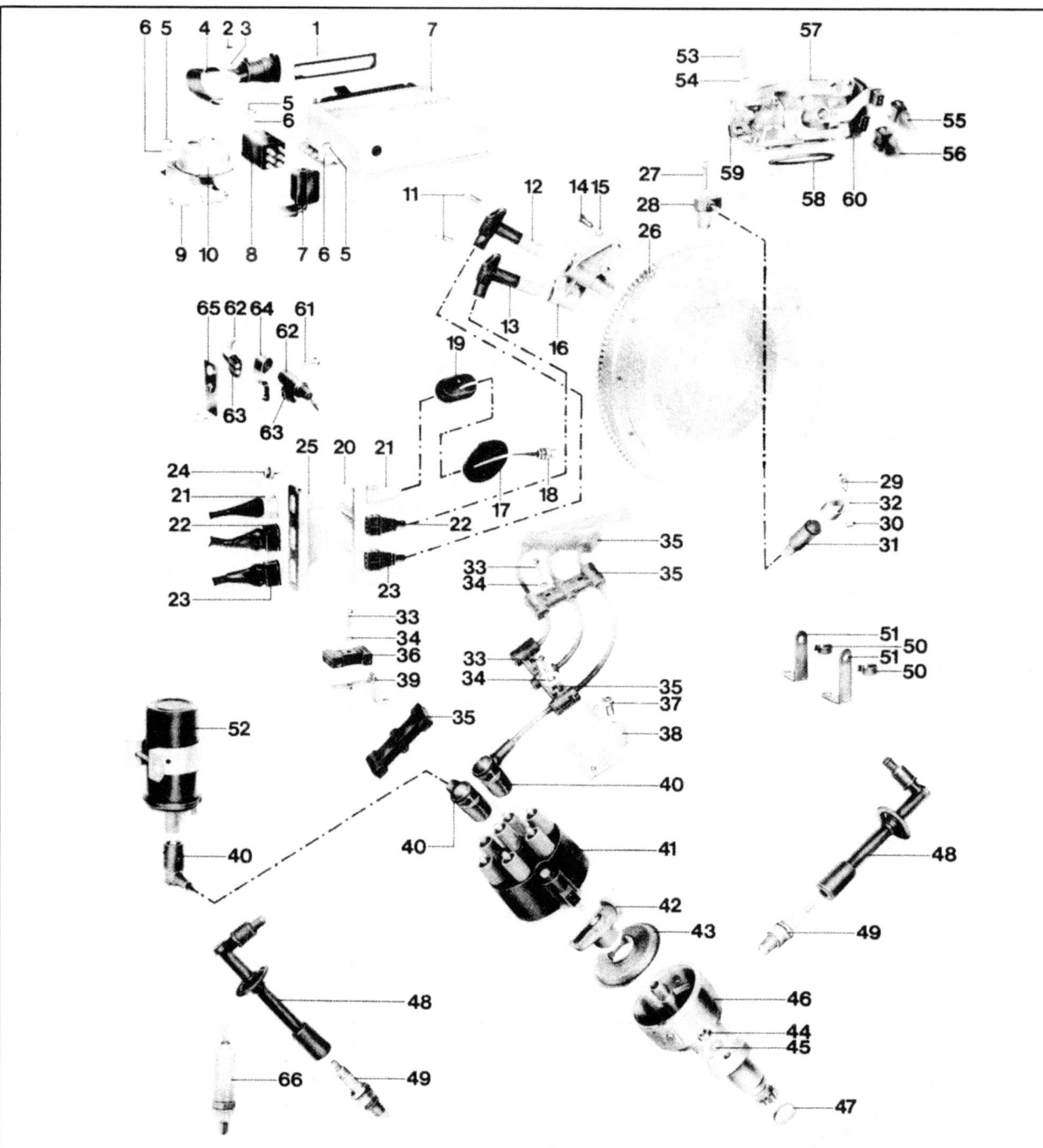

Fig. 13 Exploded view of the DME ignition control components

1 Multiple-pin plug for DME control unit	17 Grommet	34 Washer	51 Ignition lead holder
2 Nut	18 Temperature sensor II	35 Holder	52 Ignition coil
3 Washer	19 Grommet	36 Holder	53 Screw
4 Holder	20 Arrest	37 Screw	54 Washer
5 Nut	21 Plug	38 Holder	55 Plug
6 Washer	22 Plug DG	39 Holder	56 Plug
7 Plug	23 Plug BG	40 Ignition lead	57 Throttle housing
8 DME relay	24 Bolt	41 Distributor cap	58 O-ring
9 Plug	25 Holder	42 Distributor rotor	59 Idle switch
10 Altitude correction box	26 Reference mark (Flywheel)	43 Dust cap	60 Full load switch
11 Screw	27 Screw	44 Nut	61 Bolt
12 Reference mark sensor	28 TDC sensor	45 Washer	62 Oxygen sensor plug
13 Speed sensor	29 Bolt	46 Distributor	63 Heating plug
14 Screw	30 Nut	47 Seal	64 Holder
15 Washer	31 TDC sensor test connection	48 Spark plug connector	65 Holder
16 Holder	32 Clamp	49 Spark plug	66 Oxygen sensor
	33 Bolt	50 Clip	

Ground connection checks

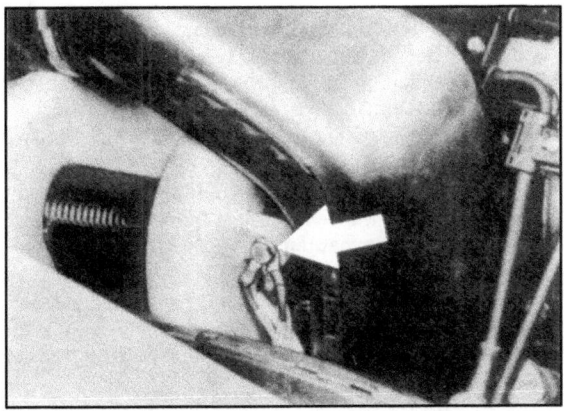

Fig. 14 Ground point on intake pipe of No. 1 cylinder

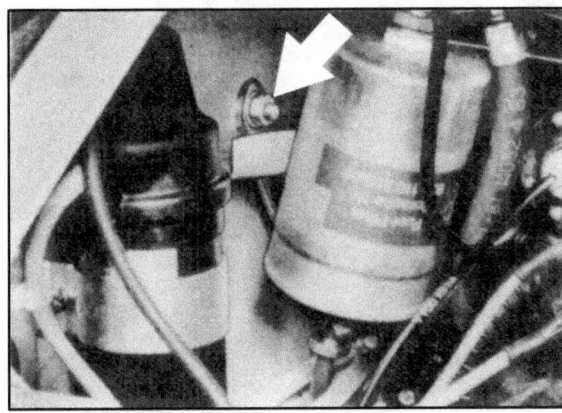

Fig. 15 Ground point next to fuel filter

Fig. 16 Connections between body/engine/transmission

Plug connection checks

Fig. 17 Fuel injector plugs

Plug connection checks (continued)

Fig. 18 Control unit plugs 1 DME control unit
2 DME relay 3 Altitude correction box

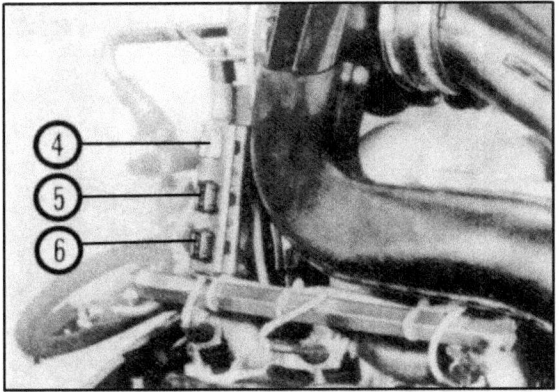

Fig. 19 Sensor rail plugs 4 Temperature sensor II
5 Speed sensor DG 6 Reference mark sensor BG

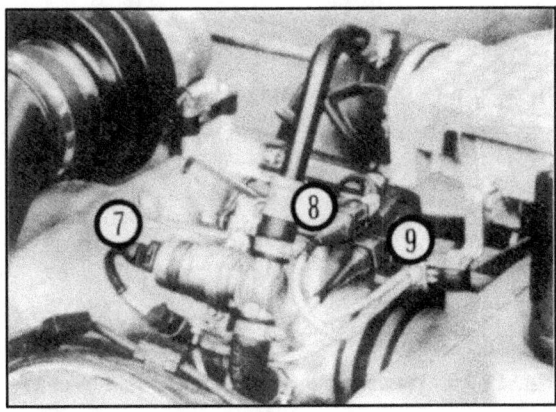

Fig. 20 Fuel injection plugs 7 Idle positioner
8 Throttle switch/idle contact 9 Full load contact

Fig. 21 Air flow sensor plug

Plug connection checks (continued)

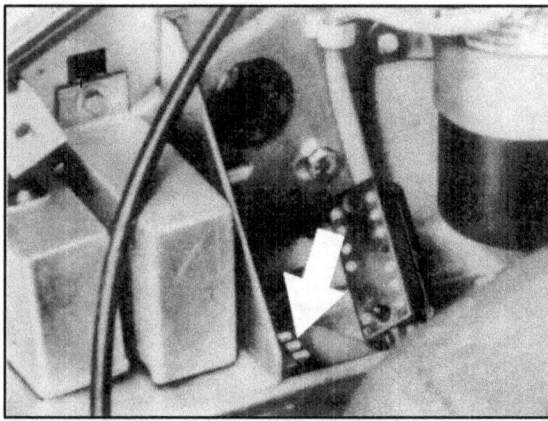

Fig. 22   Regulator plug - located under the ignition coil

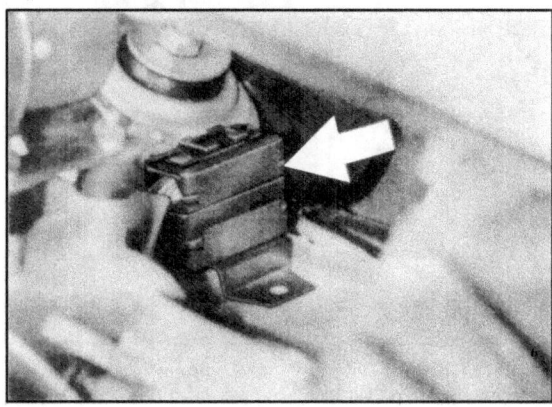

Fig. 23   Engine compartment plug - located on the front crossmember

Control unit remove and replace

1   Turn off the ignition and disconnect the negative battery cable.
2   Push back the driver's seat and fold the floor mat forward.
3   Unlock the catch on the control unit and pull off the multiple pin plug. (FIG 24)
4   Unscrew the mounting nuts on left and right sides of the control unit.
5   Installation is the reverse of the removal procedure, making sure to check the multiple pin plug for any damaged pins before reattaching it to the control unit.

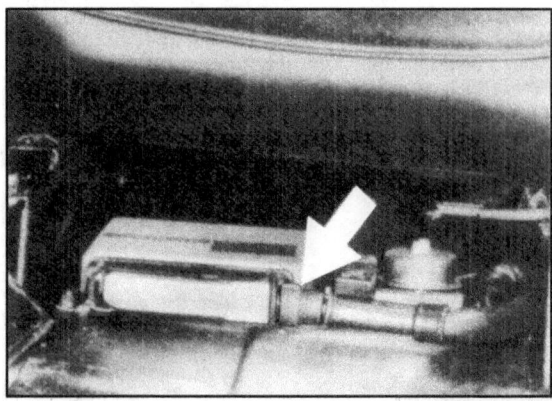

Fig. 24   Unlock the catch (arrow) on the control unit and remove the multiple pin plug

Speed and reference mark sensors remove and replace

1   Disconnect the battery negative cable.
2   Remove heated air elbow. (FIG 25)
3   Remove the plug holder next to the coil and disconnect the speed and reference mark sensors. (FIG 26)
4   Remove the sensor retaining screws and pull out the sensors while turning them back and forth. (FIG 27)
5   Remove the grommet (FIG 28) from the shield behind the sensors and pull out the sensor wires from the slotted end of the grommet. The grommet remains on the temperature sensor wire.
6   Installation is the reverse of the removal procedure.
7   After installing the sensors the clearance between the speed sensor and ring gear must be checked and adjusted if necessary.

Fig. 25   Hose clamp locations for the heated air elbow

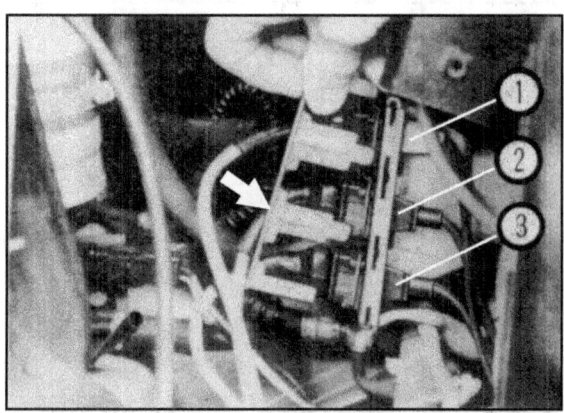

Fig. 26   Retaining clip must be removed (arrow) before disconnecting the sensor plugs
1 Temperature sensor II   2 Speed sensor DG
3 Reference mark sensor BG

Fig. 27   Speed and reference sensor retaining screws
2 Speed sensor DG   3 Reference mark sensor BG

Fig. 28 Remove the grommet (arrow) from the heat shield

Speed and reference mark sensors adjustment

Note: *Clearance between the speed sensor and ring gear must be adjusted to specification. The reference mark sensor will also be positioned correctly, if this value is adjusted correctly.*

Adjusting on removed engine

1 Make sure the speed sensor is tight in its holder.
2 Loosen the mounting screws on the holder.
3 To adjust the clearance insert a feeler gauge of the appropriate size between the ring gear and the speed sensor.
4 Position the sensor against the feeler gauge and tighten the mounting screws.

Adjusting on installed engine

1 Remove the sensor retaining screw and slide out the speed sensor.
2 If available, a faulty sensor can be used as an adjusting tool by gluing an 0.8 mm thick washer on the bottom of the sensor with a quick drying glue to use as a clearance gauge.
If a substitute sensor is unavailable the sensor installed on the car could also be used if procedures are carried out carefully. If using the installed sensor the glued surface must be kept as small as possible and an easy to remove glue must be used.
3 Loosen the screws on the sensor holder just enough so that the holder can still be pivoted on its bottom screw. (FIG 29)
4 Install the extended sensor in the speed sensor opening and tighten the retaining screw.
5 Move the holder with extended sensor against the ring gear and tighten the holder screws.
6 Remove the extended sensor.
7 If the original sensor has been used, press off the washer carefully and remove the glue.
8 Install the speed sensor.

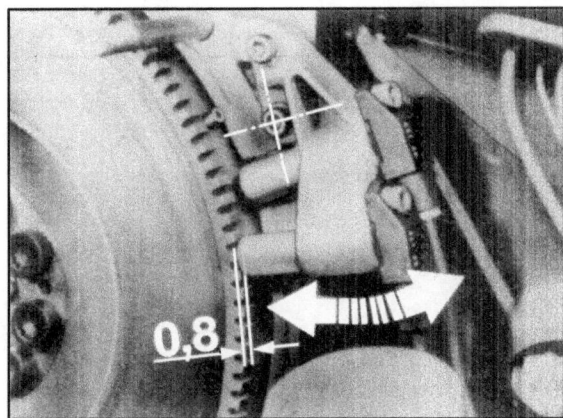

Fig. 29 With the sensor retaining screws loose the clearance can be adjusted

Distributor remove and replace

Removal

1 Set cylinder 1 at TDC (refer to **FIG 9**).
2 Remove heated air elbow. **(FIG 25)**
3 Remove the spark plug wires from their holders.
4 Unscrew and take off the distributor cap. **(FIG 30)**
5 Note where the rotor is pointing for reinstallation.
6 Remove the distributor hold down nut and pull the distributor out of the engine block.

Installation

7 Check to be sure the engine is set with the number 1 cylinder at TDC. (refer to **FIG 9**).
8 Install the distributor so the rotor is centered with the notch in the distributor housing. (FIG 31)
9 Install the distributor hold down nut and distributor cap. **Note:** *Basic ignition adjustments are not necessary. The distributor only has the task of distributing high tension voltage.*

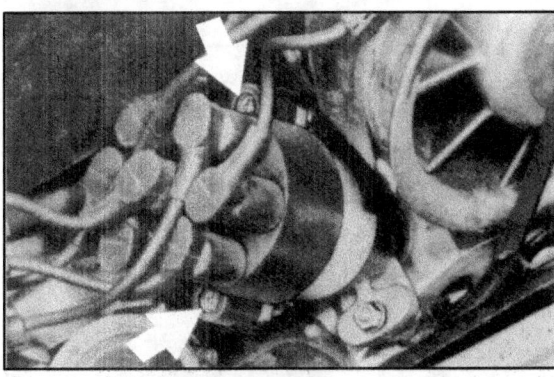

Fig. 30 Remove the distributor cap screws (arrows) using a small phillips head screwdriver

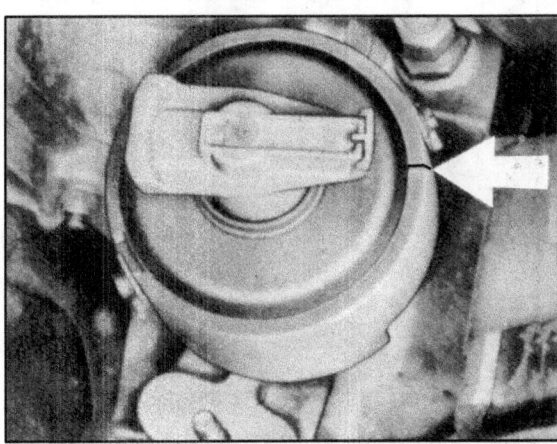

Fig. 31 The rotor must point to the reference mark (arrow) on the distributor housing when the distributor is installed

TDC sensor remove and replace

1 Remove heated air elbow and blower. (FIG 32)
2 Unscrew the TDC sensor retaining screw and pull the sensor out of its holder. (FIG 33)
3 Unscrew and remove the test connection just below the idle positioner. (FIG 34)
4 Installation is the reverse of the removal procedure, making sure that the test connection is securely plugged in.

Fig. 32 Remove heated elbow and blower motor

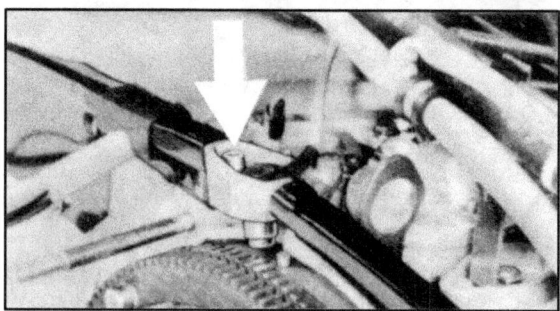

Fig. 33 Location of the TDC sensor retaining screw

Fig. 34 Remove the test connection from its holder

9 Sparking plugs and HT leads

Recommended types:

A selection of officially recommended plugs is listed in the **Technical Data** section of the **Appendix**. If the types quoted are not available, consult the manufacturer's lists for equivalent alternatives.

Cleaning, testing, and refitting:

Every 6000 miles (10,000km), have the sparking plugs cleaned on an abrasive-blasting machine and tested under pressure with the gaps correctly set at 0.55mm (0.022in). The gaps must always be adjusted by bending the earth electrode. **Do not attempt to bend the centre electrode or the insulation will be damaged.**

When refitting sparking plugs coat the plug threads with a molybdenum paste (MOLYKOTE HTP-White or similar) and torque tighten to 2.5 to 3.0kgm (18 to 22lb ft).

Plugs as a tuning guide:

Inspection of the deposits on electrodes can be helpful as a tuning guide. Normally, from mixed periods of high and low speed driving, the deposits should be powdery and range in colour from brown to greyish tan. There will also be some slight wear of the electrodes. Long periods of fairly constant speed driving or low speed city driving will produce white or yellowish deposits. Dry, black fluffy deposits are due to incomplete combustion and indicate running with a rich mixture, excessive idling and, possibly, defective ignition. Overheated plugs have a white or light grey look round the centre electrode and the electrodes themselves will appear bluish and burnt. This may be due to weak mixture, poor cooling, incorrect ignition timing or sustained high speed running with a heavily loaded vehicle. Black, wet deposits result from oil in the combustion chambers from worn pistons, rings, valve stems or guides or from worn and scored cylinder bores. Sparking plugs which run hotter may alleviate this problem temporarily but the cure is in an engine overhaul.

HT leads:

When renewing HT leads, use only the best quality of cable. Cut the cable to the **same length as the original lead** and ensure that the different lengths are connected to the relevant distributor cap positions. Check that the connections are well made at both the cap and at the plug connector.

NOTES

CHAPTER 4 - COOLING, HEATING AND EMISSION CONTROL SYSTEMS

1 The cooling system
2 The heating system
3 Exhaust emission control
4 Vapour emission control
5 Supplemental information 1976-1983
6 Supplemental information 1978 onwards
7 Fault diagnosis

1 The cooling system

The engine cooling air is produced by the rear entry, belt-driven, ducted fan blower as shown in **Chapter 1, FIG 2**. The air is blown forwards into a shroud which extends across the engine and carries it to the two banks of cylinders and cylinder heads. The profiled outline of the shroud is shown immediately above the crankcase and cylinders in **Chapter 1, FIG 1**. After passing across the fins of the cylinders and heads, a proportion of the air is deflected upwards by deflector pieces.

It will be noted that the hub of the fan is keyed to the alternator drive shaft and that the belt drives both the fan and the alternator.

Maintenance:

This is confined to adjustment of the driving belt for the blower and alternator. The method is shown in **FIG 1**.

Check the tension by pressing the belt inwards about midway between the pulleys. Light thumb pressure should deflect it 15 to 20mm (0.60 to 0.80in). A belt which is too tight puts a greater strain on the alternator bearings and is more liable to break. A slack belt may slip, causing overheating problems and lowering the output from the alternator.

To adjust the tension, remove the nut from the blower pulley shaft. A steel bar with pegs, similar to tool No P208, can be used to engage the holes in the pulley flange to hold it still. Remove the washer and any spacers which may be fitted. Remove the belt flange.

FIG 1 The tension of the blower belt is adjusted by altering the number of washers between the pulley flanges

Removal of spacers from between the pulley flanges will tighten the belt and vice versa. Spacers from between the flanges must be added to those outside so that the total number of washers remains unaltered. A belt which is so stretched or worn that only one spacer remains between the flanges must be renewed. A belt must not run on the bottom of the pulley groove.

Tighten the pulley nut to 4kgm (29lb ft) torque. Check the belt tension. If a new belt is fitted, check the tension after 50 miles of running, as the belt will stretch slightly.

Never remove a belt by levering it over the pulley with a screwdriver. Belts contaminated with oil may be cleaned in a detergent solution and rinsed in water. Any signs of cracking or of frayed edges call for renewal of the belt.

Removing and refitting blower:

The blower is mounted on the alternator shaft and the assembly must be removed complete (engine in or out of car). Details of the mounting can be seen in **Chapter 1, FIG 2**.

Proceed as follows:
1 Remove screws securing upper air channel. Remove the belt as described earlier.
2 Slacken the clip surrounding the blower housing. Pull the housing and alternator to the rear. Identify the cables for correct position before detaching them from alternator.
3 Refit in the reverse order, making sure that the dowel for the blower housing is correctly located.

Removal and fitment of shrouds, deflectors, etc:

Remove the air cleaner canister. Depending upon the fuel system, remove the intake down pipes together with the fuel pipes, vacuum pipes, controls and relevant wiring. Remove the rear coverplate and any fuel pipes which pass over the blower housing.

Remove the air hoses to the heat exchangers and the hot air ducts on both sides of the engine. Remove the front coverplates. Remove the side coverplates.

The deflector plates or shrouds between the cylinders cannot be withdrawn until the camshaft housings are removed (see **Chapter 1, Section 4**). These plates are held in place with spring clips.

When refitting the shrouds, ensure that the spring clips hold them securely. Secure the coverplates so that there are no gaps where air can leak out and reduce the cooling efficiency.

2 The heating system

The layout of the heating system is shown in **FIG 2**. Fresh air is drawn in by the engine cooling blower 2. A proportion of this air is diverted by offtake pipes 3 to the heat exchangers 4. Engine exhaust gases traverse the heat exchangers before passing to the exhaust silencers 6. Connecting hoses duct heated air to spill-valve control boxes 8 from which, depending upon the setting(s) of the hand control(s), the warmed air passes via ducts and air silencers to the various distribution points in the interior of the vehicle. The silencers, heat exchangers and ductings as fitted to later type models are shown in **FIG 3**.

Air passes through the heat exchangers whenever the engine is running. Control of its distribution to the interior of the vehicle is by manually opening or closing the control valves and allowing less or more warmed air to be spilled overboard. A single hand lever control for the spill valves is fitted to earlier models while, on later models, twin hand levers as shown in **Chapter 2, FIG 3**, are provided. Automatic control may be fitted in some models.

The auxiliary self-powered heater 16 in **FIG 2** may, when required, be switched in to supplement the primary heater system.

Silencers and heat exchangers:

The relative position of the silencer(s) and heat exchangers is shown in **FIG 3**. Reference may also be made to **Chapter 1, FIG 2**.

Note that the main silencer is supported by retaining clips. To dismount the silencer, remove the flange bolts and the bolts from the support clips. Check the unit for cracks, corrosion and deterioration. Do not attempt to salvage a defective silencer but obtain a replacement of the appropriate type. On refitment, use new gaskets and ensure that the flange joints are well made. Tighten the flange bolts gradually and alternately and, after running the engine up to full operating temperature, recheck the joints.

To remove the heat exchangers, detach their air intake pipes and the hoses which connect between the exchangers and the heater control boxes. Withdraw the exhaust flange bolts. Remove the mounting bolts and lift out the units. Inspect carefully for cracks, corrosion and damage. This inspection is particularly important to preclude the possibility of contaminated heated air being distributed to the interior of the vehicle. On refitment, use new gaskets and follow the procedure described earlier for the silencer(s).

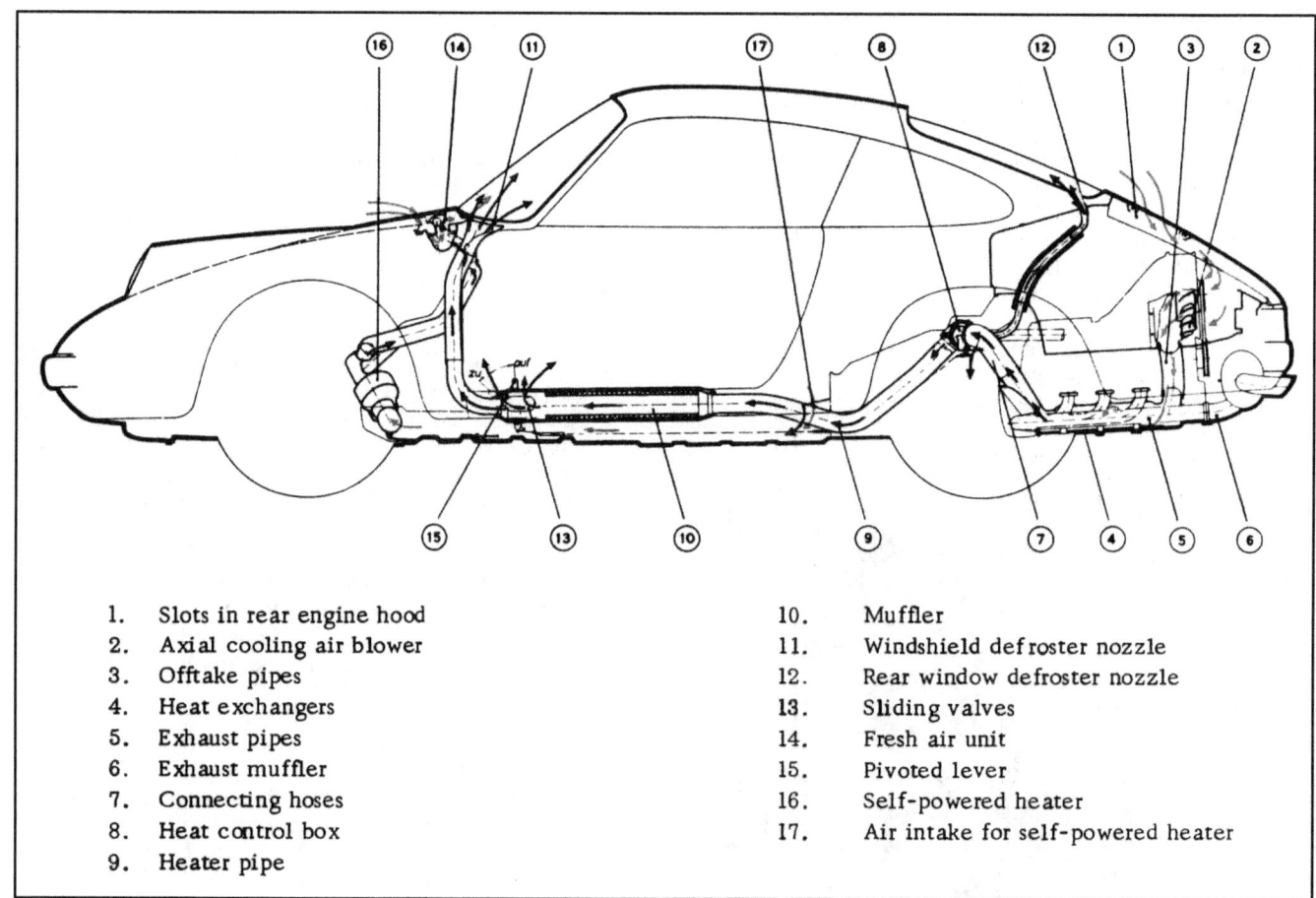

1. Slots in rear engine hood
2. Axial cooling air blower
3. Offtake pipes
4. Heat exchangers
5. Exhaust pipes
6. Exhaust muffler
7. Connecting hoses
8. Heat control box
9. Heater pipe
10. Muffler
11. Windshield defroster nozzle
12. Rear window defroster nozzle
13. Sliding valves
14. Fresh air unit
15. Pivoted lever
16. Self-powered heater
17. Air intake for self-powered heater

FIG 2 How heated air is supplied to the interior. Heavier arrows indicate hot air after it has left the heat exchangers

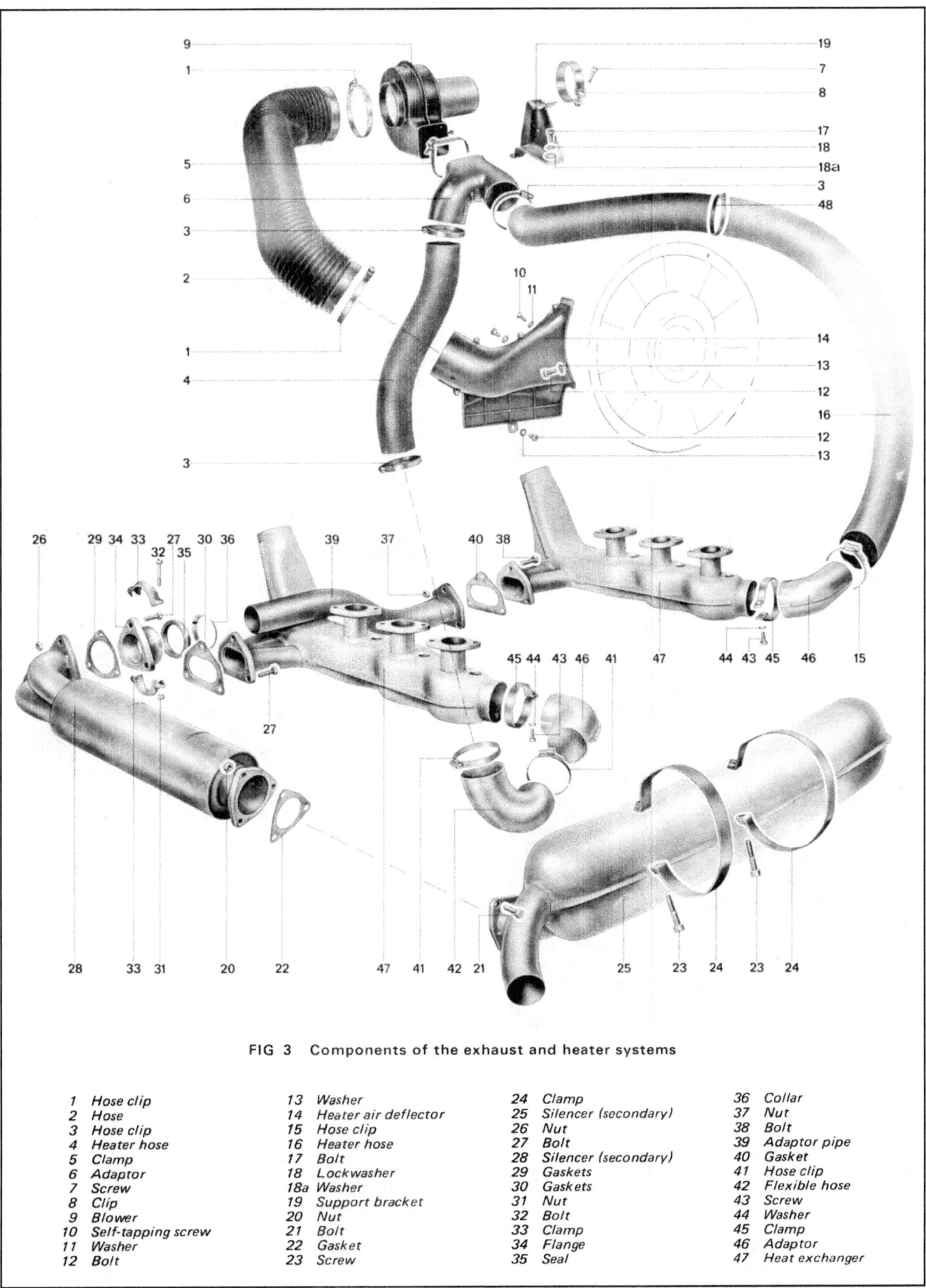

FIG 3 Components of the exhaust and heater systems

1 Hose clip	13 Washer	24 Clamp	36 Collar
2 Hose	14 Heater air deflector	25 Silencer (secondary)	37 Nut
3 Hose clip	15 Hose clip	26 Nut	38 Bolt
4 Heater hose	16 Heater hose	27 Bolt	39 Adaptor pipe
5 Clamp	17 Bolt	28 Silencer (secondary)	40 Gasket
6 Adaptor	18 Lockwasher	29 Gaskets	41 Hose clip
7 Screw	18a Washer	30 Gaskets	42 Flexible hose
8 Clip	19 Support bracket	31 Nut	43 Screw
9 Blower	20 Nut	32 Bolt	44 Washer
10 Self-tapping screw	21 Bolt	33 Clamp	45 Clamp
11 Washer	22 Gasket	34 Flange	46 Adaptor
12 Bolt	23 Screw	35 Seal	47 Heat exchanger

Heating system controls:

FIG 4 shows the arrangement on earlier models in which the single hand lever operates the cables which control the position of the spill valves. One of the spill valves is shown in **FIG 5**. On later models, each of the two hand levers operates a cable and the equaliser arrangement is eliminated.

Adjustment, if required to compensate for control cable stretch, is carried out at the spill valves by loosening the cable clamp nut, repositioning the cable and re-tightening the clamp nut. Adjustment is best carried out with the valve in the position shown in the illustration (open). Operate the hand lever and check that the valves close fully on the 'on' position(s).

The procedure for dismantling the hand control(s) is included in **Chapter 11, Section 8**. On reassembly, reset the pivotal friction of the lever(s) by tightening nut **C** in **Chapter 2, FIG 3** until a load of 10kg (22lb) applied at the clevis pin hole and at right angles to the below-floor lever(s) is required to move the hand lever in its pivot.

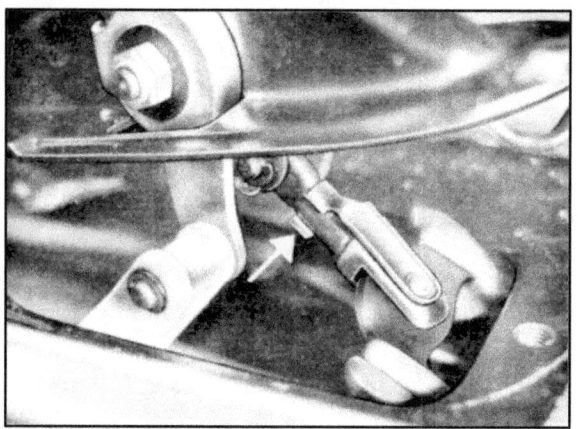

FIG 4 Control cable equaliser. Spring clip is arrowed

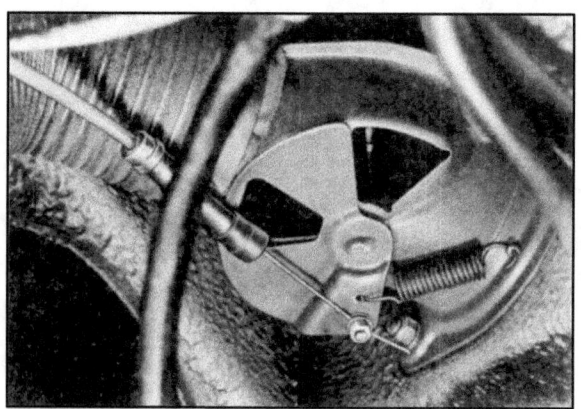

FIG 5 Heater system spill valve

3 Exhaust emission control

By injecting air into the incandescent exhaust gases immediately after they leave the engine cylinders, combustion of unburned hydrocarbons is encouraged and the final exhaust gases when they leave the exhaust pipe contain less carbon monoxide (but more of the less noxious carbon dioxide) than would be the case with untreated exhaust gases.

On earlier models the emission control air pump is driven from a pulley on the rear end of the lefthand camshaft. On later models (see **FIG 7**), the air pump is driven from a pulley attached to the alternator/cooling fan pulley.

Exhaust gas recirculation system (EGR):

On 1975 models with California equipment where the nitrogen oxide (NOx) content of the exhaust gases has to be reduced an exhaust gas recirculation system (EGR) is installed to dilute the fuel/air mixture during partial throttle positions (see **FIG 6**).

An EGR valve under control of depression in the intake manifold directs exhaust gas from the silencer through a line filter into the intake housing as required.

An elapsed mileage odometer is installed beneath the blower housing to indicate the inspection intervals. The EGR lamp will light up after 30,000 miles have been driven to indicate inspection or replacement is required.

All 1976 models for the USA are fitted with a modified switch. The indicator lamp lights when the ignition is switched on and goes out when the engine starts to indicate serviceability of the bulb.

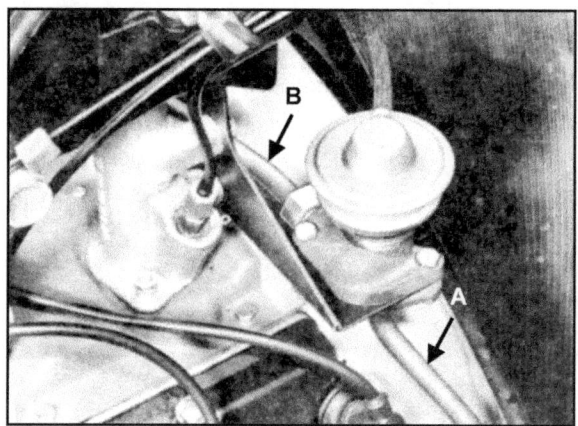

FIG 6 EGR valve outlet pipe (filter to valve): A
EGR valve outlet pipe (valve to intake housing): B

Checking: (Refer to FIG 6)

Run the engine at a fast-idle until the pipe **A** between the EGR filter and the valve feels hot. Increase engine speed to about 4000rev/min, the pipe **B** between the valve and the intake housing should also heat up. If the pipe does not heat up either the valve is defective in which case it will have to be renewed, there is a blockage in the system or a leak in the vacuum hoses.

Removing:

Disconnect the vacuum hoses. Unscrew the outlet pipe union at the valve. Remove the mounting bolts.

Refitting:

Proceed in the reverse order of removal connecting the upper chamber vacuum hose to the lefthand connection on the throttle housing looking from the rear and the lower chamber hose to the other.

Resetting EGR odometer to zero:

Disconnect the battery and remove the tachometer. Using a small tommy bar or similar, press the pin on the housing into the stop.

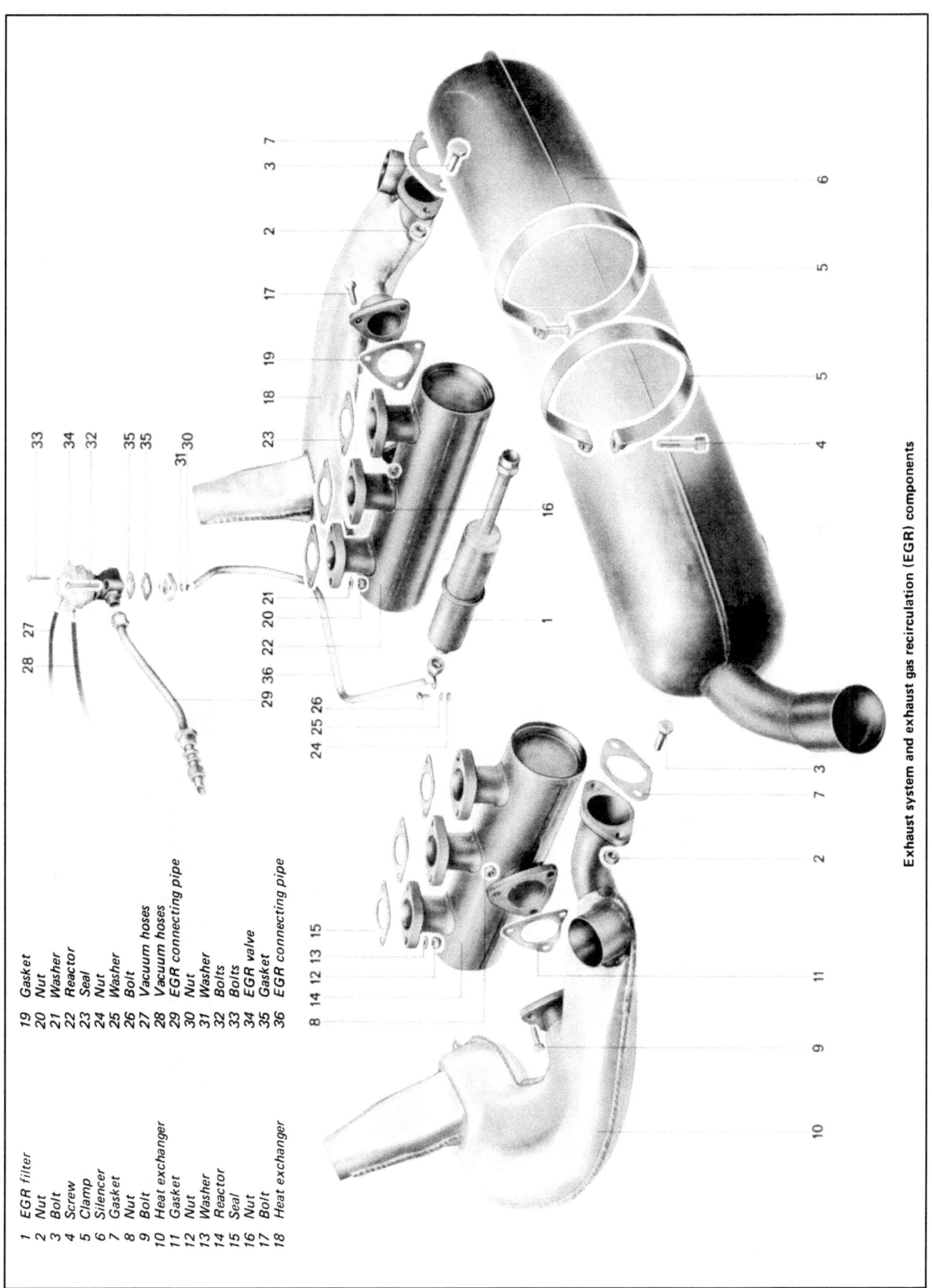

Exhaust system and exhaust gas recirculation (EGR) components

1 EGR filter
2 Nut
3 Bolt
4 Screw
5 Clamp
6 Silencer
7 Gasket
8 Nut
9 Bolt
10 Heat exchanger
11 Gasket
12 Nut
13 Washer
14 Reactor
15 Seal
16 Nut
17 Bolt
18 Heat exchanger
19 Gasket
20 Nut
21 Washer
22 Reactor
23 Seal
24 Nut
25 Washer
26 Bolt
27 Vacuum hoses
28 Vacuum hoses
29 EGR connecting pipe
30 Nut
31 Washer
32 Bolts
33 Bolts
34 EGR valve
35 Gasket
36 EGR connecting pipe

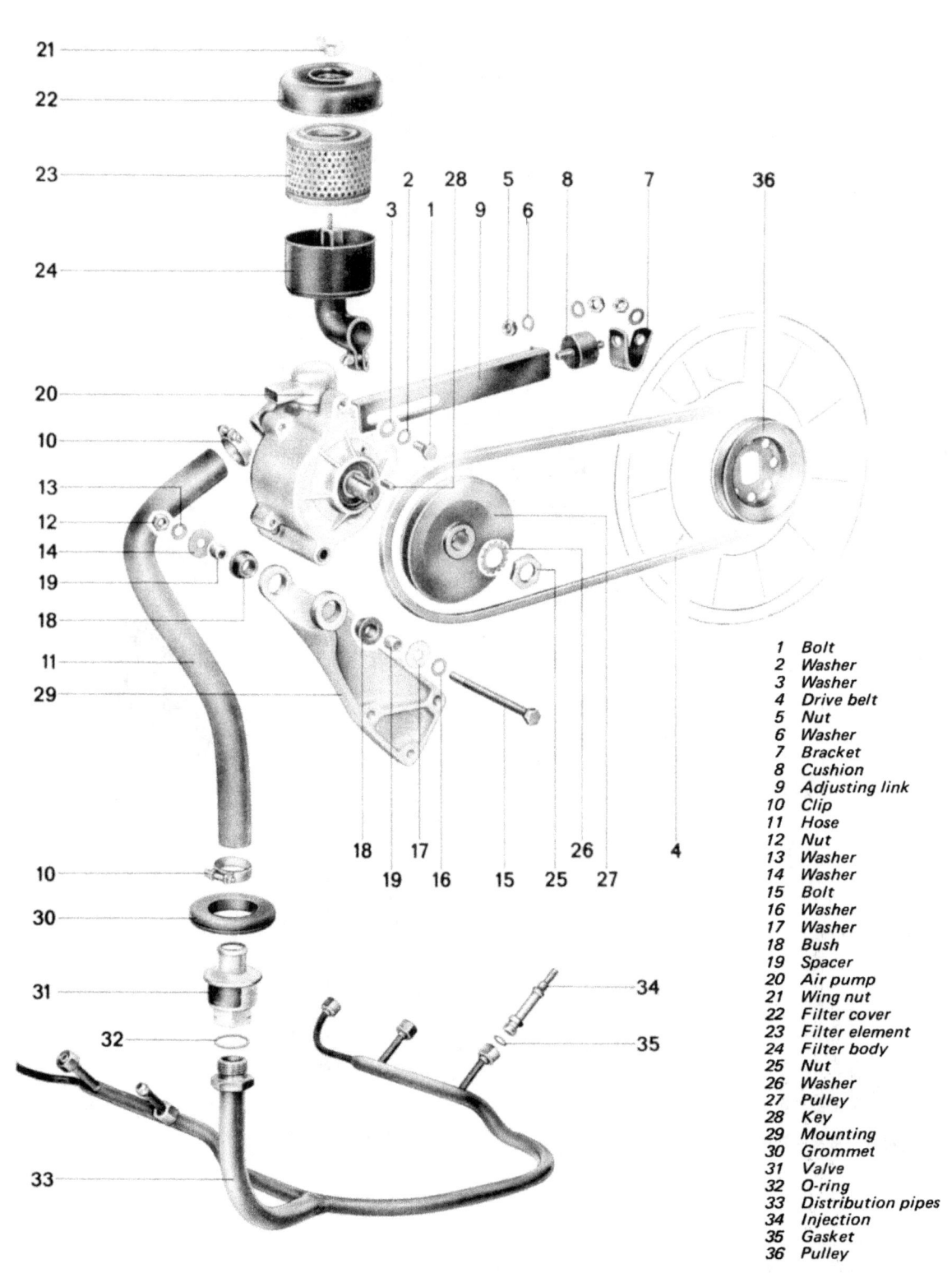

FIG 7 Components of the air injection system (later models)

Maintenance:

Adjust the belt tension if, under thumb pressure at the midway point between the pulleys, the belt can be made to yield by more than 10mm (0.4in) in the case of earlier models, or by more than 15mm (0.6in) in the case of later models. **Do not overtighten the belt**, however, as doing so will stress the pump and alternator bearings. Adjustment is made by loosening the bolt which engages the elongated slot (see **FIG 8** for earlier models and **FIG 9** for later models), swinging the pump away from the driving pulley and retightening the adjuster bolt.

Every 6000 to 12,000 miles (10,000 to 20,000km) depending upon how dusty the terrain may be in which the vehicle is operating. Follow the procedure for cleaning the filter as described in **Chapter 2, Section 3**.

Air pump removal and fitment:

No procedures are prescribed for the repair or overhaul of an air pump by an owner and an unserviceable pump should be removed and a new or an exchange replacement unit fitted.

Loosen the belt adjuster bolt and swing the pump towards the drive pulley. Remove the belt. Remove the pipe(s) from the pump. Withdraw the mounting bolt and lift out the pump. Refitment is the reverse of this sequence. Refit the belt if it is serviceable and tension it as described earlier.

Valves:

A single non-return valve 31 in **FIG 7** covers the air supply pipe to both banks of cylinders. This valve may be unscrewed from the air manifold after removing hose 11. It is a push fit in the mounting grommet 30. On refitment, use a new 'O' ring 32.

The excess pressure valve is incorporated in the pump and cannot be separately removed or renewed.

Air jets, removal and fitment:

Access to the jets requires removal of the heat exchangers as described earlier. Use new 'O' rings on refitment.

Drive pulley removal and fitment, earlier models:

1 Remove the engine transverse support and the silencer. Remove the regulation valve from the rear shield as described earlier.
2 Remove the rear shield and the pump drive belt. Do not lever the belt over the pulley flanges but slacken the pump off the camshaft extension.

When refitting the parts in the reverse order, make sure that the belt is correctly tensioned as described earlier.

Camshaft pulley bearing removal and fitment, earlier models:

This bearing is mounted in the lefthand camshaft chain cover. Remove the pulley as just explained, remove the retaining nuts and withdraw the bearing cover. Use a puller to draw the bearing off the camshaft, after removing the chain cover.

Clean the parts and check condition of bearing when unlubricated. Check the oil seal in the cover and renew if leaking. Lubricate the sealing lip after fitting. Refit the bearing on the camshaft after lubricating.

FIG 8 Adjusting the drive belt tension (early models)

FIG 9 Adjusting the drive belt tension (later models)

Fit the chain cover on a new gasket. Fit the bearing cover on a good gasket. Refit the pulley and tension the belt as described earlier.

Servicing the throttle valve compensator and vacuum pipes:

Remove the hose from the compensator (**FIG 10**). Detach the connecting rod ball joint socket, release the compensator from the mounting bracket and lift it away.

The vacuum lines are a push fit on the connections. The pipe from the compensator goes to a T-piece with branches to intake ports of cylinders 1 and 3. Branches from cylinders 1 and 4 go to a T-piece which is connected to the distributor vacuum control unit. Check that the pipes are in sound condition.

Adjusting the compensator and its linkage:

Before embarking on any adjustments, check that the ignition timing and idling speed are correctly set. Run the engine up to operating temperature and then check the compensator adjustment as follows.

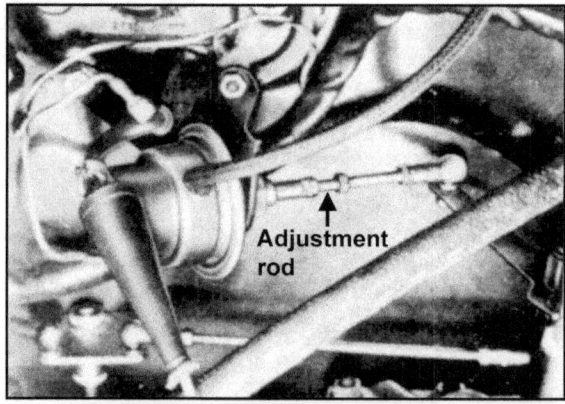

FIG 10 Throttle valve compensator
Upper arrow, adjuster   Lower arrow, clearance

Shut the throttle quickly from an engine speed of 3000rev/min. Engine speed should then fall to around 1000rev/min within 4 to 6 seconds. If this is not so, loosen the side screw which locks the adjusting screw indicated by the top arrow in **FIG 10**. Turn the adjusting screw right in.

Accelerate the engine quickly and shut off to draw the compensator rod up into the device and check the engine speed at once. It should be 2000 to 2200rev/min. If the speed is greater, lengthen the rod; if it is lower, shorten the rod, but make sure there is always slight clearance between the levers as indicated by the lower arrow when the engine is idling again.

Now adjust the time lag taken for the engine speed to drop. It must lie between 4 and 6 seconds, so turn the adjusting screw to the left to reduce the lag and to the right to increase it. In case of difficulty, check that the compensator is not sticking when the engine oil temperature is at least 90°C (200°F), or the indicator needle is in the green sector. Keeping the time lag to the upper limit will reduce exhaust backfiring to a minimum.

4 Vapour emission control

Engine breathing:

On all models the crankcase is vented to the oil tank and the oil tank is vented to the air cleaner canister (see **Chapter 1**, **FIGS 22, 23** and **24**). Oil fumes and blow-by gases are consequently consumed in the engine. A flame trap is provided at the crankcase breather outlet. The system ensures that noxious vapour is not discharged to atmosphere.

The flame trap should be cleaned in petrol at intervals of 12,000 miles (20,000km). The breather pipes should be blown through at the same time.

Fuel tank breathing (see FIGS 11 and 12):

A vented fuel tank filler cap will allow air to enter the tank as fuel is consumed but will not allow fuel vapour to leak to atmosphere. The vapour is vented via a vapour pipe to an activated carbon filter which is connected to the air cleaner canister. Accumulated vapour in the filter is drawn into the air cleaner and consumed in the engine so precluding its discharge to atmosphere. Pressure air from the cooling blower is fed to the filter to assist this flow of vapour.

Every 12,000 miles (20,000km), check that all hoses are securely connected. Every 60,000 miles (100,000km), remove and discard the activated carbon filter and fit a new replacement.

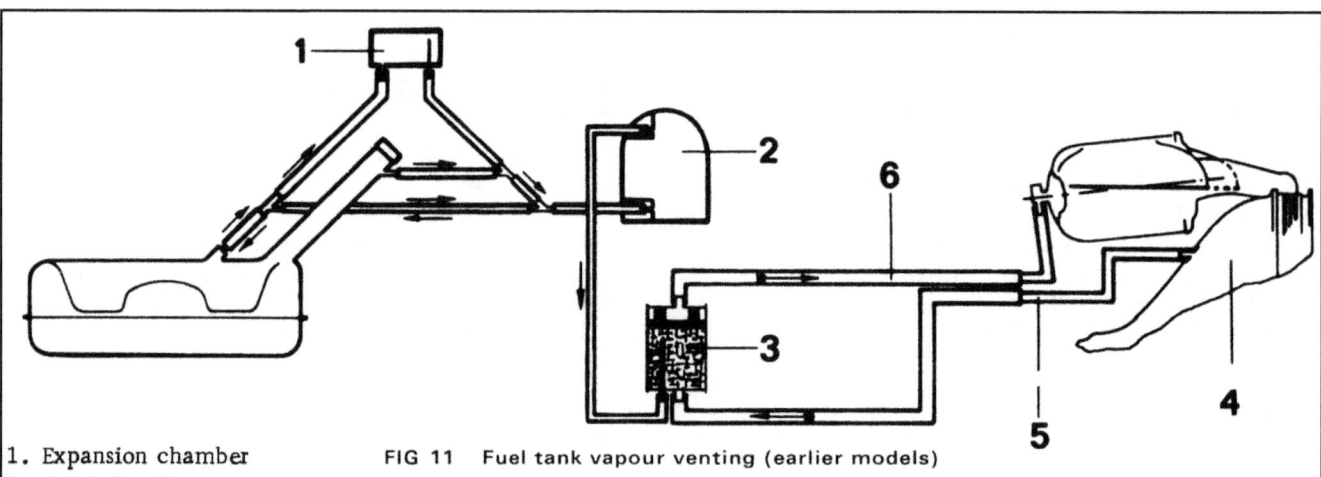

1. Expansion chamber
2. Vent chamber
3. Activated charcoal container
4. Engine fan upper shrouding
5. Pressure line from fan to activated charcoal container
6. Purging line from charcoal container to engine air cleaner

FIG 11 Fuel tank vapour venting (earlier models)

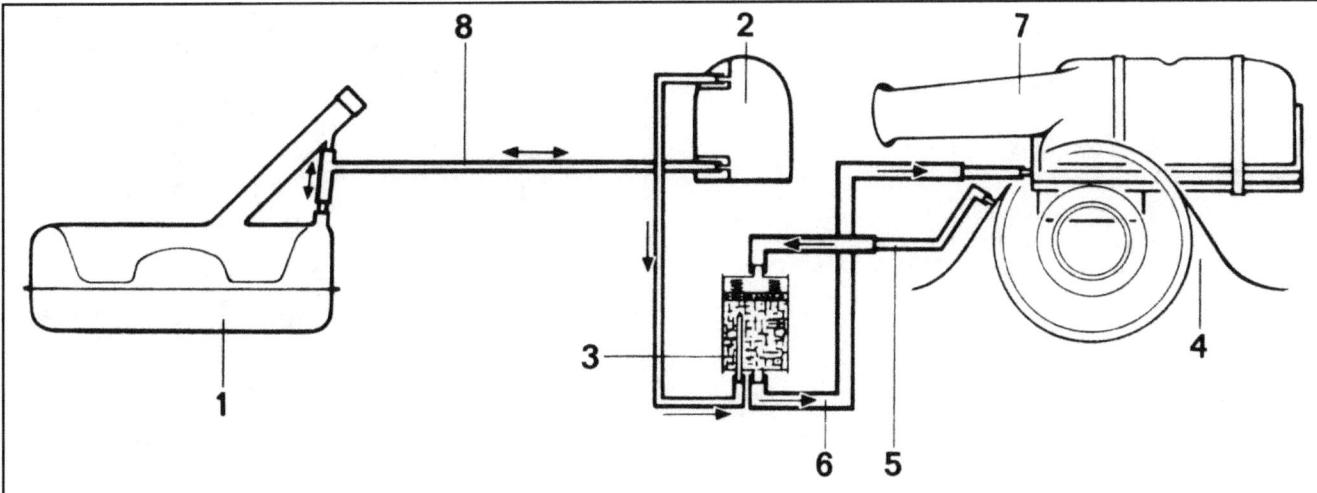

FIG 12 Fuel tank vapour venting (later models)

1 Fuel tank
2 Expansion chamber
3 Activated charcoal filter
4 Cooling fan upper shroud with hose connector
5 Hose from cooling fan to activated charcoal filter
6 Hose from activated charcoal filter to engine air filter
7 Engine air filter
8 Return hose connecting fuel tank with the expansion chamber

5 Supplemental information 1976-1983

Auxiliary air valve (remove - install):
Refer to FIG 13

1 Loosen the clamps securing the hoses to the rear of the device and pull the hoses off.
2 Remove the mounting bolts and lift away the air valve.
3 Installation is the reverse of removal.

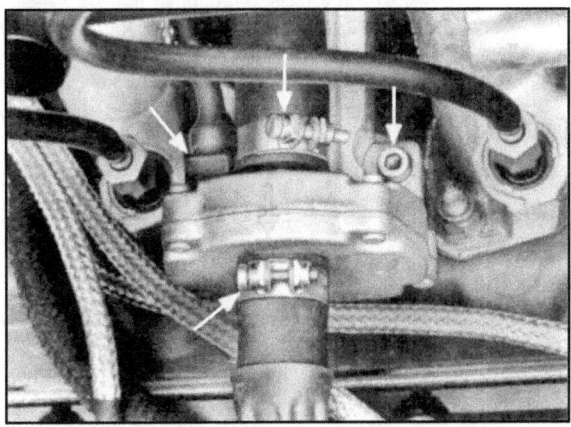

Fig. 13 Loosen the hose clamps (lower arrows) remove the mounting bolts (upper arrows)

Auxiliary air regulator (remove - install):
Refer to FIG 14

1 Disconnect the electrical leads from the air regulator.
2 Loosen both hose clamps
3 Remove the socket head mounting bolts and lift out the air regulator.
4 Installation is the reverse of removal.

Fig. 14 Electrical connector (upper left arrow) hose clamps (center two arrows) socket head mounting bolt (right arrow)

Diverter valve (remove - install):
Refer to FIG 15

1 Remove the clamps and pull the hose off the diverter valve
2 Remove the mounting bolts from the air pump carrier.
3 Disconnect the vacuum hose and lift the valve and bracket out.
4 Installation is the reverse of removal.

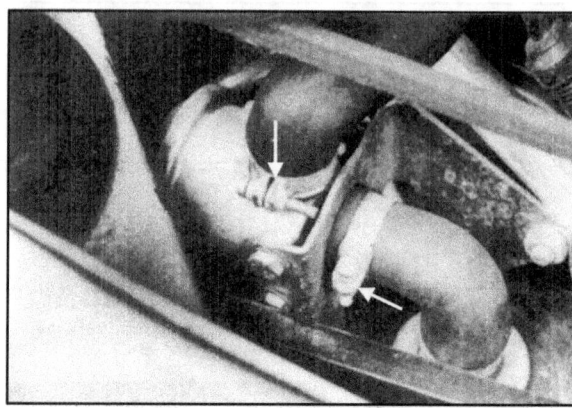

Fig. 15 Location of the diverter valve - below the distributor, in the engine compartment.

Throttle valve switch (remove - install):
Refer to FIG 16

1 Disconnect the cable from the negative terminal of the battery.
2 Remove the air cleaner assembly.
3 Disconnect the hose from the vacuum booster and the vacuum hoses for the distributor.
4 Remove the frequency valve holder.
5 Unplug the wire connector from the throttle valve switch.
6 Unscrew the throttle housing mounting bolts and remove the throttle housing.
7 Remove the throttle valve switch retaining screws and lift away the switch.
8 Installation is the reverse of removal but be sure a new O-ring is positioned properly on the throttle housing.

Fig. 16 Arrows indicate components which must be disconnected to remove the throttle valve switch

6 Supplemental information 1978 onwards

Oxygen sensor (refer to FIGS 17 through 22):

Removal and installation

1 Some later model cars have an oxygen sensor attached to the left exhaust manifold. (FIG 17)
2 Disconnect the oxygen sensor plug from the engine compartment on the left side. Push the plug and grommet downward through the engine panel.
3 Raise the rear of the vehicle and remove the left wheel.
4 Remove the shield from the left exhaust manifold. (FIG 18)
5 Lift the safety plug away from the oxygen sensor (FIG 19) and unscrew the oxygen sensor from the exhaust manifold.
6 Apply assembly paste to the threads of the oxygen sensor. Do not get any paste in the slot of the sensor.
7 Screw the sensor into the exhaust manifold as far as possible by hand then tighten it to between 36 to 43 ft-lbs (50 and 60 Nm).
8 Continue installation in the reverse order of removal.

Counter resetting

1 Anytime the oxygen sensor is replaced or every 30000 miles the counter must be reset to zero.
2 Disconnect the battery cable from the negative terminal.
3 Remove the speedometer.
4 Insert a piece of 0.12 in (3 mm) diameter wire through the speedometer hole in the dashboard and press the reset button into the stop. (FIG 20)
5 Install the speedometer and connect the negative cable to the battery.

Control unit — removal and installation (FIG 21)

1 Loosen the screws at the front and rear of the seat rails for the right seat.
2 Unplug the electrical connectors.
3 Remove the screws securing the control units for the acceleration enrichment and for the oxygen sensor.
4 Installation is the reverse of removal.

Frequency valve — testing (FIG 22)

1 Disconnect the electrical plug to the frequency valve and attach an ohmmeter to the valve.
2 Coil resistance should be between two and three ohms. If not, replace the frequency valve.

Fig. 17 Location of the oxygen sensor plug (arrow) on left side of engine compartment

Fig. 20 Reset the oxygen sensor counter located behind the speedometer

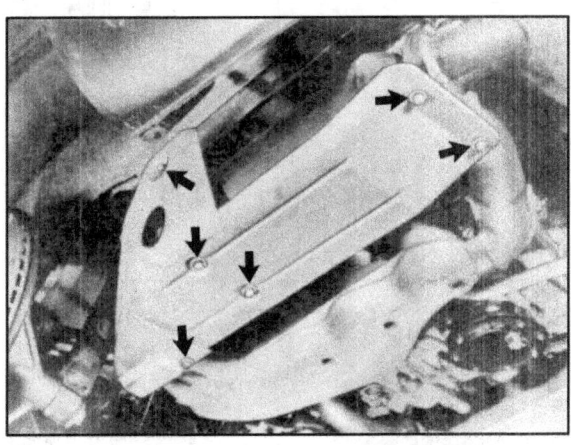

Fig. 18 Shield mounting screws (arrows) on the left exhaust manifold

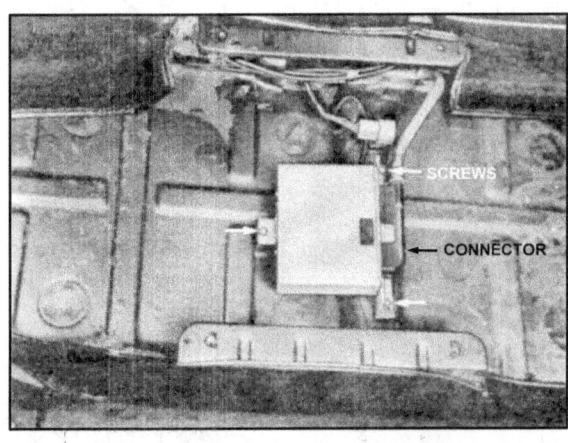

Fig. 21 Location of the control unit for the oxygen sensor under the right seat

Fig. 19 Remove the safety plug (upper arrow) from the oxygen sensor - unscrew the sensor (lower arrow)

Fig. 22 Location of the frequency valve's electrical plug (arrow)

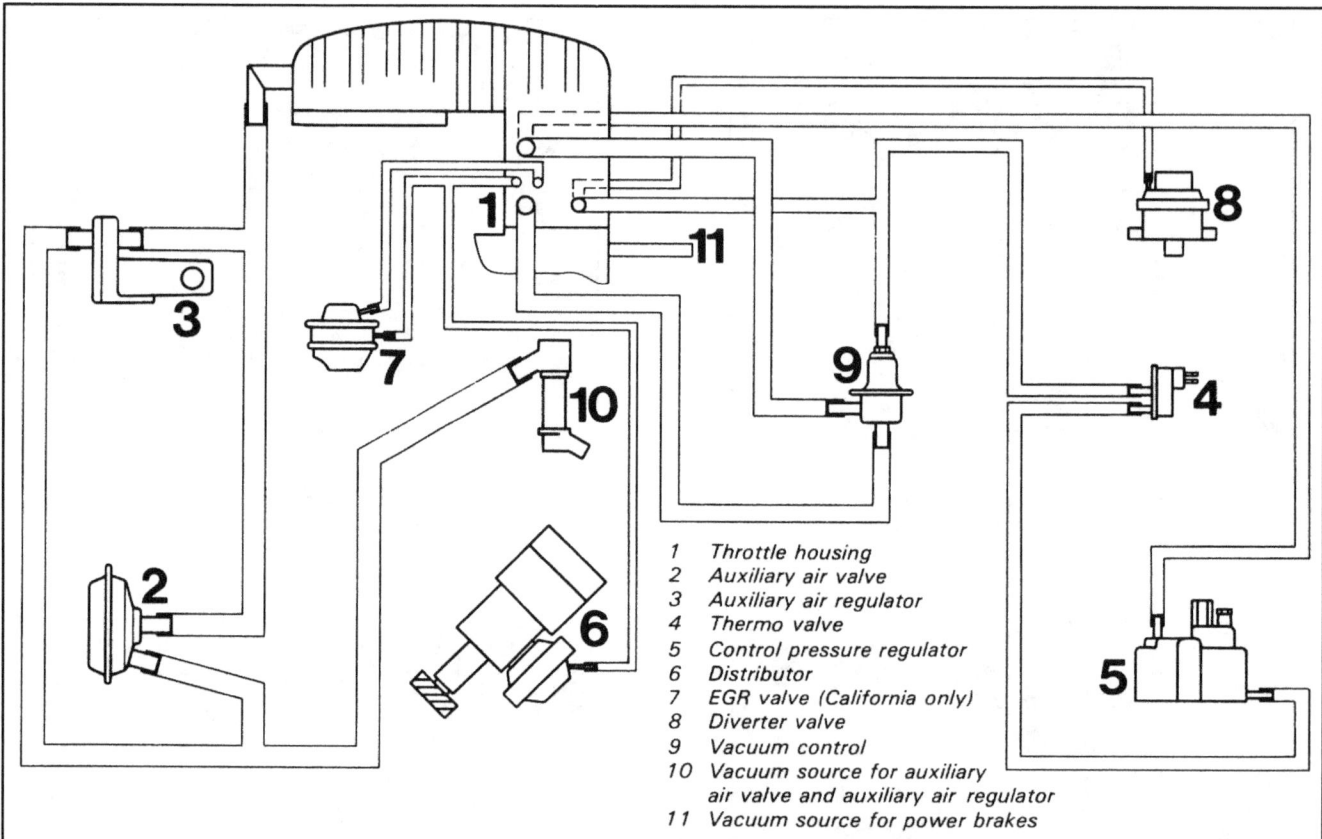

1 Throttle housing
2 Auxiliary air valve
3 Auxiliary air regulator
4 Thermo valve
5 Control pressure regulator
6 Distributor
7 EGR valve (California only)
8 Diverter valve
9 Vacuum control
10 Vacuum source for auxiliary air valve and auxiliary air regulator
11 Vacuum source for power brakes

Fig. 23 Vacuum line and emission control component layout of 1978 models

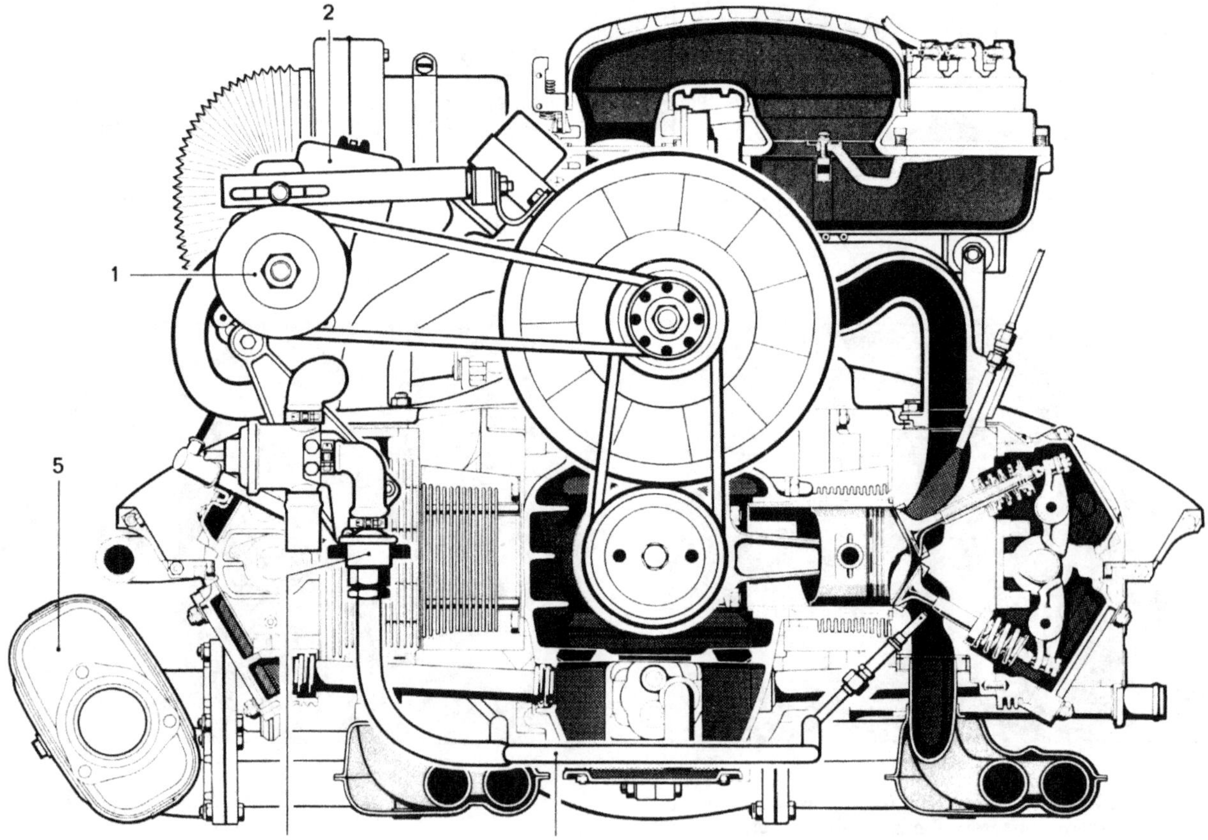

1 Air pump   2 Air pump filter   3 Check valve   4 Air line to exhaust port   5 Catalytic converter

Fig. 24 Locations of emission control devices on 1978 and 1979 models

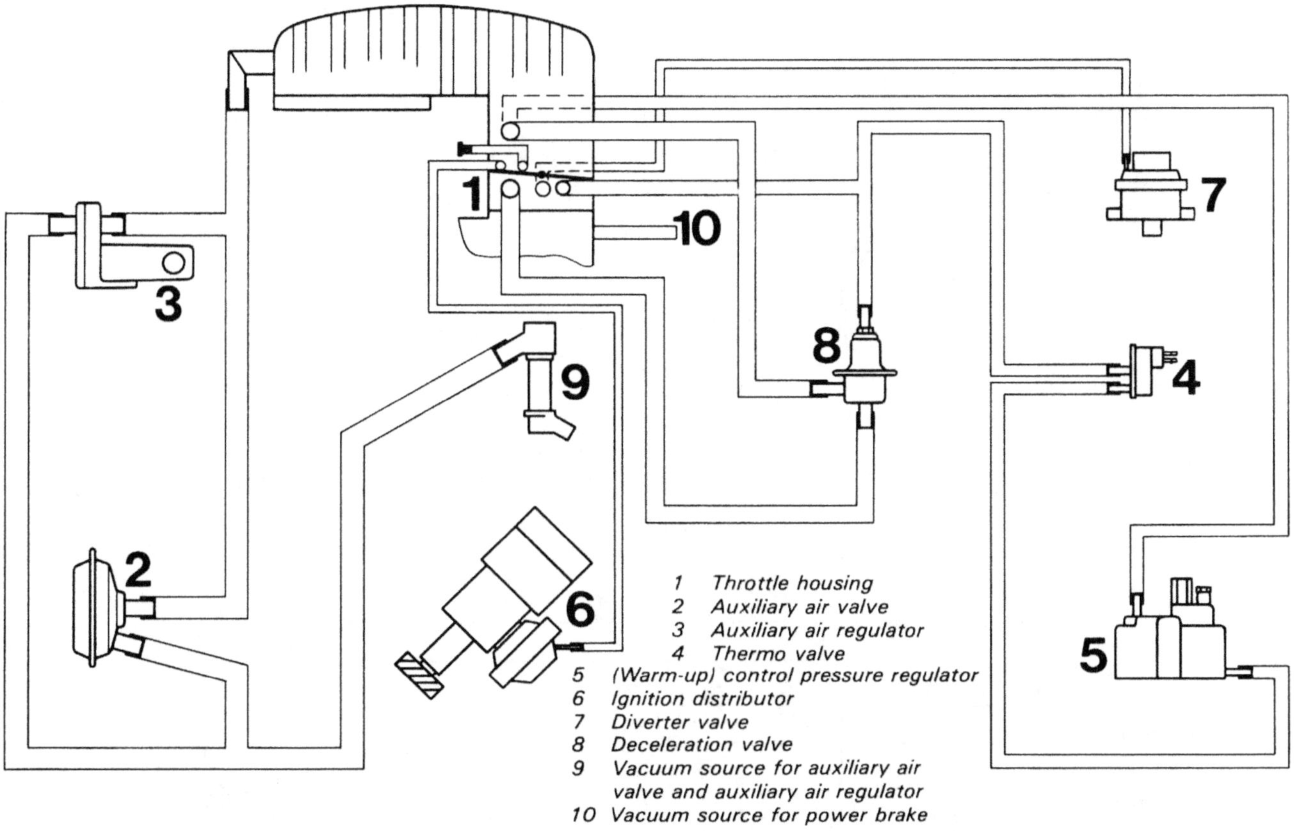

1. Throttle housing
2. Auxiliary air valve
3. Auxiliary air regulator
4. Thermo valve
5. (Warm-up) control pressure regulator
6. Ignition distributor
7. Diverter valve
8. Deceleration valve
9. Vacuum source for auxiliary air valve and auxiliary air regulator
10. Vacuum source for power brake

Fig. 25 Vacuum line and emission control component layout of 1979 models

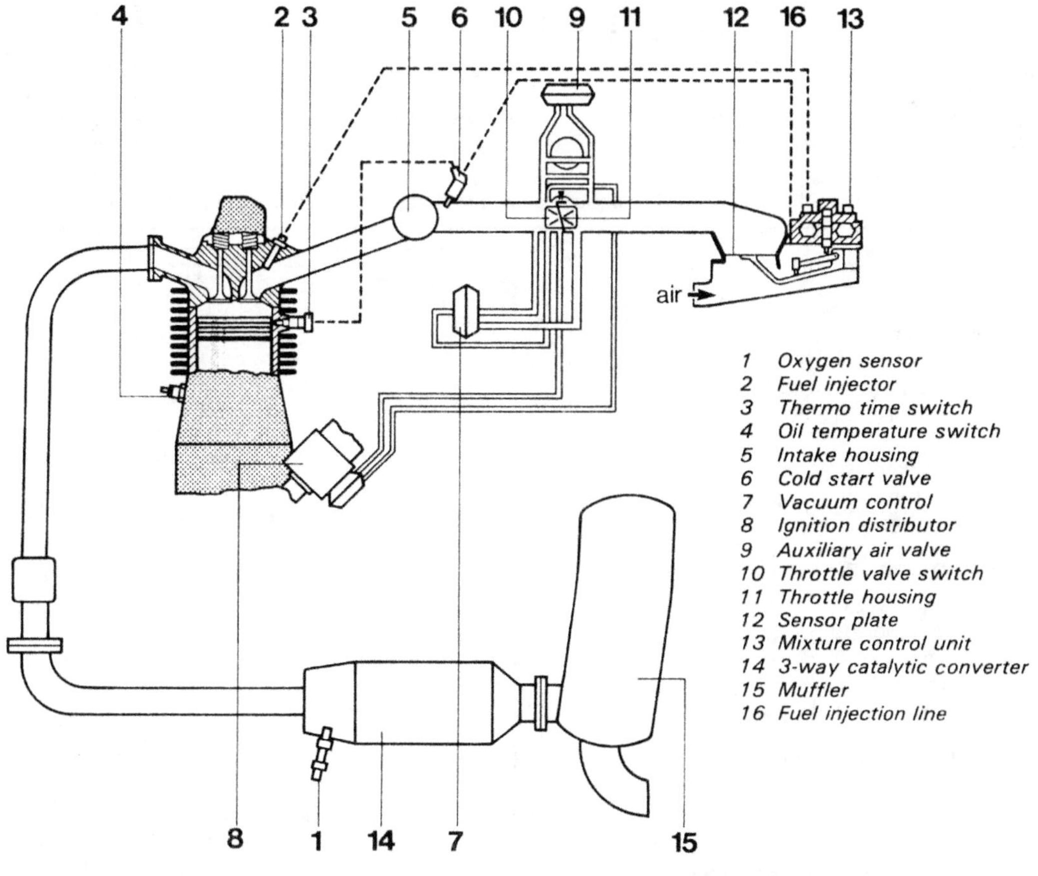

1. Oxygen sensor
2. Fuel injector
3. Thermo time switch
4. Oil temperature switch
5. Intake housing
6. Cold start valve
7. Vacuum control
8. Ignition distributor
9. Auxiliary air valve
10. Throttle valve switch
11. Throttle housing
12. Sensor plate
13. Mixture control unit
14. 3-way catalytic converter
15. Muffler
16. Fuel injection line

Fig. 26 Component layout of emission control devices on 1980 through 1983 models

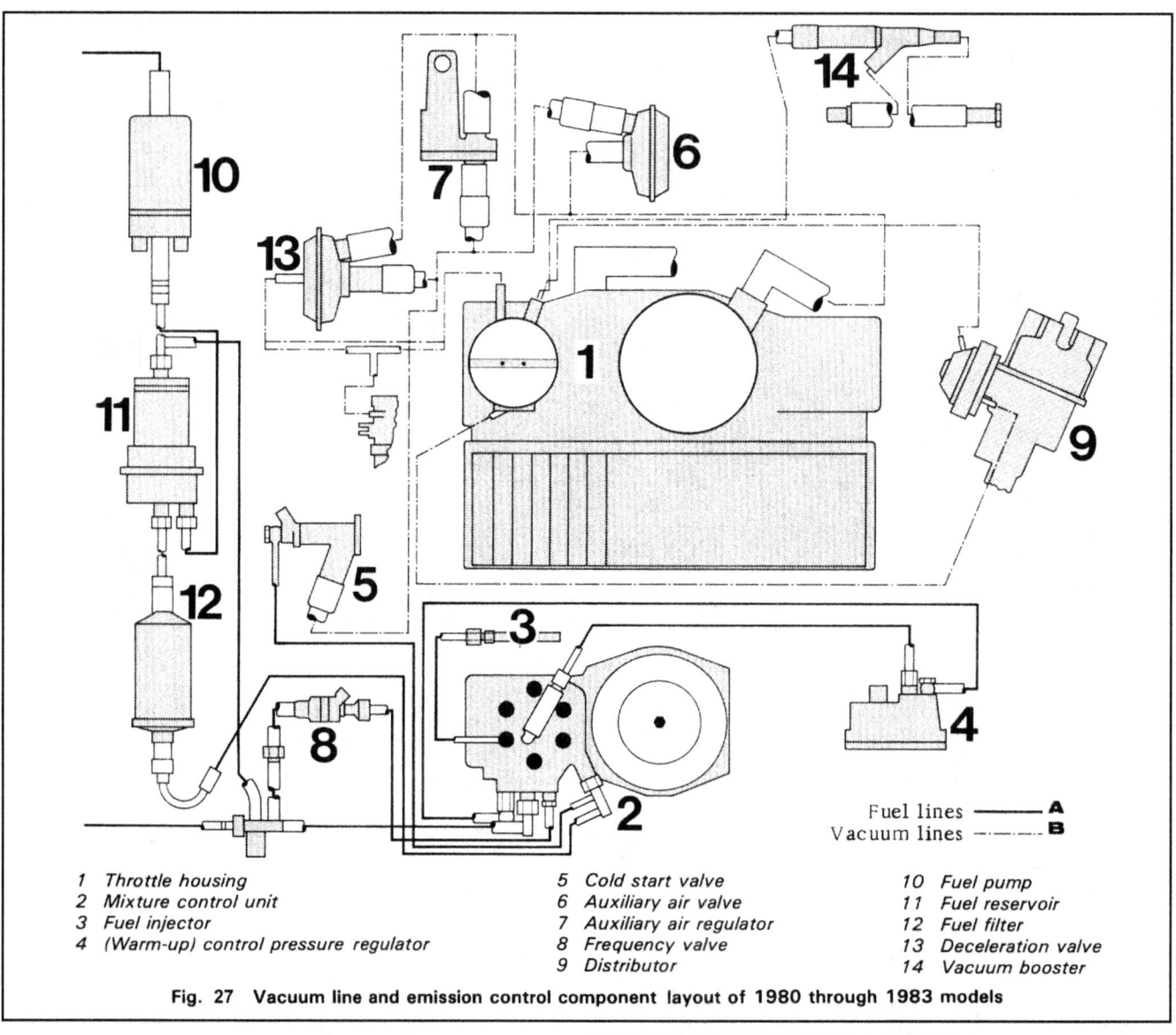

1 Throttle housing
2 Mixture control unit
3 Fuel injector
4 (Warm-up) control pressure regulator
5 Cold start valve
6 Auxiliary air valve
7 Auxiliary air regulator
8 Frequency valve
9 Distributor
10 Fuel pump
11 Fuel reservoir
12 Fuel filter
13 Deceleration valve
14 Vacuum booster

Fuel lines ——— A
Vacuum lines —·— B

Fig. 27 Vacuum line and emission control component layout of 1980 through 1983 models

7 Fault diagnosis

(a) Engine overheats

1 Blower fan belt requires tensioning
2 Cooling air spilling from joints
3 Deflectors and/or shrouds wrongly fitted
4 Cooling fins (crankcase, oil cooler, cylinder) caked with dirt
5 Exhaust system blocked
6 Fuel system out of tune
7 Ignition timing incorrect

(b) Heating system ineffective

1 Check 1 in (a)
2 Control cables broken or out of adjustment
3 Spill valves stuck open
4 Hoses disconnected or leaking
5 Auxiliary heater defective or inoperative

(c) Vapour emission system ineffective

1 Breather pipe disconnected
2 Breather pipe blocked
3 Flame trap blocked
4 Fuel vapour pipe disconnected or blocked
5 Carbon filter requires renewal

NOTES

CHAPTER 5 - CLUTCH

1 Description
2 Maintenance
3 The control cable
4 Removing and refitting the clutch
5 Servicing the clutch components
6 Modified clutch components 1977 onwards
7 Fault diagnosis

1 Description

The clutch fitted to manual transmission models is of the single dry-plate variety incorporating a diaphragm spring (see **FIG 1**). The cover 1 is bolted to the front face of the flywheel 10 and carries diaphragm spring 4 on pins and fulcrum rings. The spring bears on pressure plate 2 and spring pressure at points 14 traps driven plate 3 between the faces of the flywheel and the pressure plate. The driven plate is splined to the gearbox input shaft 7 and thus transmits drive from the flywheel to the gearbox. When the clutch pedal is depressed, release bearing 5 presses on the fingers of the diaphragm of the diaphragm spring. As spring pressure on the pressure plate is relieved, the driven plate is no longer trapped, and there is no drive from the flywheel to the input shaft and gearbox. The hub 15 of the driven plate incorporates shock-absorbing springs to eliminate clutch engagement snatch. Clutches fitted to earlier models are not identical to those fitted to later models.

The clutch is operated by a Bowden-type cable arrangement in which, on earlier models, the outer cable pushes the throwout fork lever but, on later models, the inner cable pulls the fork lever. Referring to **FIG 2** the forward end of the earlier clutch cable is attached to the pedal by an adjustable fork end, and at the rear end to an integrally cast lug on the transmission housing. The outer cable housing is adjustable and is supported at the centre tunnel rear panel and the clutch throwout fork. It is routed in an upward arc through a guide bracket that prevents the cable moving sideways but allows it to move vertically and towards the throwout fork.

When the pedal is depressed the cable is tensioned and because it is fixed firmly to the transmission housing the pressure is then exerted on the cable housing. The housing reacts against the rear wall of the centre tunnel and is forced to move in the direction of the throwout fork. As it approaches its fully extended condition it reacts also against the throwout fork pushing the end away from the centre tunnel rear panel. When the gap between the end of the fork and the tunnel rear panel has increased by about 15mm (0.60in) the clutch is fully disengaged.

In later models the throwout fork and clutch lever are mounted on a shaft which is splined on both ends and located within the transmission tunnel. The fork is located on the shaft by a roll pin and the lever is secured to the shaft by a lockring and the lever is now pulled by the inner cable instead of being pushed by the cable housing as on earlier models.

1977 models have a servo arrangement where the adjusting lever is splined to the shaft and the release lever is located by a roll pin, an adjusting screw and locknut are located in the release lever. See **Section 6**.

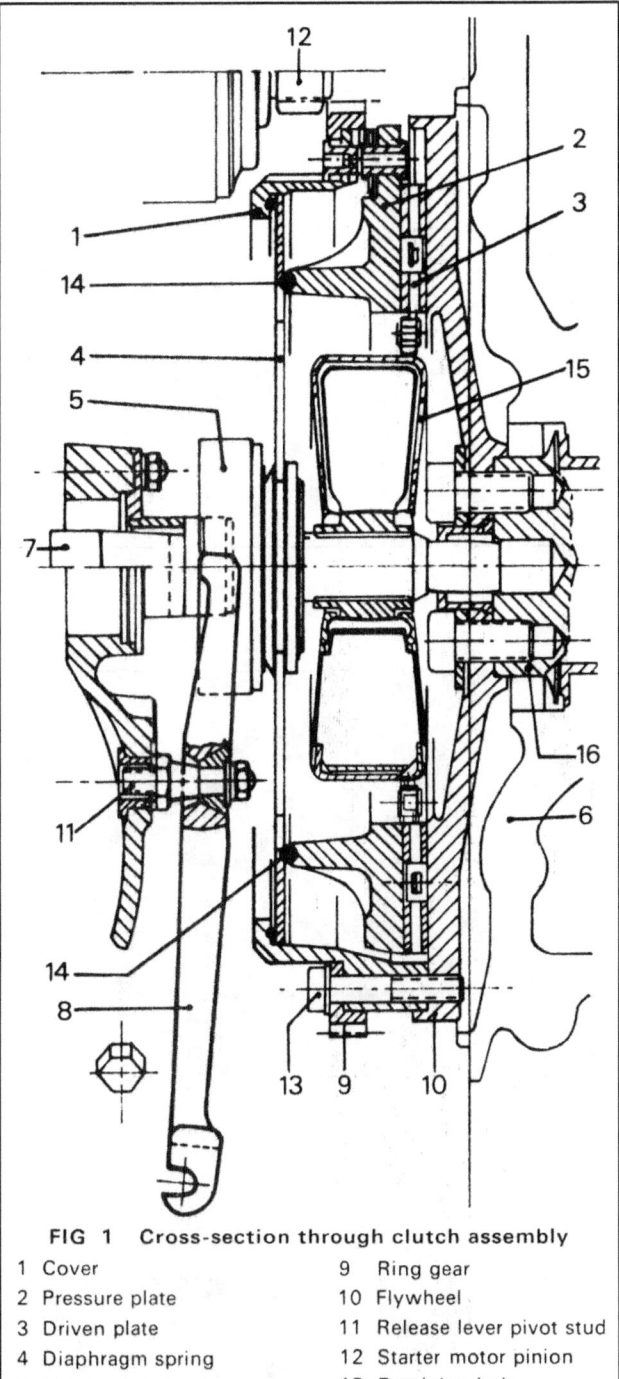

FIG 1 Cross-section through clutch assembly

1 Cover
2 Pressure plate
3 Driven plate
4 Diaphragm spring
5 Release bearing
6 Crankcase
7 Input shaft to gearbox
8 Release lever
9 Ring gear
10 Flywheel
11 Release lever pivot stud
12 Starter motor pinion
13 Retaining bolt
14 Spring loading points
15 Driven plate hub

2 Maintenance

Every 6000 miles (10,000km) in the case of earlier models and every 12,000 miles (20,000km) in the case of later models, check and adjust the clutch pedal free play if necessary. The free play at the pedal pad should be within the range of 20 to 25mm (0.80 to 1.00in) on all models. The adjustment procedures are described in **Section 3**.

When the limit of adjustment is reached, a new release bearing and/or a new driven clutch plate should be fitted.

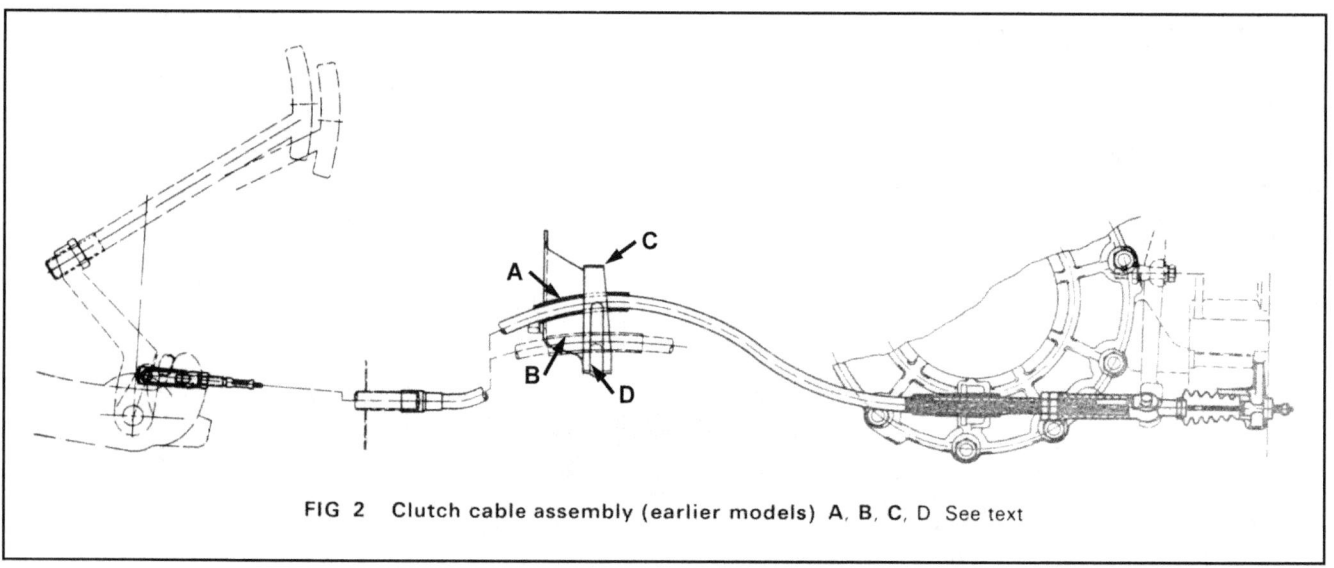

FIG 2 Clutch cable assembly (earlier models) A, B, C, D See text

FIG 3 Adjusting earlier type cable

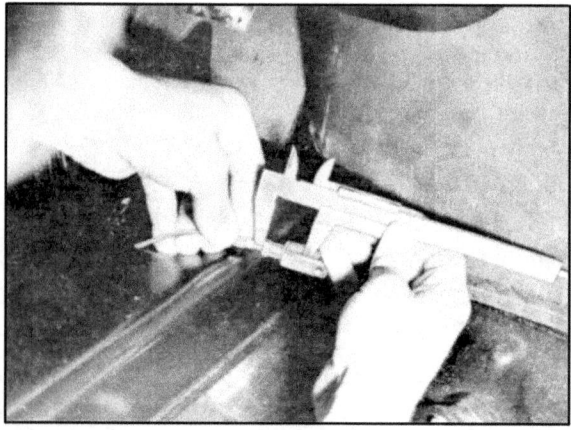

FIG 4 Measuring end of cable to outer face of locknut dimension

3 The control cable

Earlier type cable assembly:

The layout of this type of cable is shown in **FIG 2**. The cable assembly must be correctly arced so that, when the inner cable is tensioned by operation of the clutch pedal, the outer cable 'straightens' and pushes the clutch release lever. When operated, a correctly set cable assembly will move up and down in the guide bracket between positions indicated at **A** and **B**. The procedure for resetting the arc of the cable assembly is included in the following pedal free play adjustment sequence.

Free play adjustment, earlier type cables:

1 Loosen the cable housing locknut (see **FIG 3**) and turn the adjusting nut to obtain a free play in the clutch pedal of 20 to 25mm (0.80 to 1.00in). To check, measure the travel of the pedal as it is pulled upwards. Tighten the locknut without turning the cable housing.

2 When the clutch pedal is fully depressed the throwout fork should move approximately 15mm (0.60in) to disengage the clutch fully. If it does not move this distance the clutch pedal stop must be adjusted.

3 Refer to **FIG 2**. If the cable rests at D (the bottom of the guide bracket) when the pedal is fully depressed, adjust the inner cable at the fork end. To check the location of the cable in the fork end, use slide calipers and measure from the end of the cable to the outer face of the locknut as shown in **FIG 4**. The correct measurement should be between 17 and 22mm (0.70 and 0.90in).

4 If, after adjusting, the cable still rests on the bottom of the guide bracket, lengthen the inner cable at the fork end.

5 If the arc of the cable is too large with the cable coming out of the top of the guide bracket (C in **FIG 2**) in the pedal released position, the inner cable must be shortened at the fork end.

Later type cable assembly:

As indicated in **Section 1**, the inner cable is operated by the clutch pedal and actuates clutch release by pulling on the release lever. This arrangement is that usually designed for Bowden-type cables and is not illustrated.

Free play adjustment, later type cables:

Refer to **FIG 5**. Using two spanners, hold the cable end while turning the self-locking nut in the appropriate direction to obtain a free travel at the clutch pedal of 20 to 25mm (0.80 to 1.00in) when it is pulled upwards. Operate the clutch pedal a number of times and recheck the pedal free play. No adjustment is required at the pedal end of the cable. If a new cable is fitted, the cable end should be screwed fully into the clevis so that it is flush but does not protrude.

Servo type clutch:

Clutch play cannot be measured at the pedal, but is measured at the adjusting and release levers. Check that the clutch cable is tight. Release the locknut on the adjusting screw at the release lever and set the adjusting screw so that there is a clearance of 1.0 + 0.1mm (0.040 + 0.004in) between the screw and the adjusting lever. Tighten the locknut.

4 Removing and refitting the clutch

Removal:

Remove the engine and transmission assembly, as described in **Chapter 1, Section 3**. On models with the type of fork lever shown in **FIGS 2** and **3** it is necessary before separating the engine and transmission to release the tension on the throwout bearing and disengage the fork lever as follows:

1 Remove the starter and turn the flywheel to bring one of three equally spaced threaded rivet heads into sight through the starter mounting aperture.
2 Install a spacer sleeve on each of the three rivet heads secured with a M6 × 12 Allen screw. By tightening the three screws evenly, as shown in **FIG 6**, the diaphragm spring will be lifted to release the tension on the throwout bearing.
3 Refer now to **FIG 7** and with a screwdriver inserted through the opening in the transmission housing, turn the throwout bearing 90° until the throwout fork lever can be slid past the bearing. Remove the three Allen screws and spacers. If the clutch cable is loose detach the cable and adjust play between the adjusting lever and the adjusting screw to 1.2mm (0.047in). Attach the cable and tighten until play is 1.0 + 0.1mm (0.040 + 0.004in).

Support the engine and transmission assembly and remove the nuts, bolts and washers holding the two units together. Taking care not to strain the gearbox input shaft in any direction, separate the transmission from the engine and clutch. Loosen the bolts which attach the clutch assembly to the flywheel by a turn at a time. Work diagonally and evenly and gradually release the spring load. Dismount the pressure plate assembly and the clutch driven plate from the flywheel.

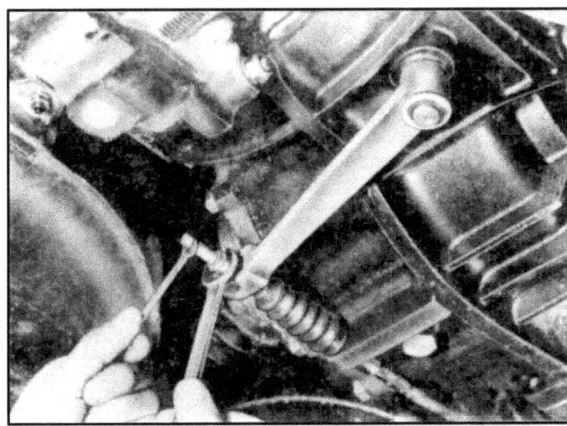

FIG 5 Adjusting later type cable

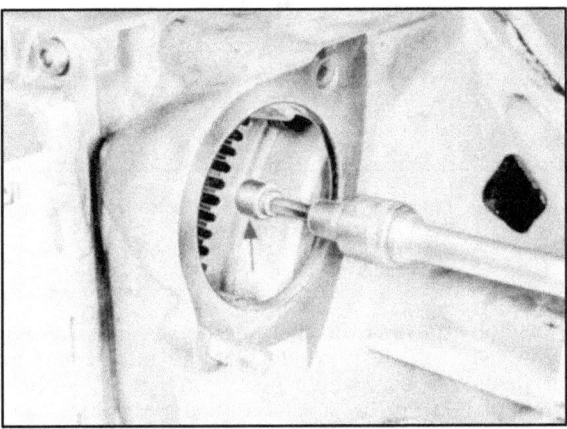

FIG 6 Relieving tension on release bearing. One of the spacers is arrowed

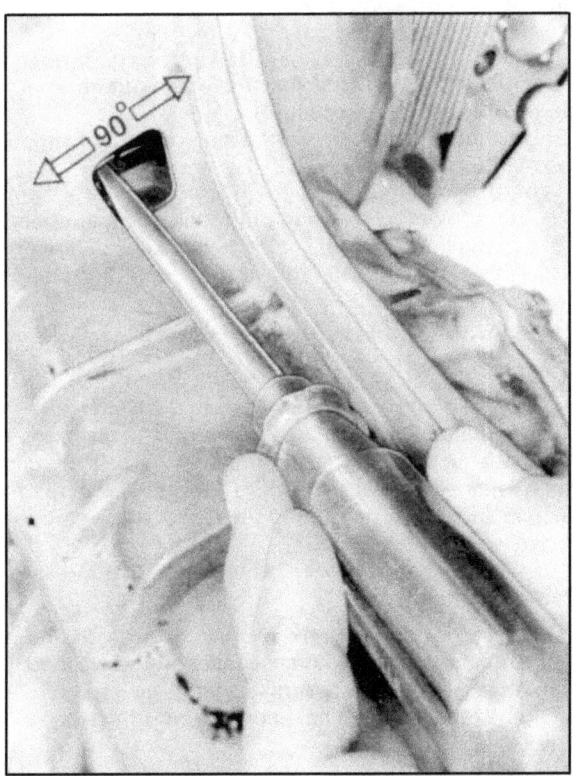

FIG 7 Turning the bearing through 90°

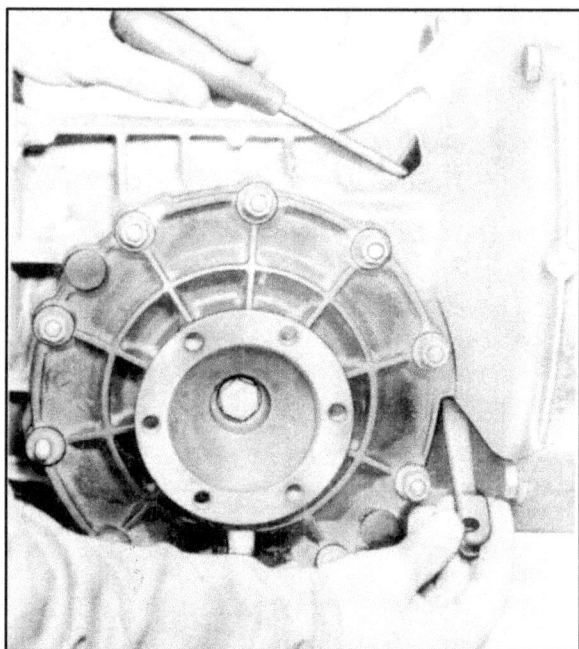

FIG 8 Turning the bearing into engagement with the fork lever

Fitment:

Position the pressure plate assembly and the clutch driven plate on the flywheel. Fit the attachment bolts and their washers but do not tighten them. Align the clutch plate using a stub shaft or a mandrel inserted through the plate hub and into the pilot bearing. Working diagonally and evenly tighten the retaining bolts and finally torque them to 3.5kgm (25lb ft). Remove the centring mandrel and press about 2cc of molybdenum disulphide grease into the bore of the pilot bearing.

On models with the earlier pattern fork lever, refit the three Allen screws and spacers used during removal (stage 2 of removal procedure).

Refit the transmission to the engine as described in **Chapter 6, Section 3**.

Where applicable, refer to **FIG 8** and use a screwdriver, as shown, to turn and guide the throwout bearing into engagement with the fork lever. Loosen the three Allen screws evenly and remove them and the spacers.

5 Servicing the clutch components

Dismantling:

Lay the clutch assembly on the bench with the pressure plate upwards. Press down on the plate and the thrust washer and, using circlip pliers, remove the circlip which retains the release bearing. Take careful note of the washers and which way round they are fitted. Remove the release bearing.

Release bearing:

Do not use petrol or any solvent to clean the release bearing as the prepacked grease must not be washed out. An excessively worn bearing cannot be repaired and should be replaced by a new component of the same part number.

Diaphragm spring:

Check for wear and cracks. Scoring and wear at the inner ends of the fingers up to a depth of 0.30mm (0.012in) is acceptable. If the spring is cracked or excessively worn, a new or exchange replacement assembly will be required. Ensure that the new clutch is the same type as that removed.

Pressure plate:

Cracks, deep scores or uneven wear dictate rejection and the fitment of a new assembly of the same type as that removed. Concavity across the operating face of up to 0.30mm (0.012in) is acceptable.

Driven plate:

Renew the plate if the linings are broken, burned or contaminated with oil. Do not attempt to clean off contamination. Check for wear and renew the plate if the thickness over the linings is down to 6.5mm (0.25in). Reject the plate if the wear is uneven.

Mount the plate on a mandrel between centres and check the run out with a dial gauge. Maximum permissible runout is 60mm (0.023in). It will be noticed that the steel disc is divided into leaves and the linings are riveted to these alternately. The leaves are bowed and offset to provide a cushioning effect and the offsetting must be evenly balanced.

Check hub splines for wear. The plate should slide freely on the input shaft without undue play. Check the hub shock absorbing springs for wear and breakage.

The linings may have a high polish and be perfectly capable of transmitting power. If the grain of the lining material is visible the linings are good, but if the linings are a dark brown with an opaque glaze, they are probably contaminated with burnt oil and the plate must be renewed. It is not advisable to attempt to rivet new linings into place.

A new replacement plate must be of the correct type. Note, in particular, that the number of splines in the bore of the hub differs between earlier and later type clutches.

Reassembly:

Follow the reverse of the dismantling sequence. Apply molybdenum disulphide grease sparingly to the diaphragm spring finger tips before fitting the release bearing.

6 Modified clutch components 1977 onwards

Adjusting auxiliary spring type clutch:

1 The clutch on models with an auxiliary spring must be adjusted at the transmission.

2 Test the clutch cable for excessive play. Adjust the tension if necessary.

3 When the cable is tight, insert a feeler gauge between the adjusting lever and the adjusting bolt. The clearance should be between 0.039 and 0.043 in (1.0 and 1.1 mm).

4 To adjust the clutch itself, loosen the cable or remove it from the holder.

5 Adjust the play in the clutch at the adjusting lever to 0.047 in (1.2 mm). Measure with a feeler gauge.

6 Install the cable and tighten it at the holder until the play at the adjusting lever is reduced to 0.039 in (1.0 mm).

7 It may be necessary to make some of the adjustment at the pedal assembly.

8 Measure the clutch cable, as shown in **FIG 9**, with the clutch released.
9 Depress the clutch pedal and measure the clutch cable again. The difference of the two measurements is the amount of clutch travel. The travel should be between 0.965 and 1.004 in (24.5 and 25.5 mm).
10 Adjust the stop on the floor plate until the specified travel is attained.

Auxiliary clutch spring (remove - install):
Removal - Refer to FIG 10

1 On some transmissions installed in vehicles produced from 1977 an auxiliary clutch spring **10** is mounted to the bottom of the transmission housing.
2 Remove the spring **1** from the adjusting lever.
3 Disengage the circlip **2** from the lever shaft **19** used to secure the adjusting lever **3**.
4 Lift the adjusting lever from the shaft.
5 Pry the release lever **6** toward the front of the transmission cover and release the auxiliary spring. The auxiliary spring will snap forward on its own when the 'dead point' is reached.
6 Use a drift of the proper size and drive out the roll pin **5** from the clutch release lever. No roll pin is used after March, 1979.
7 Lift the release lever and seal from the lever shaft. The auxiliary spring and its mounting components will remain attached to the release lever.

1977 Models - Refer to FIG 10

1 On 1977 models, place washer **11** over the pin and slide the auxiliary spring onto the pin until the upper washer and clip **8 & 9** can be attached.

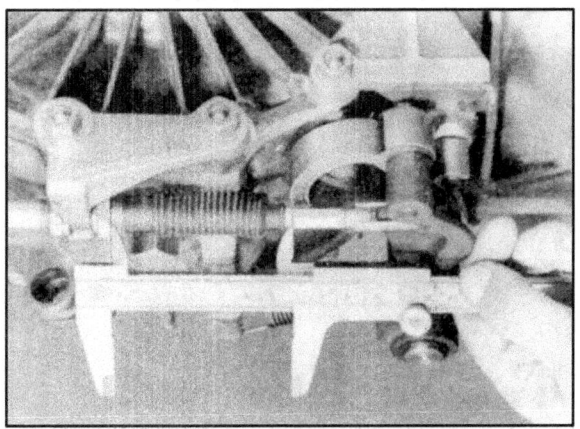

Fig. 9 Measure the clutch release travel Using a vernier caliper

2 Replace the seal **7** on the lever shaft, if necessary, and slide the release lever and auxiliary spring assembly onto the splines of the lever shaft. Secure the release lever with a roll pin **5**, if so equipped.
3 Pry the release lever until the auxiliary spring can be located on the stop pin.
4 The adjusting lever **3** should not be installed until the engine/transmission is installed in the vehicle.

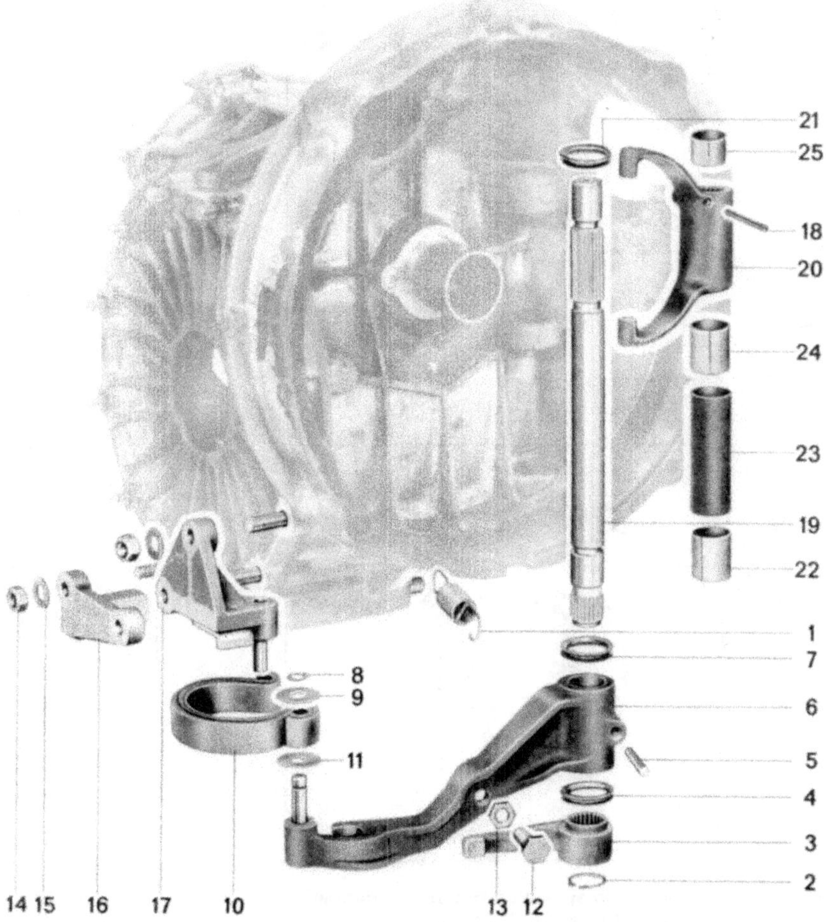

1 Adjusting lever spring
2 Circlip
3 Adjusting lever
4 Seal
5 Roll pin
6 Release lever
7 Seal
8 Circlip
9 Washer
10 Auxiliary spring
11 Washer
12 Adjusting bolt
13 Nut
14 Nut
15 Washer
16 Holder
17 Base
18 Spring pin
19 Lever shaft
20 Release fork
21 Seal
22 Bushing
23 Cover tube
24 Bushing
25 Bushing

Fig. 10 Auxiliary clutch spring components

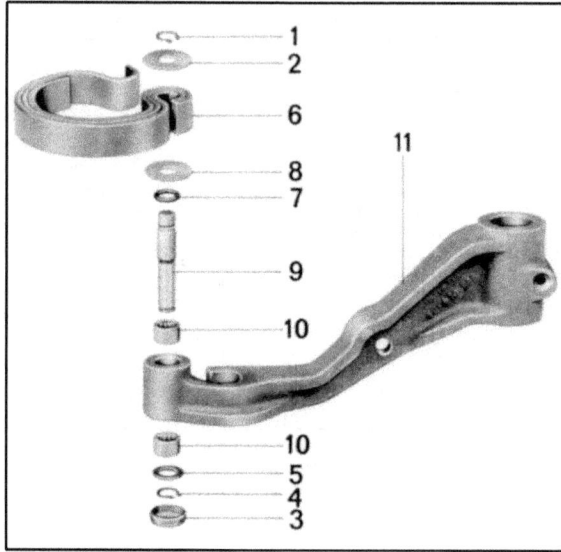

Fig. 11 Auxiliary clutch spring and release lever components (beginning 1977 model)

1 Circlip
2 Washer
3 Cover
4 Circlip
5 Washer
6 Auxiliary spring
7 O-ring
8 Washer
9 Pin
10 Needle bushing
11 Release lever

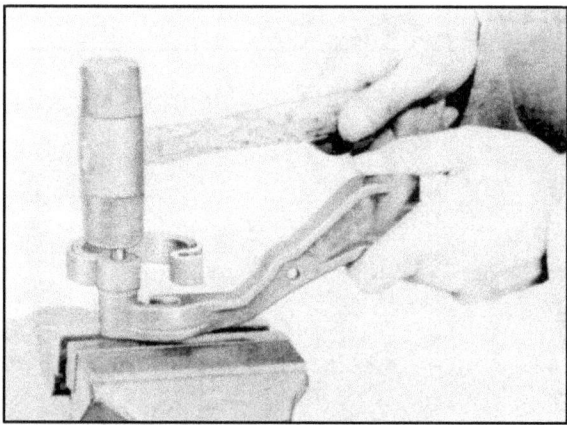

Fig. 12 Drive pin into auxiliary spring until the cover can be removed from below

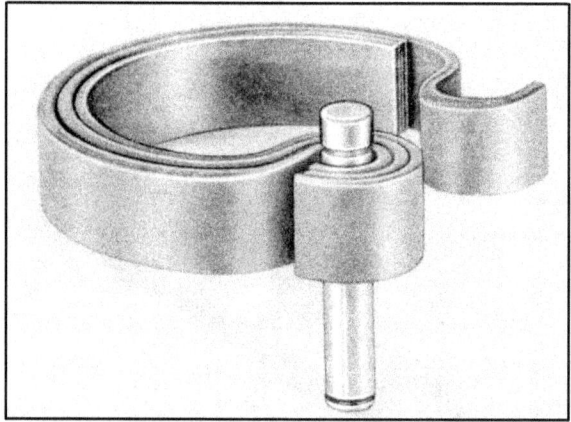

Fig. 13 Position pin in spring so the upper washer and circlip can be installed

1978 Models - Refer to FIG 11

1 To separate the auxiliary spring, remove the circlip and the washers **1 & 2** and pull the spring off the pin. On 1978 and later models the release lever is equipped with a removable pin and two needle bushings.

2 On these later models, remove the clip from the spring end of the pin and drive the pin down until the cover drops off. **(FIG 12)** Remove the lower clip and washer and lift the spring away. The pin will remain on the spring.

3 Drive the needle bushings **10** out of the release lever using an appropriate sized drift.

4 Press new needle bushings into the release lever. Refer to **FIG 14** for the correct positioning of the bushings.

5 Drive the pin into the spring enough **(FIG 13)** so the washer and clip **1 & 2** can be installed. Replace the clip if necessary.

6 Place a new washer and O-ring **7 & 8** on the pin below the auxiliary spring.

7 Apply a coat of silicone or lithium-based waterproof grease to the bore of the release lever and the needle bushings.

8 Push the spring and pin into the release lever until the washer and clip **4 & 5** can be installed.

9 Drive a new cover **3** into position.

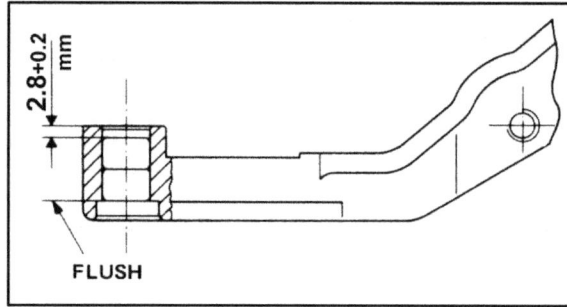

Fig. 14 Proper positioning of the needle bushings in the release lever

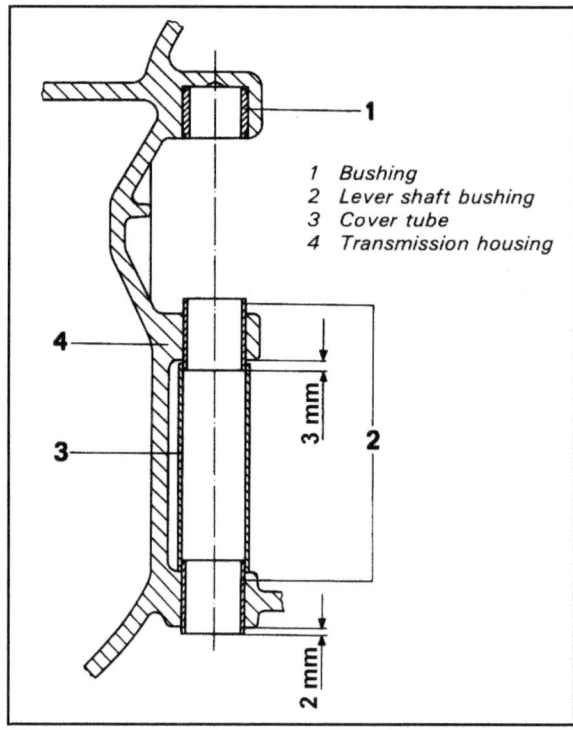

1 Bushing
2 Lever shaft bushing
3 Cover tube
4 Transmission housing

Fig. 15 Proper positioning of the lever shaft bushings in the bellhousing

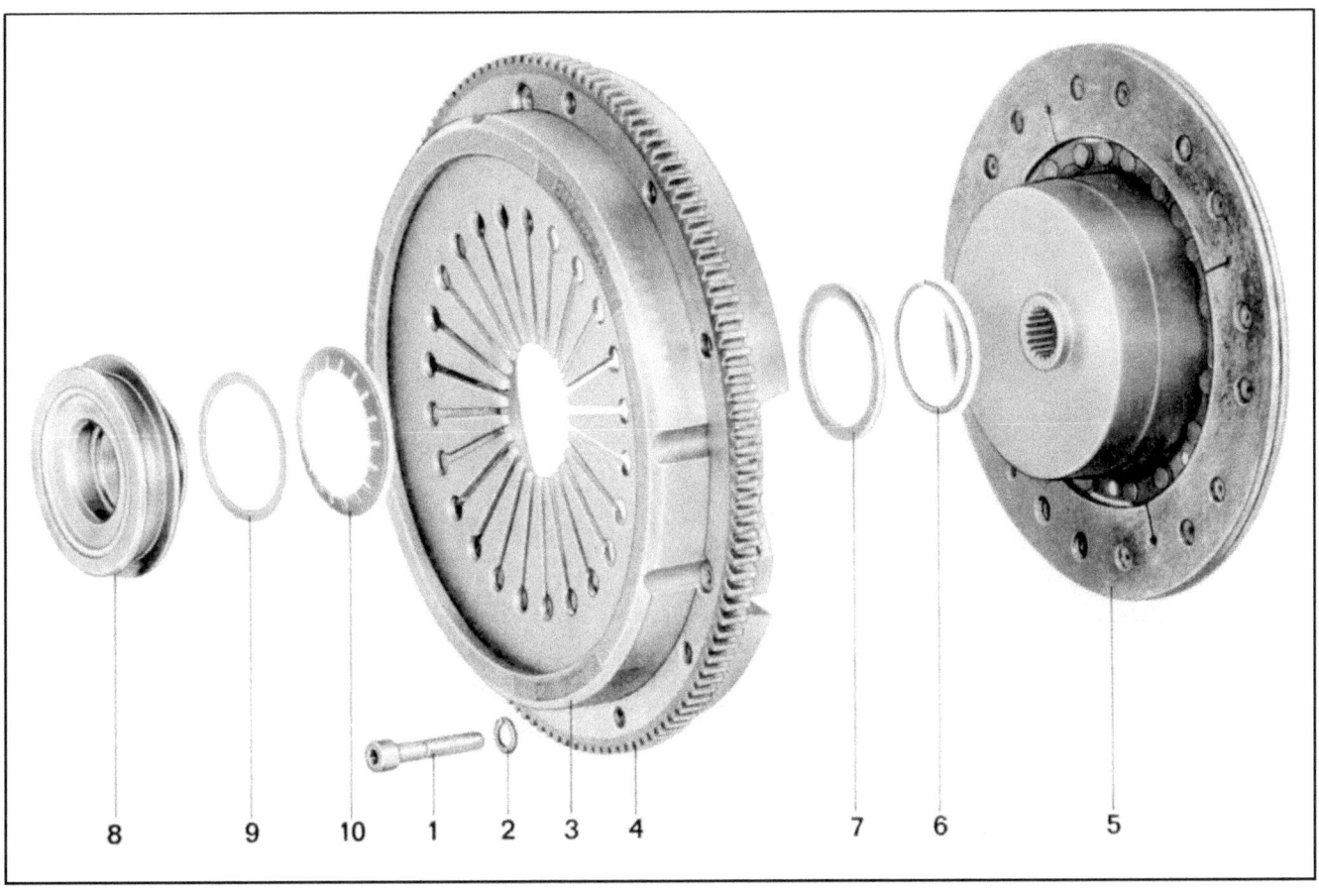

Fig. 16 Modified clutch (beginning 1978 models)

1 Socket head bolt	3 Pressure plate	5 Clutch disc
2 Lockwasher	4 Ring gear	6 Circlip
7 Thrust washer	9 Washer	
8 Release (throwout) bearing	10 Spring washer	

7 Fault diagnosis

(a) Noisy clutch

1 Worn pilot bush in flywheel boss
2 Worn release bearing
3 Broken springs in driven plate hub
4 Broken driven plate disc or linings

(b) Clutch judder

1 Defective engine and transmission mountings
2 Pressure plate face worn and uneven
3 Diaphragm spring distorted
4 Driven plate disc distorted
5 Grease or oil on linings

(c) Dragging or incomplete release

1 Excessive clutch clearance
2 Driven plate or input shaft running out of true
3 Driven plate segments or linings unevenly set
4 Input shaft spigot bearing tight
5 Stiffness of clutch pedal, cable or release mechanism
6 Sticky linings
7 Distorted clutch cover or pressure plate

(d) Slipping

1 See 3 and 5 in (b)
2 Lack of free play in clutch pedal
3 Linings burned or broken, contact faces defective

NOTES

NOTES

CHAPTER 6 - MANUAL TRANSMISSION

1 Description
2 Maintenance
3 Removing and installing the transmission
4 Dismantling the transmission
5 Servicing the gearbox shafts
6 The differential gearing
7 Gear and backlash settings
8 The front cover and intermediate plate
9 The oil pump
10 Reassembling the transmission
11 Gearchange linkage
12 Fault diagnosis

1 Description

The manual transmission operates in conjunction with the clutch which is covered in **Chapter 5**. It may have either four speeds and reverse or five speeds and reverse. All forward speeds have synchromesh engagement. Final drive to the rear wheels is through a conventional type of bevel and pinion arrangement and a differential which may be of either conventional design or of a self-locking (limited slip) type. The drive shafts are covered in **Chapter 8, Section 4**.

Either of two types of four-speed or either of two types of five-speed gearboxes may be fitted to the models covered by this manual. A cross-section through the earlier five-speed gearbox is included in **FIG 1** and through the later type five-speed gearbox in **FIG 2**. In each case the later type of gearbox is stiffened to accommodate the higher torques provided by the bigger engines installed in later models. It will be noted that a one-piece transmission casing is provided for the earlier type transmission while, on the later type, the gearbox casing and the final drive/bellhousing casing are separate components. It will also be noted that, as indicated by the position of the ballbearings, the axial location of the input and pinion shafts is, on the later type gearbox, at the front of these shafts and not, as on the earlier type, at the rear. The speedometer drive arrangement also differs notably between the earlier and later type box. On a later version of the stiffened type gearbox, pressure lubrication is provided by a pump incorporated into the gearbox front cover (see **Section 9**).

In 1976, two slightly modified transmissions were installed. They are the 915/44 4-speed and the 915/49 4-speed. 1976 models incorporate a new guide tube for the clutch release bearing, an easy to remove drive shaft seal, and an electronic speedometer transmitter.

1977 model vehicles are equipped with one of four different transmissions. There are two 4-speeds and two 5-speeds. These differ from the 1976 transmissions by utilizing different 1st and 2nd gear synchronizers, a modified 1st/2nd gear operating and guide sleeve and an asymmetric tooth profile of the 1st gear clutch body. The models 915/66 (4-speed) and 915/61 (5-speed) are both equipped with a servo clutch.

1978 and 1979 model vehicles use the 915/61 (5-speed) transmission. This transmission varies from the 1977 unit by using a modified clutch release lever and a silumin case.

The transmissions installed in 1980 and 1981 differ from the 1978/79 units only in their gear ratios.

The transmission assembly is attached to the forward face of the engine and cannot be removed from the vehicle separately. After removal of the engine and transmission as a unit, the transmission is separated from the engine.

Overall transmission ratios differ between models and special competition and racing ratios have also been produced.

NOTE: As the gearbox utilized in the semi automatic 'Sportomatic' transmission is of similar construction to the manual transmission there is a certain overlap in their maintenance and repair. Consequently, both the manual transmission and 'Sportomatic' sections may reference diagrams or procedures in the alternate chapters.

2 Maintenance

Every 12,000 miles (20,000km) drain the oil from the transmission and refill with an SAE 90 Hypoid transmission lubricants of reputable brand. In the case of limited slip differentials, refer to **Section 6** for recommended lubricants. Drain off the old oil while the transmission is hot. Clean the drain plug of any adhering steel particles.

The drain (lower) and filler/level (upper) plugs are located on the lefthand side of the transmission casing just forward of the ribbed differential cover. The correct oil level is up to the bottom of the filler plug orifice. Both plugs should be tightened to a torque of 2.0 to 2.5kgm (14.5 to 18.0lb ft).

3 Removing and installing the transmission

Removal:

Remove the engine and transmission unit as described in **Chapter 1, Section 3**, taking particular care (see operation 8 of the removal procedure) to check that all pipes, controls and wiring connections which bridge the chassis and engine have been removed, uncoupled or disconnected.

Separation of the transmission from the engine:

With both the engine and the transmission assembly supported, remove the nuts, bolts and washers which attach the transmission casing to the engine. Taking care that the gearbox input shaft is not strained in any direction, separate the transmission from the engine and clutch.

Refitting the transmission to the engine:

Lightly coat the gearbox input shaft splines with multi-purpose grease. Press about 2cc of molybdenum disulphide grease into the bore of the pilot bearing after checking that it is serviceable (see **Chapter 1, Section 9**). Ensure that the input shaft is not strained in any direction when entering it into the clutch hub and pilot bearing. Torque tighten the attachment nuts and bolts to 2.5kgm (18lb ft).

Refitting:

Refitting of the engine/transmission unit into the vehicle is the reverse of the removal sequence (see **Chapter 1, Section 3**).

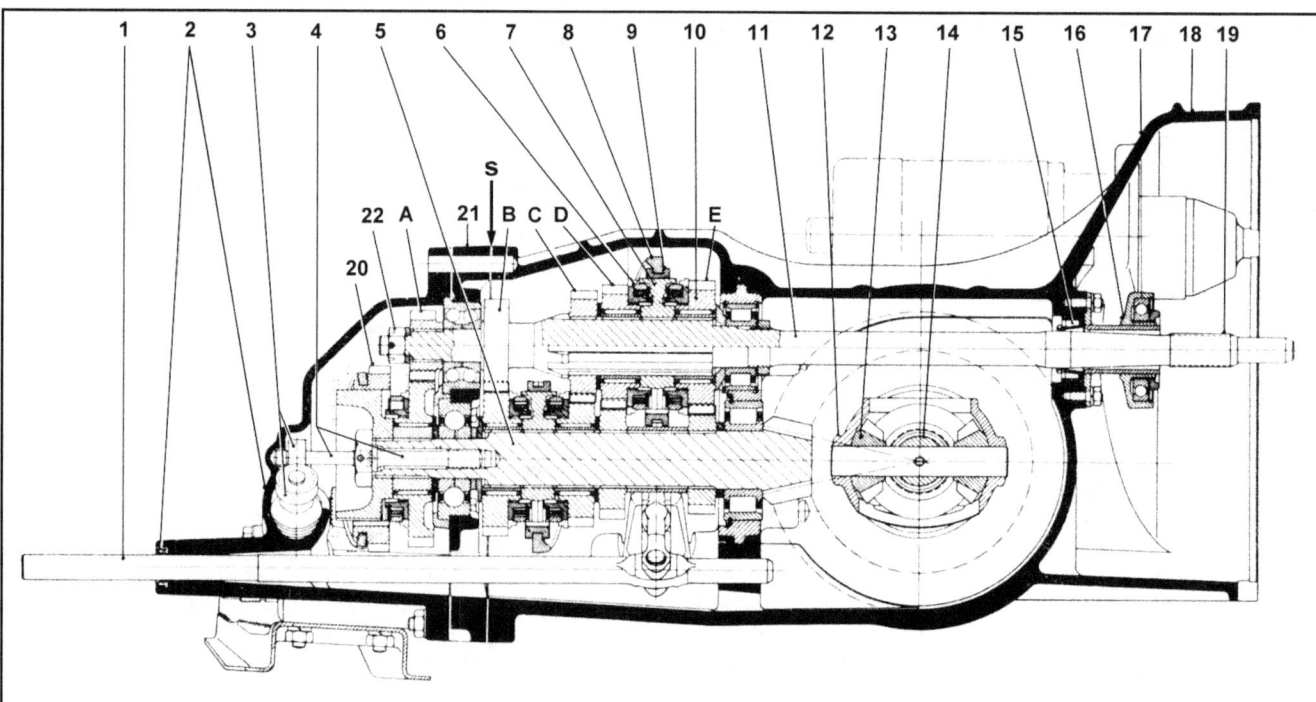

FIG 1 Longitudinal section through earlier five-speed manual transmission

1 Shift rod
2 Front cover and oil seal
3 Speedometer gears
4 Pinion shaft bolt
5 Pinion shaft
6 Synchronizing ring
7 Spider
8 Shift fork
9 Sliding sleeve
10 Fifth-speed gear
11 Input shaft
12 Differential carrier
13 Spider gear
14 Side gearshaft
15 Oil seal
16/17 Clutch release bearing
18 Housing
19 Clutch plate splines
20 Pinion shaft gear for first-speed and reverse
21 Intermediate plate
22 Castellated nut
A First-speed fixed gear
B Second-speed fixed gear
C Third-speed fixed gear
D Fourth-speed free-running gear
E Fifth-speed free-running gear
S Pinion positioning gasket

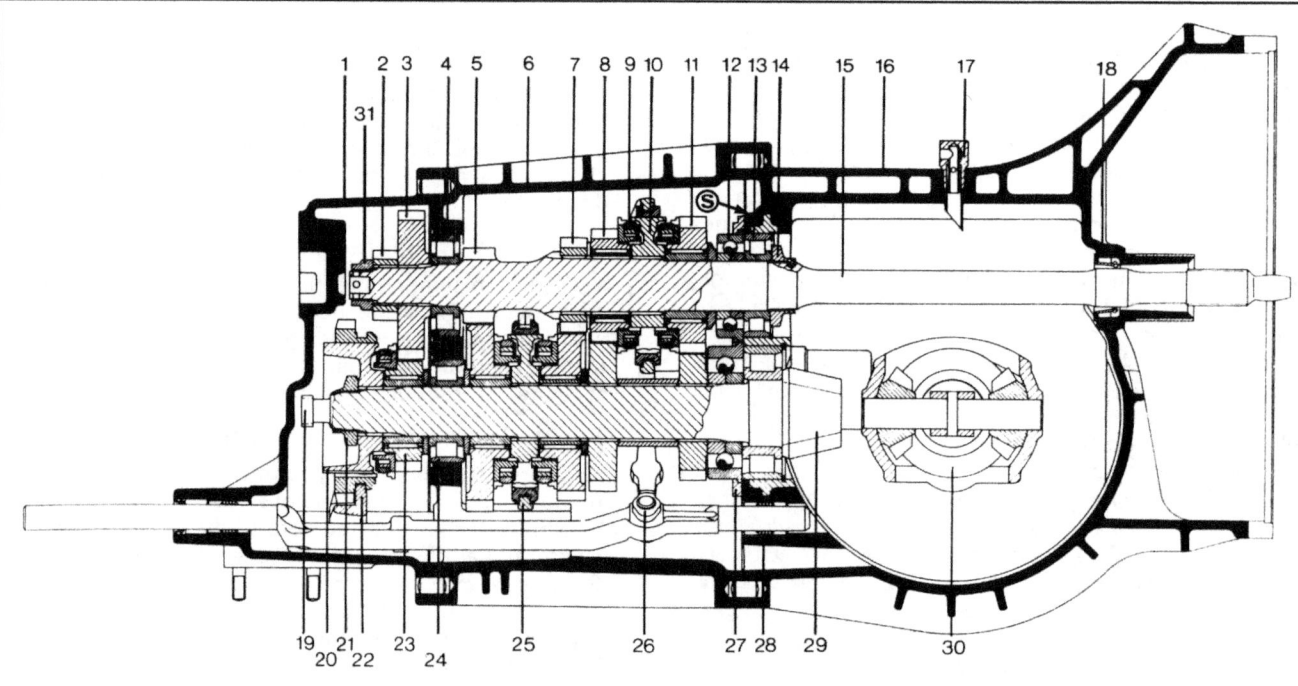

FIG 2 Longitudinal section through later five-speed manual transmission

1 Transmission front cover
2 Reverse gear
3 5th gear (fixed)
4 Roller bearing
5 1st gear (fixed)
6 Gear housing
7 2nd gear (fixed)
8 3rd gear (free-wheeling)
9 Synchronizing ring
10 Spider (synchro hub)
11 4th gear (free-wheeling)
12 Ball bearing
13 Roller bearing
14 Flange nut
15 Input shaft
16 Transmission housing
17 Breather
18 Seal
19 Speedometer gear
20 Spider (5th/reverse)
21 Flange nut
22 Shift fork (5th/reverse)
23 5th gear (free-wheeling)
24 Roller bearing
25 Shift fork (1st/2nd)
26 Selector shaft
27 Bearing retaining plate
28 Ball sleeve
29 Pinion shaft
30 Differential
31 Castellated nut
S Pinion positioning shim

84

4 Dismantling the transmissions

Servicing Porsche transmissions demands a high degree of experience and mechanical skill and the use of many special tools not normally available. The relative positions of the pinion and crownwheel (ring gear) must be set with great accuracy. Any error in these settings may lead to rapid tooth wear and noisy running.

Due to manufacturing tolerances, renewal of such parts as the easing(s), the differential carrier, the intermediate plate, the pinion shaft and its bearings and the crownwheel will upset the relative positions just mentioned and it will be necessary to go through the whole procedure for meshing the drive gears. It is possible to dismantle and reassemble the transmission without the need for adjustment, provided that all shims and spacers are refitted in their original positions. It is also possible to renew parts which obviously have no effect upon the meshing of the drive gears.

The following instructions, which are given primarily to help those who have the requisite experience, access to the necessary tools and to appropriate precision measuring equipment, must be supplemented by the operator's own notes and sketches.

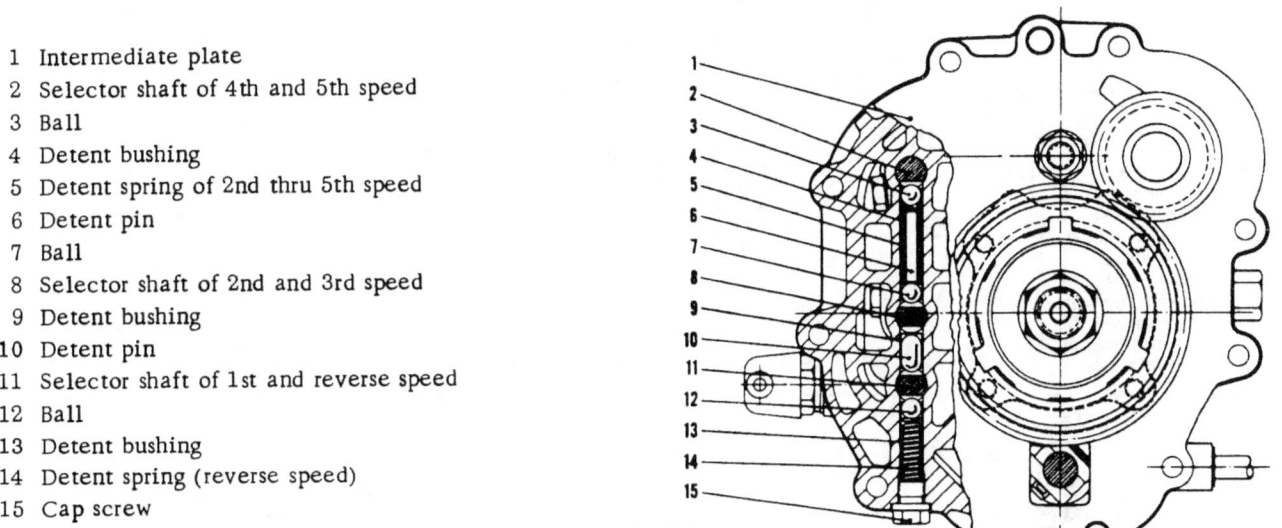

1 Intermediate plate
2 Selector shaft of 4th and 5th speed
3 Ball
4 Detent bushing
5 Detent spring of 2nd thru 5th speed
6 Detent pin
7 Ball
8 Selector shaft of 2nd and 3rd speed
9 Detent bushing
10 Detent pin
11 Selector shaft of 1st and reverse speed
12 Ball
13 Detent bushing
14 Detent spring (reverse speed)
15 Cap screw

FIG 3 Section through detent components in intermediate plate

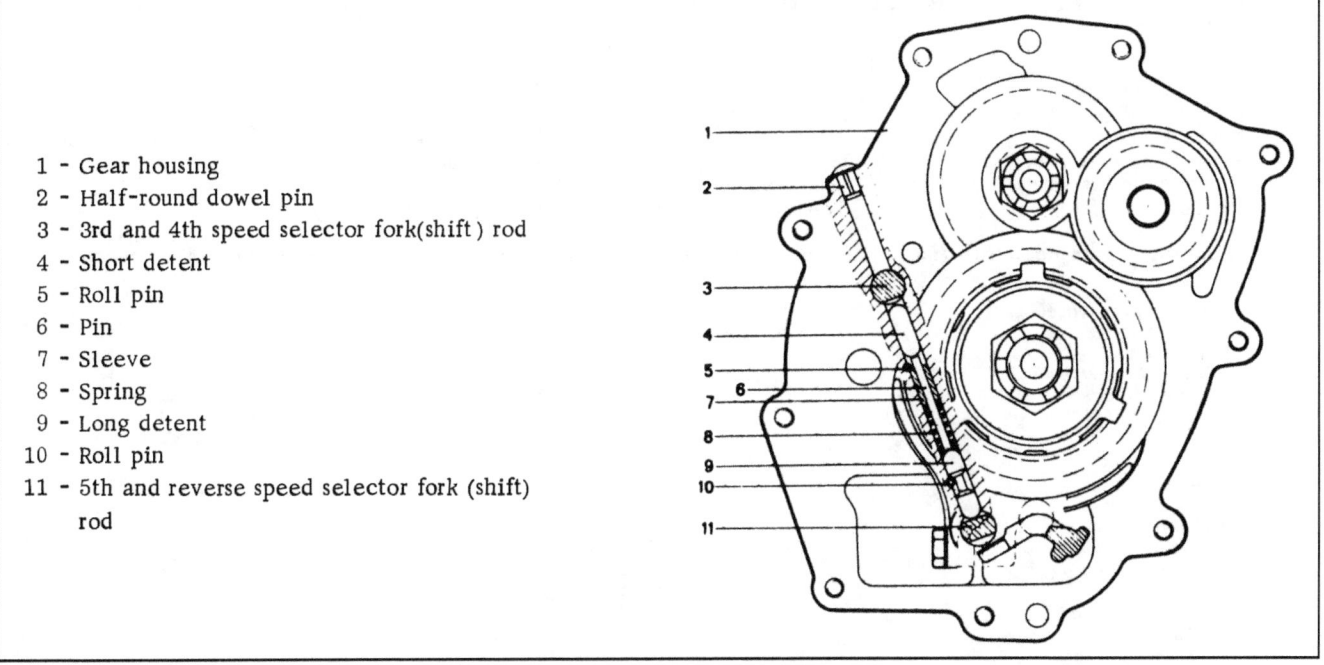

1 - Gear housing
2 - Half-round dowel pin
3 - 3rd and 4th speed selector fork(shift) rod
4 - Short detent
5 - Roll pin
6 - Pin
7 - Sleeve
8 - Spring
9 - Long detent
10 - Roll pin
11 - 5th and reverse speed selector fork (shift) rod

FIG 4 Section through detent components in gearbox casing

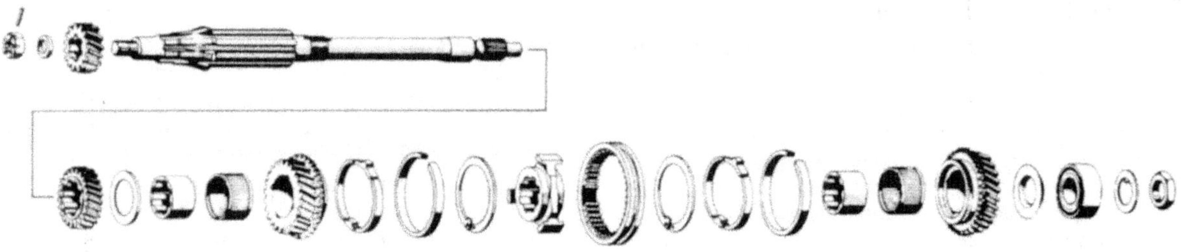

Input shaft components (earlier five-speed gearbox)

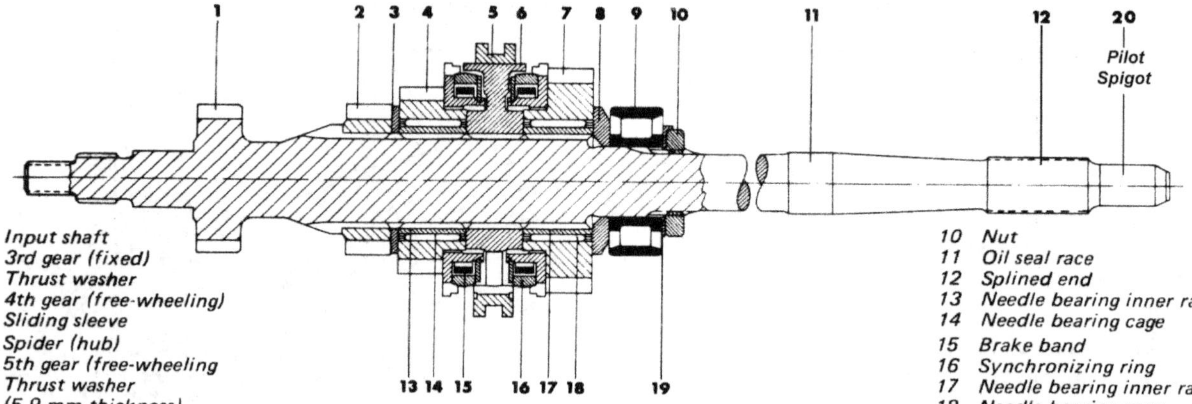

1 Input shaft
2 3rd gear (fixed)
3 Thrust washer
4 4th gear (free-wheeling)
5 Sliding sleeve
6 Spider (hub)
7 5th gear (free-wheeling)
8 Thrust washer (5.9 mm thickness)
9 Roller bearing
10 Nut
11 Oil seal race
12 Splined end
13 Needle bearing inner race
14 Needle bearing cage
15 Brake band
16 Synchronizing ring
17 Needle bearing inner race
18 Needle bearing cage
19 Lock plate
20 Pilot Spigot

FIG 5   Input shaft cross-section

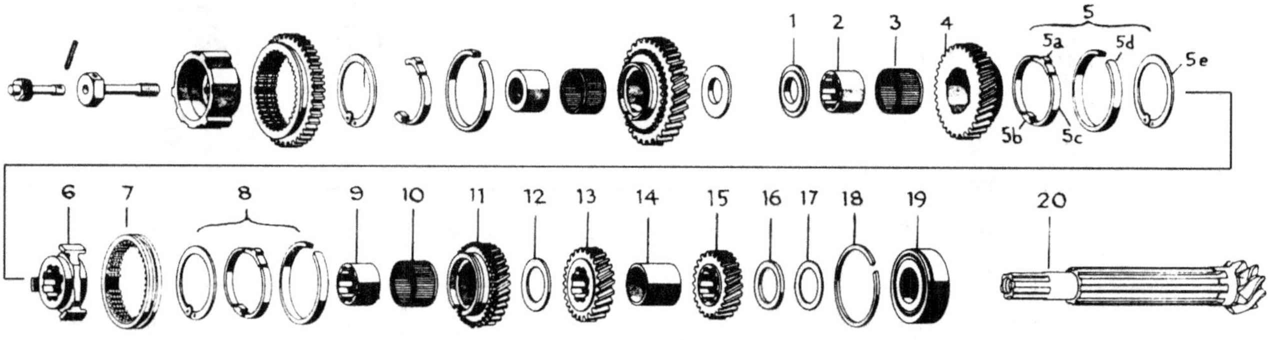

Key to Fig 9
1 Thrust washer (6.6 mm)
2 Needle bearing inner race
3 Needle bearing cage
4 Second-speed gear (free-running)
5 Synchronizing assembly
5a Energizer
5b Stop
5c Brake band
5d Synchronizing ring
5e Retainer
6 Spider
7 Sliding sleeve
8 Synchronizing assembly
9 Needle bearing inner race
10 Needle bearing
11 Third-speed gear (free-running)
12 Thrust washer
13 Fourth-speed gear (fixed)
14 Spacer bush
15 Fifth-speed gear (fixed)
16 Spacer
17 Shim
18 Retaining ring
19 Roller bearing
20 Pinion shaft

Pinion shaft components (earlier five-speed gearbox). Numbered items are to rear of intermediate plate

1 2nd gear (free-wheeling)
2 Spider (hub)
3 Brake band
4 3rd gear (free-wheeling)
5 4th gear (fixed)
6 5th gear (fixed)
7 Spacer
8 Roller bearing
9 Pinion shaft
10 Thrust washer (6.6 mm thickness)
11 Needle bearing inner race
12 Needle bearing cage
13 Sliding sleeve
14 Synchronizing ring
15 Needle bearing inner race
16 Needle bearing cage
17 Spacers
18 Retaining ring

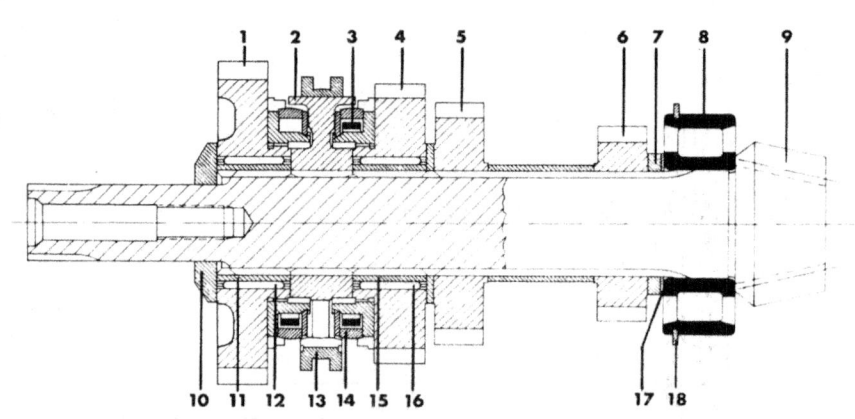

FIG 6   Pinion shaft cross-section

Earlier five-speed gearbox:

1 Drain off the oil and remove starter. Prise up flange caps if fitted. Hold input shaft splines securely and engage fifth gear. Remove the retaining bolts and withdraw the final drive flanges. Remove side cover and withdraw the differential assembly.
2 Remove the support from the front cover 2 (see **FIG 1**). Remove front cover with care as reverse gears may fall out. Remove the selector fork screw. Remove the gear and fork.
3 Engage the fifth speed and lock the pinion with tool P37. Remove pinion shaft bolt 4 and nut 22 from the input shaft. Drive out the locking pin from nut, remove the nut 22 and the first speed gear 'A'.
4 Select neutral. From the underside of the casing remove the plate and guide fork. Pull out the inner shift rod through the rear access hole. Insert a screwdriver in the guide fork hole and select fifth speed. **Gears cannot be withdrawn or inserted unless transmission is in this position.**
5 Tap the intermediate plate with a soft-faced hammer and detach it complete with gears. **Check gasket thickness for correct assembly.** Hold the plate in a vice with soft jaws and prise off the spider wheel. Remove the first speed gear and needle bearing from the pinion shaft. Shift into neutral.
6 Remove the plug and detent spring (15 & 14 **FIG 3**). Withdraw the selector shaft and detent ball for first and reverse gear 11 & 12. Mark the forks to avoid confusion and remove the shafts, forks and detents.
7 Tap the dowels forward and remove the throttle linkage. Place the intermediate plate under a press with gears downwards and press out input and pinion shafts simultaneously. Balls may fall out of input shaft bearing. Prise out the circlips from the centre web if the bearings are to be renewed.
8 Heat the casing to 120°C (248°F) and tap out the bearing races one at a time using tool P254 and a soft-faced hammer.
Clean the parts and check for damage, cracks or wear. Tooth breakage and subsequent jamming may cause casing cracks and possible damage to bearing bores. Check the bearings when clean and dry.

Later five-speed gearbox:

1 Drain off the oil and remove the starter. Use tool P37a to block the input shaft. Engage fifth gear. Refer to **FIG 2** and remove the front cover 1.
2 Remove the castellated nut 31 from the input shaft and the flanged nut 21 from the pinion shaft. Identify the needle bearing of the fifth-speed free gear which must be reassembled with the same gear. Remove the guide fork cover and gasket from the bottom of the gearbox casing. **Engage neutral.**
3 Remove the nuts from the casing. Pull the casing and selector fork rod (fifth and reverse) and the selector fork rod and selector shaft off the studs (tap lightly if necessary) noting that **fifth and reverse must be in neutral** or the casing cannot be removed.
4 Remove the third and fourth detent plug. Withdraw the spring and detent. Remove the bolt from the first and second selector fork, gently spread the clamping piece with a screwdriver.
5 Remove the input and pinion shaft retaining plates. Withdraw the input and pinion shafts complete with the third and fourth selector rod and the first and second selector fork from the final drive casing.
6 Remove the first and second detent plug. Withdraw the spring and detent. Remove the first and second selector fork. **Identify and retain the shims fitted between the casing and the retaining plates.**
7 If the detent components are to be removed, refer to **FIG 4** and drive out the roll pins 5 and 10 (since the detent components are under spring load, the roll pins must be removed before the half-round dowel pin). Drive out the half-round dowel pin 2.
8 Heat the gearbox casing to 120°C (248°F), identify and drive out the bearing races using tool US8050. Check the parts and the bearings as described earlier for the unstiffened type gearbox.

Earlier four-speed gearbox:

When dismantling the earlier type four-speed transmission, refer to the procedure for the earlier type five-speed transmission. For reference purposes it will be found that the Sportomatic four-speed gearbox closely resembles this manual four-speed box and **FIGS 1** and **4** in **Chapter 7** should be referred to.

Later four-speed gearbox:

When dismantling the later type four-speed transmission, refer to the procedure for the later type five-speed transmission. Engage fourth gear (instead of fifth) in operation 1. Differences due to there being four and not five forward gears will be self-evident.

5 Servicing the gearbox shafts

This section covers the input and pinion shafts of the earlier type five-speed gearbox in some detail and **FIGS 5** and **6** relate directly to this gearbox. When dealing with the four-speed version of this box, refer in addition to **Chapter 7, Section 9**.

FIGS 7 and **8** relate directly to the later, stiffened, five-speed gearbox. The servicing procedures for the stiffened shafts are similar to those described for the earlier types but, where relevant, notes on differences and on tool numbers are given later.

Input shaft, earlier type:

Refer to **FIG 5**. Take careful note of which way round the components are fitted.
1 Unlock and remove nut 10 after checking the shaft runout. Press the roller bearing 9 off the shaft. Mark the needlebearing cages for position and pull all components off the shaft.
2 The inner half of the front bearing race is hard against gear 1. Drift it away a little and use a puller to remove it taking care not to damage the gear.

Clean parts and check for wear or damage. Runout must be checked before shaft is dismantled because tightening nut 10 may alter it. Assemble bearings on shaft and mount in V-blocks. Check runout of pilot spigot 20. Maximum permissible is 0.10mm (0.004in). Excessive runout up to 0.30mm (0.012in) may be corrected cold under a press, using tools VW405 and VW406.

Check the spigot for wear. Check the clutch plate splines for radial play. Oil seal race 11 must be smooth and unmarked. Running surfaces of gears and bearings must be unworn. Also check those parts which are to be press fitted on the shaft. Gear 1 is integral with the shaft. If worn, renew the shaft. Check synchromesh parts for wear and renew parts, particularly if gear changing has been noisy.

Fit all components dry. Gear 2 has its small collar facing the shaft flange. Following with thrust washer 3 and inner race 13. Fit cage 14, gear 4 and spider 6. **Used bearings must be fitting in original positions.** Fit sleeve 5 followed by bearing 17 and 18 and gear 7. Fit thrust washer 8 and roller bearing 9 with the cover ring of the cage facing towards the clutch plate splines. Press the bearing into place using a tubular extension to avoid damaging the threads at the front end of the shaft. Fit a new lockplate 19 with its inner tab in the groove in the shaft and under the inner race of the bearing. Oil the face and the threads of the nut and fit it with the spherical part uppermost. Tighten to 10 to 12kgm (72 to 86lb ft). Bend up the locking tab. Check the mating numbers then press the inner half of the front bearing race into place.

Pinion shaft, earlier type:

Refer to **FIG 6**. The un-numbered components are forward of the intermediate plate. Take careful note of which way round the components are fitted.

Place the shaft, pinion downwards under a press, using tool P225 as an abutment to the roller bearing so that the shaft may be pushed through the gear and bearing assemblies. Mark the positions of the needle bearing cages for correct reassembly and take great care of the shims 17 as they control the basic location of the pinion.

After cleaning look for wear and damage. Check the shaft for the condition of the splines and the pinion for worn, cracked or broken teeth. Check synchromesh parts for wear, particularly if gear changing has been noisy. Dismantle these by removing the retaining plate 5e with circlip pliers. Make a note of the positions of the bands 5c, energisers 5a and stops 5b. When installed, diameter of ring 5d should be 76.30 ± 0.18mm (3.004 ± 0.117in).

Remember that the pinion and crownwheel (ring gear) are a matched pair and are marked as such. If no parts are renewed which affect the endwise location of the pinion shaft, there there is no problem in reassembling, but otherwise refer to **Section 7**.

1 All parts must be fitted to the pinion shaft in a dry state. Press roller bearings into place with the thin coverplate of the cage facing away from the pinion. Fit shims 17 as removed or as calculated (see **Section 7**).
2 Fit the spacer 16. Fit the fifth-speed gear 15 with the small collar facing away from the pinion. Fit the spacer bush 14, followed by the fourth-speed gear 13 with the collar against the bush.
3 Fit the thrust washer 12 and the needle bearing inner race 9. Fit the bearing cage 10. Reassemble the synchromesh parts and fit the third-speed gear 11 followed by the spider 6. **Always fit used needle-bearing cages in their original positions.**
4 Fit the inner race 2, bearing cage 3 and sliding sleeve 7. Fit gear 4. Fit the bevelled thrust washer 1 with its wide face against the needlebearing. Follow up with the thin spacer, but note that starting with transmission No 100.407, the washer and spacer were replaced by a single washer 6.60mm (0.26in) thick. Using a tubular drift, press on the inner half race for the front bearings. This must be marked with the mating number without the letter X.

Input shaft, later type:

Take careful note of which way round the components are fitted. To remove the roller bearings, use press tools VW412, VW401 and VW402 for the rear bearing and VW407 and VW415a for the forward bearing. Keep the needle bearings identified to their own gears. Use press tools VW412, VW416b and VW402 to fit the forward bearing and VW407, VW401 and VW454 to fit the rear bearing. Torque tighten the flange nut to 16 to 18kgm (116 to 130lb ft) and (on assembly) the castellated nut to 12 to 14kgm (87 to 101lb ft). Lock the flange nut by peening.

Pinion shaft, later type:

Take careful note of which way round the components are fitted; in particular on 1977 models where the asymmetrical pointed teeth of the first/second gear operating sleeve must face towards the first gear wheel.

To remove the roller bearings, use press tools VW412, P255a and VW401 for the front bearing and VW407 and VW415a for the rear bearing. Keep the needlebearings identified to their own gears. A suitable puller is required to withdraw the speedometer drive gear and the new gear must be heated to 120°C (248°F) before it is pressed into position. Refit the bearings using press tools VW412, VW244b and VW401. Torque tighten the flange nut (on assembly) to 24 to 26kgm (174 to 188lb ft) and lock by peening.

Synchronisers:

To dismantle a synchroniser assembly, remove the circlip type retainer (e.g. 5e in **FIG 6** or 1 in **FIG 9**) with circlip pliers. Note carefully which way the bands, rings, etc. are fitted and identify them to their gears. Ensure that new parts match those being rejected. Refer to **FIG 9** and note that the first-speed gear up to 1977 models has only one brake band 3 and that one of the blocks is 'hooked.' Correct assembly positioning of these parts is very important. (See examples on page following **FIG 9**).

Using a micrometer, check the diameters of the installed synchronising rings. Depending upon the transmission type and the speed gear, this diameter should be either 76.30 ± 0.18mm (3.004 ± 0.007in) or 86.37 ± 0.17mm (3.4004 ± 0.0067in).

The clearance between the first/fifth selector fork and its sleeve must not exceed 0.50mm (0.02in).

Pinion shaft positioning:

The pinion and crownwheel (ring gear) are manufactured as a matched set and cannot be renewed individually. The positioning of the pinion in relation to the ring gear is critical and, on initial assembly of the transmission, was set accurately by the fitment of shims of selected thickness at the datum casing face. The pinion is located by the ballbearing included in the shaft assembly. If no new critical components are required, the unit may be reassembled with the original shims. If the pinion/ring gear set, the ballbearing or the main casing is renewed, the pinion shaft position must be reset as described in **Section 7**.

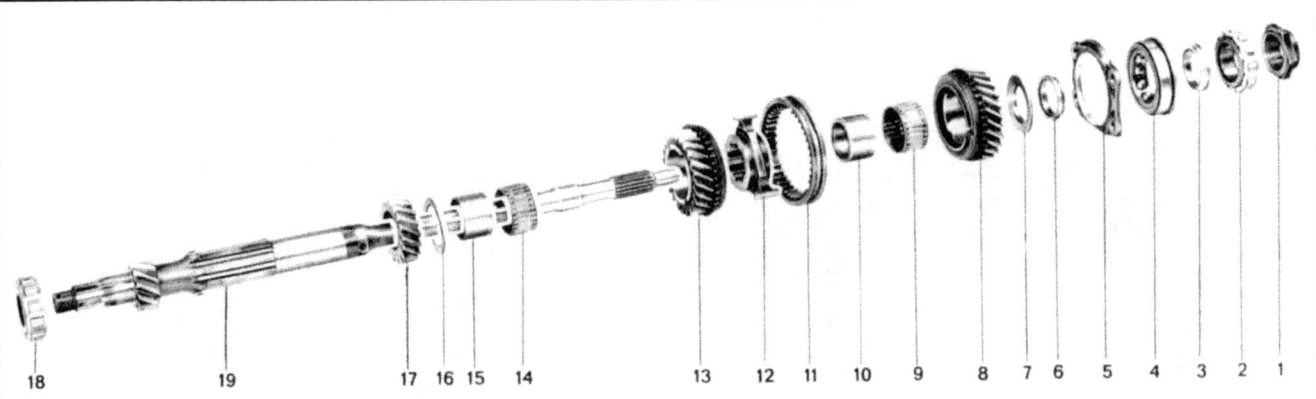

FIG 7   Input shaft and components (later five-speed gearbox)

1	Flange nut	6	Bearing inner race	11	Sliding shift sleeve	16	Thrust washer
2	Roller bearing	7	Thrust washer	12	Guide sleeve	17	2nd gear
3	Bearing inner race	8	4th gear	13	3rd gear	18	Roller bearing
4	Four point bearing	9	Needle bearing	14	Needle bearing	19	Input shaft
5	Clamping plate	10	Needle bearing race	15	Needle bearing race		

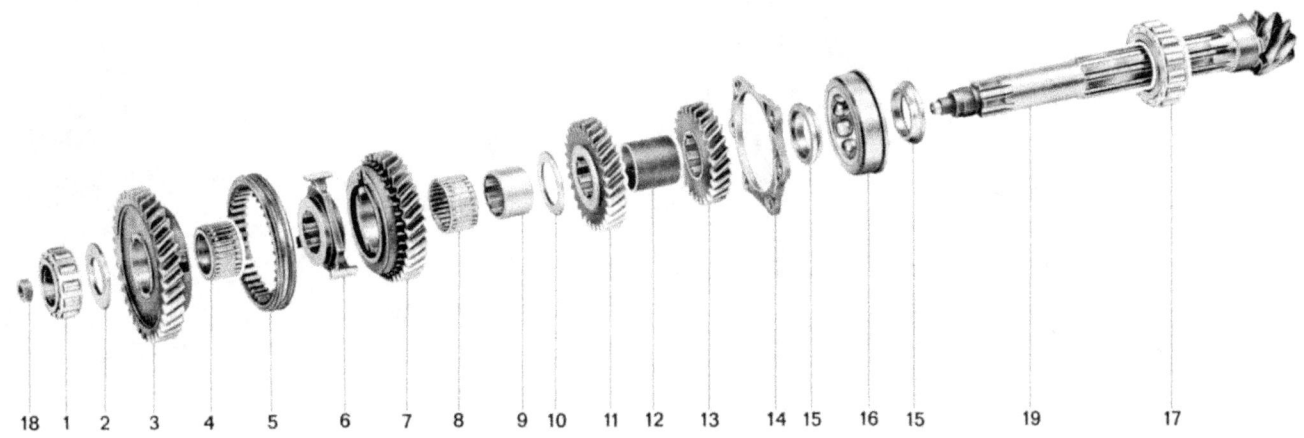

FIG 8   Pinion shaft and components (later five-speed gearbox)

1	Roller bearing	5	Shift sleeve	9	Needle bearing race	13	4th gear
2	Thrust washer	6	Synchro hub	10	Thrust washer	14	Clamping plate
3	1st gear	7	2nd gear	11	3rd gear	15	Bearing inner race
4	Needle bearing	8	Needle bearing	12	Spacer bushing	16	Four-point bearing

17 Roller bearing
18 Speedometer gear
19 Pinion shaft

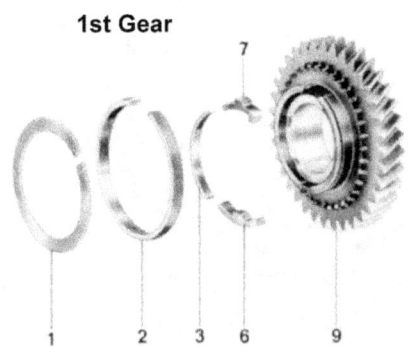
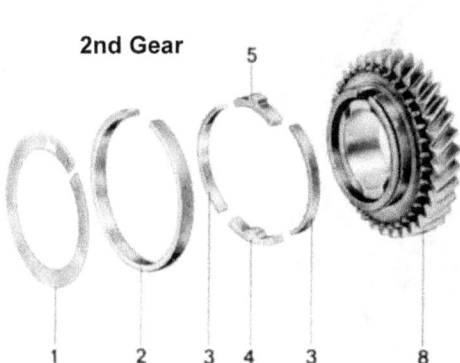

1 Circlip
2 Synchronizing ring
3 Brake band, only 1 for 1st speed
4 Brake band anchor block, 2nd speed
5 Thrust block, 2nd speed
6 Brake band anchor block, 1st speed
7 Thrust block, 1st speed
8 Gear, 2nd speed
9 Gear, 1st speed

FIG 9   Synchronising assembly components (later five-speed gearbox)

Examples of synchronising component assemblies

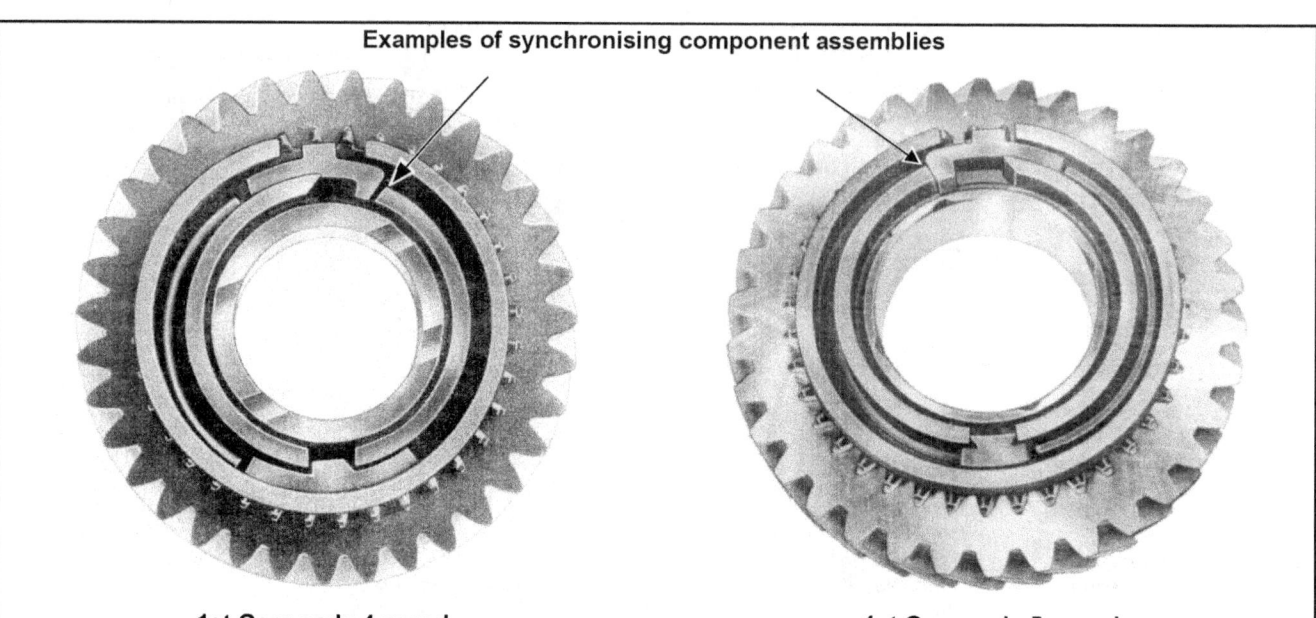

1st Gear early 4 speed   1st Gear early 5 speed

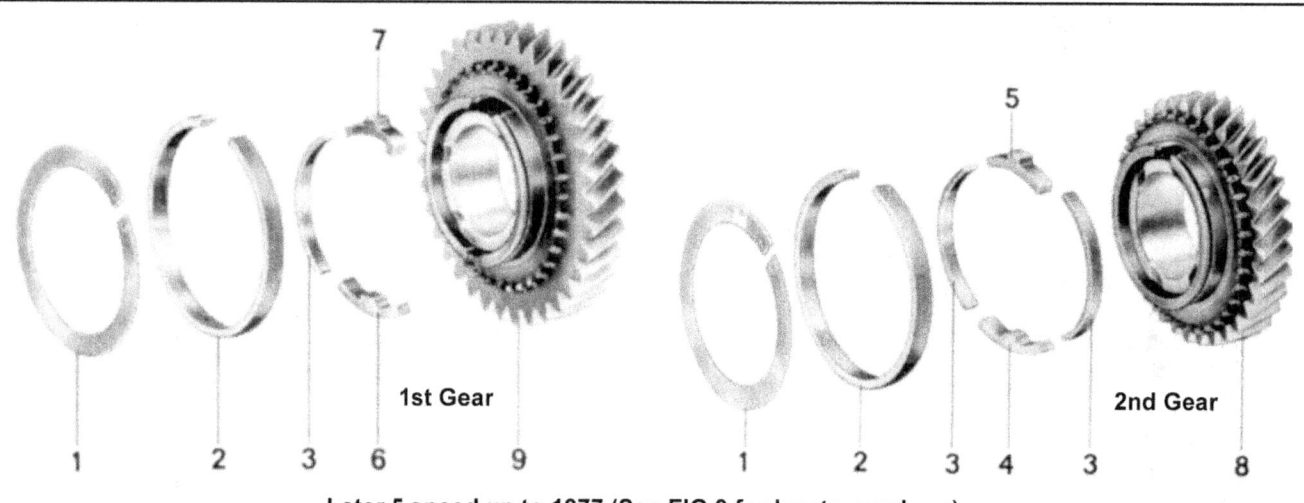

1st Gear   2nd Gear

Later 5 speed up to 1977 (See FIG 9 for key to numbers)
NOTE: The later type 5 speed 1st gear synchroniser is similar to the early type 4 speed 1st gear synchroniser

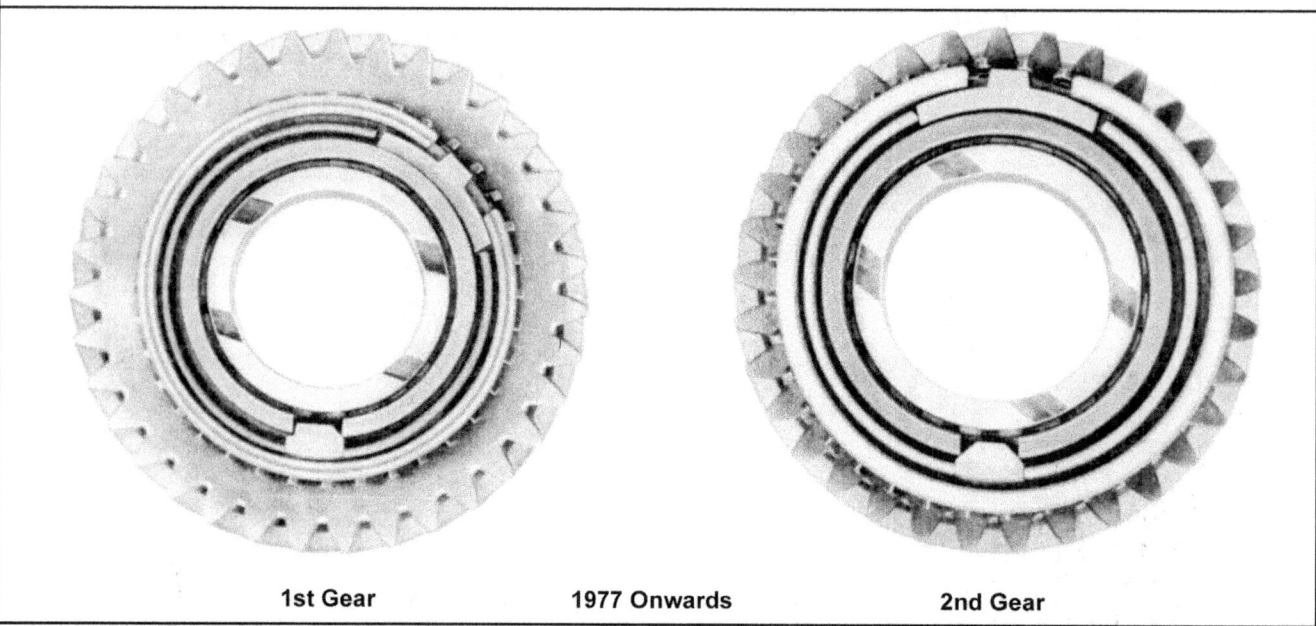

1st Gear   1977 Onwards   2nd Gear

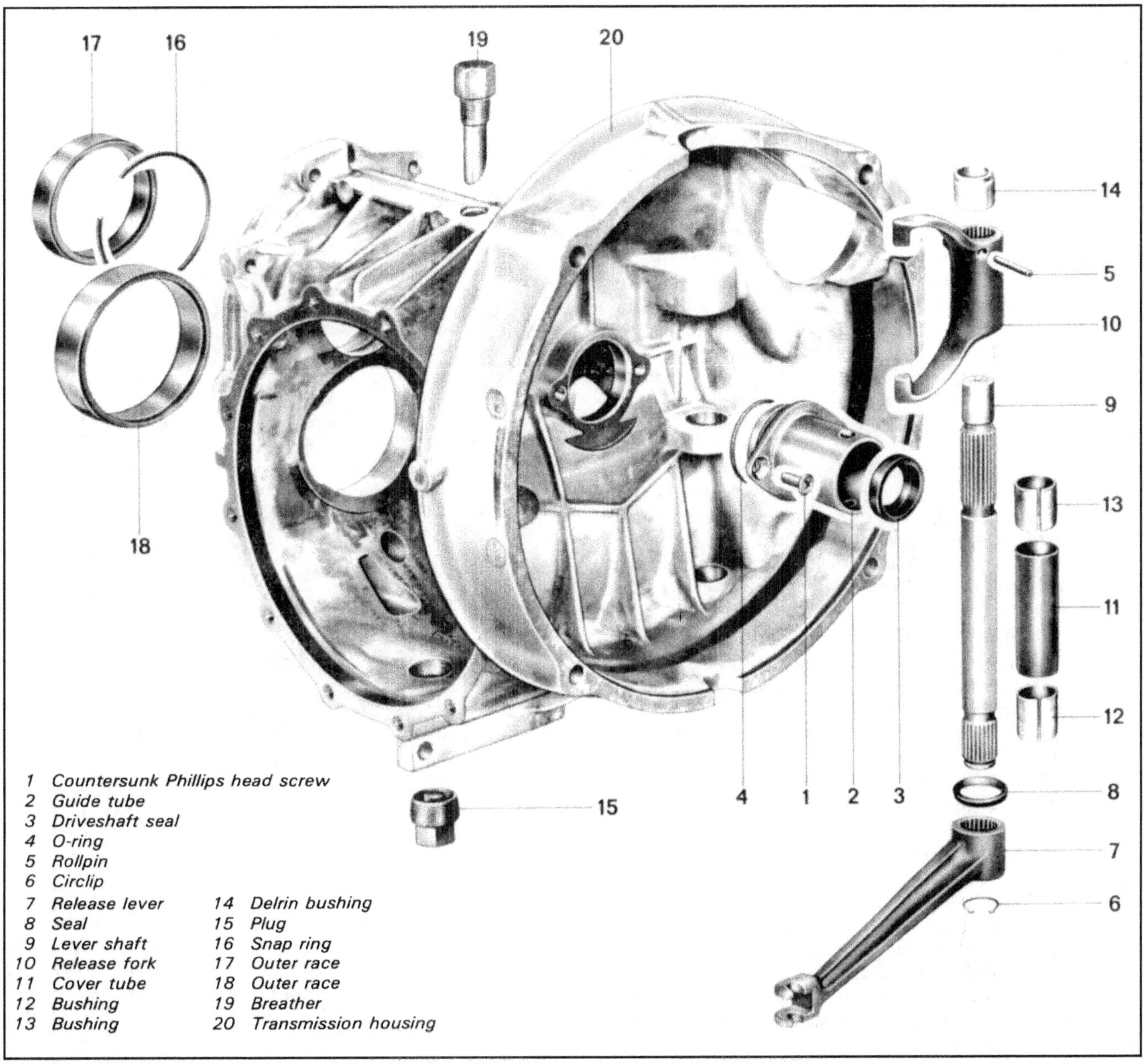

17
16
19
20
14
5
10
9
13
11
12
18
8
7
6
15
4
1
2
3
1 Countersunk Phillips head screw
2 Guide tube
3 Driveshaft seal
4 O-ring
5 Rollpin
6 Circlip
7 Release lever
8 Seal
9 Lever shaft
10 Release fork
11 Cover tube
12 Bushing
13 Bushing
14 Delrin bushing
15 Plug
16 Snap ring
17 Outer race
18 Outer race
19 Breather
20 Transmission housing

Transmission housing (beginning 1976 model)

Driveshaft seal (remove - install)

1 The driveshaft (input shaft) seal on manual transmissions installed in 1976 through 1981 models is removable without dismantling the transmission.

2 With the transmission separated from the engine, remove the countersunk Phillips-head screws **1** securing the guide tube **2**.

3 Pull the guide tube away from the transmission housing.

4 Use an appropriate-sized drift or screwdriver to pry the seal from the guide tube.

5 Drive a new seal **3** into the guide tube.

6 Install an O-ring seal **4** on the neck of the guide tube.

7 Lubricate the O-ring and the lip of the driveshaft seal with transmission oil.

8 Slide a protective sleeve over the splined driveshaft and install the guide tube. Turn the guide tube until the holes line up with the tapped holes in the transmission housing.

9 Tighten the mounting screws securely.

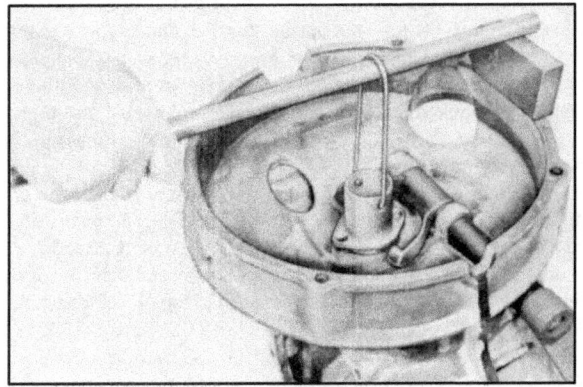

Removing the guide tube

6 The differential gearing

A cross-section through an earlier type Sportomatic differential and final drive assembly is shown in **Chapter 7, FIG 4**. The components of a later type differential are shown in **FIG 10**. The design is conventional with two side gears 6 splined to the output shafts and two mating gears 4 running on shaft 2. The carrier runs on two taper roller bearings 7 which are preloaded by washers 9 and shims 8. Bolts 11 retain the ring gear to the carrier and its meshing with the pinion is adjustable. **Chapter 7, FIG 4** shows that the output flanges 5 are retained by bolts 4 which engage with retainers 6 (5 in **FIG 10**). Note that, in this case, an extension on each bolt locates with the cross-shaft and that there is no anchor piece 3 or pin 1 (see **FIG 10**) as in the later type unit. Items 14, 15 and 16 are only fitted in conjunction with the electronic speedometer.

Removal:

1 It is possible to remove the differential with the transmission installed in the car. However, where any replacement parts or adjustment are required, it may be advantageous to remove the engine/transmission, as described in Chapter 1. If the differential is removed with the transmission installed, detach the driveshafts as described in Chapter 8. Also detach the clutch cable and rear throttle linkage.

Refer to **Chapter 7, FIG 4**:

2 Install two bolts in one of the driveshaft flanges and arrange a bar, so that as the expansion bolt is loosened, the turning effect of the flange will wedge the bar against the bolts and the transmission housing. Remove the bolt 4 completely, and withdraw the flange 5 and stub shaft.
3 Repeat this operation for the other flange.
4 Mark the installed position of the differential side cover 24, then remove it from the housing.
5 Lift out the differential assembly.

Dismantling:

6 The only remaining job which can readily be done is renewal of the oil seals. If it is found that the bearing outer races (and the bearings on the differential) require renewal, these jobs can be done by reference to paragraphs 7 to 12, but it is possible that re-shimming of the bearings will be required. This will need to be checked by a Porsche dealer or transmission specialist.

Refer to **FIG 10**. Drive out and discard pin 1 (if fitted). Drive out shaft 2. Remove the anchor piece 3 (if fitted). Withdraw the gears 6 and retainers 5
7 Where necessary, drive out the bearing outer races from the transmission housing and cover.
8 Where necessary, pull off the differential bearings using a universal puller. Do not mix up the shims 8 and spacer washers 9 from side-to-side. Untab and withdraw bolts 11. Remove ring gear 12.
9 Inspect the parts for obvious damage whilst removed. If a new ring gear is required, a new matching pinion shaft must also be fitted.
10 Press on new bearings using a suitable diameter tube, applying loads to the inner race only.
11 To install new outer races it will be necessary to heat the cover and housing to approximately 120°C (250°F) in an oven (do not use a naked flame). The bearing races can then be pressed in.
12 When the housing and cover have cooled, install new input shaft and differential case oil seals. (see images to top of next column).

Driving the input shaft seal into position

Installing differential casing oil seal

Assembly:

This is the reverse of the dismantling sequence. Use Molykote or an equivalent lubricant on the spherical surfaces of the side and mating gears. Centre the side gears by temporarily fitting the drive flanges. Use a new pin 1 (if fitted). Torque tighten bolts 11 to 12kgm (86lb ft) and lock by tabbing.

13 Position the differential into the housing.

Installing differential

14 Install the cover using a new O-ring lubricated with transmission oil. Install the washers and nuts, and tighten to the specified torque

Installing differential cover

15 Install the flange and stub shaft.

Installing the flange and stub shaft

16 Lock the universal flanges, as described in paragraph 2, and tighten the expansion bolts to the specified torque. Lubricate with oil as specified for the type of transmission.

Torque settings:

Side cover retaining nuts 2.2 to 2.5kgm (16 to 18lb ft), drive flange retaining bolts 4.5 to 5.0kgm (32.5 to 36.0lb ft) on unstiffened type transmissions and 2.6 to 3.0kgm (19 to 22lb ft) on later, stiffened, transmissions.

Differential 1977 and later models (remove - install):

1 Beginning with the 1977 model year a slightly different procedure must be followed from that described above.
2 Proceed with the operation as described in 2 through 11 in the previous section.
3 At this point, install the breather to the top of the housing. Be sure the opening faces toward the front cover of the transmission.
4 Place the input shaft seal in position with the sealing lip facing the bellhousing. Drive it into its seat with the appropriate tool.
5 Using a drift of the proper size, drive the lever shaft bushings into position. Apply silicone or lithium grease to the bushings.
6 Proceed with the operation as described in 12 through 16 in the previous section.
7 Connect the controls for the clutch. To achieve the proper lever travel, the throwout lever and fork must be adjusted on the lever shaft splines.
8 After the transmission is completely reassembled, the entire outside of the housing should have a protective undercoating applied to it.

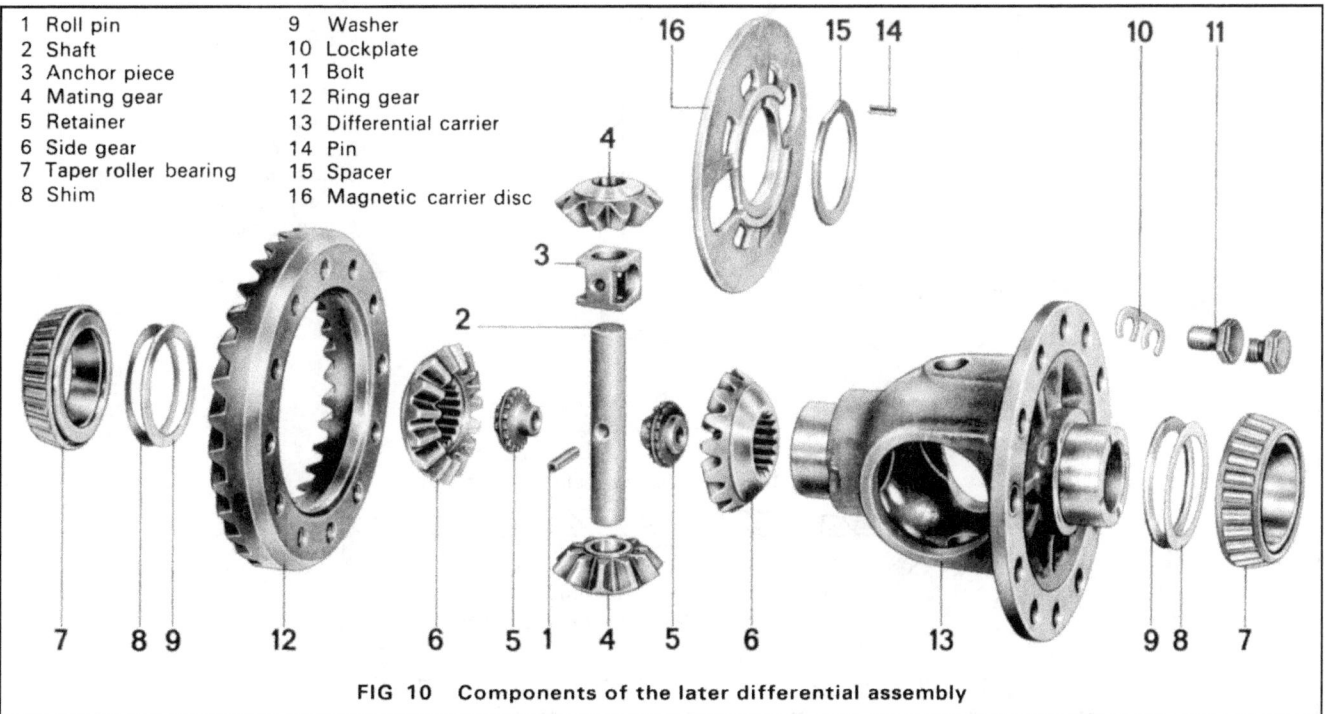

1 Roll pin	9 Washer
2 Shaft	10 Lockplate
3 Anchor piece	11 Bolt
4 Mating gear	12 Ring gear
5 Retainer	13 Differential carrier
6 Side gear	14 Pin
7 Taper roller bearing	15 Spacer
8 Shim	16 Magnetic carrier disc

FIG 10 Components of the later differential assembly

Limited slip differential:

A cross-section through a limited slip differential is shown in **FIG 11**. The disc sequence shown (one dished profile outer disc, two inner discs, two outer discs, one inner disc—reading inwards at each side) provides a 50% locking effect. The locking effect can be modified to 40%, 75% or 80% by changing the 'mix' of inner and outer discs and, if a different % is required, the appropriate discs should be obtained from a Porsche agent together with their fitment sequence.

To dismantle, remove the ring gear and the two Allen type screws. **Note the sequence of the discs.** They must be refitted in the same order or the locking effect will not be the same. On reassembly, apply Molykote G or LM348 to all disc surfaces, pressure rings and differential shafts. Ensure that each dished profile outer disc is next to the casing or to the casing cover. When assembled but before fitting the ring gear, hold the flange section in a soft-jawed vice and measure the torque required to turn a drive flange. This torque should be 4 to 8kgm (30 to 57lb ft) for a 50% and a 40% assembly or 6 to 12kgm (43 to 85lb ft) for a 75% and an 80% assembly. If the torque is outside the relevant range, fit thicker or thinner disc(s) to bring the torque within the specified range. Torque tighten the ring gear retaining bolts to 15kgm (108lb ft).

Recommended lubricant for limited slip transmissions is Shell Transmission Oil S 1747A. The equivalent in other countries is: USA, Shell HDR Gear Oil 90EP; Canada, Shell HDR Gear Oil 90; Australia, Shell SCL Gear Oil 90.

Adjustments:

If either new bearings, a new carrier or a new casing have been fitted, adjust the bearing preload. If any of these parts or if a new gear ring and pinion have been fitted, adjust the backlash after setting the pinion position. The procedures are described in **Section 7**.

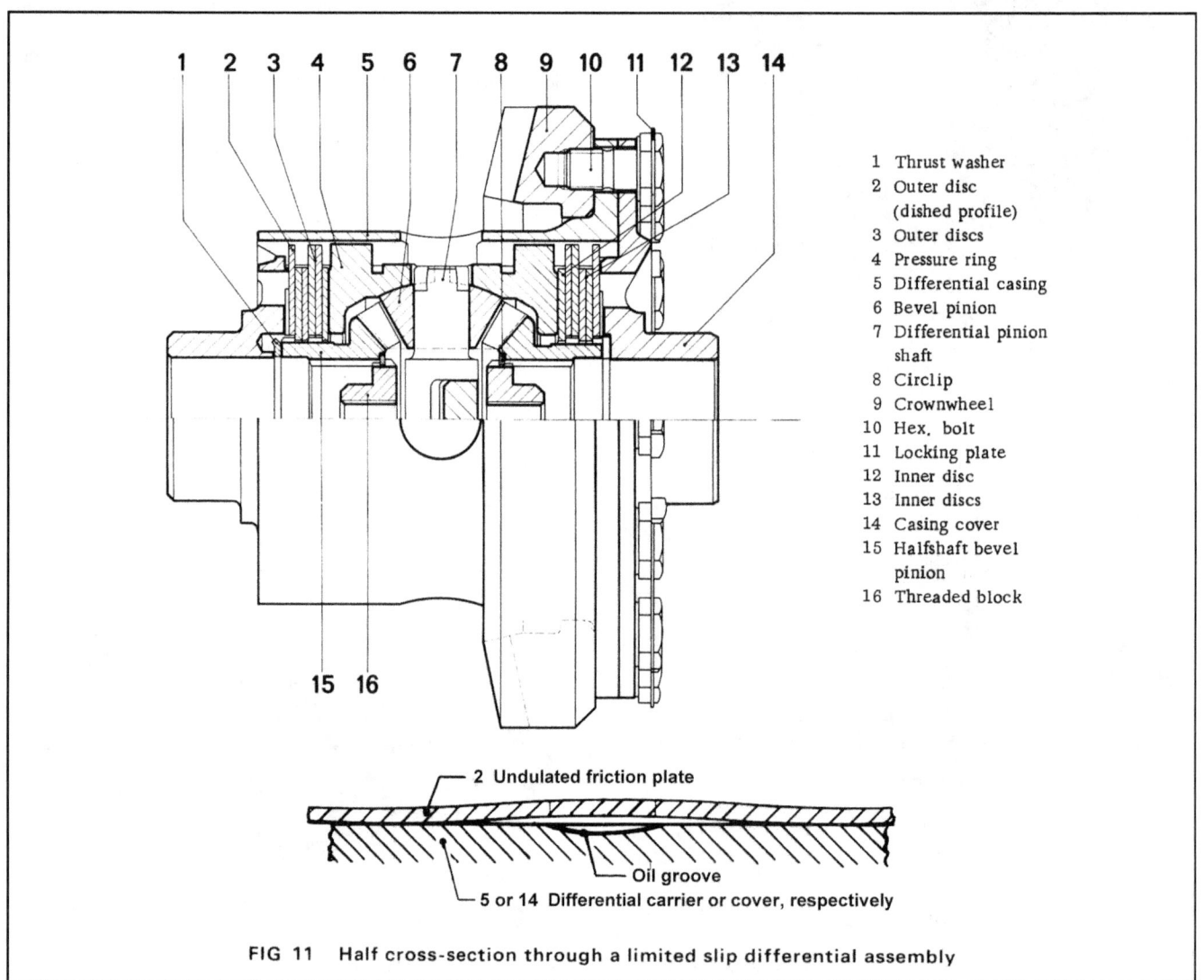

1. Thrust washer
2. Outer disc (dished profile)
3. Outer discs
4. Pressure ring
5. Differential casing
6. Bevel pinion
7. Differential pinion shaft
8. Circlip
9. Crownwheel
10. Hex. bolt
11. Locking plate
12. Inner disc
13. Inner discs
14. Casing cover
15. Halfshaft bevel pinion
16. Threaded block

- 2 Undulated friction plate
- Oil groove
- 5 or 14 Differential carrier or cover, respectively

FIG 11 Half cross-section through a limited slip differential assembly

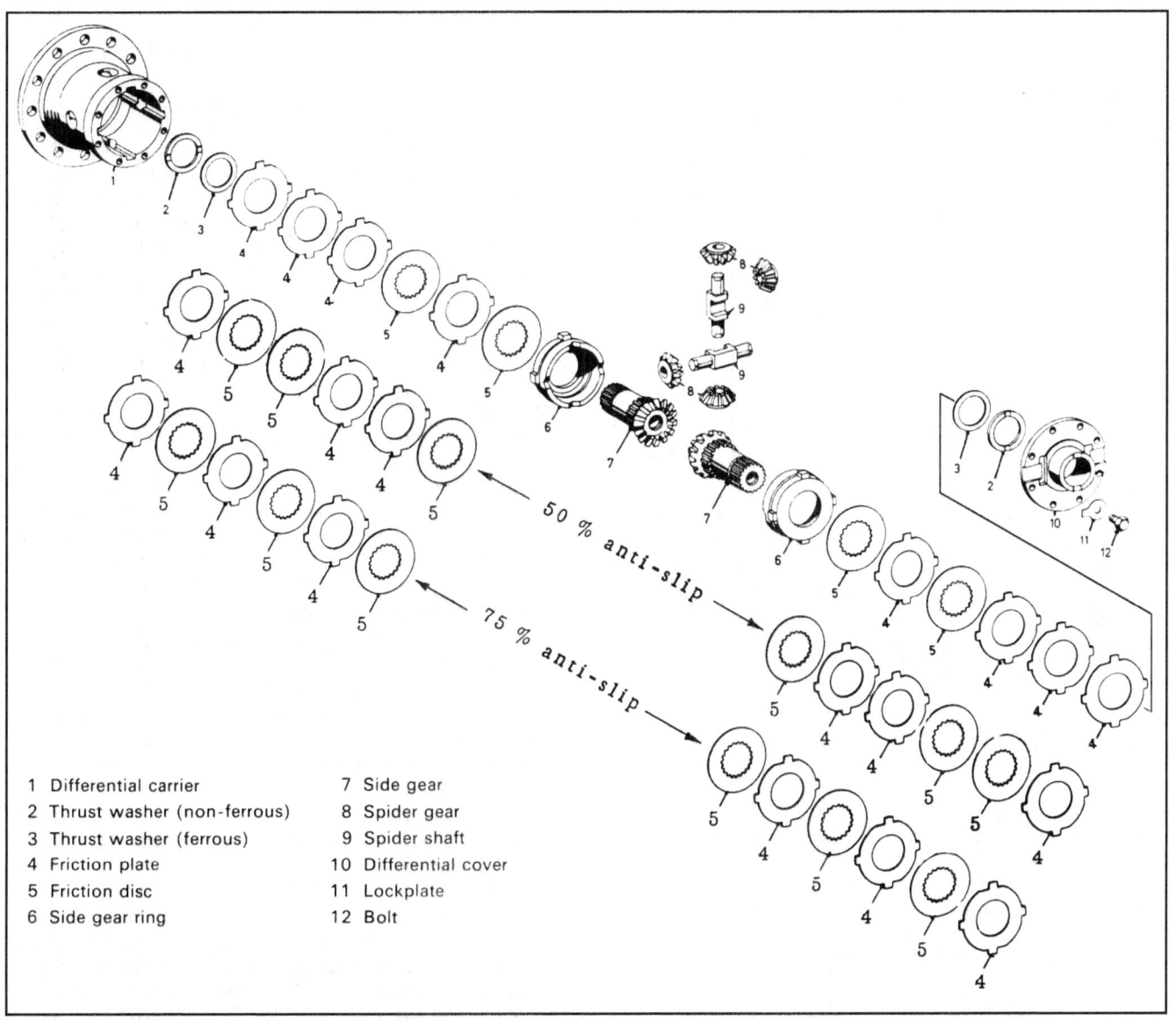

Components of ZF self-locking differential with standard assembly of plates and discs in top row.
Plate and disc assemblies for 50 per cent and 75 per cent anti-slip effectiveness are also shown

1 Differential carrier
2 Thrust washer (non-ferrous)
3 Thrust washer (ferrous)
4 Friction plate
5 Friction disc
6 Side gear ring
7 Side gear
8 Spider gear
9 Spider shaft
10 Differential cover
11 Lockplate
12 Bolt

Inspecting:

Check carrier and cover thrust faces for wear and scoring. Check plate grooves for wear. Side gear rings must slide freely in carrier. The locating tabs and thrust faces must not be worn or grooved. Thrust washer faces must be smooth and unworn. Friction discs must slide freely on side gear splines. Check plates for worn tabs and spline teeth.

Reassembling:

Fit non-ferrous thrust washer 2 with machined recess downwards. Fit steel washer 3, then plates and discs in order of removal, starting and finishing with a plate. Differentials fitted with pre-loaded disc and plate assemblies must have the undulated plate fitted first and last, and so arranged that a space exists between the oil groove in the carrier and the cover and the bow in the plate as shown by the insert in **FIG 11**. Check that plates and discs are correctly assembled (as above illustration).

Continue assembling the side gear, spider shafts and gears, and second side gear and the second set of plates and discs. Fit the steel washer followed by the non-ferrous one with the groove facing upwards. Secure the cover, tightening the bolts on new lockplates to a torque of 2.5 mkg or 18 lb ft. Turn up locking tabs.

The assembled differential must turn freely under a torque of 1 to 1.5 mkg (7.2 to 10.8 lb ft) without binding.

Note that slight noises may be heard when driving through sharp curves under power. These are inherent in the design and are not the result of defects.

Note also that the ZF self-locking differential must always be used in conjunction with NADELLA halfshafts.

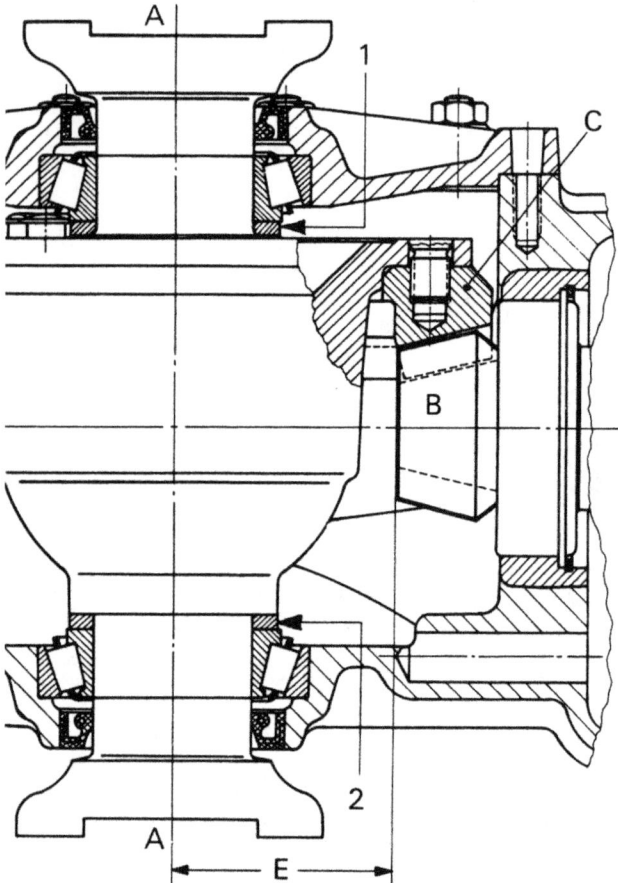

AA Differential centreline
B Pinion
C Ring gear
E Pinion setting dimension (see text)
1 Shims and washer (**S1**)
2 Shims and washer (**S2**)

FIG 12 Bearing preload and ring gear backlash adjustment

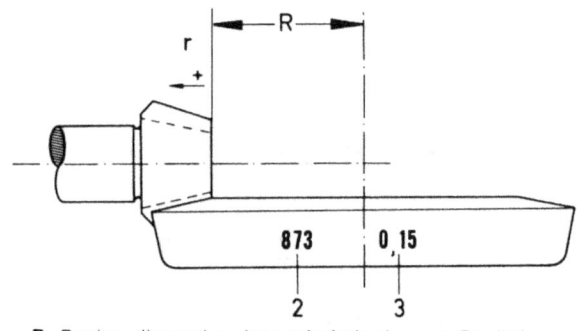

R Design dimension (see tabulation)   **r** Deviation

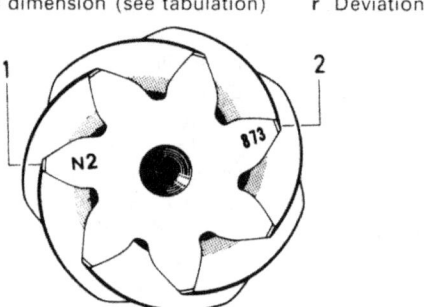

1 Actual deviation in 0.01mm units
2 Pinion and ring gear matching set no.
3 Desired backlash (mm)

FIG 13 Pinion setting data

7 Gear and backlash settings

This section is applicable to both the manual and to the Sportomatic transmissions.

Refer to **FIG 12**. The total thickness of shims 1 and 2 determines the preload on the taper roller bearings in which the differential unit runs. The individual thicknesses of 1 and 2 determines the backlash between the ring gear **C** and the pinion **B**. **E**, the position of the pinion in relation to the ring gear centre line **AA**, is a calculated dimension and the pinion is set to this by selecting the appropriate thickness of the gasket or shim at the face arrowed **S** in **FIGS 1** or **2** or in **Chapter 7, FIGS 1, 2, 3** and **4**. **FIG 13** illustrates diagrammatically the geometry of the pinion and ring gear engagement.

Manufacturing tolerances preclude **E** in **FIG 12** from being precisely equal to the design dimension **R** in all cases. The difference (**r**) between **R** and **E** is marked on the matched pinion as shown at 1. The **N** figure is always positive (since 1970) and indicates, in 0.01mm units, the amount by which **E** deviates from **R**. The values of **R** are tabulated later in this section. **E** is **R** + **r**. The pinion shaft is positioned by selecting the appropriate thickness of **S** so that the measured value of **E** is equal to the calculated value.

Pinion shaft positioning:

Refer to this heading in **Section 5** and, if new critical components have been fitted, proceed as follows. Refer to **FIGS 12** and **13**. Check that the pinion and ring gear numbers match. Note **r** and **N** figure. Read off **R** (which differs for different types of transmission) from the following tabulation. Calculate **E** which equals **R** plus **r**.

Transmission and type No.	R
Earlier manual, type 911	63.20mm (2.488in)
Earlier Sportomatic, type 905	54.20mm (2.134in)
Later manual, type 915	66.30mm (2.610in)
Later Sportomatic, type 925	59.70mm (2.350in)

In place of the differential assembly, install dummy carrier tool P258 with its dial gauge set to measure **E**. As a datum use the thickness of **S** (see **FIGS 1** and **2** or **Chapter 7, FIGS 1, 2, 3** and **4**) originally fitted.

Measure the deviation of **E** from the calculated figure and increase or decrease the thickness of **S** by the amount of the divergence. Recheck the setting.

Determining the total thickness of S1 plus S2:

So that the pinion is not engaged with the ring gear, the gearbox must be separated from the main casing for the following procedure. The oil seal must be removed from the side cover.

Check that the outer races are fully seated in the casing and in the side cover. On later (stiffened) models note whether SKF or FAG bearings are fitted. Select shims 8 in **FIG 10** so that the thickness of these shims plus that of the spacer 9 is 3.5mm (0.138in) and fit them to the ring gear side of the carrier. These are 1 (**S1**) in **FIG 12**. On the opposite side fit a spacer plus shim thickness of 3mm (0.118in). These are 2 (**S2**). Fit the bearings and install the differential. Fit the side cover without a gasket. Lightly tighten it down using only two nuts opposite each other and, using feeler gauges, measure the gap between the cover and the casing. The required gap is 0.15mm (0.006in). If it differs from this, reduce or increase the **S1** thickness until the required gap is obtained. Fit all the cover retaining nuts and tighten down to 2.3kgm (17lb ft). Fit the drive flanges and their retaining bolts torque tightened to the figure quoted in **Section 6**.

Using a torque meter on the drive flange at the cover side, measure the drag of the differential/final drive assembly. This should be within the range of 18 to 24kgcm (16 to 21lb in) on unstiffened transmissions and 25 to 35kgcm (22 to 30lb in) on stiffened transmissions fitted with SKF bearings or 40 to 65kgcm (35 to 57lb ft) if fitted with FAG bearings. If necessary, adjust the preload shim thickness to bring the drag within the relevant specified range.

Backlash basic setting:

Remove the differential assembly. Withdraw the bearings and identify the spacing washers to their respective sides. Measure the total thickness (**S1** plus **S2**) and proportion the shims so that **S1** is 0.10mm (0.004in) thinner than half the total of **S1** plus **S2**. **S2** will now be 0.10mm (0.004in) thicker than half the total of **S1** plus **S2**. Round off **S1** and **S2** if necessary but do not depart from the total thickness of **S1** plus **S2**.

Backlash, final setting:

Reassemble and fit the differential (with the oil seal fitted to the side cover). Fit the drive flanges and torque tighten the retaining bolts. Fit the gearbox less its front cover but with the pinion shaft correctly positioned. Use clamping tool P259 (earlier models), P259a (later manual), or P357a (later Sportomatic) on the forward end of the pinion shaft to block it. Using a suitable dial gauge set up at the radius of the ring gear tooth mid-face (the official dial gauge holder, etc. are part of the clamping tool toolset) measure the pinion/ring gear backlash. This should be within the range of 0.12 to 0.18mm (0.0047 to 0.0071in). This is ± 0.03mm (0.0012in) of the 0.15mm (0.006in) nominal backlash shown at 3 in **FIG 13**. If the backlash is outside this range, transfer shimming from **S1** to **S2** or vice versa but, again, do not depart from the **S1** plus **S2** total.

8 Front cover and intermediate plate

Earlier type front cover:

The front cover (2 in **FIG 1**) fitted to earlier type gearboxes is similar to the front cover fitted to Sportomatic transmissions and reference may be made to **Chapter 7, Section 9**.

Later type front cover:

The front cover fitted to later type manual gearboxes (1 in **FIG 2**) is shown in **FIG 14**. This shows the components of the speedometer drive and the location of the reversing light switch. If the bush 13 has to be renewed, heat the cover to 120°C (248°F) and drive out the bush with a suitable mandrel. With the cover again at this temperature, drive in the new bush. If a new seal 3 is being fitted, use tool P374. If a new seal 11 is being fitted, use tool P369.

The oil pump which is incorporated into the front cover is covered in **Section 9**.

Intermediate plate:

A separate intermediate plate (21 in **FIG 1**) is only relevant to earlier type manual transmissions and is equivalent to that fitted to Sportomatic transmissions. Reference may consequently be made to **Chapter 7, Section 9**.

1	Backup light switch
2	Actuating pin
3	Seal
4	Retainer
5	Thrust washer
6	Speedometer drive
7	Retainer
8	O-ring
9	Positioning piece
10	Worm shaft
11	Seal
12	Shift rod bushing
13	Bushing
14	Transmission front cover

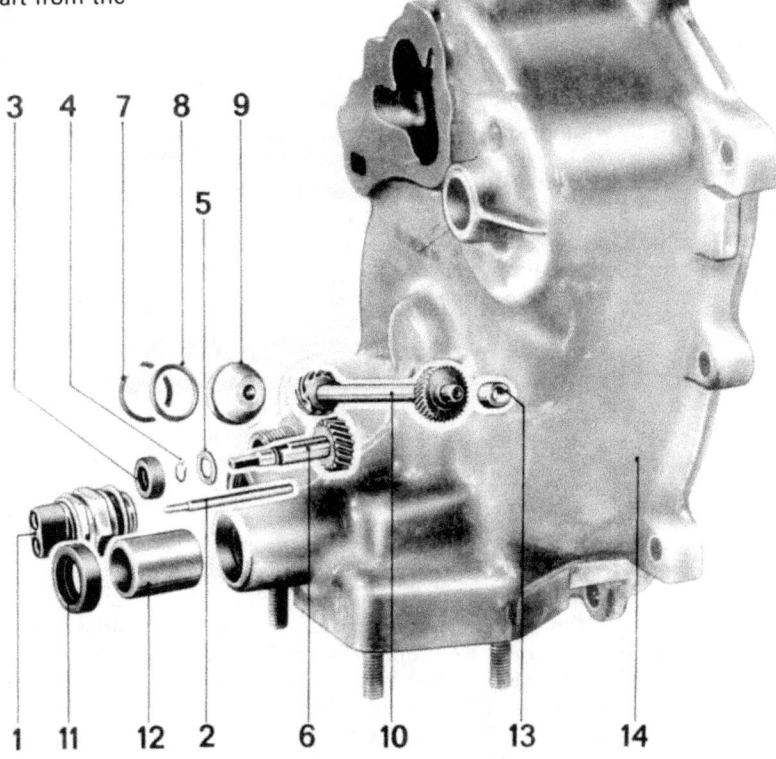

FIG 14 Front cover (later transmissions) and speedometer drive components

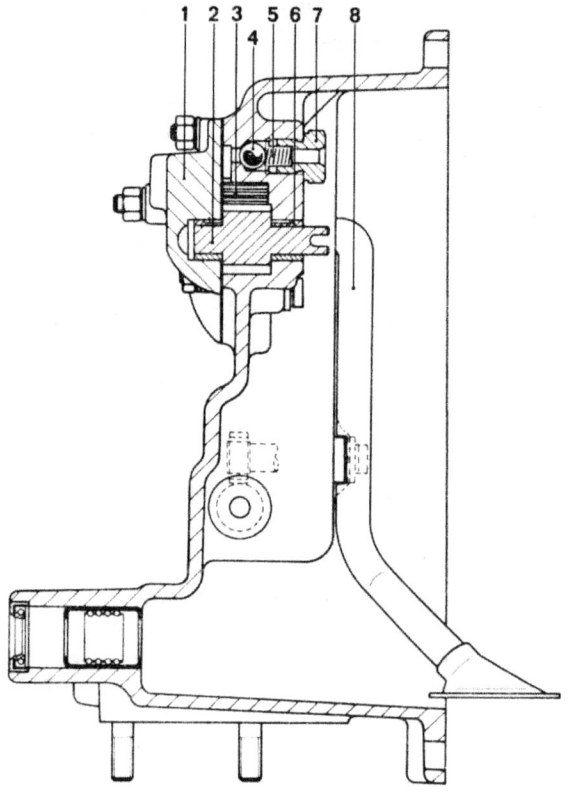

1 - Oil pump cover
2 - Oil pump gear I
3 - Oil pump gear II
4 - Ball for pressure relief valve
5 - Spring for pressure relief valve
6 - Bushing
7 - Plug for pressure relief valve
8 - Pickup tube

FIG 15 Gearbox front cover oil pump (2.7 litre Carrera)

9 The oil pump

If fitted, the pump is incorporated into the front cover as shown in **FIG 15**. It is driven from the forward end of the input shaft by a simple dog arrangement.

Dismantling and reassembling:

Remove the cover 1. Carefully remove and retain the gasket(s). Withdraw the gears. The relief valve assembly 4, 5 and 7, the suction tube 8 and the delivery tube can only be removed after the cover has been separated from the gearbox.

If the bushes have to be renewed, note their orientation and mark the alignment of the oil holes. Use mandrel P368 to drive in the new bushes which must be correctly positioned and fully entered. The milled ends of the oil pockets must point towards the pressure chamber or oil pump gears respectively.

When fitting the pump cover, tighten the retaining nuts diagonally and keep checking that the pump gears remain free. If necessary, reduce or increase the thickness of the gasket(s) to give an axial clearance of 0.05mm (0.002in) between the gears and the cover. Finally, torque tighten the cover nuts to 1kgm (7lb ft). Torque tighten plug 7 to 2.5kgm (18lb ft). If the suction tube was removed, ensure that the 'O' ring is refitted. Torque tighten the Allen retaining bolts to 0.9kgm (6.5lb ft).

On refitment of the front cover to the gearbox, ensure that the pressure line passes through the hole in the third/fourth gearchange fork.

10 Reassembling the transmission

General:

Reassembly of the transmission is substantially the reverse of the dismantling sequence and the following notes will augment the operator's own notes and sketches made during dismantling. It is assumed that the **Section 5, 6, 7, 8** and **9** procedures (as may have been relevant or necessary) have been correctly carried out. As the work proceeds, lubricate parts and assemblies with the correct oil specified for the type of transmission.

Earlier (unstiffened) transmission:

Torque tighten bolt 4 in **FIG 1** to 11 to 12kgm (80 to 86lb ft) while blocking the input shaft with P37. Torque tighten the detent plug 15 in **FIG 3** to 2.5kgm (18lb ft). Use plasticine to check that there is clearance of at least 1mm (0.04in) between the teeth of the first speed and reverse gears under the conditions which bring them closest together. Check that the first and reverse selector control forks have a side clearance of 2 to 3mm (0.08 to 0.12in) with those for the second and third. Torque tighten the first and reverse selector fork screw to 2.5kgm (18lb ft).

It is not possible to set the remaining forks accurately without supporting the shafts with tool P260 as shown in **FIG 16**. Adjust the position of the second and third and fourth and fifth speed forks so that the sliding sleeves are exactly central between the sychronising rings. After a shift test, tighten the fork screws to 2.5kgm (18lb ft), making sure that the control forks clear each other by 2 to 3mm (0.08 to 0.12in).

Take shift rod 1 in **FIG 1** and assemble the shift lever and pin, making sure that the pin and hole tapers are correct. Fit the cotterpin.

Insert the shift rod into the casing and install the intermediate plate and gears, fitting the correct gaskets under the plate as determined in **Section 7**. It is essential to select fifth speed for this operation and care must be taken not to damage the input shaft oil seal. Shift back into neutral. Set the shift lever between the selector control forks and pushrod into the rear bore. Fit a new gasket and install the guide fork, locating the lever in the fork correctly. Fit the front cover. The hole in the breather must point forward at an angle of 45° from the transmission centre line.

If the reversing light switch was removed, make sure when refitting it, that the operating pin is fitted with the rounded end entering first.

Later (stiffened) transmissions:

The torque tightening figure specified for the differential side cover, the front cover and the guide fork cover is 2.2 to 2.5kgm (16 to 18lb ft). The figure for the guide fork nut is 0.8 to 0.9kgm (5.8 to 6.5lb ft); for the detent nut (transmission casing) is 1.5 to 1.8kgm (11 to 13lb ft); and for the fork nuts, 2.4 to 2.6kgm (17 to 19lb ft). Torque tighten the bearing retaining plate nuts to 2.1 to 2.3kgm (15 to 17lb ft) and ensure that the correct thickness of shimming is fitted to suit the pinion shaft positioning. Adjustment of the selector forks is described later. When installing the idler gear shaft, turn the shaft until the pin in the casing prevents it from turning further. Use tool P37a to block the input shaft and engage fifth gear so that the input shaft castellated nut and the pinion flange nut may be tightened to the figures specified in **Section 5**.

To adjust the selector forks, install mounting plate P260a as shown in **FIG 17**. Block the input shaft with P37a, engage fifth speed and torque tighten the input shaft nut. Turn the first/second fork rod left to the stop and then slightly back until the unmachined flat inner surface is almost vertical. Do not turn back beyond the middle point or fully to the right. Position the first/second selector fork so that the sleeve is exactly in the middle between the synchronising rings and tighten the bolt. Adjust the third/fourth fork in the same way. Position the third/fourth guide flush with the fork and check that this is 2 to 3mm (0.08 to 0.12in) clearance between third/fourth and first/second guides. They must not touch.

11 Gearchange linkage

The components of a manual transmission lever and linkage are shown in **FIG 18**. The lever knob is pressed onto the lever.

Uncoupling and removing the linkage:

Pull off the knob, lift off boot 3 and the tunnel cover and release the base 4. Remove the tunnel cover in the rear compartment, push the boot 18 forwards, loosen clamp bolt 19 and drive rod 17 off the coupling 23. Pull off the clamp and boot. Cut the locking wire and remove screw and socket 15. With the engine/transmission unit removed, rod 17 may be withdrawn.

Installation:

This is the reverse of the uncoupling and removal sequence. Torque tighten screw 16 to 1.5kgm (11lb ft) and relock with wire.

Coat the working faces of coupling 23 with lithium grease. Tighten the bolts for gearlever base to 2.5kgm (18lb ft). Tighten the bolts securing guide bracket 10 to 1kgm (7lb ft). Adjust the linkage as described later.

Adjusting the linkage:

Through the aperture in tunnel, loosen bolt 19. Put the gearlever in neutral and press it to the right as far as it will go. With the transmission in neutral, move coupling 23 as far to the left as it will go and tighten the clamp bolt to 2.5kgm (18lb ft), using a serrated lockwasher under the nut.

Try all gears and check for play in the linkage. Gear lever play should be the same in all gears in every direction.

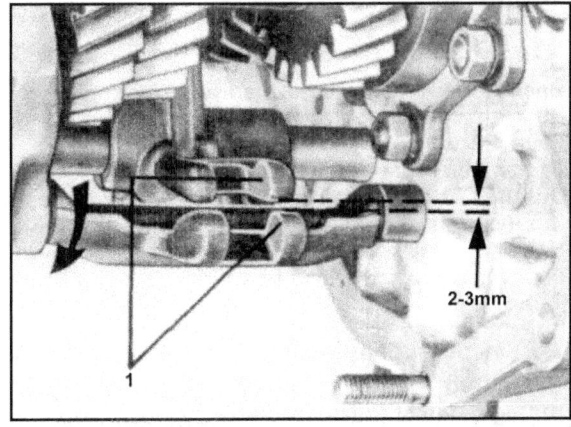

FIG 17 Adjusting the selector forks (later gearboxes)
See text: 1 Install flush 2 Mounting plate P260a

FIG 16 Supporting the shafts with tool P260 (earlier gearboxes)

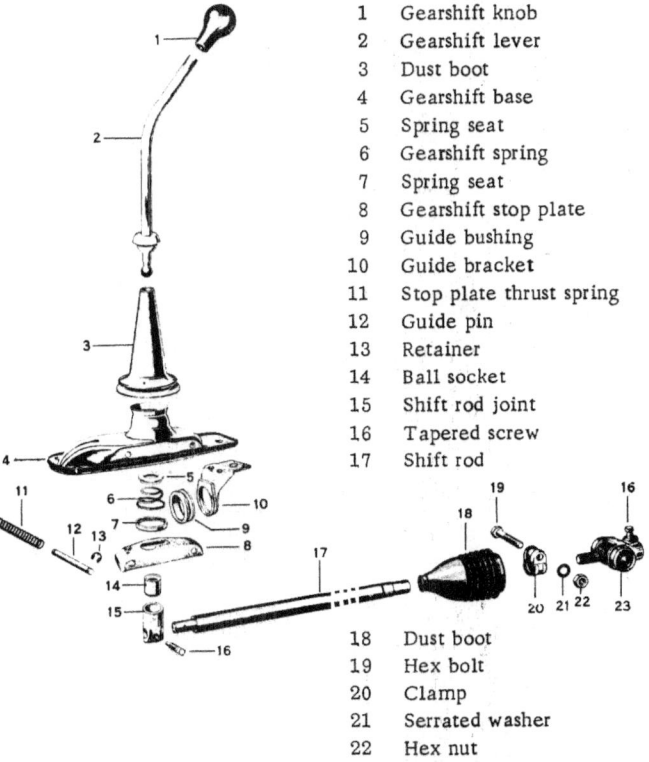

1	Gearshift knob
2	Gearshift lever
3	Dust boot
4	Gearshift base
5	Spring seat
6	Gearshift spring
7	Spring seat
8	Gearshift stop plate
9	Guide bushing
10	Guide bracket
11	Stop plate thrust spring
12	Guide pin
13	Retainer
14	Ball socket
15	Shift rod joint
16	Tapered screw
17	Shift rod
18	Dust boot
19	Hex bolt
20	Clamp
21	Serrated washer
22	Hex nut
23	Shift rod coupling

FIG 18 Components of gearlever and linkage

12 Fault diagnosis

(a) Difficulty in changing gear
1 Bent or worn gearshift mechanism
2 Shift rod coupling wrongly set
3 Faulty or worn synchronising mechanism
4 Faulty clutch or release bearing
5 Stiffness of clutch pedal, cable or release mechanism
6 Input shaft spigot bearing tight
7 Excessive clutch clearance
8 Faulty selector rod detent or springs

(b) Noisy gearchanging
1 Check 3 to 7 in (a)
2 Wrong grade of transmission oil

(c) Slipping out of gear
1 Check 8 in (a)
2 Excessive end float of free running gears
3 Worn synchronising teeth
4 Selector fork wrongly positioned
5 Gearshift mechanism worn
6 Worn bearings

(d) Noisy transmission
1 Check 2 and 6 in (c)
2 Incorrect or insufficient lubricant
3 Worn drive gears and differential
4 Insufficient preload on differential bearings
5 Drive gears incorrectly meshed

NOTES

CHAPTER 7 - SPORTOMATIC TRANSMISSION

1 Description
2 Maintenance
3 Removing and installing the transmission
4 Separating and refitting the transmission
5 Servicing the control valve and sensor
6 Servicing the gear lever and microswitch
7 Servicing the torque converter and clutch
8 Servicing the clutch controls
9 Overhauling the transmission
10 The torque converter pump
11 Fault diagnosis

1 Description

The Sportomatic semi-automatic transmission is alternative to the manual transmission covered in **Chapter 6**. The differential and final drive is substantially the same as for manual transmission models. **Chapter 6**, **Sections 6** and **7** are relevant to both types of transmission.

The Sportomatic transmission comprises an engine driven three-element hydraulic torque converter, a single dry plate clutch (which operates automatically) and either a four-speed and reverse or a three-speed and reverse gearbox. The gearbox itself is non-automatic and the four-speed versions are similar to the unstiffened and stiffened versions of the four-speed manual gearboxes.

Cross-sections through three versions of earlier and later type Sportomatic transmissions are shown in **FIGS 1, 2** and **3**. **FIG 4** shows a horizontal cross-section through the earlier four-speed gearbox and differential. The clutch and torque converter are not included in this illustration. Later transmissions are stiffened to accommodate the higher torques provided by the bigger engines installed in later models. The three-speed gearbox is available only in the stiffened version.

The engine drives the torque converter casing which, internally, carries impeller blading. This (via stator blading) directs oil against the turbine blading and transmits torque to the driven rotor. The clutch is interposed between the turbine and the gearbox input shaft. The pneumatically operated 'automatic' clutch is arranged to disengage while a gearchange is being made. The clutch operation is triggered by the driver's initial movement of the manual gearchange lever. This, electrically, actuates an air valve and powers a vacuum-servo unit which operates the clutch. Pneumatic power for the vacuum-servo is provided by the difference between atmospheric pressure and the partial vacuum derived from the engine induction manifold. The system is shown diagrammatically in **FIG 5**.

The torque converter provides intermediate 'gear ratios' between the mechanical ratios of the gearbox. Maximum torque multiplication occurs when the turbine is stationary and the impeller is being driven at increasing engine speed (vehicle moving off). The stator element redirects the oil flow from the turbine so that it re-enters the impeller at the most effective angle. The stator hub incorporates a one-way drive and, as the turbine picks up speed and the slip between it and the impeller becomes less, the torque multiplication reduces progressively until, when their speeds become substantially equal, the unit acts as a fluid coupling and the free wheel stator hub permits it to rotate with the other two elements.

Oil for the torque converter is common to the engine lubrication system and is fed to it under pressure from a pump driven by the lefthand camshaft. The gearbox lubrication is entirely separate and operates on the same transmission oil as that for manual transmission gearboxes.

Gearlever symbols are: **P** (Parking lock), **R** (Reverse), **L** (Low), **D** (for city driving), **D3** (for normal highway speeds) and **D4** (for high-speed motorways) or, in the case of the three-speed gearbox, **D3** combines normal and high-speed driving. A gear may remain engaged for brief stops but, otherwise, engage P. **Do not touch the gearlever except when actually changing or engaging gear. Do not change down when the engine speed is very high or overspeeding will occur.** If the oil temperature warning light comes on, change down to a lower gear. An inhibitor (bypass) switch prevents the starter motor from operating except when P is engaged. **Engage P only when the vehicle is stationary** and then apply the handbrake.

The transmission assembly is attached to the forward face of the engine and cannot be removed from the vehicle separately. After removal of the engine and transmission as a unit, the transmission is separated from the engine.

2 Maintenance

Gearbox lubrication:

Refer to **Chapter 6, Section 2** and renew the oil at the same mileage intervals as those specified for the manual transmission models.

Torque converter oil:

Renewal of the engine oil (**Chapter 1, Section 2**) also includes the torque converter oil. Note, however, that if the torque converter has been drained, some 4 pints (2.3 litre) of additional engine oil will be required to refill the system (see **Section 7**).

Clutch free play:

Check this every 6000 miles (10,000km) and adjust as described in **Section 7**.

Control valve and air filter:

Every 6000 miles (10,000km) adjust the control valve and clean the filter as described in **Section 5**.

Gearlever microswitch:

Every 6000 miles (10,000km), clean and, if necessary, adjust the contacts as described in **Section 6**.

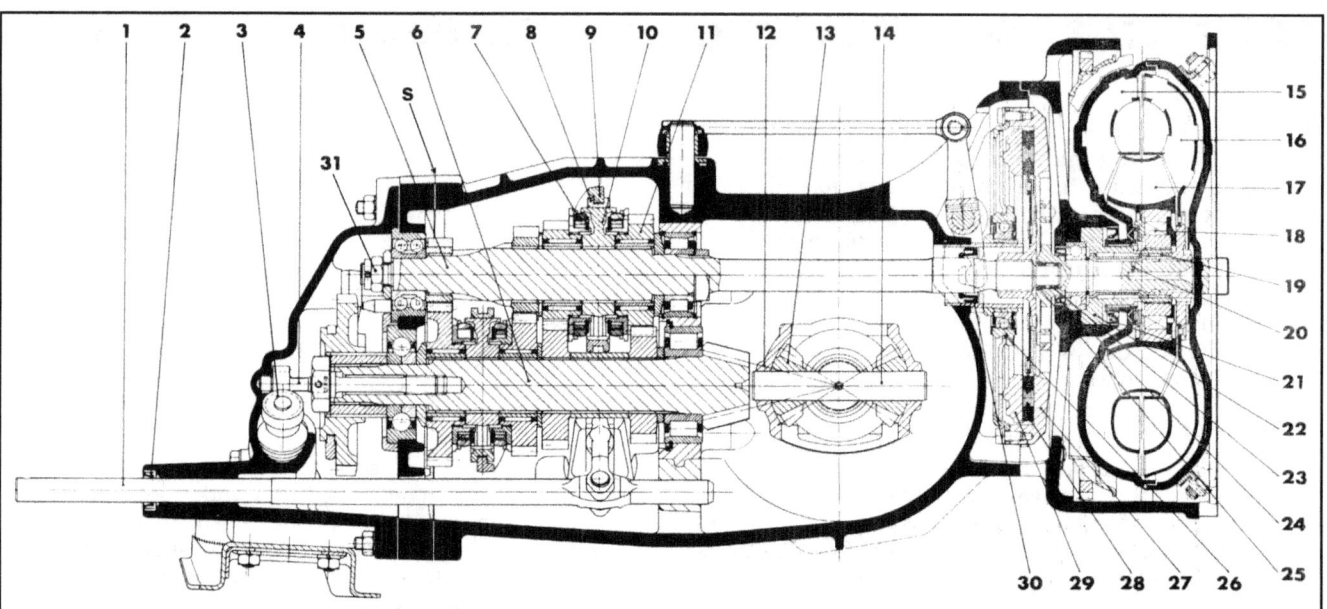

FIG 1 Cross-section through earlier four-speed transmission

1 Selector shaft
2 Oil seal
3 Speedometer gear shaft
4 Speedometer drive gear
5 Input shaft
6 Pinion shaft
7 Synchronizing ring
8 Sliding sleeve-coupling
9 Selector fork
10 Spider
11 Gear 1, 4th speed
12 Differential case
13 Pinion gear
14 Pinion gear shaft
15 Pump
16 Turbine
17 Stator
18 Freewheeling unit
19 Turbine shaft bush
20 Oil restrictor in turbine shaft
21 Oil seal
22 Freewheeling unit support
23 Clutch pilot needle bearing
24 Oil seal
25 O-ring
26 Clutch throwout bearing
27 Clutch carrier and turbine shaft
28 Clutch disc
29 Clutch pressure plate
30 Oil seal
31 Nut
S Gasket(s) see text

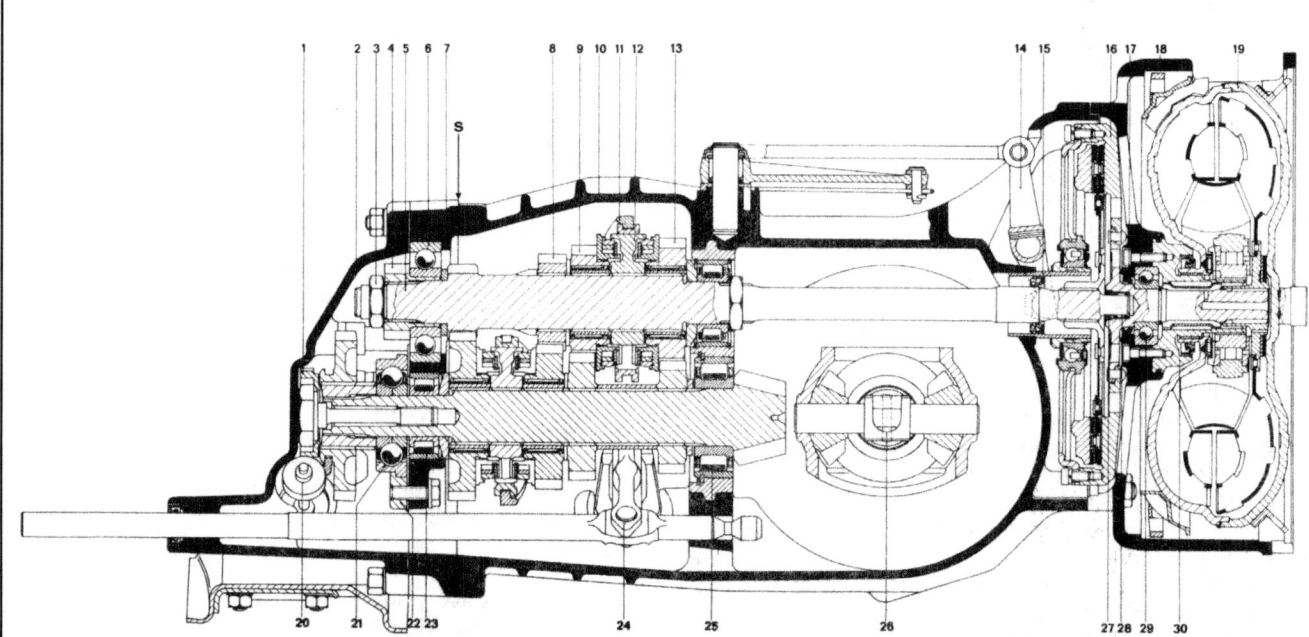

FIG 2 Cross-section through later four-speed transmission

1 Speedometer drive
2 Front cover
3 Flange nut
4 Gear I, reverse gear
5 Input shaft
6 Ball bearing race
7 Intermediate plate
8 Gear I, 2nd gear
9 Gear I, 3rd gear
10 Transmission housing
11 Shift fork, 3rd and 4th gear
12 Shift sleeve, 3rd and 4th gear
13 Gear I, 4th gear
14 Throwout fork
15 Oil seal
16 Clutch plate / turbine shaft
17 Oil seal
18 Torque converter housing
19 Torque converter
20 Speedometer gear shaft
21 Four point ball bearing
22 Clamping plate
23 Roller bearing
24 Selector shaft
25 Roller bearing
26 Anchor block
27 Oil seal
28 Needle bearing sleeve
29 Ball bearing
30 Stator support
S Gasket(s) see text

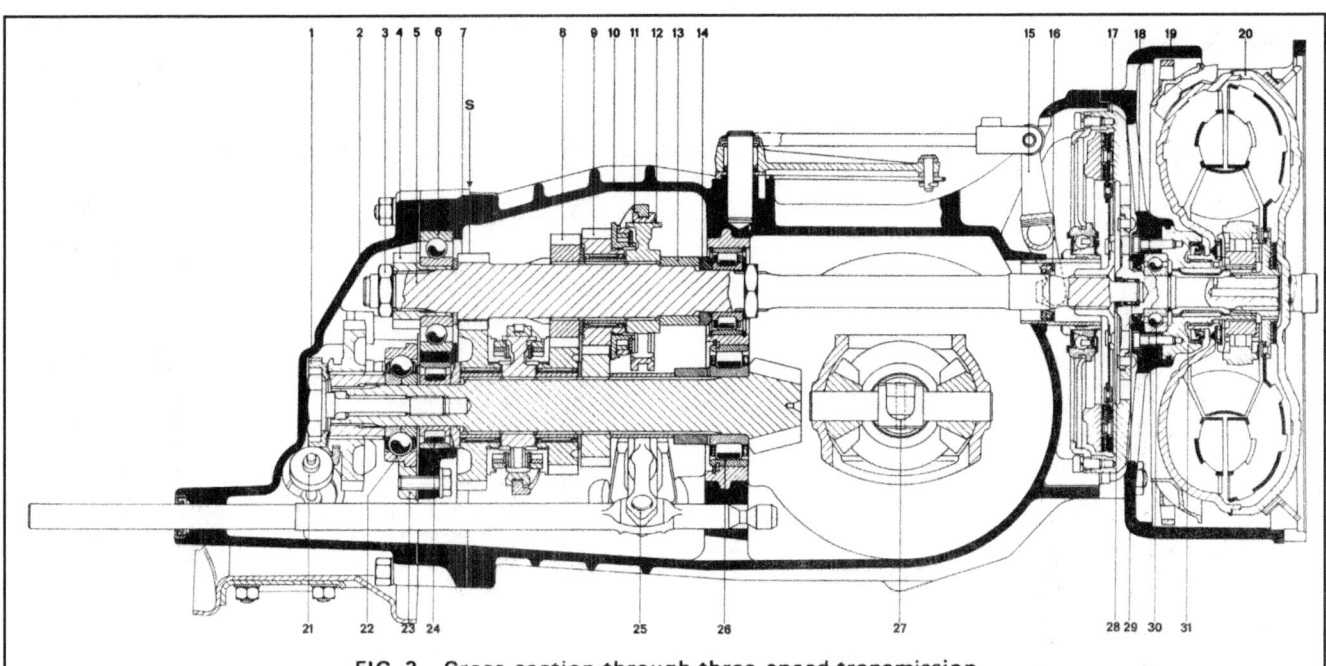

FIG 3 Cross-section through three-speed transmission

1	Speedometer drive gear	9	3rd gear (27:25 V)	17	Turbine shaft
2	Front transmission cover	10	Transmission case	18	Oil seal
3	Flanged nut	11	3rd gear shift fork	19	Torque converter housing
4	Reverse gear	12	3rd gear shift sleeve guide	20	Torque converter
5	Main shaft	13	Spacer	21	Speedometer drive shaft
6	Ball bearing	14	Washer	22	Four-point ball bearing
7	Intermediate plate	15	Release lever	23	Clamping plate
8	2nd gear (22:29 M)	16	Oil seal	24	Roller bearing

25	Inner shift lever
26	Roller bearing
27	Anchor block
28	O-ring
29	Needle bearing
30	Ball bearing
31	Stator support
S	Gasket(s) see text

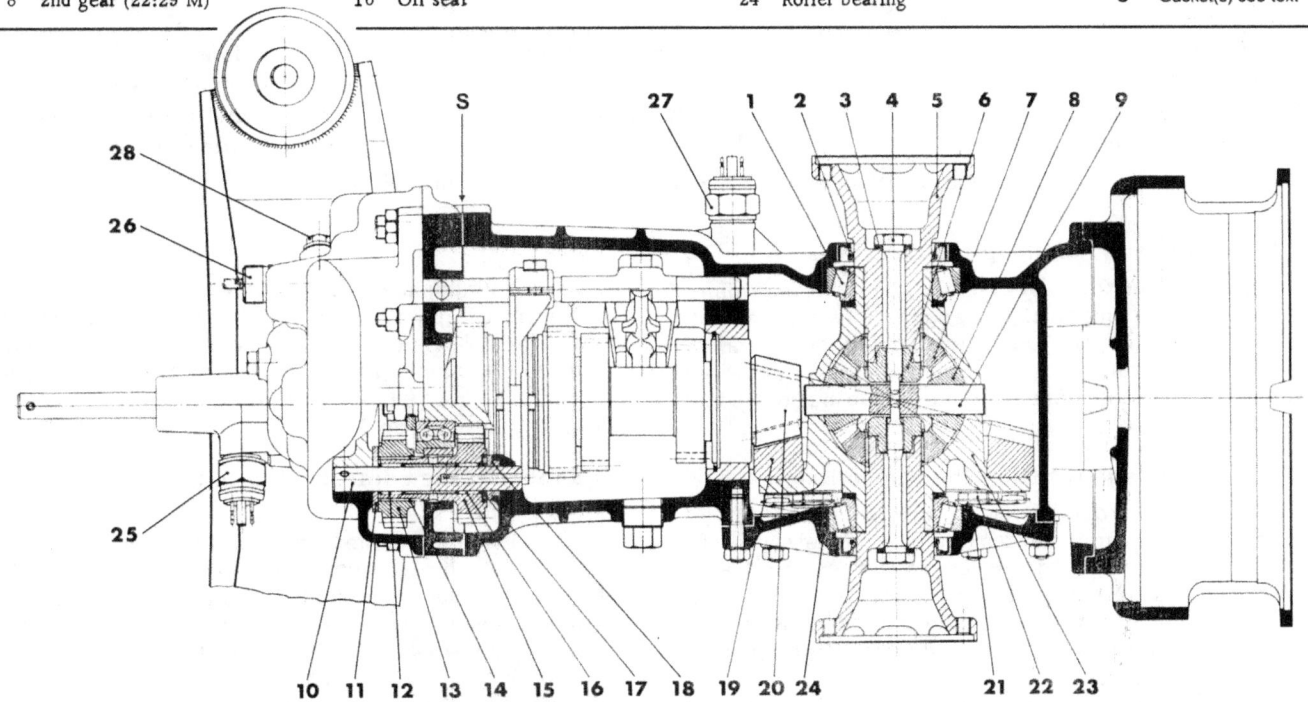

FIG 4 Horizontal cross-section through earlier four-speed transmission

1	Side bearing	8	Pinion gear	15	Gear 2 for reverse speed
2	Oil seal	9	Pinion gear shaft	16	Caged needle bearing
3	Washer	10	Reverse gear shaft	17	Thrust needle bearing
4	Stretchbolt	11	Thrust washer	18	Thrust ring
5	Axle flange	12	Caged needle bearing	19	Ring gear
6	Threaded piece	13	Gear 3 for reverse speed	20	Pinion shaft
7	Side gear	14	Retaining ring	21	Transmission side cover

22	Hex bolt
23	Differential case
24	Side cover
25	Bypass switch
26	Speedometer drive
27	Reverse light switch
28	Parking lock cap
S	Gasket(s) see text

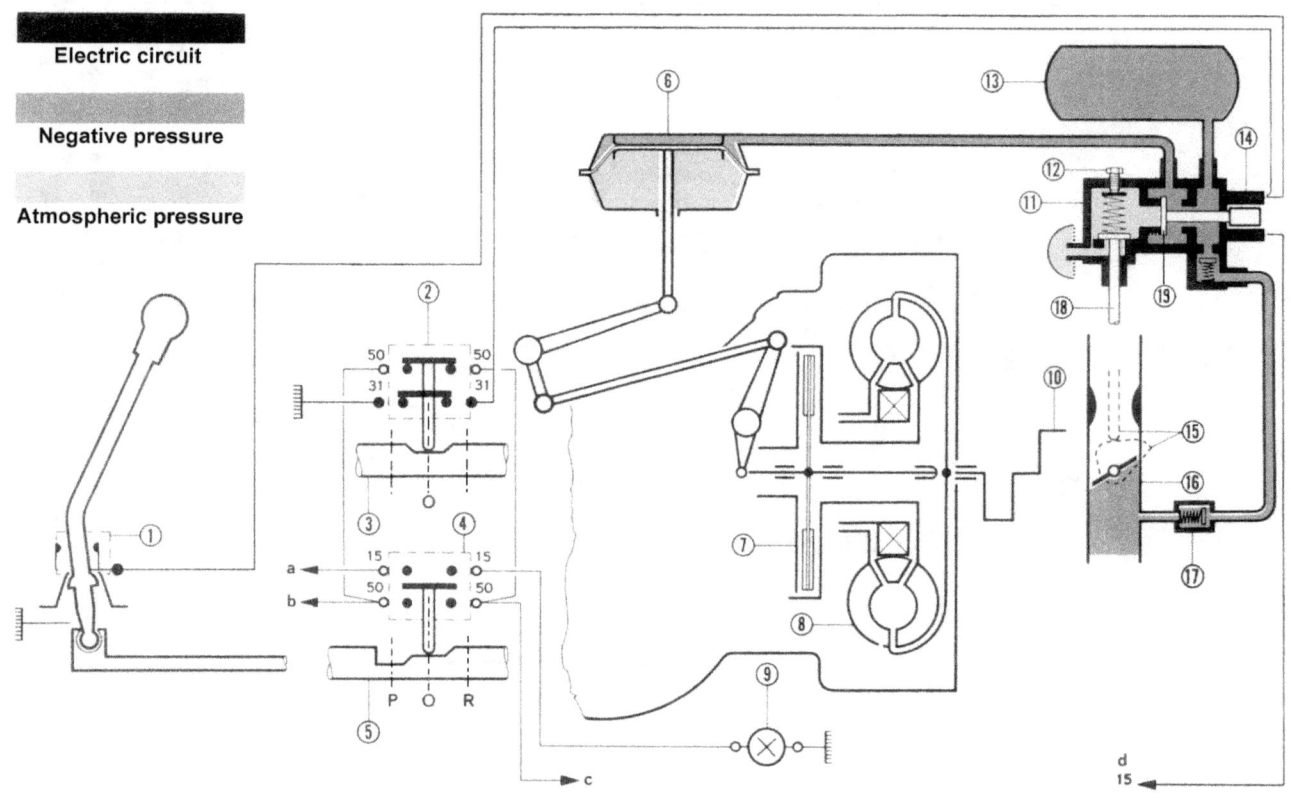

1 Microswitch in gearshift lever
2 Bypass switch
3 Gear selector shaft
4 Backup light switch and park position contact
5 Shift rod P and R
6 Vacuum servo unit
7 Transmission clutch
8 Torque converter
9 Backup light
10 Crankshaft
11 Control valve
12 Adjusting screw
13 Vacuum reservoir
14 Electric solenoid switch
15 Cam and plunger
16 Intake manifold
17 Check valve
18 Auxiliary valve
19 Main valve

a Wire from fuse 1
b Wire from ignition switch
c Wire to starter terminal 50
d Wire to intermediate fuse 8/15 A

FIG 5 Diagrammatic layout of Sportomatic transmission

3 Removing and installing the transmission

Refer to **Chapter 6, Section 3**. The notes regarding removal and refitment of the engine/transmission unit are also relevant to models with Sportomatic transmissions. Separation of the Sportomatic transmission from the engine and refitment to the engine are covered in **Section 4** below.

4 Separating and refitting the transmission

On earlier models, refer to **FIG 6**. Remove the electrical wiring from the temperature gauge sensor **A** and the temperature switch **B**. Loosen hose clamp 1 and uncouple hose 2 and pipe 3 from the sensor unit **C**. Detach the vacuum hose 4 from the clutch vacuum-servo unit. On later models the sensor and switch are fitted to the torque converter casing.

Unhook and withdraw the rear throttle control rod. Through the large apertures in the torque converter casing, remove the angled 12-point bolts which secure the torque converter to the coupling plate. Remove the bolts and nuts joining the engine to the transmission. As the units are separated, take care that the torque converter remains in its housing. A short length of flat steel strip may be bolted to one of the casing bolt holes to keep the torque converter in place.

When refitting the engine to the transmission, use a torque of 4.7kgm (34lb ft) on the attaching nuts and bolts. The 12-point bolts for securing the torque converter to the coupling plate must be tightened to 2.4 to 2.6kgm (17 to 19lb ft). Set the clutch free play as described in **Section 7**.

5 Servicing the control valve and sensor control valve:

No procedures are prescribed for the overhaul or repair of this unit and a faulty valve must be renewed. To remove it, detach the battery leads. Remove the air cleaner assembly after detaching the oil tank breather hose and the small hose for the breather valve. Refer to **FIG 6**. Withdraw the rubber cap from solenoid 6. Remove the splitpin and pull off the wire connector.

Detach the hoses from the valve and release the bracket from its support.

When fitting a control valve, coat the sliding surface of the cam, and drag spring where fitted, with molybdenum disulphide grease. Adjust the valve as described later. Make sure the cable connector is well seated. Redrill the splitpin hole if necessary.

Cleaning the air filter:

Remove the filter 7 in **FIG 6**. Refit after washing off in petrol and drying thoroughly with compressed air.

Control valve adjustment:

Do this every 6000 miles (10,000km) or when required as in preceding notes. Control linkage and engine idling speed must be correctly adjusted first.

Upshift on acceleration is adjusted as follows:

Where CIS equipment is fitted, it will be necessary in order to gain access to remove the following after disconnecting the battery: the air cleaner cover, the heater blower, holder, and detach number 3 cylinder injection line at the injector, and remove number 3 cylinder intake pipe.

1 Refer to **FIG 7**. Clearance at 3 must be 1.5mm (0.06in) when the throttles are set for idling. Cam 6 must be fully returned. (Adjust by slackening bolt 4)
2 Put a 4mm (0.16in) shim under the lefthand idling stop screw (see illustration). Adjust the cam so that the cam or the drag spring where fitted just touches the control valve plunger 1.
3 Remove the shim. In this position the original clearance of 1.5mm (0.06in) may be different, but a minimum clearance of 1.0mm (0.04in) must be maintained.

Downshift on deceleration is adjusted as follows:

1 Drive the car or run it onto a roller stand. As a rough guide on a standing vehicle, set the handbrake, let the engine idle and engage a gear. The time lag between releasing the gear lever and the perceptible impact of engagement must be 0.30 to 0.50 seconds.
2 Check under driving conditions by running at 4500rev/min in 'D'. Take the foot off the throttle and shift down to 'L'. The clutch should engage without a time lag, but the rear wheels must not lock. If necessary, adjust the time lag as follows:
3 Remove the plastic cover from the control valve adjusting screw 10 in **FIG 6**. Turn the screw in to give a softer, delayed clutch engagement. Turn the screw anticlockwise to give a harder and more instantaneous clutch engagement. Do not turn more than $\frac{1}{4}$ to $\frac{1}{2}$ a turn at a time. Refit the plastic cover.

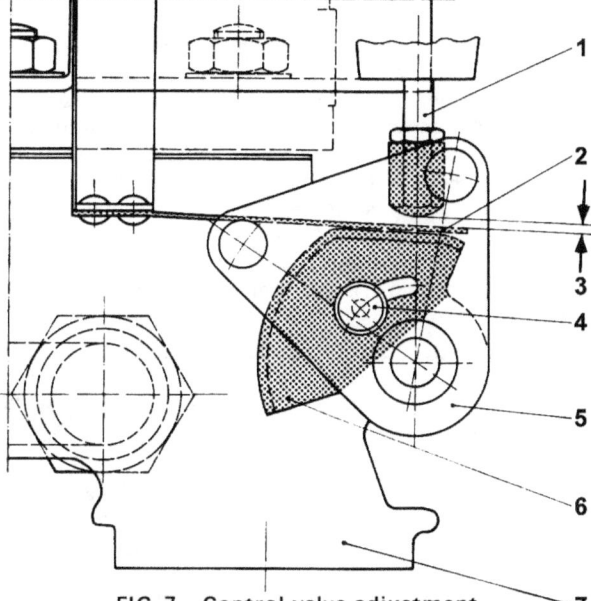

FIG 7 Control valve adjustment

1 Control valve plunger 5 Throttle cross-shaft
2 Drag spring, early models 6 Cam
3 Clearance of 1.5mm (0.059in) 7 Inlet manifold
4 Socket head bolt

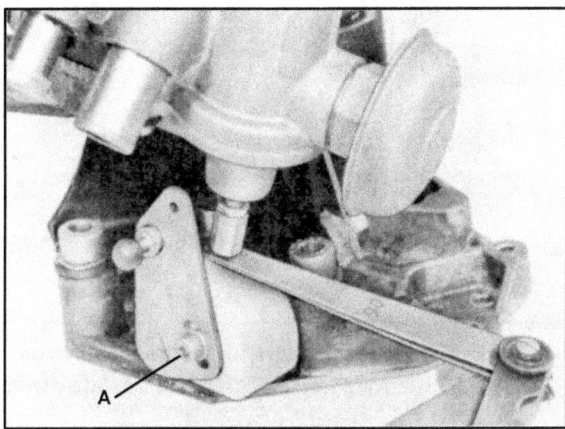

Adjust the cam by slackening bolt A to allow the plunger to have 0.060 in. (1.5 mm) of clearance

FIG 6 Control valve and earlier location of temperature sensor and switch

A Temperature sensor 2 Hose 6 Solenoid
B Temperature switch 3 Pipe 7 Air cleaner
C Housing 4 Hose 8, 9 Hoses
1 Hose clamp 5 Valve 10 Adjusting screw

Partially open the throttle using a 0.160 in. (4 mm) shim

Temperature switch and gauge sensor:

The location of these on earlier models is shown in **FIG 6**. They may be removed without taking the power unit out of the car by following the instructions for removing the engine and transmission as described in **Chapter 1** up to the point where the unit is lowered a little. The switch and sensor are then accessible from above. Pull the cables off and remove the unit.

When refitting, heat and quench the copper gaskets to anneal them. Tighten the switch and sensor to 4.5 to 5.0kgm (33 to 36lb ft). On later models the switch and sensor are fitted to the torque converter housing.

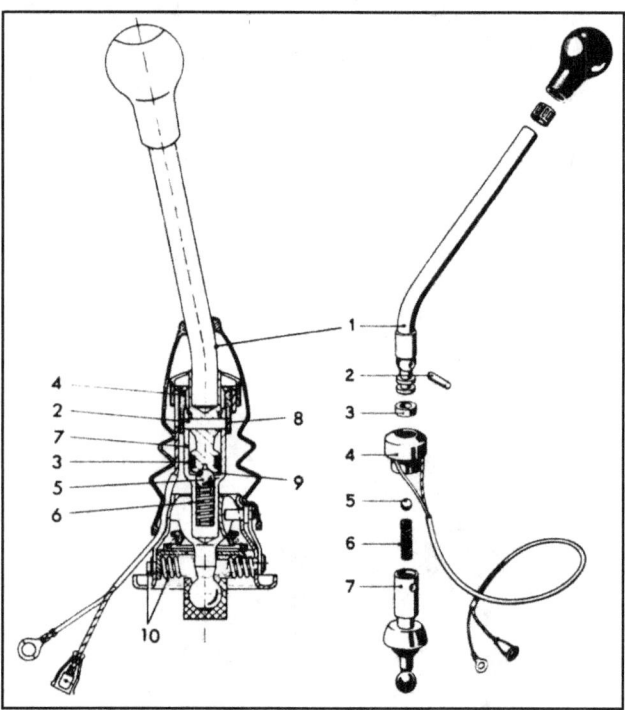

FIG 8 Details of the gearlever and microswitch

1 Gearlever 2 Retaining pin 3 Stop ring 4 Microswitch
5 Ball 6 Spring 7 Gearlever lower part
8 Position of switch when engaged with pin
9 Parts to be lightly lubed 10 Spring and guide pin

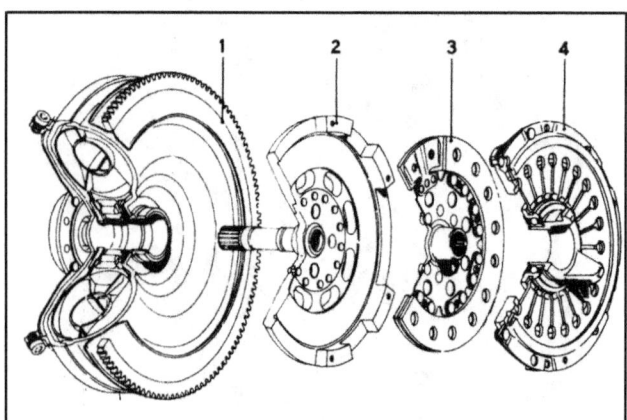

FIG 9 Clutch and torque converter components

1 Torque converter 2 Turbine shaft and clutch carrier plate
3 Clutch driven plate 4 Clutch pressure plate

6 Servicing the gearchange lever and microswitch

Refer to **FIG 8**. Remove and refit the microswitch as follows:

1 Lift the rubber boot and remove the tunnel covering. Release the base flange from the tunnel and lift slightly.
2 Detach the microswitch cables in the tunnel and lift away the lever and base.
3 Drive off the gear lever knob and pull the boot and switch off the lever.

Clean dirty switch contacts or, if unserviceable, renew the switch. Reassemble by pushing the switch on to the lever with the split facing forward. Push far enough to engage pin 2. Check the contact gap with the lever in neutral. The gap must be 0.30 to 0.40mm (0.012 to 0.016in). Adjust the gap by bending the outer contact tabs. Fit the switch top and boot. Refit the knob. Connect the cable connectors and fit the assembly to tunnel. The earth lead from the switch goes under the front lefthand bolt. Tighten the 8mm bolts to 2.5kgm (18lb ft) and the 6mm bolts to 1kgm (7.2lb ft).

Overhauling the gearchange lever base:

Apart from the microswitch, the rest of the assembly resembles that for the manual gearbox lever, so refer to **Chapter 6**, **Section 11** for instructions. Having fitted the plastic ball socket to the lever, lightly grease the stop ring 3 and push onto the lever. Grease spring 6 and insert it into lower part 7, grease the ball and lever and insert it into the lower part. Fit the retaining pin 2. It must enter easily to prevent the switch malfunctioning. Install the switch and knob.

7 Servicing the torque converter and clutch

Cross-sections through the torque converter and clutch are included in **FIGS 1**, **2** and **3**. Cut-away sections are shown in **FIG 9**.

FIGS 10 and **11** are relevant to the clutch controls.

FIG 10 Components of the clutch operating mechanism

1 Mounting stud 2 Intermediate lever 3 Clevis
4 Servo unit 5 Clutch rod

Clutch free play:

Check this every 6000 miles. Depressurise the vacuum-servo unit by pressing the accelerator linkage operating lever towards full throttle. Push the clutch intermediate lever 2 towards the righthand rear wheel (see **FIG 7:10**). Free play at this point should be at least 5mm (0.20in). If play is less, readjust as follows:

1. Remove engine/transmission unit (see **Section 3**). Remove the clevis pin from fork 3.
2. Pull the actuating rod of vacuum-servo unit 4 right out to the stop. Push the intermediate lever 2 towards the servo unit as far as possible.
3. The holes in the fork must be further away from the servo unit than the hole in the intermediate lever by 12 to 15mm (0.47 to 0.59in). Refit the clevis pin, using a new splitpin. Tighten the locknut on the rod. Check the control valve adjustment as described in **Section 5** then refit power unit.

Removing the torque converter and clutch:

With the engine detached from transmission as described in **Section 4**, withdraw the torque converter. **Oil will run out.** Cover the converter to keep out dirt. Remove the external and internal nuts securing the converter housing to the transmission casing. Release the front end of the clutch rod 5 from the intermediate lever 2 (see **FIG 10**). Part the housing from the casing while disengaging the clutch release bearing from its fork.

Remove the socket head bolts from the clutch pressure plate flange, loosening them a turn at a time diagonally to prevent distortion. Withdraw the pressure plate, noting that the release bearing may fall out. Remove the clutch driven plate. Remove the socket head bolts from the freewheel support, insert two long bolts in opposite holes and drive out the support with the oil seal.

Remove the circlip from turbine shaft 2 in **FIG 9**. Support the housing on blocks and drive out the turbine shaft. Using a punch at alternating points, drive out the shaft bearing and push out the oil seal.

Inspecting converter and clutch:

Refer to **Chapter 5** for instructions on checking the clutch condition, but note that the minimum thickness over the linings (uncompressed) is 5.5mm (0.217in). Lateral runout must not exceed 0.50mm (0.02in).

Torque converters cannot be repaired. Renew a damaged or unserviceable unit.

Check the clutch face of turbine shaft and carrier assembly. Renew the assembly if it is heavily scored. Check the needle bearing and inspect the hub seat and oil passage. If worn, the needle bearing and oil seal may be extracted with a puller and a new bearing driven in with tool P361. The oil seal is fitted with tool P362.

Grease the bearing with molybdenum disulphide grease, using it sparingly so that the clutch plate will not be contaminated.

Check the ballbearing in its housing when it is dry after cleaning. To fit a new bearing, heat the housing to 120°C (248°F) and drive it in with tool P359. Renew the smaller oil seal by driving it in with tool P359. Oil the sealing lip.

Check the freewheel support and turbine shaft bushing for wear. Check the oil passages. A defective support must be renewed as an assembly complete with bushing and sealing sleeve.

Reassembling:

Secure the freewheel support with three bolts and drive in the turbine shaft using tool P362. Remove the bolts and support and fit the circlip onto the shaft. Refit the freewheel support, tightening the sockethead bolts diagonally to 1.4kgm (10lb ft). Fit new 'O' rings to the bolts. Refit the seal and oil its lip.

Centre the clutch driven plate with a suitable mandrel (see **Chapter 5**). Lightly coat both sides of the diaphragm spring segments with molybdenum disulphide grease and work the release bearing in diagonally from the inside. Fit the clutch pressure plate, tightening the bolts diagonally a turn at a time to 1.4kgm (10lb ft). Make sure plate is seating on the dowels and that the release bearing is free.

Refitting:

Use molybdenum disulphide grease to coat the contact faces of the clutch release fork and bearing, also the pilot at the rear end of the gearbox input shaft. Fit the engine mounting bolt and spring washer into housing adjacent to temperature sensor body. **The vacuum-servo unit prevents the fitting of the bolt later on.** Bring the mounting flanges together while guiding the clutch release bearing into the fork. Tighten the large nuts to 4kgm (29lb ft) and the smaller nuts to 2.2kgm (16lb ft).

The torque converter must hold a small quantity of oil during assembly. Put about 0.50 litres of engine oil in a new converter. The equivalent is 1 US pint and slightly less than 1 Imp. pint. Slide the converter on to the freewheel support and turbine shaft. Refit the engine to the transmission.

Refilling the torque converter with oil:

On completion of a torque converter and clutch overhaul it is necessary to fill the torque converter and the oil pipes. The converter must be full of engine oil before checking the tank level by dipstick. If there is any doubt about this, detach the oil return pipe from the converter at the tank, run the engine and check that oil flows from the pipe.

8 Servicing the clutch controls:

Intermediate lever:

Components of the lever are shown in **FIG 11**. To remove the lever, detach the clutch rod and actuating rod clevis. Remove circlip 1, washer 2, grommet 3, spacer 4 and lever 6. Lift off 'O' ring 7, thrust ring 8 and spring 9.

Renew the pivot shaft and bush 5 if worn. Renew the lever pin if its eyes are worn. To remove and refit the shaft and dowel pin, heat the casing to 120°C (248°F). Install to dimensions given in **FIG 11**. Coat the shafts with molybdenum disulphide grease. Fit the spring as shown at A. Fit the thrust ring with the cavity over the dowel pin and the end of the spring. Fit the 'O' ring, the lever and the remaining parts. Install the circlip.

Clutch fork:

Detach the rear end of the clutch rod 5 from the release fork lever (see **FIG 10**). The fork is carried on the shaft located in the transmission casing. holes being covered on outside by caps. Prise out the caps with two screwdrivers. Drive out the roll pin securing the fork to the shaft. Drift out the shaft and remove the fork and washers.

If worn, renew the shaft bushes, driving them below the outer surface so that the caps may be refitted. Reassemble the fork and shaft so that the holes for the roll pin are aligned. Fit the roll pin. Use molybdenum disulphide grease on the shaft and its bushes.

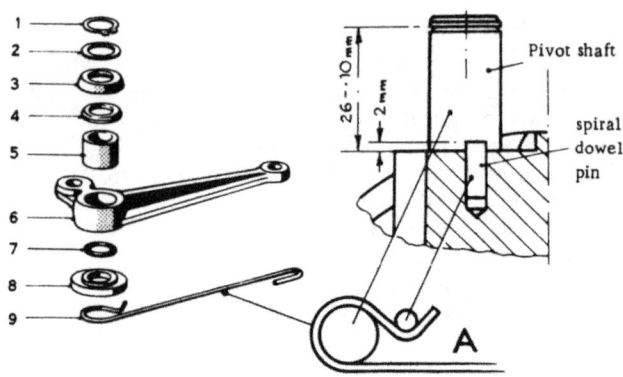

FIG 11 Clutch intermediate lever

1 Lock ring 4 Spacer 7 O-ring
2 Washer 5 Bushing 8 Thrust ring
3 Grommet 6 Intermediate lever 9 Spring

FIG 12 Earlier type gearbox (front cover removed)

1 Reverse selector fork 4 Roll pin
2 Parking lever and pawl 5 Reverse sliding gear
3 Pinion shaft bolt 6 Circlip

Key to Fig 13

1 Input shaft
2 Gear I of 1st speed (fixed)
3 Gear I of 2nd speed (fixed)
4 Thrust washer
5 Gear I of 3rd speed (freewheeling)
6 Sliding sleeve-coupling
7 Spider
8 Gear I of 4th speed (freewheeling)
9 Thrust washer (5.9 mm thick)
10 Roller bearing
11 Hex nut
12 Oil seal race
13 Splined seat for clutch plate
14 Needle bearing inner race
15 Needle bearing cage
16 Brake band
17 Synchronizing ring
18 Needle bearing inner race
19 Needle bearing cage
20 Nut lock plate

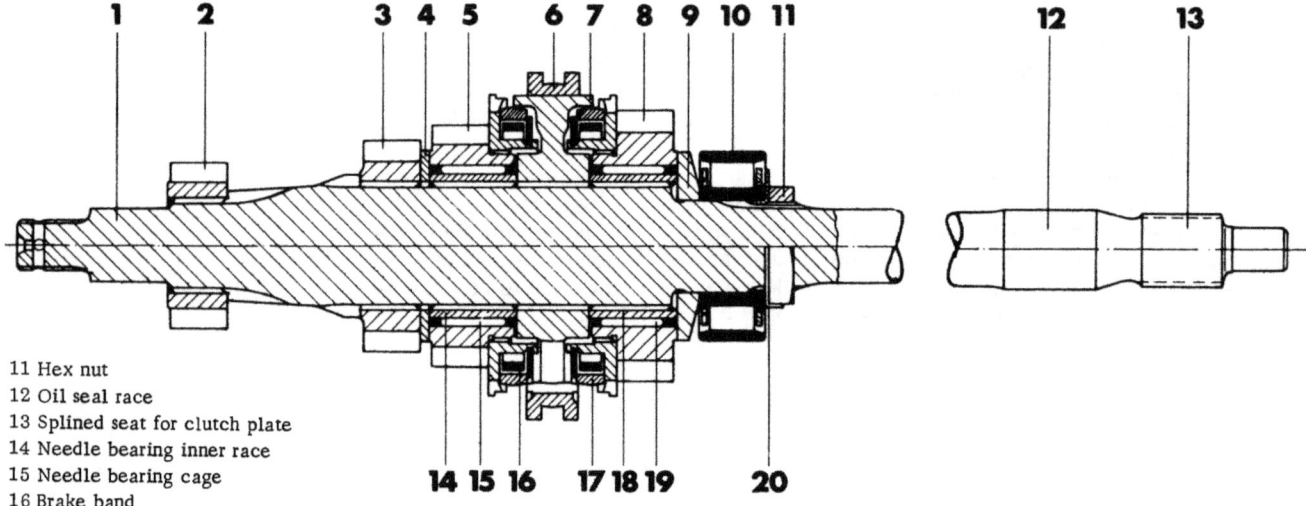

FIG 13 Cross-section through earlier four-speed input shaft

9 Overhauling the transmission:

Refer to the opening paragraphs of **Chapter 6, Section 4**. These apply with equal force to the Sportomatic transmissions and the following instructions are given to assist those who have the requisite experience, access to the necessary tools, a press, an oven and to appropriate precision measuring equipment. Make notes and sketches to supplement the text. In particular note which way round components are fitted. Do not transpose shims or washers (see **Chapter 6, Section 5**).

Dismantling, all transmissions:

The following initial dismantling operations (which assume that the transmission is to be completely dismantled) are common to the three-speed and to the earlier and later types of four-speed transmissions.

1 Release the clutch intermediate lever from the vacuum-servo clevis (see **FIG 10**). Release the servo unit and bracket from the transmission casing.
2 Remove the transmission front support. Remove the parking lock cap screw from just above the tachometer elbow drive. Withdraw the spring and ball. Remove the bypass switch. Remove the front cover.
3 Remove the torque converter and clutch as described in **Section 7**. Remove and dismantle the differential and final drive as described in **Chapter 6, Section 6**.

Dismantling the earlier four-speed gearbox:

FIGS 1 and **4** relate to this gearbox.

1 Refer to **FIG 12** and remove the parking lockpin and ball from reverse selector fork 1. Remove circlip 6 and pull off the reverse sliding gear 5 and fork. Detach the springs and lift off the parking lock lever and pawl 2.
2 Select fourth speed by turning the selector rod clockwise and pulling it forward. Fit tool P37 to the splines at the rear end of the input shaft to prevent turning and unscrew bolt 3. Remove the splined muff.
3 Remove roll pin 4 and unscrew the castellated nut. Remove the reversing light switch and the actuating pin. Remove the selector shaft guide fork and continue with removal of the intermediate plate as described for the earlier five-speed gearbox in **Chapter 6, Section 4**. Identify and retain the gasket(s) **S** in **FIGS 1** and **4**.
4 Carry on dismantling as instructed for the five-speed transmission. When identifying the gears, remember there is one speed less, so that called a second-speed gear in the five-speed transmission is the first-speed gear in the four-speed gearbox, and so on.
5 A cross-section through the input shaft is shown in **FIG 13**. The gear for first-speed is splined to the shaft and is mounted to the rear of the intermediate plate, the shaft carrying no gear in front of the plate as it does in the five-speed box. The gear may be pressed off the shaft together with the inner race half of the ballbearing. When refitting this gear, its small collar faces outward.
6 A cross-section through the pinion shaft is shown in **FIG 14**. The relevant **R** dimension (see **Chapter 6, FIG 13**) is tabulated in **Chapter 6, Section 7** and the pinion positioning procedure is as described in **Chapter 6, Sections 5** and **7**.

Key to Fig 14
L Pinion shaft ball bearing location
1 Gear II for 1st speed (freewheeling)
2 Spider
3 Brake band
4 Gear II for 2nd speed (freewheeling)
5 Gear II for 3rd speed (fixed)
6 Gear II for 4th speed (fixed)
7 Spacer
8 Roller bearing
9 Pinion shaft
10 Thrust washer (6.6 mm or .260" thick)
11 Needle bearing inner race (1st thru 4th gear)
12 Needle bearing cage (1st thru 4th gear)
13 Sliding sleeve-coupling
14 Synchronizing ring
15 Needle bearing inner race
16 Needle bearing cage
17 Spacers
18 Retaining ring

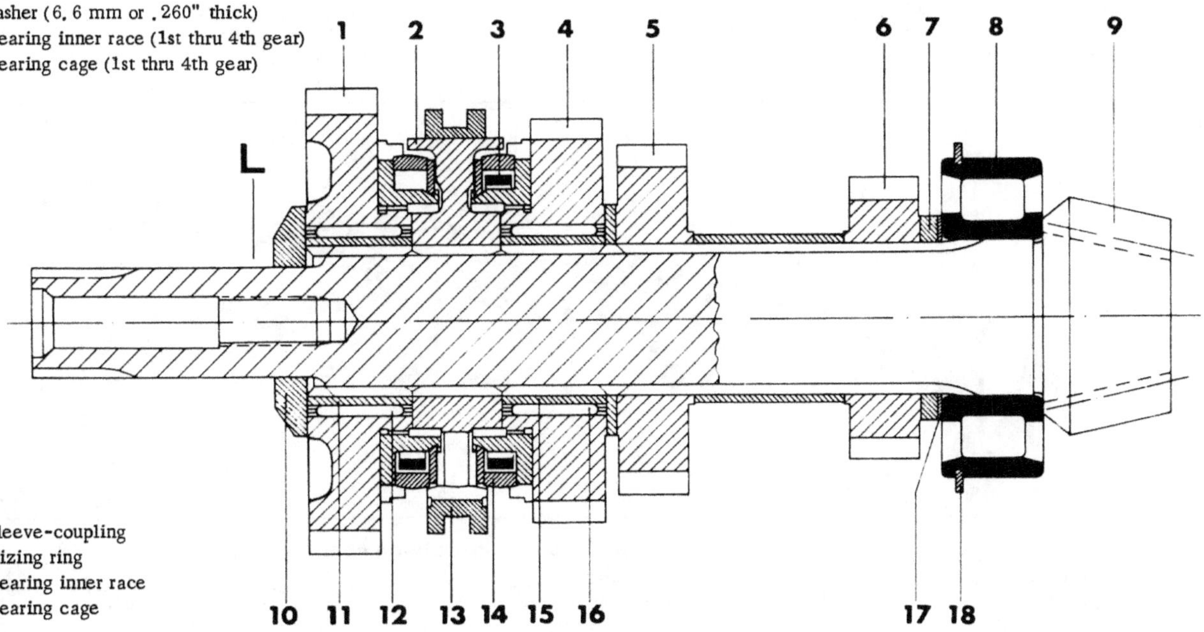

FIG 14 Cross-section through earlier four-speed pinion shaft

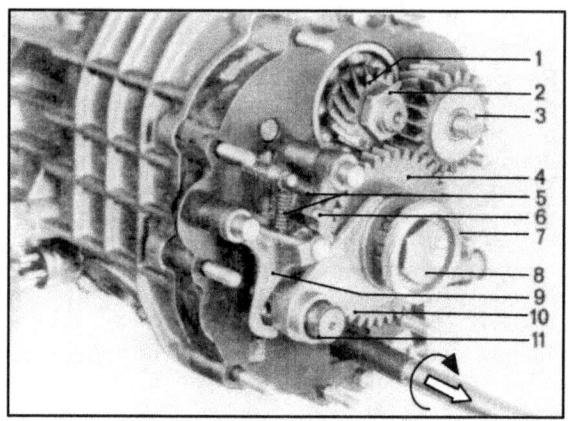

FIG 15 Later type gearbox with front cover removed

1. Gear I, reverse gear
2. Flanged nut
3. Reverse idler gear assembly
4. Reverse selector gear
5. Parking lock springs
6. Speedometer drive gear
7. Speedometer drive gear
8. Expansion bolt
9. Parking lock lever
10. Shift fork, reverse gear
11. Snap ring

Dismantling the later four-speed and the three-speed gearboxes:

FIGS 2 and 3 relate to these gearboxes.

1 Refer to FIG 15. Engage fourth gear by turning the selector rod to the right and pulling it forwards (see arrows). Detach the parking lock springs and remove the pawl and lever.

2 Use tool P37 to block the input shaft. Remove bolt 8 and gear 7. Remove ring 11. Remove parking lock 9. Push in the detent pin and remove the reverse gear selector and fork 10.

3 Remove the splined bush and the reverse idler gear assembly 3 together with the needle bearing cages and thrust bearing cage. Remove nut 2. Remove the bypass and reversing light switches and their contact plungers.

4 Withdraw the shaft assemblies and intermediate plate. Identify and retain the gasket(s) S in FIG 2 or 3. Using tool P353a, press the pinion and input shaft assemblies from the intermediate plate as described in Chapter 6, Section 4 for the earlier five-speed box.

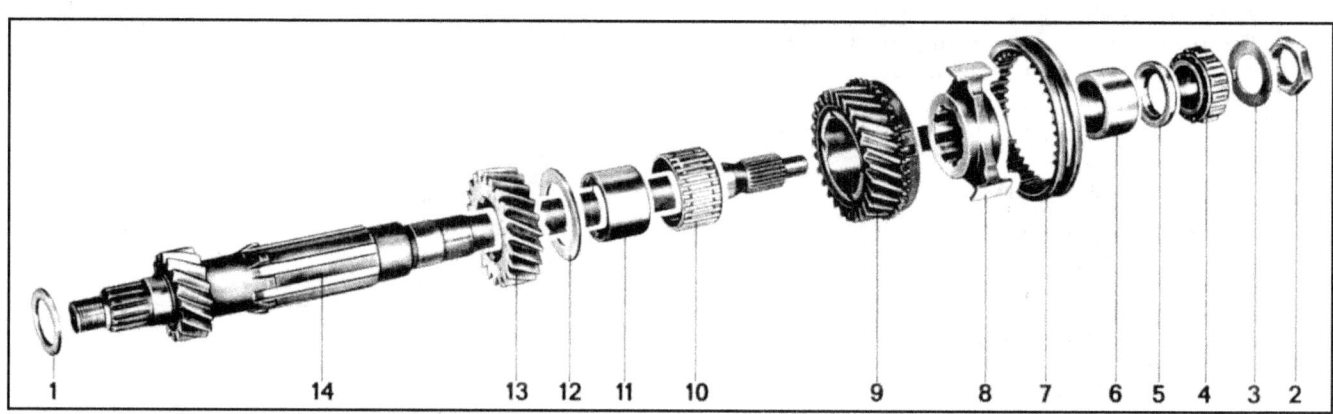

FIG 16 Three-speed gearbox input shaft

1 Spacer
2 Nut
3 Lockplate
4 Roller bearing
5 Washer
6 Spacer
7 Sliding sleeve
8 Sleeve guide
9 Third-speed free running gear
10 Needle bearing
11 Needle bearing race
12 Thrust washer
13 Second-speed fixed gear
14 Input shaft with integral first-speed gear

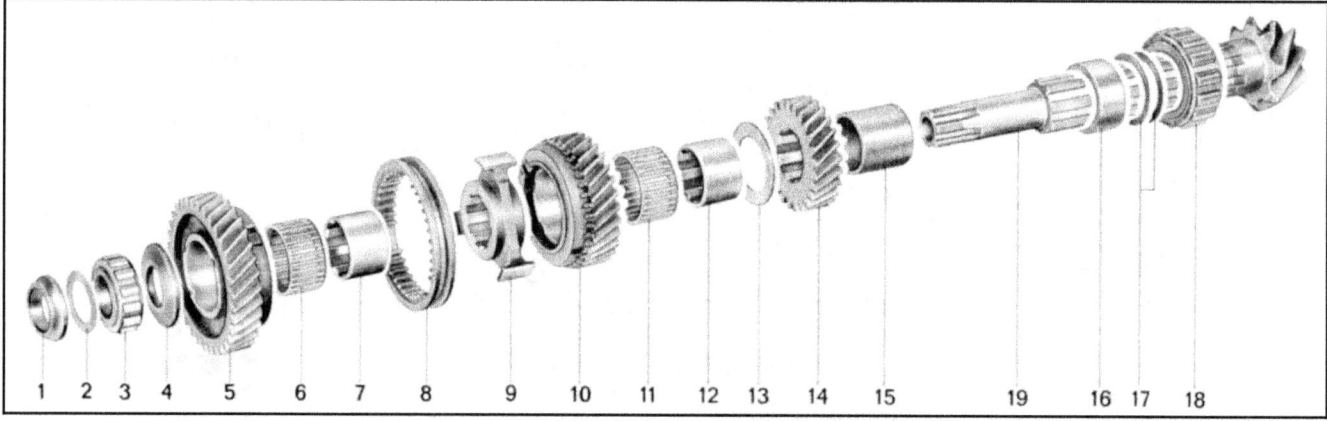

FIG 17 Three-speed gearbox pinion shaft

1 Ballbearing inner race
2 Spacer
3 Roller bearing
4 Thrust washer
5 First-speed free running gear
6 Needle bearing cage
7 Needle bearing race
8 Sliding sleeve
9 Sleeve guide
10 Second-speed free running gear
11 Needle bearing
12 Needle bearing race
13 Thrust washer
14 Third-speed fixed gear
15 Spacer
16 Spacer
17 Shim(s)
18 Roller bearing
19 Pinion shaft

5 The components of the three-speed input and pinion shafts are shown in **FIGS 16** and **17** respectively. The components of the four-speed version will be identified from **FIG 2** in conjunction with these illustrations. The relevant **R** dimension (see **Chapter 6, FIG 13**) is tabulated in **Chapter 6, Section 7** and the pinion positioning procedure is as described in **Chapter 6, Sections 5** and **7**.

Synchronisers:

Refer to **Chapter 6, Section 5**. Take particular care to note which way round the single brake band in the first-speed gear is fitted as **this is not the same for all boxes.**

Front cover:

Refer to **FIG 18**. This shows a later Sportomatic version. Differences between this and other models will be self-evident. To withdraw the speedometer drive, remove retaining bolt 1. Remove the reverse idler thrust washer 6 by prying it out. Extract bush 7 after heating the cover to 120°C (248°F). Heat the cover to this temperature before pressing in a new bush or, using tool P362, driving in washer 6. When reassembling, ensure that the blind hole in bush 3c aligns with the hole for the retaining bolt 1. If seal 5 is being renewed, use P218 to drive in the new part. Torque tighten bolt 1 to 1.6 to 1.8kgm (12 to 13lb ft).

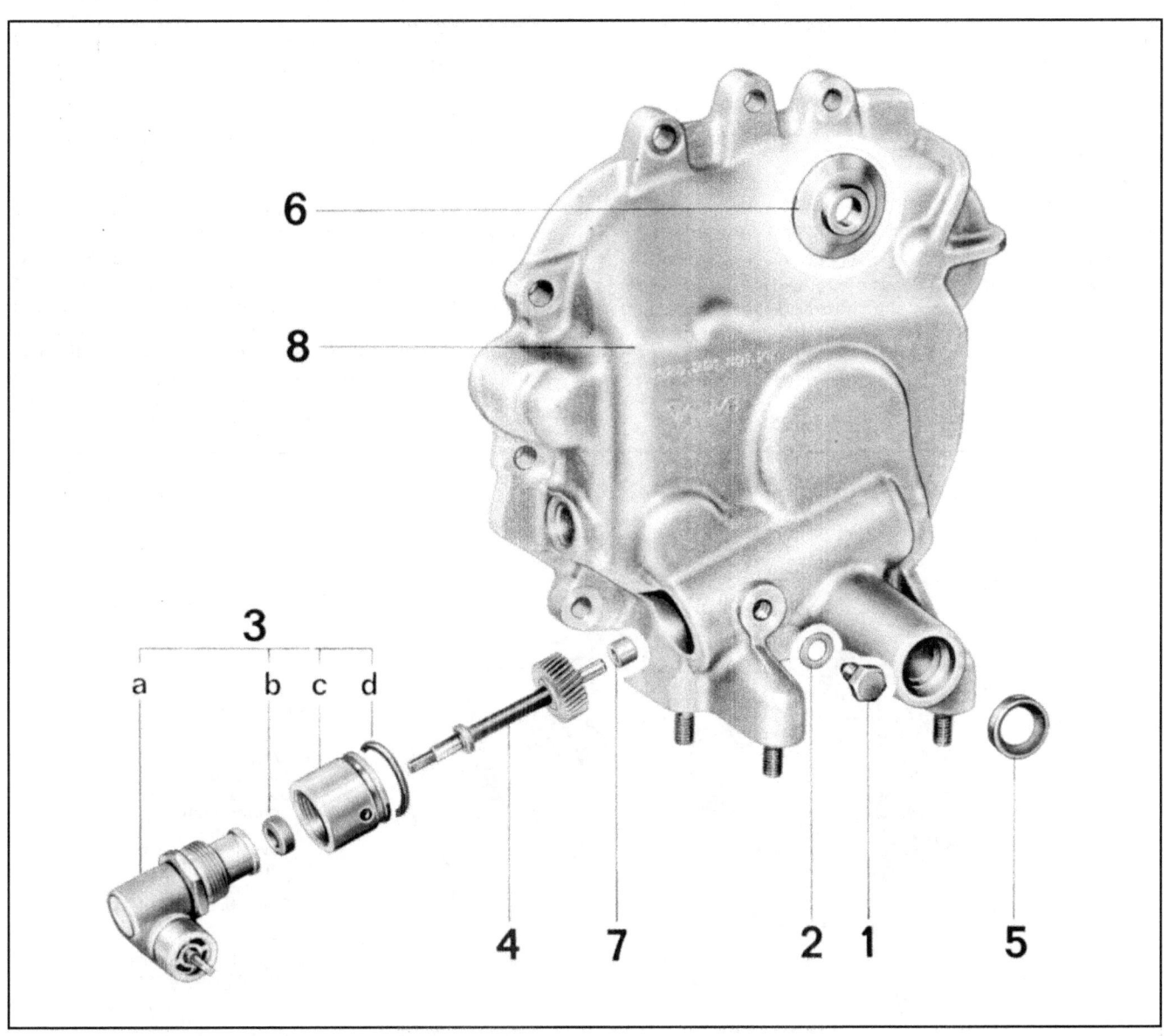

FIG 18 Front cover

1 Speedometer drive retaining bolt
2 Washer
3a Elbow adaptor
3b Seal
3c Guide bush
3d 'O' ring
4 Gearshaft
5 Seal
6 Thrust washer
7 Bush
8 Front cover

Intermediate plate:

Refer to **FIG 19**. This shows a later Sportomatic version. Differences between this and other models will be self-evident. Heat the plate to 120°C (248°F) before removing shaft 7, bearing/reverse gear 9, roller bearing outer race 10 or dowels 11. Heat the plate again to this temperature before fitting those new parts. If new detent bushes are being fitted, use mandrel P262 and drive in bush 15 until the mandrel bottoms. Drive in bush 14 to the second mark on the mandrel and bush 13 to the first mark on the mandrel. Use tool P372 to align bearing 4 and torque tighten the bolts which retain clamping plate 3 to 2.1 to 2.3kgm (15.0 to 16.5lb ft). Bolts 1 should also be tightened to this torque. Dowels 11 should protrude by 5.5mm (0.22in) on each side of the plate. Use press tools VW407 and P255 to assemble the reverse gear into a new bearing to form assembly 9.

The differential gearing:

Refer to **Chapter 6, Section 6**.

Gear and backlash settings:

Refer to **Chapter 6, Section 7**.

Reassembling the earlier four-speed gearbox:

Reverse the dismantling procedure. Torque tighten the reversing light and bypass switches to 4.5 to 5.0kgm (33 to 36lb ft), the input shaft nut and the pinion shaft bolt to 11 to 12kgm (80 to 87lb ft), the input shaft castellated nut to 10kgm (72lb ft), and also refer to **Chapter 6, Section 10** (earlier five-speed box). Also refer to **Sections 5, 6, 7 and 8** (this chapter).

Reassembling the later three & four-speed gearboxes:

Reverse the dismantling procedure. Use tools VW401, VW426 and VW412 when pressing the input and pinion shafts into the intermediate plate. Use tools P360 and P364 to fit a new input shaft seal. Note the following torque tightening figures. Reversing light and bypass switches, 3.5 to 4.0kgm (25 to 29lb ft); input shaft flanged nut and pinion shaft bolt, 11 to 12 kgm (80 to 87 lb ft); input shaft front nut, 10 to 12kgm (72 to 87lb ft); selector fork bolts, 2.2 to 2.6kgm (16 to 19lb ft), and refer to **Sections 5, 6, 7 and 8** (this chapter).

10 The torque converter pump

The dual rotor pump is driven by the lefthand camshaft. A non-adjustable relief valve is incorporated. The function of the pump is to keep the torque converter full of oil drawn from the main oil tank. This oil is drawn from the tank at a 30mm higher level than is the engine oil supply. The difference in level ensures that a leaking converter will not result in failure of the engine lubrication. Functioning of the pump may be checked by disconnecting the oil return line from the converter at the oil tank while the engine is running.

Access to the pump requires removal of the lefthand road wheel and the lefthand heat exchanger. Spare rotors and shaft are only supplied in sets. Check that the 'O' ring is in good condition and use new gaskets when reassembling the pump. Assemble with internal parts wetted with engine oil and ensure that the outer rotor is fitted with the bevelled diameter into the pump body. The alignment dowel should project from the housing face by 4mm (0.157in). The driving roll pins should project by 8mm (0.315in) from the end face of the camshaft.

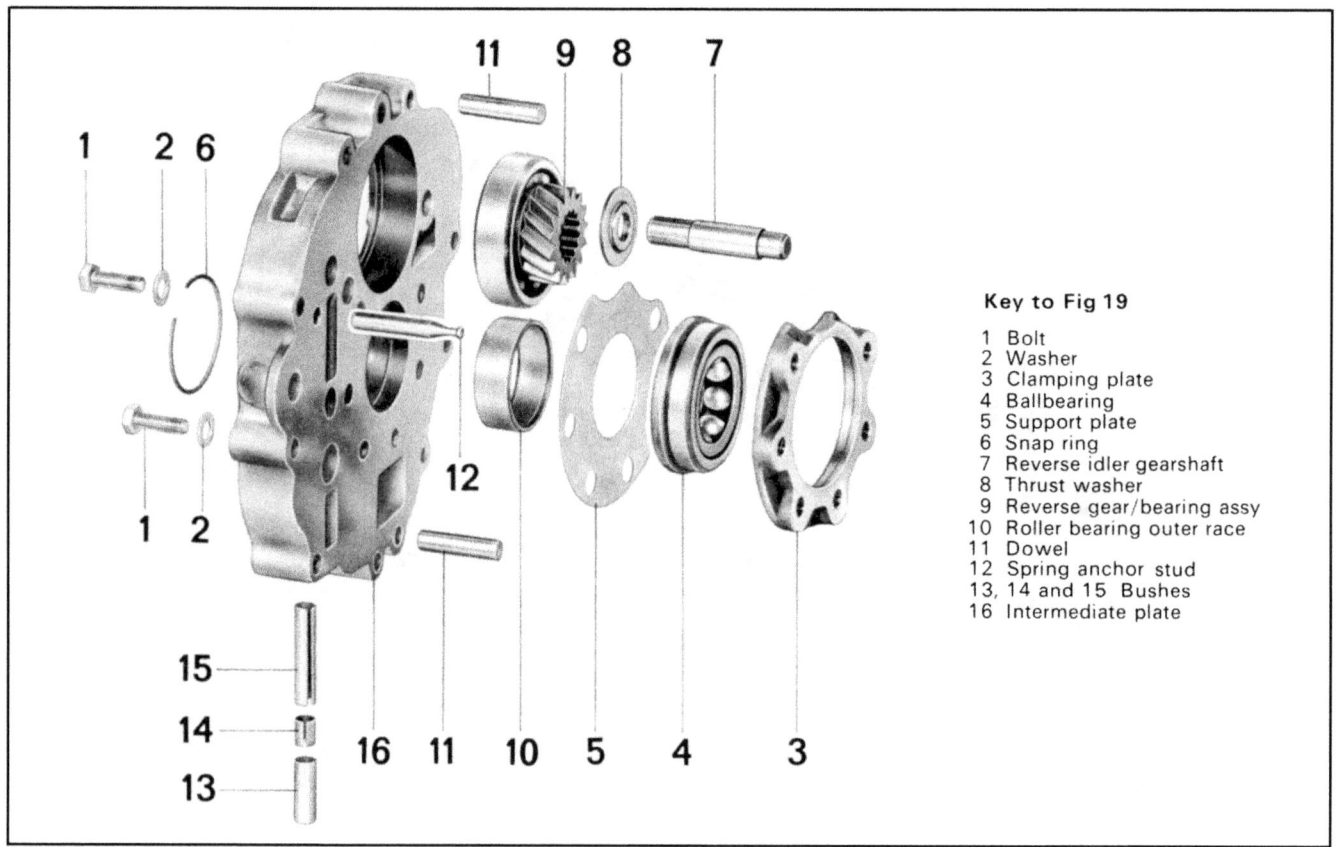

Key to Fig 19

1 Bolt
2 Washer
3 Clamping plate
4 Ballbearing
5 Support plate
6 Snap ring
7 Reverse idler gearshaft
8 Thrust washer
9 Reverse gear/bearing assy
10 Roller bearing outer race
11 Dowel
12 Spring anchor stud
13, 14 and 15 Bushes
16 Intermediate plate

FIG 19 Intermediate plate

11 Fault diagnosis

Malfunction	Cause	Remedy
1. Clutch slipping under full throttle although not only upon completion of a shift	Oily clutch linings	Replace clutch plate, eliminate oil leak
	Defective clutch	Replace clutch
	Improperly adjusted clutch linkage	Readjust linkage (basic adjustment), check clutch free play, check clutch
2. Excessive clutch slippage under open throttle upon completion of a shift	Improperly adjusted control valve	Readjust control valve for acceleration upshift
3. Harsh or delayed clutch engagement upon completion of a downshift	Improperly adjusted control valve	Readjust control valve for deceleration downshift
4. Clutch does not disengage	Improperly adjusted clutch linkage	Check adjustment, reaccomplish basic adjustment if necessary, possibly check the clutch
	Leaks in connecting hoses or vacuum reservoir	Eliminate leaks
	Defective diaphragm in vacuum servo unit	Replace vacuum servo unit
	Defective needle bearing in pilot seat of input shaft inclutch	Replace needle bearing and oil seal in turbine shaft
	Break in electric solenoid circuit	Repair damage, possibly by replacing the fuse
	Dirty or oxidized contact points in gearshift lever switch, poor ground to chassis	Clean contacts or install new switch, as appropriate; check ground connection to chassis
	Defective solenoid in control valve	Replace control valve
	Crimped or flattened hoses (blocked air passage)	Replace defective hoses
5. Engine dies when a shift is made, idle speed cannot be adjusted	Leak in hose between control valve and vacuum servo unit	Replace hose
	Defective diaphragm in vacuum servo unit	Replace vacuum servo unit
	Leaking check valves in intake manifold	Replace check valves
	Loose or defective hose between control valve and vacuum reservoir	Tighten or replace hoses
	Leak in vacuum reservoir	Eliminate leak

Malfunction	Cause	Remedy
6. Clutch does not engage upon completion of a downshift, but engages harsh when throttle is opened	Gearshift switch contacts sticking, or shorting due foreign matter in switch	Clean switch, free contacts, or replace the switch
	Short circuit in wire between switch and solenoid	Repair damage, install new wire if necessary
	Sticking solenoid in control valve	Replace control valve
7. Car leaps when gearshift lever is released while engine is idling and gear engaged (engagement jerk)	Idle speed too high	Readjust idle speed
	Improperly adjusted control valve	Readjust control valve (for deceleration shift)
8. Noisy torque converter (high-pitch whining)	Not enough oil in torque converter	Replenish oil in oil tank
	Oil pressure too low	Check oil pump
	Torque converter losing oil through pump hub	Replace oil seal in pump hub
	Oil leaking through weld seam between pump and turbine	Replace torque converter unit
9. Poor acceleration characteristics despite well performing engine and Sportomatic system	Defective torque converter: check stall speed by setting handbrake, depressing footbrake, shifting into D4, and opening the throttle. Engine speed should be between 2400 and 2800 rpm under the above conditions Caution: When performing the above test, watch the temperature gauge. Do not let the temperature rise to the red field on the dial	If the engine speed is higher than stated here, and possibly continues to rise, it will be necessary to replace the clutch. If the lower value (2400 rpm) cannot be attained, the torque converter will have to be replaced.

CHAPTER 8 - REAR AXLE & SUSPENSION

1 Description
2 Maintenance
3 Dampers
4 Drive shafts
5 Removing and refitting a control arm
6 Servicing a control arm
7 Removing, refitting and adjusting torsion bar
8 Radius arms
9 Anti-roll bar
10 Wheel alignment
11 Height adjustment
12 Fault diagnosis

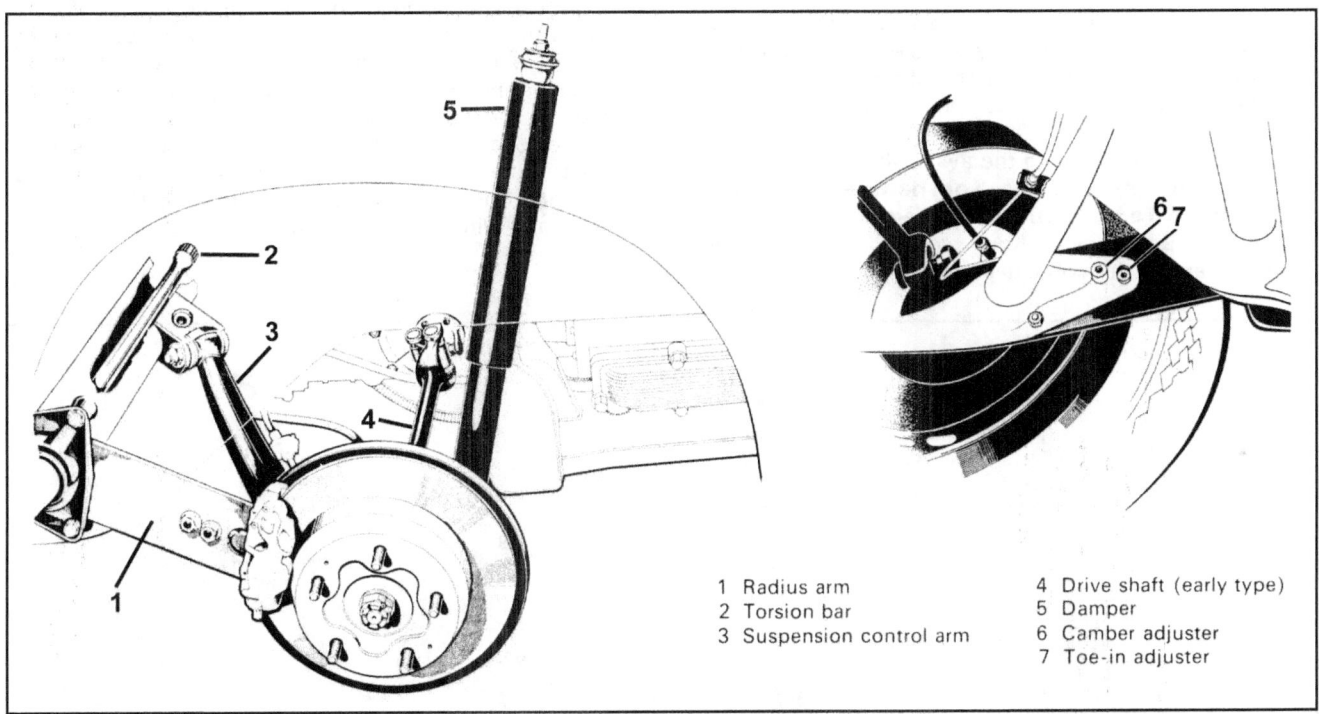

1 Radius arm
2 Torsion bar
3 Suspension control arm
4 Drive shaft (early type)
5 Damper
6 Camber adjuster
7 Toe-in adjuster

FIG 1 Layout of the rear suspension system and camber and toe-in adjusters

1 Description

The layout of the system is shown in **FIG 1**, each independent suspension unit consisting of a radius arm 1 bolted at the rear end to the flange of control arm 3. The front end of the radius arm is coupled to the outer splined end of torsion bar 2, the inner end of the bar being fixed.

Triangulated control of the suspension is maintained by arm 3, the inner end being pivoted in a bracket on the body. Drive from the transmission is taken through drive shaft 4, each shaft being provided with two constant speed joints. Telescopic hydraulic dampers 5 are fitted. These straddle the body and each rear suspension assembly. Depending upon the vehicle model and whether a different make may have been optionally selected for fitment, dampers of Boge, Koni or Bilstein manufacture may be installed. Note, however, that dampers of Koni manufacture cannot be installed on Targa models. Eccentric bolts 6 and 7 allow adjustments to be made to wheel camber and toe-in as described in **Section 10**. An anti-roll bar is not standard but may have been fitted as an optional extra.

2 Maintenance

Wheels and tyres:

Regularly check and re-inflate the tyres to the pressure tabulated in **Technical Data** in the **Appendix**. Periodically check the treads and sidewalls of the tyres for damage. A damaged tyre should be renewed; this is particularly vital if the car is to be driven at high speeds.

Suspension:

Every 6000 miles (10,000km), check over the suspension generally. Ensure that the dampers are securely mounted and that all rubber bushes are serviceable.

Drive shafts:

No routine maintenance to the drive shafts is required except for checking that the rubber boots are not torn or perished.

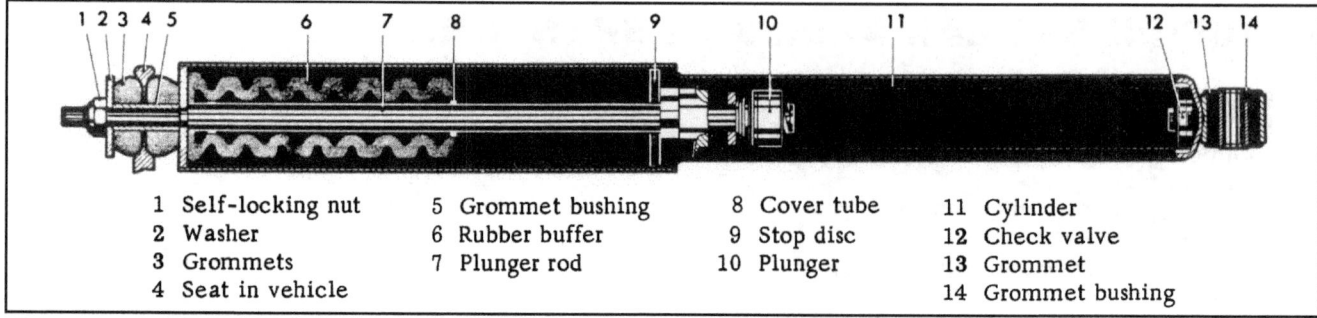

1 Self-locking nut	5 Grommet bushing	8 Cover tube	11 Cylinder
2 Washer	6 Rubber buffer	9 Stop disc	12 Check valve
3 Grommets	7 Plunger rod	10 Plunger	13 Grommet
4 Seat in vehicle			14 Grommet bushing

FIG 2 Cross-section through a rear damper, top end to the left

3 Dampers

Dampers fitted to later models are of larger diameter and increased length and are not interchangeable with those fitted to earlier models. Defective dampers cannot be overhauled or repaired by an owner and must be replaced by new units. Ensure that the new dampers are the same make and type as those originally fitted. If dampers of another manufacture are to be fitted, consult a Porsche agent regarding the availability of the acceptable alternative(s) noting that **Koni dampers cannot be installed on Targa models**. Dampers are colour coded as follows: Boge, black; Koni, red; and Bilstein, green. A cross-section through a damper is shown in **FIG 2**.

Damper removal:

The car should preferably be standing on its wheels. If it is on stands, lift the suspension arm with special tool P289 or use a jack at the rear of the arm. From inside the engine compartment, remove the mounting cap, hold the damper rod with a spanner fitted to the flats and remove the retaining nut, washer and grommet. Release the lower end from the suspension arm by removing bolt 12 in **FIG 3** or nut and bolt 13 and 14 in **FIG 4** and withdraw the damper.

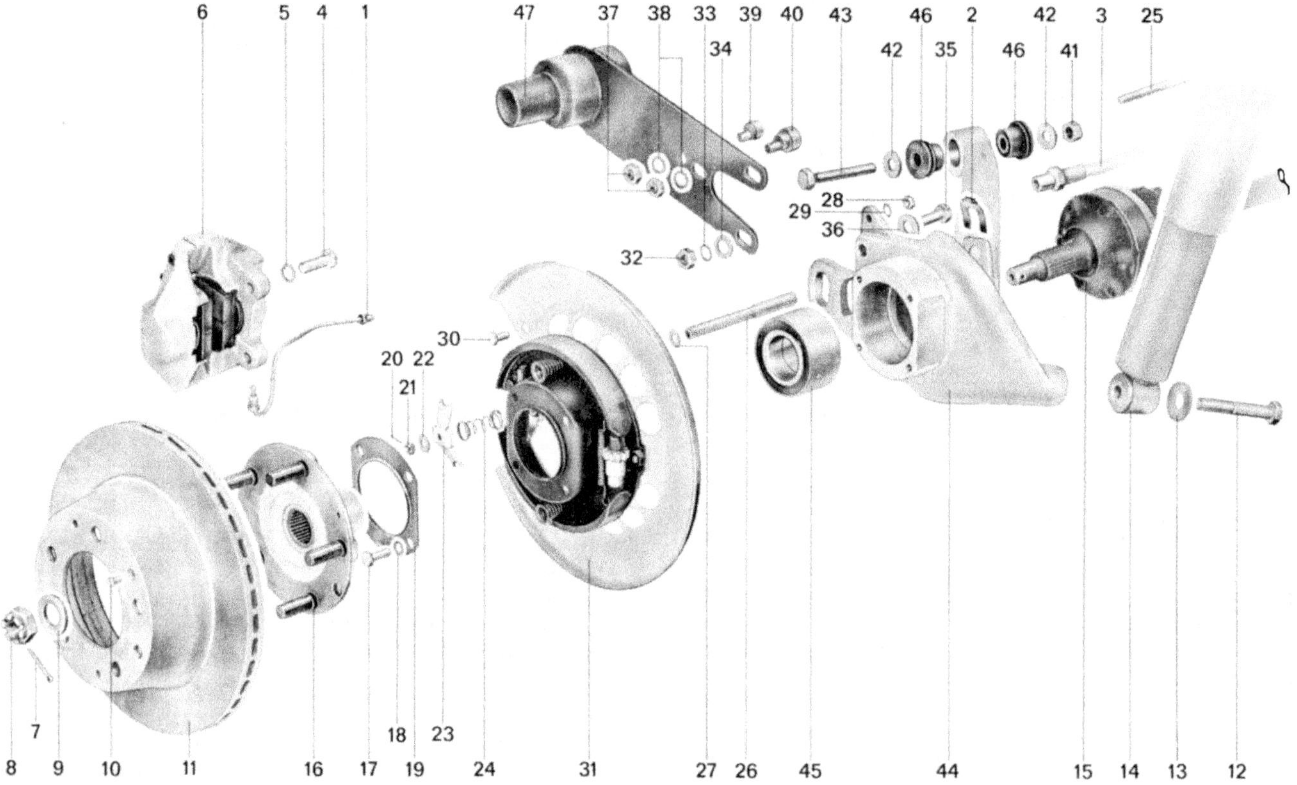

1 Brake line	9 Washer	16 Hub	24 Spring	32 Nut	40 Camber adjuster
2 Clip	10 Screw	17 Bolt	25 Handbrake cable	33 Toothed washer	41 Nut
3 Brake hose	11 Brake disc	18 Lockwasher	26 Spacer tube	34 Washer	42 Washers
4 Bolt	12 Bolt	19 Cover	27 Washer	35 Bolt	43 Bolt
5 Lockwasher	13 Washer	20 Splitpin	28 Nut	36 Washer	44 Control arm
6 Brake caliper	14 Damper	21 Nut	29 Spring washer	37 Nuts	45 Ballbearing
7 Splitpin	15 Drive shaft splined stub	22 Washer	30 Bolt	38 Toothed washers	46 Rubber mounts
8 Nut		23 Expander	31 Backing plate with handbrake shoes	39 Toe-in adjuster	47 Radius arm

FIG 3 Components of a hub and suspension assembly (later type)

Damper fitment:

Hold the new damper vertically in a vice and reciprocate the top end several times to 'bleed' the unit. Fitment is now the reverse of the removal sequence. If the original damper is being refitted, ensure that the buffer 6 in **FIG 2** is serviceable and that all grommets are in good condition. Torque tighten the nut and bolt (**FIG 4**) to 7.5kgm (54lb ft) or the bolt (**FIG 3**) to 12.5kgm (90lb ft). Tighten the upper retaining nut to 2.5kgm (18lb ft). This will partially compress the grommet.

4 Drive shafts

Later type drive shafts are lighter than those fitted to earlier models and have narrower constant velocity joints of 32mm (1.26in) width. The later type of shaft may be fitted to earlier models but new supporting plates and new bolts will be required to match.

Removal:

1 Raise the car and remove the rear wheels. Refer to **FIG 4**. Remove and discard the splitpin 16 and remove nut 15. The flange should be held with tool P36b and the nut removed with tools P296, P44a and P42a.

2 Remove the bolts 11 from both flanges and dismount the shaft. Discard the gaskets 7.

Dismantling and reassembling:

Remove the clips from the rubber boots and the circlips from the shaft ends. Press the constant velocity joints from the shafts. Clean all parts and check for wear.

Fit new dust boots. Slide the wire retainer and joint onto the shaft and fit new circlips. Fill each joint with 70g (2.5oz) of molybdenum disulphide grease. Apply any surplus to the flange side. Clean the boot and flange face from grease. Apply MMM EC.750M.2G51 adhesive between the flange and large boot diameter. To fit the boot clips, drill 2mm (0.08in) holes at each end and draw together with pliers. Lock by bending the tab over. Tap down flat.

Refitting:

Fit new gaskets 7. Lightly oil the stub shafts and insert them into the wheel hubs. Check that the flange faces are free of grease. Use only bolts marked either 130-140 or 12K on Schnorr washers that have their hollow sides facing the base plates. Torque tighten the bolts to 4.3kgm (30lb ft) on earlier shafts or to 8.3kgm (60lb ft) on later, lighter joint, shafts. Tighten the axle nut to a torque of 30 to 35kgm (220 to 250lb ft) and lock with a new splitpin.

5 Removing and refitting a control arm

It is officially specified that, on earlier models (those fitted with fabricated arms), the engine/transmission assembly should be removed (see **Chapter 1, Section 3**) before carrying out the following procedure. Depending, however, upon the experience of the operator and the equipment available, removing the pivot bolt (see **Removal** section 5) may be carried out after releasing the relevant mountings, pipes, controls, etc. and raising the engine/transmission assembly sufficiently to provide the necessary clearance. The engine/transmission assembly removal requirement is not specified for models fitted with the type of arm shown in **FIG 3** (cast aluminium arms).

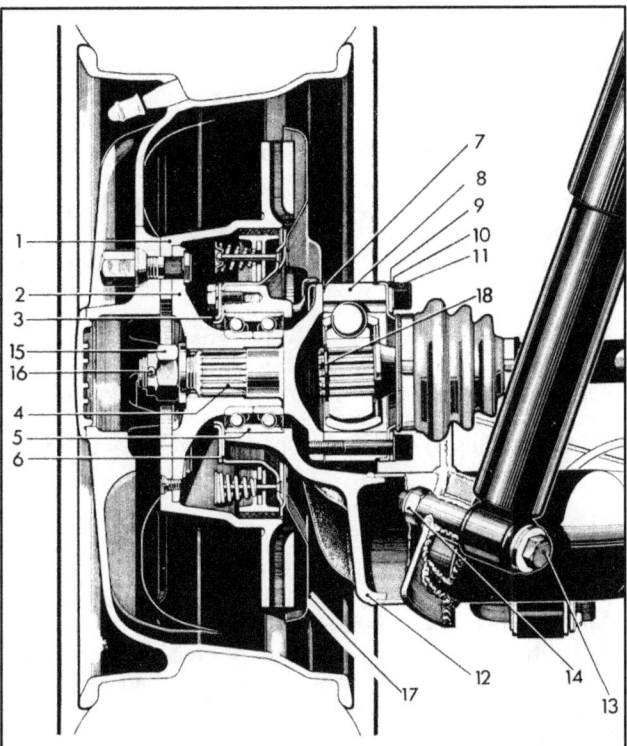

1 Brake disc	10 Schnorr washer
2 Wheel hub	11 Bolt
3 Cover	12 Suspension control arm
4 Stub shaft	13 Bolt
5 Ballbearing	14 Nut
6 Handbrake carrier plate	15 Nut
7 Gasket	16 Splitpin
8 Constant velocity joint	17 Shroud
9 Plate	18 Circlip

FIG 4 Cross-section through a rear hub

Removal:

1 Mount the rear of the car on stands and remove the road wheels. Remove the brake caliper and brake disc as described in **Chapter 11, Section 5**.

2 Using tool P289, refer to **Section 3** and uncouple the lower end of the damper from the control arm. Dismount the drive shaft as described in **Section 4**. Drive out the wheel hub (2 in **FIG 4**) using tool P297 and, if necessary, remove the bearing inner race of bearing 5.

3 Remove the splitpin and nut from the handbrake cable and withdraw the cable. Remove the retaining bolt from the shield plate. Remove the retaining bolts and dismount the carrier plate and shield plate. Remove the handbrake cable guide.

4 Remove the hexagon nuts and washers 32, 33 and 34 from the bolts which attach the radius arm 47 in **FIG 3** to the control arm 44. Remove the bolts. Remove the nuts and washers 37 and 38 from the eccentric bolts 39 and 40. Remove the bolts.

5 Remove the self-locking nut 41 and remove the pivot bolt 43. Dismount the control arm assembly. Service the arm and hub as described in **Section 6**. If necessary, remove the radius arm as described in **Section 8**.

Refitment:

Follow the reverse of the removal sequence. Raise the control arm until its lower edge is in line with the upper edge of the radius arm and, **in this position**, fit a new nut 41 and tighten it to a torque of 12kgm (87lb ft). Connect the control and radius arms and torque tighten the retaining nuts and bolts to 9kgm (65lb ft). Tighten the camber adjustment nut to 6kgm (43lb ft) and the toe-in adjustment nut to 5kgm (36lb ft). Tighten the brake support and the shield plate retaining bolts to 2.5kgm (18lb ft). Use new splitpins where applicable. The refitment procedure for the drive shafts is covered in **Section 4**. The procedure for refitment of the brake caliper, bleeding the system and adjustment of the handbrake are described in **Chapter 11, Sections 5, 7** and **8**. Adjust the wheel camber and toe-in as described in **Section 10**.

6 Servicing a control arm

An unserviceable hub bearing (45 in **FIG 3**, 5 in **FIG 4**) may be renewed without dismounting the control arm. After removing the drive shaft, brake disc and hub and knocking out the old bearing, press in a new bearing using tool P298b and the drive shaft as shown in **FIG 5**. Once removed, a hub ballbearing must not be refitted.

For full servicing, dismount the arm as described in **Section 5**. An unserviceable hub bearing may be removed and a new bearing pressed in. If a suitable press is not available, use tool P298b as described earlier.

Possible accident distortion of an arm may be checked using gauges P295b and P295c. Do not attempt to salvage an arm which is distorted or cracked.

The flanbloc pivot bearings (fabricated type arms) can only be removed by breaking them up. Always renew radial ball thrust bearings on fabricated type arms noting that the housing must be heated to approximately 120°C (250°F) before inserting the new bearing. The rubber mounts (46 in **FIG 3**) fitted to the pivots of later type aluminium arms cannot (if pressed out) be refitted and new mounts must be obtained.

7 Removing, refitting and adjusting torsion bar

The torsion bar, shown at 2 in **FIG 1** may be removed as follows:

1 Raise the car and remove the rear wheel. Lift the radius arm with a jack or with the aid of tool P289 as shown in **FIG 6**. Release the damper lower mounting bolt or bolt and nut (see **Section 3**).
2 Refer to **FIG 3**. Release the radius arm from the control arm 44 by removing the bolts 35 (2 off) and the adjusting bolts 39 and 40. All these bolts are attached by nuts and washers 32, 33, 34, 37 and 38.
3 Refer to **FIG 6** and remove the four cover bolts shown and withdraw the single spacer fitted to the lowermost bolt. Prise off the cover with a screwdriver.
4 Lower the jack or remove the lifting tool P289. Remove the body plug from inside the body and withdraw the radius arm.
5 Withdraw torsion bar taking care not to damage its protective coating.

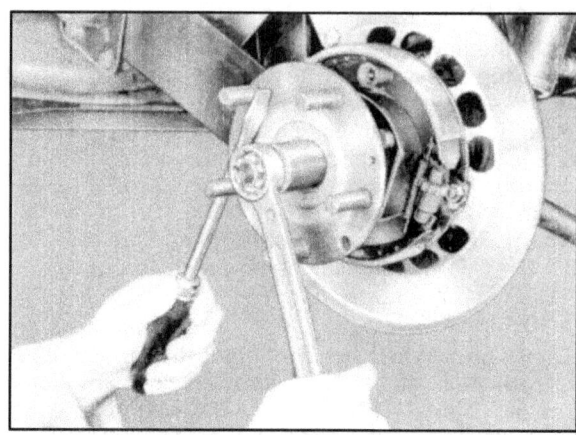

FIG 5   Pressing in a new hub bearing

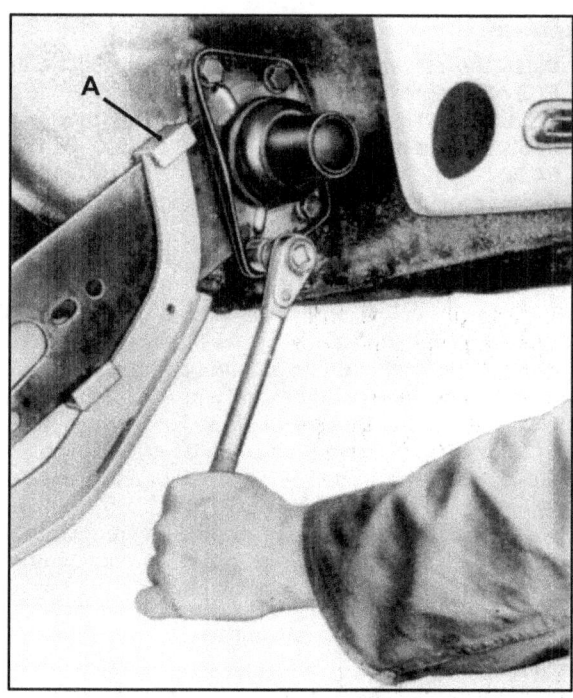

A   Special tool P289

FIG 6   Removing a radius arm cover

A broken bar is removed by withdrawing opposite bar and pushing out parts with a steel rod. **Do not attempt to identify the bar by scratches or centre-punch marks.** Check the rubber support for deterioration. Check the torsion bar for cracks, rust or worn splines. Renew if necessary. Ends of bars are stamped 'R' for righthand side and 'L' for lefthand side. **They are pre-stressed and must not be interchanged.**

When refitting, coat the bar and its splines with multi-purpose lithium grease. Adjust as described later. Coat the rubber support with rubber grease and fit it. Refit the radius arm and cover and start the three bolts which can be reached. Lift the radius arm until the fourth bolt and spacer can be fitted. Tighten these bolts to 4.7kgm (34lb ft). Refit to the control arm as described in **Section 5**. Adjust the wheel tracking and camber as in **Section 10**.

Adjusting a torsion bar:

The car must be standing level. Check with a spirit level on door sill. The radius arm must be hanging free and detached from the control arm. Check the angle of the radius arm with a clinometer placed along the top edge.

The correct angle is 39°. Adjustment is by vernier splines on the torsion bar. There are 40 splines at the inner end and 44 at the outer end. If the bar is turned one spline onwards at the inner end, the change in angle is 9°. If the radius arm is reset in the opposite direction by one spline, the change is 8° 10'. The total movement of the radius arm is thus only 50'. This is the minimum re-adjustment possible. Adjust to the nearest degree. After completing the assembly of the control arm, adjust the rear wheel tracking and camber as described in **Section 10**.

8 Radius arms

Lefthand radius arms are shown 1 in **FIG 1** and 47 in **FIG 3**. They link the 'springing' function of the torsion bars with the suspension control arms. Radius arms are bolted to the control arms. The procedure for uncoupling and recoupling the radius arms to the control arms is included in **Section 5**. The procedure for dismounting and refitting a radius arm is included in **Section 7**.

9 Anti-roll bar

Rear anti-roll (stabiliser) bars are not standard equipment on the models covered by this manual. As an optional extra, a bar may or may not have been fitted to the model being dealt with. If installed, the bar is fitted transversely and forward of the suspension control arms.

Removal and fitment:

The outer ends of the bar are connected by shackles to ball-studs on the arms. To remove the bar, prise the upper eyes of the shackles off the ball-studs with a large screwdriver. Remove the bearing caps (four bolts) and lift away the bar. Check the rubber bearing bushes for wear. Place the bar on a flat surface and check that the ends lie in the same plane. Look for cracks and rust which may lead to premature failure. Check shackle bushes and fit new ones dry, making sure they are the right size for the bar diameter. There are grommets in the upper eyes and these may be renewed by lightly lubricating new ones and pressing them in with a vice. When installing the shackles make sure that they are correctly angled to point as shown in **FIG 7**. Lubricate the grommets with molybdenum disulphide grease.

To refit bar, reverse the dismantling procedure, pressing the upper eyes of the shackles into place with a screwdriver.

10 Rear wheel alignment

Checking alignment must be carried out in association with front wheel alignment, the total effect giving the best road-holding and cornering characteristics to the car.

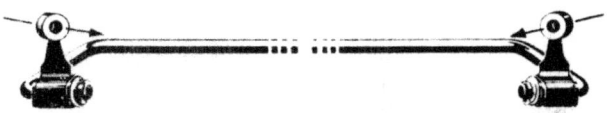

FIG 7 Anti-roll bar. Arrows show correct angle for top shackle eyes

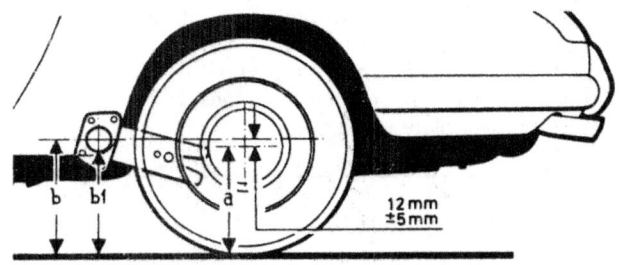

a, b, b1 See text

FIG 8 Rear height adjustment

It is desirable to have the checking and setting made on accurate equipment and with the car properly prepared. The fuel tank must be full and the spare wheel fitted. All parts of the suspension must be in good mechanical condition and adjustment. Wheel rims must not runout excessively, tyres must not be unevenly worn and they must be correctly inflated. It is assumed that the rear torsion bars are correctly set as described in **Section 7**.

Refer to **FIG 1** and slacken the eccentric bolt nuts 6 and 7 and the retaining nuts, one of which can be seen to the left of the eccentric bolts. Turn the tracking and camber eccentric until the values specified in **Technical Data** in the **Appendix** are obtained on the equipment.

When installing the camber eccentric, make sure it points downwards so that there is adequate clearance for adjustment. If it is found that the eccentric binds at one end or the other of the slot, turn it through 180°. After adjustment, tighten the nuts.

11 Height adjustment

Refer to **FIG 8**. Have car correctly prepared as described in **Section 10** and standing on level ground. Bounce the car at the rear several times to allow suspension to settle naturally. Note that dimension 'b' cannot be measured directly because the torsion bar is eccentrically mounted in its bush and cover. Dimension 'b1' is calculated as follows: Measure wheel centre height 'a' and add 12mm (0.47in) to give value 'b'. Subtract from this figure half the diameter of the radius arm cover (30mm or 1.18in). The result is 'b1'.

The measured height 'b1' must not differ from the calculated height by more than ± 5mm (0.197in), and the height difference between the righthand and lefthand sides must not exceed 8mm (0.315in). If the correct setting cannot be obtained, check both the height adjustment of the front suspension and the adjustment of the rear torsion bar.

12 Fault diagnosis

(a) Noise from axle

1 Worn wheel bearings
2 Worn constant velocity joints
3 Worn axle splines
4 Loose axle nuts
5 Damper mountings defective (or loosely fitted)
6 Broken stabiliser bar or faulty mountings.
7 Loose radius or control arm
8 Control arm pivot mounting worn
9 Worn torsion bar splines or bushes
10 Brake backplate loose

(b) Poor handling, bad road holding

1 Check 6, 7, 8 and 9 in (a)
2 Torsion bars 'settled' or broken
3 Radius arm setting incorrect
4 Incorrect wheel alignment
5 Incorrect height adjustment
6 Dampers inoperative, rubber buffers worn
7 Faulty transmission mountings

NOTES

CHAPTER 9 - FRONT SUSPENSION

1 Description
2 Maintenance
3 Suspension struts
4 Hubs
5 Control arms
6 Crossmember
7 Torsion bars
8 Anti-roll bar
9 Suspension height
10 Wheel alignment
11 Fault diagnosis

Key to Fig 1

1 Boot
2 Strut top location
3 Self-levelling hydro-pneumatic strut
4 Boot
5 Steering gearbox
6 Brake caliper
7 Triangulation link
8 Crossmember (fabricated type)
9 Ball joint
10 Brace
11 Tie rod
12 Tie rod clamp

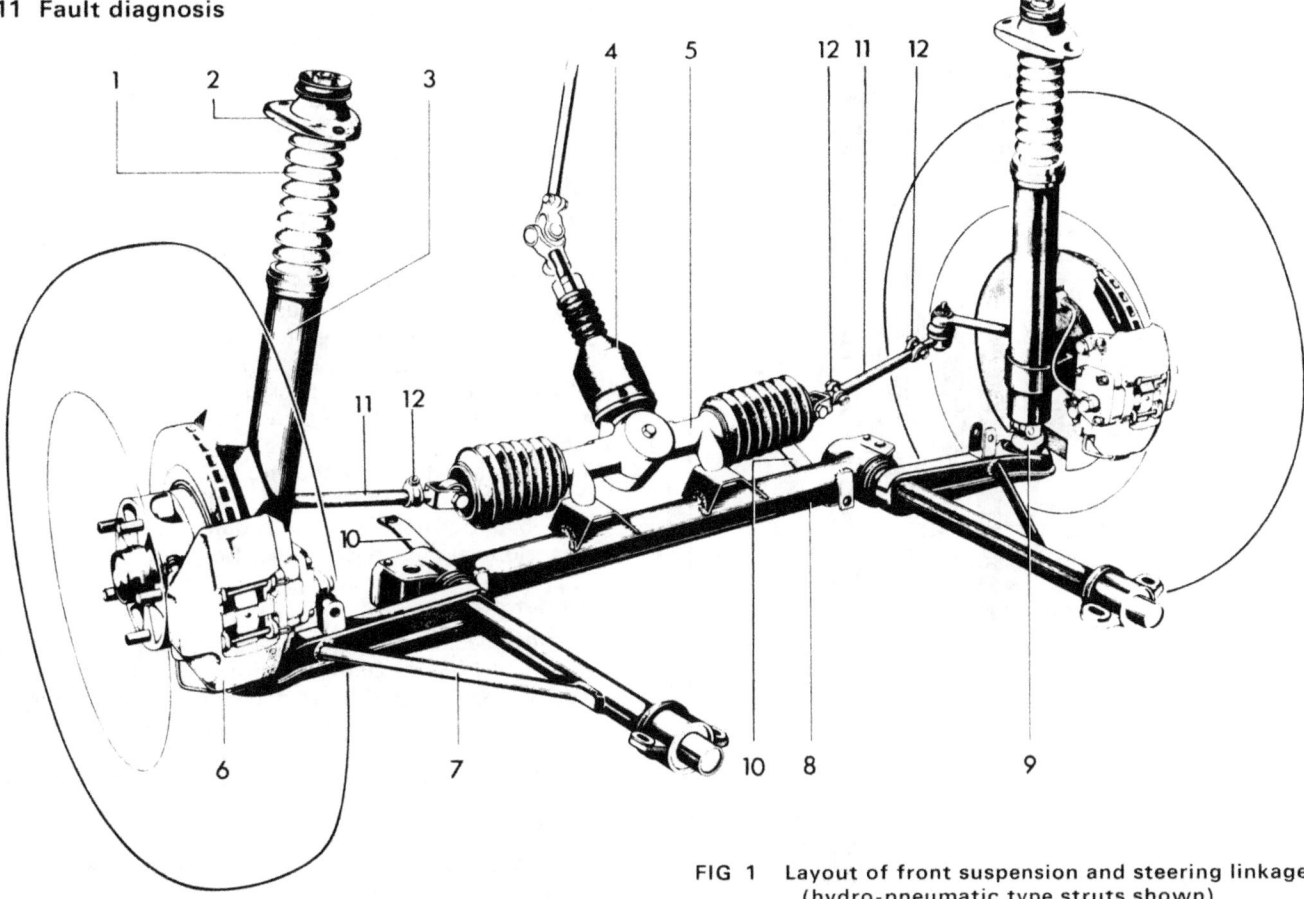

FIG 1 Layout of front suspension and steering linkage (hydro-pneumatic type struts shown)

1 Description

Two types of front suspension are fitted to models covered by this manual. In both types the layout incorporates MacPherson type struts with forward facing steering arms. Earlier models are provided with telescopic self-levelling struts with which torsion bars are not incorporated. Later models are provided with torsion bars and conventional dampers unless the self-levelling type of struts have been optionally ordered on relevant models. Road bumps cause the pump to transfer oil through valves 7 and 9 (**FIG 2**) from the low pressure cylinder to the high pressure cylinder. The pressurised gas is further compressed, which raises the car to a predetermined level.

Self-levelling type suspension:

This system is shown in **FIG 1**. The strut provides the suspension 'spring' function and also acts as a damper. A cross-section through this type of hydro-pneumatic strut is shown in **FIG 2**.

Gas in the high pressure chamber is isolated from the oil by a diaphragm shown as a thick black line. Oil and gas are not separated in the low pressure chamber. Gas pressure acting on the piston rod area takes 90% of the weight of the empty car. Pump rod 12 forms a hydraulic pump in conjunction with piston rod 11.
The pump action also acts as a damper. At a predetermined height, port 5 is cleared by the damping piston and normal suspension movements continue, the ports being too small to affect them. The pump rod is reduced in diameter higher up so that no pumping can take place. This prevents excessive raising of the suspension.

The struts will bring the car up to normal level within 300 to 1500 yards on smooth roads and much shorter distances on rough roads. The level remains constant if the load is not altered after parking.

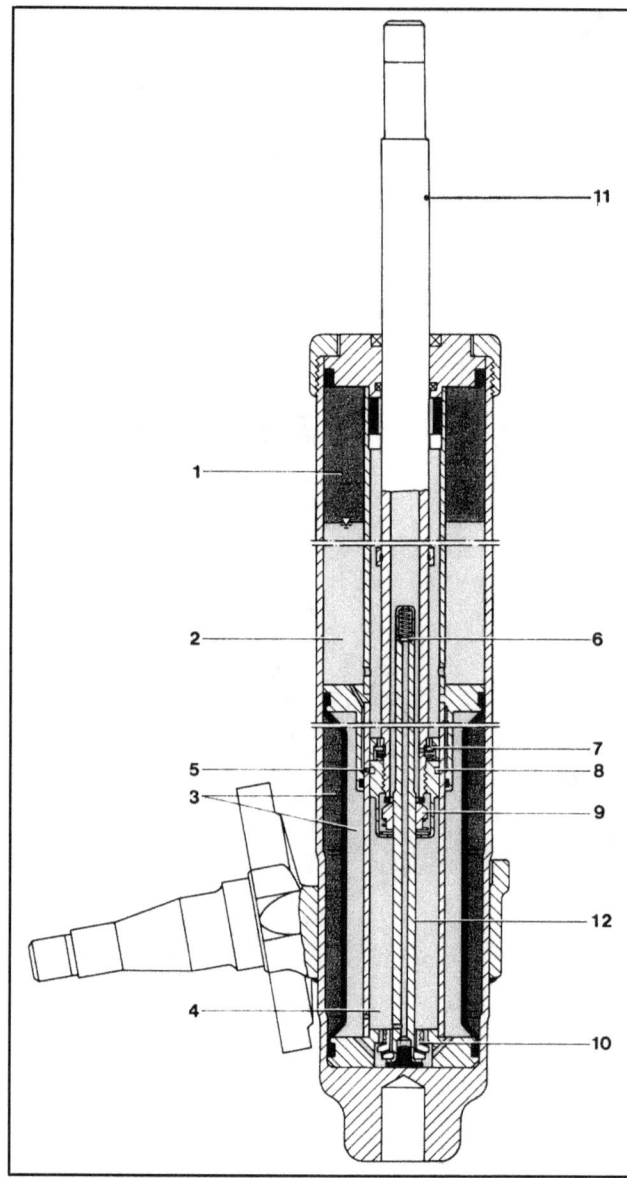

1 Low pressure chamber
2 Low pressure cylinder
3 High pressure chamber
4 High pressure cylinder
5 Relief port orifice
6 Overload valve
7 Suction valve
8 Piston ring seal
9 Pressure valve
10 Damping valve
11 Piston rod
12 Pump rod

FIG 2 Self-levelling hydro-pneumatic strut cross-section

Torsion bar suspension:

In this system each suspension strut incorporates a single function telescopic hydraulic damper (see **FIG 3**) and torsion bars provide the 'springing' function.

Hubs and suspension control arms:

The wheel hub stub axles are integral with the struts. Each strut unit is ball jointed at its lower end to a transverse suspension control arm which is 'keyed' to a control arm. Struts are located at their upper ends in body mountings which can be moved to allow adjustment of wheel camber and caster angles. Wheel toe-in is adjusted by altering the 'lengths' of the steering linkage tie rods. Each wheel hub runs on two taper roller bearings.

Anti-roll bar:

Depending upon the model, an anti-roll bar may or may not be fitted and may be of differing diameters. **FIG 4** shows the location of an anti-roll bar.

2 Maintenance

Wheels and tyres:

Regularly check and re-inflate the tyres to the pressure tabulated in the **Technical Data** section of the **Appendix**. Periodically check the treads and sidewalls of the tyres for damage. A damaged tyre should be renewed.

Suspension and hubs:

Every 6000 miles (10,000km), look over the suspension generally. Check the wheel bearings for play and, if necessary, adjust as described in **Section 4**.

3 Suspension struts

Self-levelling struts:

A cross-section through a self-levelling hydro-pneumatic suspension strut is shown in **FIG 2**. Their operation is described in **Section 1**.

As there are no height adjusters on this system, wheel alignment must be entrusted to a Porsche service station. The agent must also be consulted if the strut gives trouble.

It is most important to check ground clearance during servicing operations. If the car is lifted so that the wheels are clear of the ground, pressure in the struts is equalised. When the car is lowered, the strut will then support only the basic load and the car will drop below the normal static load position. The procedure for checking the suspension height is described in **Section 9**.

Damper struts:

A cross-section through a damper suspension strut is shown in **FIG 3**. Damper struts may be of Boge, Bilstein or Koni manufacture depending upon the model or which make of damper may have been optionally selected. Note, however, that **dampers of Koni manufacture cannot be installed on Targa models.**

Suspension strut removal and fitment:

1 Remove the brake caliper as described in **Chapter 11, Section 4**. Remove the wheel hub as described in **Section 4** (this chapter). Remove the brake shield plate.
2 Uncouple the tie rod ball joint from the strut steering arm as described in **Chapter 10, Section 6**. On cars fitted with the damper type struts, refer to **Section 7** and **FIG 8** and remove the torsion bar and adjusting lever 6.
3 Uncouple the suspension strut from the suspension arm and separate them by pushing the arm downwards. If the strut is fitted with the type of ball joint shown in **FIG 5**, unscrew the nut 1 and tap out the double wedge bolt 3 to separate the strut from the suspension control arm. The other type of fitting is that shown in **FIG 6**, which consists of three bolts securing the lower end of the strut to the control arm. From inside the luggage compartment, remove the retaining nut, etc. and withdraw the strut downwards. If necessary, pull off the spacer ring.

If accident damage to a suspension strut of either type is suspected, have the geometry and function serviceability checked on the relevant gauges by a Porsche agent.

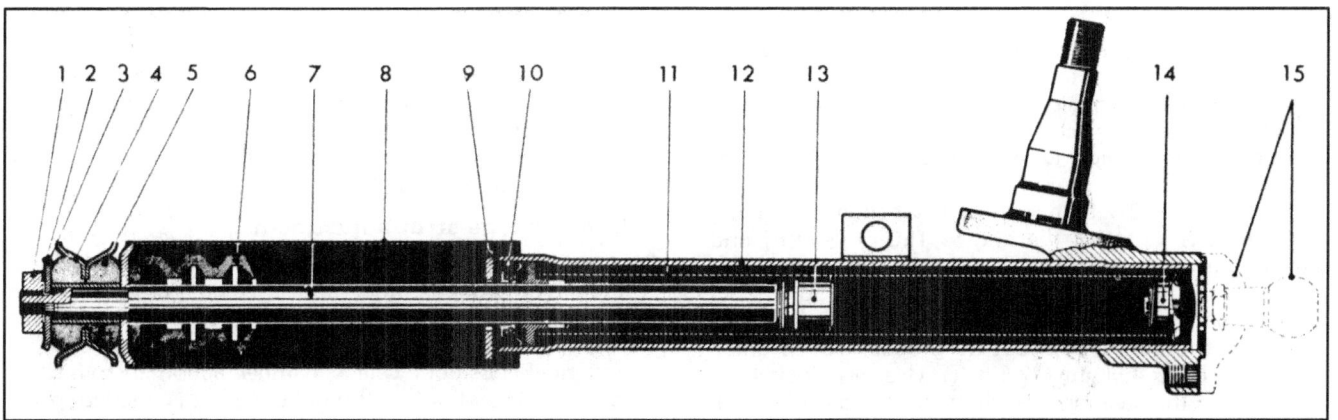

FIG 3 Section through the damper strut fitted to torsion bar suspension models

Key to Fig 3
1 Hex nut
2 Safety plate
3 Washer
4 Bracket (on vehicle)
5 Rubber bushing
6 Rubber buffer
7 Piston rod
8 Shielding tube
9 Stop disc
10 Oil seal
11 Cylinder
12 Strut tube
13 Piston
14 Bottom valve
15 Steering lever & ball

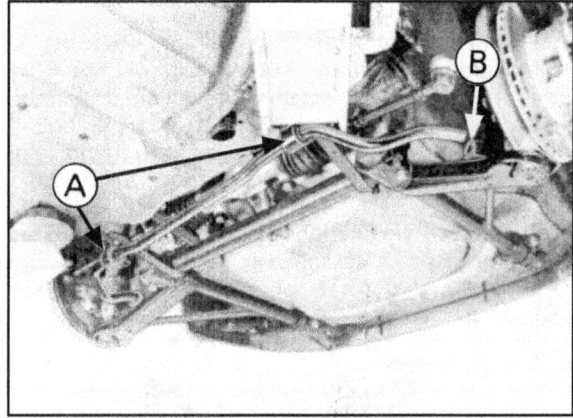

A Crossmember brace clamp   B Control arm location
FIG 4 Front anti-roll bar

Do not attempt to salvage a strut with a damaged, cracked or distorted stub axle, steering arm or strut body. Renew torn or perished rubber parts.

From chassis No 301800, damper repair kits can be installed in damper type struts. This saves a renewal of the whole strut, but it entails the local or home manufacture of a suitable peg tool to open the damper.

1972 models have a modified ball joint mounting which is attached to the strut by a double-wedge arrangement as shown in **FIG 5**. The former clamping arrangement is no longer used. A special adaptor tool with four lugs spaced at 90° is necessary to remove the nut 6. The part number is P2806. To remove the ball joint, refer to **FIG 5** and proceed as follows:

1 Separate the suspension strut from the control arm as detailed in the preceding instructions.
2 From beneath the control arm, extract splitpin 4, remove lockplate 5 and, with the special adaptor tool and a wrench, unscrew nut 6. Using a soft-faced mallet, tap out the ball joint and remove it from the control arm.
3 Reassemble in the reverse order and coat the double-wedge bolt with multi-purpose grease before assembling. Install it so that the retaining nut 1 is forward and the notch on the face of the double-wedge and the wedge contour are directed towards the stub axle. Renew splitpin 4 and lockwasher 5.
4 Tap the double-wedge with a hammer before finally tightening the nut to a torque of 2.2kgm (16lb ft).

Key to Fig 5
1 Nut M 8
2 Washer
3 Double-wedge bolt
4 Cotter pin
5 Lock plate
6 Nut
7 Ball joint
8 Strut

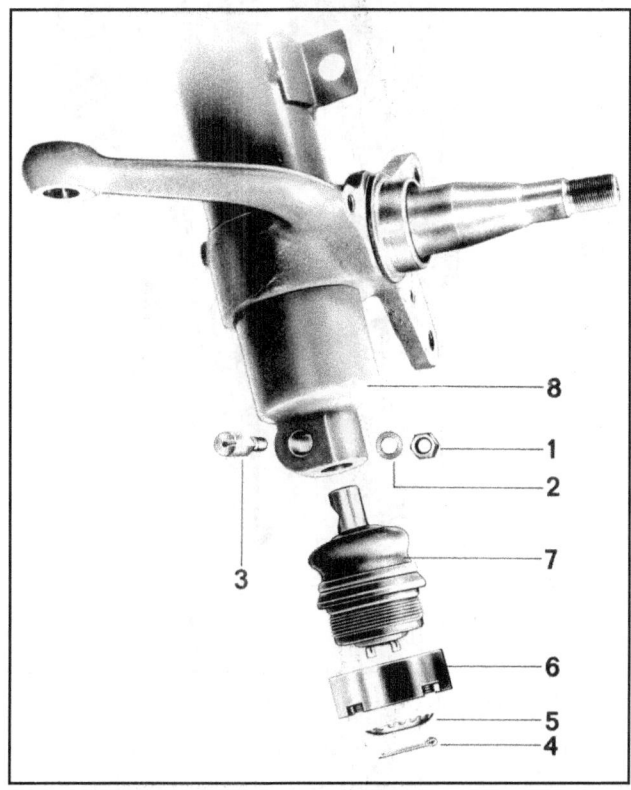

FIG 5 Front axle ball joint (later type)

Refitting the strut:

This is the reverse of removal, noting the following points where relevant to the type of strut used.

NOTE: Beginning with the 1975 models, a spacer is installed between the support bracket and the guard tube. This spacer must be installed in order to keep the height adjustment of the vehicle correct.

Fit 'O' ring R32-2.5 on to the axle when installing ring 10 (see **FIG 6**). Heat the ring to 150°C (300°F) and push it into place.

Fill rubber boots on new ball joints with 6.5g (0.2oz) of multipurpose molybdenum disulphide grease. **The taper of the ball stud must be grease-free.** Tighten the stud nut to 4.5kgm (32.5lb ft). Use new lockplates and tighten the steering lever bolts to 4.7kgm (34lb ft). Fit the rubber buffer dry. Fit the top nut of strut on a new safety plate with its tab upwards. Tighten the nut to 8kgm (58lb ft).

Use the following torques:

Ball joint to control arm nuts 7.5kgm (54lb ft). Use washers and new splitpins. Tie rod ball joint nut 4.5kgm (32.5lb ft) using a new splitpin. Brake carrier plate bolts on new lockplates 4.7kgm (34lb ft). Caliper bolts on spring washers 7kgm (50.5lb ft). Gland nut for brake pipe at caliper 2kgm (14.5lb ft). Shroud bolts 2.5kgm (18lb ft).

Adjust the wheel bearings as described in **Section 4**. Bleed the brakes as described in **Chapter 11, Section 7** and check the wheel alignment as described in **Section 10**.

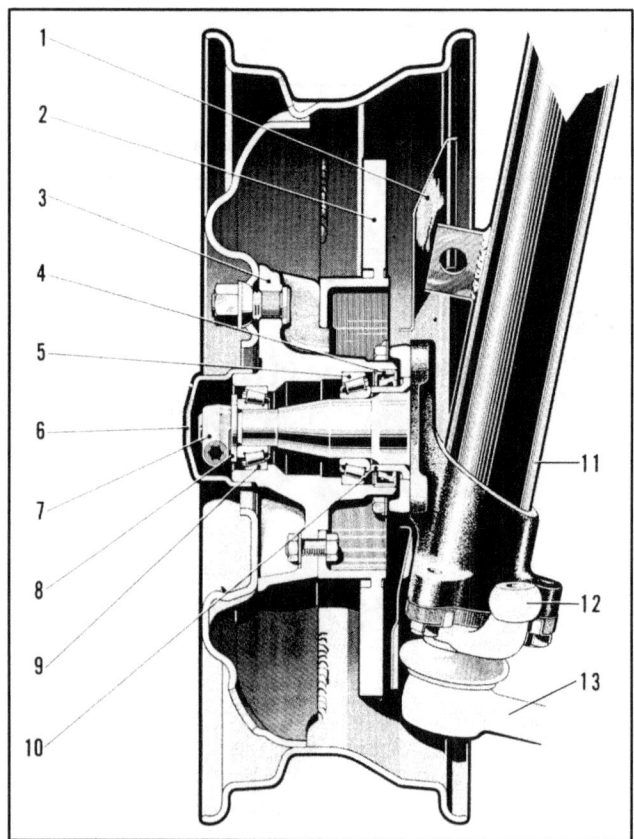

FIG 6 Front hub sectioned, showing bearings and seal

Key to Fig 6
1 Shield plate
2 Brake disc
3 Hub
4 Seal
5 Taper bearing
6 Cap
7 Clamping nut
8 Washer
9 Taper bearing
10 Distance ring
11 Damper strut
12 Steering lever
13 Ball joint (earlier type)

Checking the strut:

Alignment of the damper and stub axle is checked on special tool P.286. Renew the strut if the outside is covered in oily dirt. Hold strut vertically in a vice and pump it a few times. Then give long full strokes up and down and check for free play at any point. Excessive free play calls for strut renewal.

Damper type strut adjustment:

Koni adjustable dampers are standard on 911S cars and are optional on other models except Targa. To adjust outside car, mount vertically, press top end right down and turn gently to left until lugs engage inside damper and mark position. Check damper action by pumping top end up and down. If more damping is needed, press down and engage lugs at mark and then turn top tube to left for harder setting and to the right for a softer setting. Make sure both dampers have the same setting. To adjust Koni dampers when installed in car, raise front end and remove wheels. Hold up control arm with a jack and remove nut from top end of strut (inside luggage compartment). Adjust as just described. When finished, fit top nut on a new safety plate with tab upwards. Tighten nut to 8kgm (58lb ft).

4 Hubs

A cross-section through a hub is shown in **FIG 6**.

Removal:

Remove the brake caliper as described in **Chapter 11, Section 4**. Prise off cap 6, loosen the socket-headed screw and remove nut 7 and washer 8. Pull off the hub 3. Press out and discard the bearing outer races and the inner oil seal. If the brake disc is to be removed, mark it so that it may be refitted in its original relative position. Removal of the bearing may be eased by heating the hub to 120° to 150°C (250° to 300°F).

Clean out the old grease from the hub and check the flange for cracks, distortion or loose studs. Clean the bearings and check them in a dry state. Renew if rough, but note that renewed parts must be of same manufacture if mixed with original parts. Various makes of bearing have been fitted, such as SKF, FAG or Timken. **Do not mix parts of one make with those of another.**

Reassembly:

Heat the hub to 120° to 150°C (250° to 300°F) and press in the outer race of the inner bearing. Insert the inner race and press in the oil seal until it is flush with hub. Fit the outer race of the outer bearing.

Refit the brake disc with the marks made earlier, align and fit the bolts from the inside. Tighten the nuts on the spring washers to 2.3kgm (16.5lb ft). Fill the hub with 50cc or 43g (3cu in or 1.5oz) of multipurpose lithium grease, pressing it well into the bearings. Smear grease on both lips of the oil seal. Refit the hub to the axle stub.

Tighten the clamping nut to about 1.5kgm (10.8lb ft) while turning the hub to seat the rollers in their races. Slacken the nut until it is possible to move the washer 8 in **FIG 6** with a screwdriver (see **FIG 7**). There must be no free play in the bearings. Lock the nut by tightening the socket-head screw to 2.5kgm (18lb ft). Check that the adjustment is still correct.

Coat the nut and washer with lithium grease. Fit the cap without filling it with grease. Refit the caliper as described in **Chapter 11, Section 4**. Bleed the brakes as described in **Chapter 11, Section 7**.

FIG 7   Adjust front hub clamping nut such that the thrust washer can be moved sideways under light pressure from the screwdriver without any axial play in the hub

5 Control arms

A control arm, fabricated type crossmember and associated parts are shown in **FIG 8**.

Control arm removal:

1 Refer to **Section 8** and remove the anti-roll bar if one is fitted. Remove the torsion bar adjusting screw 5 in **FIG 8**.
2 Refer to **Section 3** and uncouple the lower end of the suspension strut from the control arm. Withdraw the torsion bar adjusting lever 6 from the bar and remove the OWA-seal 4.
3 Remove bolt 3a. Remove the bolts which retain the control arm rubber mount cover bracket 1. Dismount the bracket. Press the control arm and torsion bar out of the reinforcing support member.

4 If distortion of the arm is suspected, have it checked in gauge P288. Inspection of the torsion bar is covered in **Section 7**.

Control arm fitment:

If a new torsion bar is being fitted or if both arms have been removed, confirm that the correctly handed bar (L, lefthand; R, righthand) is being fitted. Lightly coat the bar with lithium grease (particularly the splines) and fit the bar into the arm. Ensure that the end cap 7 in **FIG 8** is in position. Proceed by reversing the removal sequence and referring to **Sections 7** and **3**. Torque tighten bolts 10 to 4.7kgm (34lb ft) and bolts 3a to 9kgm (65lb ft). Adjust the suspension height as described in **Section 7** and check the wheel alignment as described in **Section 10**.

6 Crossmember

1974 Carrera models are provided with light-alloy crossmembers with detachable braces. The fabricated type of crossmember (with welded on braces) fitted to other models is 3 in **FIG 8**. Removal of the crossmember will normally only be necessary if, following an accident, distortion is suspected.

Removal and fitment:

Remove the control arms as described in **Section 5**. Detach the axle shield. Remove the two bolts which retain the steering gearbox (see **Chapter 10, Section 7**) to the crossmember. Remove the bolts which retain the crossmember to the body and dismount the crossmember.

A cracked or distorted crossmember should be renewed.

Fitment is the reverse of the removal sequence. Make sure that the crossmember is correctly seated in the alignment studs in the body. Torque tighten the steering gearbox bolts (use new spring washers) to 4.7kgm (34lb ft).

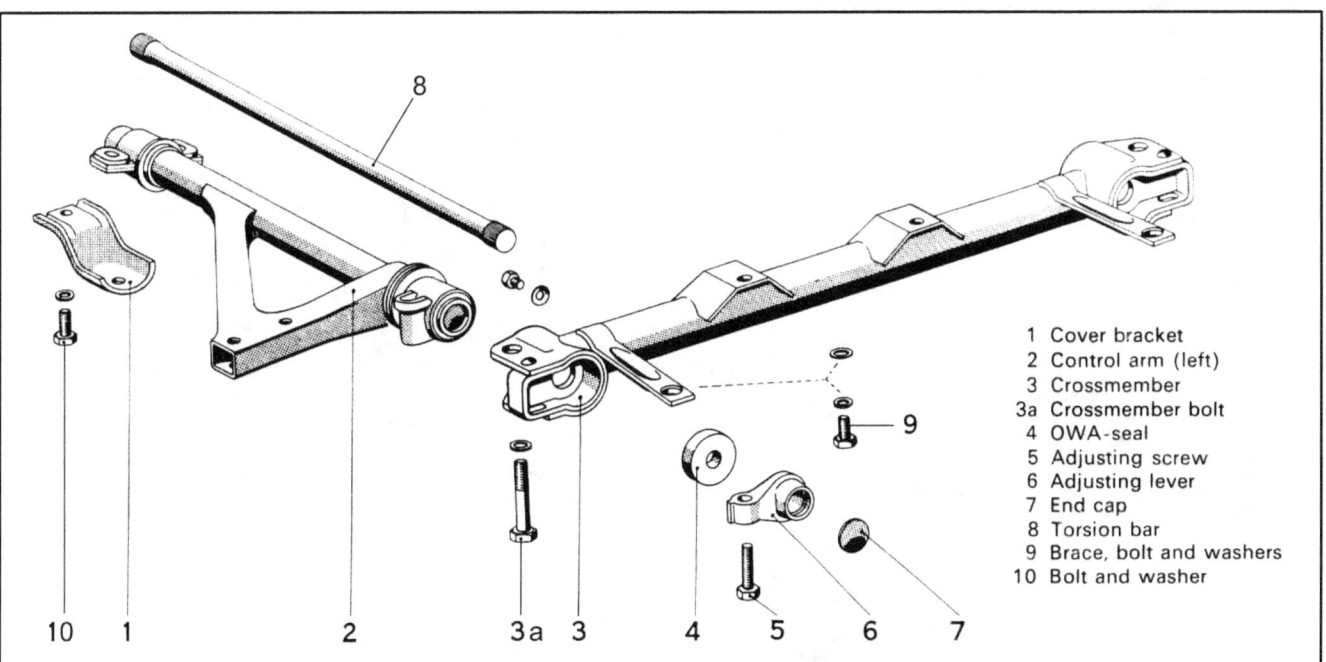

1 Cover bracket
2 Control arm (left)
3 Crossmember
3a Crossmember bolt
4 OWA-seal
5 Adjusting screw
6 Adjusting lever
7 End cap
8 Torsion bar
9 Brace, bolt and washers
10 Bolt and washer

FIG 8   A modified crossmember and control arm fitted with integral rubber mounts was first introduced on the 1968 models. This modification, with minor design changes, was used up to 1989 - see illustration on following page for later models.

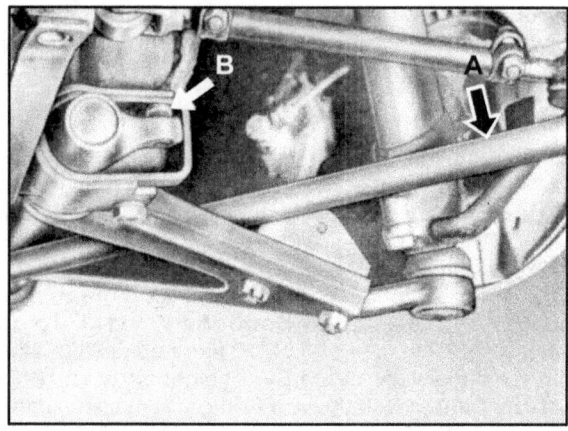

A Levering the control arm downwards **B** See text

FIG 9 Fitting a torsion bar adjusting lever

7 Torsion bars

Torsion bars are prestressed. They are handed and marked L and R. Do not fit a lefthand bar to a righthand control arm or vice versa.

Removal:

Remove the adjusting screw 5 in **FIG 8**. Pull the adjusting lever 6 off the torsion bar and withdraw the OWA-seal 4. Remove the bolts 10 and dismount the bracket 1. Using an appropriate punch and taking care not to damage the splines, drive the bar forwards out of the control arm.

Check the bar for damaged splines, rust or chipped lacquer finish and renew if necessary.

Fitment:

Lightly coat the bar (particularly the splines) with lithium grease, check that the correctly handed bar is being fitted and insert the bar into the control arm from the front. Fit the OWA-seal. Refer to **FIG 9** and lever (see arrow **A**) the arm downwards as far as the suspension strut will allow. With the end cap 7 in **FIG 8** fitted, slide the adjusting lever 6 onto the bar leaving as little clearance at **B** in **FIG 9** as possible. Coat the adjusting bolt threads with molybdenum disulphide grease and lightly tighten it in place. Check that the end cap is properly seated. Fit the cover bracket and torque tighten the retaining bolts to 4.7kgm (34lb ft).

Adjustment:

Refer to **Section 9**. The bolt 5 in **FIG 8** is screwed inwards until the suspension height specified for the model is achieved.

8 Anti-roll bar

The anti-roll bar fitted to later models is shown in **FIG 4**. The bar is mounted in rubber bushes and is clamped to the braces of the crossmember. The bar diameter differs between Carrera (20mm) and other models (16mm). If a replacement bar is required, ensure that it is of the same diameter as that removed.

To dismount the anti-roll bar, remove the stone guard, dismount both clamps **A** and withdraw the bar rearwards from the locations **B**. Fitment is the reverse of this sequence. Use rubber lubricant in the bushes.

9 Suspension height

The front suspension 'height' is dimension **C** in **FIG 10**. It is the difference between the wheel centre to ground dimension **A** and the control arm pivot centre (centre of the torsion bar if fitted) to ground dimension **B**. When measuring the suspension height it will be advantageous to use conical plugs as shown in **FIG 11**.

Vehicles fitted with damper struts and torsion bars:

On models produced up to 1974, **C** should be 108 ± 5mm (4.25 ± 0.2in) and on models produced in 1974 and onwards, **C** should be 113 ± 5mm (4.45 ± 0.2in). The difference in **C** between the lefthand and righthand sides should be kept to within 5mm (0.2in).

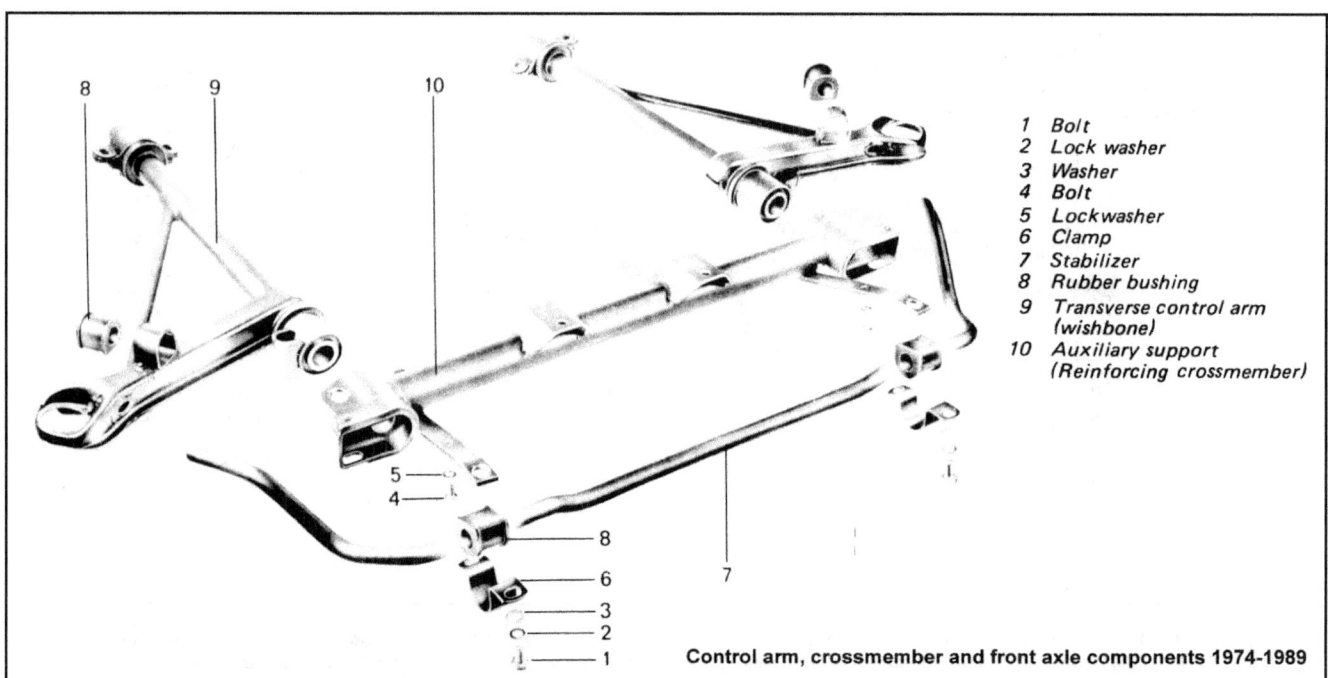

1 Bolt
2 Lock washer
3 Washer
4 Bolt
5 Lockwasher
6 Clamp
7 Stabilizer
8 Rubber bushing
9 Transverse control arm (wishbone)
10 Auxiliary support (Reinforcing crossmember)

Control arm, crossmember and front axle components 1974-1989

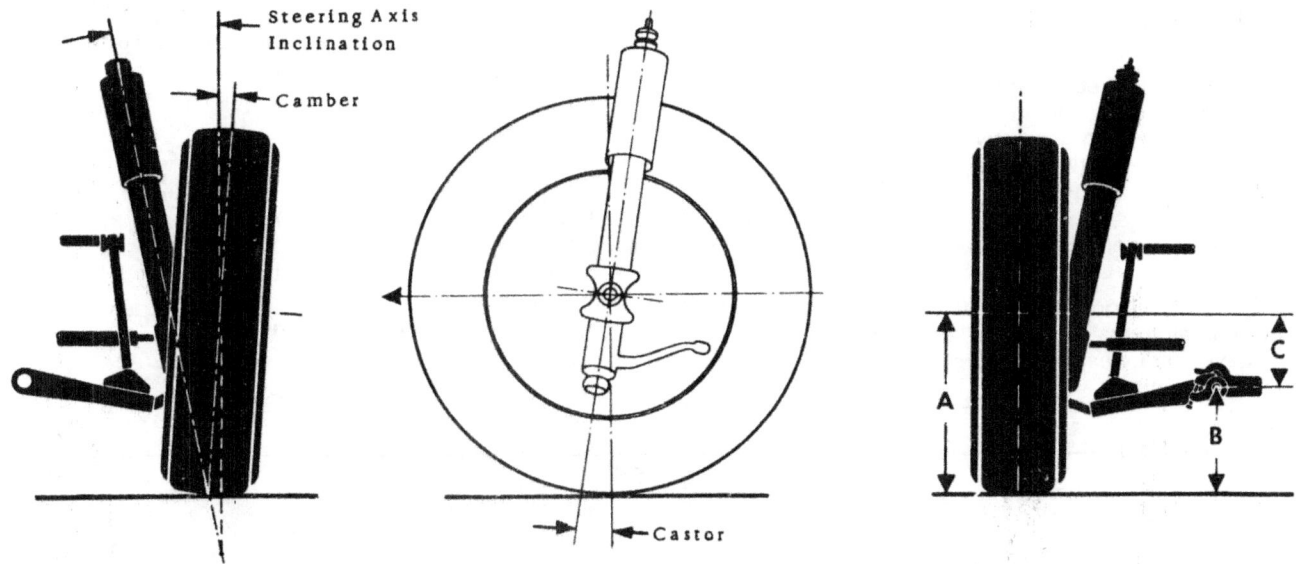

A, B and C See text
FIG 10 Measuring the suspension 'height'

Vehicles fitted with self-levelling hydro-pneumatic struts:

1 Distribute a load of 100kg (220lb) in the luggage compartment so that both front wheels are evenly weighted.
2 Drive the car onto a level surface and, referring to **FIG 10**, measure the distance **A** from the ground to the front wheel centre. Distance **B** should be equal to **A** minus 124mm (5in), that is **C**, the distance between wheel centre and the mounting point centre of the traverse control arm. Special cone-shaped plugs (P301b) are used by the service agents which fit into the box section as shown in **FIG 11** to give an accurate datum point. Work on both sides of the vehicle.
3 Raise the car with a jack under the front centre until distance **B** is attained. Now measure, and make a note of the reading, the distance between ground and the bottom edge of the front fender on both sides. To eliminate tyre deflection when the jack is lowered, measure also the distance between the wheel flange and ground; measure again when the jack has been lowered and deduct the difference from that obtained between ground and fender.
4 Remove the ballast from the boot, load the car with passengers and drive the vehicle on a straight but rough road for a distance of 2km (1.25 miles), without hard braking.
5 The driver and passengers must stay in the car, which is also parked on a level surface, and another person must measure the distance between lower edge of wing and the ground. The values should not have differed by more than 10mm (0.4in) either way.

10 Wheel alignment

First class gauges and optical equipment is essential for accurate measurement and adjustment of toe-in and camber and caster angles. Specification figures are quoted in the **Technical Data** section of the **Appendix**.

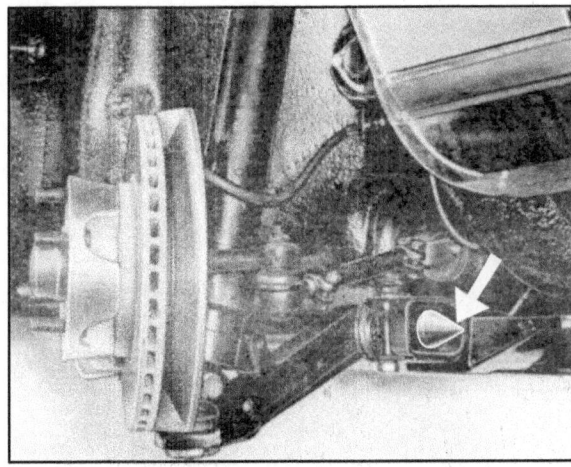

FIG 11 Using cone-shaped plugs (arrowed) to measure centre point to ground dimension

Toe-in adjustment:

Toe-in is adjusted by altering the 'lengths' of the tie rods. Loosen the clamps 12 in **FIG 1** and rotate the tie rods 11 in the appropriate direction. Maintain symmetry by adjusting both tie rods by equal amounts until the specified toe-in is achieved. Retighten the clamps to a torque of 2.5kgm (18lb ft).

Caster and camber angles:

Adjustment is made by repositioning the suspension strut top location. From inside the luggage compartment mark the position of the single-hole and double-hole plates, loosen the retaining screws using tool P291 and reset the dish ring together with the strut end. Movement **across the direction of vehicle travel adjusts the camber angle** and movement of 1mm (0.04in) corresponds to 0.1° of strut attitude. Movement **along the direction of vehicle travel (fore and aft) adjusts the caster angle**. Retighten the screws to a torque of 4.7kgm (34lb ft).

11 Fault diagnosis

(a) Wheel wobble
1 Unbalanced wheels and tyres
2 Worn steering ball joints
3 Incorrect steering geometry
4 Weak or incorrectly set torsion bar
5 Worn hub bearings

(b) Erratic steering
1 Check (a)
2 Bent suspension components
3 Worn ball joints and control arm mountings
4 Uneven tyre wear or pressures
5 Defective strut

(c) Excessive pitching, rolling or 'bottoming'
1 Check 4 in (a) and 5 in (b)
2 Buffer rubbers missing or faulty
3 Broken anti-roll or torsion bar

(d) Rattles
1 Check 3 in (b) and 3 in (c)
2 Loose strut
3 Loose crossmember or control arm

(e) Incorrect suspension 'height'
1 Check 4 in (a)
2 Defective hydro-pneumatic strut

NOTES

CHAPTER 10 - STEERING

1 Description
2 Maintenance
3 The steering wheel
4 The steering column
5 The intermediate shaft and couplings
6 The steering linkage
7 The steering gearbox
8 Fault diagnosis

1 Description

The layout of the steering gearbox, its linkage to the steering arms and the coupling of the column shaft to the gearbox unit are included in **Chapter 9, FIG 1**.

The steering gearbox unit is a rack and pinion type in which the pinion is actuated by the steering column assembly and slides the rack in the selected direction. The ends of the rack are linked with the steering arms by tie rods. It will be noted that the front suspension/steering design does not incorporate a kingpin and that what would be the kingpin inclination is the inclination of the line through the top of the support of the suspension strut and the suspension arm ball joint.

The steering gearbox unit is mounted directly onto a supporting crossmember the ends of which carry the suspension arm pivots. The steering shaft couples to the centre of the gearbox unit and lefthand or righthand drive mounting of the steering column is accommodated via substantial angulation of the intermediate shaft. The tie rods are adjustable to allow adjustments to be made to wheel alignment (see **Chapter 9, Section 10**).

2 Maintenance

As the steering gearbox is packed with a special grease at the time of manufacture, or after a complete overhaul, there is no provision for subsequent extra lubrication. The same applies to the universal joints and ball joints in the steering system. There is no need for routine adjustment at any point.

Every 12,000 miles (20,000km), look over the steering gear generally. Ensure that all couplings and joints are secure and tight. Check the condition of the rubber boots as, apart from age deterioration these are subject to being damaged by road surface debris. Cracked or torn boots should be renewed at the earliest opportunity.

The procedure for the adjustment of wheel alignment is described in **Chapter 9, Section 10**.

3 The steering wheel

FIG 1 shows a cross-section through the steering wheel.

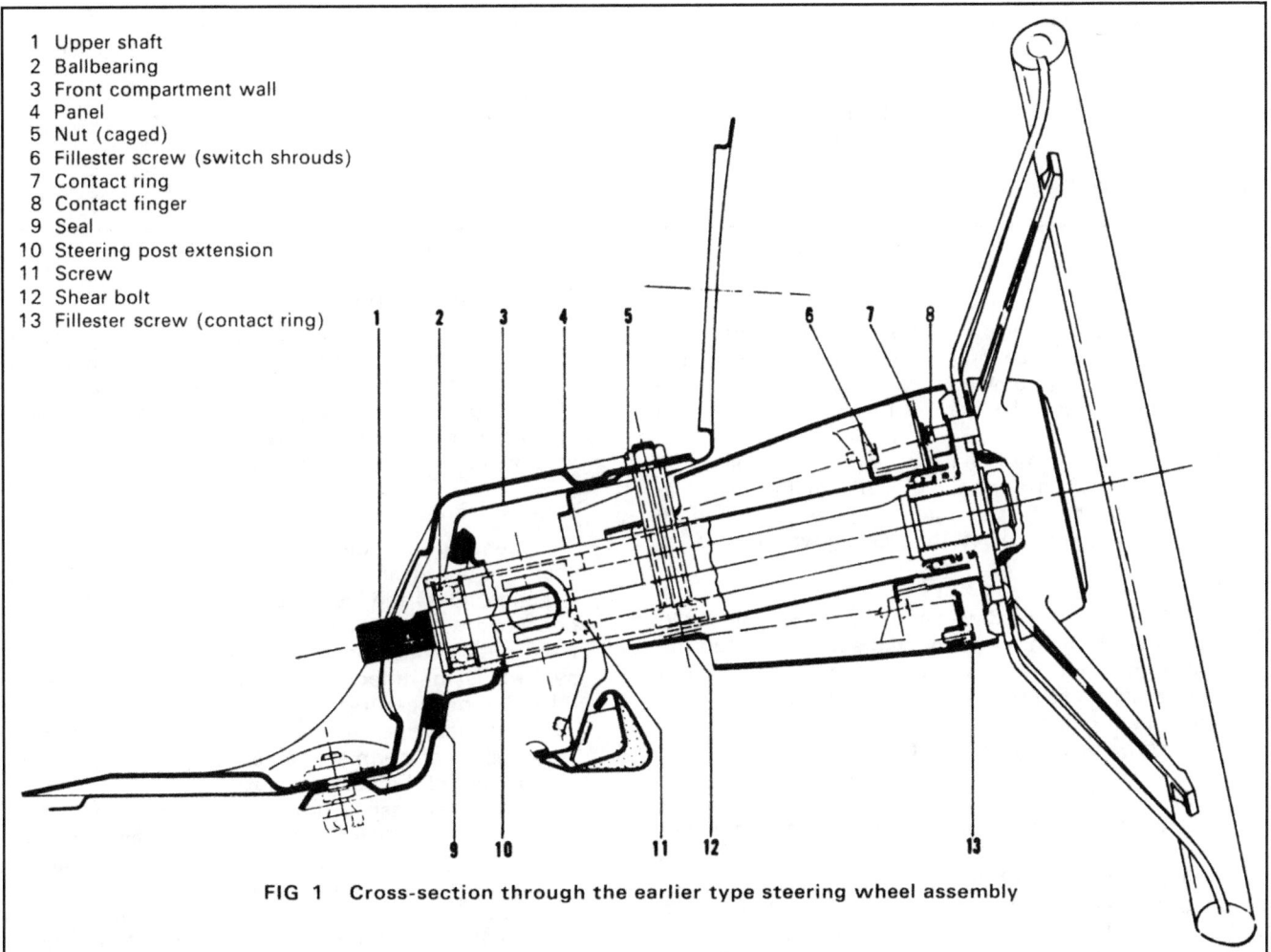

1 Upper shaft
2 Ballbearing
3 Front compartment wall
4 Panel
5 Nut (caged)
6 Fillester screw (switch shrouds)
7 Contact ring
8 Contact finger
9 Seal
10 Steering post extension
11 Screw
12 Shear bolt
13 Fillester screw (contact ring)

FIG 1 Cross-section through the earlier type steering wheel assembly

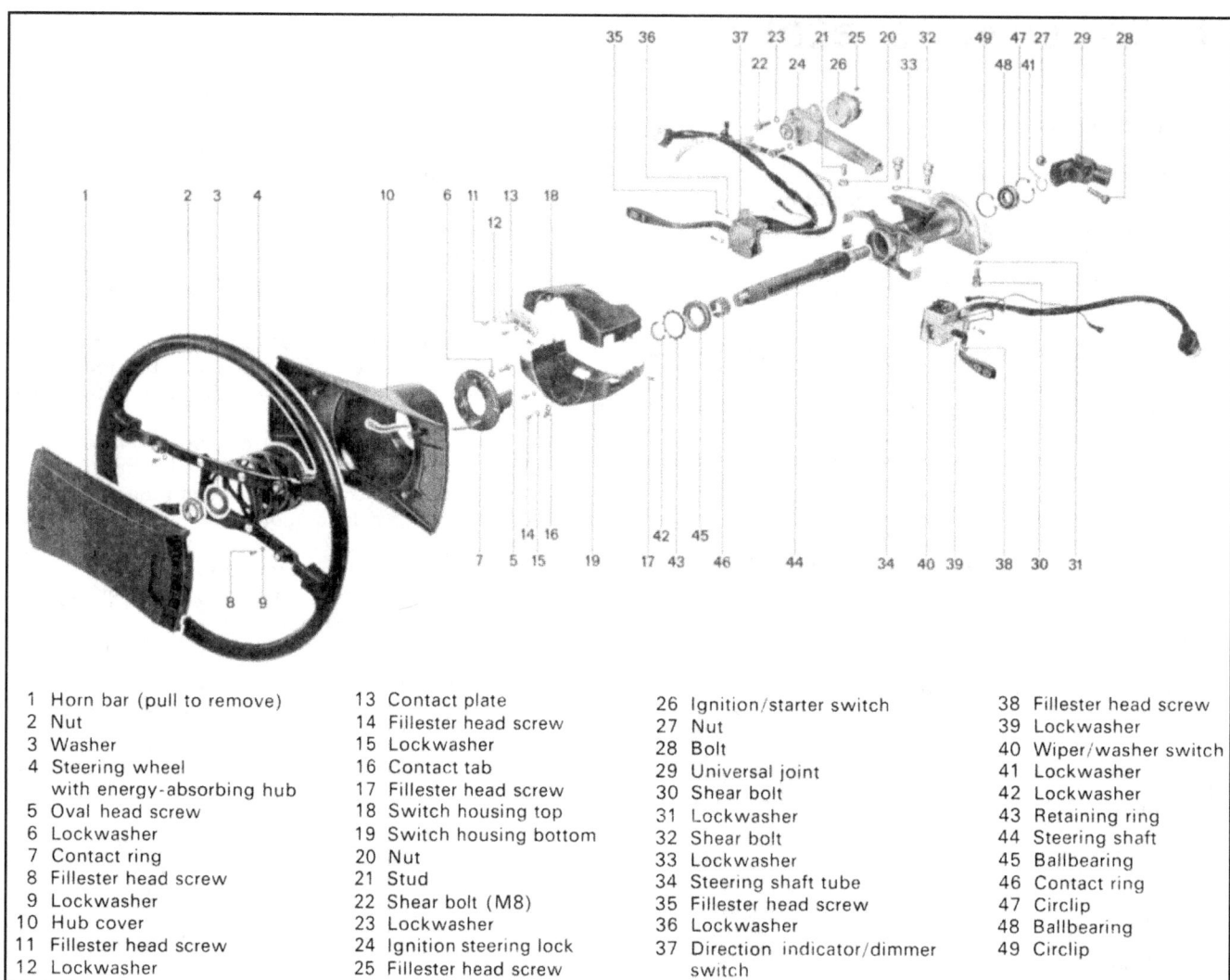

1 Horn bar (pull to remove)	13 Contact plate	26 Ignition/starter switch	38 Fillester head screw
2 Nut	14 Fillester head screw	27 Nut	39 Lockwasher
3 Washer	15 Lockwasher	28 Bolt	40 Wiper/washer switch
4 Steering wheel with energy-absorbing hub	16 Contact tab	29 Universal joint	41 Lockwasher
	17 Fillester head screw	30 Shear bolt	42 Lockwasher
5 Oval head screw	18 Switch housing top	31 Lockwasher	43 Retaining ring
6 Lockwasher	19 Switch housing bottom	32 Shear bolt	44 Steering shaft
7 Contact ring	20 Nut	33 Lockwasher	45 Ballbearing
8 Fillester head screw	21 Stud	34 Steering shaft tube	46 Contact ring
9 Lockwasher	22 Shear bolt (M8)	35 Fillester head screw	47 Circlip
10 Hub cover	23 Lockwasher	36 Lockwasher	48 Ballbearing
11 Fillester head screw	24 Ignition steering lock	37 Direction indicator/dimmer switch	49 Circlip
12 Lockwasher	25 Fillester head screw		

FIG 2 Components of the later type steering wheel assembly

Removal:

1 Set the road wheels in the straightahead position. Disconnect the battery earth lead(s). Release the horn button by turning it anticlockwise or, on later models, release the horn bar. Withdraw the horn contact pin.

2 Remove the wheel retaining nut and collect the washer. Mark the relative position of the wheel in relation to the shaft so that it may be refitted in its original position. Pull off the steering wheel.

Refitment:

1 Confirm that the road wheels are in the straightahead position. Position the spring and support ring on the wheel hub and fit the steering wheel with the wheel and shaft marks aligned. The wheel spokes should be horizontal and the direction indicator flasher striker should be pointing towards the switch.

2 Fit the washer and tighten the retaining nut on earlier models (those with a horn button) to a torque of 8kgm (58lb ft) or, on later models (those with a horn bar), to 7.5kgm (54lb ft). Check that the flasher return striker operates correctly.

3 Lightly grease the horn contact ring, insert the contact pin and fit the horn button by turning it clockwise or, on later models, refit the horn bar.

4 The steering column

A cross-section through the earlier type steering column is shown in **FIG 1**. The components of the later type steering column (with collapsible, energy-absorbing hub) are shown in **FIG 2** and it may be noted that models not initially fitted with this collapsible type of column may have it fitted retrospectively.

Column removal:

Depending upon the model, access to the intermediate shaft and universal couplings requires removal of air box, ductings, hoses and blower unit and associated electrical connections. The following procedure relates to models fitted with normal equipment. **If an air conditioning system is installed, refer to Chapter 13, Section 8 before proceeding.**

1 Disconnect the battery earth lead(s). Remove the luggage compartment carpet. Remove the panel from the front of the fresh air box.

2 Remove the fresh air box by: pulling out the frame and grille after removing four crosshead screws; removing the two crosshead screws which retain the box; detaching the control box hoses, the electrical connections from the air box and the wire cable from the flap lever on the air box; pushing off the retaining clip from the outer cover.

3 Remove the intermediate shaft coverplate. Remove the **upper** nut and bolt from the intermediate shaft **upper** universal joint. Remove the **lower** nut and bolt from the intermediate shaft **lower** universal joint.

4 Remove the fillester headed bolts (see **FIG 3**) which retain the lower steering shaft bearing cap and remove the bearing cap. Withdraw the lower universal joint from the lower steering shaft and dismount the intermediate shaft complete with the upper and the lower universal joints.

5 Remove the steering wheel as described in **Section 3**. Using a suitable extractor as shown in **FIG 4**, withdraw the column sleeve. Remove the circlip from the steering shaft and drive the shaft out upwards.

6 Remove the circlip from the grooved ballbearing/steering outer tube and drive out the bearing downwards.

Note that if the steering/ignition switch and/or the steering shaft tube is to be dismounted, the light switch and the tachometer must be removed. Refer to **FIG 5** and drill or grind off the shear bolts. Access to the bolts which retain the steering tube (later model illustrated) is shown in **FIG 6**.

Column refitment:

Follow the reverse of the removal sequence. Refer to **Section 5** when refitting the intermediate shaft and couplings. Note the following points. Pack bearings with a lithium based multi-purpose grease. On the later type column, drive the bearing into place with a piece of pipe of 24mm (0.945in) internal diameter by 28mm (1.102in) external diameter and ensure that the pipe section only contacts the bearing inner race. Adjustment of heater valves is described in **Chapter 4, Section 2**. Tighten the new shear bolts until their heads break off.

5 The intermediate shaft and couplings
Removal:

The procedure for the removal of the intermediate shaft and its universal couplings is covered by operations 1 to 4 of the steering column removal sequence described in **Section 4**.

1 Universal joint lower bolt   2 Bearing cap nuts
FIG 3   Uncoupling the lower universal joint

Refitment:

Do not attempt to salvage a bent or damaged shaft. If there is any backlash in a universal joint, it should be renewed.

To refit the intermediate shaft assembly, reverse the removal sequence. Use new self-locking nuts and torque tighten them and the fillester headed bearing cap retaining nuts to 2.5kgm (18lb ft). Tighten the bearing cap retaining nuts before tightening the universal joint clamping nuts and bolts.

FIG 4   Withdrawing the bearing sleeve
(earlier type column)

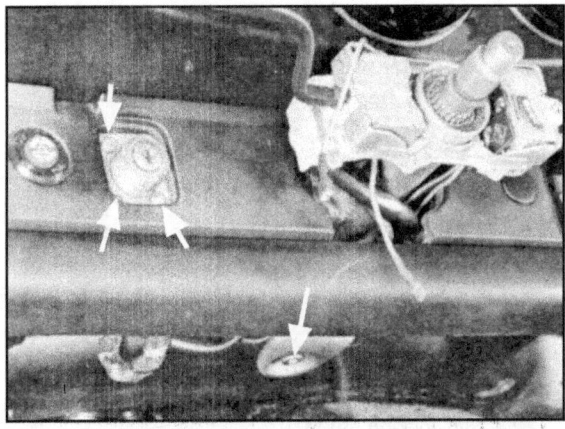

FIG 5   The shear bolts (later type column)

FIG 6   Access to the steering tube bolts
(later type column)

6 The steering linkage

A tie rod couples each steering arm to each end of the steering unit rack. The arrangement is shown in **Chapter 9, FIG 1**. Alteration of the effective 'length' of the tie rods allows wheel alignment to be adjusted. The steering arm to tie rod connection is through a ball joint and the tie rod to steering unit is through a yoke coupling.

Removal:

Unlock and remove the castellated nut which retains the ball joint to the steering arm. Using a suitable extractor (the official tool is VW266h), separate the ball joint stud from the arm. Unlock and remove the coupling bolt from the tie rod yoke. Withdraw the tie rod. If necessary the ball joint or the yoke may be removed after loosening the relevant clamp bolt.

Refitment:

To refit the tie rod, follow the reverse of the removal sequence. Torque tighten the ball joint retaining nut to 4.5kgm (32.5lb ft). Apply molybdenum disulphide grease to the yoke coupling bolt and torque tighten it to 4.7kgm (34lb ft). Use new splitpins.

If the 'length' of either tie rod was disturbed, adjust the wheel alignment as described in **Chapter 9, Section 10**.

7 The steering gearbox

Removal:

Refer to **Section 4** and uncouple the lower universal joint from the lower steering shaft. Remove the rubber boot from the lower steering shaft, unlock and remove the two bolts which retain the pinion flange to the coupling. Withdraw the lower steering shaft and coupling.

Separate the tie rod ball joints from the steering arms as described in **Section 6**. Remove the bolts which retain the steering gearbox to the crossmember 8 in **Chapter 9, FIG 1**. Remove the righthand crossmember brace. Dismount the steering gearbox by withdrawing it to the right.

Dismantling:

1 Hold the assembly between the padded jaws of a vice to avoid cracking the casing. Release the rubber bellows outer clamps to expose the tie rod bushing holders. Use a 42mm wrench to unscrew the bushing holder. It will be advisable here to use two wrenches, one to unscrew a holder, the other to hold the holder on the opposite side to prevent the steering rack from turning. Remove the tie rods and bushes.

2 Refer to **FIG 7** and dismantle in the numerical sequence shown; 1 to 20 is fairly straightforward.

3 Use a puller to extract the rack bushing 21. Withdraw the bearing 17 from the pinion 18 by removing the snap ring 15 and thrust washer 16 and forcing the pinion through the bearing under a flypress or any other small press.

4 Drive the needle bearing 22 out of the housing with special drift P362 or an equivalent tool.

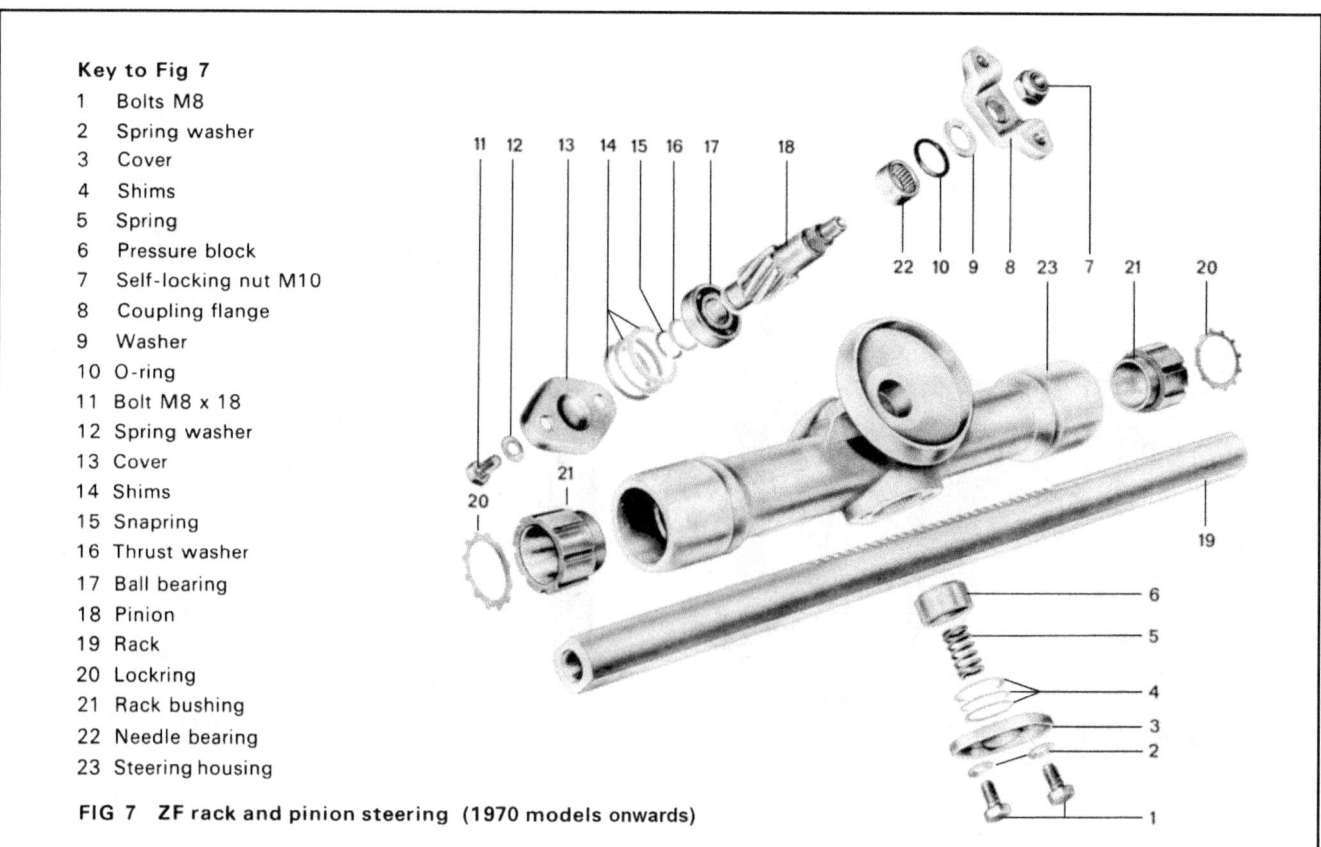

Key to Fig 7
1. Bolts M8
2. Spring washer
3. Cover
4. Shims
5. Spring
6. Pressure block
7. Self-locking nut M10
8. Coupling flange
9. Washer
10. O-ring
11. Bolt M8 x 18
12. Spring washer
13. Cover
14. Shims
15. Snapring
16. Thrust washer
17. Ball bearing
18. Pinion
19. Rack
20. Lockring
21. Rack bushing
22. Needle bearing
23. Steering housing

FIG 7 ZF rack and pinion steering (1970 models onwards)

Reassembly:

1 Fill the steering and rack housing with multi-purpose molybdenum disulphide grease and drive in the needle bearing until the top edge of the bearing is 3mm (0.12in) below the top edge of the housing (see **FIG 8**).

2 Fit the pinion 18 complete with bearing 17 thrust-washer and snap ring and measure the distance between ballbearing and contact face of housing (see **FIG 9**). This clearance must be taken up by the shims 14. Free play between the cover 13 and bearing should be not more than 0.05mm (0.002in).

3 Continue the reassembly and measure the distance between pressure block 6 and the housing flange face (see **FIG 10**). This clearance must be taken up by the shims 4 but allow for a maximum free play between the block and cover 3 of 0.2mm (0.008in).

4 Temporarily fit the shims and covers and check the gear drag over the entire working length of the steering rack (see **FIG 11**). A drag of 6 to 8kgcm (5 to 7lb in) must be attained. If the drag cannot be attained renew the spring 5.

5 Remove the covers and smear the contact surfaces with gasket compound. Tighten the bolts 1 and 11 to a torque of 1.5kgm (10lb ft).

6 Lubricate 'O' ring 10 when fitting and fit a new self-locking nut 7 (size M10), tighten to a torque of 4.7kgm (33lb ft). Ensure the lockplates 20 seat correctly when refitting.

7 Refit the tie rod bushing holders and tighten them to 7kgm (50lb ft).

8 Check the eyebolts for faulty bushes and look for cracks and deterioration of the bellows. **FIG 12** shows the correct settings for the eyebolts, and although this may be done by measurement it is better to use the setting fixture P.285a. The angles are important to ensure free movement of the tie rods.

9 Fit the bellows to the housing. Put gasket compound on the eyebolt threads, the end faces of the rack and on both faces of the stop plate and lockwasher. Fit eyebolts, set them correctly and tighten nuts to 6.5kgm (47lb ft), locking them when secure.

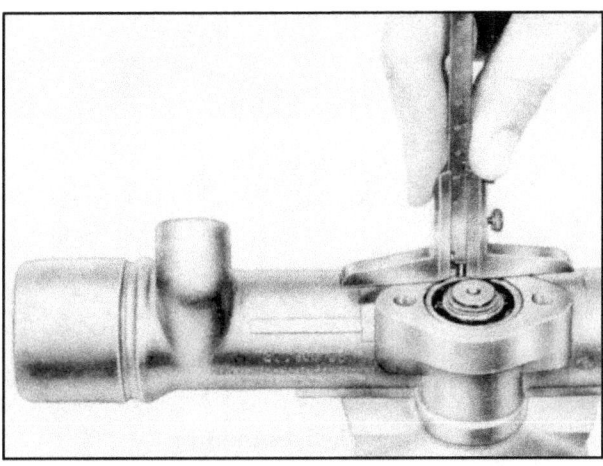

FIG 9   Measure distance from top of ball bearing to contact surface of housing to determine shim pack

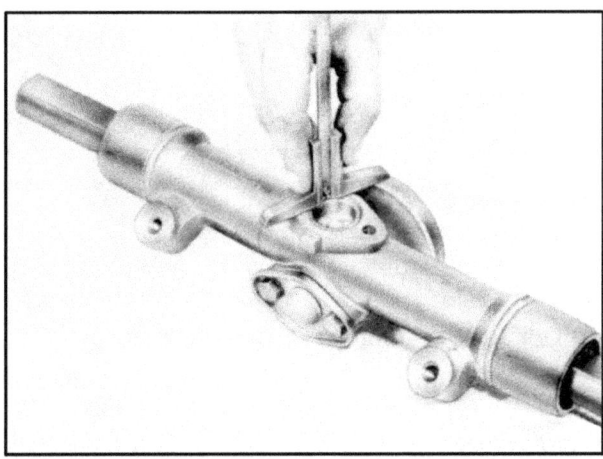

FIG 10   Measure distance from top of pressure block to contact surface of housing to determine shim thickness. This measurement minus .20 mm (.008 inch) will give correct end float

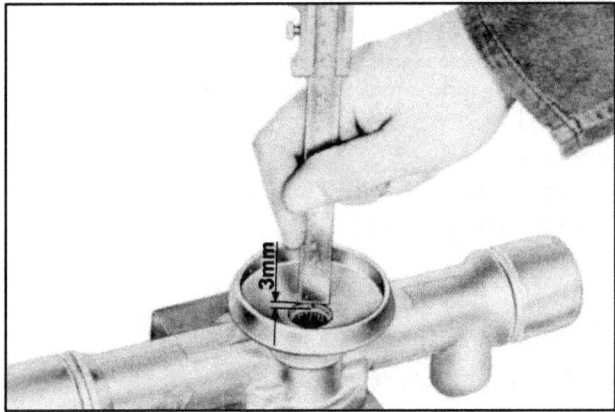

FIG 8   Measure distance from top of bearing to top of housing to determine correct position of bearing

FIG 11   Using torque meter on pinion flange nut to check steering drag

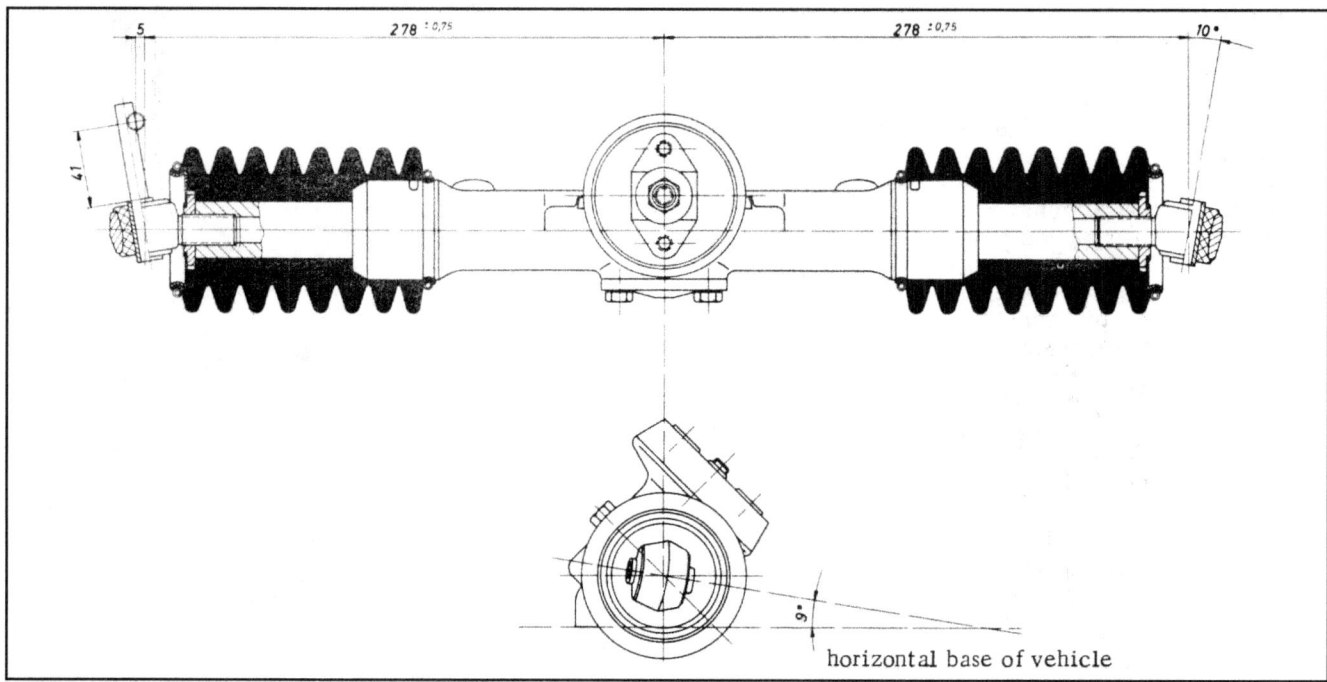

FIG 12 Correct positioning of the rack eyebolts relative to the centre line and mounting bosses (1970 models onwards)

Installing:

Reverse the sequence of operations followed when the steering gearbox was removed but do not, at this stage, reconnect the tie rods to the steering arms. Remove the horn button or the horn bar and, using a torque meter on the steering wheel retaining nut, measure the drag in a similar manner to that shown in **FIG 11**. The drag should be about 10kgcm (8.75lb in) with the tie rods disconnected. If this check is satisfactory, connect the tie rods to the steering arms as described in **Section 6**. The steering unit retaining bolts should have new lockwashers fitted and torque tightened to 4.7kgm (34lb ft). Fit the crossmember brace without strain and torque tighten the nut to 6.5kgm (47lb ft) and the bolt to 4.7kgm (34lb ft). Adjust the wheel alignment as described in **Chapter 9**, **Section 10** if new parts were fitted to either the steering unit assembly or to the tie rods.

8 Fault diagnosis

(a) Wheel wobble

1 Unbalanced wheels and tyres, uneven pressures
2 Free play in steering gear and connections
3 Front end damaged, incorrect steering angles
4 Incorrect toe-in adjustment
5 Worn or slack hub bearings
6 Faulty damper strut
7 Insufficient drag in steering gear

(b) Steering wander

1 Check 2, 3, 5 and 7 in (a)
2 Smooth front tyres, pressures too high or too low

(c) Heavy steering

1 Check 3 in (a)
2 Low or uneven tyre pressures
3 Too much drag in steering gear
4 Insufficient lubricant
5 Steering gearbox mountings out of line
6 Weak or broken torsion bars
7 Faulty steering shafts and joints
8 Defective bearing assembly in post extension

(d) Lost motion

1 Check 2 in (a)
2 Loose steering wheel
3 Worn ball joints
4 Steering gearbox loose on mountings
5 Worn steering gearbox
6 Universal joints loose on steering shafts

(e) Steering pulls to one side

1 Check 3 in (a) and 2 in (c)
2 One front brake binding
3 Broken or sagging front or rear suspension

CHAPTER 11 - BRAKES

1. Description
2. Maintenance
3. Brake pad renewal
4. Front brakes
5. Rear brakes
6. The master hydraulic cylinder
7. Bleeding the hydraulic system
8. The handbrake
9. Servo unit
10. Fault diagnosis

1 Description

The layout of the braking system is shown diagrammatically in **FIG 1**. A dual line hydraulic system is employed. This operates the front brakes (via lines 4 and 5) and the rear brakes (via lines 15, 16 and 5) from the tandem piston master cylinder 2. In the event of a rear brake line failure, the front brakes can be temporarily operated normally and vice versa. Each hydraulic system has its own fluid supply source. These supplies are amalgamated into a two-part reservoir 3 which is topped up through a single filler orifice.

Both front and rear brakes are disc type. Each disc is straddled by a twin piston caliper in which each piston actuates a friction pad. Compensation for pad wear down to the pad wear limit thickness is automatic and does not require routine attention. Pads are renewed when the wear limit thickness of the friction material is reached. Each caliper is provided with a fluid bleed nipple and the procedure for bleeding the system when this operation is necessary is described in **Section 7**. Discs are provided with air cooling passages to ensure that they do not heat up excessively under heavy and continuous use of the brakes.

The handbrake is mechanically actuated by a system of cables and operates on the rear wheels only. The cable mechanism expands two brake shoes on each wheel onto the internal diameter of a drum which is integral with each rear brake disc. Pull-off springs retract the shoes when the handbrake lever is released. Routine adjustment is required to compensate for wear of the shoe friction linings. The hand throttle lever and the heater control lever(s) are incorporated in the handbrake lever mounting.

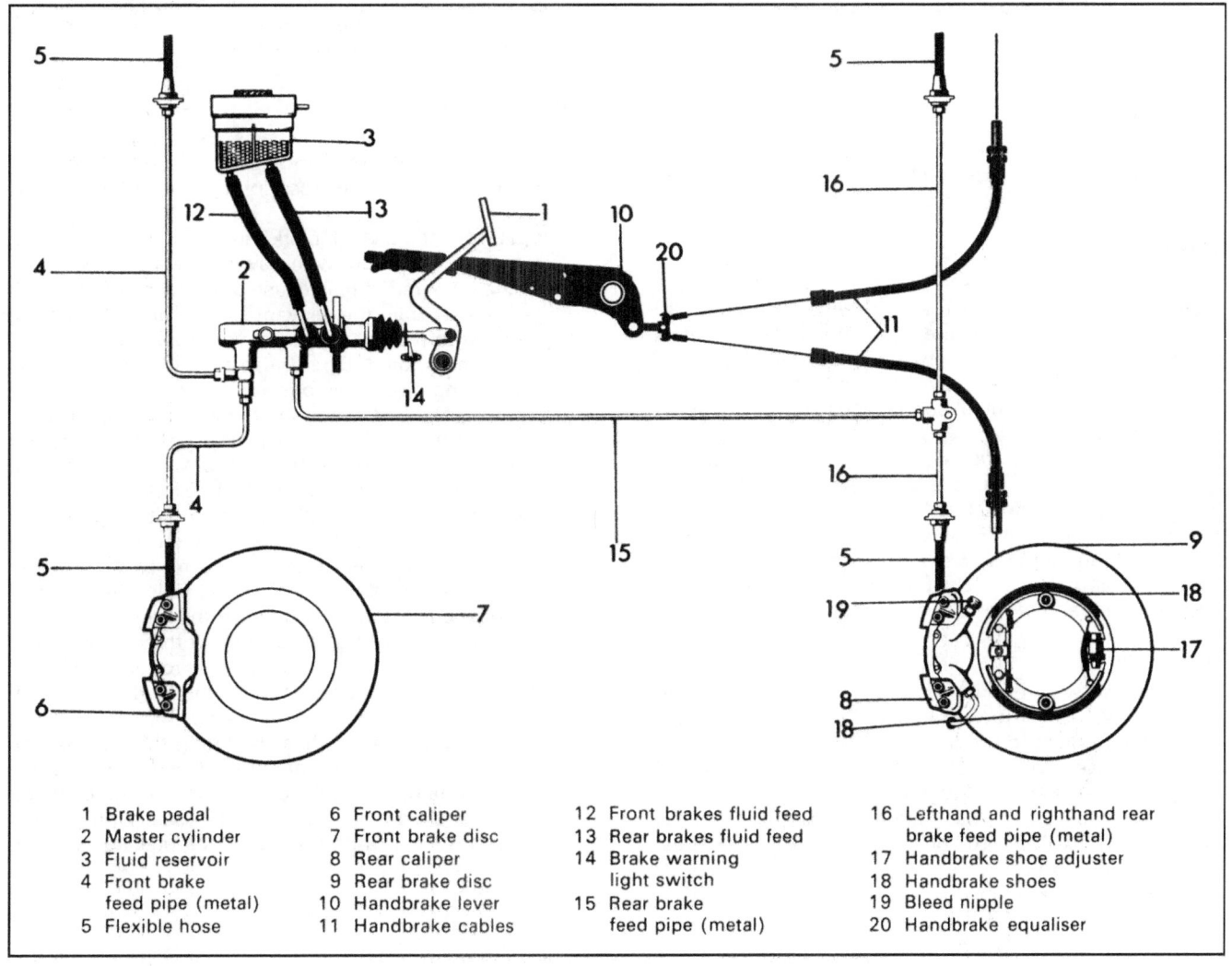

1. Brake pedal
2. Master cylinder
3. Fluid reservoir
4. Front brake feed pipe (metal)
5. Flexible hose
6. Front caliper
7. Front brake disc
8. Rear caliper
9. Rear brake disc
10. Handbrake lever
11. Handbrake cables
12. Front brakes fluid feed
13. Rear brakes fluid feed
14. Brake warning light switch
15. Rear brake feed pipe (metal)
16. Lefthand and righthand rear brake feed pipe (metal)
17. Handbrake shoe adjuster
18. Handbrake shoes
19. Bleed nipple
20. Handbrake equaliser

FIG 1 Diagrammatic layout of the braking system

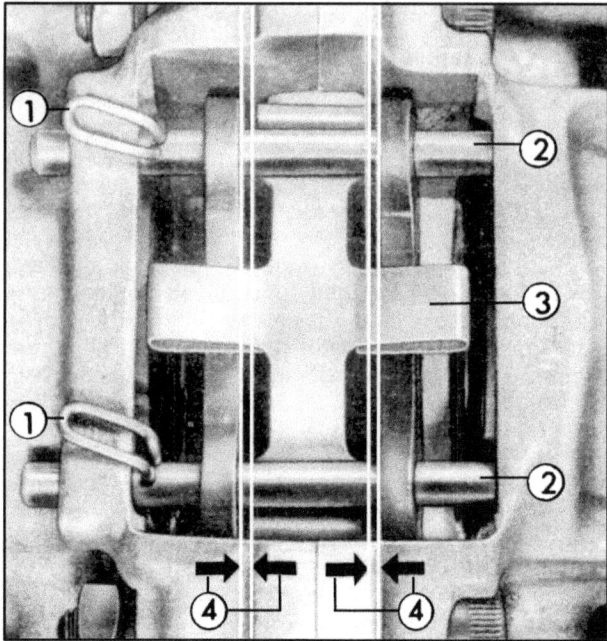

1 Spring pins 3 Cross spring
2 Retaining pins 4 Arrows indicate pad wear limit

FIG 2 Wear limit of caliper pads

2 Maintenance

General:

At least every 12,000 miles (20,000km), check the system for damaged pipes and hoses and confirm that the warning devices are operative.

Reservoir fluid level:

The fluid level in the reservoir will drop as the caliper pistons take up progressively advanced positions to compensate for wear of the pad friction linings. It is important to distinguish between this normal drop in fluid level and any excessive drop which results from leaks from seals or pipe connections which must be corrected without delay.

At least every 12,000 miles (20,000km), check the fluid level and top up as necessary. The correct fluid level is approximately 2cm (0.80in) below the top ridge of the reservoir. Use only ATE Blue fluid or an equivalent of reputable brand and be careful not to spill fluid onto the paintwork as it has solvent properties. Clean off round the reservoir cap before unscrewing it.

Brake pads:

The rate of wear of the pad friction linings will depend greatly upon the driving conditions and methods employed. Subject to the severity with which the brakes have been used, visually check the thickness of the pad linings at least every 12,000 miles (20,000km).

Renew pads when the friction lining thickness has worn down to 2mm (0.08in). The procedure is described in **Section 3**.

Handbrake:

When, due to wear of the shoe linings, the travel of the handbrake lever becomes excessive, adjust as described in **Section 8**.

Brake pedal free play:

Every 12,000 miles (20,000km) or more frequently if necessary, check and, if necessary, adjust the pedal free play. The procedure is described in **Section 6**.

3 Brake pad renewal:

The wear limit of pads is reached when the pad backing plate touches the cross spring or when the pad friction lining has worn down to 2mm (0.08in) as indicated between the arrows in **FIG 2**.

The overall thickness, the friction lining plus the backing plate, of a new pad is approximately 15mm (0.60in). Pads with different types of linings (touring, competition, etc.) are available and all pads in both the front or in both the rear calipers should be of the same type. Although it is possible to renew one pad only, it is recommended that all four front pads or all four rear pads are renewed together. Front and rear pads are not identical and are not interchangeable.

Serviceable pads which are being withdrawn as part of a caliper removal procedure must be marked so that they may be refitted in their original positions. It is not permissible to change their positions.

Changing pads:

1 Jack up car and remove wheels. Extract spring pins 1 and push out retaining pins 2 (see **FIG 2**), pressing down on the cross spring 3 and pushing pins inwards.
2 If pads are still usable, mark their positions for correct re-installation before withdrawing them.
3 The next operation may cause overflowing of the fluid reservoir so drain the relevant section of it. Press both pistons into their bores, either with tool P83 or with a lever of hardboard. Do not use steel tools which may damage the disc or pistons.
4 Clean out the pad cavities with methylated spirits and a soft-edged tool. **Do not use other solvents.** Check the condition of the dust cover and clamping ring. Renew hardened or cracked covers.
5 Polish the brake discs with fine emerycloth and smooth out any inner and outer ridges on each face.
6 Fit the pads and check that they are free to move in the cavities. Reassemble in the reverse order, fitting new spring pins in the retaining pins if the original pins are distorted or worn. Put clean fluid in the reservoir and depress the brake pedal several times to set the pistons in the correct positions. Recheck the fluid level in the reservoir.

Do not use the brakes heavily during the first 200km (125 miles) if new pads are fitted. Condition the pads by moderate pedal pressure, with intervals for cooling, unless an emergency occurs. The pads, with careful bedding in, will then give effective braking without fade.

4 Front brakes

Removing a caliper and disc:

1 Remove the pads (operations 1 and 2 in **Section 3**). Block brake pedal in slightly depressed position, then detach fluid pipe at the banjo connection behind the caliper.
2 Remove the two caliper mounting bolts on the inner side of the brake assembly and pull off the caliper.
3 Prise off the hub cap. Slacken the socket head screw in the clamping nut on the end of the axle, unscrew the nut and remove the thrust washer. Parts are shown in **Chapter 9**, **FIG 6**. Pull off the disc and hub. If tight, do not hammer on the disc but use a puller.
4 From behind the axle remove the disc shroud. Unlock and remove the bolts and lift off the brake carrier (see **FIG 3**).

Dismantling a caliper:

1 Do not separate the caliper halves unless there has been leakage. Loosen bleed screw arrowed in **FIG 4** and use gentle air pressure (1 atm or 14 lb/sq in) to eject any residual fluid from the caliper.
2 Remove the clamping ring and dust cover (see **FIG 5**). Depress one piston with tool P83 or use a clamp. Place a block of wood in the slot and blow out the opposite piston with air pressure of 2 atm or 29 lb/sq in, raising the pressure if necessary. **Serious injury may result if fingers are not kept out of slot during this operation.**
3 Remove the piston seal from inside the cylinder bore with a plastic or wooden tool, so that the groove and bore are not damaged. Restore the removed piston and seal and the clamp in order to remove the opposite piston. Clean all parts in methylated spirit (industrial alcohol). **Do not use any other type of solvent or the rubber seals will be damaged.** Check the cylinder bores and pistons for wear, scoring or pitting, and renew faulty parts. **Renew all seals as a matter of course.** It is dangerous to refit any doubtful parts. The components of the automatic pad adjustment cannot be renewed. Always fit a new piston if the automatic action is defective.

1 Disc
2 Intermediate plate (between the caliper halves)
3 Disc shroud
4 Caliper base housing
5 Pad segment
6 Cross spring
7 Spring pin
8 Retaining pin
The bleed nipple is arrowed

FIG 4 A front caliper and brake disc assembly

FIG 3 Removing the bolts which secure the brake carrier to the front axle

FIG 5 Prising out spring ring that secures caliper piston dust cover

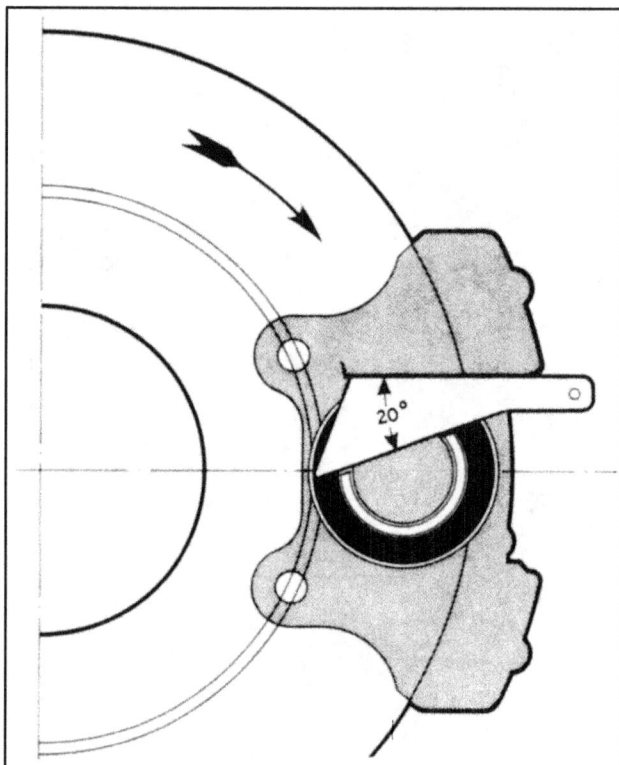

FIG 6 Using 20° plate to set piston step in relation to caliper and to disc rotation

FIG 7 Handbrake assembly with drum removed. Dotted lines show correct alignment of coils of right-hand spring

Key to Fig 7
1 Nut for cable
2 Brake shoe expander
3 Shoe retainer
4 Shoe adjuster
5 Interrupted return spring

Reassembling a caliper:

1 Use ATE brake cylinder paste to coat the cylinder and piston parts. Insert the seals in the cylinder grooves.
2 Note the cut-away step on the piston pressure face. Use aligning tool P84, or make up a thin sheet metal gauge with an included angle of 20°, as shown in **FIG 6**, to set the piston correctly. Insert the piston carefully so that it does not tilt or jam, and align it so that the stepped down part faces the disc rotation as shown. Use a clamp to press the piston into place. The aligning tool must rest against the upper edge of the brake pad slot. If the caliper is installed, a piston may be turned by clamping the opposite piston and ejecting the required piston until it can be turned by hand.
3 Wipe off surplus assembly grease and fit the dust covers dry.
4 If the caliper was separated into halves because of 'O' ring leakage, clean the faces with methylated spirit (industrial alcohol), fit new rings and assemble with new bolts, nuts and spring washers, using genuine Porsche spares. Tighten to half the required torque and then fully tighten. Torque for front calipers is 3.5kgm (24.5lb ft). Do not omit the packing plate from between the halves of the caliper.
5 Fit the disc to its hub, if it was removed, with the marks aligned and tighten the nuts to 2.3kgm (16.5lb ft). Refit the hub as described in **Chapter 9** and adjust the bearings. Use a dial gauge to check the lateral runout of the disc faces as described in **Section 5**.
6 Fit the caliper using new spring washers and tighten the retaining bolts to 7kgm (50.5lb ft). Fit the brake pads in their original positions (see **Section 3**). Bleed the hydraulic system (see **Section 7**).

Brake discs:

If necessary, separate the disc from its hub after marking for correct reassembly.

The servicing of both front and rear brake discs is covered at the end of **Section 5**.

5 Rear brakes

Removing:

1 Jack up the car and remove the rear wheels after chocking the front wheels and releasing the handbrake.
2 Remove the brake pads (see **Section 3**). From behind, remove the disc shrouds. Block the brake pedal in a slightly depressed position and detach the fluid pipe from the caliper. Detach the caliper.
3 Remove the two countersunk screws adjacent to the wheel studs and pull off the disc.
4 Refer to **FIG 7**. Remove the castellated nut 1 and its washer. From behind, pull out the handbrake cable. Remove the expander 2 and its spring.
5 Turn the retainer 3 to release it from its pin, remove the spring and pull out the pin from rear. Lift the upper shoe with a screwdriver, withdraw the adjuster 4 and unhook the spring from between the shoes.
6 Release the retainer from the lower shoe. Remove both shoes in a forward direction and unhook the second return spring.

Servicing a caliper:

For this operation, follow the instructions for front brake calipers in **Section 4**. There is a packing plate 10.6mm (0.417in) thick between the caliper halves. Bolt torque for the caliper halves retaining bolts is 1.8kgm (13lb ft).

Checking parts:

Clean and examine all mechanical parts for wear. Renew any broken or distorted springs and check that the adjuster works freely. Discard oily brake linings as it is not possible to clean them satisfactorily. Worn linings must be replaced by Porsche-approved makes.

Reassembling:

1 Insert the handbrake cable and fit the washer against the spacer tube. Fit the inner expander struts. Fit the special return spring 5 to both shoes with coils pointing inwards (see **FIG 7**).
2 Slide the shoes rearwards onto the brake carrier plate and fit the retaining pins, springs and retainers 3. Fit the inner expander of the handbrake into the seats in the shoes.
3 Lift the upper shoe with a screwdriver and fit the adjuster 4. The sprocket should be downwards in the righthand brake and upwards in the lefthand brake. Fit the return spring at the adjuster end of the shoes.
4 Slacken the adjusting nut on the handbrake cable fully back. Fit the expander spring, the second half of the expander 2 and tighten the castellated nut, until one of its slots clears the splitpin hole. Fit a new splitpin. Make sure the expander struts are correctly seated in the shoes.
5 Refit the disc and check for runout as described later. Fit the intermediate plate between the caliper and the rear axle control arm. Fit the caliper and tighten the retaining bolts to 6kgm (43.5lb ft). Fit the pads in their original positions. Bleed the hydraulic system (see **Section 7**) and adjust handbrake (see **Section 8**).

Handbrake carrier plate:

Removal and refitment of the carrier plate are covered in **Chapter 8 Section 5**.

Brake discs:

A ventilated disc is shown in **FIG 4**. Note the plate 2 between the caliper halves. Disc thickness is 19.8 to 20.0mm (0.780 to 0.787in) both front and rear.

Smooth, rounded concentric scoring is normal, but sharp ridges, cracking and pitting call for disc renewal or regrinding. This is also the remedy for excessive runout or excessive variation in thickness.

When regrinding, remove no more than 0.70mm (0.028in) equally from each side, the minimum permissible disc thickness being 18.6mm (0.732in). Surface finish must be within 0.006mm (0.0002in). Deviation in thickness 0.03mm (0.001in) maximum. Runout up to 0.05mm (0.002in) measured on faces 10mm (0.4in) inside the outer edge.

Wear limit of disc thickness is 1mm (0.04in) from each face. If worn symmetrically, the lowest limit of disc thickness is 18mm (0.71in).

To check front disc runout when installed, remove the brake pads (see **Section 3**) and adjust the front

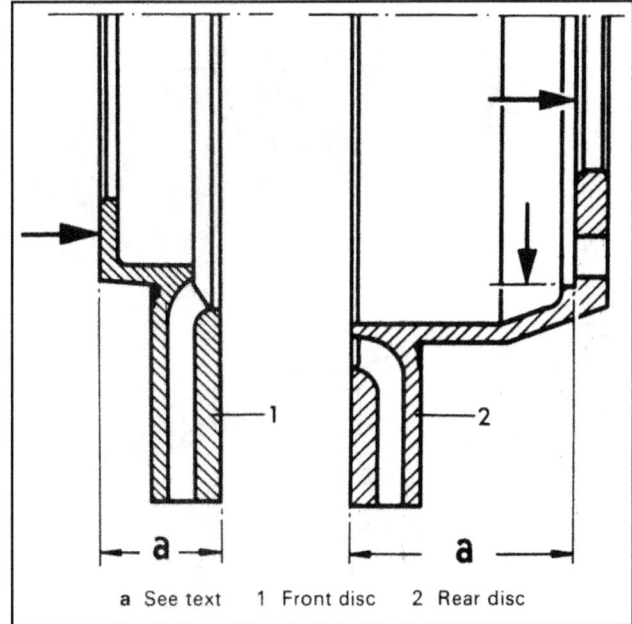

FIG 8 The disc regrind datum faces are arrowed

a See text   1 Front disc   2 Rear disc

wheel bearings. Set up a dial gauge so that its plunger bears on the disc face about 10 to 15mm (0.40 to 0.60in) below the outer edge. It is advisable to check both faces. Maximum permissible runout when mounted in 0.20mm (0.008in), and discs with excessive runout must be reground or renewed.

To check the rear discs, remove the pads and fit up a dial gauge as before. The disc must be fully tightened onto the hub by refitting the wheel nuts on steel spacers, so that the nuts may be tightened to 10kgm (12.25lb ft). To avoid warping, tighten evenly and diagonally. Runout must not exceed the figure given for front discs.

When regrinding discs it is most important to preserve the original symmetry. This is the reason for taking an equal amount off each side. To ensure that this may be checked by the operator, the following dimensions are given. Measurement 'a' in **FIG 8** is tabled together with the original disc thickness, and a simple calculation will enable the check to be made.

When the thickness of a new front disc is 19.8 to 20.0mm (0.780 to 0.787in), dimension 'a' is 35.0 ± 0.10mm (1.378 ± 0.004in).

With the same thickness of a new rear disc, dimension 'a' is 65.0 ± 0.10mm (2.559 ± 0.004in).

Pad thickness:

All the preceding limits for wear and regrinding apply only if the pad thickness is not allowed to fall below 2mm (0.08in). **This is important if the brakes are to function correctly.**

Disc balance:

Discs are balanced at the factory by inserting spring clips into the ventilating slots. **Do not remove these clips.**

Disc cleanliness:

Using the car on dirty roads may lead to clogging of the ventilating slots. When washing the car, use a hose to clear the slots to ensure adequate cooling.

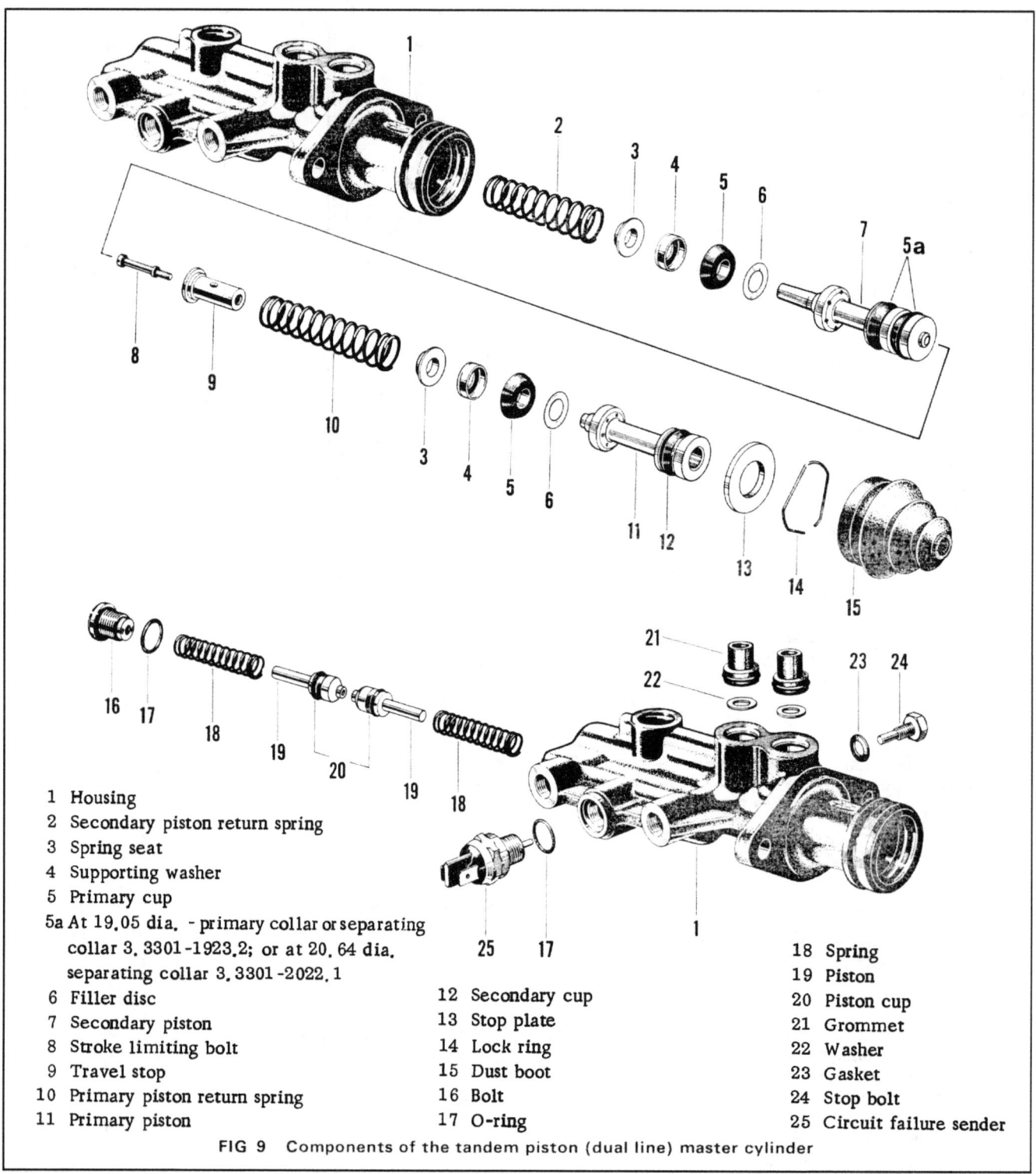

1 Housing
2 Secondary piston return spring
3 Spring seat
4 Supporting washer
5 Primary cup
5a At 19.05 dia. - primary collar or separating collar 3.3301-1923.2; or at 20.64 dia. separating collar 3.3301-2022.1
6 Filler disc
7 Secondary piston
8 Stroke limiting bolt
9 Travel stop
10 Primary piston return spring
11 Primary piston
12 Secondary cup
13 Stop plate
14 Lock ring
15 Dust boot
16 Bolt
17 O-ring
18 Spring
19 Piston
20 Piston cup
21 Grommet
22 Washer
23 Gasket
24 Stop bolt
25 Circuit failure sender

FIG 9 Components of the tandem piston (dual line) master cylinder

6 The master cylinder

Observe scrupulous cleanliness when working on any part of the hydraulic system and use only ATE Blue Fluid or an equivalent of reputable brand. Note that **brake fluid will damage paintwork.**

The components of the tandem piston dual line master cylinder are shown in **FIG 9**. Each piston serves a separate hydraulic section. One section operates the front brakes and the other operates the rear brakes. In the event of a pipe or seal failure in one section, the other section will continue to operate normally. Note that each section of the master cylinder is separately connected with the partitioned reservoir. A disc on the master cylinder pushrod operates the brake warning lights.

On certain models a brake circuit failure sender (25 in **FIG 9**) is provided. This device closes an electrical circuit to a warning light in the event of either front or rear brake hydraulic circuits becoming inoperative. This device is obligatory fitment on vehicles imported into the USA and must be checked every 6000 miles (10,000km) as described later.

Removing the master cylinder:

1 Jack up the car. Detach the accelerator pedal from the rod by pulling the pedal back. Remove the mat and floorboard. From behind the brake pedal, pull rubber boot off the master cylinder (see part 15 in **FIG 9**).
2 Drain both sections of the brake fluid reservoir (see **FIG 1**) beneath car, remove the shield from the suspension crossmember. Detach the pipes and switch wires from the master cylinder.
3 Loosen the clamps and withdraw the hoses connecting the reservoir to the cylinder. Release the cylinder flange from body (2 nuts) and withdraw the cylinder.

Dismantling:

Refer to **FIG 9**. Hold cylinder lightly in a vice fitted with soft jaws.

1 Prise out ring 14. Remove stop plate 13 and piston 11 complete with all cups, washers, spring and stop 9.
2 Remove the stop bolt 24 of secondary piston 7 and use gentle air pressure of 1atm (15lb/sq in) to blow out the piston and cups. Cover any holes in the cylinder which would allow air to escape. Remove spring 2 and the associated washers.
3 Hold the neck of the primary piston 11 between soft jaws in a vice and unscrew the stroke limiting bolt 8, keeping the spring compressed to reduce the load on the threads. Separate the parts.
4 On relevant cars, remove the warning sender 25 and the cap screw 16 and blow out parts 19 and 20 with gentle air pressure blocking any air escape holes.

Cleaning and inspection:

Wash all parts in methylated spirit (industrial alcohol). **Use no other solvents as they may lead to rapid deterioration of the rubber parts.** Dry the housing and clear all parts with compressed air. Renew all rubber parts at every overhaul. They are available in kit form.

Check the piston and cylinder bore surfaces for wear, scoring or corrosion. Renew if not smooth and highly polished.

Reassembling the master cylinder:

Do not let mineral oil contact any of the internal parts. Observe absolute cleanliness at all times. Reassemble in the reverse of the dismantling order. Lightly coat the bore, the piston and the cups with ATE brake cylinder paste. When inserting the cups, take care not to turn back the sealing lips. Make sure that the cups face correctly as shown in the illustration, with the lips entering first, except for the rear cup of piston 7 where the lip faces the opposite direction (towards the rear of the master cylinder).

Insert the secondary piston and filler disc, primary cup, supporting washer, spring seat and spring, with the large coil of the spring entering first. Using a piece of clean plastic rod, push the piston down the bore until it clears the hole for the stop bolt. Fit the bolt and washer, tightening to 1.0 to 1.2kgm (7.2 to 8.7lb ft). Check that the bolt is properly seated ahead of the piston and that the piston moves freely to the bottom of the bore.

Fit the filler disc, primary cup and supporting washer to the primary piston. Use the stroke limiting bolt to secure the spring, spring seat and stop sleeve to the piston. Insert the assembly into the bore and fit the lock ring, making sure that it is well seated.

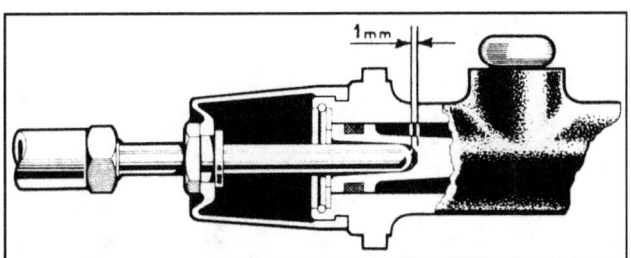

FIG 10 Correct clearance between master cylinder piston and pedal pushrod is 1 mm (.04 inch)

On relevant models, coat the warning system plungers with ATE brake cylinder paste before fitting. Use a new 'O' ring under the cap screw and tighten to 1.5kgm (11lb ft). Fit a new 'O' ring to the sender unit and tighten to the same torque.

Installation:

Apply sealer to the cylinder mounting flange and check that the pushrod enters the cylinder. Attach the flange to body, using new spring washers. Tighten the retaining nuts to 2.5kgm (18lb ft). Inside the car, check the pushrod clearance shown in **FIG 10**. To adjust to 1mm (0.04in) specified, loosen the locknut and turn the pushrod as necessary, then tighten the locknut. Reconnect pipes and switch wires.

Check that the vent hole in the reservoir cap is clear. Fill the reservoir (see **Section 2**). Bleed the brake system (see **Section 7**). Check the operation of the brakes, check for leaks with the pedal depressed firmly and check the stoplights. Refit the undershield, tightening nuts to 6.5kgm (47lb ft) and the bolts to 4.7kgm (34lb ft).

Circuit failure sender:

On relevant models, check the warning system every 6000 miles (10,000km) or whenever the hydraulic system has been disturbed. Confirm that the warning lamp is operative by switching on the ignition and applying the handbrake. If the lamp does not light up, check the bulb. Test the sender as follows.

Depress the brake pedal to the brake actuation point. A second operator must now simulate failure of one braking circuit by slackening a bleed screw on one of the brake calipers. Further depression of the brake pedal to actuation point for the other brake circuit should cause the control lamp to light up. Tighten the bleed screw and release pedal.

Repeat the operation but select a bleed screw in the second circuit. If the lamp does not light up during one of the tests, check the sender unit on the master cylinder and renew if necessary. If the sender unit is found to be serviceable, check the wiring continuity and correct the fault.

Stoplight switch:

This is mounted on a bracket to one side of the brake pedal and pushrod. Remove the two screws and detach the wires to release the switch.

To adjust the switch, place a packing piece 4mm (0.157in) thick under the pedal stop. This will be equivalent to a pedal pad travel of 21mm (0.827in). Adjacent to the cable connections on the switch is a screw and locknut. Slacken the nut and turn the screw to the point where the stoplights just go on. Tighten the locknut and recheck the action.

7 Bleeding the hydraulic system

This procedure, for which two operators are required, is only necessary if air has entered the system. This may result from the level of the fluid in the reservoirs having fallen too low; because the system has been drained of old fluid or because part of the system has been dismantled. It is important to keep the reservoirs topped up during the bleeding procedure to avoid further air from entering the system. Do not re-use fluid which has been bled from the system as it will have become aerated. Use fresh fluid straight from the supply tin. The bleed screws are shown in **FIGS 1** and **4**. Proceed as follows.

Sequence:

If only one caliper has been disconnected, bleed at that point. If the master cylinder has been disconnected or if the system has been drained, bleed in the following sequence: righthand rear, lefthand rear, righthand front and, finally, lefthand front.

Procedure:

1 Remove the cap from the bleed screw and attach a length of rubber or plastic tubing. Submerge the free end of the tubing in a container which is partially filled with brake fluid. Loosen the relevant bleed screw by approximately half-a-turn.
2 Depress the brake pedal through its full travel, close the bleed screw and release the pedal slowly. Repeat this sequence until the fluid from the drain tube is free from air bubbles.
3 Close the bleed screw, remove the drain tube and refit the cap. Repeat this procedure, if relevant, on the other calipers in the order specified earlier.

FIG 11 Slackening handbrake cable adjuster behind rear brake (top). Using screwdriver to turn brake shoe adjuster for handbrake (bottom)

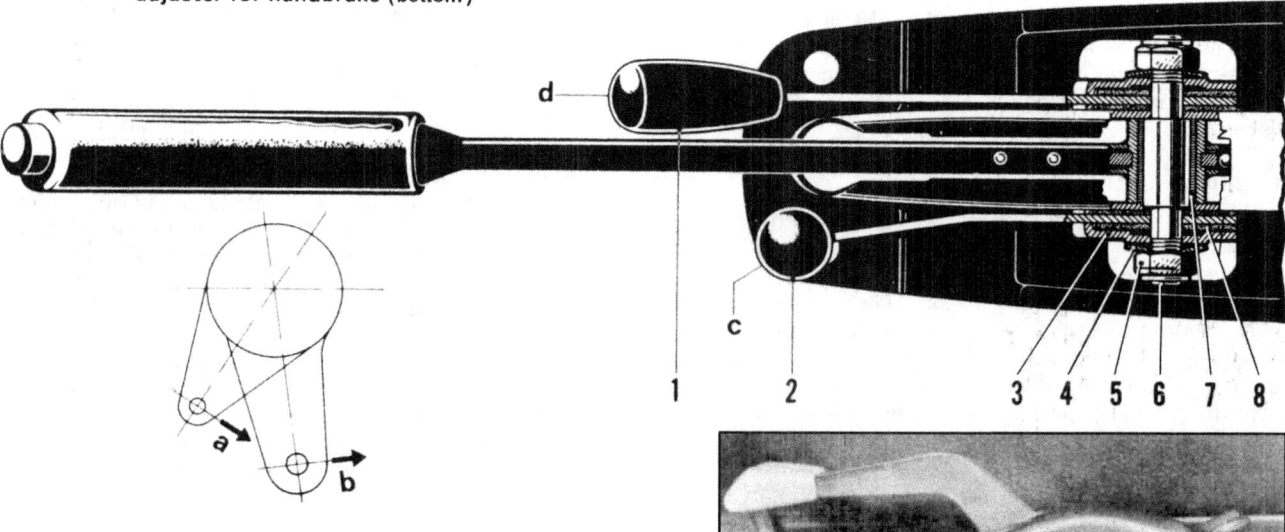

FIG 12 Handbrake mounting and throttle and heater control levers (pre 1975 models)

1 Heater control lever
2 Hand throttle lever
3 Pressure disc
4 Cup spring
5 Self-locking nut
6 Pivot
7 Spacer sleeve
8 Friction disc

a Friction limit of heater lever is 10 kg (22 lb)
b Friction limit of hand throttle lever is 6 kg (13 lb)
c Hand throttle lever knob is pressed on
d Heater lever knob is screwed on

FIG 13 Removing the handbrake mounting assembly (arrowed) 1975 onwards models

8 The handbrake

Adjustment:

When the lever movement is excessive, adjust the handbrake as follows:

1 Raise the car and remove the rear wheels. Release the handbrake. Push back the pads of the rear disc brakes so that the discs rotate freely.

2 Behind the shrouds, loosen the cable adjusting nuts to relieve cable tension (see upper view, **FIG 11**). Insert a screwdriver as in the lower view and turn the adjusting sprocket until the shoes lock inside the drum and the disc is immoveable. Sprocket can be seen at 4 in **FIG 7**. Repeat adjustment on the opposite wheel.

3 Remove the cable slack at the adjusting nuts (see **FIG 11**, top). Pull back the cover round the handbrake lever mounting and note two holes in the flange near the rear bolt. Looking vertically downwards, the ends of the cable equaliser should be visible. The equaliser should be at right angles to the car centre line. If not, adjust at the nuts behind the shrouds. Tighten the adjusting nut locknuts.

4 Now back off the two sprockets by about four or five teeth so that the discs can be turned freely. Check that the handbrake is applied when pulled up about four teeth, but is quite free when the lever is released. Finally, depress the brake pedal several times to set the pads and then check the fluid level in the reservoir.

Handbrake lever and mounting:

The handbrake lever mounting assembly also incorporates the hand throttle lever and the heater control lever(s). **FIG 12** relates to earlier models in which the heater control has a single lever. Later models are provided with twin heater control levers (see **Chapter 2, FIG 3**) and further lever pressure plates and friction discs is consequently incorporated into the mounting assembly.

Removing the handbrake mounting:

1 Remove the tunnel cover and lever dust boot. Remove the knob from the heater control lever 1. Release the support housing from the tunnel.

2 Remove nut 5 and withdraw cup spring 4, pressure disc 3, friction disc 8 and heater control lever 1. Note that the numbered parts are actually at the opposite end, so work on the end adjacent to the heater lever.

3 Lift the housing a little. The cable and equaliser beam can be seen attached to a clevis, the clevis pin being secured by a spring clip arrowed in **FIG 13**. Release the clip and pull out the pin.

4 Remove the wiring from the control lamp switch and lift away the handbrake mounting assembly.

Dismantling the handbrake mounting:

1 Remove the locking ring and withdraw the drag link and washer from the lower end of the hand throttle lever. Remove the nut from the pivot shaft 6 and lift off the hand throttle lever and friction disc assembly. Pull out the pivot shaft.

2 Remove the screw to the rear of the pivot and withdraw the control switch. Push the handbrake lever slightly to the rear and out of the housing to remove the ratchet plate.

3 Grind the rivet head off the ratchet pawl stud, drive out the stud and remove the pawl. If it is necessary to remove the handbrake lever, pull off the hand grip which is glued on. This will release the button and rod, the ring and the spring.

Reassembling the handbrake mounting:

1 After fitting the handbrake control button, glue the grip in place, making certain that no surplus glue interferes with the action of the button.

2 Grease the ratchet plate pawl and pivot shaft with multi-purpose lithium grease and insert it into place.

3 Fit the hand throttle friction discs dry. All friction assembly surfaces must be free from grease. Tighten the self-locking nut.

Installing the handbrake mounting:

Do this in the reverse order of dismantling. Do not forget to attach the wiring to the control lamp switch. Fit the heater control lever in the housing. Install the cable beam and check that the cables are correctly seated. Fit the housing to the tunnel and tighten the bolts to 2.5kgm (18lb ft). Reassemble the friction parts for the heater lever in the manner described for the hand throttle lever. Tighten the self-locking nut until the lever does not feel too stiff to move, but does not slip back when the heater is fully on. Check the adjustment of heater flaps as in **Chapter 4**. Check the adjustment of the hand throttle control as in **Chapter 2**. Check handbrake adjustment as described earlier.

Removing the handbrake cables:

1 Chock the front wheels, release the handbrake and raise the rear of the car. Remove the rear wheels.

2 Remove the handbrake housing from the tunnel. Detach the cables from the equaliser beam.

3 Block the brake pedal in a slightly depressed position to prevent draining of fluid from system and remove the pipe line from the rear caliper. Detach the caliper from its mounting.

4 Remove the countersunk screws and pull off the brake disc and spacer. Release the cable from the expander (see **Section 5**). Pull the cable out from the rear of the brake. Pull the other end out of the conduit tube in the tunnel.

Refitting the handbrake cables:

1 Feed the cable into the conduit tube while coating it with multipurpose lithium grease. Refit the cable end to the brake expander as described in **Section 5**.

2 Refit the caliper, tightening the bolts to 6kgm (43lb ft) on new spring washers. Refit the handbrake housing to tunnel. Bleed the brake system (see **Section 7**). Adjust the handbrake as described earlier.

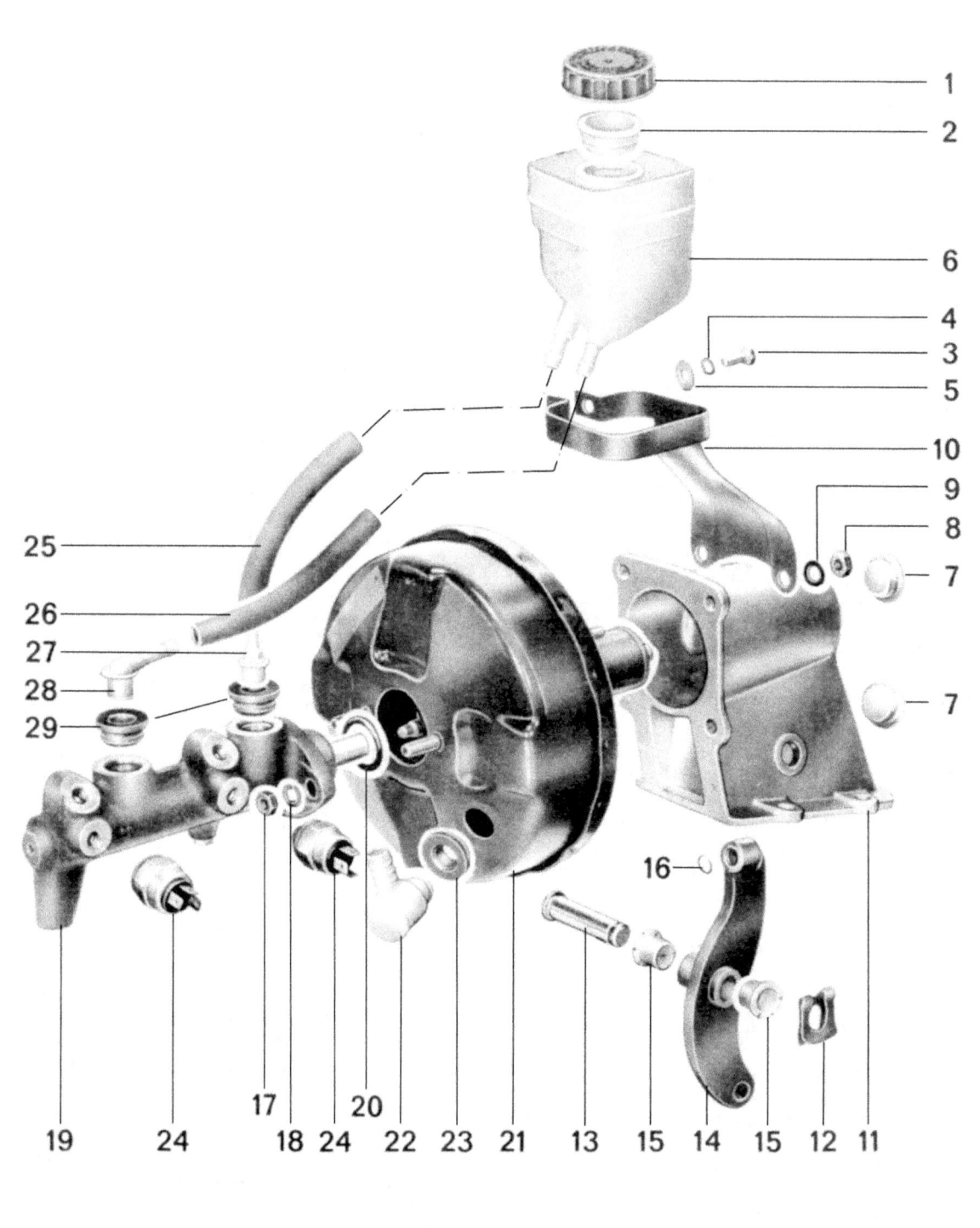

1 Cap	7 Plug	13 Pivot pin	19 Tandem master cylinder	24 Stop light switch
2 Filter screen	8 Nut	14 Operating lever		25 Hose
3 Bolt	9 Spring washer	15 Bushing	20 Seal	26 Hose
4 Lock washer	10 Holder	16 Snap-ring	21 Brake booster	27 Elbow
5 Washer	11 Bracket	17 Nut	22 Check valve	28 Elbow (75°)
6 Reservoir	12 Lock clip	18 Lock washer	23 Sealing plug	29 Sealing plug

FIG 14 Brake servo unit components

9 Servo unit

The servo unit where fitted cannot be repaired and if defective must be renewed.

Checking servo unit:

Depress the brake pedal several times until all vacuum is exhausted from the unit, with the pedal depressed fully start the engine, the pedal will move further as vacuum takes effect if the servo unit is functioning correctly.

Malfunction of the unit can be caused by leaking vacuum line connections, a sticking check valve 22 (see **FIG 14**) or master cylinder defects. If attention to these does not correct the fault renew the unit.

Removing and refitting:

Remove the lockpin connecting the operating lever 14 to the pressure rod. Remove the screw, lockwasher and plain washer attaching the master cylinder to the luggage compartment floor plate. Drain the brake fluid carefully to avoid spillage. Disconnect the stoplight connections at the plugs 24. Disconnect the vacuum hose and brake lines. Unscrew the bolt securing the top of the strut to the unit and the securing nuts of the unit and lift away. If the unit 21 is to be renewed unscrew the nuts 17 and spring washers 18 and separate the master cylinder from the unit, discard the 'O' ring 20. Remove the nuts 8 and spring washers 9 and separate the base 11, remove the circlip 16 and lift the unit 21 away.

Reassemble and refit in the reverse order renewing the 'O' ring 20. Adjust the pressure rod and bleed the brakes (see **Section 7**).

Adjusting the pressure rod:

Pull the pedal back to the stop. Loosen the locknuts on the pressure rod and adjust the length of the rod so that the pin can enter the clevis and operating lever 14 without force with the operating lever just touching the pushrod of the servo unit without moving it and the pedal on the stop. Tighten the pressure rod locknuts.

Check the play in the unit by bleeding the brakes and with the engine stopped there should be at least 10mm (0.40in) pressure rod play at the pedal.

10 Fault diagnosis

(a) 'Spongy' pedal action

1 Leak in hydraulic system
2 Worn master cylinder
3 Leaking caliper cylinders
4 Air in the fluid
5 Insufficient fluid in reservoir

(b) Excessive pedal movement

1 Check 1, 4 and 5 in (a)
2 Excessive pad wear
3 Too much free movement in pedal pushrod
4 Defective cups and valve in master cylinder
5 Wheel bearings slack
6 Disc or caliper mountings loose
7 Excessive runout or thickness variation of discs

(c) Brakes grab or pull to one side

1 Check 5, 6 and 7 in (b)
2 Oily pads or mixed grades
3 Worn suspension or steering connections

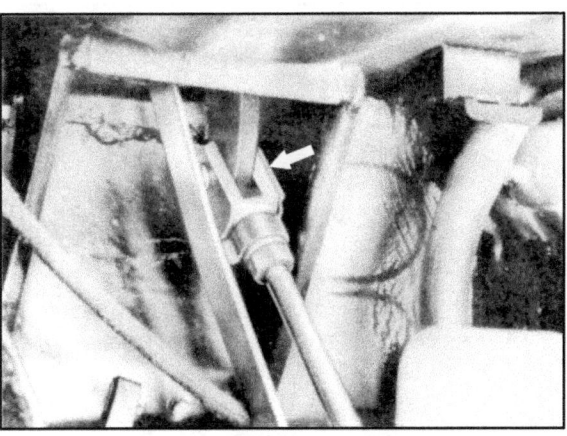

Spring clip pin (arrow) attaching the control rod to the operating lever (see text)

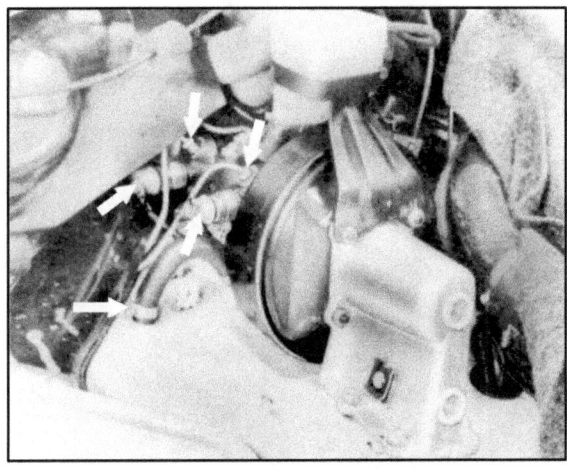

Clamp on vacuum hose (lower arrow), electrical connections (center arrows) and brake lines (upper arrows) must be disconnected from the master cylinder for removal (see text)

4 Uneven tyre pressures
5 Dirt in pad slots, dust covers defective
6 20° piston step wrongly set
7 Seized piston in caliper cylinder

(d) Pedal must be pumped to get braking

1 Check 2, 4 and 5 in (a) and 4 in (b)

(e) Brakes get hot when not used

1 Check 4 and 5 in (b); 5 and 7 in (c)
2 Reservoir supply port in master cylinder blocked by piston cup
3 Insufficient free play in pedal pushrod
4 Rubber cups swollen due to wrong fluid
5 Handbrake adjusted too tightly, cables seized (rear)
6 Handbrake shoe return springs weak or broken (rear)

(f) Frequent topping up of fluid required

1 Check pipes, connections and cylinders for leaks

(g) Only front brakes or only rear brakes operate

1 One section of reservoir empty
2 One section of master cylinder defective
3 Broken pipe in front or in rear system

NOTES

CHAPTER 12 - ELECTRICAL

1 Description
2 The battery
3 Fuses and relays
4 The starter motor
5 The alternator
6 The alternator regulator
7 Headlights
8 Safety belt warning system
9 Flasher unit
10 Windscreen wiper and washer
11 Horns
12 Instruments
13 Steering column switches
14 Automatic speed control
15 Clutch pedal switch
16 Automatic heater control
17 Automatic antenna
18 Alarm
19 Fault diagnosis

1 Description

All models covered by this manual have 12-volt electrical systems in which the negative battery terminal is earthed. A selection of wiring diagrams is included in the **Technical Data** section of the **Appendix**. Depending upon the model, a single 12-volt battery or a pair of 12-volt batteries (connected in parallel) may be fitted.

The starter motor is mounted on the transmission casing. It incorporates positive engagement of the drive pinion. The starter motor switch is combined with the ignition switch and operates a solenoid which is integral with the starter motor assembly.

The generator is housed in the hub of the engine air cooling fan which is keyed to the generator shaft. The generator and cooling fan are consequently driven by the same belt. The generator is a three-phase AC machine and incorporates a transistorised rectifier. An electronic regulator is incorporated into the charging circuit.

Headlamps may have renewable bulbs or sealed-beam or halogen lights. Flasher and reversing lights are fitted. Instrument lights may be dimmed by turning the switch knob. The revolution indicator is transistorised and is driven by electrical impulses from the ignition system. Electrical sender units operate the fuel, oil temperature and, in relevant models, the oil pressure gauges.

Although instructions for the servicing of certain of the electrical equipment units are given in this chapter, it must be accepted that it is not sensible to attempt repairs to units which are seriously defective, electrically or mechanically. Such defective equipment should be replaced by new or exchange replacement units. The testing of certain equipment requires specialist equipment, facilities and services.

2 The battery

Depending upon the model, a single 12-volt battery or two 12-volt batteries (connected in parallel) may be fitted. The system is negative earth. **Do not, under any circumstances, reverse the battery terminal connections.** The connections must be tight on the battery posts and a light coating of non-metallic grease should be applied to the terminal clamps and posts to retard corrosion and oxidisation. If the connections are corroded, remove the clamps and wash them in bicarbonate of soda. Dry them thoroughly, apply non-metallic grease and refit the terminal clamps tightly.

Keep the fluid in each cell topped up to about 10mm (0.4in) above the plates and separators by adding distilled water. **Never use undiluted acid. If it is necessary to prepare a new solution of electrolyte due to spillage or loss, add the acid to the distilled water. It is highly dangerous to add water to acid.**

If the charge state of a battery is suspect, test the electrolyte with a hydrometer. The indications from the specific gravity readings given by the hydrometer are approximately as follows:

	Specific gravity
Cells fully charged	1.240 to 1.260
Cells half charged	1.170 to 1.190
Cells discharged	1.100 to 1.120

The above readings will apply when the battery temperature is about 20°C (68°F). For the same cell condition, specific gravity will increase when the electrolyte temperature is more than 20°C and vice versa. Add 0.002 for every 3°C (5°F) above 20°C and subtract 0.002 for every 3°C (below 20°C).

If the state of a battery is low, take the car for a long daylight run or put the discharged battery on charge at 4 to 5amps. If this does not correct the battery state, have the individual cells voltage tested to ascertain whether the battery should be replaced by a new one. If a battery is to be put on charge without dismounting it from the vehicle, **disconnect both leads from the battery.**

If a battery is to stand for a long period, give it a freshening-up charge every month. If it is left discharged, it will deteriorate and be ruined.

From 1974 through 1987, all models have a single battery mounted in the front left of the luggage compartment.

Standard batteries have a capacity of 66 Ah but an 88 Ah battery is optional.

1981 and later models are equipped with the 88 Ah battery. To service the battery, special tools are used to tighten or loosen the battery hold down bolts.

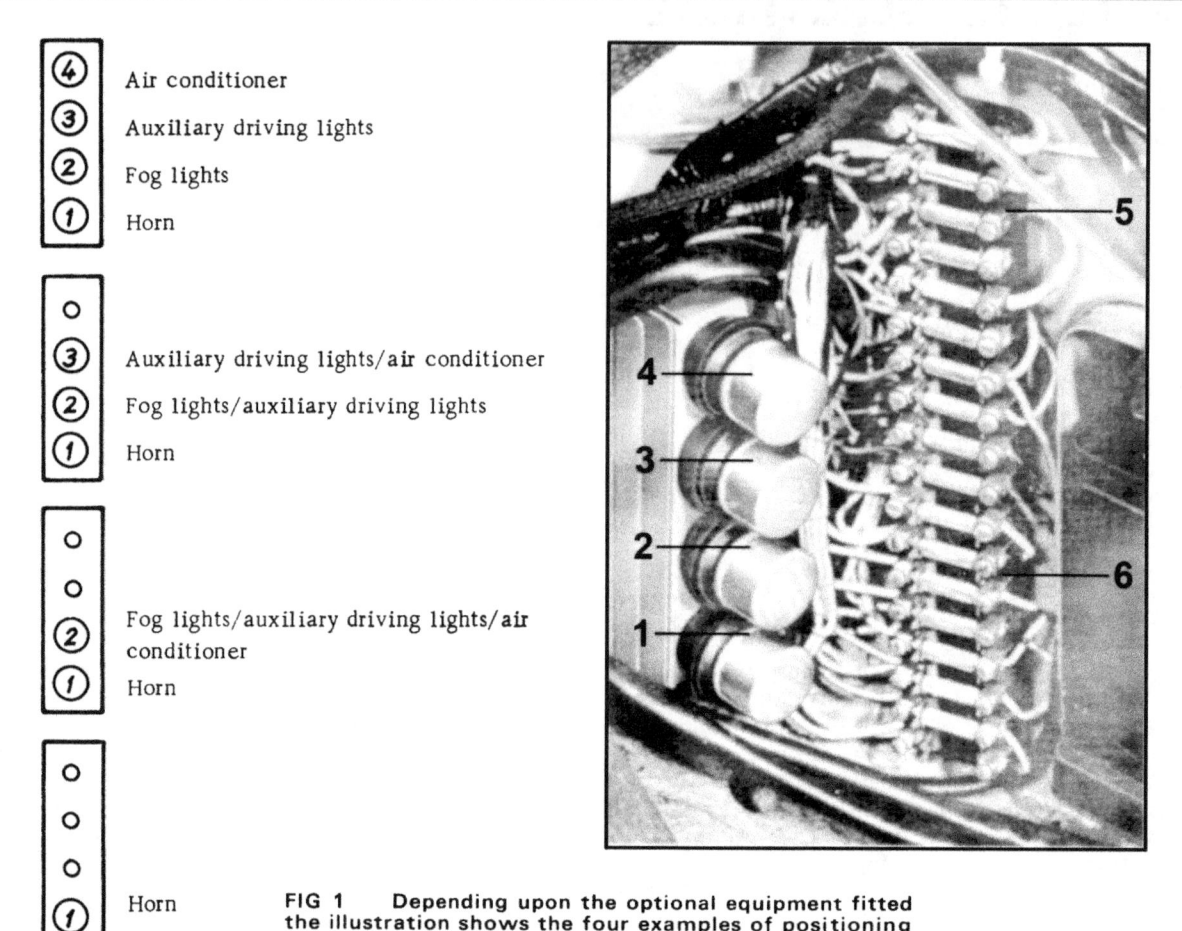

FIG 1 Depending upon the optional equipment fitted the illustration shows the four examples of positioning standard relays (5 Fuse box 1, 6 Fuse box 2)

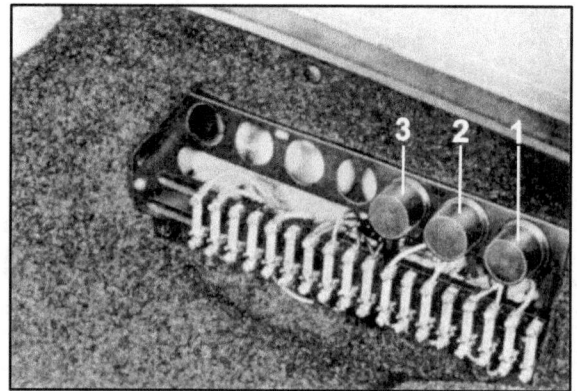

1 Air conditioning 2 Fog lights 3 Horn

FIG 2 Fuses and relays (later models)

3 Fuses and relays

The main fuse box(es) are located in the lefthand side of the luggage compartment and it will be noted from **FIGS 1** and **2** that their configuration is not identical in all models. On relevant models a further three fuse positions are located in the engine compartment as shown in **FIG 3**.

Depending upon the model and the equipment installed, relays are located in both the luggage compartment (see **FIGS 1** and **2**) and in the engine compartment (see **FIGS 3**, **4** and **5**).

Depending upon the model, the special equipment fitted and the optional extra equipment installed, certain fuse and relay positions may not be in use. On earlier models fuses are identified in the fuse box cover(s). On later models they are identifiable by number (No 1 is the foremost) in the relevant wiring diagram.

Never fit a replacement fuse of greater capacity than that originally fitted since, by doing so, the protection of the relevant circuit may be jeopardised. If a fuse blows repeatedly, trace the reason for it doing so without delay. A failed relay should be replaced by one of the same type.

If additional electrical equipment is being installed, it should be wired up through a fuse and, if relevant, an appropriate relay fitted to the relevant position(s). Do not connect such equipment directly across the battery posts.

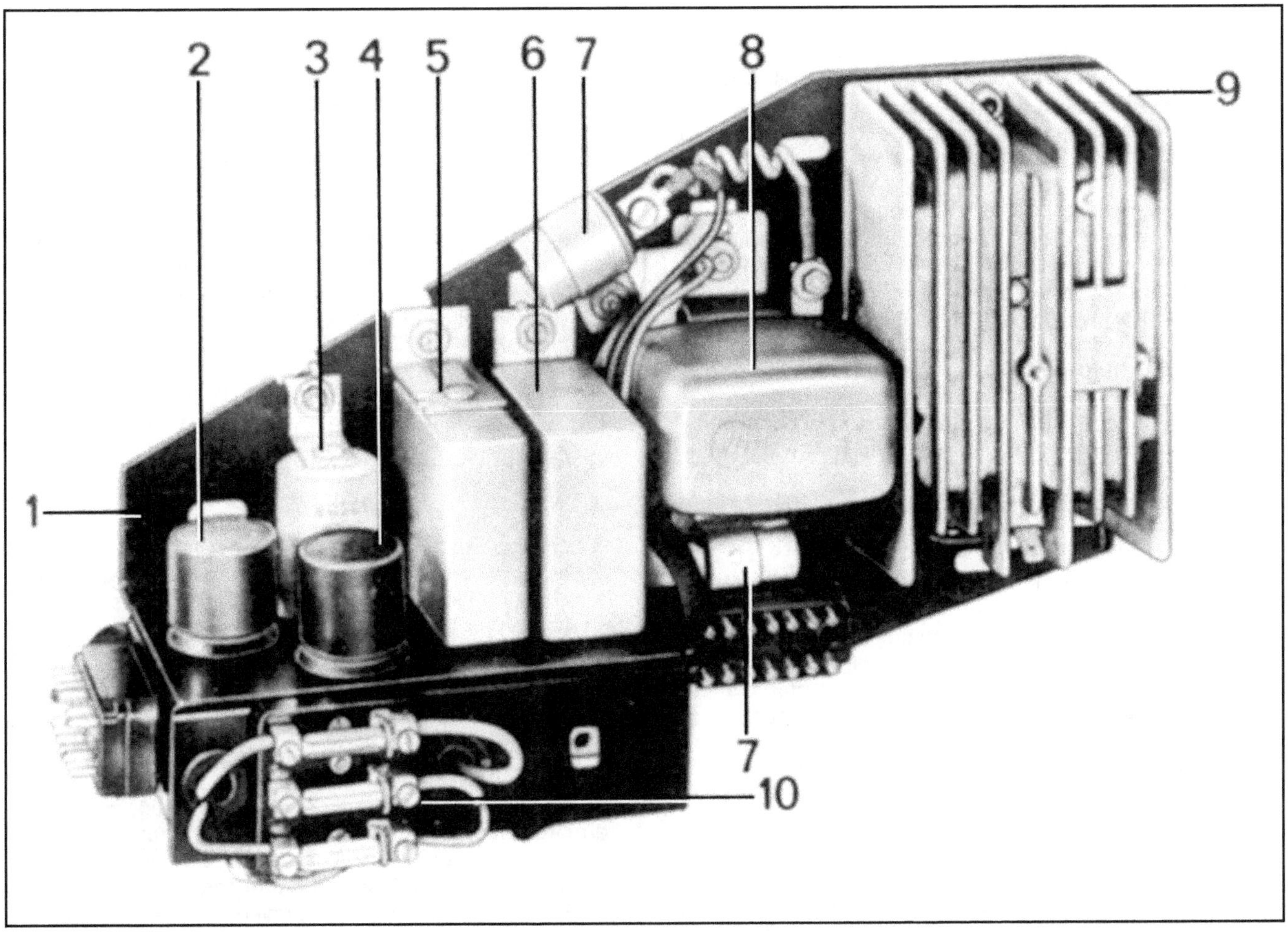

1 Console
2 Relay switch for single stage rear window defroster (not used with two stage)
3 Rev/min sensor
4 Relay switch for start enrichment (not used in carburetter engines)
5 Rev/min transducer (not used in carburetter engines except 911T USA model)
6 Control relay for two stage rear window defroster (not used for single stage)
7 Radio noise suppression
8 Regulator
9 Ignition trigger unit
10 Fuse box 3

FIG 3   Engine compartment console

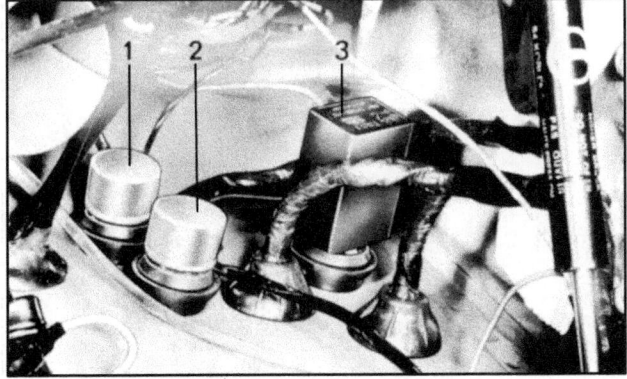

1 Headlight dimmer switch relay
2 Windshield defogger relay
  (not valid for USA)
3 Turn signal relay

FIG 4   Relays (earlier models)

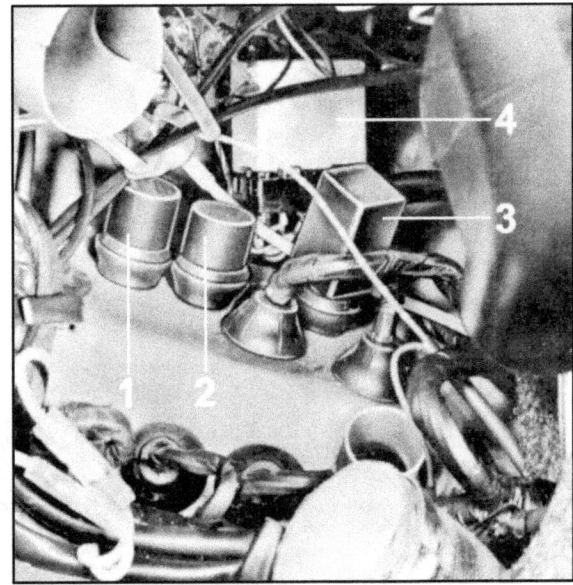

1 Optional equipment
2 Heated windshield
3 Emergency flasher
4 Safety belt warning system (logic relay)

FIG 5   Relays (later models)

4 The starter motor

Components of the starter motor are shown in **FIG 6**. When the ignition key is turned to the start position, the solenoid is energised, the plunger is drawn in and the actuating lever starts to move the actuating sleeve. When the associated locking ring has moved about 2mm or 3mm ($\frac{1}{8}$in) the balls round a groove in the shaft are freed and allow the pinion to move into engagement with the flywheel ring gear. The solenoid plunger has simultaneously closed a switch which passes current to the motor. If the engine fires, it may run up to a speed which would drive the motor by way of the pinion. To prevent this, a one-way clutch is provided. When the switch is released, the solenoid return spring starts to retract the pinion, and pressure from the engagement spring pushes the locking ring over the balls and a braking disc comes into action to slow down the armature. The one-way clutch consists of five spring-loaded rollers confined in cam-shaped recesses.

Tests for a starter which does not operate:

Check the condition of the battery and its connections. If these are in order, switch on the lights and operate the starter switch. Current is reaching the starter if the lights go dim. If the lights do not go dim, check with a voltmeter or test light if there is voltage at the solenoid when the switch is operated. If there is, suspect a defective solenoid. If there is not, suspect the ignition switch or the wiring continuity. If these are in order, remove the starter motor for further investigation and to check the brush gear.

Removal:

Disconnect the battery earth cables. Detach the cables from the starter and the solenoid. Remove the flange bolts and disconnect the starter.

Removing and refitting the solenoid:

Remove the connector from the terminal next to the motor body. Remove the solenoid from the drive housing. Pull the pinion out a little and withdraw the solenoid, while disconnecting the plunger from the actuating lever. Solenoids are not repairable and a defective one must be renewed.

Install the solenoid in reverse order. Hold the cable terminals when tightening the nuts so that the studs cannot turn. If the solenoid is new, adjust the plunger so that the distance from the centre of the hole in the clevis to the mounting flange is 32.4mm ± 10mm (1.276in ± 0.004in) when the plunger is in position.

When the solenoid is energised, the travel of the plunger must be 10mm ± 0.2mm (0.394in ± 0.008in), of which 3mm (0.118in) is engagement reserve.

Checking the brushes and the commutator:

1. Remove the cover from the end of the starter opposite to the pinion.
2. Lift the brush springs and pull the brushes out of the holders by their flexible leads. If the length of a brush allows a lead to touch the holder, then it is too worn for further use and must be renewed.
3. Clean the commutator with a stick wrapped in a petrol-soaked cloth. Keep dirt and excess petrol from the end bearing.

Check brush springs for tension. Renew brushes if worn, oil-soaked or if their leads are loose or frayed. Always renew brushes in sets.

If a commutator is badly scored or burned, remove the armature and skim the commutator in a lathe. Use fine sandpaper for polishing. Do not use emerycloth. Undercut as explained in 'Inspection and Testing'.

When refitting the brushes, make sure that they are free in their holders and check that the flexible leads are out of the way.

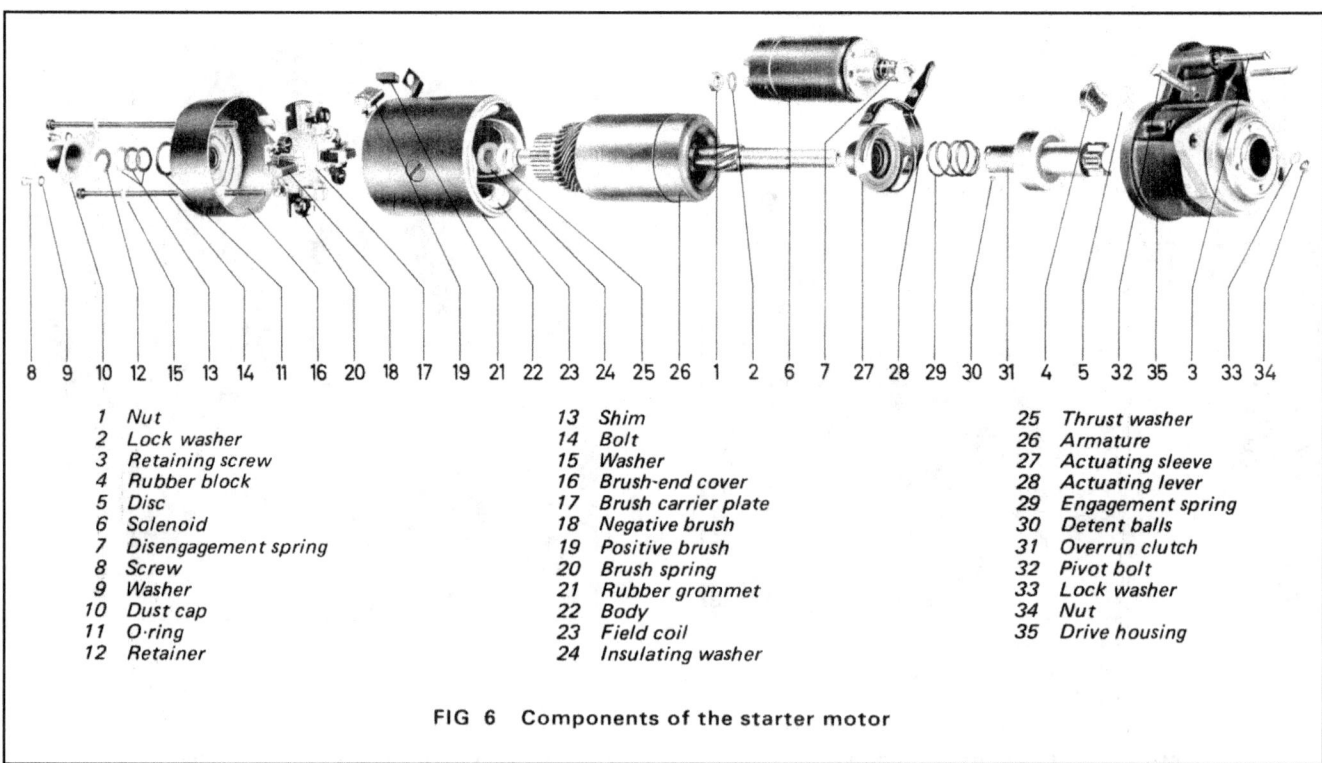

1 Nut	13 Shim	25 Thrust washer
2 Lock washer	14 Bolt	26 Armature
3 Retaining screw	15 Washer	27 Actuating sleeve
4 Rubber block	16 Brush-end cover	28 Actuating lever
5 Disc	17 Brush carrier plate	29 Engagement spring
6 Solenoid	18 Negative brush	30 Detent balls
7 Disengagement spring	19 Positive brush	31 Overrun clutch
8 Screw	20 Brush spring	32 Pivot bolt
9 Washer	21 Rubber grommet	33 Lock washer
10 Dust cap	22 Body	34 Nut
11 O-ring	23 Field coil	35 Drive housing
12 Retainer	24 Insulating washer	

FIG 6 Components of the starter motor

Dismantling the starter:

1 Remove the dust cap from the end opposite to the pinion. Remove the 'O' rings, the lock ring on the shaft and the spacers.

2 Detach the cable from the inner terminal of the solenoid. Remove the solenoid mounting screws and withdraw the solenoid while unhooking the plunger from the actuating lever.

3 Remove the two long through bolts and the end cover or armature support. Withdraw the brushes, making a note of their locations. Positive brushes have leads which are soldered to the field windings, negative brush leads going to the brush holders.

4 Remove the brush carrier plate and the metal and insulating washers from the armature shaft. Pull the complete field frame off the drive housing, taking care of the rubber seal and the metal plate.

5 Remove the actuating lever pivot bolt and withdraw the armature and lever. Hold the armature in a vice with soft jaws. Refer to **FIG 6** and press actuating sleeve 27 towards the overrun clutch 31 and catch the detent balls 30 as they fall out. Release the sleeve and spring 29.

6 When cleaning the parts, do not put the armature or the overrun clutch in solvent and keep the solvent away from the self-lubricating bearing bushes. Normally, during a major overhaul, it is advisable to renew these bushes. Clean off all carbon dust from the armature and from the brush carrier.

Inspecting and testing:

Check the action of the actuating lever, sleeve and clutch. Renew parts if the sleeve and lever do not move freely, or if the lever is bent. If necessary renew the brake disc. Renew the pinion and shaft if the teeth are worn.

Check the field windings for signs of excessive heat or melted solder. They must not protrude beyond the pole-pieces. Check for continuity and shorting to earth, using a 40-volt AC test lamp.

Test the armature and brush carrier plate for short to earth in the same way. The insulated brush holders must not be shorting to earth. Apply test prods to the cylindrical body of the armature and to each commutator segment in turn. The test lamp should not light.

Check the condition of the commutator. Minimum diameter is 33.5mm (1.319in) and maximum runout should not exceed 0.05mm (0.002in). Clean out excessive wear and pitting by skimming the commutator in a lathe, providing the diameter is not reduced below the stipulated figure. The mica insulation between the commutator segments must be undercut to a depth of about 0.8mm (0.03in) using a piece of fine hacksaw blade ground on the sides to the correct width. Take care not to damage the segments or the soldered joints.

Brushes which are worn, broken or which have defective leads must be renewed. Always fit a complete set. Unsolder the leads one at a time to avoid confusion, and when soldering the new leads into place do not let the solder run too far up the flexible part.

Armature shaft bushes are of the self-lubricating type, so make sure that the new bushes are well impregnated with oil. At the pinion end, drill out the rivets to release the seal and press out the bush. Press a new bush into place with a shouldered mandrel having a pilot the same diameter as the shaft until it is flush on the inside. Do not ream this type of bush after fitting. Centre a new seal with a suitable mandrel and secure the retainer with small screws, nuts and spring washers. Peening the screw ends to prevent loss of the nuts.

Reassembling:

Hold the armature in the vice and stick balls into the locking ring with grease such as Bosch Ft 2v3. Fit the actuating sleeve, brake disc and spring to overrun clutch and locking ring and push the assembly onto the shaft until balls engage the groove in the shaft. Check that the pinion and the clutch are properly seated and that the mechanical engagement parts move freely when released. Grease all parts.

Fit the actuating lever to the sleeve and push the armature and lever into the drive housing. Grease and fit the lever pivot stud. Fit the rubber seal between the solenoid and the field recesses so that its tabs seat correctly in the cutout provided. Push the field frame over the armature. Fit greased metal and insulating washers to the shaft. Fit the brush carrier plate, aligning the notch which prevents turning, in the correct position.

Seat the rubber grommet for the field lead correctly and refit the end cover. Earthing points between the brush carrier plate and the cover and between the cover and the field housing must be clean and bright. Secure the two through bolts. Fit the spacer washers and locking ring to the end of the shaft and check that the end float lies between 0.1 and 0.3mm (0.004 and 0.012in). Secure the flange of the end cap. Fit the solenoid and connect the field lead to the inner terminal.

Replacement starter motors:

Starter motor types are not identical on all models. If a new or exchange replacement starter is required, ensure that it is of the same type as that originally fitted.

5 The alternator

The alternator may be either of Bosch or of Motorola manufacture. The alternator generating capacity is not identical for all vehicle models and, if a replacement alternator is required, ensure that the new or exchange replacement machine is of the same type as that originally fitted.

The servicing of Bosch and Motorola alternators is covered separately in this section.

Servicing a Bosch alternator:

Before carrying out alternator tests, it is important to understand that it must not be run without connection to the battery, neither must the cables be removed during a running test. Be careful not to reverse the battery connections. Entrust major repairs to a Bosch service station.

Testing the system:

The control lamp should light up with the ignition switched on. If it does not, the bulb may be broken or a wire disconnected. If the lamp stays on with the ignition switched off, it indicates a defective rectifier. Disconnect the battery at once to prevent damage to the alternator and battery.

Start the engine. If the control lamp does not go out with increasing engine speed or lights up at certain speeds, the rectifier is defective.

For a quick test with the alternator installed, run the engine at a steady 3000rev/min. Switch on lamps and accessories to bring the load to 28 to 30amp. The voltage between terminals B+ and D− should lie between 13.5 and 14.5 volts.

Removing the alternator:

Remove the air cleaner. Release the clips from the upper shroud. Remove the alternator pulley nut and take off the belt (see **Chapter 4, Section 1**). Release the blower housing strap, pull the assembly rearwards and identify and detach the wires.

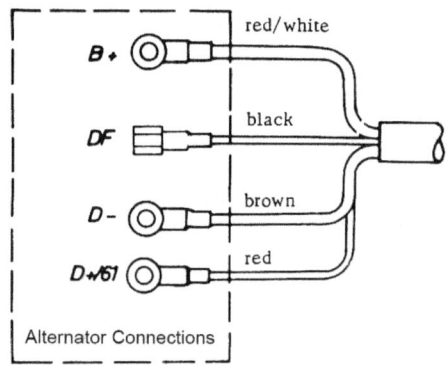

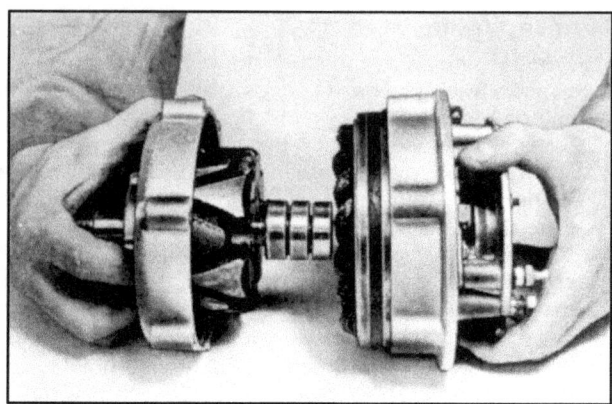

FIG 8 Separating rotor and end frame from stator housing (Bosch alternator)

Using the same test voltage, check the rotor coils for earthing, putting one probe on a slip ring and the other on the pole piece. Connect an ohmmeter across the slip rings to check the rotor coil resistance. It must be 4 ohm + 10 per cent. If the slip rings are worn and pitted, skim them in a lathe, taking off the minimum amount of metal. When finished, check that runout does not exceed 0.03mm (0.001in). Minimum slip ring diameter is 31.5mm (1.24in) and maximum vertical runout of the rotor is 0.05mm (0.002in).

Bearings:

Renew bearings which are rough when spun without lubricant. In any case, renew bearings which have seen 60,000 miles (100,000km) of service. Adequately support the end frame and rotor when pressing bearings into place. Coat one side of the bearing with Bosche FT1V33 grease and fit to the end frame with the closed side entering first. Fit the retaining plate.

FIG 7 Removing brush plate and brushes (Bosch)

Cleaning:

Parts must not be soaked in solvents. Momentary exposure to solvents is permissible for cleaning purposes. Always relubricate the bearings after cleaning.

Reassembling:

Do this in the reverse order of dismantling. Check that the rotor turns freely after fitting the brushes.

Installation:

Fit the alternator to the blower housing with the marks aligned. Seat the blower housing on the dowel in the crankcase after connecting the wires to their identified connections. After fitting the pulley and belt, tighten the retaining nut to 4kgm (29lb ft).

Brushes:

Removing the brush plate is shown in **FIG 7**, but first check the brushes for freedom in their housings. Hook up the springs and check the brush length if no further dismantling is required. The minimum length is 14mm (0.55in). Unsolder the brush leads to renew brushes. Check that the brushes slide freely, rubbing the sides on a smooth file if necessary. Resolder the leads with resin-cored solder, taking care not to let solder run up the stranded, flexible connector.

Rotor:

To continue dismantling, remove the brush plate complete. Remove the six long screws and part the rotor from the stator housing (see **FIG 8**). The rotor may now be pressed out of the end frame for attention to the bearings and slip rings. It is not advisable to attempt repairs to the rectifier diodes which are mounted on plates at the same end as the brushes.

If the stationary windings are removed from the housing the coils may be tested. Use 40VAC and a pair of probes and check for continuity and earthing. Also check for resistance using an ohmmeter. The correct resistance is 0.26 ohm + 10 per cent.

Servicing a Motorola alternator:

The component parts are shown in **FIG 9**. An alternator is not self-exciting so that the necessary field current has to reach the unit by way of the generator control lamp 8 (see **FIG 10**) and the voltage regulator. For this reason it is important that the lamp is not burned out or of the wrong wattage. The field current is only about 2amp and is conducted to the field coils by brushes 4 and slip rings 3. An isolation diode 7 protects the alternator against overloading and also allows current to flow to the control lamp. The rectifier consists of three positive and three negative diodes 12. These pass current from the alternator to the battery or load but not in the reverse direction, so that there is no need for a cut-out.

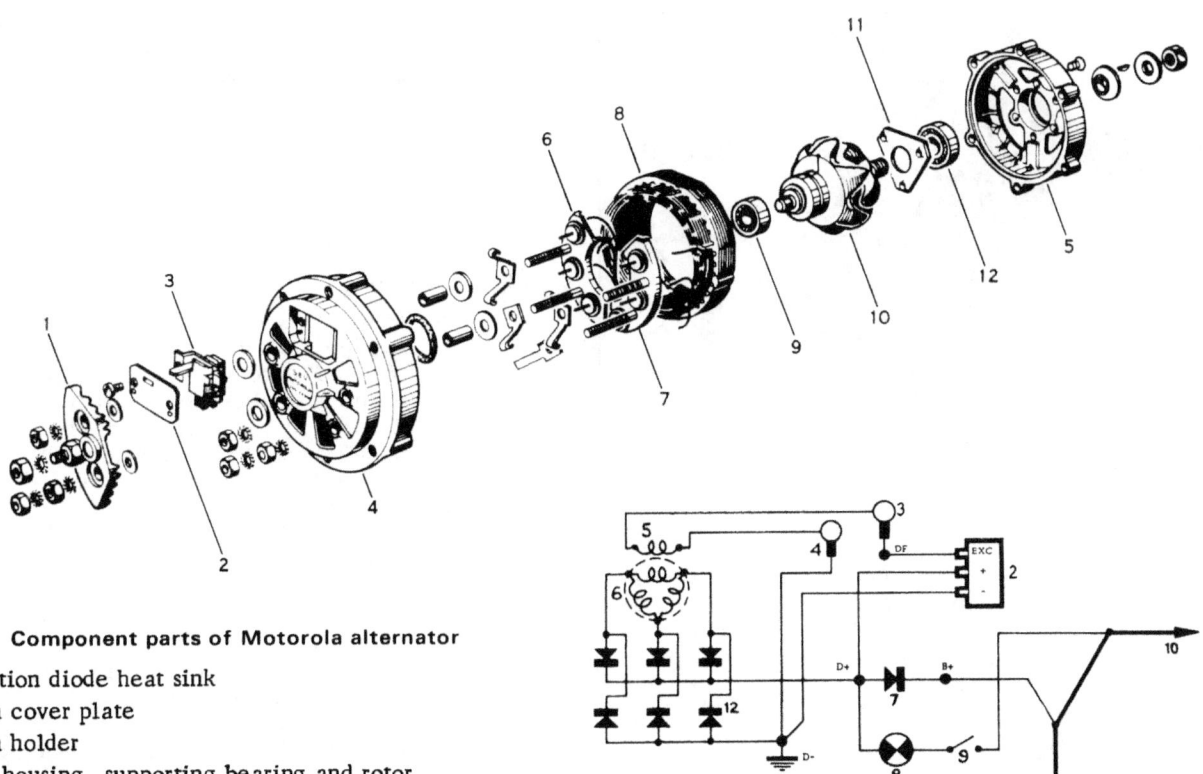

FIG 9 Component parts of Motorola alternator

1 Isolation diode heat sink
2 Brush cover plate
3 Brush holder
4 Rear housing, supporting bearing and rotor
5 Front housing, supporting bearing and rotor
6 Positive diode heat sink
7 Negative diode heat sink
8 Stator
9 Ball bearing
10 Rotor
11 Bearing cover plate
12 Ball bearing

FIG 10 Circuit diagram of Motorola alternator, regulator and battery

1 Battery
2 Regulator
3 Slip rings
4 Brushes
5 Rotor
6 Stator
7 Isolation diode
8 Generator control lamp
9 Ignition/starter switch
10 To accessories
11 To starter
12 Diodes

Precautions:

Observe the following:

1 Do not earth the field exciter terminals DF of the alternator, regulator or the connecting wire.
2 Do not wrongly connect the voltage regulator and do not disconnect the regulator or the battery when the regulator is running.
3 Disconnect the battery before removing the alternator.
4 The voltage regulator must always be connected to the alternator earth.
5 For alternator tests the battery must be in good condition and fully charged. When running the alternator in the car, the battery must always be connected.
6 Disconnect the battery before carrying out any arc welding on the car.
7 Heat damaged diodes. Use pliers as heat sink when unsoldering or soldering. Wrong connections will cause damage to diodes.
8 Detach the battery leads when charging the battery in the car.

Maintenance:

Apart from checking the belt tension (see **Chapter 4, Section 1**) no routine maintenance of the alternator or the voltage regulator is required. Bearings are lubricated for life.

Testing an alternator:

Connect the voltage regulator leads so that blue and red go to D+, black goes to DF and brown goes to D−. The location of the regulator is shown at 8 in **FIG 3**.

For a quick test with the alternator installed, run the engine at 2500 ± 150rev/min with lamps and accessories switched on to give a load of 28 to 30amp. The voltage between terminals B+ and D− must be between 13.4 and 14.6 volts.

Removing an alternator:

Do this as described earlier for the Bosch alternator.

Checking the brush gear:

Remove the brush holder (two bolts, see **FIG 11**). Use an ohmmeter and probes to check for continuity, the insulated brush with the DF terminal and the earthed brush with the holder. Resistance should be nil. Resistance should be infinitely high when the probes are touching the brushes only.

FIG 11 Removing brush holder on Motorola alternator

Checking the rotor:

Test for shorting to D− by connecting one ohmmeter probe to D− and the other to one of the slip rings. Resistance should be infinite.

Test the rotor coil for continuity by connecting one ohmmeter probe to each slip ring. The circuit resistance should be 4.5 to 6.5ohm. Renew the rotor is faulty.

Testing the isolation diode:

First test the heat sink for earthing by connecting one ohmmeter probe to D+ 61 and the other D− on the alternator and then in reverse. Resistance should be infinite in one direction and less than 50 ohm in the other. If readings differ from these, check the heat sink insulation behind the housing.

Test the diode by connecting one ohmmeter probe to terminal B+ and the other D+ 61 and then reversing them. Resistance should be infinite in one direction and less than 50 ohm in the other.

Testing the rectifier diodes:

Positive diodes are marked red and negative diodes black. Test negative diodes by connecting an ohmmeter across the diode terminal and D−. Reverse the connections and note the result, which should be the same as that described for the isolation diode. For positive diodes connect the ohmmeter to D+ 61 and the diode and then reverse the connections to get the same results as for the isolation diode.

Testing the stator coil:

This is done by connecting one ohmmeter probe to one end of a coil and the other to the stator frame. Resistance must be infinite. Check all coil ends and renew the stator if any test shows a lower resistance.

Dismantling the alternator:

1 Remove the brush assembly (see **FIG 11**). Remove the isolation diode assembly 1 in **FIG 9** (two outer nuts).
2 Remove the through bolts and separate the front housing 5 and rotor 10 from the stator and rear housing 4.
3 The rotor may be pressed out of the front housing and the ballbearing pulled off the rear end. To remove the bearing in the front cover, remove the bearing cover (three screws) and press out the bearing.

4 Release the diode assembly 6 and 7 from the rear housing and withdraw together with the stator 8. Mark the negative and positive diode leads if the diodes are to be removed. It would be best to leave servicing the diodes to a service station, but the method is as follows:
5 Hold each lead with a pair of pliers on the diode side so that heat cannot travel into the diode, and quickly unsolder the connections.

Reassembling:

1 If the stator leads were unsoldered from diodes, pull them through the clips so that they lie correctly and will not need bending after soldering. Make sure connections are correct, noting that positive diodes are marked red and negative diodes black.
2 Hold diode leads with pliers which will act as a heat sink. **Use a hot iron and solder the leads as quickly as possible.**
3 Fit the stator and diode assemblies into the housing after placing an insulating washer and sleeve on each fixing stud of the positive diode assembly.
4 After fitting the stator and diode assemblies, put insulating washers on the two positive diode studs and secure both assemblies with nuts. Make sure the stator leads are properly arranged.
5 Press the rotor into front bearing in housing. Press the other ballbearing into place up to the stop on the rear end of the rotor shaft.
6 Make sure that the bore in the rear housing is clear and that the 'O' ring is in good condition. Join the two housings together and tighten the six bolts evenly and diagonally.
7 Secure the isolation diode assembly in position and attach the brush assembly. Install the alternator as described earlier for the Bosch alternator.

6 The alternator regulator

The voltage regulator is mounted as shown at 8 in **FIG 3**. It is a single unit controlling the field circuit of the alternator and there is no current regulator or cut-out. As there is no provision for servicing, it is important to consult a service station if the regulator gives trouble. A defective unit should be replaced by one of the same type.

Great care must be taken to ensure that the connections to the regulator are correctly fitted. The blue and red leads go to D+, the black lead to DF and the brown lead to D−.

Symptoms of regulator trouble may be no charge, or too low or too high an output from the alternator.

7 Headlights

The headlamp rims are secured by a screw at the lowest point indicated at c in **FIG 12**. Whatever the type of light unit fitted, avoid touching the reflecting surface or the light unit when working on a headlight or renewing a light unit.

Alignment:

Professional facilities are required for a complete and accurate alignment of the main and dipped beams but if a temporarily acceptable setting has to be carried out by an owner, the procedure is as follows:

Refer to **FIG 13**. Select a piece of level ground and mount a board as shown, distance 'd' being about 5m

(16.5ft). The tyres must be properly inflated and the car bounced to normalise the suspension. The board must be central on the car axis.

Mark the height of the headlamp centres at 'b'. Mark a line 'c' on the board at 1 per cent of the distance 'd'. If 5m (16.5ft), 'c' will be 50mm (2in). Mark the width between the headlamp centres (value 'a') on line 'c' centrally about the axis. Make a cross at the intersection.

Cover one headlamp while setting the other. First adjust horizontally to bring the point of the angle between the dark and light areas onto the cross on the board. Make horizontal adjustments by turning screw 'a' in **FIG 12**.

Adjust vertically by turning screw 'b' until the horizontal plane of the dark and bright areas lies on the line marked at 'c' (see **FIG 13**). After setting vertically, check the horizontal setting again.

8 Safety belt warning system

From the beginning of 1972 onwards, all vehicles exported to the USA are equipped with a safety belt warning system. The fitment is obligatory to conform with the federal laws on safety.

The system comprises, two inertia reel safety belts with automatic locking retractions; a control lamp with the inscription 'Fasten Seat Belt'; a built-in passenger seat contact switch; a new parking brake switch and a modified warning buzzer. The modified buzzer is a three-pole type which can be used, if necessary, to replace the existing two-pole type.

A switch is built into each safety belt buckle, it remains closed when the belts are not worn and provides an earth contact for terminal 'G' in the control lamp. The handbrake switch provides an earth connection to the buzzer terminal 50a when the handbrake lever is fully released. Terminal 86 is energised when the ignition is switched on. To avoid activating the system when there is no passenger in the front seat a two-pole connector is located under the seat which breaks the independent earth contact when the seat is unoccupied.

The control lamp lights up and a simultaneous warning from the buzzer will operate when:

1 The ignition is switched on.
2 The drive (and passenger) have not put on their seat belts.
3 The parking brake is not fully released.

From 1974 models, the circuits were modified and each seat had a contact in conjunction with a logic relay and integrated buzzer, but the system was completely modified in 1975 with a timer relay and built in buzzer, the passenger seat being divorced from the warning system.

European models from 1977 are equipped with a seat belt indicator lamp mounted in the centre of the instrument panel with the parking brake and brake failure warning lamps. It lights for 8sec after the ignition is switched on whether seat belts are fastened or not.

9 Flasher unit

This is located under the luggage compartment mat adjacent to the steering column. It is a push fit in a three-pronged connector. There is an indicator lamp to show when a flasher bulb has failed, a magnetic switch breaking the earth connection to the lamp. The flasher unit cannot be repaired and it must be renewed in the event of failure.

FIG 12 To set headlamp beam vertically, turn screw 'a' to right to lower and to left to raise it. Turn screw 'b' for horizontal setting, turning to right sets beam to left, turning to left sets beam to right. Screw 'c' secures rim

10 Windscreen wiper and washer

No procedures are prescribed for the repair or overhaul of the windscreen wiper motor or the washer pump. In the event of either of these units becoming unserviceable it should be removed and a new or an exchange replacement unit fitted.

Removing the wiper motor and linkage:

Pull the luggage compartment mat forward and remove the front ventilating case after releasing the clip and air duct. These are located just below the grille in front of the wiper blades. Pull off the five cables from the wiper motor. Remove the wiper arms and the rubber grommets, unscrew the large nuts to release the spindles and withdraw the motor and linkage downwards. The linkage joints are service-free.

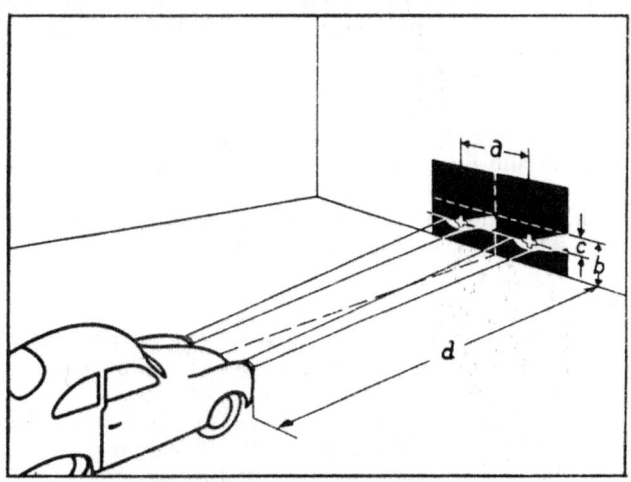

a, b, c and d See text

FIG 13 Headlamp beam setting

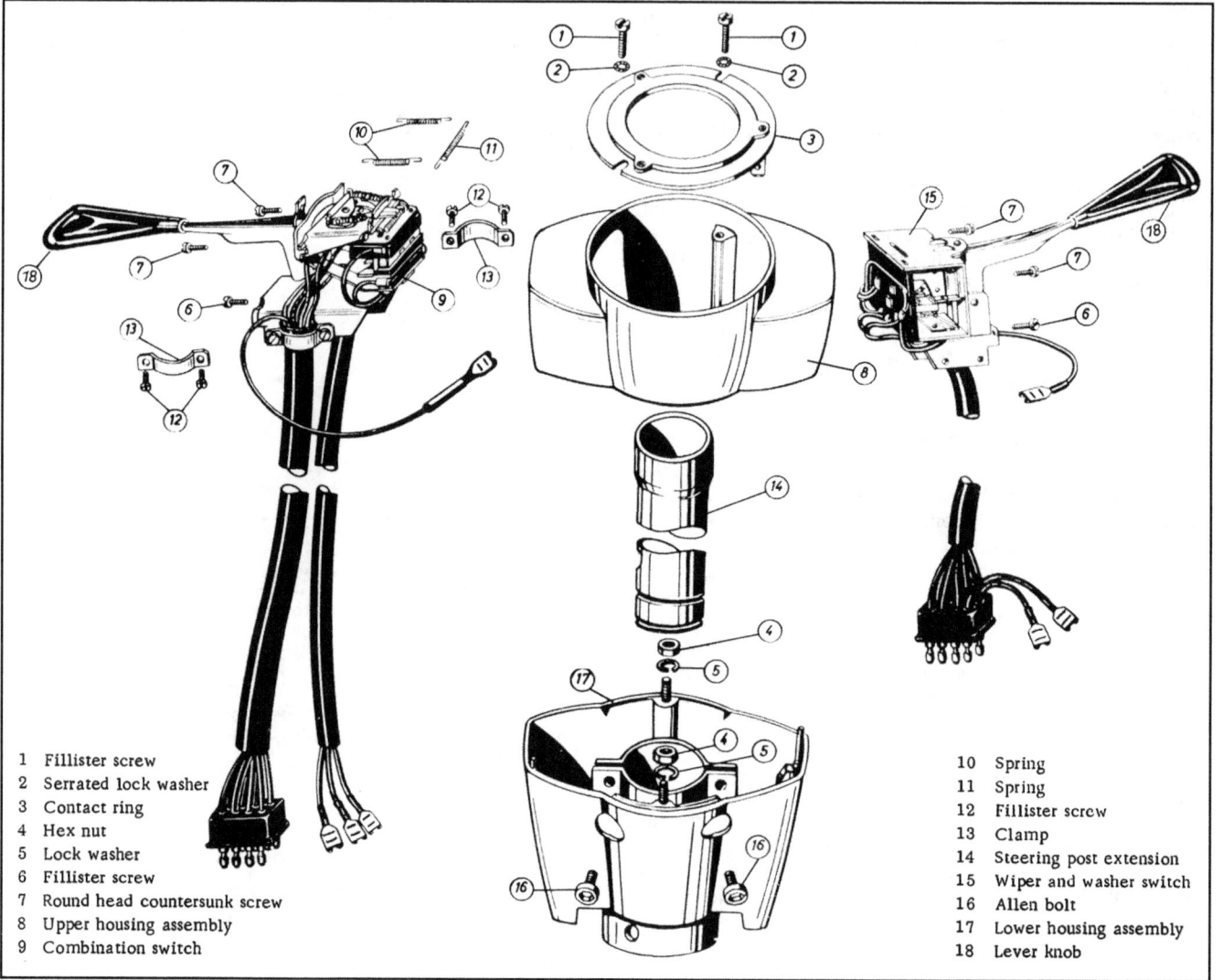

1 Fillister screw	10 Spring
2 Serrated lock washer	11 Spring
3 Contact ring	12 Fillister screw
4 Hex nut	13 Clamp
5 Lock washer	14 Steering post extension
6 Fillister screw	15 Wiper and washer switch
7 Round head countersunk screw	16 Allen bolt
8 Upper housing assembly	17 Lower housing assembly
9 Combination switch	18 Lever knob

FIG 14 Components of combination switches fitted to steering column

When refitting the assembly, make sure the wire connections are correctly made. Check that the linkage moves freely. Fit the wiper blades so that they wipe a symmetrical arc.

Windscreen washer:

To remove the pump, detach the wiring cables and suction and pressure hoses. Loosen the retaining straps and lift out the pump. Note, that in the case of later models, access for the removal of the washer reservoir requires removal of the lefthand front wheel.

11 Horns

No procedures are prescribed for the adjustment or repair of the horns and a defective unit should be removed and a new or an exchange replacement fitted.

Horns operate through a relay. The location of this relay is shown in **FIGS 1** and **2**. If the horns do not operate, check that the relevant fuse is intact, that the horn button is serviceable and that the relay is also serviceable before suspecting the horns themselves.

12 Instruments

Withdraw an instrument by prying against the back of its protruding ring. The leads, etc. may then be disconnected.

Speedometer, mechanical:

The speedometer is mechanically driven by a flexible cable from the transmission. If the speedometer becomes inoperative, check that the drive cable is intact and correctly coupled at both ends before suspecting the instrument itself. On California equipped cars with EGR the cable is coupled to the elapsed mileage odometer switch (see **Chapter 4**). An unserviceable speedometer should be passed to a specialist for repair.

Speedometer, electronic 1976-1987:

The sensor can be checked by removing the tunnel cover in front of the emergency seats and disconnecting the flat male plugs at the connector.

Connect a test buzzer to the wires leading to the rear.

Jack up the righthand rear wheel. The buzzer should sound eight times for each two revolutions of the wheel, or with a limited slip differential eight times for each revolution, if not change the sensor.

Turn on the ignition and touch the wires together quickly that lead to the front, there should be a deflection of the speedometer needle, if not and the connections to the speedometer are correctly fitted change the speedometer.

Speedometer sensor

Disconnect the battery cable from the negative terminal of the battery.
Raise the rear of the vehicle and remove the right wheel.
Separate the holder from the sensor after removing the hex head screw.
Remove the sensor wires from the holders.
Pull the sensor out of the transmission housing.
Remove the cover from the tunnel in front of the rear seats.
Unplug the flat male electrical connector in the tunnel.
Pull the sensor wire out of the tunnel from the rear.
Installation is the reverse of removal.

Tachometer:

The tachometer is electronically operated and is wired into the ignition system. If the tachometer becomes inoperative, check the wiring continuity before having the instrument itself tested.

Level, pressure and temperature gauges:

These are electrically operated from fuel level, oil pressure and oil temperature transmitters. If a gauge becomes inoperative, check the relevant fuse. If this is intact, check the wiring continuity. If this is in order, have the transmitter checked or carry out a cross-check by substituting a transmitter which is known to be serviceable. If the gauge still does not record, remove it and fit a replacement.

Warning lights:

If, when the ignition is switched on but before the engine is started, a warning light fails to light up, check the bulb. If the bulb has not failed, check the wiring continuity, the fuse, the relevant switch (if applicable) or other reason for the warning light being inoperative.

13 Steering column switches

The steering wheel must be removed as described in **Chapter 10, Section 3** before the combination switch assembly can be dismounted. With the steering wheel removed, refer to **FIG 14**, identify and separate all the wiring connections. Remove the horn contact ring 3. Remove the nuts and pull the upper housing assembly 8 upwards, pushing the leads and connectors through the holes provided. Remove combination switch 9 (three screws).

Faulty switch units are best renewed as an assembly, but a broken flasher return spring may be renewed separately. Check all electrical contacts for firm seating and cleanliness. Refit the parts in the reverse of the dismantling order, making sure the connections are correctly made.

14 Automatic speed control

Engagement switch:

Disconnect the battery cable from the negative terminal of the battery.
Remove the steering wheel as described in Chapter 10.
Remove the steering column switch housing as described in Section 13.
On air conditioned models, loosen the duct on the driver's side of the vehicle.
Unplug the electrical connector to the engagement switch.
Remove the mounting screws and lift away the switch.
Installation is the reverse of removal.

Servo:

Remove the hose from between the blower motor and the air connection for the heater.
Disconnect the negative lead from the battery.
Unplug the electrical connectors from the solenoid and the servo.
Remove the small vacuum hose from the servo.
Unscrew the servo mounting bolts.

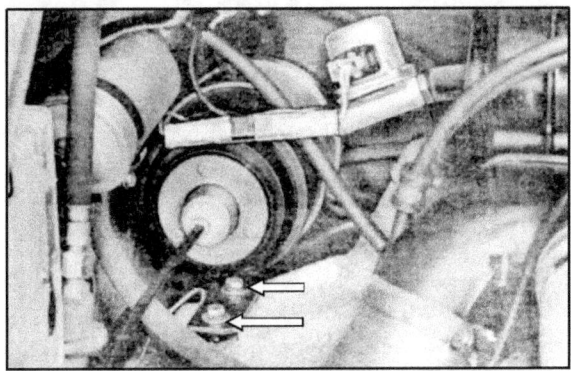

Speed control servo mounting screws (arrows)

Unscrew the cable holder from the throttle lever.
Pull the cable securing spring clip from the holder upward.
Separate the cable from the throttle and remove the servo and cable together.
Remove the screws securing the cap to the front of the servo.
Pull the cap away from the servo.
Squeeze the black clip with needle-nose pliers. Push in on the cable until it is detached, then remove the cable downward through the slot.
From inside the cap, squeeze the white clip and push it out of the cap.

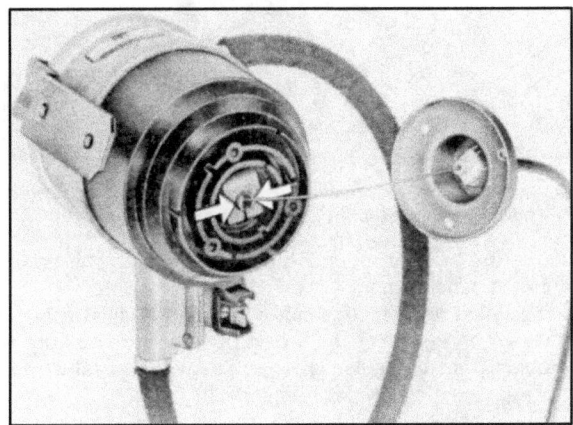

Squeeze the clip (arrows) together to release the cable from the servo

Installation is the reverse of removal. Be sure there is only a minimum amount of play between the holder and the nipple and that the cable is not frayed or bent.
Adjust the free play of the cable with the adjusting nut on the cable holder.

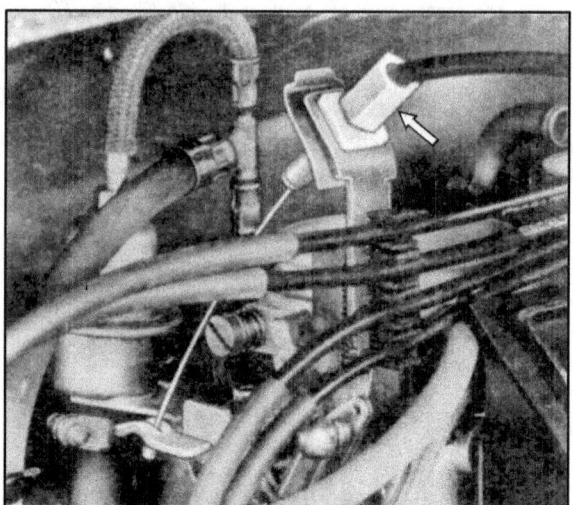

Turn the hex nut (arrow) to adjust the speed control cable

Note: Do not allow the cable to have any tension on it while the engine is off.

Brake light switch:

An extra wire is attached to the brake light switch on models with automatic speed control.

15 Clutch pedal switch

Remove the cover from the front of the tunnel.
Disconnect the negative lead on the battery.
Unplug the electrical connectors from the front of the switch in the tunnel.

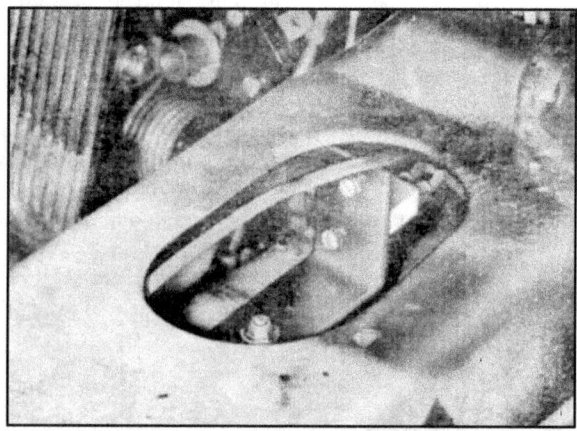

Disconnect the electrical plug on the back of the clutch pedal switch bracket before removing the switch

Remove the bracket mounting nuts and lift out the bracket and clutch pedal switch.
The mounting bracket uses slotted holes for adjustment purposes. When installing the bracket and switch be sure the switch will not be damaged when the clutch pedal is pulled on to adjust the clutch pedal free play.
With the bracket in position, plug the electrical leads onto the switch then tighten the mounting nuts securely.

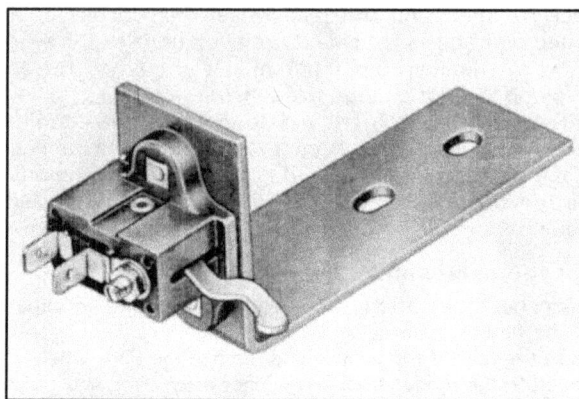

The clutch pedal switch can be adjusted by sliding the mounting bracket along the elongated holes

16 Automatic heater control

Control unit

Pry the covers from both sides of the control unit.
Unhook the connecting rod from the heater lever, by detaching the clamp at the ball socket, with a screwdriver.

The connecting rod to the heater lever is accessible through the opening in the side of the heater control unit

Unscrew the bolts securing the control unit to the tunnel.
Carefully lift the control unit until the electrical connections can all be unplugged.
Remove the rubber seal from the front of the control unit and slide the unit forward to remove it.
Installation is the reverse of removal.
Check the adjustment of the heater cables by turning the heater off with the ignition on. See that the heater flaps are completely closed. If they aren't closed, adjust the cables so there is no play.

Heat sensor

Loosen the control unit as previously described. Lift the unit until the front two-pole male connector can be unplugged.
Lift the carpet away from the tunnel until the cable is accessible up to the grommet in the kick panel.
Depress the terminal retainer and remove both wires from the male electrical connector.
Push the grommet out of the kick panel.
Remove the adapter from the heater flap housing, on the left side.
Pull the cable out.
Using the proper size drill bit, drill the rivets out of the adaptor.

Place the new heat sensor in position on the adaptor and rivet it into place.
With the heater flaps equally adjusted on both sides, install the adapter.
Attach the plug housing to the cable with the black wire on the tabbed side of the connector housing.
Route the cable back into position in the vehicle.
Glue the carpet to the tunnel and install the control unit.

Interior sensor

Remove the Phillips head screws securing the sensor.
Carefully pull the sensor out of position.

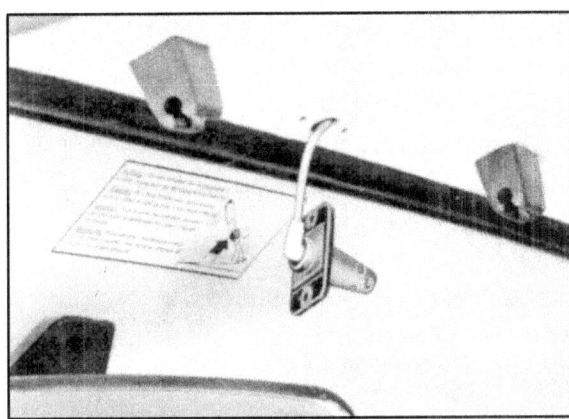

Lower the heat sensor carefully to gain access to the electrical lead

Unplug the angled electrical connector.
Installation is the reverse of removal.

Power supply to control unit

Pry off the right side panel of the control unit.
Unplug the three-pole connector.
Connect a test lamp between the red/white and the brown wires as well as between the gray/blue and brown wires.
Turn the parking lights and the ignition on.
The test lamps should illuminate in both cases.
If the test lamps illuminate but the heater controls don't work correctly, the control unit is defective.

17 Automatic antenna

Disconnect the negative lead from the battery.

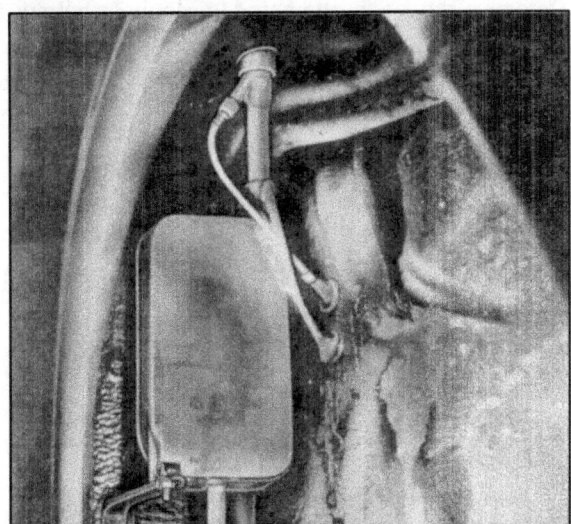

Location of automatic antenna inside the right wheelwell

Pull the wire from the light switch and ground the wire under the dashboard.
Unplug the antenna wire from the radio.
Disconnect the antenna control wire from the radio.
Remove the mat from the luggage compartment and disconnect the front trim piece.
Pull the wires for the antenna, into the right wheelwell.
Remove the antenna mounting nut from on top of the wiring and remove the antenna from below.
Installation is the reverse of removal.
Be sure the base of the antenna is grounded well to the fender.

18 Alarm

Alarm horn

Disconnect the negative lead from the battery.
Remove the front axle guard, under the car.
Unplug the electrical connector from the horn.
Unscrew the alarm horn mounting bolts and remove the horn.
Installation is the reverse of removal.

Alarm switch

Remove the door panel from the left door as described in Chapter 13.
Pry the rubber trim piece from the switch.
Unscrew the nut securing the switch to the door.
Pull the switch through the inside of the door.
Unplug the flat electrical connectors from the switch.
Installation is the reverse of removal.

Alarm control unit

Open the luggage compartment and remove the carpet and the rear trim piece.
Remove the air vent hoses and the fresh air blower.
Pull the control unit toward the instrument panel to disengage it from its securing clip.

The alarm control unit is attached by a spring clip on the back of the instrument panel

Installation is the reverse of removal.

Alarm system test

Remove the alarm switch from the door as previously described.
Attach an ohmmeter to the electrical terminals of the switch.
With the key in the off position (vertical), the ohmmeter should register between 4.0 and 5.5 K-ohms.
Turn the key horizontal (to the On position). The ohmmeter should read between 2.0 to 3.0 k-ohms.
If either of these readings don't fall into the specified range the switch must be replaced with a new one.
Install the switch in the door after attaching the electrical connectors.
Remove the control unit and unplug the electrical connectors as previously described.

Use a double contact test lamp with no more than a 3 W bulb to test the connections.

Test the alarm control unit with a test lamp of less than 3 watts

Attach the test lamp leads to the 'Hn' terminal and terminal '30'. The lamp should illuminate, indicating a good connection to the horn and that there is battery voltage.

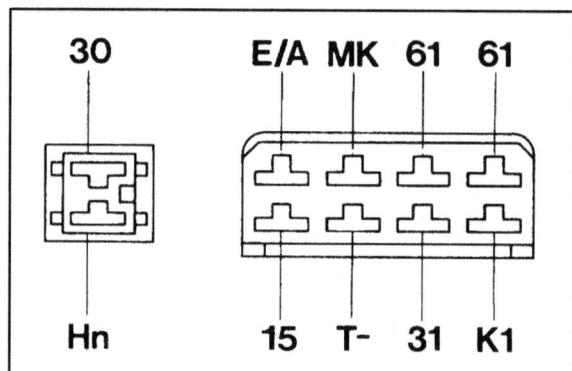

Alarm control unit terminals

With one lead of the test lamp connected to terminal '30', connect the other lead to terminal 'K1' then to terminal '31'. In both instances the test lamp should come on.

Connect the test lamp to terminals '15' and '31' and turn the ignition on. The lamp should light up.

Connect the test lamp to terminals T and 30. Open and close each door separately. When the door is open the lamp should be on.

Attach the test lamp to terminal '31' and to the left terminal '61'. The lamp should light up. Turn the ignition on, the lamp should go out. The lamp should come on then go out when the engine is started and run at an accelerated speed.

Disconnect the lamp from the left terminal '61' and connect it to the terminal '61' on the right. Perform the same tests as in the previous paragraph.

Connect the test lamp between terminals '30' and 'MK'. Push the contact switch for the trunk light, on and off. The test lamp should illuminate only when pushing in on the switch.

Connect an ohmmeter between terminals '31' and 'E/A' and take readings with the alarm switch in the on and off positions. The ohmmeter should read between 2.0 and 3.0 K-ohms with the switch on and between 4.0 and 5.5 k-ohms with the switch off. Plug the eight-pin connector into the control unit.

Use a jumper wire to connect terminal '30' to the red wire in the two-pin connector. Attach the test lamp between the red/white wire in the plug and terminal 'Hn' on the control unit. Open the driver's door with the alarm switched on. The test lamp should flash. Repeat this test on the passenger door and the trunk lid.

After the alarm is set off shut the door and observe that the alarm continues for about 30 seconds. Open the door again. The alarm should go off again.

When the alarm has stopped, attempt to start the engine. The test lamp should flash and the engine should not start.

If the above tests do not produce the required results, replace the control unit.

Plug the two-pin connector into the control unit, after removing the jumper wire and test lamp.

Turn the alarm on to check that the alarm horn operates.

19 Fault diagnosis

(a) Battery discharged

1 Terminals loose or dirty
2 Battery internally faulty
3 Shortcircuits in system
4 Alternator not charging
5 Regulator defective

(b) Insufficient charging current

1 Check 1, 4 and 5 in (a)
2 Driving belt slipping

(c) Battery will not hold charge

1 Low level of electrolyte
2 Battery plates sulphated
3 Electrolyte leakage from cracked case or top seal
4 Plate separators ineffective

(d) Battery overcharged

1 Check 5 in (a)
2 Poor connections between regulator and alternator

(e) Alternator output low or nil

1 Check 3 and 5 in (a) and 2 in (b)
2 Faulty brushes, rotor coil or isolation diode

(f) Noisy alternator

1 Worn belt, loose pulley
2 Defective bearings

(g) Control lamp not lighting with ignition on

1 Defective bulb or broken connection

(h) Control lamp stays on with ignition switched off

1 Defective diodes in alternator (disconnect battery at once)

(i) Starter motor lacks power or will not operate

1 Battery discharged, loose connections
2 Solenoid switch contacts worn or dirty
3 Brushes worn or sticking, springs weak or broken
4 Commutator, armature or field coils defective
5 Engine abnormally stiff

(j) Starter motor runs but does not turn engine

1 Pinion or flywheel gear defective

(k) Starter pinion stays in mesh

1 Bent armature shaft, dirty or defective pinion
2 Solenoid switch faulty

(l) Lamps inoperative or erratic

1 Battery low, bulbs burned out
2 Switch faulty, poor earthing, loose connections, broken wires

CHAPTER 13 - BODY

1. Bodywork finish
2. Engine and luggage compartment lids
3. Doors, locks, fittings and glass
4. Sliding and folding roofs
5. Windscreen and backlight glass
6. Bumpers
7. Front wings
8. Air conditioning
9. Targa door window adjustment
10. Reflective rear panel
11. Electric cross arm window controls

1 Bodywork finish

Large-scale repairs to body panels are best left to expert panel beaters. Even small dents can be tricky, as too much hammering will stretch the metal and make things worse instead of better. Filling minor dents and scratches is probably the best method of restoring the surface. Use a modern filling compound and work to the manufacturer's instructions. The touching-up of paintwork is well within the ability of most owners, particularly as self-spraying cans of the correct colours are now readily available. Use an air-drying enamel rather than a cellulose lacquer.

Before spraying, remove all traces of wax polish with white spirit. More drastic treatment will be required if silicone polish has been applied. Use a primer surfacer or a paste stopper or a filler according to the amount of filling required. When dry, rub down with 400 grade (or equivalent) 'Wet or Dry' paper until the surface is smooth and flush with the surrounding area. Spend time on getting a good finish as this will control the final effect. Apply the retouching paint and, when dry, use a cutting compound to remove the dry spray. Finish off with a liquid polish.

2 Engine and luggage compartment lids

Two operators are required to dismount and refit either of these lids. The procedures are similar for both lids.

Removal:

Open the lid and scribe round the hinge brackets on the underside of the lid so that, on refitment, the minimum of adjustment will be needed. While the lid is being held firmly, uncouple the prop from the lid and remove the bolts which retain each hinge bracket to the lid. Lift off the lid.

Fitment:

Fitment of a lid is the reverse of the removal sequence. Before finally tightening the bolts which secure the hinge brackets to the lid, position the lid to the scribed marks made before removal. When finally fitted, the gap between the lid and the body aperture should be equal and even all round. This gap should be 3.5 to 5.0mm (0.14 to 0.20in). The height of a lid in relation to the body may be adjusted by fitting (or removing) washers between the lid and the hinge brackets and, if necessary, adjusting the vertical position of the lock striker.

Reconnect the prop to the lid noting that, if it was removed for any reason, it should be fitted with the piston end of the prop attached to the lid.

3 Doors, locks, fittings and glass

Malfunctioning of the locks and window winding mechanisms can only be corrected by dismantling a door as far as may be necessary to gain access to the broken spring, pin, rod, clip or lever. Full dismantling will be necessary to renew the door glass. Unless accident damage has occurred, it will not normally be necessary to dismount a door from its hinges. To cover the model and modification standard variants, supplement the following procedure descriptions by making appropriate notes and sketches. If new units (locks, glass, winding mechanism) are required, ensure that they are identical with those being replaced. If they are not identical, new associated parts may have to be obtained in addition.

FIG 1 Removing the hand pull (earlier models)

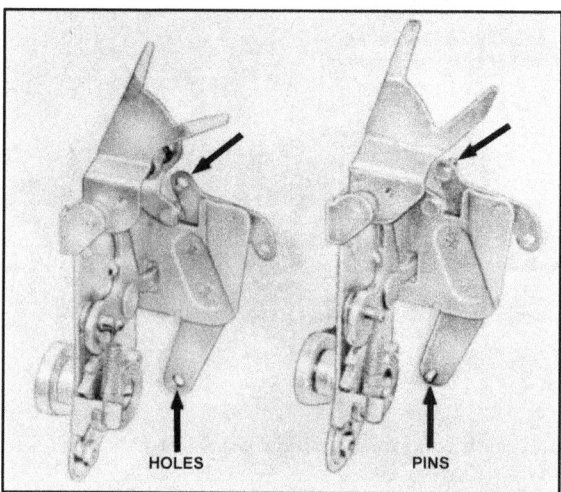

FIG 2 Two types of door lock

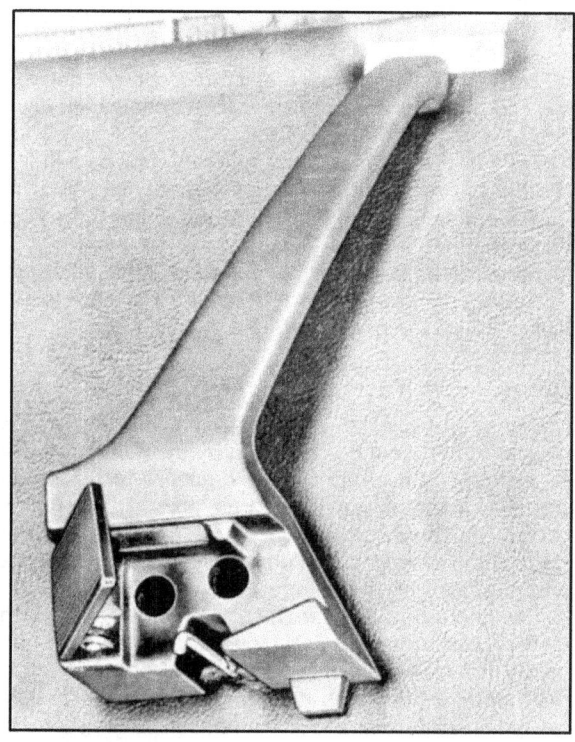

FIG 3 Removing the hand pull (later models)

Dismantling and dismounting a door (earlier models):

1 Unscrew the decorative strip and the internal door lock knob. Remove the padded cover and unscrew the window winder.
2 Remove the rubber surround from the folding storage box, detach the box from its retaining spring and unscrew the box. Dismount the armrest after removing the retaining bolts and detaching the lock operating lever from its linkage.
3 Loosen the plastic sheet (note where adhesive was used) and, from inside as shown in **FIG 1**, remove the door pull rear retaining screw. Remove the front screw and unscrew the pocket at the bottom.
4 Separate the door panel from the frame, unscrew the spring plate, pull off the window aperture seal and the plastic sheet and lift off the chrome strip. Unscrew all the threaded connections for the window frame or, in the case of Targa models, the window guide rails and pull the frame up and out.
5 In the case of coupé models, push the glass forwards until the sliding block can be freed from the lift rail and remove the glass. Unscrew the window lift regulator. In the case of Targa models, first detach the window lift screws and then remove the window.
6 Unscrew the outside door handle. Remove the lock retaining screws and withdraw the door lock complete with the inside locking mechanism and the remote control device. **FIG 2** shows two lock variants.
7 Unscrew the external mirror. Detach the door stay at the hinge pillar. Using tool P290, drive out the hinge pins and lift off the door.

Dismantling and dismounting a door (later models):

1 Dismount the storage compartment after removing the screws from below, from each end and from below the cover. Unscrew the door lock button, the screws from both ends and remove the door ledge cover.
2 Remove the storage compartment after detaching at the rear. Detach the connecting rod at the handle (see **FIG 3** and **4**), unscrew the fasteners from the top and bottom of the hand grip. Remove the window winding crank.
3 Remove the supporting brackets, unhook the door panel, remove the control lever from the door inner panel and disconnect the spring.
4 Further operations are as described earlier for the dismantling and dismounting of a door from earlier models. When removing the door stop roll pin, use tool P290 with tool P290a.

Door refitment and reassembly:

Follow the reverse of the dismantling and removal sequence. If new glass is being fitted, ensure that it is the same size and thickness as that originally fitted. Attach the rubber pad to the base with adhesive. Torque tighten window regulator 6mm screws to 1.2kgm (8.7lb ft) and window frame 6mm screws to 0.9kgm (6.5lb ft). 8mm screws should be torque tightened to 2.2kgm (16lb ft).

On Targa models, wind up the window glass fully, adjust the position of the stop angle (see **FIG 5**) and then tighten firmly. Check the condition of the window frame corner pieces to ensure that they will make good joints with the folding roof.

Use sealing compound where shown arrowed in **FIG 6**. Ensure that the door pocket and armrest holes align with those in the inner panel.

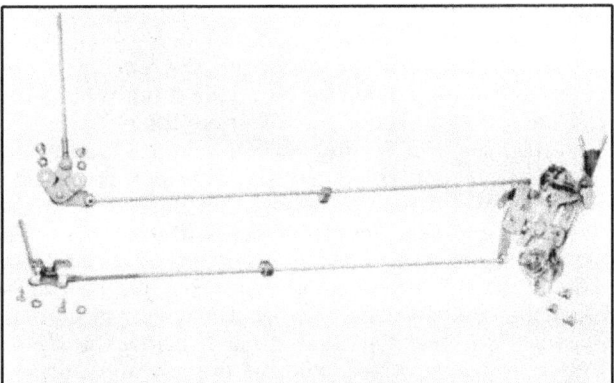

FIG 4 Remote control mechanism (later models)

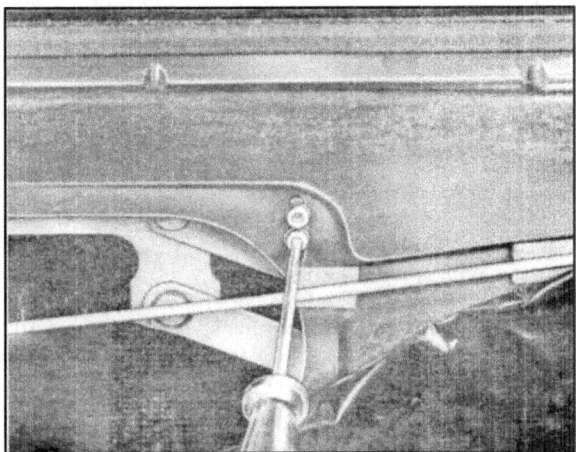

FIG 5 Window glass adjustment (Targa models)

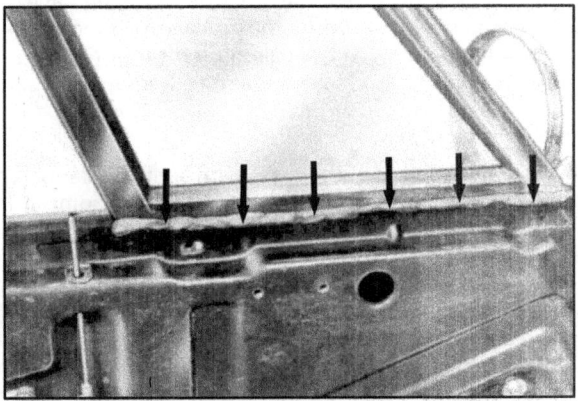

FIG 6 Apply sealing compound where arrowed

4 Sliding and folding roofs

Manual operation of sliding roof:

If the electric motor drive fails, the roof can be operated by means of an emergency manual crank which is fitted as follows:

Open the zip. Detach the plastic cap from the gear and remove the screw with the screwdriver end of the manual crank as shown in **FIG 7**. Remove and **retain the spacing washers**. Screw the manual crank into the gear by means of the knurled nut. The teeth on the crank must locate in the groove in the gear before the knurled nut is tightened. The sliding roof can now be operated by the crank.

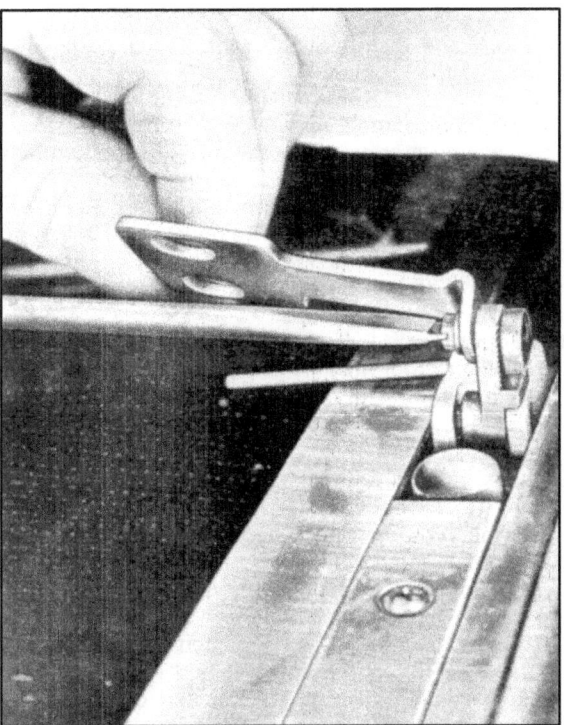

FIG 7 Fitting the manual winding crank

Sliding roof motor drive removal and fitment:

If the drive does not operate, confirm that the battery is not flat, that the fuse is intact and that all connections are tight and that there is no discontinuity in the wiring. If these are in order, remove the motor drive as follows:

Open the zip and disconnect the wiring from the motor. Remove the screws which retain the gear (see **FIG 8**). Unbolt the motor and its bracket from the roof frame and separate the motor from the bracket.

Renew the motor complete with the gear and flexible drive and, following the reverse of the removal sequence, refit the drive assembly. No procedures are prescribed for the repair or overhaul of the sliding roof motor.

Sliding roof guides and guide rails:

Renewal of the guides, rails and cable requires removal of the complete sliding roof. This work is best carried out by a Porsche agent. On completion, check that the height of the sliding roof has been satisfactorily adjusted.

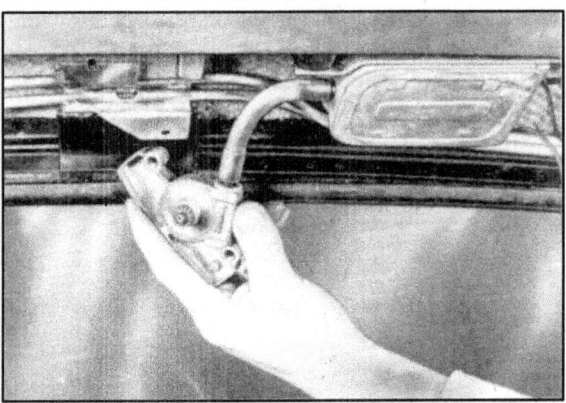

FIG 8 Removing the sliding roof motor drive

Folding roof dismantling and reassembling:

1 Unlock and dismount the roof. Collapse the braces and fold the roof.
2 Place the roof on soft pads to preclude damage to the outer material and to reinforce the braces. Pry out the plastic stopper from the front hinge pin which retains the upholstery pads.
3 Remove the screws from the side covers. Remove the covers and cover strips. Remove the circlips from the outer hinge pins. Press out the pins. Separate the centre hinge in the same manner. Renew worn hinge pins.
4 Pry out the roof lock grip mouldings. Carefully remove the glued on upholstery pads from the forward frame and at the same time, remove the plastic rivet from the frame. Remove the lock moulding screws and remove the locks.
5 Check the front locating studs for signs of wear. Remove the circlips from the rear hinge pins. Press out the pins and separate the rear frame sections. Check all hinge joints. If necessary, remove burrs from the edges and lubricate lightly.
6 Remove the screws from the aluminium rear cover. Remove the covers and unfasten the roof covering from the pins in the lefthand and righthand frames. The brackets can now be adjusted or, if necessary, renewed.

Reassembly is the reverse of the dismantling sequence. Since modifications have introduced differences between earlier and later type roofs, check that any new parts obtained are suitable for the model being worked on.

Folding roof front to frame:

To dismantle this unit, proceed as follows:

Remove the four countersunk screws from the roof side frame. Renew any damaged weatherstrip by removing the screws in the rear part of the frame and separating the glued on ends of the weatherstrip. If the water drain strip is damaged, remove the retaining screws and discard the strip.

Reassembly is the reverse of the dismantling sequence. Use waterproof adhesive to fix the ends of the weatherstrip. With the roof installed and locked, adjust the weatherstrip so that it seals against the door windows and fasten in place. If adjustment is required, unlock the roof before adjusting as necessary (adjustment, front, 42.5mm [1.67in]; rear, 43.5mm [1.71in]).

5 Windscreen and backlight glass

The procedure for renewing a windscreen or a backlight glass is similar except, where applicable, for the threading and connection of heater cables. If the windscreen is being dealt with, remove the wiper blade arms and position a protective covering over the luggage compartment lid and over the dashboard. **A new moulding will be required.**

Removing the original glass:

1 In the case of a windscreen, push a thin blade or knife carefully between the glass and the interior mirror base plate until it can be dismounted from the glass. Clean off all traces of adhesive from the plate.
2 In the case of a **Targa** backlight, remove the folding roof before proceeding to unscrew the box clamps and rear bulkhead lining. Remove the upper rear panel section and seat decorative strips. Detach the inner treadle panel and remove upwards. Detach the sealing frame at the front along the roll bar. Remove the screws on the chrome treadle panel. Unscrew the chrome panel. Unscrew the chrome panel below the wings and remove upwards. Pull off the seal upwards. In the case of **other models**, take out the rear bulkhead lining.
3 On all models, cut round the moulding on the outside of the glass. Remove the trim strips. Disconnect the electrical heater connections (if applicable) and dismount the glass.
4 If the glass was shattered, remove sections until the remains and the moulding can be pulled away from the aperture.
5 If the glass is heated, retain the moulding so that it may be used as a pattern for the position of the slots and/or holes in the new moulding through which the heater cables will be threaded.
6 Thoroughly clean the body aperture and remove old moulding, sealer glass particles, etc. It is important that the aperture should be thoroughly clean as any remnants left behind may induce breakage of the new glass.
7 Check the body aperture for bumps and irregularities and, if there are any, file them away as they too may induce breakage of the new glass. If accident damage could have distorted the aperture profile, have the contour checked with the relevant gauge by a Porsche agent. It will not be prudent to attempt to fit a new glass to a distorted aperture frame.

Fitting new glass:

1 Moisten the edge of the glass with soapy water or with turpentine. Position the moulding with its joint at the top centre and fit it round the glass. Using the old moulding as a pattern, make apertures for the heater cables (if applicable).
2 Thread the cables into position and connect up. Thread a strong cord all round the moulding recess which will be fitted over the body aperture. The cord ends should overlap by about 40cm (16in) at the top in the case of a windscreen or at the bottom in the case of a backlight.
3 Lubricate the trim groove with soapy water or with turpentine, fit the trim frame. Make sure that there is a gap of about 1cm (0.4in) between the ends before pushing on the connecting clip.

4 Fit the assembly to the body aperture. With one operator supporting the glass and maintaining hand pressure from outside the vehicle (see **FIG 9**), a second operator pulls the cord along the edge of the aperture so that the moulding lip is forced over the projecting edge. The first operator assists by lightly striking the glass with the palm of the hand at the point where the cord is being pulled.

5 Check, where applicable, that the heated glass is operating correctly. If this is in order, proceed to seal the glass to the moulding and to the body aperture. Use a pressure gun fitted with a copper nozzle (which will not scratch the glass) and, round the outside, inject sealer between the glass and the moulding and between the moulding and the body flange.

6 Remove excess sealer with a rag and white spirit. Do not use thinners as this will damage the paintwork. The remaining operations are the reverse of those carried out before removing the original glass.

FIG 9 Fitting a backlight glass

6 Bumpers

A damaged front or rear standard type bumper may be removed by an owner for possible repair or for replacement by a new unit. In the case, however, of energy-absorbing type units which incorporate deformation tubes or hydraulic absorption struts, it is advisable to entrust the work to a Porsche agent. The following procedures refer to standard types of bumpers.

Refitting a front bumper:

Straighten the surface below the front edge of the lid to get an even gap between the bumper and the lid. Fit the bumper without the rubber strip and check the distance to the flasher housing and adjust if necessary. Fit the flasher lens.

Adjust the bumper brackets so that there will be considerable tension during reassembly. Bend the rear bracket forward for this purpose.

Secure the bumper braces so that there will be as much preload tension on the bumpers as possible. Cement the sealing rubber to the body and install the bumper.

Refitting a rear bumper:

Fit the bumper side pieces and straighten the attaching tabs. Fit the bumper centre piece, insert the bumper horns and adjust to equal height. File the gap between the bumper and horn if necessary.

Cement the sealing rubber strip and cut off the edges. Fit the bumper parts and horns and cover the holes with plastic caps.

7 Front wings

A damaged front wing may be removed for repair or replacement by a new wing but, unless an owner has experience of this type of work (see **Section 1**) or can be assisted by someone who has, the work is best entrusted to a specialist. Note the following points.

Before fitting the lefthand wing, install the fuel filler cover if applicable. Apply body sealer strip to the mounting flange of the wing and then fit the snap nuts. Fit the wing, and screw in the bolts finger tight. While guiding the wing into place make sure the cable conduit for the filler cover release is correctly positioned. Do not, at this stage, install the sealing strip as it may be necessary to apply body solder in places. As a result, the gap between the wing and the door may be wider at the top edge by 1mm (0.04in).

Tighten the second bolt in from the rear end first and lightly tighten one at the front. Do the rearmost top bolt followed by the lowest one by the door sill, then tighten the remaining bolts on the vertical flange starting at the top. Finally, work along the top flange, starting at the rear.

When satisfied with the fit, drill two 4mm (0.16in) holes through the attaching flanges at front and rear locations, insert steel rivets in the holes and weld the heads to the body panel. These will act as dowels so that when the wing is removed for painting and then refitted it can be restored to its correct position and be properly aligned.

8 Air conditioning

The installation features of the Behr air conditioning system are shown in **FIG 10** and its wiring diagram is shown in **FIG 11**. The compressor is belt driven from the engine. For control purposes an electro-magnetic clutch is positioned between the compressor and its drive pulley. Hot compressed refrigerant vapour passes under pressure to the condensers in which the vapour is cooled and liquefied. The refrigerant then passes to the receiver which acts as a storage tank. Refrigerant passes through the expansion valve to the evaporator core. Cold, low pressure refrigerant is drawn through the core by the suction of the compressor. Warm air, passing over the evaporator core, is cooled by the refrigerant vapour while the vapour, heated by the air, passes again to the compressor. The cooled air is circulated to the interior of the vehicle.

This description and the installation feature illustration is given for information purposes only. **It is dangerous for an unqualified person to attempt to disconnect any part of the refrigeration circuit.** Units may be dismounted from their locations without the assistance of a qualified refrigeration engineer **provided that pipe connections are not disturbed.** An owner must enlist specialist assistance if it is necessary to discharge, evacuate or recharge the system. If such assistance is not available, arrange for a Porsche agent to carry out the work.

The three-speed switch turns the system on or off and also controls the volume of conditioned air. The temperature switch provides thermostatic control of the temperature of the conditioned air. If the system does not operate, check that the compressor drive belt is intact and correctly tensioned. If it is in order, check that the fuses (see **FIG 11**) are intact and that the relays (see **Chapter 12, FIGS 1** or **2** and also **FIG 11** this **Chapter**) are operative. If these are in order, check that the switches are serviceable and that there is no wiring discontinuity. If all these appear to be in order but the system is still inoperative, consult a Porsche agent.

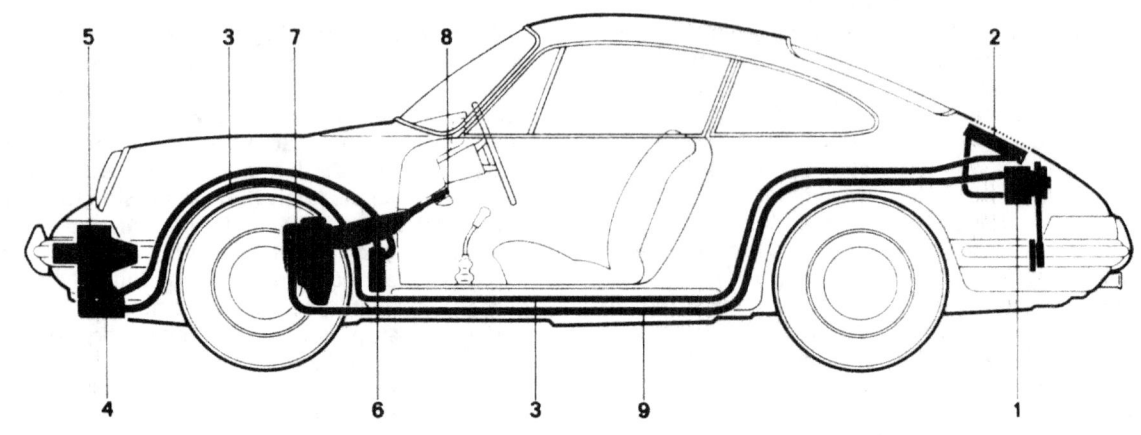

1 Compressor with electromagnetic clutch
2 Condenser, rear
3 Liquide hose, left
4 Condenser, front
5 Fan for condenser
6 Receiver-drier with filter
7 Evaporator with expansion valve
8 Cold air outlet housing with temperature and blower switch
9 Suction hose, right

FIG 10   Air conditioning installation features

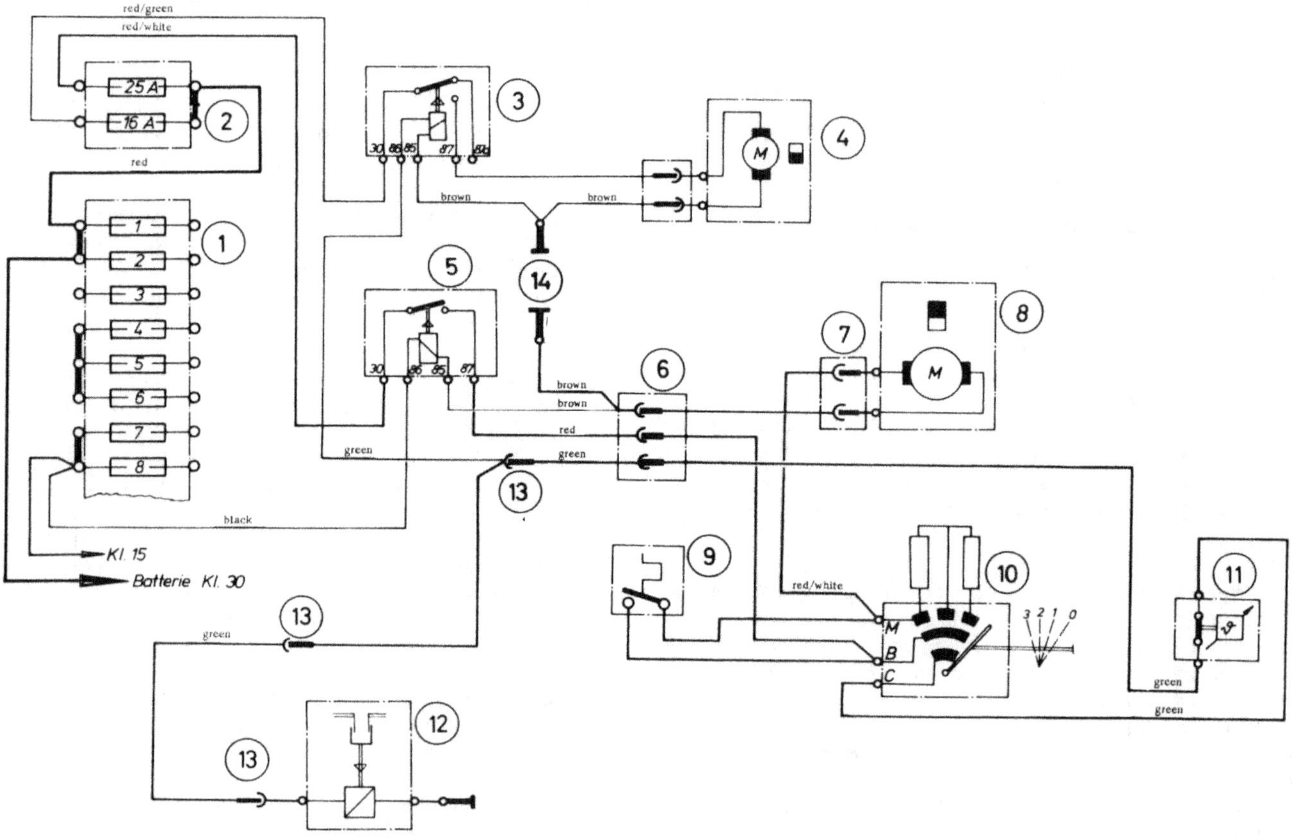

1 Fusebox I (10 terminal)
2 Fusebox (2 terminal)
3 Standard relay
4 Fan motor (front condenser)
5 Working contact relay
6 Plug coupling (3 terminal)
7 Plug coupling (2 terminal)
8 Blower motor (evaporator)
9 Thermostat
10 Blower switch
11 Temperature switch
12 Electromagnetic clutch
13 Plug connection (single terminal)
14 Ground connection - body

FIG 11   Air conditioning system wiring diagram

9 Targa door window adjustment

Beginning with the 1980 models, Targas use two adjustable stop brackets for the door windows.

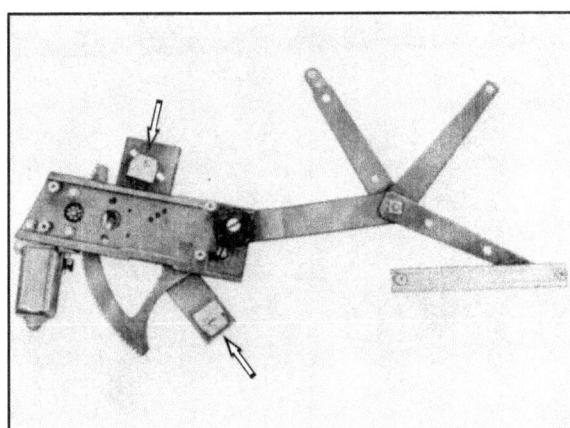

Window control unit for a Targa with two stop brackets (arrows)

Check the position of the installed top and the gap between the rear fender and the rear of the door. These adjustments must be corrected before adjusting the window.

If adjustment is required, remove the hinge strip, the door pocket with its cover, the door handle, the inside trim piece and the plastic sheeting.

Lower the window until the stop bracket can be adjusted through the opening in the door panel.

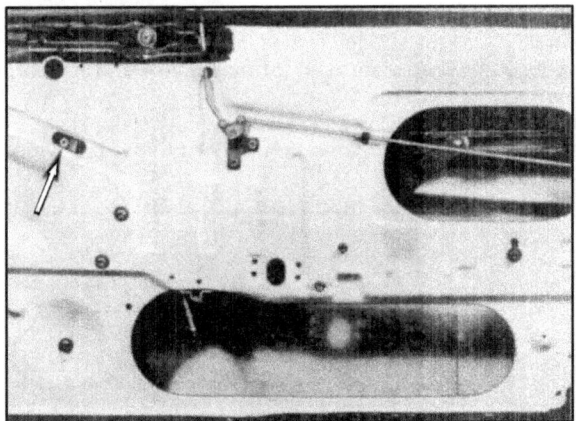

Window height adjustment on Targa models

Adjust the stop bracket until the window fits snugly against the entire length of the seal and the height is in alignment with the roof seal.

If the window sags at the rear during operation, adjustment of the guide rail will correct it. It may be necessary to elongate the access hole in the door, upward.

10 Reflective rear trim panel

The trim panel is attached with 10 clips to the rear cross panel on 1978 through 1981 models.

Open the engine compartment lid and attach some thick tape (adhesive duct tape) on the cross panel above the reflective trim panel.

Pry the top of the trim panel away from the securing clips. Use a screwdriver or putty knife. Only pry on the trim panel at the reinforced areas. Do not scratch the reflective finish on the back of the trim panel.

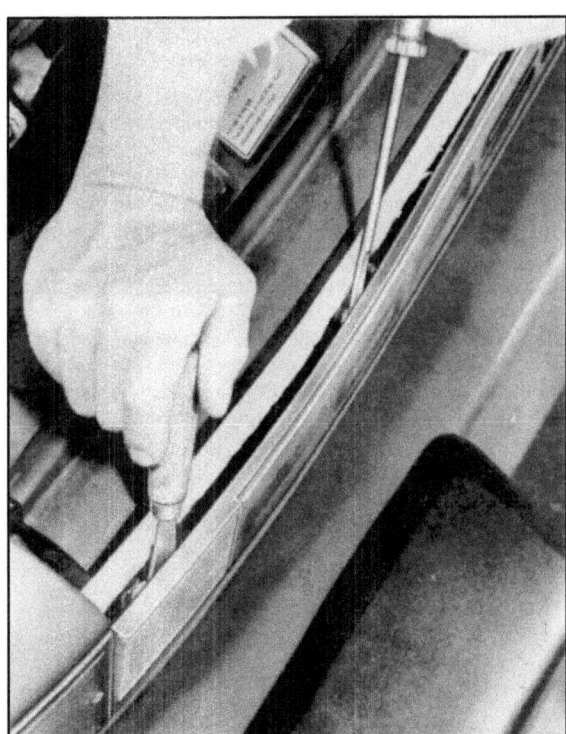

Carefully pry the reflective trim piece from the rear end at the reinforcement points

When all of the top clips are loose, pry the lower clips out of position and lift the trim panel away.

If any clips are damaged, replace them with new ones.

Remove the adhesive tape and touch up the paint where necessary.

Attach clips to the relective trim panel. Press the trim panel onto the cross panel until the clips are into their stops.

11 Electric cross-arm window controls

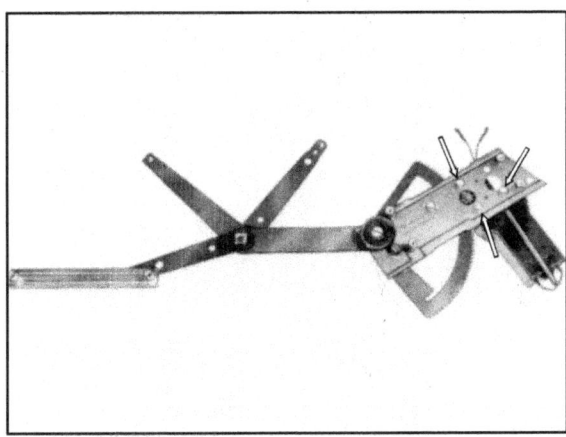

Electrical motor attachments (arrows) on the cross arm window control

Cross-arm window controls became standard equipment in 1980. Earlier models use parallel control arms. To modify earlier models to use cross arm controls proceed as follows.

Remove the trim panel on the inside of the door as previously described.

Unplug the electrical connectors for the mirror and the window control.

Pry off the water shields for the door window.
Remove the frame for the door window.
Disconnect the parallel arm window control then separate the window from its guide. Remove the window.
Remove the electric motor and the window control.
On Targa models, remove the height adjusting screw.
Lightly tap on the old window channels to remove them.
Lightly press the new lift channel and rubber insert onto the window glass. Position the lift channel eight millimeters behind the front edge of the glass on Coupe models.
Special rain molding cement must be applied in the groove of the plastic part of the lift channels on Targa models.
Position the window glass firmly in the channel and guide groove.
Attach the electric motor to the cross arm window control.
Position the wire harness away from any moving parts.
Install the assembly in the door with the window control at its center position.
Drill two 9/32 inch (7.0 mm) holes in the door panel.

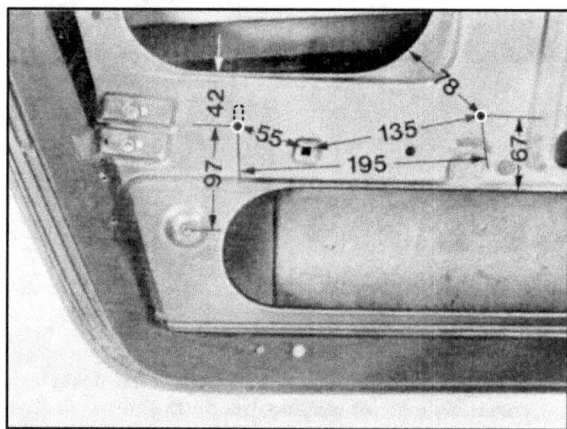

Measurements (in millimeters) for the locations of holes needed to adapt a cross arm window control to an earlier model vehicle

The rear hole may need to be elongated upward (see broken line) if the window does not go all the way up at the rear.
On Targa models a slot must be placed in the door panel to gain access to the height control stop bracket.

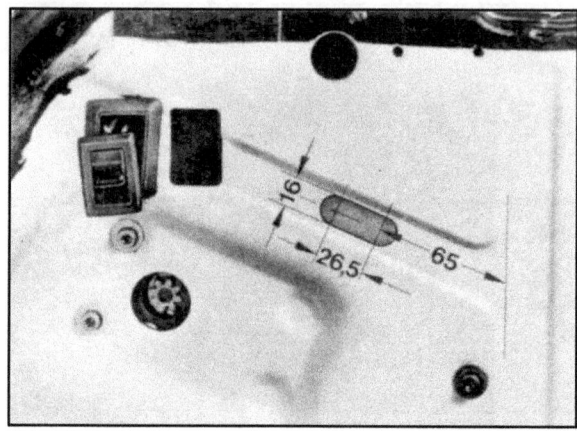

Measurements (in millimeters) of the slot required on Targa models for access to the height control stop bracket

If the velvet in the window guides is worn it must be replaced. When installing them to the door frame, apply glue at the top.
Install the window control and secure the base plate in position.
Attach the wire harness to the switch.
Install the window glass and place the window control plastic rollers in the lift channel.
Attach the short guide rail with bolts (6 x 10 mm) and washers, to the inside door panel.
Apply multi-purpose grease to all moving parts.
Securely install the window frame in the door.
Inspect the window for ease of movement and for proper adjustment.
Attach the water shields and install the door trim panel.
Check the operation of the mirror switch and the window controller.

NOTES

CHAPTER 14 - APPENDIX

TECHNICAL DATA

Due to the year end introduction of new models (for the following year) plus the introduction of mechanical modifications for existing models (at that same time), there can be significant overlap in both the model and technical specifications for the 1973-1978 series of 911 automobiles. For example, while fuel injection did not become standard equipment until the introduction of the 2.7 Litre engine, some 1973 2.4 Litre cars destined for the U.S.A., Australia, Japan and Canada were fitted with Bosch mechanical fuel injection (FIP), instead of carburetters, in order to bring them into compliance with emission requirements. In addition, in 1975 the (1976 model) Carrera was equipped with the 3.0 Litre engine but that engine was not available in any other 911 until the 1978 models were released. Therefore, in an attempt to avoid confusion and duplication of information, we have separated out 'General Specifications' that are common to the 1973 to 1984 models in addition to specific data for the 2.7 Litre and the 3.0 and 3.2 Litre cars. Therefore, it is recommended that the reader review the 'General Specifications' information in conjunction with the specific data for their vehicle.

2.7 Litre Specifictions - pages 170 to 172

3.0 & 3.2 Litre Specifications - pages 173 to 176

General Specifications - all models - pages 177 to 180

WIRING DIAGRAMS

NOTE: Space limitations prevent the inclusion of every wiring diagram that Porsche has produced for the various models covered by this manual. However, we have included diagrams for the 1973, 1974, 1975, 1977, 1981, 1982, 1984 and 1985 models. Should your car have been manufactured in one of the years not included one of the earlier and/or later diagrams should be accurate enough for all practical purposes.

CURRENT FLOW DIAGRAMS: Were introduced by Porsche for the later models in order to simplify computer diagnostic checks and may initially appear more difficult to follow than a conventional wiring diagram. However, the track number at the bottom of the diagram, when referenced to the key allows any component to be easily located. The connections between each component on that track, is shown by heavy lines that includes a color code for that wire. Thin lines show internal connections or that the component is connected directly to ground.

1973 Models - pages 181 to 188

1974 Models - pages 189 to 191 and 193 to 198

1975 Models - pages 189 to 191 and 199 to 201

1977 Models - pages 202 to 207

1981 Models - pages 208 to 218

1982 Models - pages 219 to 225

1984 Models - pages 226 to 233

1985 Models - pages 234 to 247

2.7 LITRE SPECIFICATIONS

Unless otherwise stated, dimensions are in mm but, where relevant, non-metric equivalents are given in brackets

Capacity:
    Nominal, litres 2.7
    Actual, cc 2687
Bore and stroke .. .. 90 × 70.4
Compression ratio .. .. 8.0 (S) 8.5

Crankshaft:
    Main journal diameters:
        Nos 1 to 7 .. .. 56.990 to 56.971
        No 8 .. .. 30.993 to 30.980
        Undersizes .. .. −0.25, −0.50 and −0.75
        Running clearance:
            Nos 1 to 7 .. .. 0.030 to 0.088
            No 8 .. .. 0.048 to 0.104
    End float .. .. 0.10 to 0.02
    Crankpin diameters:
        2.7 and 3.0 litre .. .. 51.990 to 51.971
        Undersizes .. .. −0.25, −0.50 and −0.75
        Running clearance .. .. As main journals 1 to 7
    Interference fits:
        Timing and distributor gears .. .. 0.002 to 0.038
        Flywheel .. .. Zero to 0.049

Connecting rods:
    Big-end running clearance .. .. .. As main journals 1 to 7
    Gudgeon pin running clearance .. .. 0.020 to 0.039
    Wear limit 0.050

Pistons:
    Clearance in cylinder bores .. .. .. See tabulation in **Chapter 1 : 10**
    Measurement position .. .. .. See tabulation in **Chapter 1 : 10**
    Wear limit on diameter 0.10 (0.004in)
    Weight variation per set .. .. .. 6 to 8gr (0.21 to 0.28oz)
    Piston diameter:
    2.7 litre and Carrera
      Make   *Mahle*
      Standard sizes:
        0 .. .. 83.95
        1 .. .. 83.96
        2 .. .. 83.97
      Oversizes:
        0.KD1 .. .. 84.20
        1.KD1 .. .. 84.21
        2.KD1 .. .. 84.22

Cylinders:
    Cylinder/piston clearances .. .. .. See tabulation in **Chapter 1 : 10**
    Wear limit on diameter 0.10 (0.004in)
    Maximum ovality 0.04 (0.0016in)
    Height tolerance .. .. See **Chapter 1 : 10**

Continued :

Camshafts:
- Bearing diameters .. .. 46.926 to 46.942
- Running clearance .. .. 0.025 to 0.066
- Wear limit 0.100
- End float .. .. 0.15 to 0.20
- Sprocket clearance on shaft .. .. .. Zero to 0.034

Camshaft housing:
- Bores for camshaft .. .. 46.967 to 46.992
- Bores for rocker shafts .. .. .. 18.000 to 18.018
- Rocker shaft diameter .. .. .. 17.992 to 18.00
- Clearance .. .. 0.016 to 0.035
- Wear limit 0.080
- End float .. .. 0.100 to 0.350
- Wear limit 0.500
- Clearances (timing case):
  - Carrier shaft/tensioner housing .. .. 0.016 to 0.045
  - Carrier shaft/sprocket housing .. .. 0.016 to 0.045
  - Sprocket carrier/sprocket shaft .. .. Zero to 0.029
  - Sprocket to shaft .. .. .. 0.032 to 0.061
  - Shaft to chain guide rail .. .. 0.105 to 0.129
  - Shaft to chain housing .. .. −0.014 to −0.037
  - Sprocket alignment .. .. .. Maximum deviation 0.25

Intermediate shaft:
- Bearing 1 diameter .. .. .. 29.767 to 29.780
- Bearing 2 diameter .. .. .. 23.967 to 23.980
- Running clearance .. .. .. 0.020 to 0.054
- Wear limit 0.100
- End float .. .. 0.080 to 0.150
- Sprocket mounting diameter .. .. 36.020 to 36.037
- Interference fit .. .. 0.010 to 0.037

Crankcase .. .. See **Chapter 1:11**
- Oil spray jets (if fitted) .. .. .. Open at 42 to 56lb/sq in

Valves:
- Head diameter, inlet .. .. .. 46.00 ± 0.10, 3 litre 49.00
- exhaust .. .. .. 40.00 ± 0.10, 3 litre 41.50
- Stem diameter, inlet .. .. .. 8.97 − 0.012
- exhaust .. .. .. 8.95 − 0.012
- Length, inlet .. .. 114.00 ± 0.10
- exhaust .. .. .. 113.50 ± 0.10
- Seat angle .. .. 45°

Valve springs .. .. 2 per valve
- Installed lengths .. .. See tabulation in **Chapter 1:8**
- Loaded length .. .. 42.0 to 42.5 under 20kg load

Valve clearance:
- Inlet and exhaust (cold) 0.10 (0.004in)

Valve guides:
- Interference fit in head .. .. .. 0.03 to 0.06
- Ream bore diameter to .. .. .. 9.000 + 0.015

Valve seats:
- Interference fit in head .. .. .. 0.14 to 0.18
- Seat width, inlet valve .. .. .. 1.25 ± 0.10
- exhaust valve .. .. 1.55 ± 0.10

Continued:

Valve timing (degrees):

	IO/BTC	IC/ABC	EO/BBC	EC/BTC
1973 Carrera	0	32	30	10
1974 Carrera	38	50	40	20
911	1 (ATC)	35	29	7
911S	6 (ATC)	50	24	2

*Inlet valve lift:
  1974 models:
    911 .. .. 0.7 to 0.9 (0.028 to 0.035in)
    911 (model 75) .. .. 0.5 to 0.7 (0.020 to 0.028in)
    911S .. .. 0.4 to 0.54 (0.016 to 0.021in)
    Carrera .. .. 5.0 to 5.4 (0.197 to 0.213in)
  1975 models:
    911S and Carrera (USA) .. .. 0.4 to 0.54 (0.016 to 0.021in)
  1976 models:
    911, 911S (USA) .. .. .. 0.4 to 0.54 (0.016 to 0.021in)

* Measured at overlap TC with 0.1 (0.004in) valve clearance

Flywheel:
  Bore for crankshaft .. .. .. 65.00 to 65.03
  Clearance in bore .. .. .. Up to 0.049
  Lateral runout at clutch mounting .. 0.040 max.
  Lateral runout at clutch face .. .. 0.040 max.
  Pilot bearing running clearance .. 0.075 to 0.229

Lubrication .. .. Dry sump
  Engine oil .. .. SAE 30
  Oil pressure (relief valve opens) .. 78lb/sq in
  Thermostats open at .. .. 83°C (182°F)

Torque wrench settings	lb f ft	kg fm
Crankcase section bolts	25	3.5
Crankcase nuts (M8)	18	2.5
Flywheel securing bolts	66	14.6
Crankshaft pulley bolt	56	7.7
Connecting rod bolts	36	5.0
Cylinder head nuts	21	2.9
Camshaft sprocket nuts	71	9.8
Rocker arm shaft nuts	13	1.8
Pulley to alternator nut	28	3.9
Spark plugs	18	2.5
Blower housing clamp bolts	6	0.8

NOTES

3.0 & 3.2 LITRE SPECIFICATIONS

Engine (General 3.0 Litre - 1978 through 1983)
Bore	3.74 in (95.0 mm)
Stroke	2.77 in (70.4 mm)
Displacement	182.7 cu in (2994 cc)
Compression ratio	
1978 and 1979	8.5:1
1980 and 1981	9.3:1

Engine (General 3.2 Litre - 1984 onwards)
Bore	3.74 in (95.0 mm)
Stroke	2.93 in (74.4 mm)
Displacement	190.6 cu in (3125 cc)
Compression ratio	9.5:1

Pistons (Mahle)
Early piston diameter	
Cylinder marking 0	3.7379 to 3.7385 in (94.943 to 94.957 mm)
1	3.7383 to 3.7389 in (94.953 to 94.967 mm)
2	3.7387 to 3.7393 in (94.963 to 94.977 mm)
From engine no 666 0446 or 666 9091:	
Cylinder marking 0	
cylinder bore	3.7402 to 3.7404 in (95.000 to 95.007 mm)
piston diameter	3.7388 to 3.7392 in (94.965 to 94.975 mm)
Cylinder marking 1	
cylinder bore	3.7404 to 3.7407 in (95.007 to 95.014 mm)
piston diameter	3.7391 to 3.7394 in (94.972 to 94.982 mm)
Cylinder marking 2	
cylinder bore	3.7407 to 3.7410 in (95.014 to 95.021 mm)
piston diameter	3.7393 to 3.7397 in (94.979 to 94.989 mm)
Cylinder marking 3	
cylinder bore	3.7410 to 3.7413 in (95.021 to 95.028 mm)
piston diameter	3.7396 to 3.7400 in (94.986 to 94.996 mm)
Piston to cylinder clearance	0.0010 to 0.0017 in (0.0250 to 0.0420 mm)

Piston rings (1975 onwards)
End gap	
compression ring	0.0039 to 0.0079 in (0.1 to 0.2 mm)
wear limit	0.0315 in (0.8 mm)
Oil control ring	0.0059 to 0.0118 in (0.15 to 0.3 mm)
wear limit	0.0394 in (1.0 mm)
Three-piece oil control ring	0.0158 to 0.0552 in (0.4 to 1.4 mm)
wear limit	0.0788 in (2.0 mm)
Side clearance	
top compression ring	0.0028 to 0.0040 in (0.070 to 0.102 mm)
wear limit	0.0079 in (0.2 mm)
second compression ring	0.0016 to 0.0028 in (0.040 to 0.072 mm)
wear limit	0.0079 in (0.2 mm)
oil control ring	0.0008 to 0.0020 in (0.020 to 0.052 mm)
wear limit	0.0039 in (0.1 mm)

Valves
Timing	
Inlet opens	
1978/80 UK	7° BTDC
1981/83 UK and 1978/80 NA	1° BTDC
1981/83 NA	4° BTDC
Inlet closes	
1978/1980 UK	47° ABDC
1981/83 UK and 1978/80 NA	53° ABDC
1981/83 NA	50° ABDC
Exhaust opens	
1978/80 UK	50° BBDC
1981/83 UK and 1978/80 NA	43° BBDC
1981/83 NA	46° BBDC

Continued:

Exhaust closes
- 1978/80 UK .... 3° BTDC
- 1981/83 UK and 1978/80 NA .... 3° ATDC
- 1981/83 NA .... at TDC

Timing (No. 1 inlet valve lift) *Measured at overlap TC with 0.1 (0.004in) valve clearance*
- 1978/80 NA and 1981 UK
  - ideal .... 0.0394 in (1.0 mm)
  - permissible .... 0.0354 to 0.0433 in (0.9 to 1.1 mm)
- 1978/80 UK and 1981 NA
  - ideal .... 0.0610 in (1.55 mm)
  - permissible .... 0.0551 to 0.0669 in (1.4 to 1.7 mm)

Valve spring installed height
- Intake
  - 1976 and 1977 .... 1.366 to 1.390 in (34.7 to 35.3 mm)
  - 1978 through 1980 .... 1.35 to 1.37 in (34.2 to 34.8 mm)
  - 1981 on .... 1.35 to 1.36 in (34.2 to 34.5 mm)
- Exhaust
  - 1976 and 1977 .... 1.39 to 1.40 in (35.2 to 35.8 mm)
  - 1978 through 1980 .... 1.35 to 1.37 in (34.2 to 34.8 mm)
  - 1981 on .... 1.35 to 1.36 in (34.2 to 34.5 mm)

Torque specifications

	Ft-lbs	kg-fm
Flywheel bolts	66	9.0
Crankshaft pulley bolts	59	8.0
Cylinder head nuts	24	3.3
Camshaft hex bolt	89	12.0
Camshaft nut	111	15.0
Crankshaft pulley bolt (with A/C)	125	17.0
Oxygen sensor to catalytic converter	40	5.5
Oil drain plug (oil tank)	31	4.2
Oil drain plug (crankcase)	28	4.3

Fuel injection systems

System pressure (CIS injection systems)
- Test valve .... 64.17 to 74.15 psi (4.5 to 5.2 bar)
- Adjusting valve .... 67.02 to 69.87 psi (4.7 to 4.9 bar)
- Injection valve opening pressure .... 35.65 to 51.34 psi (2.5 to 3.6 bar)

System pressure (DME injection system)
- Fuel pressure
  - engine stopped .... 36 ± 3 psi (2.5 ± 0.2 bar)
  - engine at idle .... approximately 29 psi (2.0 bar)

Idle speed
- North America
  - Pre-1977 with M/T .... 850 to 950 rpm
  - 1977 through 1979 .... 900 to 1000 rpm
  - 1977 California and high-altitude .... 950 to 1050 rpm
  - 1980 through 1983 .... 850 to 950 rpm
  - 1984 on .... 780 to 820 rpm
- United Kingdom
  - Pre-1977 with M/T .... 850 to 950 rpm
  - Pre-1977 with Sportomatic .... 900 to 1000 rpm
  - 1977 through 1980 .... 850 to 950 rpm
  - 1981 through 1983 .... 800 (preferred) to 950 rpm
  - 1984 and 1985 .... 780 to 820 rpm

CO setting
- North America
  - 1973 (2.4 liter) .... 1.5 to 2.0%
  - 1974 (2.7 liter) .... 1.5 to 2.5%
  - 1975 .... 1.7 to 2.0%
  - 1975 California and high altitude .... 1.5 to 2.0%
  - 1976 (air pump disconnected) .... 2.0 to 4.0%
  - 1977 (air pump disconnected) .... 1.5 to 3.0%
  - 1978 and 1979 (air pump disconnected) .... 1.5 to 3.5%
  - 1980 on (oxygen sensor disconnected — measured in front of the catalytic converter) ... 0.4 to 0.8%

Continued:

United Kingdom
  1975 . . . . 2.0 to 2.5%
  1976 and 1977 . . . . 1.0 to 1.5%
  1978 and 1979 (air pump disconnected) . . . . 2.0 to 4.0%
  1980 (air pump disconnected) . . . . 1.5 to 2.5%
  1981 thru 1983 (air pump disconnected) . . . . 1.0 (preferred) to 2.0%
  1984 and 1985 . . . . 1.0 to 1.5%
Leak test
  Minimum pressure after 10 minutes . . . . 18.54 psi (1.3 bar)
  Minimum pressure after 20 minutes . . . . 15.69 psi (1.1 bar)
Warm control pressure
  1974 through 1979 (no vacuum) . . . . 38.50 to 44.21 psi (2.7 to 3.1 bar)
  1980 through 1983 . . . . 48.48 to 54.19 psi (3.4 to 3.8 bar)

Torque specifications   Ft-lbs   Kg-fm
Plug-in fuel distributor 11   1.52
Pressure hose to fuel pump 15   2.07
Check valve on fuel pump 14   1.93
Cap nut on fuel pump 14   1.93
Oxygen sensor to exhaust manifold 40   5.52

Ignition system
Spark plugs (North America)
  1976
    make/number . . . . Bosch W235P21 — Beru 235/14/3p
    gap . . . . 0.022 in (0.55 mm)
  1977
    make/number . . . . Bosch W225T30 — Beru 225/14/13A
    gap . . . . 0.028 in (0.70 mm)
  1978 and 1979
    make/number . . . . Bosch W8D, W145T30 — Beru 14-8C, 145/14/3A
    gap . . . . 0.031 in (0.80 mm)
  1980 through 1983
    make/number . . . . Bosch W5D, W225T30 — Beru 14-5D, 225/14/3A
    gap . . . . 0.028 in (0.70 mm)
  1984 on
    make/number . . . . Bosch WR7DC, W7DC or Champion N7YC
    gap . . . . 0.028 in (0.70 mm)
Spark plugs (United Kingdom)
  1977
    make/number . . . . Bosch W225T30 — Beru 225/14/3A
    gap . . . . 0.028 in (0.70 mm)
  1978 through 1980
    make/number . . . . Bosch W200T30 — Beru 200/14/3A
    gap . . . . 0.031 in (0.80 mm)
  1981 through 1983
    make/number . . . . Bosch W4C1, W260T2 — Beru 14-4C1, 260/14/3
    gap . . . . 0.031 in (0.80 mm)
  1984 and 1985
    make/number . . . . Bosch WR44CC
    gap . . . . 0.028 in (0.70 mm)
Ignition timing (North America)
  1977 (California) . . . . 13° to 17° ATDC @ 950 to 1050 rpm
  1977 (all except California) . . . . Z1 mark (0 + 2°) @ 900 to 1000 rpm
  1978 (vacuum line connected) . . . . 5° BTDC @ 900 to 1000 rpm
  1978 (vacuum line disconnected) . . . . 24 to 28° BTDC @ 6000 rpm
  1980 (vacuum line disconnected) . . . . 5° BTDC @ 900 to 1000 rpm
                                                                                                                          15 to 20° BTDC @ 3000 rpm
                                                                                                                          19 to 25° BTDC @ 6000 rpm
  1981 thru 1983 (vacuum line disconnected) . . . . 3 to 5° BTDC @ 850 to 950 rpm
                                                                                                                          25° BTDC @ 4000 rpm
Ignition timing (United Kingdom)
  1977 . . . . 5° ATDC @ 850 to 950 rpm
  1978 through 1980 . . . . 5° BTDC @ 850 to 950 rpm
  1981 thru 1983 (vacuum line disconnected) . . . . 3 to 5° BTDC @ 850 to 950 rpm
                                                                                                                          25° BTDC @ 4000 rpm

Speed and reference sensor (1984 on)
  Air gap (bet. sensor and ring gear) . . . . 0.025 in (0.8 mm)
  Sensor tightening torque . . . . 6 Ft-lbs (8 Nm)

Continued:

Clutch
Torque specifications   **Ft-lbs**
Pressure plate cover bolts 1977 and later 15-18

Rear suspension and driveshafts
Rear suspension geometry
  1976 through 1981
    camber .... 0° ± 10'
    toe-in (each wheel) .... +10° ± 10'
  1984 on
    camber .... -1° ± 10'
    toe-in (each wheel) .... +10° ± 10'

Torque specifications	Ft-lbs	Kg-fm
Radius arm to spring plate	69	9.5
Shock absorber to arm	90	12.5
Lug bolts	94	13
Adjuster lever to spring strut	177	24.5
CV flange attachment		
10 mm Allen bolt	60	8.3
8 mm Allen bolt	30	4.2

Front suspension and steering

Torque specifications	Ft-lbs	Kg-fm
Balljoint to wishbone	180	25
Strut to upper mounting plate	58	8
Upper mounting plate to body	34	4.7
Steering unit attachment	34	4.7
Lug bolts	94	13

Braking system, wheels and tires
Disc thickness (minimum)
  1976 and 1977 (front) .... 0.709 in (18.0 mm)
  1978 through 1983 (front) .... 0.728 in (18.5 mm)
  1976 through 1983 (rear) .... 0.709 in (18.0 mm)
  1984 on (front and rear) .... 0.890 in (22.6 mm)

NOTES

GENERAL SPECIFICATIONS - ALL MODELS

Where noted refer to engine specifications for additional data appropriate to the later model cars

FUEL SYSTEM - See FUEL INJECTION Section in 3.0 & 3.2 engine specifictions also

Fuel injection pump (FIP) models .. .. Bosch injection pump
    Idling speed, manual transmission .. .. 850 to 950rev/min
        Sportomatic .. .. .. 900 to 1000rev/min

Continuous injection system (CIS) .. Bosch, K-Jetronic
    Idling speed, manual transmission up to 1977
        models .. .. 850 to 950rev/min
        Sportomatic up to 1977 models .. 900 to 1000rev/min
    From 1977 models:
        Europe .. .. 850 to 950rev/min
        USA (except California) .. .. 900 to 1000rev/min
        California, high altitude States .. 950 to 1050rev/min

IGNITION - See IGNITION Section in 3.0 & 3.2 engine specifications also

	Marelli	*Bosch*
Distributor:		
Type	S 112BX	JFDRG
2.7 litre	61015155	0231169011
Breaker points gap	0.4 (0.016in)	0.35 (0.014in)

  Speed limiter cut-off speed:
    2.7 litre .. .. 6500 ± 200rev/min
    2.7 litre Carrera 7300rev/min

Basic ignition timing:
  2.7 litre .. .. 5° ATC at 900rev/min
  2.7 litre Carrera .. .. TC at 900rev/min
  1977 North America:
    911S (not California) .. .. .. TC ± 2° at 950 ± 50rev/min *
    911S (California) .. .. .. 15° ATC ± 2° at 1000 ± 50 rev/min *

* Oil temperature 80°C and vacuum hose connected

Sparking plugs:
  2.7 litre:
    Pre-1976 .. .. Bosch W265/P21 or W260/T2
                                                                                                                                Beru 265/14/3P or 260/14/3
    1976 (not USA) .. .. .. Bosch W225/T30
                                                                                                          Beru 225/14/3A
    USA .. .. Bosch W235/P21
                                                                                         Beru 235/14/3P

Plug gaps:
  Plugs numbered in 260 series 0.7 (0.028in)
  Other types 0.55 (0.022in)

Firing order 1, 6, 2, 4, 3, 5

CLUTCH - See CLUTCH Section in 3.0 & 3.2 engine specifications also

Type .. .. Single dry plate, diaphragm spring

Driven plate:
  Thickness (uncompressed) .. .. 10.1 − 0.4 (0.397 − 0.015in)
  Maximum runout 0.60 (0.023in)

Pedal free play .. .. 20 to 25 (0.80 to 1.00in)

Continued :

TRANSMISSION

Manual transmission:

Forward ratios:

	1st	2nd	3rd	4th	5th
911	3.091	1.631	1.040	0.759	—
911	3.091	1.778	1.217	0.926	0.759
915	3.182	1.778	1.125	0.821	—
915	3.182	1.834	1.261	0.962	0.759
915/16	3.182	1.600	1.040	0.724	—
915/06, 08	3.182	1.833	1.261	0.926	0.724
915/18	3.182	1.600	1.040	0.759	—
915/45, 49, 65, 66	3.182	1.600	1.080	0.821	—
915/40, 44, 60, 61	3.182	1.833	1.261	1.000	0.821

Reverse ratio:
- 911 .. 3.147
- 915 series .. 3.325

Final drive ratio:
- 911S and 1975 USA models .. 3.875
- Other models .. 4.428

Sportomatic transmission:

Forward ratios:

	1st	2nd	3rd	4th
905, 925, 925/01	2.400	1.550	1.125	0.857
925/02	2.400	1.550	1.125	0.821
925/10	2.125	1.318	0.926	—
925/09, 12, 13	2.400	1.429	0.926	—

Reverse ratio .. 2.534

Final drive ratio:
- 905, 925, 925/01, 02 .. 3.857
- 925/09, 10, 12, 13 .. 3.375

Torque converter stall speed (rev/min):

1974 and earlier:

Transmission type	905, 925	925/01	925/02	925/10
911TV	2600*	—	—	—
911E, 911S	2600*	3000*	1950	—
911	—	—	2050	—
911, 911T (USA)	2600*	—	—	1900

1975 models:
- 911 .. 2000
- 911S, 911 (USA) .. 1900
- 911 (California) .. 1850

1976, 1977 all models .. 1900

*These speeds ± 100rev/min; all others ± 200rev/min

Backlash:
- Pinion to ring gear .. Adjust to 0.12 to 0.18
- Gearbox mating gears:
  - New .. 0.06 to 0.12
  - Wear limit .. 0.22

End play:
- 1st speed gear .. 0.3 to 0.4
- Wear limit .. 0.5
- Other gears .. 0.2 to 0.3
- Wear limit .. 0.4

Lubrication:
- Gearbox and standard differential .. SAE 90 Hypoid
- Gearbox and limited slip differential .. Shell S 1747A or equivalent
- Torque converter .. Pressure engine oil

Continued:

STEERING

Type	Rack and pinion
Ratio	1:17.78
Wheel turns lock to lock	3.1 approx.
Turning circle	10.7m (35ft) approx.

SUSPENSION - See SUSPENSION Section in 3.0 & 3.2 engine specifications also

Front — MacPherson type struts with transverse arms
   Springing — Torsion bars or self-levelling hydropneumatic dampers
   Dampers:
      Torsion bar springing — Hydraulic, telescopic
      Self-levelling — Hydropneumatic
   Anti-roll bar — Fitted to 2.2 and 2.4 litre S models and to 2.7 and 3.0 litre models. Optional on other models

Rear — Independent, triangulated control arms
   Springing — Transverse torsion bars
   Dampers — Hydraulic, telescopic
   Anti-roll bar — Fitted to 2.2 and 2.4 litre S models, to 2.7 and 3.0 litre and to Carrera models. Other models optional

Geometry

	Front	Rear
Toe-in, 2.7 litre	0°	0° + 20' per wheel
Caster	6° ± 15'	—
Pivot inclination	10° 55'	—
Camber, 2.7 litre	0° ± 10'	− 1° ± 10'
USA models 1975 on	—	0° ± 10'

Tyre pressures (cold):

	Front	Rear
2.7 litre	29lb/sq in	35lb/sq in

BRAKES - See BRAKES Section in 3.0 & 3.2 engine specifications also

Type:
   Foot — Dual circuit hydraulic
   Handbrake — Mechanical on rear (drum) hubs

Discs — Ventilated
   Diameter, front — 282.5
           rear — 290
   Thickness, new — 19.8 to 20.0
           wear limit — 18.0 (0.71in)

Pad lining thickness:
   Wear limit — 2.0 (0.08in)

Pedal free play — 1.0 (0.04in)

Brake fluid — ATE Blue or equivalent

Brake servo:
   Type — T52, 7in

Continued:

ELECTRICAL EQUIPMENT

Batteries	12-volt, negative earth
Starter	Bosch
2.7 and 3.0 litre	1.5 HP
Commutator diameter	33.5 (1.319in) min.
Brush wear limit	See **Chapter 12:4**
Alternator	Bosch or Motorola
Rectifier and capacity	Integral diodes, 770 W
Brush wear limit	14.0 (0.55in)
Fuses and relays	See **Chapter 12:3**

CAPACITIES

	Litres	Imperial	USA
*****Fuel tank:**			
2.7 litre (1973)	85	18.7 galls	22.5 galls
1974 and later models	80	17.6 galls	21.0 galls

Inclusive of approx. 10% reserve

	Litres	Imperial	USA
Oil tank:			
1974 models T, E	11	19.2 pints	23.2 pints
S and 1977 models**	13	22.9 pints	27.5 pints
Sportomatic models:			
Extra to refill converter***	2.5	4.4 pints	5.2 pints

*** With additional oil cooler*
****** Not required for normal oil change*

	Litres	Imperial	USA
Transmission:			
Gearbox and differential:			
2.7 and 3.0 litre	3.0	5.2 pints	6.3 pints
Brakes:			
Master reservoirs	0.2	0.35 pints	0.42 pints

	1970-73	1974 on
Windscreen washer:		
Capacity, litres	2.0	8.5

DIMENSIONS

	Front track	Rear track	Wheelbase
Wheelbase/track:			
2.7 litre, T and TV	1360	1342	2271
E and S	1372	1354	2271
2.7 litre Carrera 1973	1372	1368	2271
2.7 litre Carrera 1974	1372	1394**	2271
2.7 litre Carrera 1976	1321	1397	2271
1977 models	1369	1354	2271

**10mm less with alloy wheels*
***** With spacers on each rear wheel*

	Length	Width	Height
Overall:			
2.7 litre:			
1973 Carrera	4147	1652	1320
1975 Carrera	4291	1652	1320
Other models	4291	1610	1320
3.0 litre	4291	1652	1320

Ground clearance:
  Depending on model and loading .. .. 120 to 180

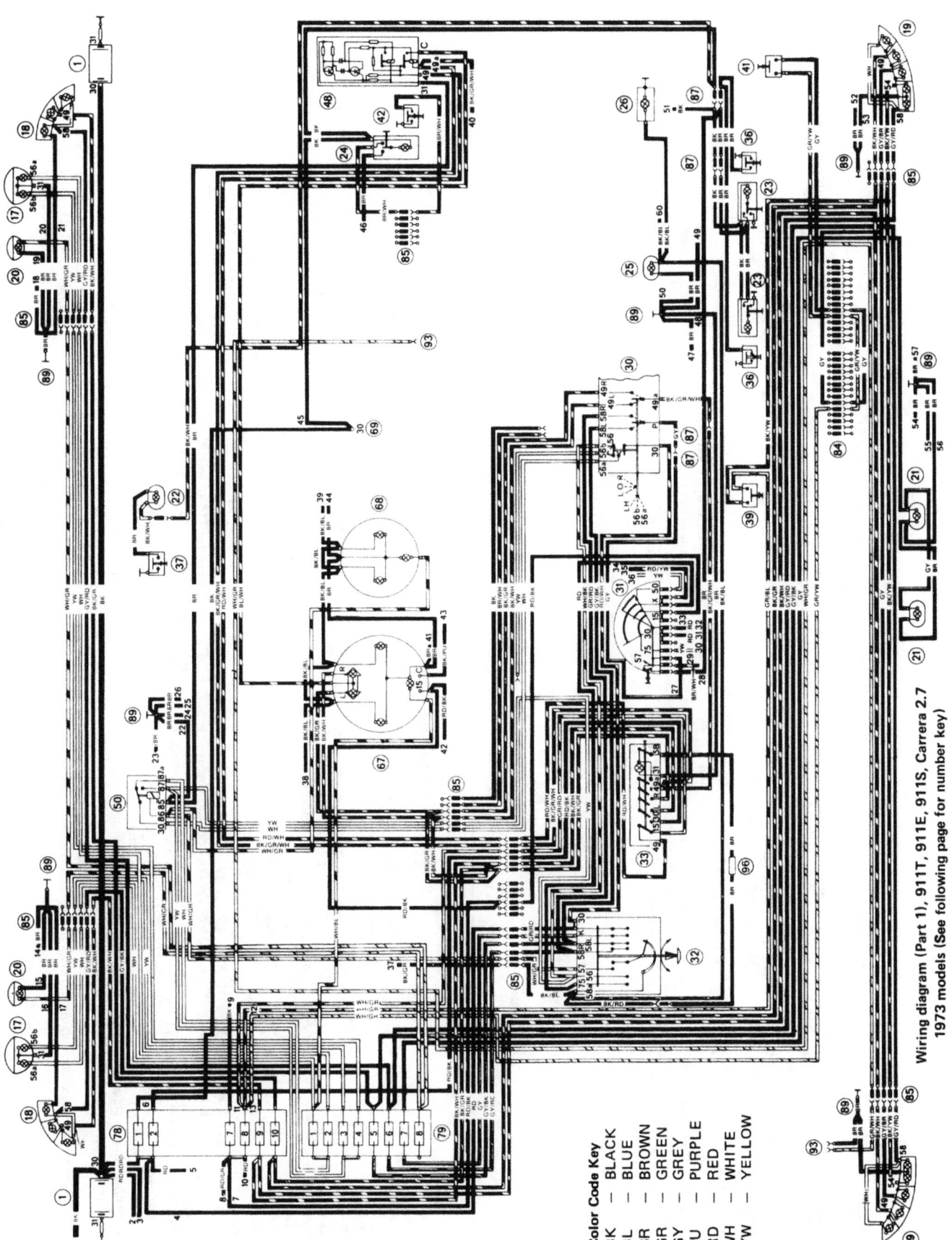

Key to Wiring Diagram (Part 1), 911T, 911E, 911S, Carrera 2.7 - 1973 models

1 Battery
17 Headlights
18 Turn signal, parking and side marker lights (side marker lights USA only)
19 Tail, stop, turn, backup and side marker lights (side marker lights USA only)
20 Fog lights (optional)
21 License plate light
22 Luggage compartment light
23 Interior light
24 Glove compartment light
25 Ashtray light
26 Illumination for heating lever (USA only)
30 Flasher, dimmer, wiper-washer switch with horn ring on steering column
31 Ignition starter switch and steering lock
32 Light switch
33 Emergency flasher switch (not applicable in Italy and France)
36 Door contact switch
37 Switch for luggage compartment light
42 Switch for glove compartment light
48 Turn signal/emergency flasher unit
50 Headlight relay
67 Tachometer
68 Speedometer
69 Electric clock
78 Fuse box I (10 terminal)
79 Fuse box II (8 terminal)
84 Multi-connector (14 terminal)
85 Multi-connector (6 terminal)
87 Connector (single contact)
89 Earth connection-body
93 Rear fog light (optional)
96 Resistor (USA only)

FUSES:

Fuse box I:
1 Interior light, clock, luggage compartment light
2 Emergency flasher
7 Fresh air fan
8 Stop, turn and backup lights
9 Left front turn signal light
10 Right front turn signal light

Fuse box II:
1 High beam, left
2 High beam, right
3 Low beam, left
4 Low beam, right
5 Side marker, left
6 Side marker, right
7 License plate light
8 (Fog lights)

Key to Wiring Diagram (Part 2) 911T, 911E, 911S, Carrera 2.7 - 1973 models

1 Battery
2 Starter
3 Alternator
4 Governor
5 Distributor
6 Ignition transformer
7 Spark plugs
8 Fuel pump
9 High tension ignition unit
11 Speed switch
12 Cold start solenoid (except 911 TV)
13 Shut-off solenoid (911 TV: solenoid valve)
14 Thermo-time switch (except 911 TV)
15 Micro switch
30 Flasher, dimmer, wiper-washer switch with horn ring on steering column
31 Ignition starter switch and steering lock
34 Switch for fan and auxiliary heater
35 Rear window defogger switch
38 Parking brake control
40 Brake warning light switch (USA only)
43 Safety belt contact, driver side (USA only)
44 Safety belt contact, passenger side (USA only)
45 Buzzer contact (USA only)
46 Seat contact, passenger side (USA only)
49 Horn relay
51 Rear window defogger relay
52 Axiliary starting relay (except 911 TV)
53 Buzzer (USA only)
56 Oil temperature indicator
57 Oil pressure indicator
58 Oil lever indicator
59 Indicator for fuel gauge
60 Safety belt warning light (USA only)
65 Fuel gauge dial
66 Oil temperature gauge dial
69 Electric clock
73 Wiper motor
74 Washer pump
75 Horns
77 Cigarette lighter
78 Fuse box I (10 terminal)
80 Fuse box III (3 terminal)
81 Fan motor
82 Rear window defogger element
83 Sportomatic (optional)
84 Multi-connector (14 terminal)
85 Multi-connector (6 terminal)
86 Multi-connector (4 terminal)
87 Connector (single contact)
88 Gear lever contact SPM (optional)
89 Earth connection-body
90 Optional horn
92 Auxiliary combustion heater (optional)
94 Radio (optional)

FUSES:

Fuse box I:
1 Interior light, clock luggage compartment light
2 Emergency flasher
3 (Electric windows)
4 Cigarette lighter
5 (Sliding roof)
6 Windshield wiper, washer pump
7 Fresh air fan
8 Stop, turn and backup lights
9 Left front turn signal light
10 Right

Fuse box II:
1 (Sportomatic)
2 Shut-off solenoid, solenoid valve, Solenoid for cold starting unit
3 Rear window defogger

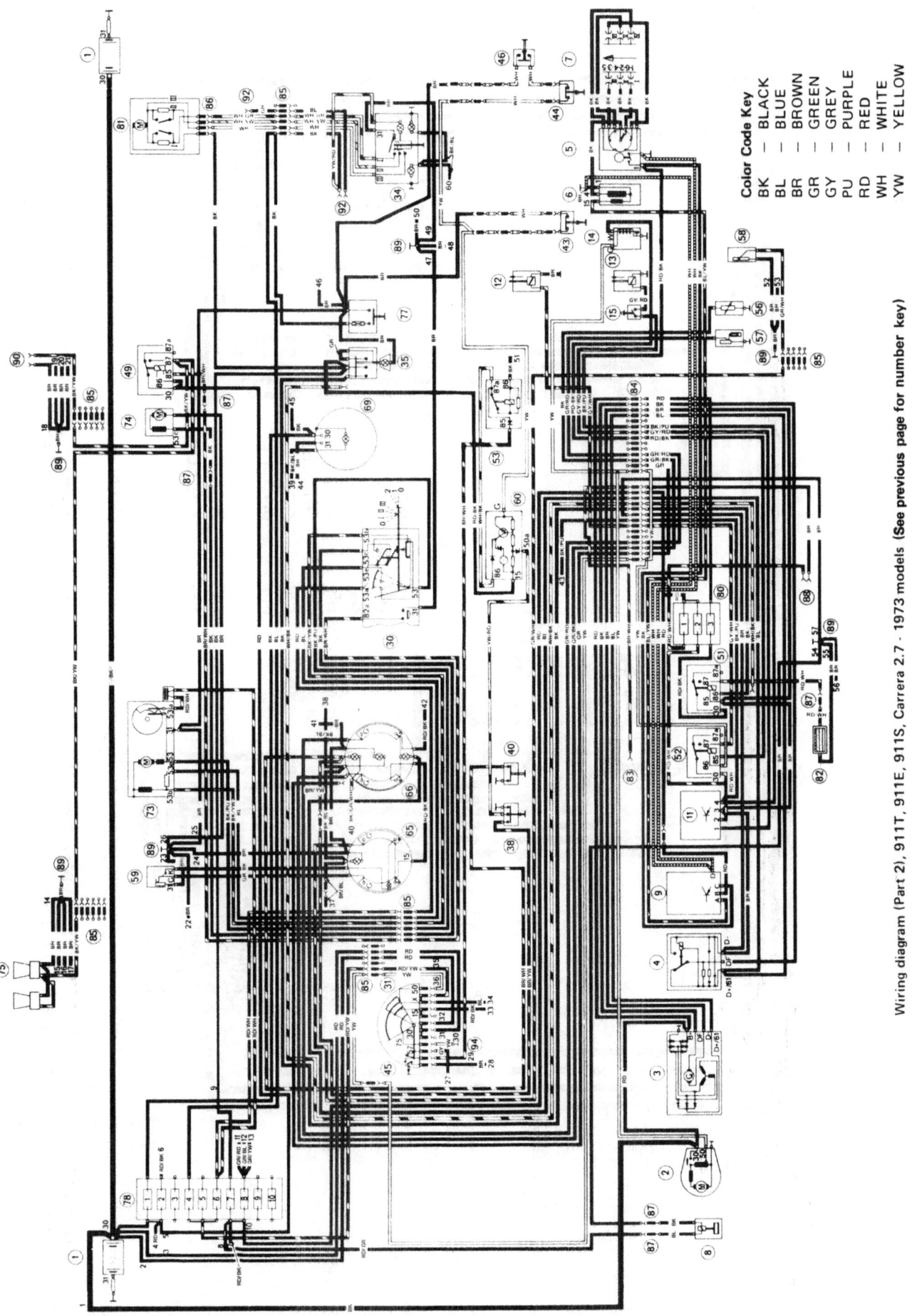

Wiring diagram (Part 2), 911T, 911E, 911S, Carrera 2.7 - 1973 models (See previous page for number key)

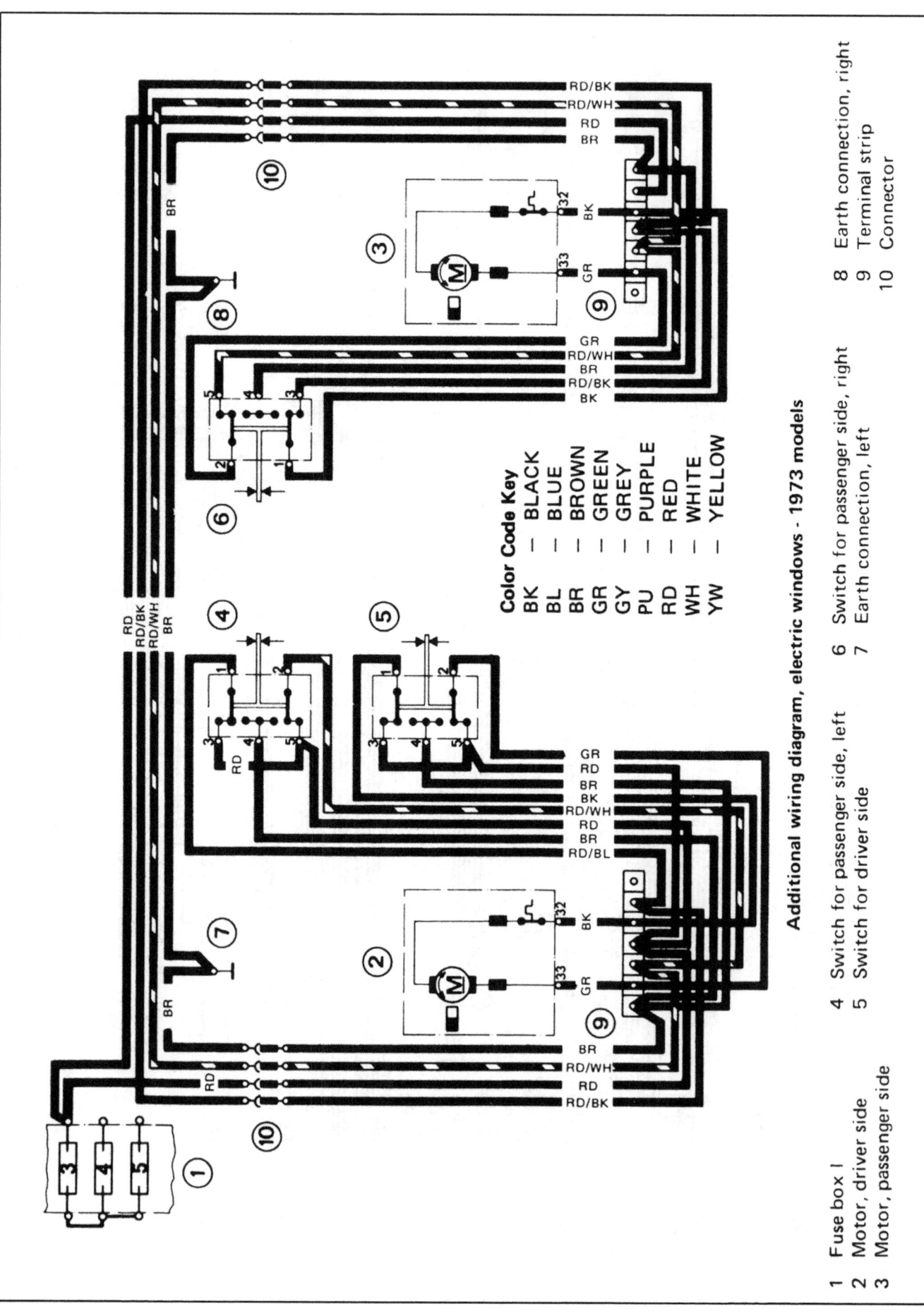

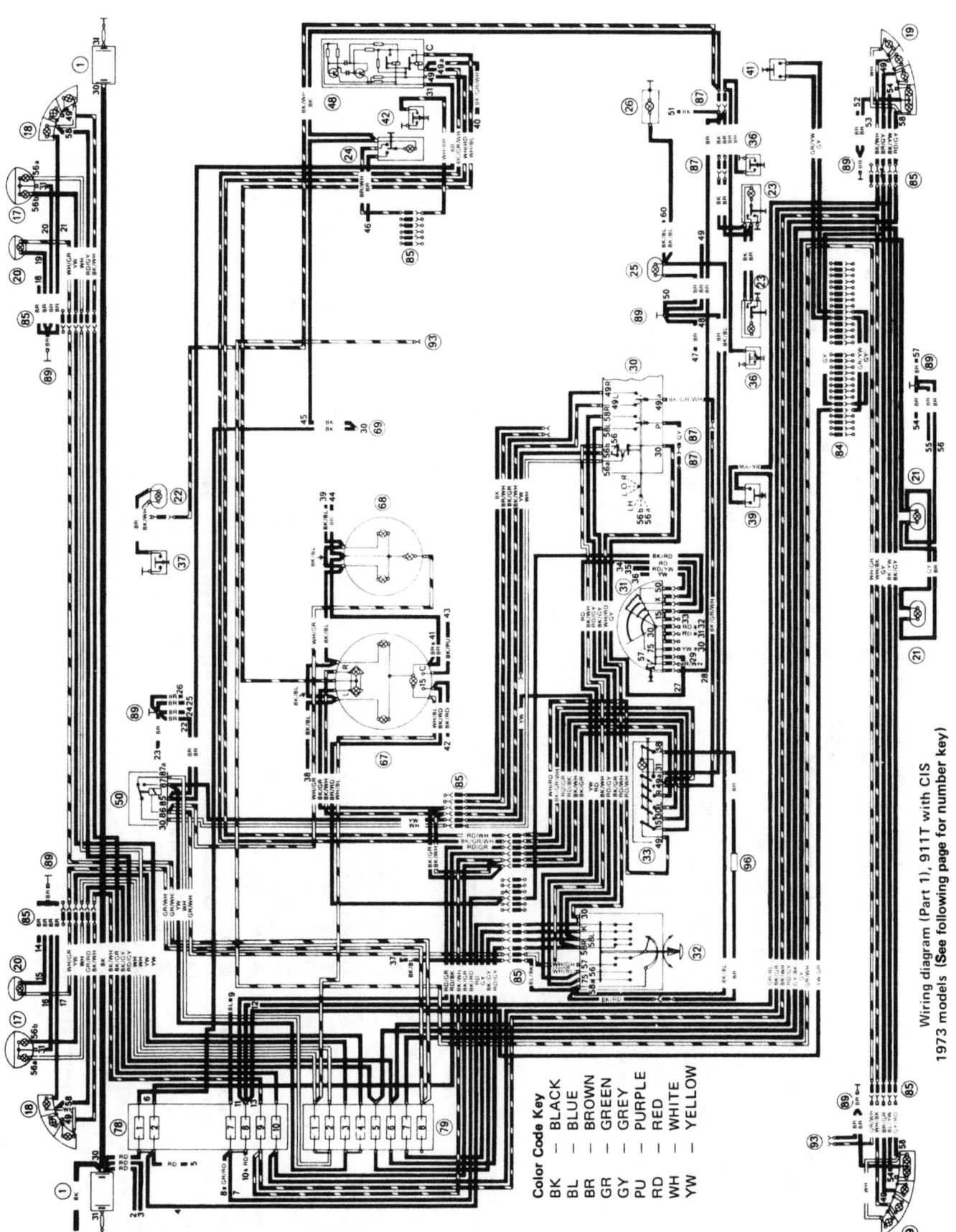

Wiring diagram (Part 1), 911T with CIS 1973 models (See following page for number key)

Key to Wiring Diagram (Part 1). 911T with C1S - 1973 models

1. Battery
17. Headlights
18. Turn signal, parking and side marker lights (side marker lights USA only)
19. Tail, stop, turn, backup and side marker lights (side marker lights USA only)
20. Fog lights (optional)
21. License plate light
22. Luggage compartment light
23. Interior light
24. Glove compartment light
25. Ashtray light
26. Illumination for heating lever (USA only)
30. Flasher, dimmer, wiper-washer switch with horn ring on steering column
31. Ignition starter switch and steering lock
32. Light switch
33. Emergency flasher switch (not applicable in Italy and France)
36. Door contact switch
37. Switch for luggage compartment light
39. Stop light switch
41. Back up light switch
42. Switch for glove compartment light
48. Turn signal/emergency flasher unit
50. Headlight relay
67. Tachometer
68. Speedometer
69. Electric clock
78. Fuse box I (10 terminal)
79. Fuse box II (8 terminal)
84. Multi-connector (14 terminal)
85. Multi-connector (6 terminal)
87. Connector (single contact)
89. Earth connection-body
93. Rear fog light (optional)
96. Resistor (USA only)

FUSES:

Fuse box I:
1. Interior light, lock, luggage compartment light
2. Emergency flasher
7. Fresh air fan
8. Stop, turn and backup lights
9. Left front turn signal light
10. Right front turn signal light

Fuse box II:
1. High beam, left
2. High beam, right
3. Low beam, left
4. Low beam, right
5. Side marker, left
6. Side marker, right
7. License plate light
8. (Fog lights)

Key to Wiring Diagram (Part 2) 911T with C1S - 1973 models

1. Battery
2. Starter
3. Alternator
4. Governor
5. Distributor
7. Ignition transformer
8. Spark plugs
9. Fuel pump
10. High tension ignition unit
12. Cold start solenoid
13. Control pressure regulating valve with warm-up compensation
14. Micro-switch
30. Flasher, dimmer, wiper-washer switch with horn ring on steering column
31. Ignition starter switch and steering lock
34. Switch for fan and auxiliary heater
35. Rear window defogger switch
38. Parking brake contact
40. Brake warning light switch (USA only)
43. Safety belt contact, driver side (USA only)
44. Safety belt contact, passenger side (USA only)
45. Buzzer contact (USA only)
46. Seat contact, passenger side (USA only)
49. Horn relay
51. Rear window defogger relay
53. Buzzer (USA only)
56. Oil temperature indicator
57. Oil pressure indicator (optional)
58. Oil level indicator (optional)
59. Indicator for fuel gauge
60. Safety belt warning light (USA only)
65. Fuel gauge dial
66. Oil temperature gauge dial
69. Electric clock
73. Wiper motor
74. Washer pump
75. Horns
77. Cigarette lighter
78. Fuse box I (10 terminals)
80. Fuse box III (3 terminal)
81. Fan motor
82. Rear window defogger element
83. Sportomatic (optional)
84. Multi-connector (14 terminal)
85. Multi-connector (6 terminal)
86. Multi-connector (4 terminal)
87. Connector (single contact)
88. Gear lever contact SPM (optional)
89. Earth connection-body
90. Optional horn
92. Auxiliary combustion heater (optional)
94. Radio (optional)

FUSES:

Fuse box I:
1. Interior light, lock, luggage compartment light
2. Emergency flasher
3. (Electric windows)
4. Cigarette lighter
5. (Sliding roof)
6. Windshield wiper, washer pump
7. Fresh air fan
8. Fresh air fan
9. Left front turn signal light
10. Right front turn signal light

Fuse box III:
1. (Sportomatic)
3. Rear window defogger

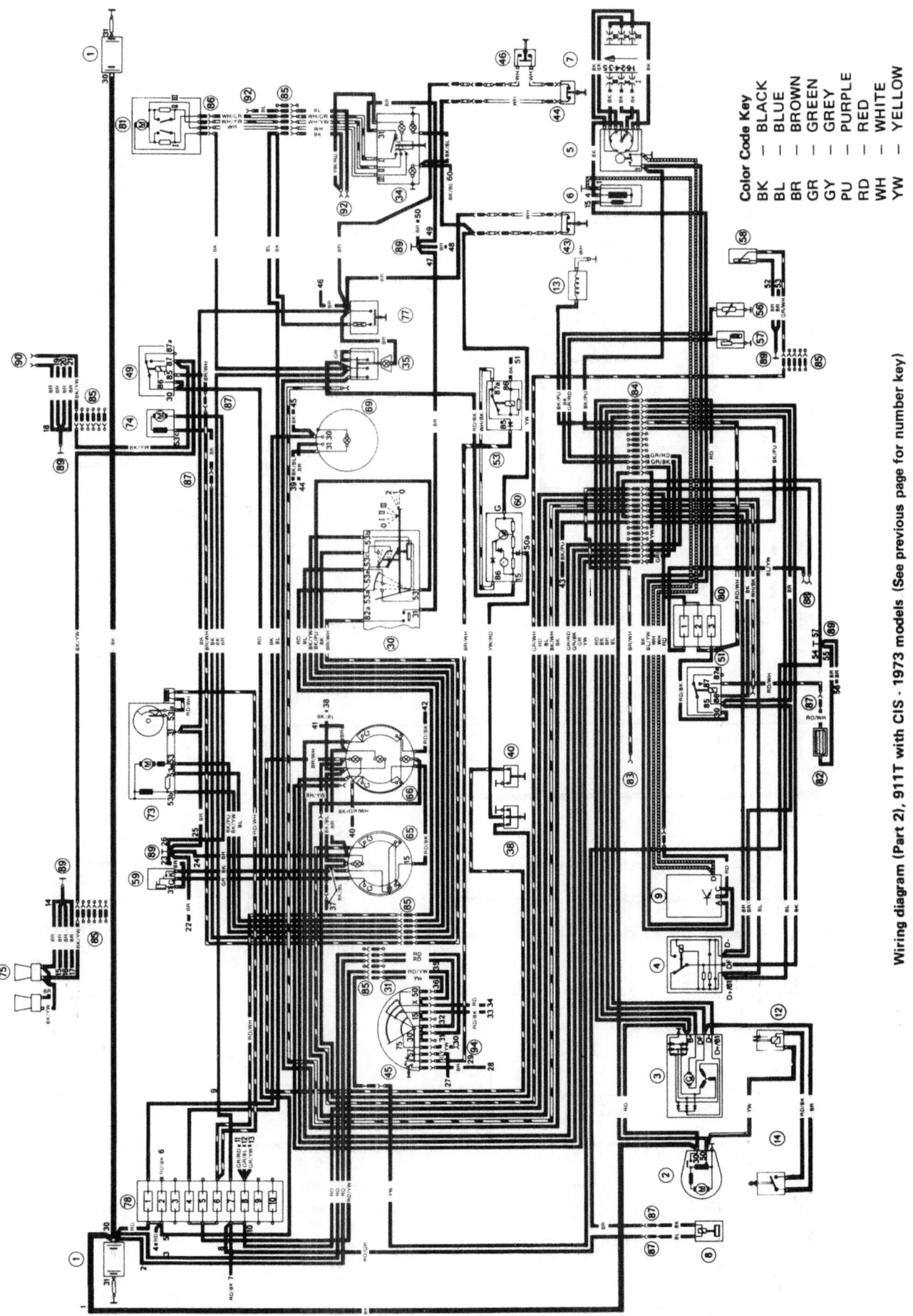

Color Code Key
BK – BLACK
BL – BLUE
BR – BROWN
GR – GREEN
GY – GREY
PU – PURPLE
RD – RED
WH – WHITE
YW – YELLOW

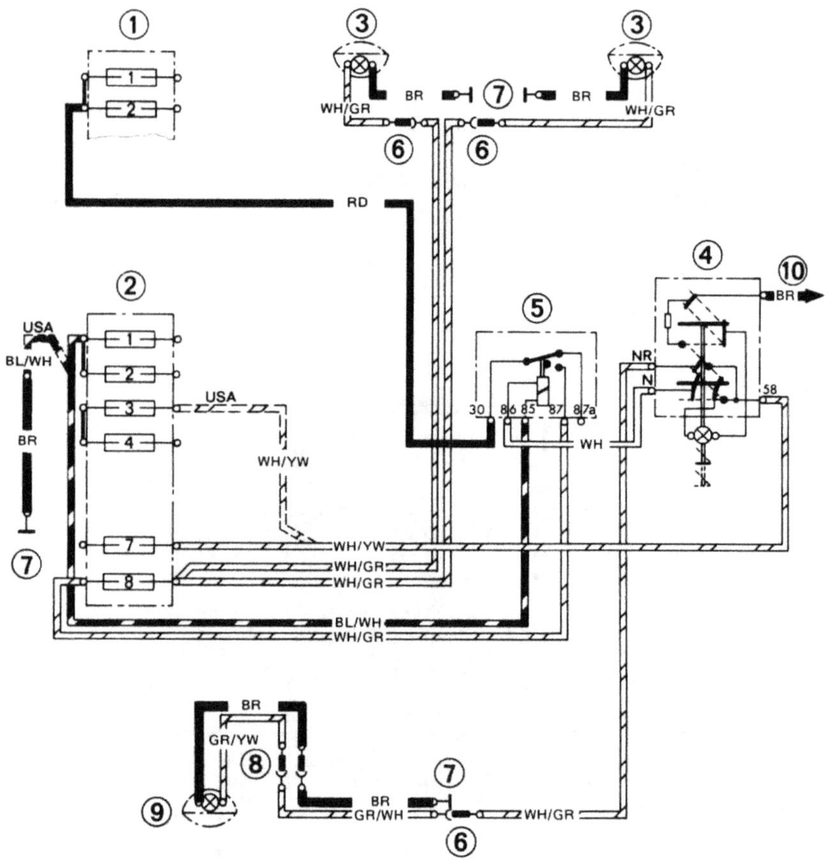

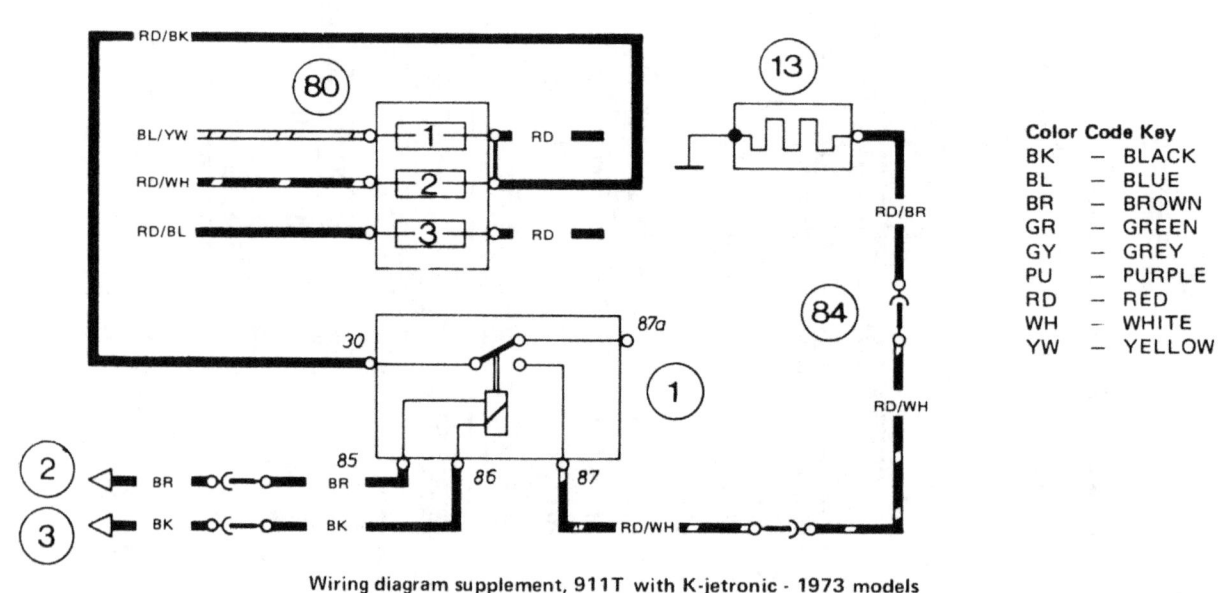

Additional wiring diagram, front and rear fog lights - 1973 models

1 Fuse box I
2 Fuse box II
3 Fog lights
4 Fog lights switch
5 Relay
6 Multi-connector (6 terminal)
7 Earth connection-body
8 Connector (double-contact)
9 Rear fog light
10 Ground connection (cigarette lighter)

Color Code Key
BK – BLACK
BL – BLUE
BR – BROWN
GR – GREEN
GY – GREY
PU – PURPLE
RD – RED
WH – WHITE
YW – YELLOW

Wiring diagram supplement, 911T with K-jetronic - 1973 models

1 Solenoid switch
2 To voltage regulator, terminal D- (earth)
3 To voltage regulator, terminal D+/61
13 Warm-up regulator
80 Fuse box III
84 14-pole connector, connector No 10

Key to Current flow diagram (Part 1 - A & B) - 1974 and 1975 onwards models

		Current track
E1	Headlight switch	6,8,9,11, 15,20
E2	Turn signal switch	28
E3	Emergency flasher switch	24,25 28,31,34
E4	Dimmer switch	6,39
E5	Headlight flasher switch	4
E19	Parking light switch	13
E20	Instrument panel illumination potentiometer	20
E26	Switch for glove compartment light	41
F	Stop light switch	50
F2	Left door switch	45
F3	Right door switch	46
F4	Back-up light switch	48
F5	Switch for luggage compartment light	42
F9	Parking brake switch	33
H	Horn switch	39
H2	Horns	36,38
J1	Hazard/turn signal flasher	33,34,35
J4	Horn relay	36,37
J25	Headlight relay	4,5
K1	High beam indicator light	2
K4	Parking lights indicator light	1
K5	Turn signal indicator light	27,29
K6	Hazard flasher indicator light	24
K14	Parking brake indicator light	34
L1	Left headlight	3,7
L2	Right headlight	4,8
L6	Speedometer illumination light	22
L7	Fuel gauge illumination light	22
L8	Clock illumination light	22
L15	Ashtray illumination light	20
L24	Oil temperature indicator illumination light	22
L26	Tachometer illumination light	22
L27	Oil pressure indicator illumination light	22
M1	Left parking light	11
M2	Right stop/rear light	17,50
M3	Right parking light	15

		Current track
M4	Left stop/rear light	13,51
M5	Left front turn signal	25
M6	Left rear turn signal	26
M7	Right front turn signal	31
M8	Right rear turn signal	30
M16	Left back-up light	48
M17	Right back-up light	49
S2 to S11	Fuses on the fuse box	9,15,11 8,7,4 3,31,25,48
S17		34
S18		40
T1	Cable connector single	
a	near regulator panel	14
b	behind sealed beam unit, left	11,25
c	behind sealed beam unit, right	15,31
d	behind fuse box	37
e	on luggage compartment floor	22,42,44 45,46
f	behind instrument panel	6,22,24,28
h	near left rear lights	24
T6	Cable connector, six way	
a	in the engine compartment, rear left	9,13,24, 26,48,51
b	in the engine compartment, rear right	10,17, 30,49,50
d	below instrument panel	4,6,26, 30,39
e	below instrument panel	25,31,32,34
g	below instrument panel	8,9,11, 15,22
h	below instrument panel	41
T14	Cable connector, fourteen way	
a	on regulator panel, front	48
b	on regulator panel, rear	48
W	Interior light	45,46
W3	Luggage compartment light	42
W6	Glove compartment light	41
X	License plate light	9,10
Y	Clock	40

NOTES

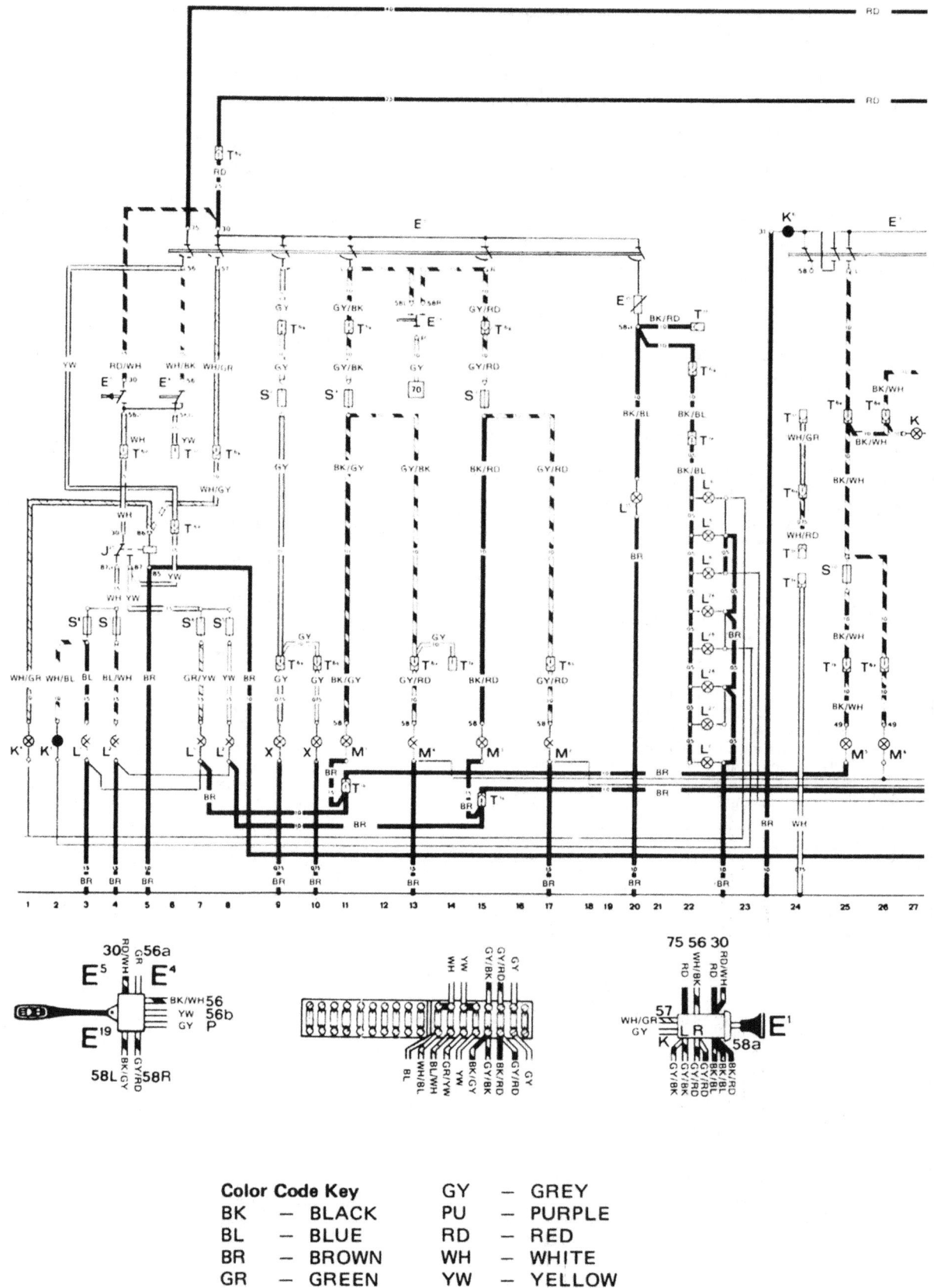

Color Code Key

BK	– BLACK	GY	– GREY
BL	– BLUE	PU	– PURPLE
BR	– BROWN	RD	– RED
GR	– GREEN	WH	– WHITE
		YW	– YELLOW

Current flow diagram (Part 1A) - 1974 and 1975 onwards models (See previous page for key)

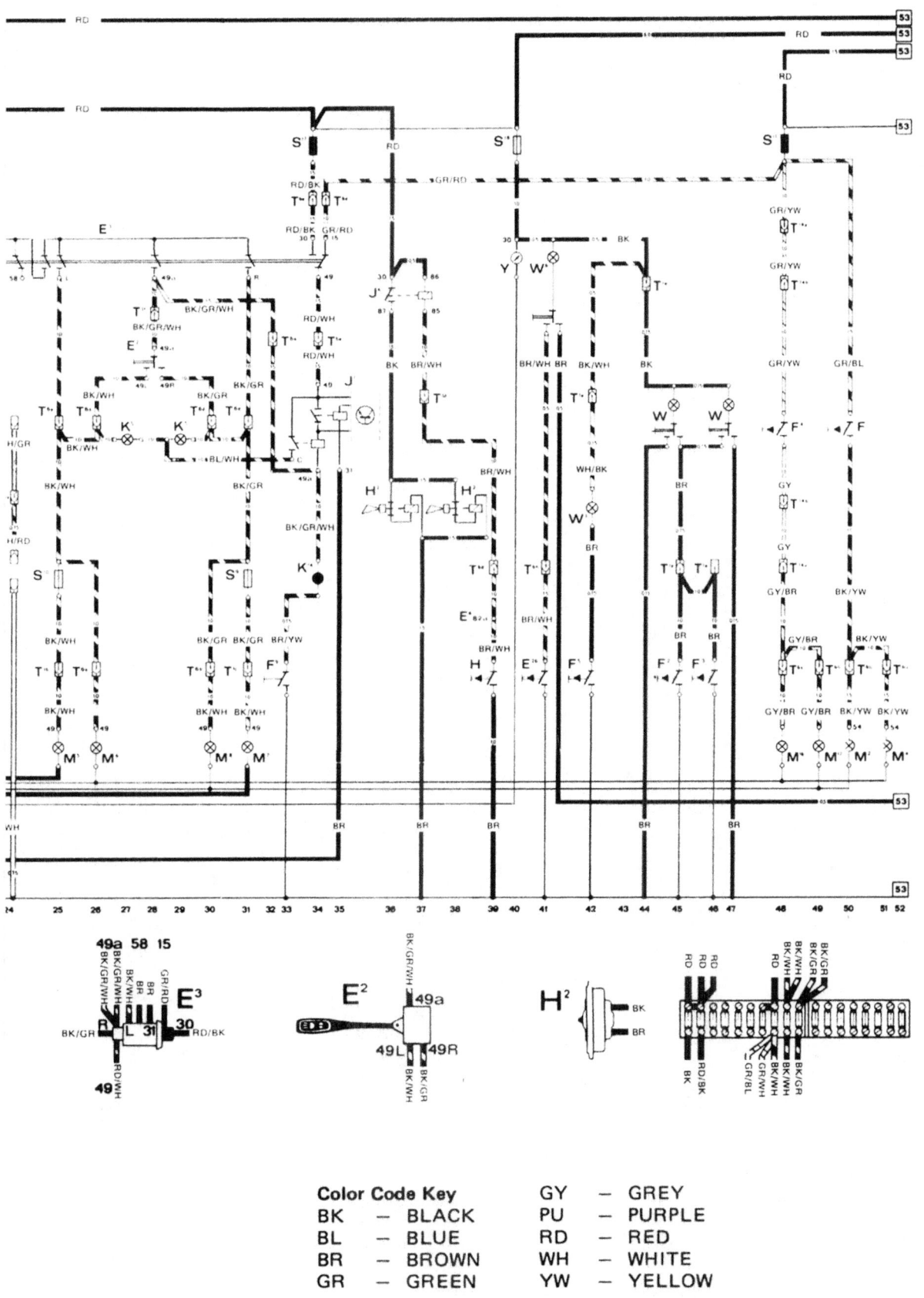

Current flow diagram (Part 1B) - 1974 and 1975 onwards models

NOTES

Key to Current flow diagrams (Part 2 - C & D) - 1974 models

		Current track
A	Battery	89
B	Starter	86,87
C	Generator	81,82,83,84
C2	Voltage regulator	81,82,83
D	Ignition/starter switch	68,69,70,71,72
E	Windshield wiper switch	63,64,65
E9	Fresh air blower switch	60
E15	Rear window defogger switch	55,56
F1	Oil pressure switch	79
G	Fuel sender unit	75
G1	Fuel gauge	76
G5	Tachometer	78
G6	Fuel pump	54
G8	Oil temperature sender unit	77
G9	Oil temperature indicator	77
G10	Oil pressure sender unit	80
G11	Oil pressure indicator	78
G12	Oil level sender unit	74
G13	Oil level gauge	74
J9	Rear window defogger relay	56,57
K2	Generator charge indicator light	77
K3	Oil pressure indicator	78
K8	Blower indicator light	61
K10	Rear window defogger indicator light	55
K16	Low fuel warning light	75
N	Ignition transformer	90
N15	High tension ignition unit	90
O	Distributor	91,92,93,94,95,96,97
P	Spark plug connector	92,93,94,95,96,97
Q	Spark plug	92,93 94,95,96,97
S12	Fuses	55,63
to	on the	62
S15	fuse box	61
S22	Fuses on the rear fuse box	99
S24	(regulator panel)	57
T1	Cable connector, single	
	a near regulator panel	56,57,58,79,83,99
	d behind fuse box	65
	e on luggage compartment floor	60,73,100
	f behind instrument panel	58,60,61,69,70
	g below shift lever housing	99
T2	Cable connector, double	
	a below regulator panel	99
	b in engine compartment, left	54
T6	Cable connector, six way	
	b in engine compartment, right	74
	c below instrument panel	63,64,65
	f below instrument panel	66,67,72,88,89
	h below instrument panel	60,61
T14	Cable connector, fourteen way	
	a on regulator panel, front	56,58,73,77, 80,85,98,99,100
	b on regulator panel, rear	57,77,80,81, 83,86,98,100
U1	Cigar lighter	62
V	Windshield wiper motor	63,64
V2	Blower motor	60
V5	Washer pump	65
Z1	Rear window defogger	57

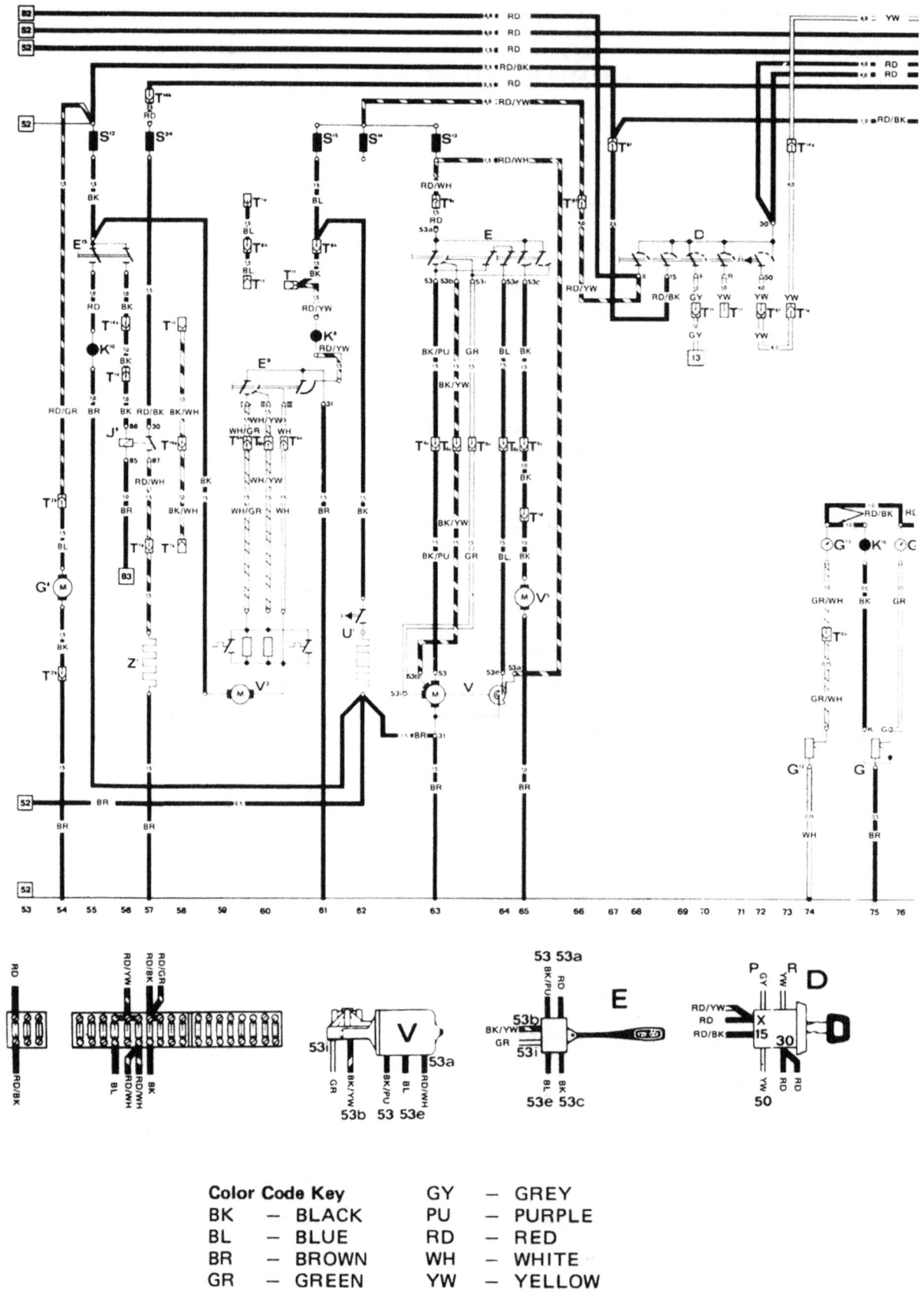

Current flow diagram (Part 2C) - 1974 models (See previous page for key)

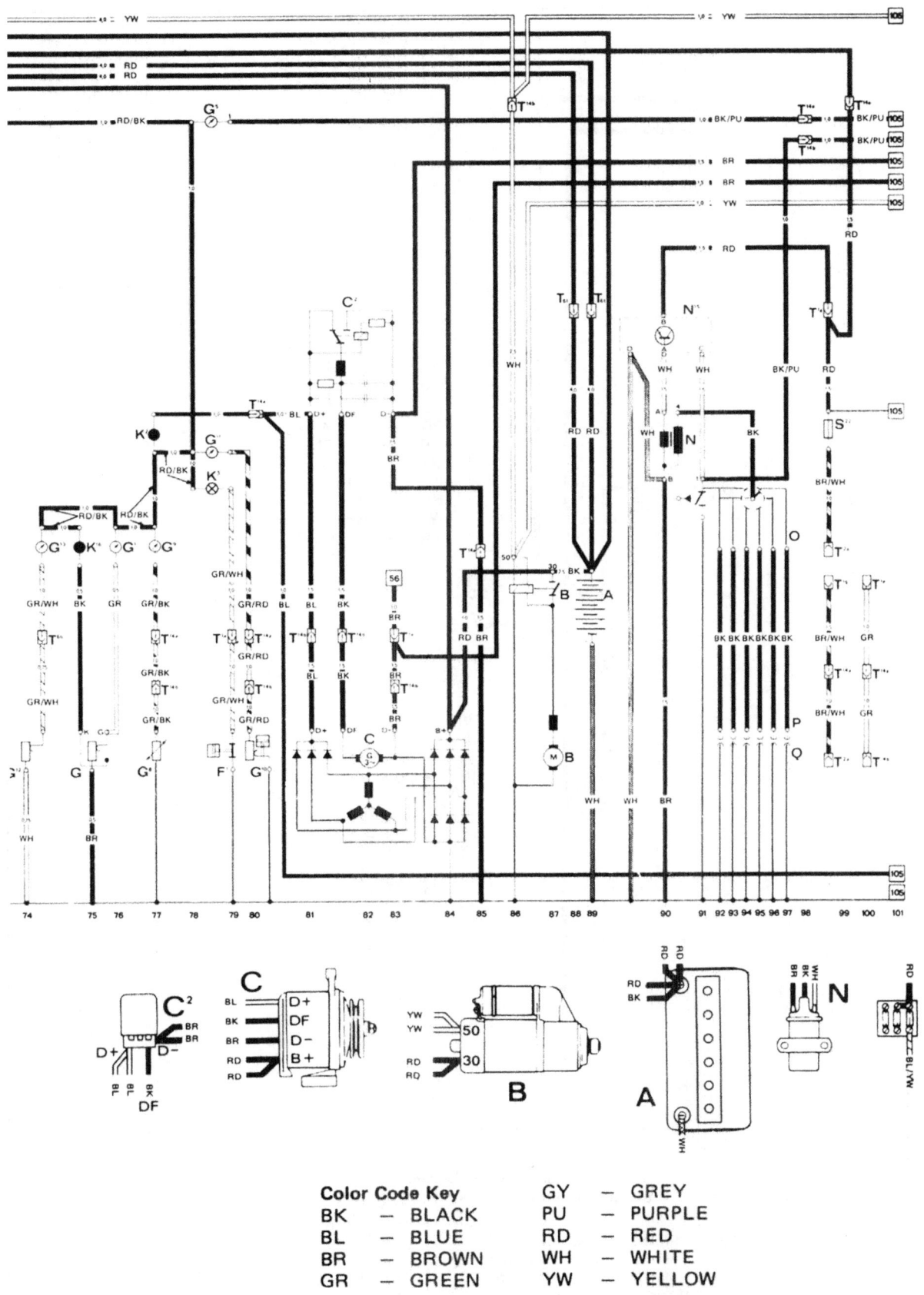

Current flow diagram (Part 2D) - 1974 models

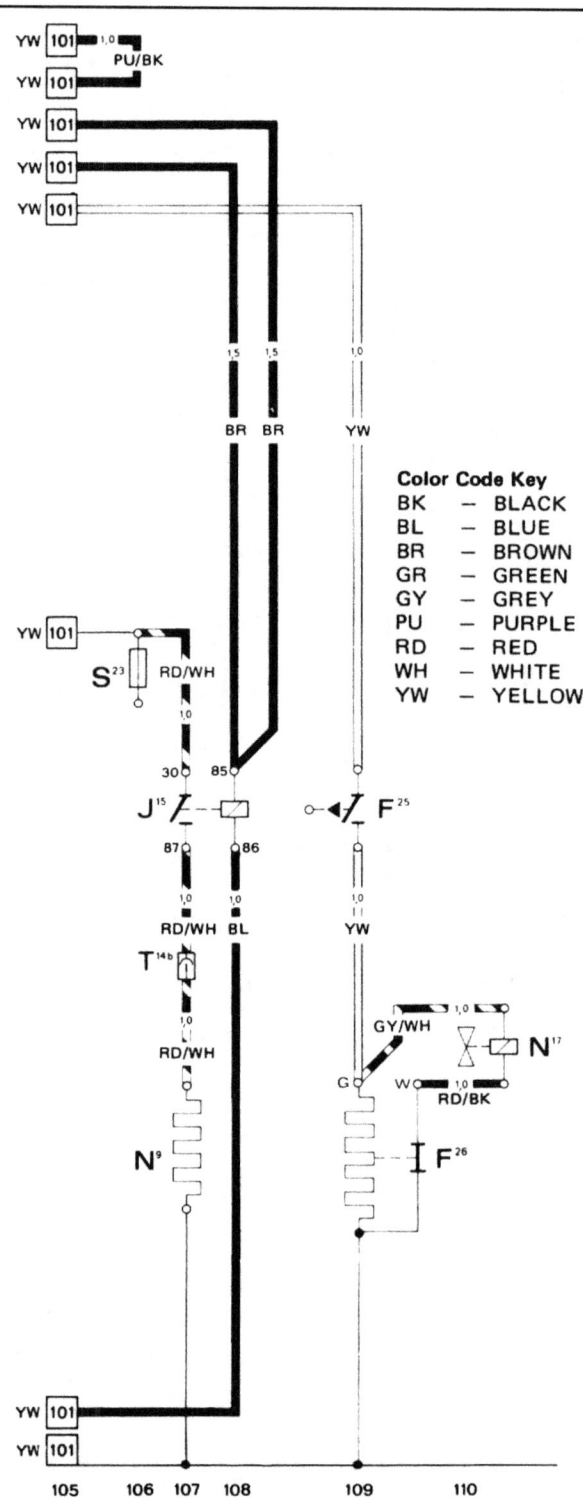

**Additional current flow diagram,
911 with K-jetronic - 1974 models**

		Current track
F25	Throttle valve switch	109
F26	Thermo-switch for cold start valve	109
J15	Relay for warm-up regulator	107, 108
N9	Warm-up regulator	107
N17	Cold start valve	110
S23	Fuse on the rear fuse box	106
T14b	Cable connector, fourteenway on regulator panel, rear	107

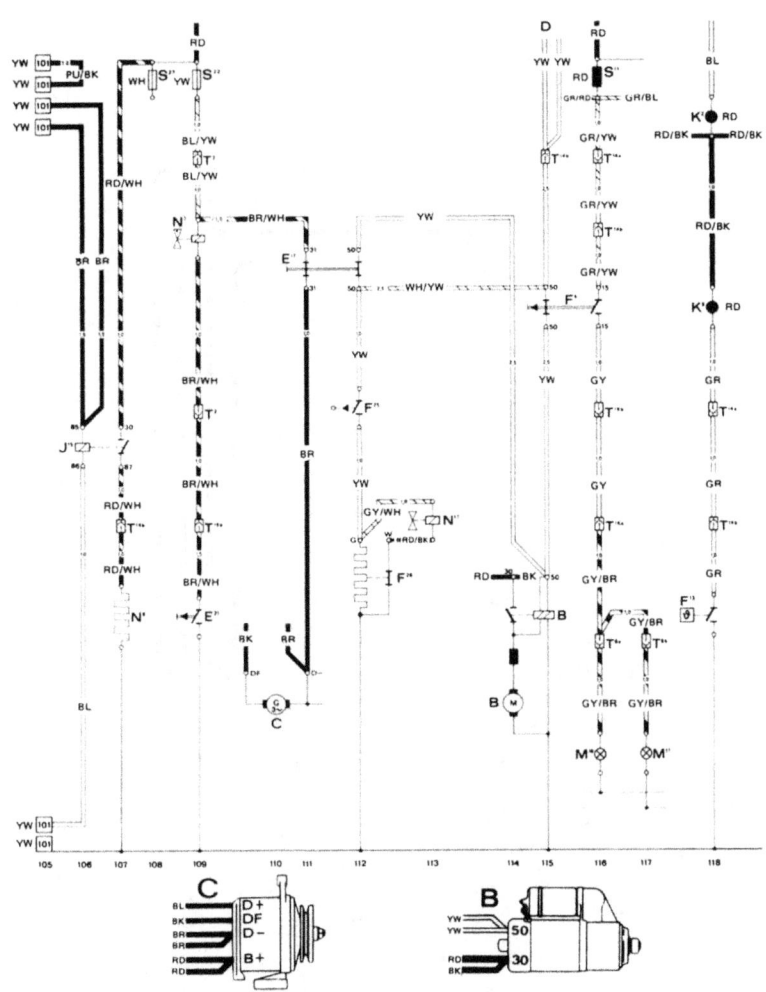

Additional current flow diagram, Carrera - 1974 models

		Current track
B	Starter	114,115
C	Generator	110,111
D	to ignition/starter switch	115
E17	Starter cutout switch (bypass switch)	111,112
E21	Selector lever contact	109
F4	Back-up light switch	115,116
F13	Oil temperature switch	118
F25	Throttle valve switch (micro switch)	112
F26	Thermo-switch for cold start valve	112
J15	Relay for warm-up regulator	106,107
K2	Generator charge indicator light	118
K9	Oil temperature indicator light	118
M16	Left back-up light	116
M17	Right back-up light	117
N7	Control valve	109
N9	Warm-up regulator	107
N17	Cold start valve	113
S11	Fuse on the fuse box	116
S22	Fuse on the rear fuse box (regulator panel)	109
S23	Fuse on the rear fuse box (regulator panel)	108
T2	Cable connector, double, below regulator panel	109
T6	Cable connector, sixway	
	a in engine compartment, rear left	116
	b in engine compartment, rear right	117
T14	Cable connector, fourteenway	109,116,118
	a on regulator panel, front	107,115,116,118
	b on regulator panel, rear	118

Color Code Key

BK	–	BLACK
BL	–	BLUE
BR	–	BROWN
GR	–	GREEN
GY	–	GREY
PU	–	PURPLE
RD	–	RED
WH	–	WHITE
YW	–	YELLOW

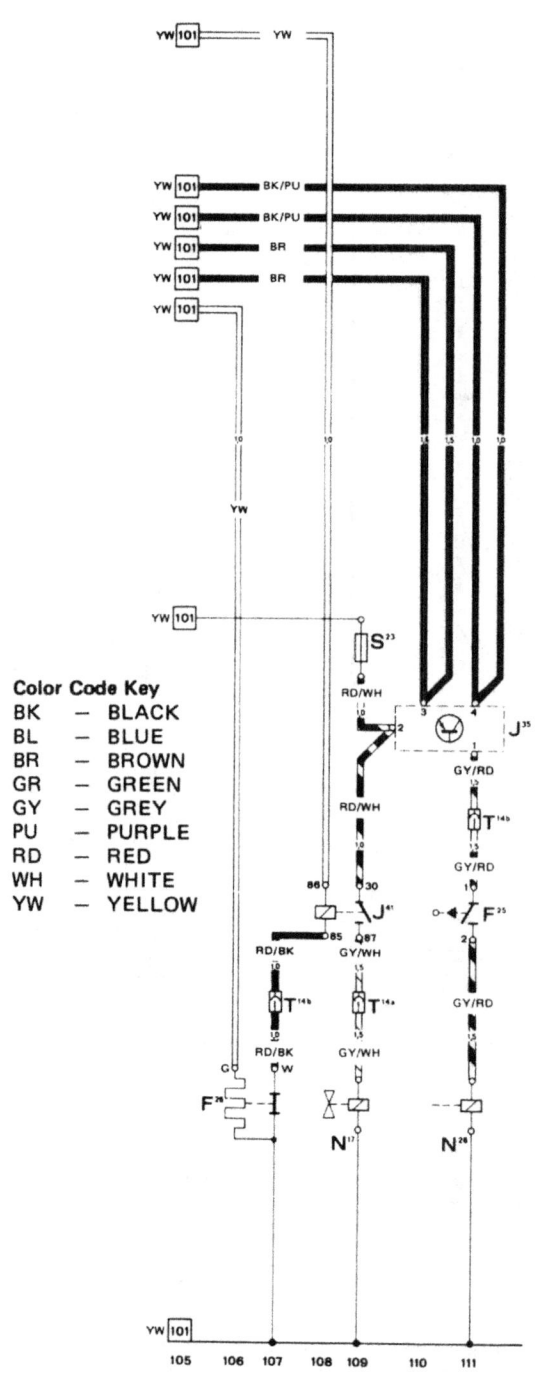

Additional current flow diagram, K-jetronic and Sportomatic - 1974 models

		Current track
F25	Throttle valve switch	111
F26	Thermo-switch for cold start valve	106, 107
J35	Speed switch	110, 111
J41	Auxiliary starting relay	108, 109
N17	Cold start solenoid	109
N26	Shut-off solenoid	111
S23	Fuse on the rear fuse box	109
T14	Cable connector, fourteenway	
	a on regulator panel, front	109
	b on regulator panel, rear	107, 111

Key to Current flow diagrams (Part 2 - E & F) - 1975 onwards models

		Current track
A	Battery	89
B	Starter	86,87
C	Generator	81,82,83,84
C2	Voltage regulator	81,82,83
D	Ignition/starter switch	68,69,70,71,72
E	Windshield wiper switch	63,64,65
E9	Fresh air blower switch	60
E15	Rear window defogger switch	55,56
F1	Oil pressure switch	79
G	Fuel sender unit	75
G1	Fuel gauge	76
G5	Tachometer	78
G6	Fuel pump	54
G8	Oil temperature sender unit	77
G9	Oil temperature indicator	77
G10	Oil pressure sender unit	80
G11	Oil pressure indicator	78
G12	Oil level sender unit	74
G13	Oil level gauge	74
J9	Rear window defogger relay	56,57
K2	Generator charge indicator light	77
K3	Oil pressure indicator	78
K8	Blower indicator light	61
K10	Rear window defogger indicator light	55
K16	Low fuel warning light	75
N	Ignition transformer	90
N15	High tension ignition unit	90
O	Distributor	91,92,93,94,95,96,97
P	Spark plug connector	92,93,94,95,96,97
Q	Spark plug	92,93 94,95,96,97
S12	Fuses	55,63
to	on the	62
S15	fuse box	61
S22	Fuses on the rear fuse box	99
S24	(regulator panel)	57
T1	Cable connector, single	
a	near regulator panel	56,57,58,79,83,99
d	behind fuse box	65
e	on luggage compartment floor	60,73,100
f	behind instrument panel	58,60,61,69,70
g	below shift lever housing	99
T2	Cable connector, double	
a	below regulator panel	99
b	in engine compartment, left	54
T6	Cable connector, six way	
b	in engine compartment, right	74
c	below instrument panel	63,64,65
f	below instrument panel	66,67,72,88,89
h	below instrument panel	60,61
T14	Cable connector, fourteen way	
a	on regulator panel, front	56,58,73,77,80,85,98,99,100
b	on regulator panel, rear	57,77,80,81,83,86,98,100
U1	Cigar lighter	62
V	Windshield wiper motor	63,64
V2	Blower motor	60
V5	Washer pump	65
Z1	Rear window defogger	57

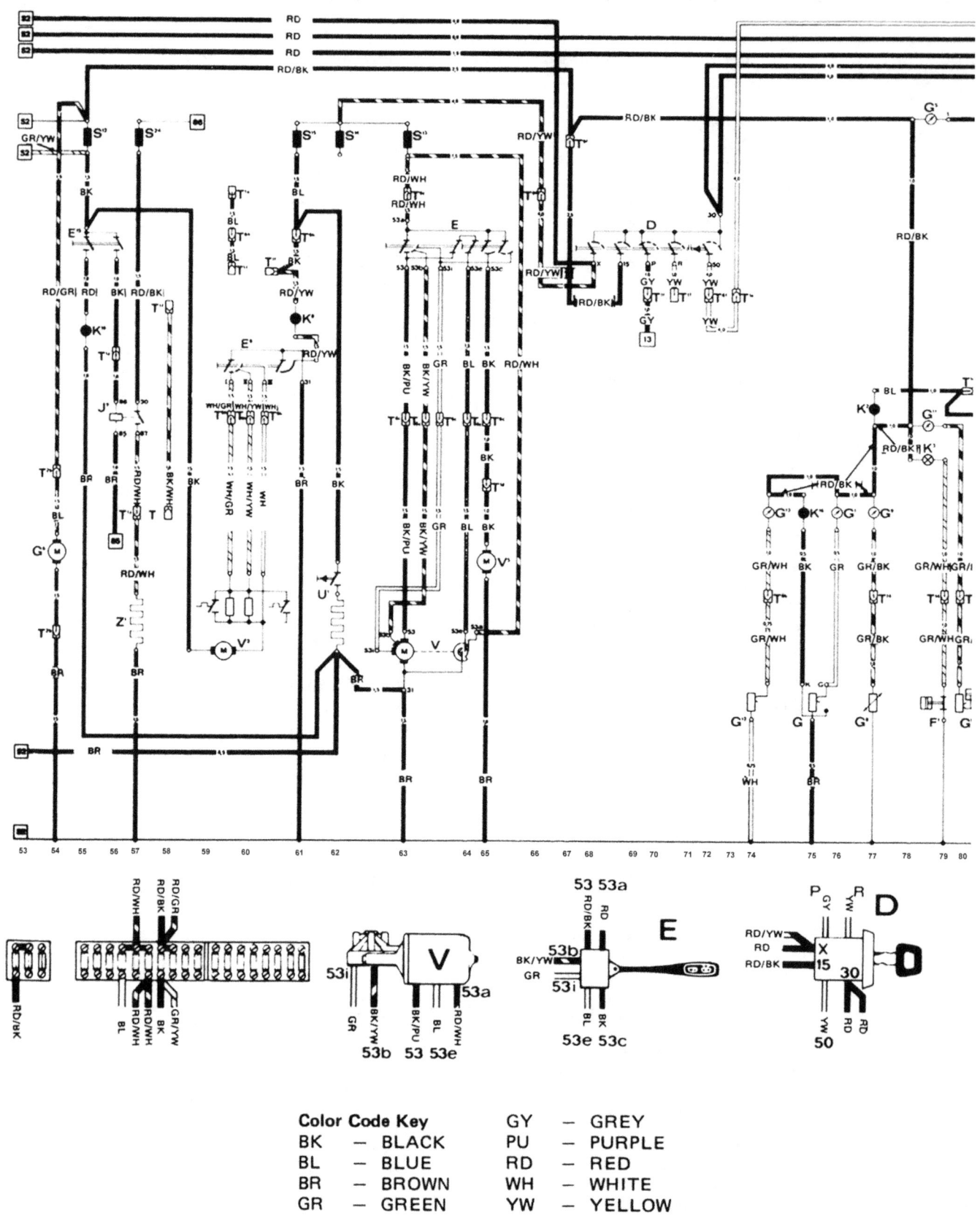

Current flow diagram (Part 2E) - 1975 models (See previous page for key)

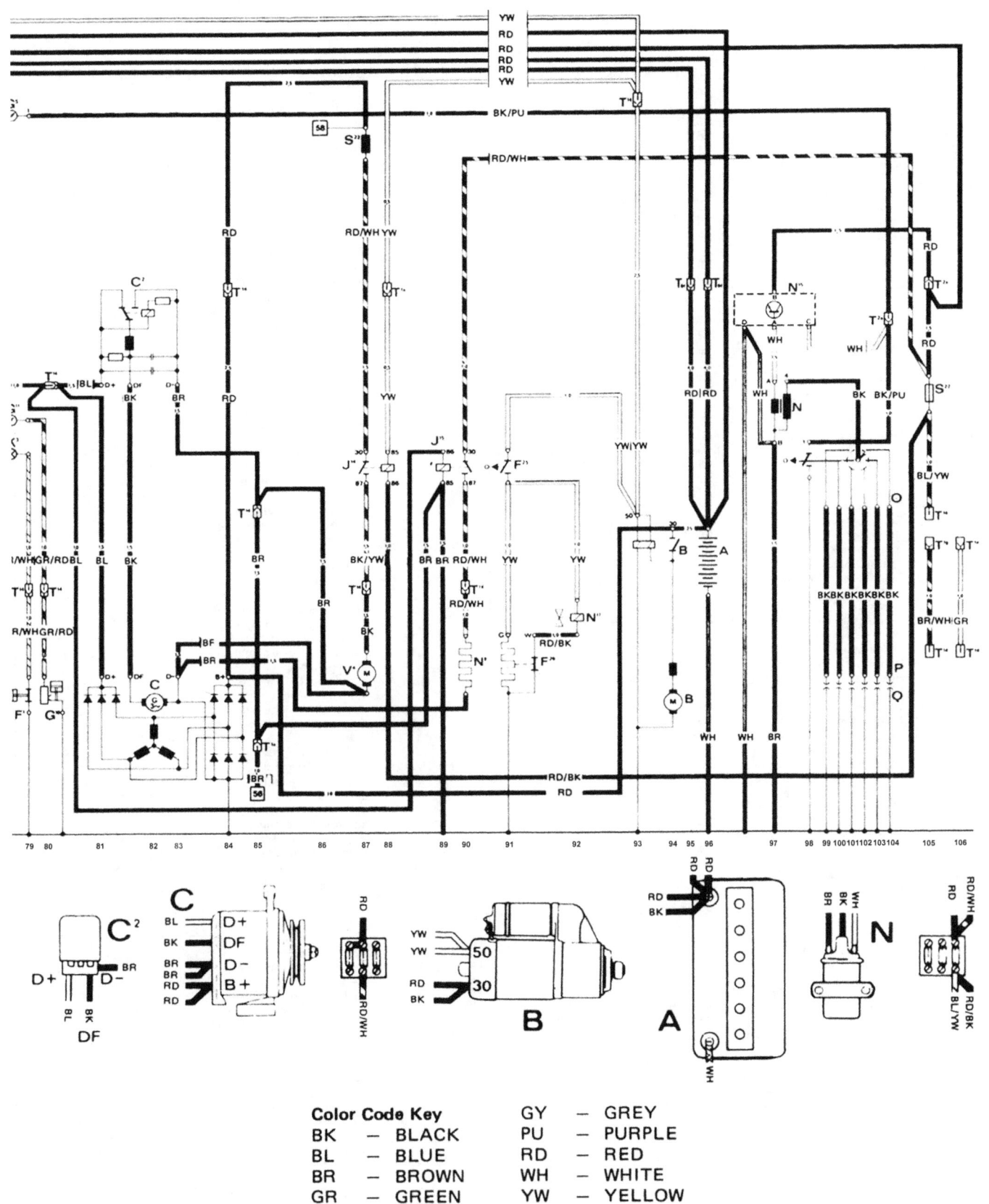

Current flow diagram (Part 2F) - 1975 models

Key to current flow diagram for 911 and Carrera, 1977 models

Description			Current track
A	=	Battery	105
B	=	Starter	102,103
C	=	Generator	88,89,92
C2	=	Voltage regulator	88,89,90
C12	=	Capacitor for ignition unit	116
D	=	Ignition/starter switch	73,74,75,76,77
E	=	Windscreen wiper switch	69-77
E9	=	Fresh air blower switch	60
E15	=	Rear window demister switch	55,56
E14	=	Heater blower switch	99
E43	=	Outside mirror control switch	64,65
F1	=	Oil pressure switch	86
F6	=	Brake warning switch	79
F9	=	Parking brake switch	79
F26	=	Thermo-switch for cold start valve	100
G	=	Fuel sender unit	82
G1	=	Fuel gauge	83
G5	=	Tachometer	85
G6	=	Fuel pump	96
G8	=	Oil temperature sender unit	84
G9	=	Oil temperature indicator	84
G10	=	Oil pressure sender unit	87
G11	=	Oil pressure indicator	85
G12	=	Oil level sender unit	80
G13	=	Oil level gauge	80
G19	=	Air meter contact	95
G21	=	Speedometer	67
G22	=	Speedometer sensor	67
J9	=	Rear window demister relay	56,57
J14	=	Relay for heater blower	98,99
J16	=	Relay for fuel pump	95,96
J31	=	Relay for intermittent wiper operation	72-76
J34	=	Relay for seat belt warning system	77,78
K2	=	Generator charge indicator light	84
K3	=	Oil pressure indicator light	85
K7	=	Parking brake/brake warning indicator light	61
K8	=	Blower indicator light	61
K10	=	Rear window demister indicator light	55
K16	=	Low fuel warning light	81
K19	=	Seat belt warning light	79
N	=	Ignition transformer	106
N9	=	Warm-up regulator	93
N15	=	High tension ignition unit	106,107
N17	=	Cold start valve	101
N21	=	Supplementary air valve	94
N35	=	Magnetic clutch for mirror control	66
N43	=	Thermo-valve for cold starting device	94
O	=	Distributor	107-113
P	=	Spark plug connector	108-113
Q	=	Spark plug	108-113
S12 to S16	=	Fuses on fuse box	55,68,63,61,96
S22 to S24	=	Fuses on rear fuse box (regulator panel)	114,99,57
T1	=	Cable connector, single	
		a – near regulator panel	56,57,58,95,99,116
		b – behind fuse box	77,93
		e – on luggage compartment floor	72,76,77,115
		f – behind instrument panel	58,75,76,79
		g – below gear lever housing	114
T2	=	Cable connector, double	
		a – below regulator panel	113,114
		b – in engine compartment, left	91,98
		i – in tunnel, rear	67
		k – below regulator panel	95,96
T4	=	Cable connector, quadruple in outside mirror housing	63,64
T6	=	Cable connector, sixfold	
		b – in engine compartment, right	80
		c – below instrument panel	69,70,71,72,77
		f – below instrument panel	70,71,72,77,104,105
		h – below instrument panel	60,61
T14	=	Cable connector, fourteenfold on regulator panel	84,86,87,92 93,98,102,114,115

Colour code		
Wh	–	White
Gn	–	Green
Bu	–	Blue
Bn	–	Brown
Y	–	Yellow
Bk	–	Black
R	–	Red
Gy	–	Grey
Pu	–	Purple

Description			Current track
U1	=	Cigar lighter	62
V	=	Windscreen wiper motor	69,70,71,72
V2	=	Blower motor	60
V4	=	Heater blower	98
V5	=	Washer pump	77
V17	=	Outside mirror control motor	64
Z1	=	Rear window demister	57
Z4	=	Outside mirror demister	63
E	=	Windscreen wiper switch	39
E1	=	Headlight switch	6,8,9,11,15,20
E2	=	Turn signal switch	28
E3	=	Emergency flasher switch	24,25,28,31,34
E4	=	Dip switch	6,39
E5	=	Headlight flasher switch	4
E19	=	Parking light switch	13
E20	=	Instrument panel illumination rheostat	20
E26	=	Switch for glove compartment light	41
F	=	Stop light switch	50
F2	=	Left door switch	45
F3	=	Right door switch	46
F4	=	Reversing light switch	48
F5	=	Switch for luggage compartment light	42
H	=	Horn switch	39
H2	=	Horns	36,37,38
J1	=	Hazard/turn signal flasher	33,34,35
J4	=	Horn relay	36,37
K1	=	High beam indicator light	2
K4	=	Parking lights indicator light	1
K5	=	Turn signal indicator light	27,29
K6	=	Hazard flasher indicator light	24
L1	=	Left headlight	3,7
L2	=	Right headlight	4,8
L6	=	Speedometer illumination light	22
L7	=	Fuel gauge illumination light	22
L8	=	Clock illumination light	22
L15	=	Ashtray illumination light	20
L16	=	Heater control assembly illumination light	18
L24	=	Oil temperature indicator illumination light	22
L26	=	Tachometer illumination light	22
L27	=	Oil pressure indicator illumination light	22
M1	=	Left parking light	11
M2	=	Right stop/rear light	17,50
M3	=	Right parking light	15
M4	=	Left stop/rear light	13,51
M5	=	Left front turn signal	25
M6	=	Left rear turn signal	26
M7	=	Right front turn signal	31
M8	=	Right rear turn signal	30
M16	=	Left back-up light	48
M17	=	Right back-up light	49
S2	=	Fuses on the fusebox	9,15,11,8,7,4,3,31,25,48
S17	=	Fuse on fusebox	34
S18	=	Fuse on fusebox	40
T1	=	Cable connector, single	
		a – near regulator panel	14
		b – behind sealed beam unit, left	11,25
		c – behind sealed beam unit, right	15,31
		d – behind fuse box	37
		e – on luggage compartment floor	22,42,44,45,46
		f – behind instrument panel	6,22,24,28
		h – near left rear lights	24
T6	=	Cable connector, sixfold	
		a – in the engine compartment, rear left	9,13,24,26,48,51
		b – in the engine compartment, rear right	10,17,30,49,50
		d – below instrument panel	4,6,26,30,39
		e – below instrument panel	25,31,32,34
		g – below instrument panel	8,9,11,15,22
		h – below instrument panel	41
T14	=	Cable connector, fourteenfold on regulator panel, front	48
W	=	Interior light	45,46,47
W3	=	Luggage compartment light	42
W6	=	Glove compartment light	41
X	=	Number plate light	9,10
Y	=	Clock	40

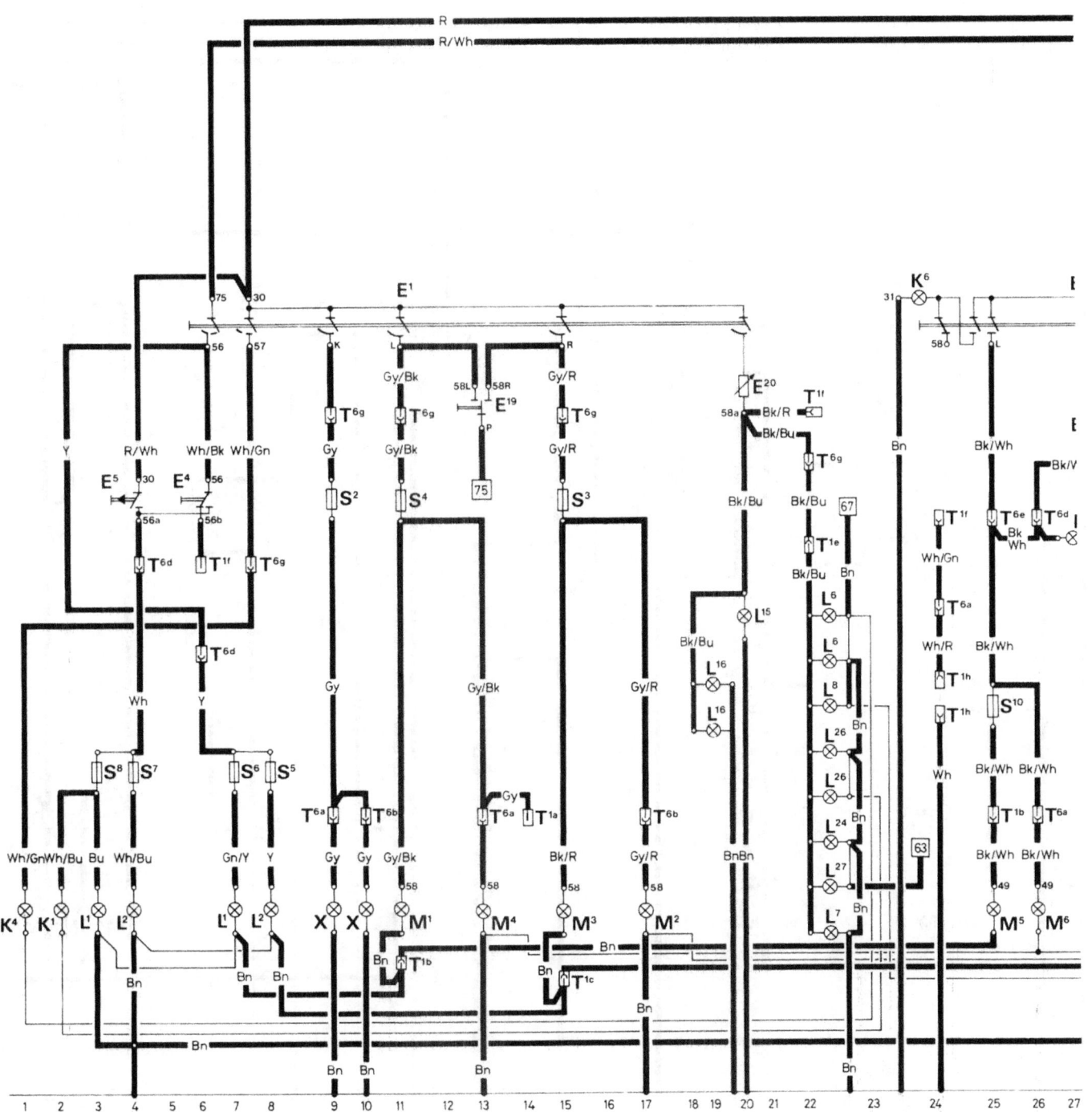

Current flow diagram for 911 and Carrera, 1977 models (diagram 1 of 5)

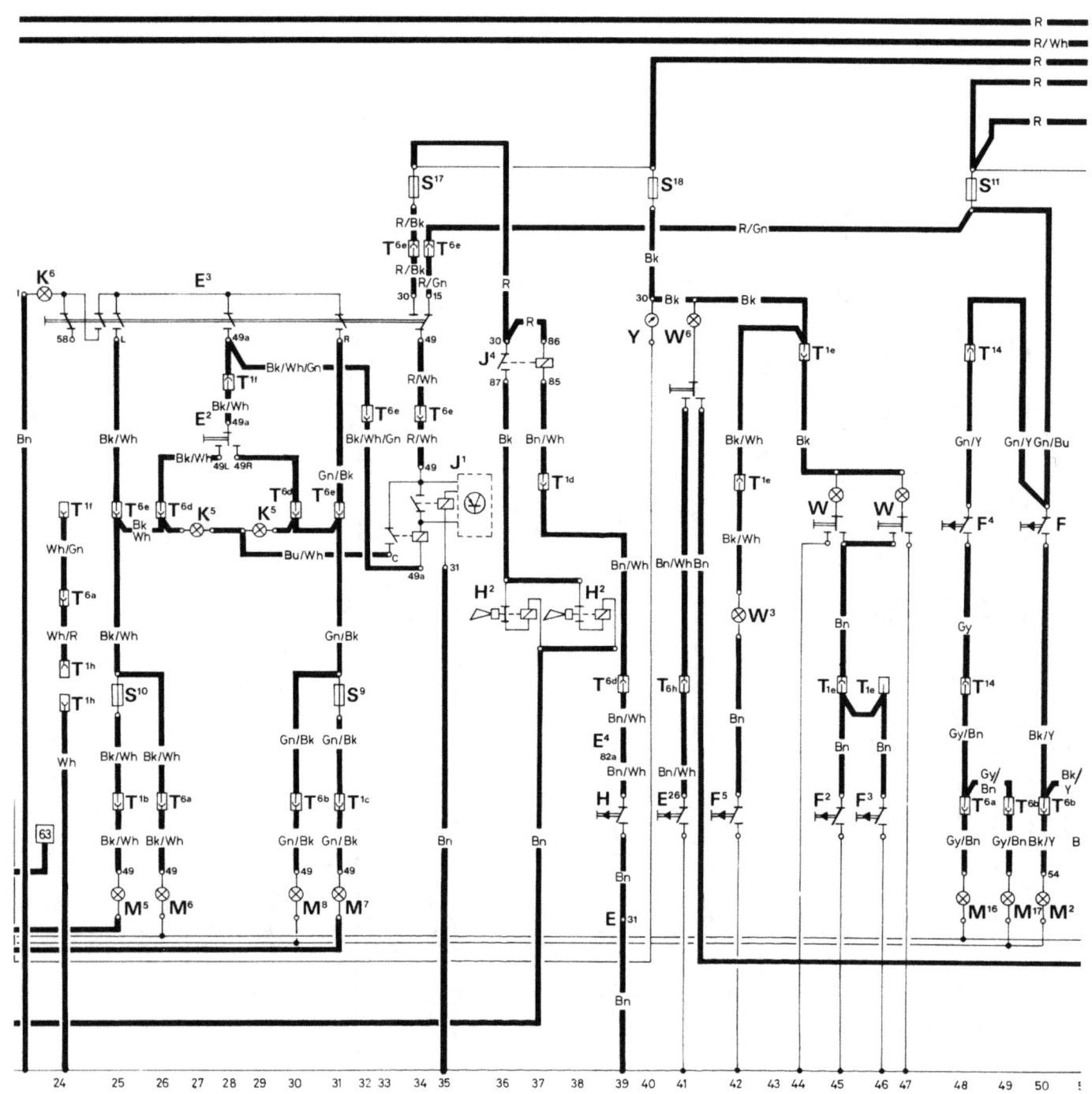

Current flow diagram for 911 and Carrera, 1977 models (diagram 2 of 5)

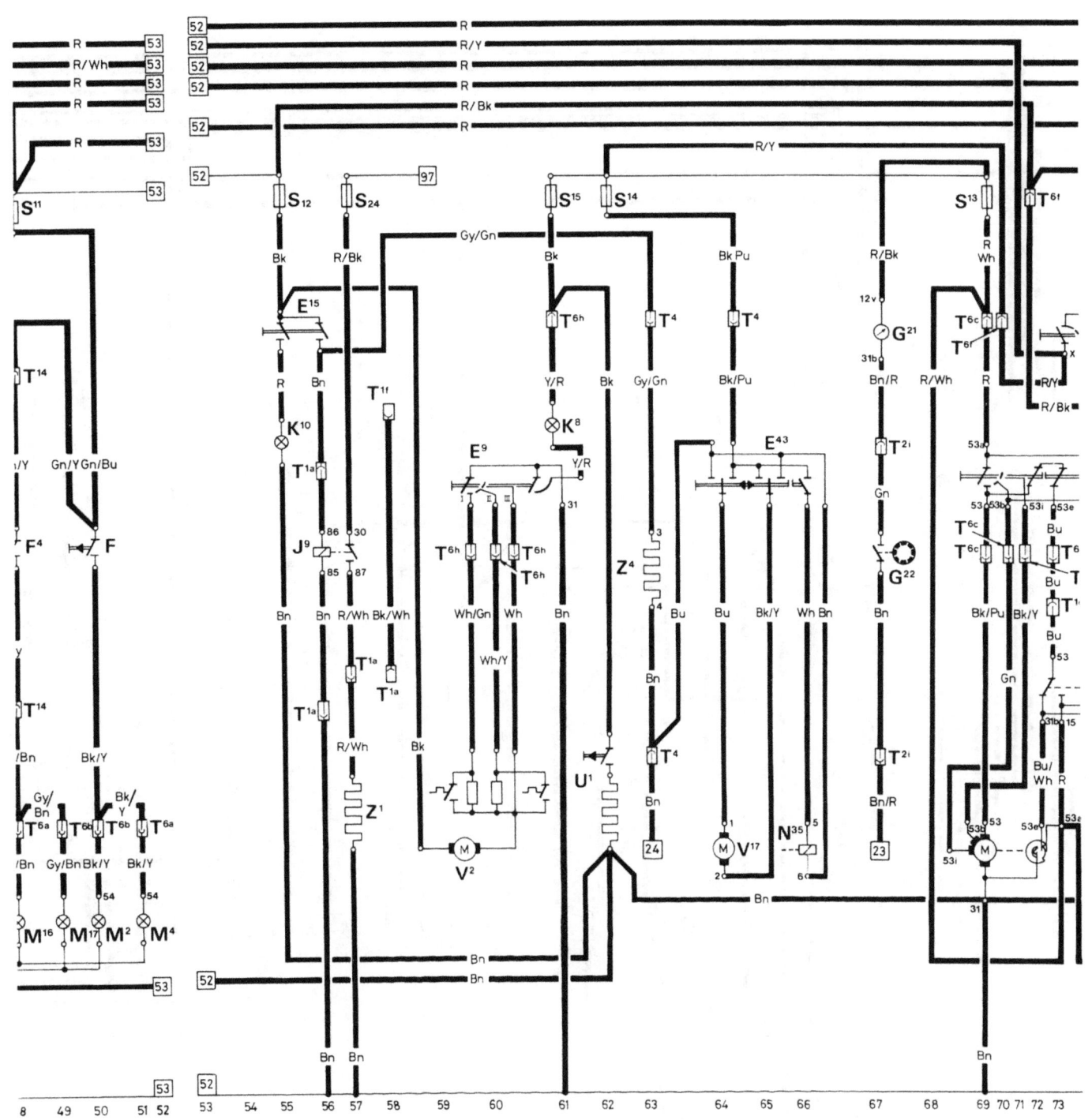

Current flow diagram for 911 and Carrera, 1977 models (diagram 3 of 5)

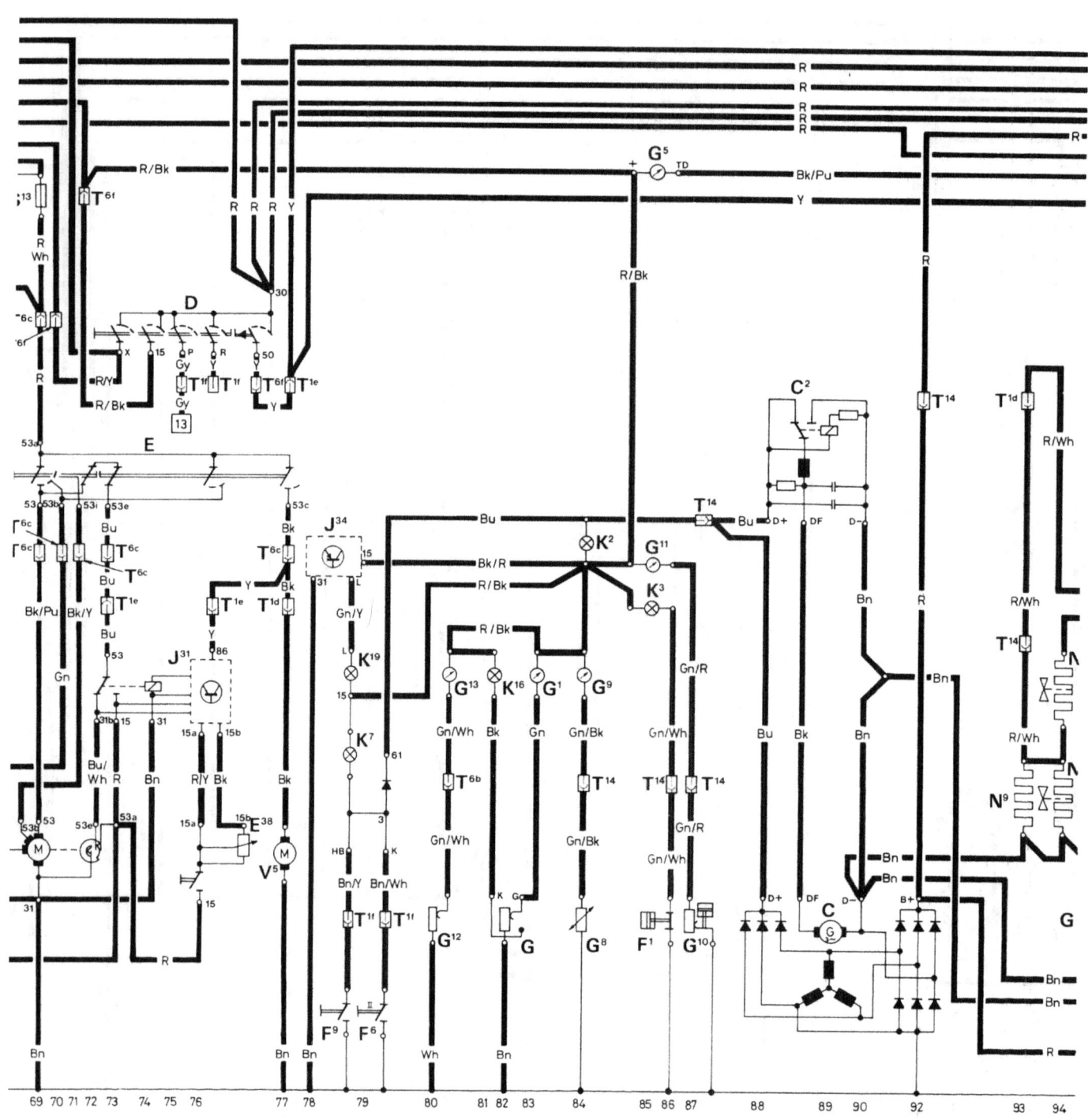

Current flow diagram for 911 and Carrera, 1977 models (diagram 4 of 5)

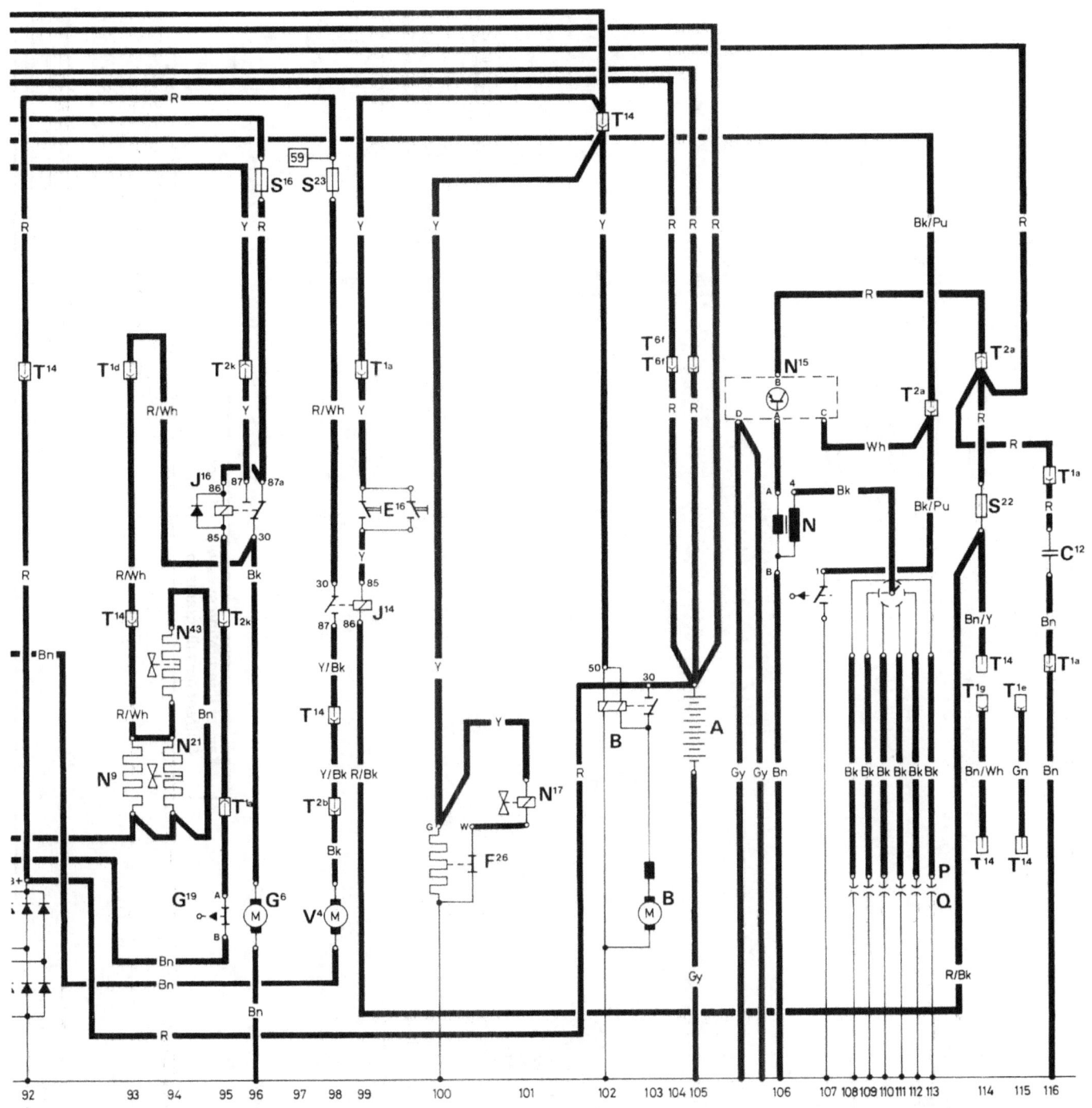

Current flow diagram for 911 and Carrera, 1977 models (diagram 5 of 5)

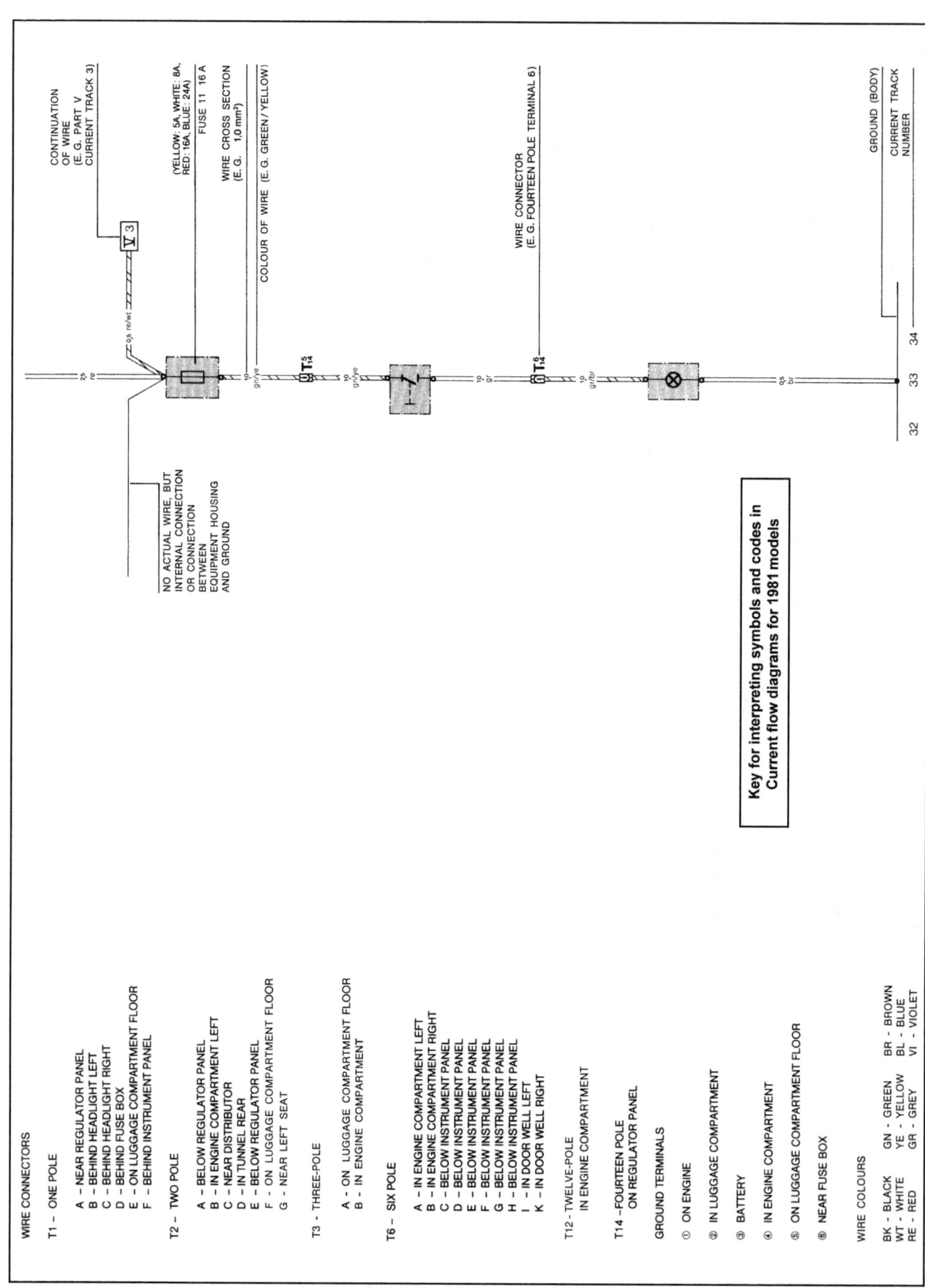

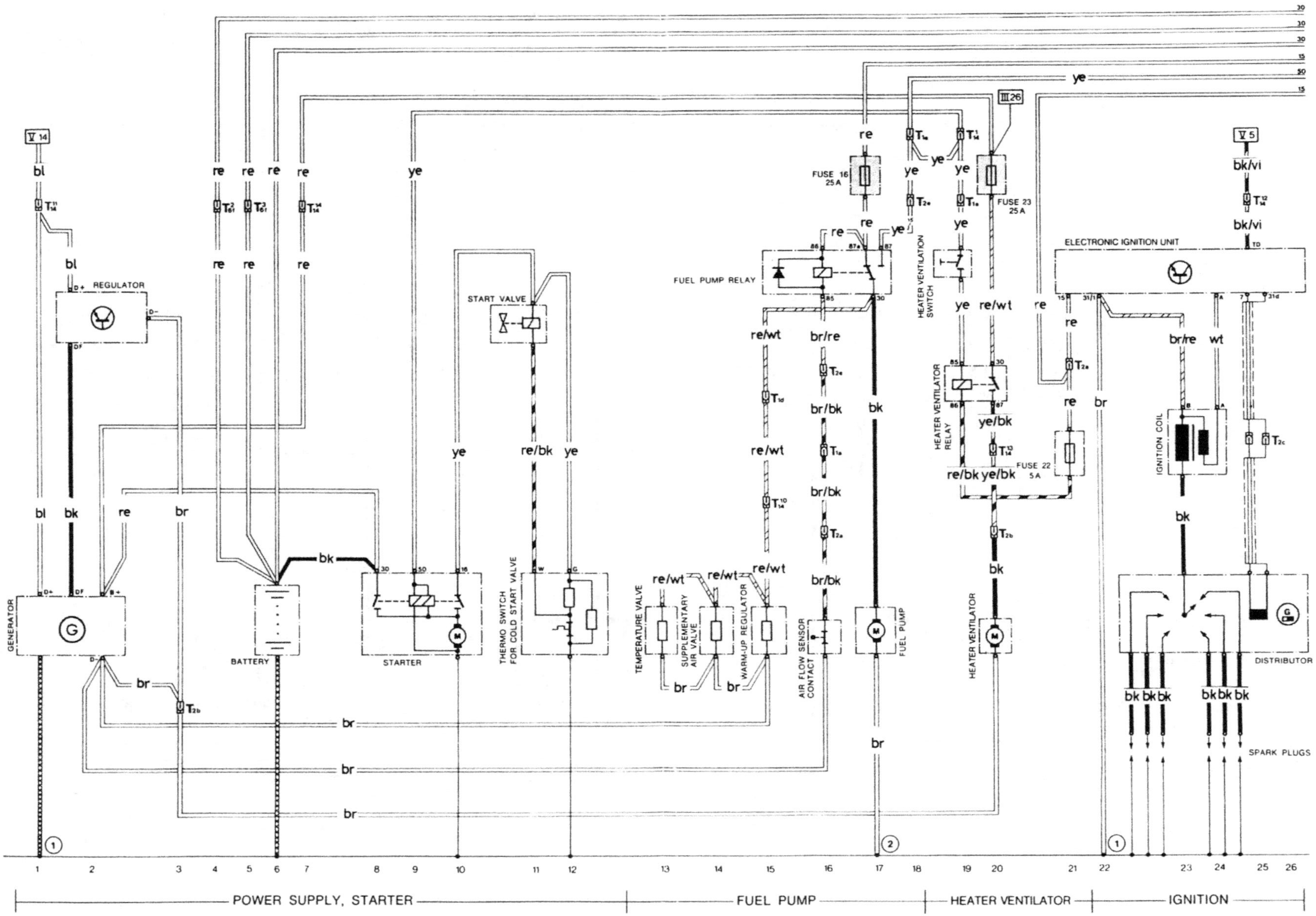

Colour code

wt	– white	br	– brown	re	– red		
gn	– green	ye	– yellow	gr	– grey		
bl	– blue	bk	– black	vi	– violet		

Current flow diagram for 911 SC, 1981 models (diagram 1 of 5)

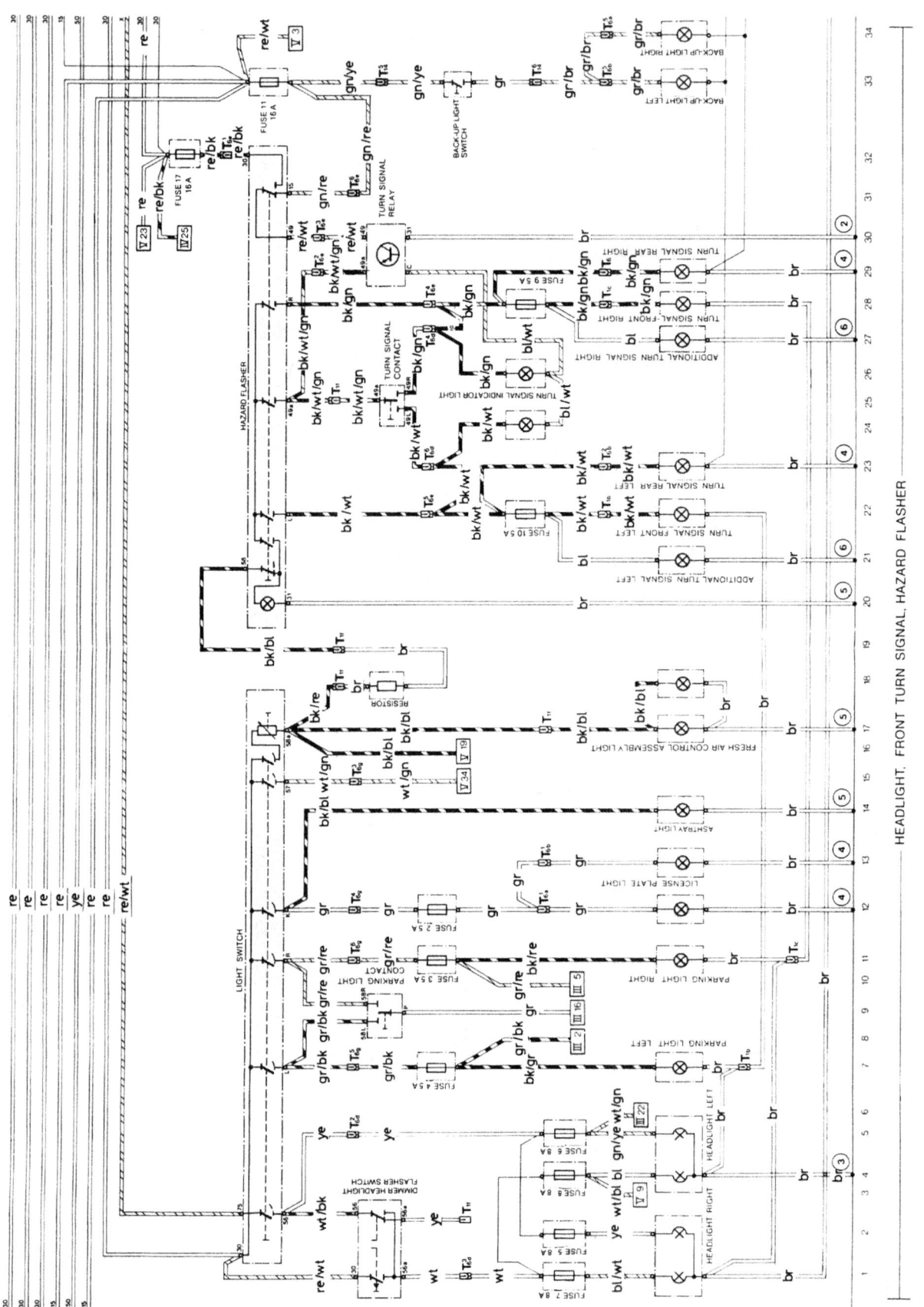

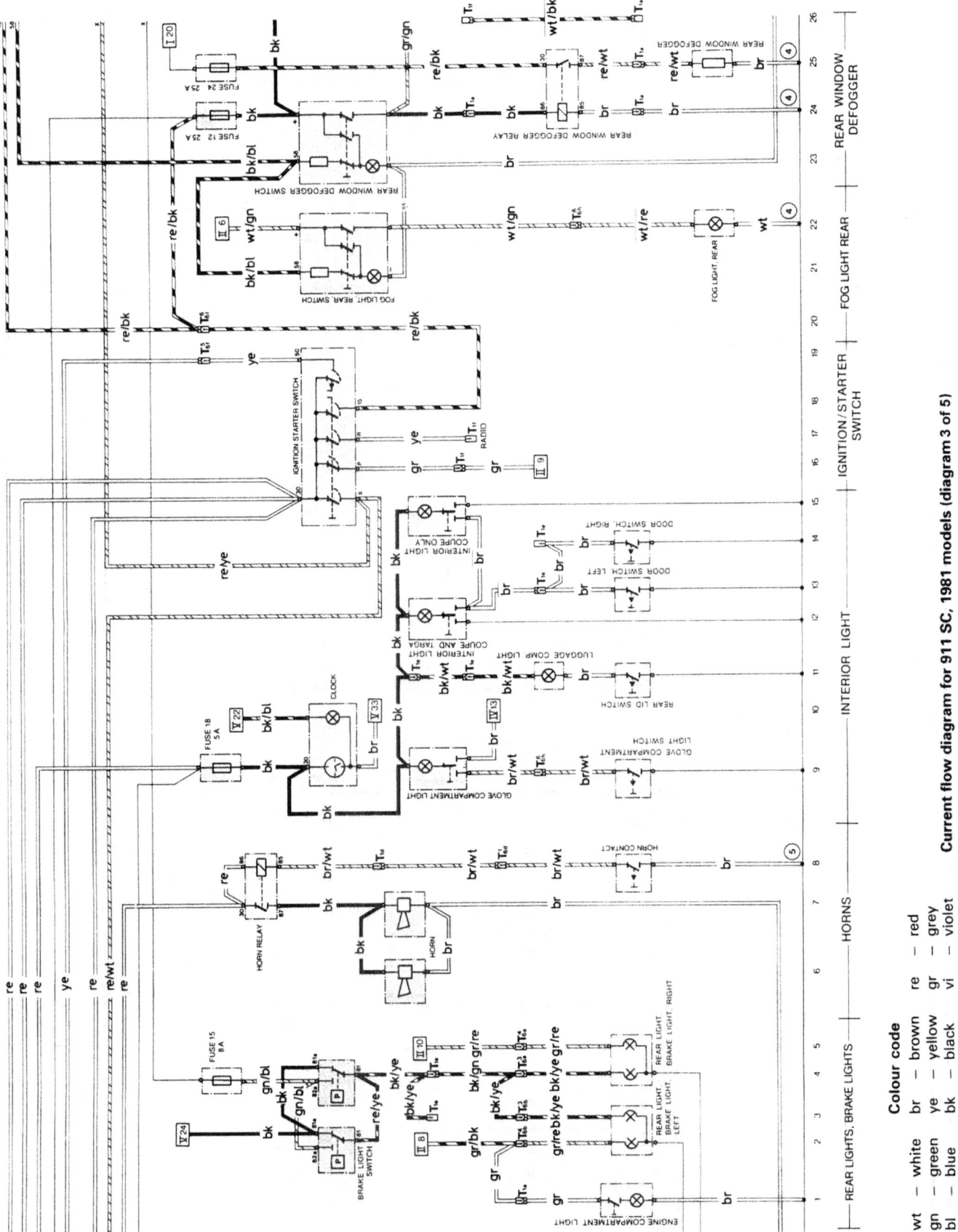

Current flow diagram for 911 SC, 1981 models (diagram 3 of 5)

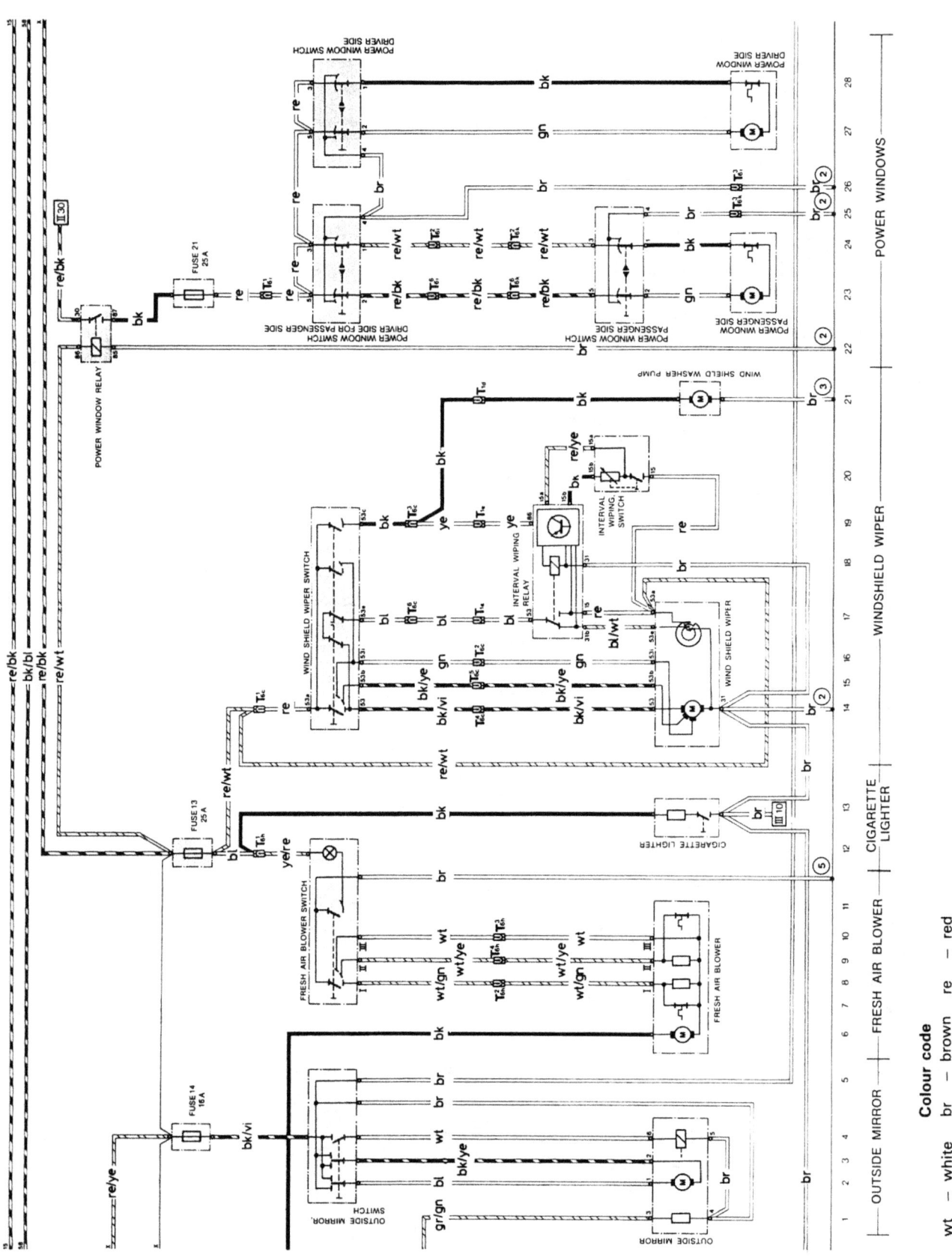

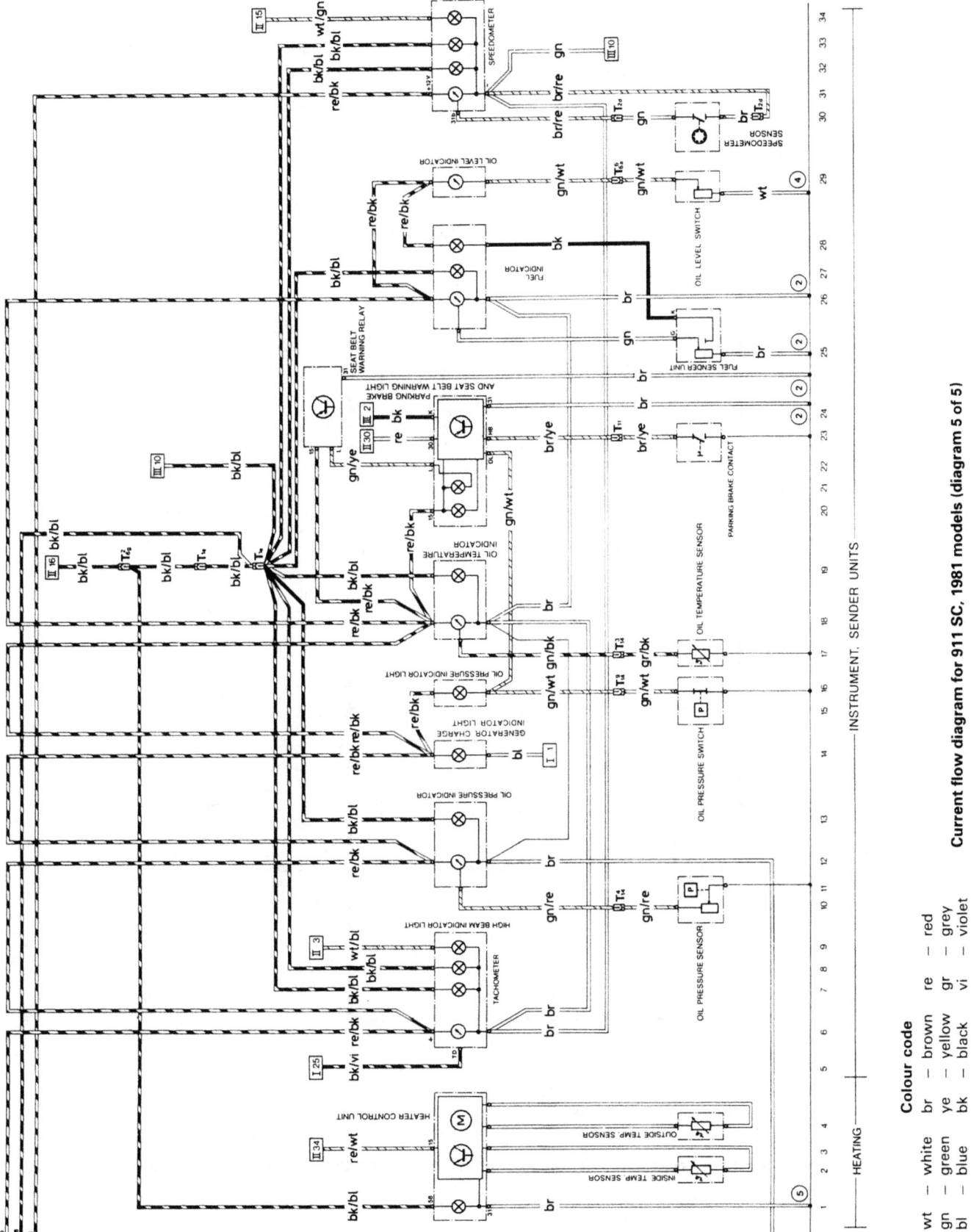

Current flow diagram for 911 SC, 1981 models (diagram 5 of 5)

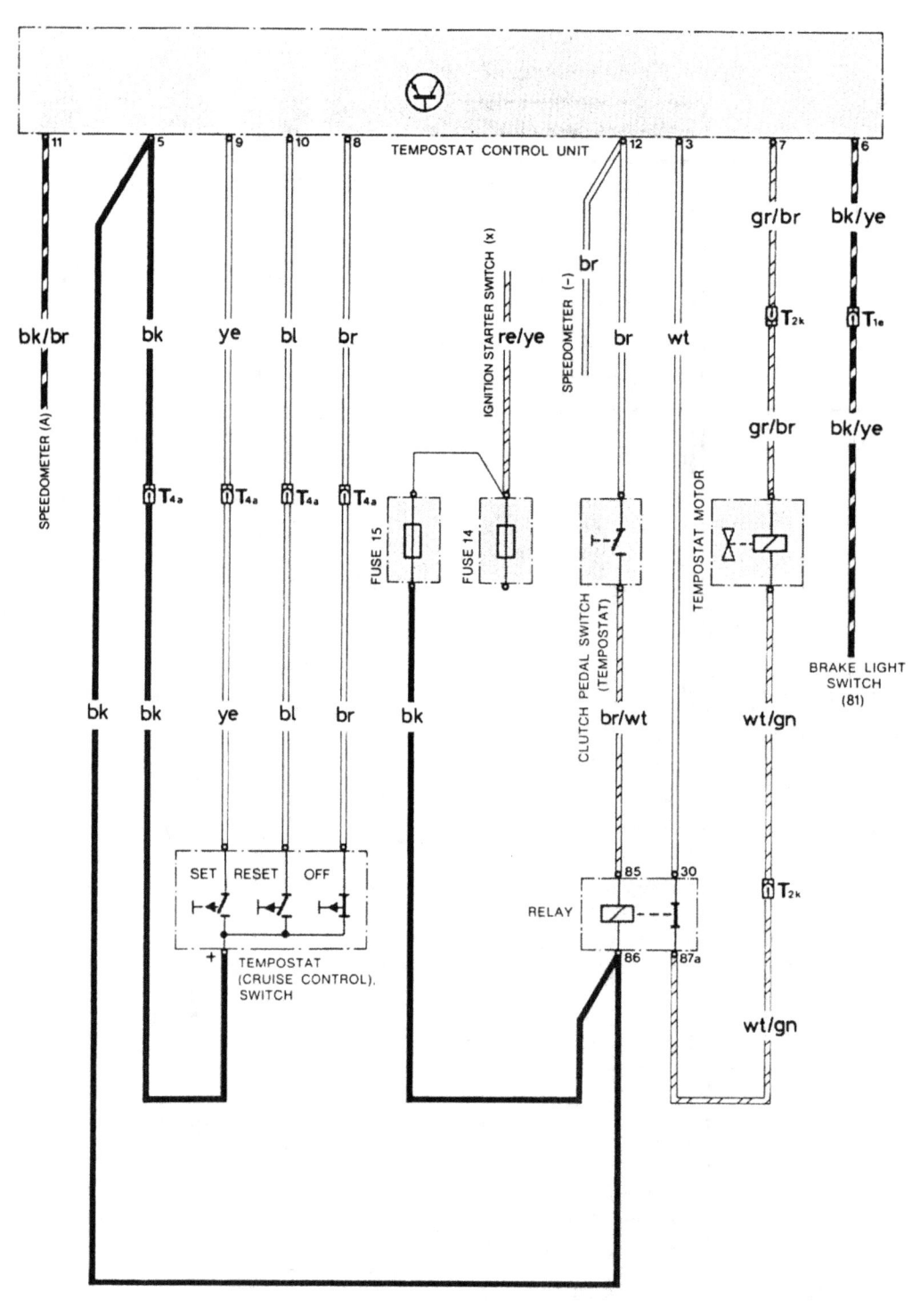

Additional current flow diagram for cruise control (tempostat) fitted to 911 SC, 1981 models

Colour code

wt – white
gn – green
bl – blue

br – brown
ye – yellow
bk – black

re – red
gr – grey
vi – violet

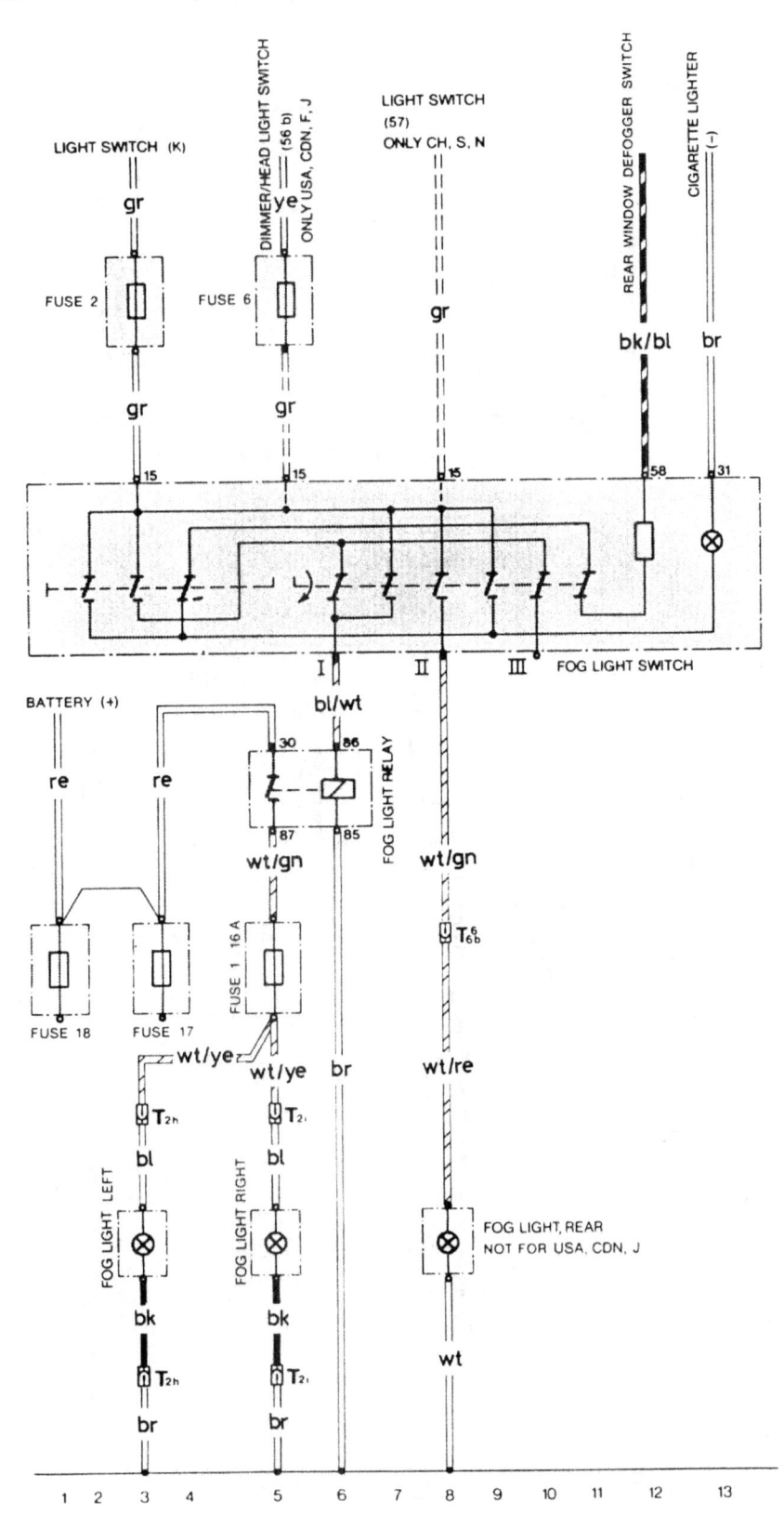

Additional current flow diagram for foglights fitted to 911 SC, 1981 models

Colour code

wt – white	br – brown	re – red
gn – green	ye – yellow	gr – grey
bl – blue	bk – black	vi – violet

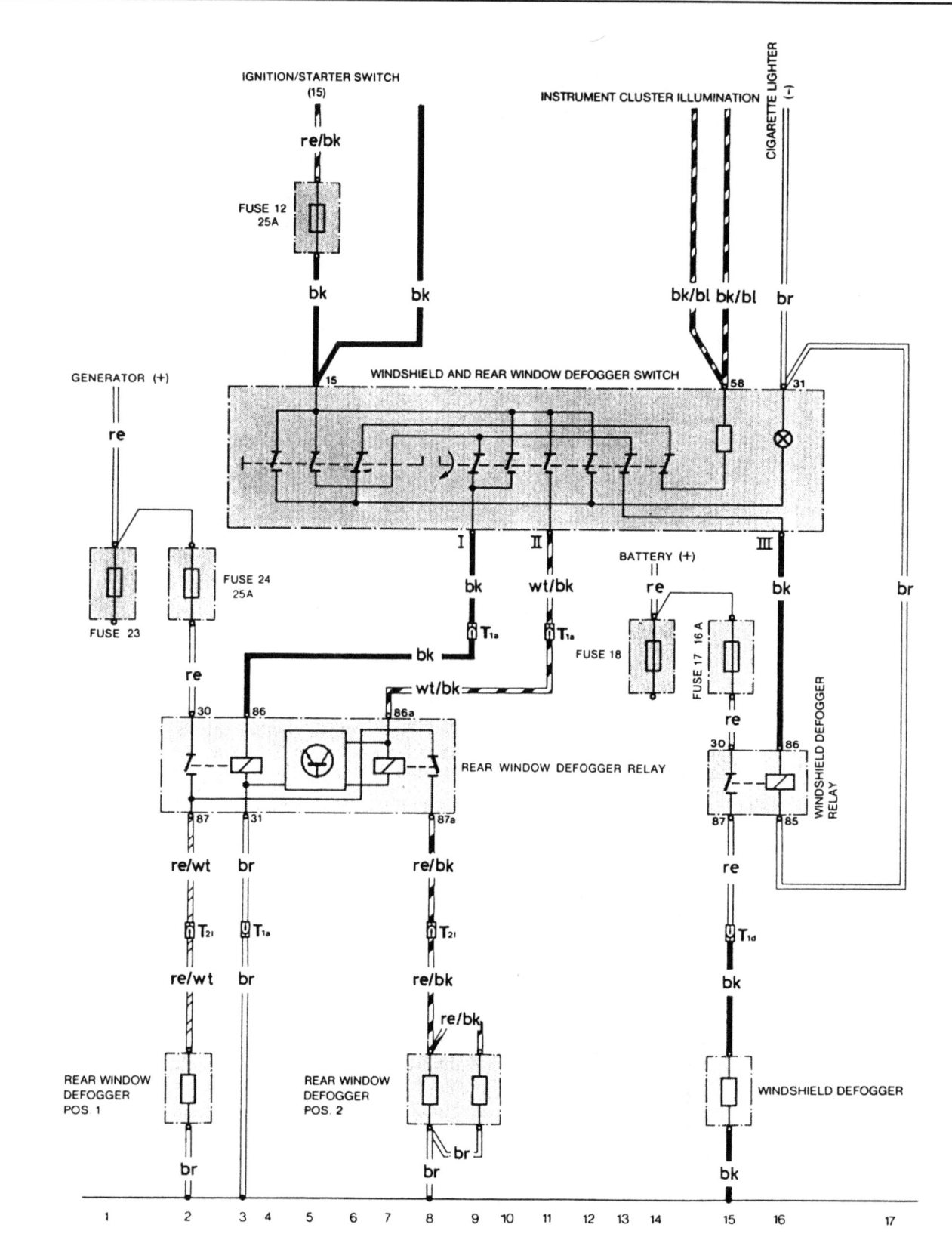

Additional current flow diagram for windshield and rear window defogger fitted to 911 SC, 1981 models

Colour code

wt – white	br – brown	re – red
gn – green	ye – yellow	gr – grey
bl – blue	bk – black	vi – violet

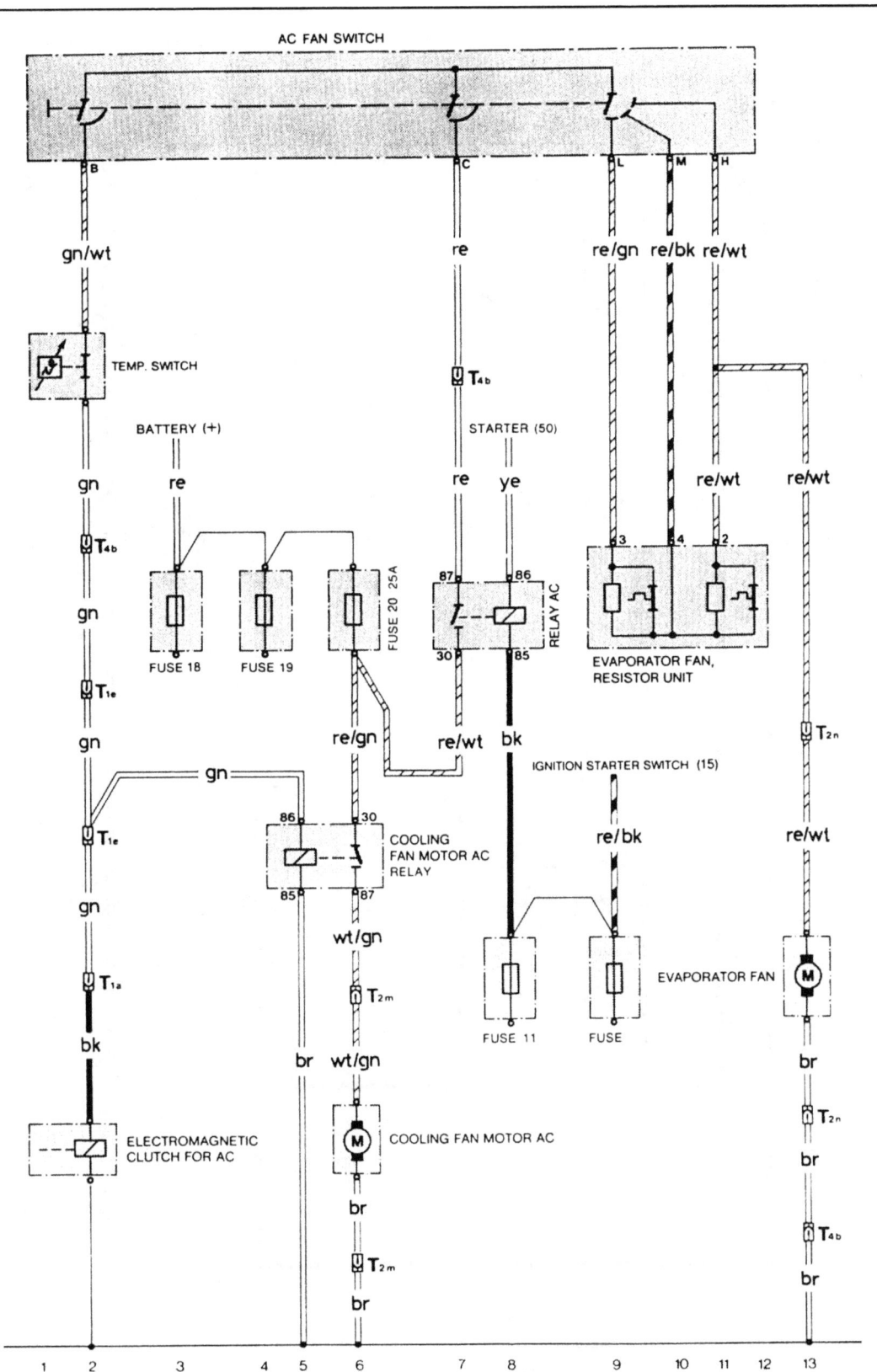

Additional current flow diagram for air conditioning fitted to 911 SC, 1981 models

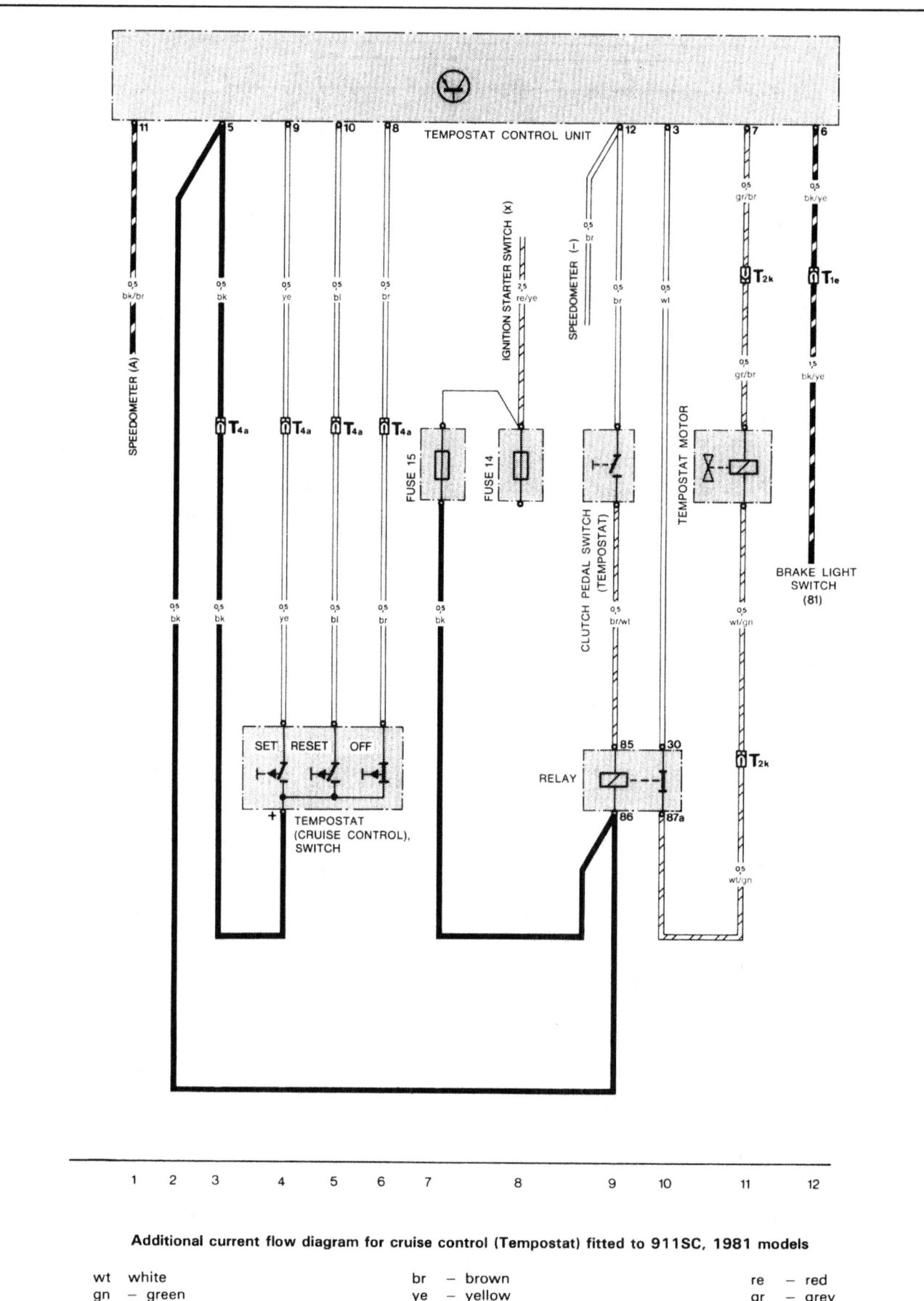

Additional current flow diagram for cruise control (Tempostat) fitted to 911SC, 1981 models

wt — white	br — brown	re — red
gn — green	ye — yellow	gr — grey
bl — blue	bk — black	vi — violet

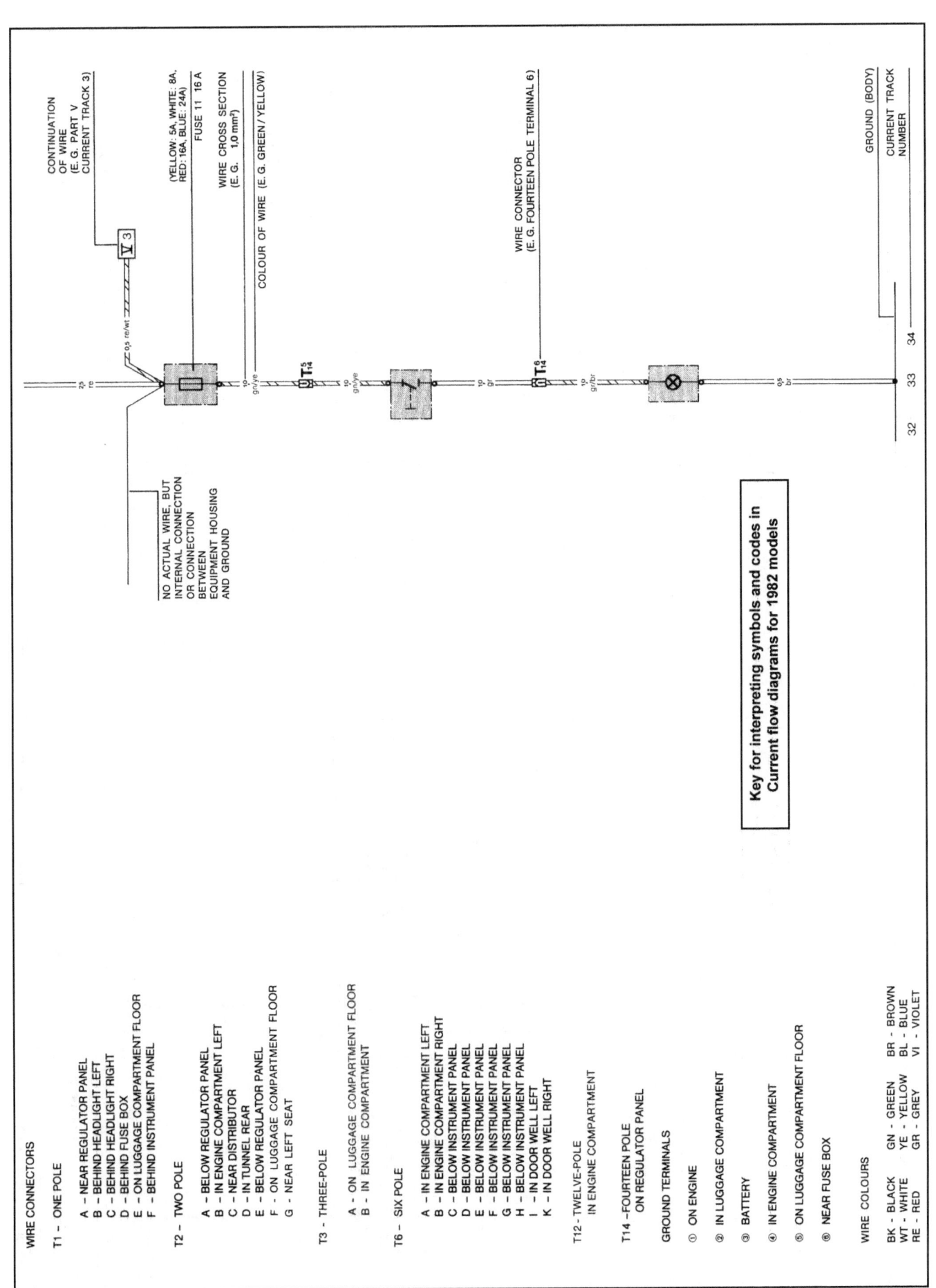

Key for interpreting symbols and codes in Current flow diagrams for 1982 models

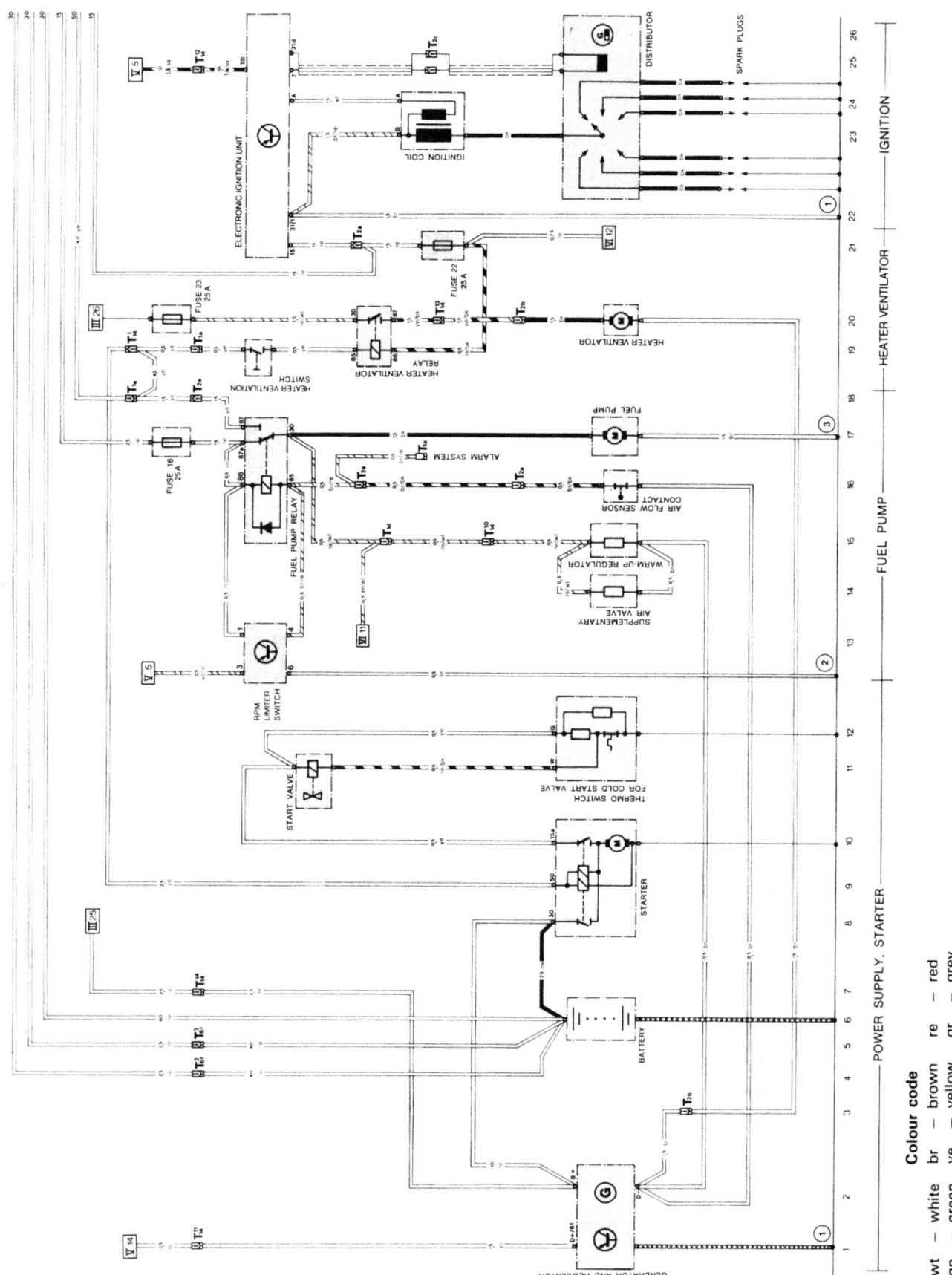

Current flow diagram for 911 SC (USA), 1982 models (diagram 1 of 6)

Current flow diagram for 911 SC (USA), 1982 models (diagram 2 of 6)

HEADLIGHT, FRONT TURN SIGNAL, HAZARD FLASHER

Colour code

wt	– white	br	– brown
gn	– green	re	– red
bl	– blue	gr	– grey
		ye	– yellow
		bk	– black
		vi	– violet

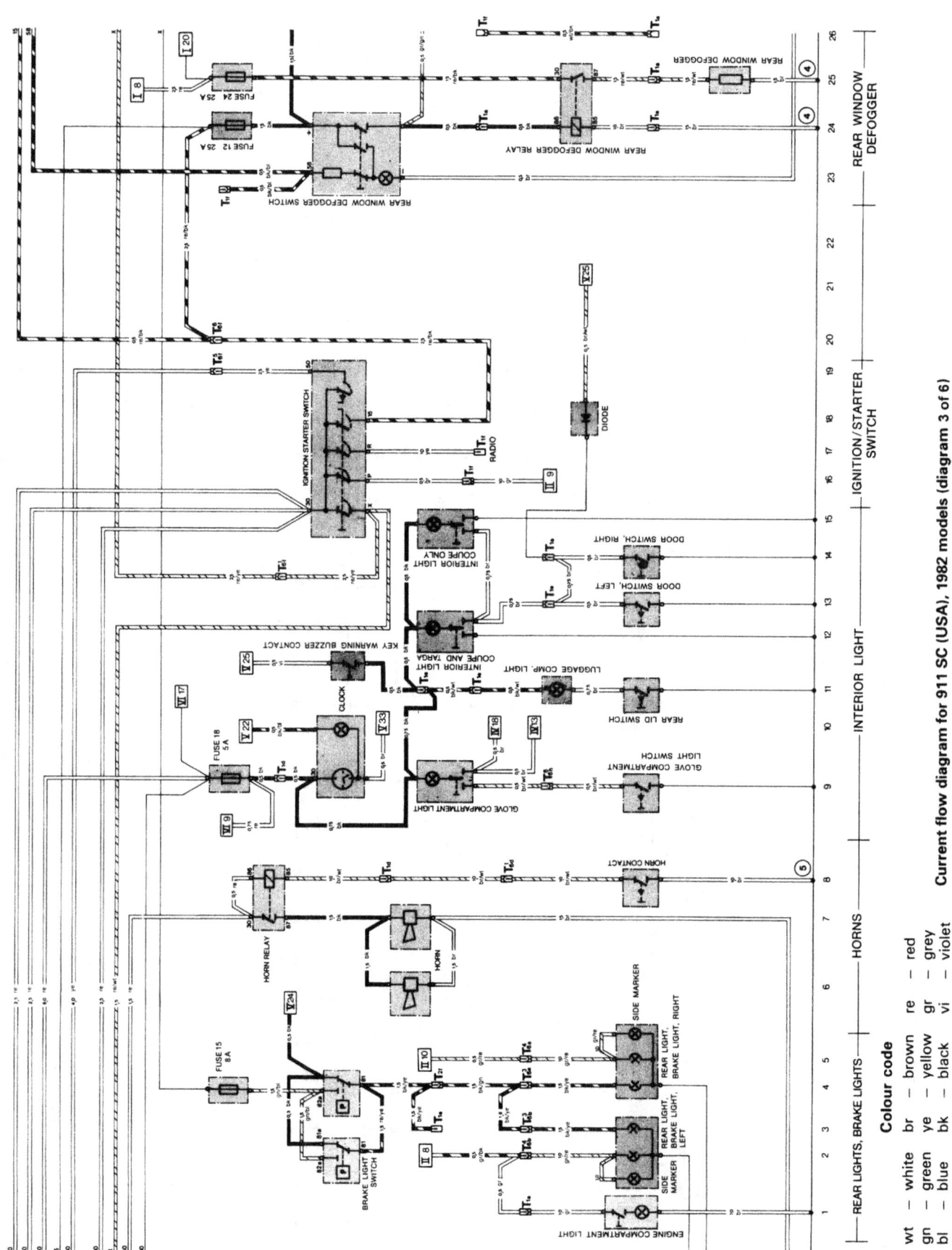

Current flow diagram for 911 SC (USA), 1982 models (diagram 3 of 6)

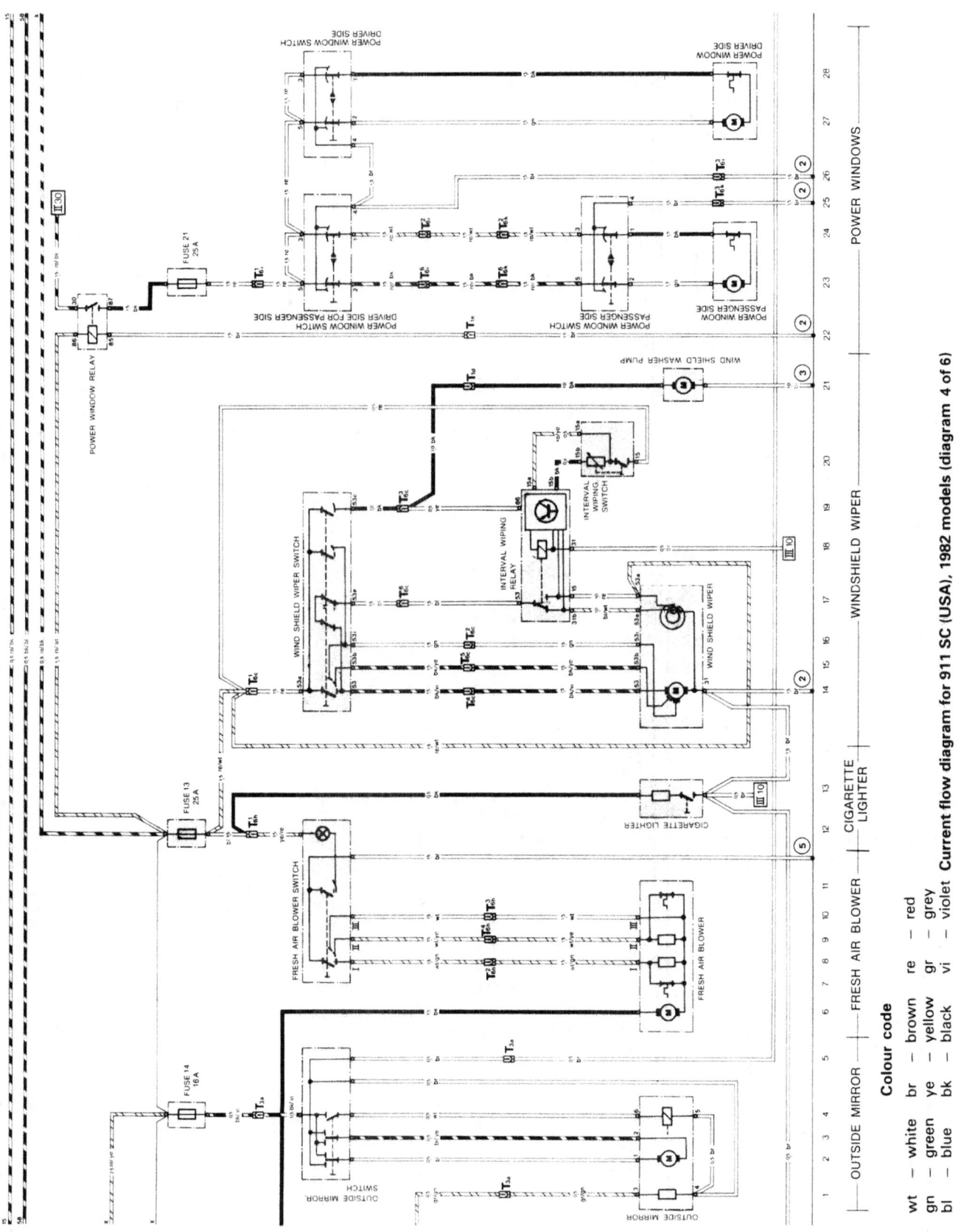

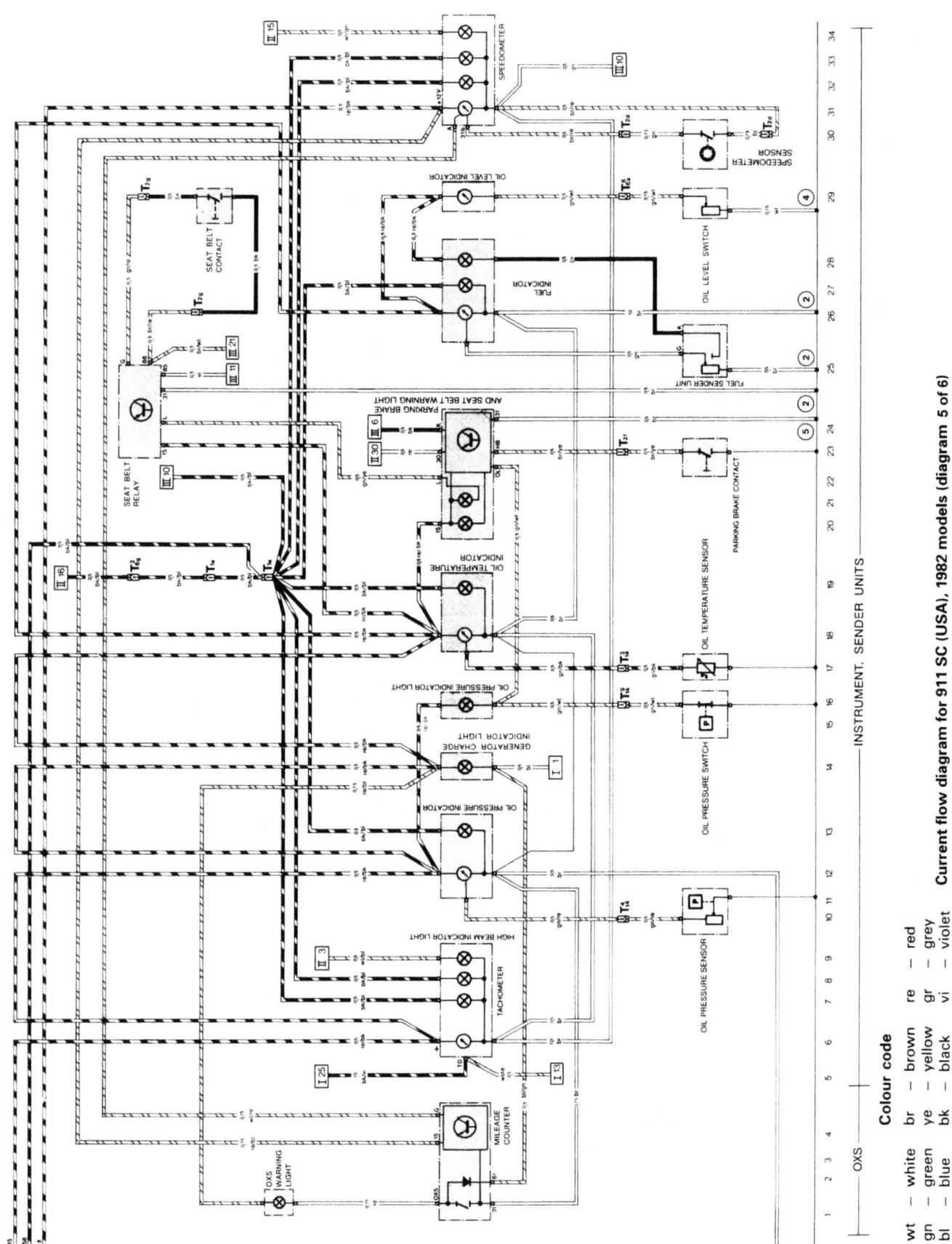

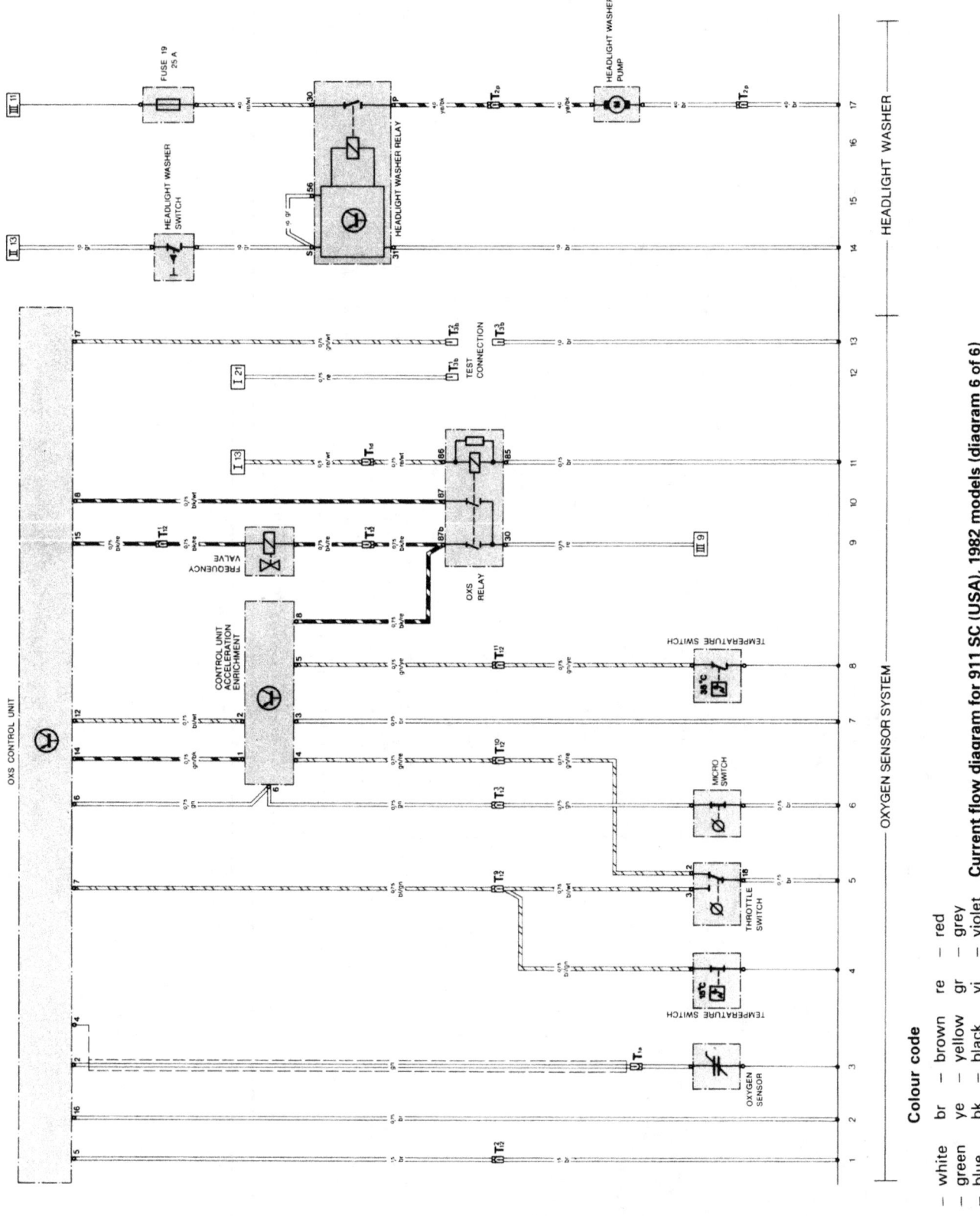

SERIAL NR.	DESCRIPTION	FIELD	PAGE
1	HEADLIGHT	A 2, A 9	3
2	TURN SIGNAL	A 1, A 10	3
3	ADDITIONAL TURN SIGNAL	A 1, A 10	3
4	FRONT LIGHT ASSEMBLY	A 1, A 10	4
5	SIDE MARKER LIGHT	A 4, A 5	3/4
6	FOG LIGHT	C 7	3/4
7	FOG LIGHT RELAY	C 2	3/4
8	TURN SIGNAL/HEADLIGHT DIMMER SWITCH	D 2	3/4
9	EMERGENZY FLASHER SWITCH	E 2	3/4
10	LIGHT SWITCH	G 2	3/4
11	FOG LIGHT SWITCH	E 4	3/4
12	ASHTRAY LIGHT	G 7	3/4
13	BACK-UP LIGHT SWITCH	E 6	3/4
14	TURN SIGNAL SWITCH	H 2, H 6	3/4
15	DOOR CONTACT SWITCH	K 3, G 4, K 4	3/4
16	INTERIOR LIGHT	I 6	3/4
17	DOOR CONTACT SWITCH		3/4
18	LUGGAGE COMPARTMENT LIGHT	H 6	3/4
19	GLOVE COMPARTMENT LIGHT SWITCH	H 5	3/4
20	GLOVE COMPARTMENT LIGHT	K 5	3/4
21	BRAKE LIGHT SWITCH I	H 8	3/4
22	BRAKE LIGHT SWITCH II	H 7	3/4
23	ENGINE COMPARTMENT LIGHT	I 8	3/4
24	TAIL LIGHT ASSEMBLY	K 5, K 10	3/4
25	LICENCE PLATE LIGHT	K 5, K 6	3/4
26	FOG LIGHT REAR	K 7	3/4
27	FUSE BOX I 10	F 9	3/4
28	FUSE BOX II 8	C 9	3/4
29	FUSE BOX GROUND SCREW		3/4
30	TRUNK FLOOR PLATE GROUND PLUG		
31	GROUND SCREW ENGINE COMP.		
32	WIRE CONNECTORS 6 PIN		
33	WIRE CONNECTORS 14 PIN		
34	FUSE BOX 3 PIN		
35	BATTERY	A 29	5
36	GENERATOR	B 29	5
37	STARTER	C 29	5
38	DISTRIBUTOR	E 33	6/7
39	SPARK PLUG	D 33	6/7
40	IGNITION COIL	A 25	6/7
41	IGNITION STARTER SWITCH	D 24	5
42	HORN CONTACT	E 27	5
43	HORN RELAY	D 28, D 29	5
44	HORN	E 24	5
45	SWITCH HEADLIGHT WASHER	E 26	5
46	RELAY " "		
47	PUMP	E 29	5
48	WINDSHIELD WIPER SWITCH	F 24	5
49	PULSE TRANSMITTER	G 27	5
50	WINDSHIELD WIPER MOTOR	F 29	5
51	POTENTIOMETER	G 29	5
52	WINDSHIELD WASHER PUMP	H 29	5
53	POWER WINDOW RELAY	I 22	
54	POWER WINDOW SWITCH	I 24, K 24	
55	POWER WINDOW MOTOR	K 27	
56	GROUND SCREW LUGGAGE COMP.		
57	GROUND SCREW BATTERY		
58	GROUND MOTOR		
59	WIRE CONNECTORS 3 PIN		
60	DME CONTROL UNIT	F 35	6/7
61	DME RELAY	B 34	6/7
62	OXYGEN SENSOR HEATING	C 34	6/7
63	ALTITUDE CORRECTION BOX		6/7
64	FUEL INJECTORS	A, B, C 39	6/7
65	IDLE POSITIONER	E 39	6/7
66	THROTTLE VALVE SWITCH	E 39	6/7
67	NTC II	G 39	6/7
68	REFERENCE MARK TRANSMITTER	H 39	6/7
69	SPEED TRANSMITTER	H 39	6/7
70	AIR FLOW SENSOR	I 39	6/7
71	FUEL PUMP	K 39	6/7
72	CARRIER PLATE GROUND SCREW		
73	OXYGEN SENSOR	D 33	6/7
74	WIRE CONNECTORS		
75	GROUND SCREW BODY		
76	WIRE CONNECTORS		
77	TACHOMETER	A 54	9
78	3 WARNING LIGHT	C 54	9
79	COMBINATION INSTRUMENTS ø 100	E 54	9
80	COMBINATION INSTRUMENTS ø 80	G 54	9
81	SPEEDOMETER	I 54	9
82	CLOCK	K 54	9
83	CLOCK RELAY	C 56	9
84	BRAKE PAD WEAR LEAD	A 58, B 59	9
85	PARKING BRAKE CONTACT	C 59	9
86	BRAKE FLUID LEVEL WARNING SWITCH	C 59	9
87	OIL PRESSURE SENDER UNIT	D 59	9
88	OIL PRESSURE SWITCH	E 59	9
89	OIL TEMPERATURE SENSOR	F 59	9
90	FUEL SENDER UNIT	G 59	9
91	OIL LEVEL SWITCH	H 59	9
92	SPEED TRANSMITTER	I 59	9
93	TEMPERATURE SWITCH FAN	G 69	10
94	OUTSIDE MIRROR SWITCH	A 64	10/11
95	OUTSIDE MIRROR	A 69	10/11
96	"	C 64	10/11
97	FRESH AIR BLOWER	B 69	10/11
98	CIGARETTE LIGHTER	D 69	10/11
99	ADDITIONAL FAN RELAY	D 66	10/11
100	ADDITIONAL FAN	E 64	10
101	HEATING CONTROL UNIT	E 69	10
102	RESISTOR	F 66	10/11
103	RELAY HEATING CONTROL UNIT	F 69	10
104	ENGINE COMPARTMENT FAN	H 67	11
105	WINDSHIELD DEFOGGER RELAY	H 69	10/11
107	PULL TURN SWITCH REAR WINDOW	I 64	10/11
106	WINDSHIELD DEFOGGER		
108	DEFOGGER	I 67	10/11
109	REGULATING RELAY REAR WINDOW DEFOGGER	K 69	10/11
110	REAR WINDOW DEFOGGER		
111	GROUND CARRIER PLATE UPPER	H 69, G 69	10/11
112	INSIDE TEMP. SENSOR		
113	TEMPERATURE SENSOR ON HEATER	H 69	10/11
114	FLAP BOX	E 64	11
115	ADDITIONAL FAN SWITCH	F 69	11
116	MICROSWITCH		
117	WIRE CONNECTORS 5 PIN		
118	SIGN LIGHT	E 5	4
119	BELT CONTACT	C 57	9
120	REAR WINDOW WIPER SWITCH	D 25	5
121	REAR WINDOW WIPER MOTOR	D 29	5
122	ELECTRONIC IGNITION UNIT HKZ	B 42	
123	DELAYED ACTION RELAY	C 45	8
124	FUEL PUMP RELAY I	H 45	8
125	FUEL PUMP RELAY II	G 45	8
126	AIR FLOW SENSO MANIFOLD PRESSURE RELAY	F 46	8
127	PRESSURE TRANSMITTER MANIFOLD PRESSURE	D 49	8
128	START VALVE	C 49	8
129	THERMO SWITCH FOR COLD START VALVE	E 49	8
130	SUPPLEMENTARY AIR VALVE	E 49	8
131	WARM-UP REGULATOR	F 49	8
132	AIR FLOW SENSO SWITCH	F 49	8
133	CONTROL UNIT	G 49	8
134	MANIFOLD PRESSURE LIMITING SWITCH	K 55	9
135	TEMPERATURE SENSOR	K 57	9
	WARNING LIGHT EX	K 59	9
	CONNECTION RAIL	G, K 22	5

Key to current flow diagrams for 911 Carrera, 1984 models

NOTES

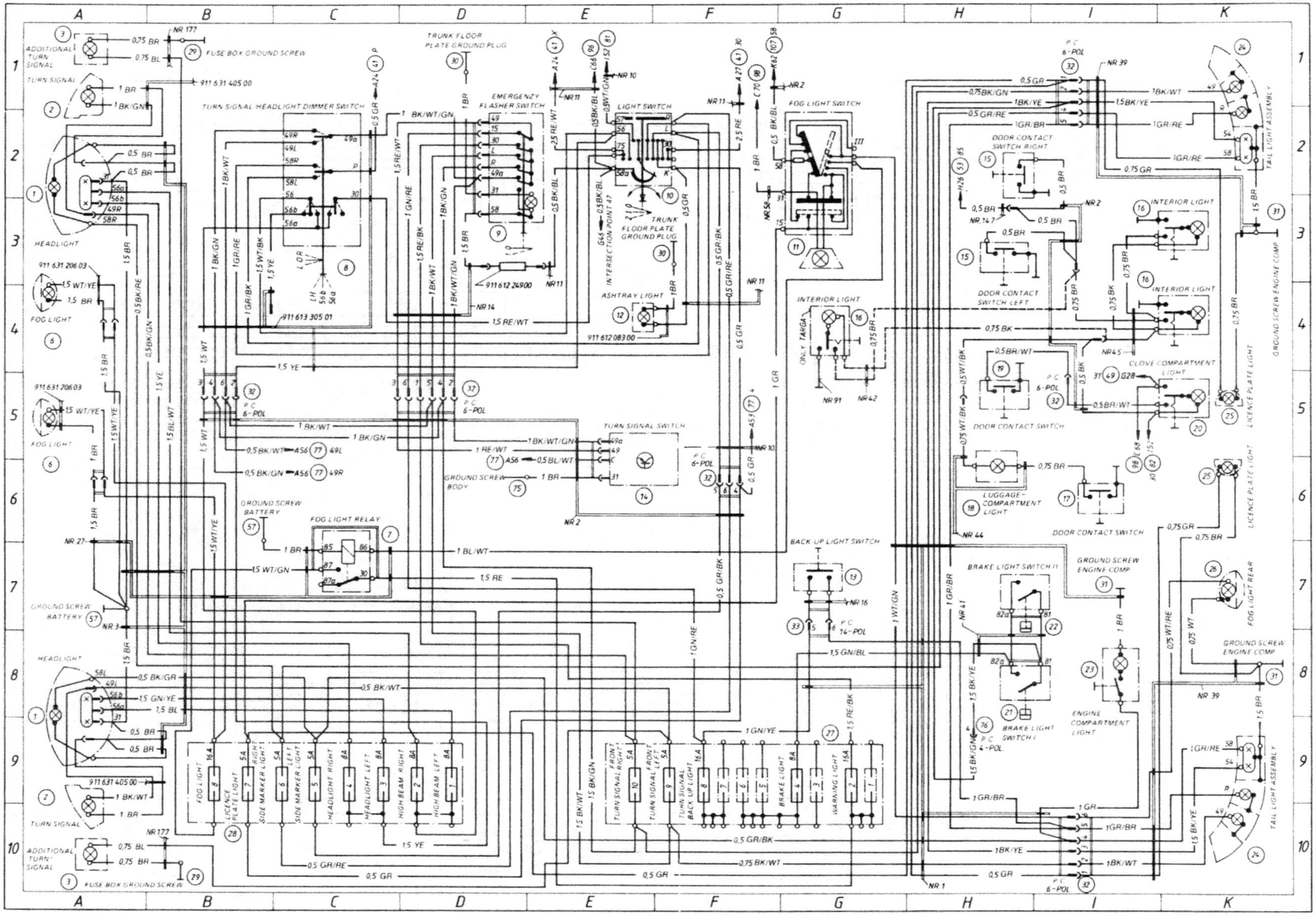

Colour code

wt	white	br	– brown	re	– red
gn	– green	ye	– yellow	gr	– grey
bl	– blue	bk	– black	vi	– violet

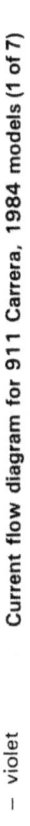

Current flow diagram for 911 Carrera, 1984 models (1 of 7)

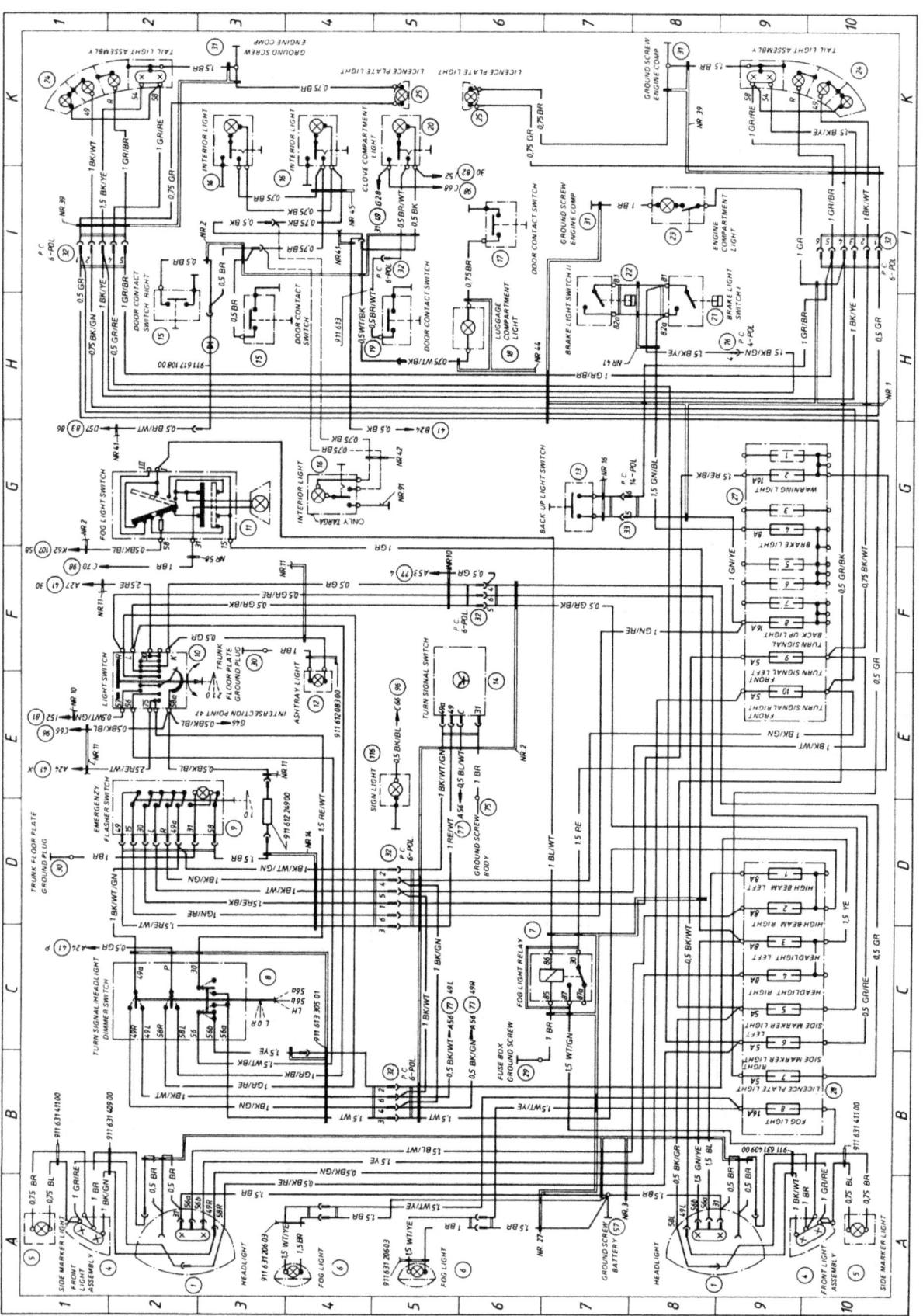

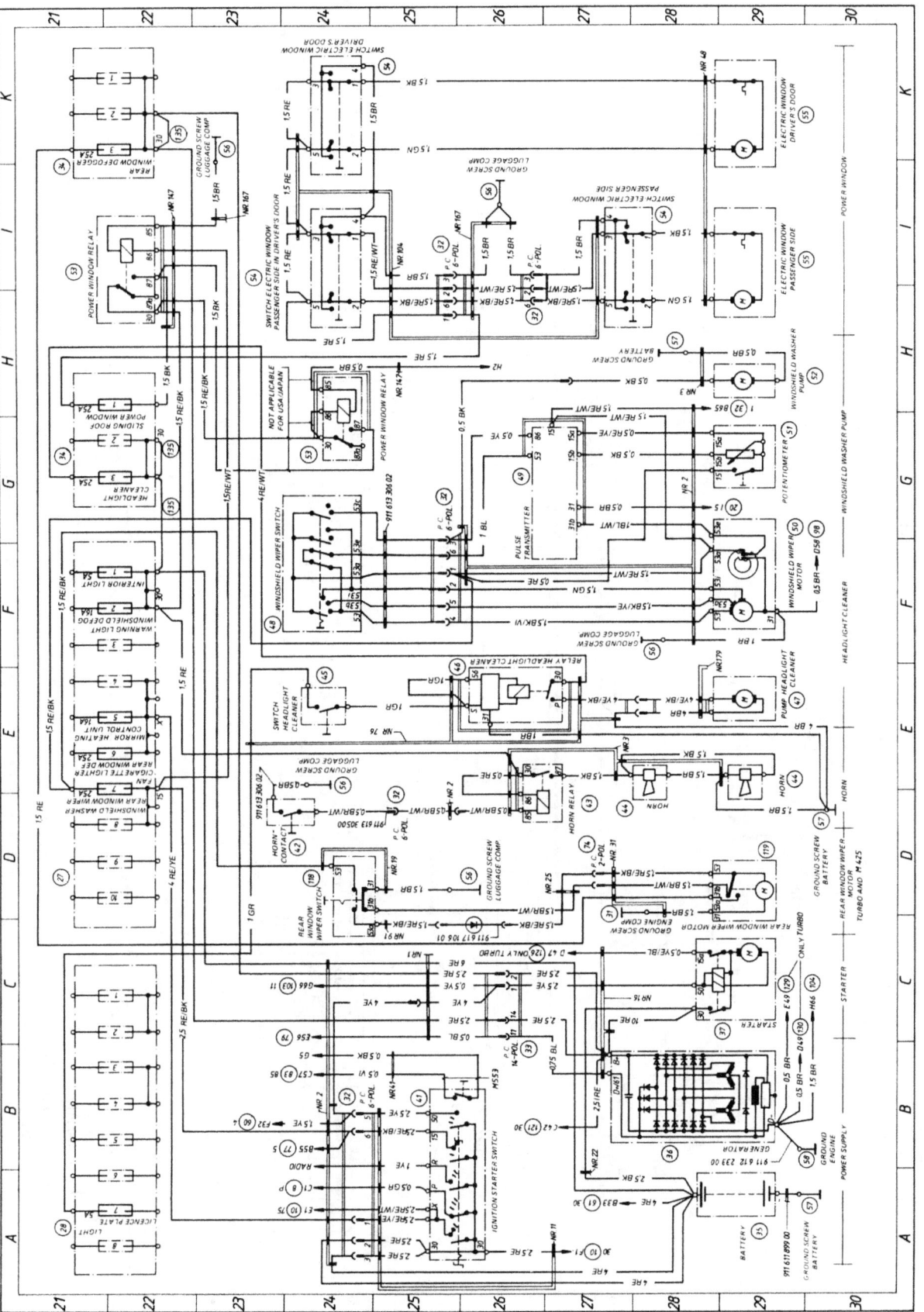

Current flow diagram for 911 Carrera, 1984 models (3 of 7)

Colour code

wt – white br – brown re – red
gn – green ye – yellow gr – grey
bl – blue bk – black vi – violet

Current flow diagram for 911 Carrera, 1984 models (4 of 7)

Colour code

wt	– white	re	– red
gn	– green	gr	– grey
bl	– blue	vi	– violet
br	– brown		
ye	– yellow		
bk	– black		

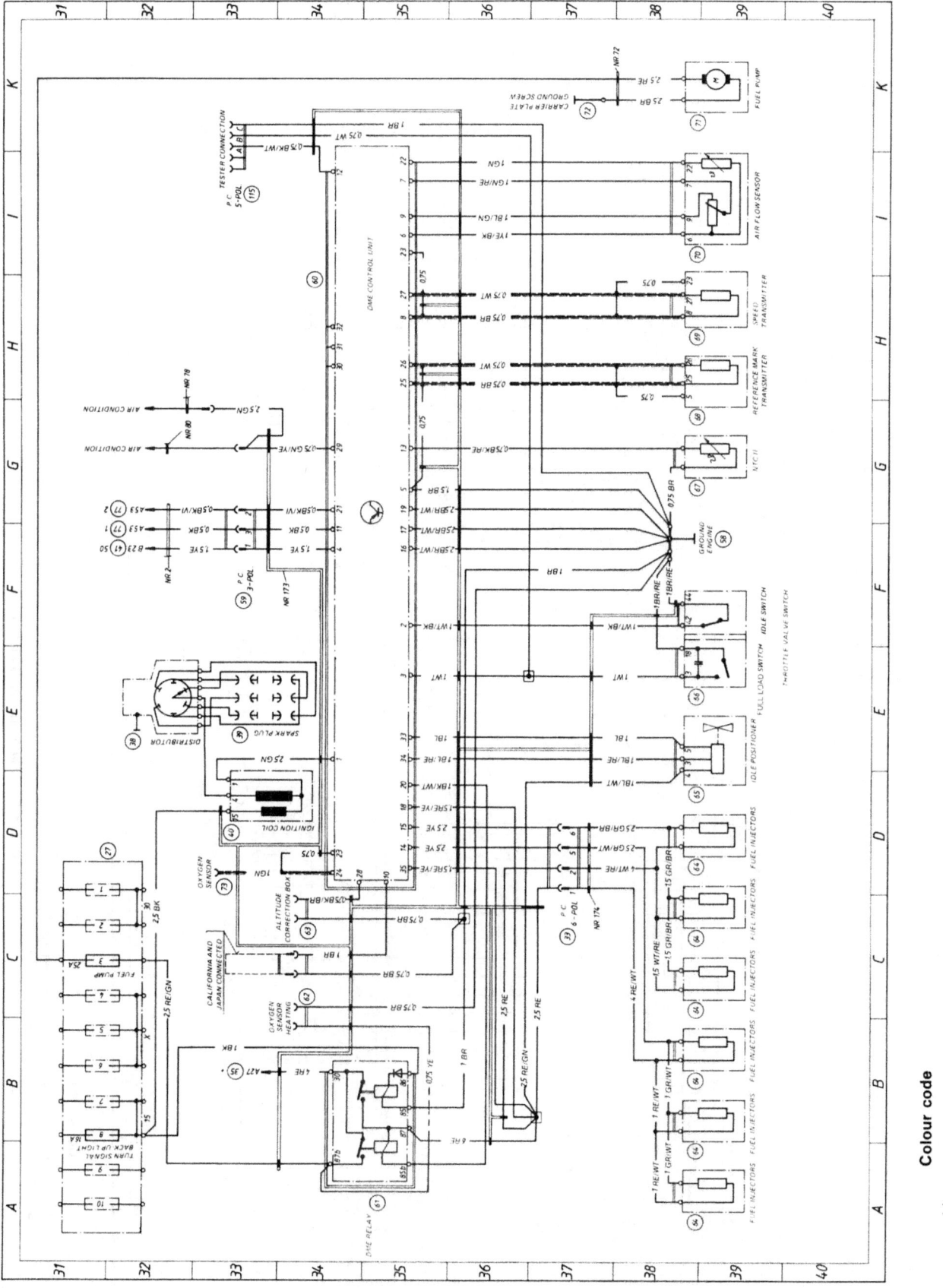

Current flow diagram for 911 Carrera, 1984 models, USA, Japan (5 of 7)

Colour code

wt — white br — brown re — red
gn — green ye — yellow gr — grey
bl — blue   bk — black   vi — violet

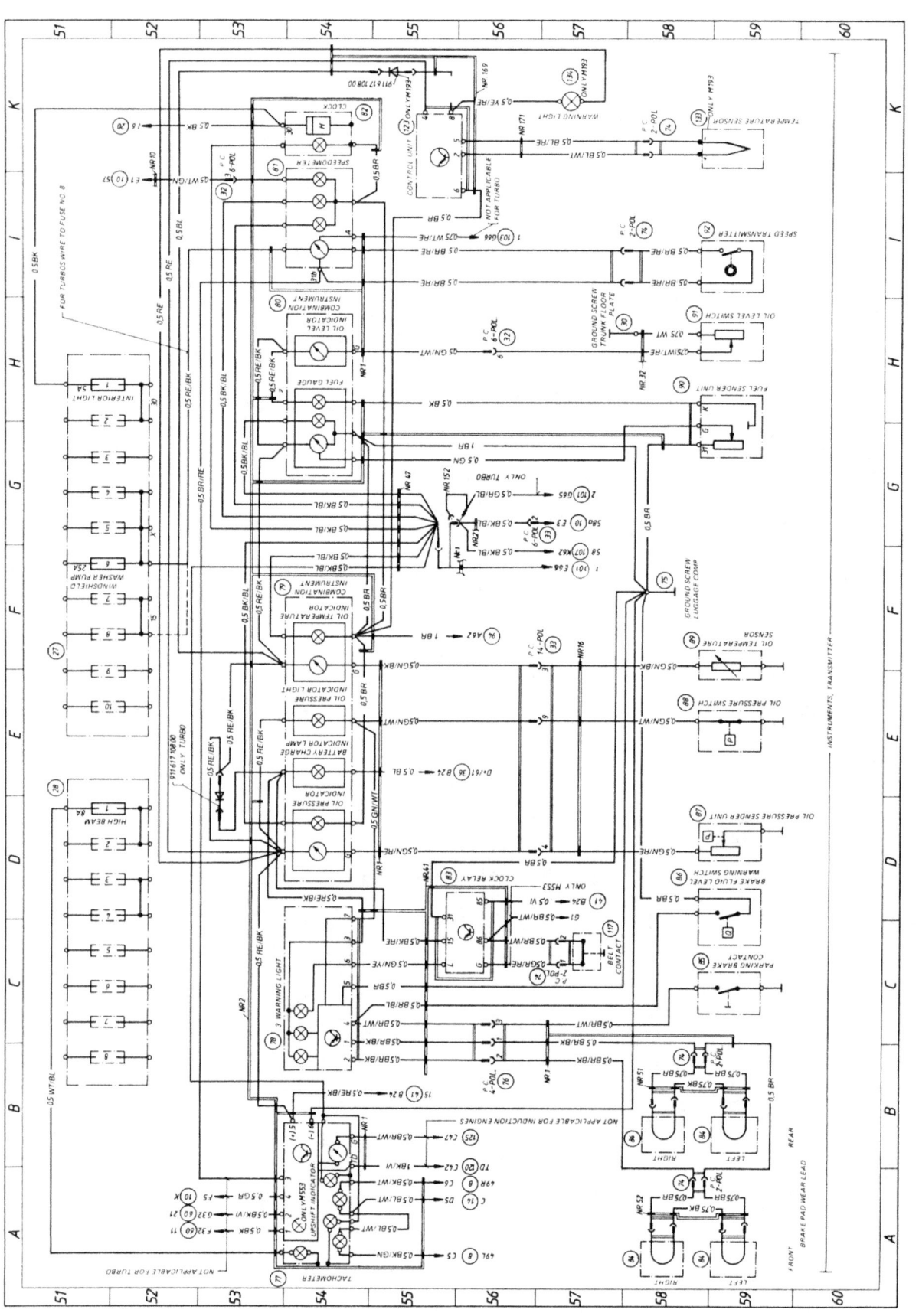

Current flow diagram for 911 Carrera, 1984 models (6 of 7)

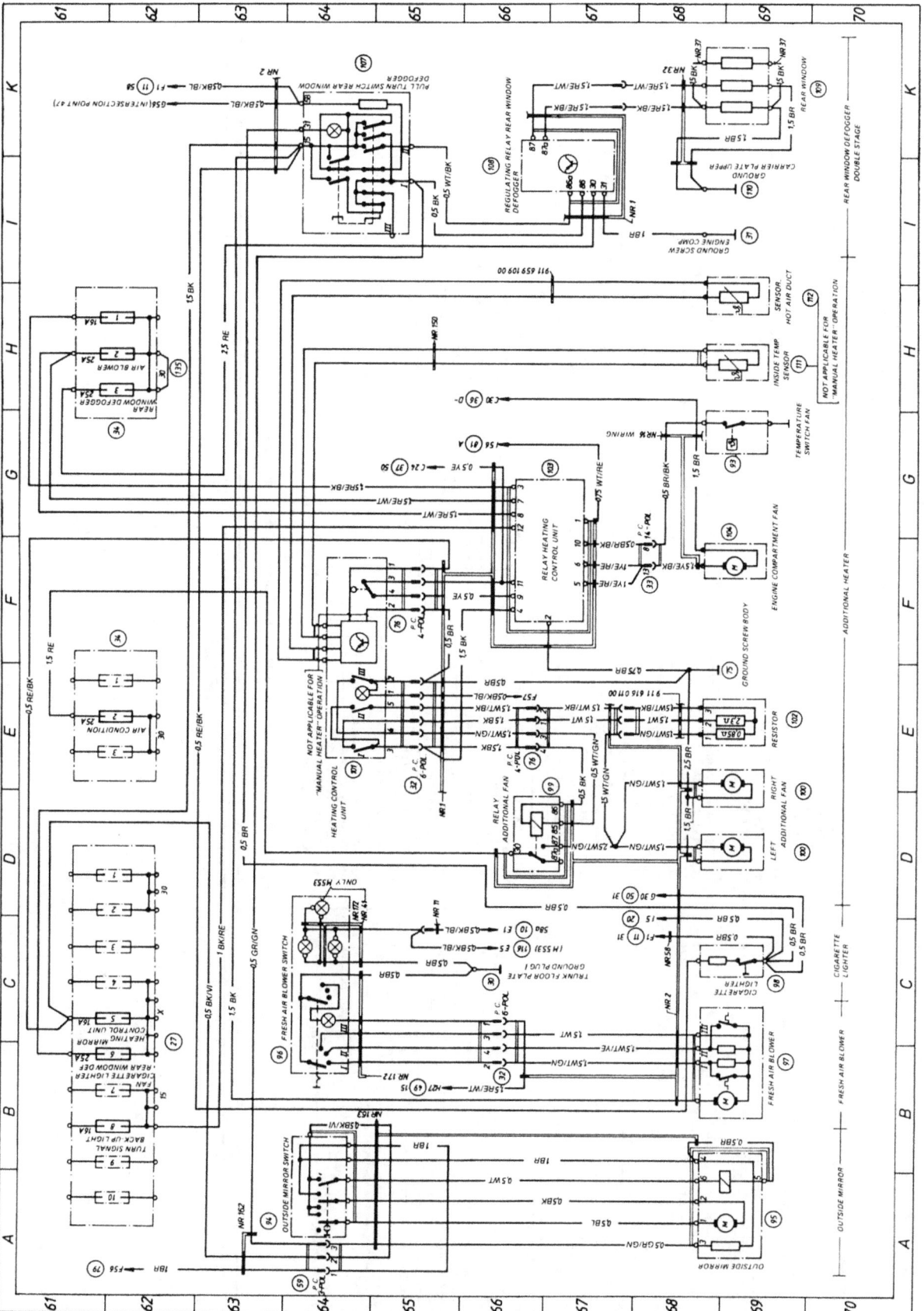

Current flow diagram for 911 Carrera, 1984 models (7 of 7)

SERIAL NR.	DESCRIPTION	FIELD	PAGE
1	HEADLIGHT	A 2, A 8	3/4
2	TURN SIGNAL	A 1, A 9	3
3	ADDITIONAL TURN SIGNAL	A 1, A 10	3
4	FRONT LIGHT ASSEMBLY	A 1, A 9	4
5	SIDE MARKER LIGHT	A 1, A 10	4
6	FOG LIGHT	A 4, A 3	3/4
7	FOG LIGHT RELAY	F 6	3/4
8	TURN SIGNAL/HEADLIGHT DIMMER SWITCH	C 3	3/4
9	EMERGENZY FLASHER SWITCH	D 2	3/4
10	LIGHT SWITCH	E 3	3/4
11	FOG LIGHT SWITCH	G 1	3/4
12	ASHTRAY LIGHT	G 4	3/4
13	BACK-UP LIGHT SWITCH	H 8	3/4
14	TURN SIGNAL SWITCH	E 4	3/4
15	DOOR CONTACT SWITCH	H 5/	3/4
16	INTERIOR LIGHT	K 4/K 5/K 6	3/4
17	DOOR CONTACT SWITCH	H 7	3/4
18	LUGGAGE COMPARTMENT LIGHT	I 7	3/4
19	CLOVE COMPARTMENT LIGHT SWITCH	H 3	3/4
20	CLOVE COMPARTMENT LIGHT	K 5	3/4
21	BRAKE LIGHT SWITCH I	G 6	3/4
22	BRAKE LIGHT SWITCH II	G 4	3/4
23	ENGINE COMPARTMENT LIGHT	I 9	3/4
24	TAIL LIGHT ASSEMBLY	K 1, K 10	3/4
25	LICENCE PLATE LIGHT	K 5	3/4
26	FOG LIGHT REAR	K 7	3/4
27	FUSE BOX I 10		
28	FUSE BOX II 8		
29	FUSE BOX GROUND SCREW	A 29	5
30	TRUNK FLOOR PLATE GROUND PLUG	B 28	5
31	GROUND SCREW ENGINE COMP.	C 29	5
32	WIRE CONNECTORS 6	E 32/B 47	6/7
33	WIRE CONNECTORS 14	E 33	6/7
34	FUSE BOX 3	D 33/B 45	6/7/8
35	BATTERY	B 26	
36	GENERATOR	C 5	3/4
37	STARTER	C 6	3/4
38	DISTRIBUTOR	A 5/A7	3/4
39	SPARK PLUG		
40	IGNITION COIL	E 24	5
41	IGNITION STARTER SWITCH	E 26	5
42	HORN CONTACT	E 29	5
43	HORN RELAY	F 24	5
44	HORN	G 26	5
45	SWITCH HEADLIGHT WASHER		
46	RELAY		
47	PUMP		
48	WINDSHIELD WIPER SWITCH		
49	PULSE TRANSMITTER		
50	WINDSHIELD WIPER MOTOR	G 29	5
51	POTENTIOMETER	G 29	5
52	WINDSHIELD WASHER PUMP	H 29	5
53	POWER WINDOW RELAY	H 21	5
54	POWER WINDOW SWITCH	I 24, K 28, K 25	5
55	POWER WINDOW MOTOR	I 30/K 30	5
56	GROUND SCREW LUGGAGE COMP.		
57	GROUND SCREW BATTERY		
58	GROUND MOTOR		
59	WIRE CONNECTORS		
60	DME CONTROL UNIT	H 34	6/7
61	DME-RELAY	A 35	6/7
62	OXYGEN SENSOR HEATING	C 34	6/7
63	ALTITUDE CORRECTION BOX	C 34	6/7
64	FUEL INJECTORS	A, B, C 38	6/7
65	IDLE POSITIONER	D 38	6/7
66	THROTTLE VALVE SWITCH	E 38	6/7
67	NTC II	G 38	6/7
68	REFERENCE MARK TRANSMITTER	H 38	6/7
69	SPEED TRANSMITTER	I 38	6/7
70	AIR FLOW SENSOR	GH 49/K 38	6/7/8
71	FUEL PUMP		
72	CARRIER PLATE GROUND SCREW	D 33	7
73	OXYGEN SENSOR		
74	WIRE CONNECTORS		
75	GROUND SCREW BODY		
76	WIRE CONNECTORS		
77	TACHOMETER	A 53	9
78	3 WARNING LIGHT	E 53	9
79	COMBINATION INSTRUMENTS φ 100	F 53	9
80	COMBINATION INSTRUMENTS φ 80	H 53	9
81	SPEEDOMETER	K 54	9
82	CLOCK	D 55	9
83	CLOCK RELAY	A 58, B 58	9
84	BRAKE PAD WEAR LEAD	C 58	9
85	PARKING BRAKE CONTACT	C 58	9
86	BRAKE FLUID LEVEL WARNING SWITCH	D 58	9
87	OIL PRESSURE SENDER UNIT	E 58	9
88	OIL PRESSURE SWITCH	F 58	9
89	OIL TEMPERATURE SENSOR	H 58	9
90	FUEL SENDER UNIT	I 58	9
91	OIL LEVEL SWITCH	G 69	10
92	SPEED TRANSMITTER		
93	TEMPERATURE SWITCH FAN	B 99/F 99	13
94	OUTSIDE MIRROR SWITCH	A 64	10/11
95	OUTSIDE MIRROR	A 69	10/11
96	FRESH AIR BLOWER SWITCH	C 69	10/11
97	FRESH AIR BLOWER	D 66/F 64	10/11
98	CIGARETTE LIGHTER	D 69	10/11
99	ADDITIONAL FAN RELAY		
100	ADDITIONAL FAN		

SERIAL NR.	DESCRIPTION	FIELD	PAGE
101	HEATING CONTROL UNIT	D 65/G 64	10/11
102	RESISTOR	E 69	10/11
103	RELAY HEATING CONTROL UNIT	G 66	10
104	ENGINE COMPARTMENT FAN	G 69	10
105	WINDSHIELD DEFOGGER RELAY	H 67	11
106	WINDSHIELD DEFOGGER	H 69	11
107	PULL TURN SWITCH REAR WINDOW	K 64	10/11
108	REGULATING RELAY REAR WINDOW DEFOGGER	I 67	10/11
109	REAR WINDOW DEFOGGER	K 70	10/11
110	GROUND CARRIER PLATE UPPER		
111	INSIDE TEMP. SENSOR	H 69, G 69	10/11
112	TEMPERATURE SENSOR ON HEATER	I 69/G 69	10/11
113	FLAP BOX		
114	ADDITIONAL FAN SWITCH	D 63	11
115	MICROSWITCH	G 65	11
116	WIRE CONNECTORS 5		
117	SIGN LIGHT	C 67	10/11
118	BELT CONTACT	C 57	9
119	REAR WINDOW WIPER SWITCH	D 24	5
120	REAR WINDOW WIPER MOTOR	D 29	5
121	ELECTRONIC IGNITION UNIT HKZ	C 42	8
122	DELAYED ACTION RELAY	D 45	8
123	FUEL PUMP RELAY I	H 45	8
124	FUEL PUMP RELAY II	G 45	8
125	AIR FLOW SENSOR MANIFOLD PRESSURE RELAY	F 46	8
126	PRESSURE TRANSMITTER MANIFOLD PRESSURE	C 49	8
127	START VALVE	D 49	8
128	THERMO SWITCH FOR COLD START VALVE	E 49	8
129	SUPPLEMENTARY AIR VALVE	E 49	8
130	WARM-UP REGULATOR	F 49	8
131	AIR FLOW SENSOR	F 49	8
132	CONTROL UNIT	G 49	8
133	TEMPERATURE SENSOR	K 55	9
134	WARNING LIGHT	K 58	9
135	CONNECTION RAIL	K 57	9
136	CONNECTION POINT I	G, K 22	5
137	CONNECTION POINT II		
138	CONNECTION POINT III		
139	CONNECTION POINT IV		
140	CHANGE OVER SWITCH (LEFT/RIGTH)	F 69	10/11
141	HEATING NOZZLE	C 96	13
142	CONNECTION POINT V	C 69/B 69	10/11
143	WIRINGS	D 63	10
144	CONNECTION POINT VI	G 24	5
145	WIRINGS	H 25	5
146	WIRE CONNECTORS 1 PIN	G 55	9

Key to current flow diagrams for 911 Carrera, 1985 models

NOTES

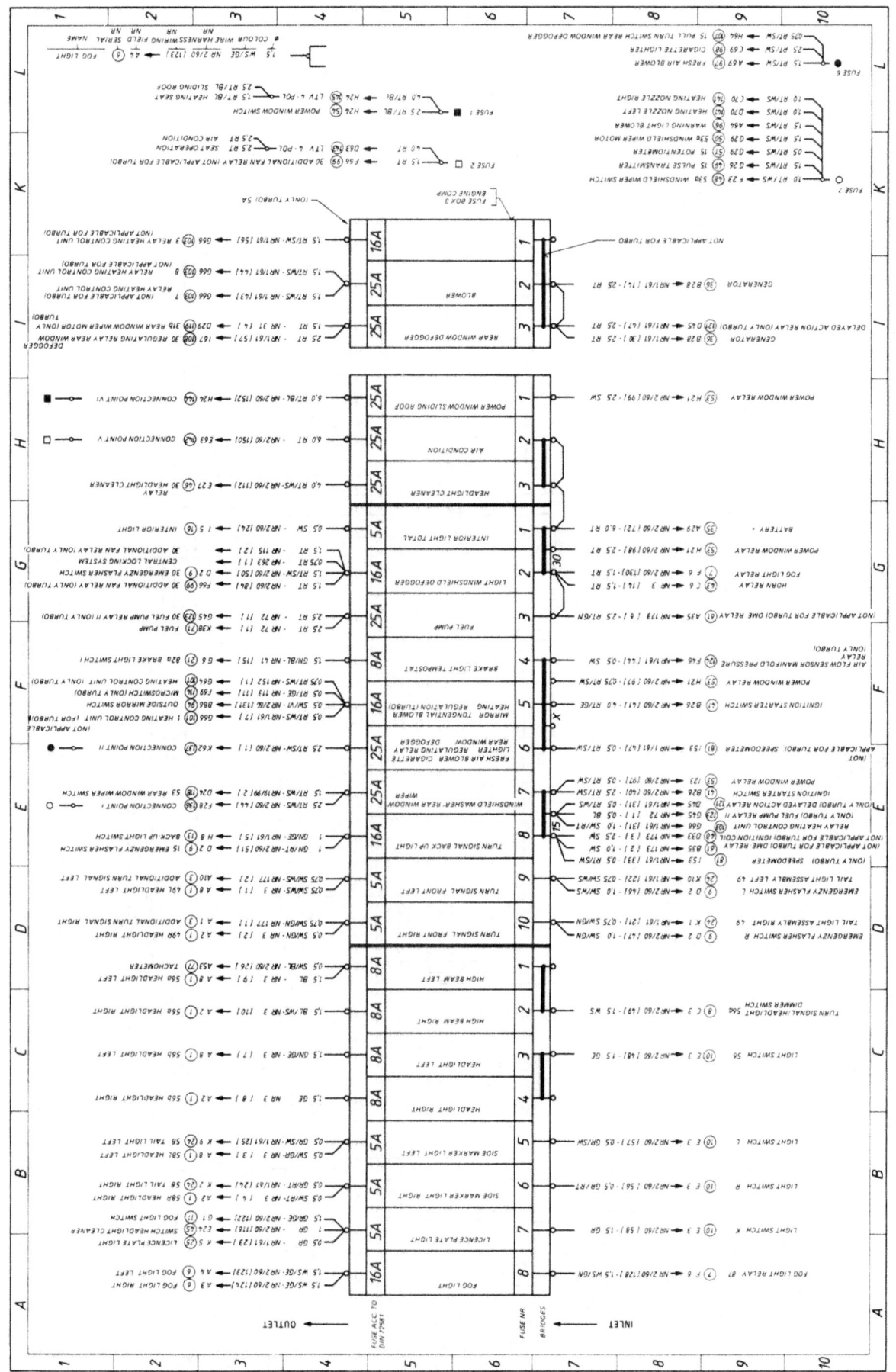

Current flow diagram for 911 Carrera, 1985 models (1 of 13)

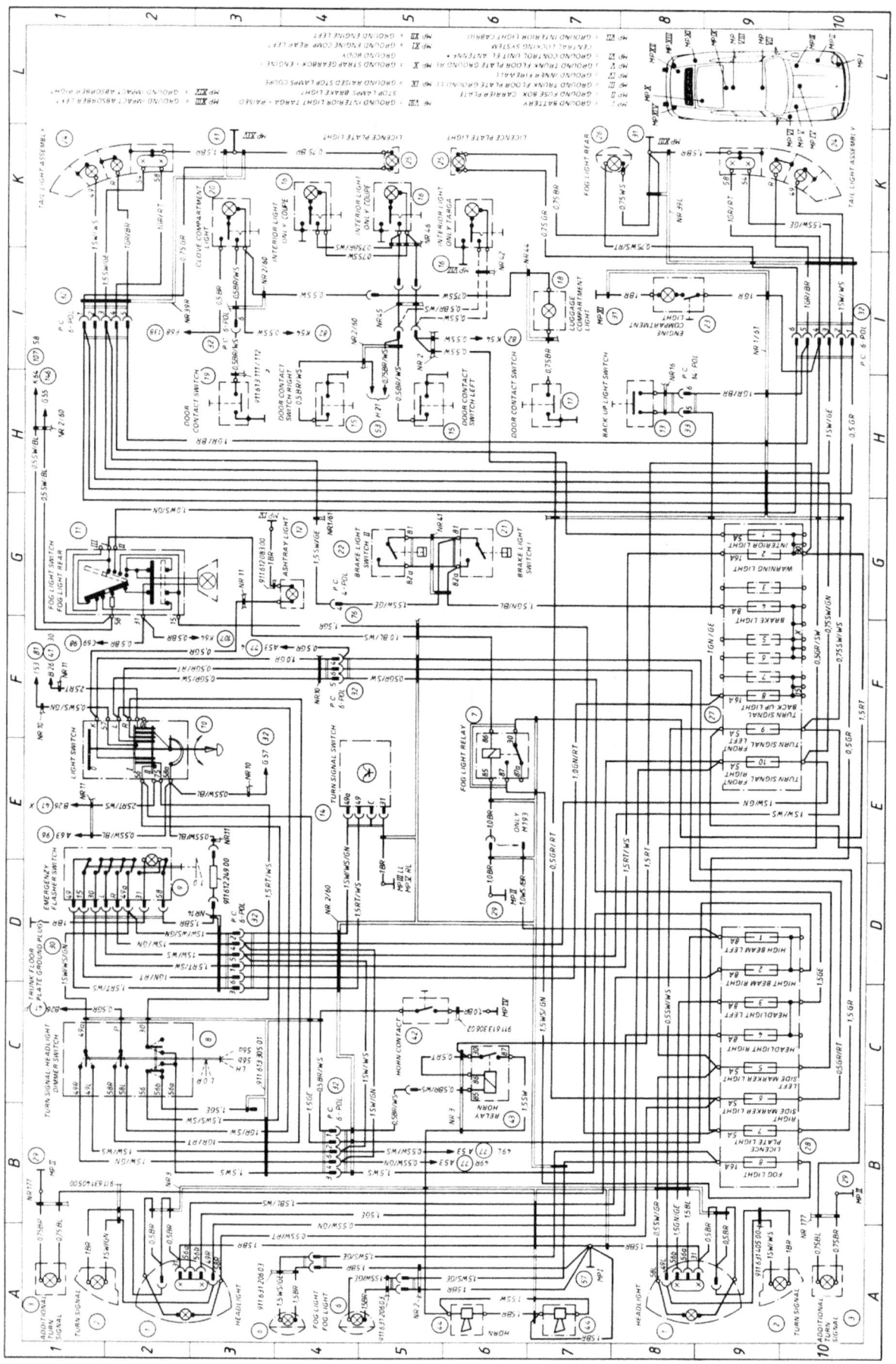

Current flow diagram for 911 Carrera, 1985 models (2 of 13)

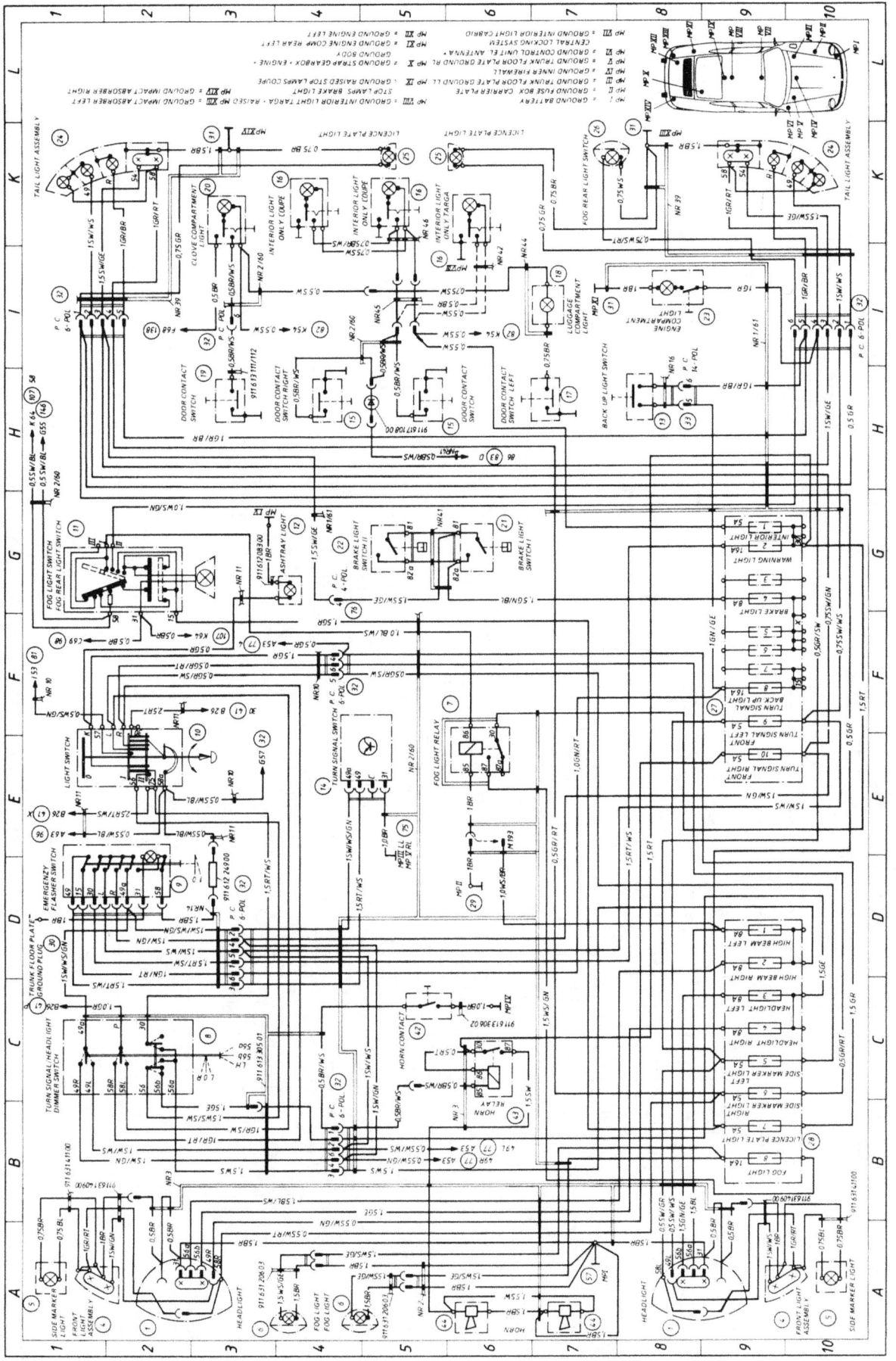

Current flow diagram for 911 Carrera, 1985 models (3 of 13)

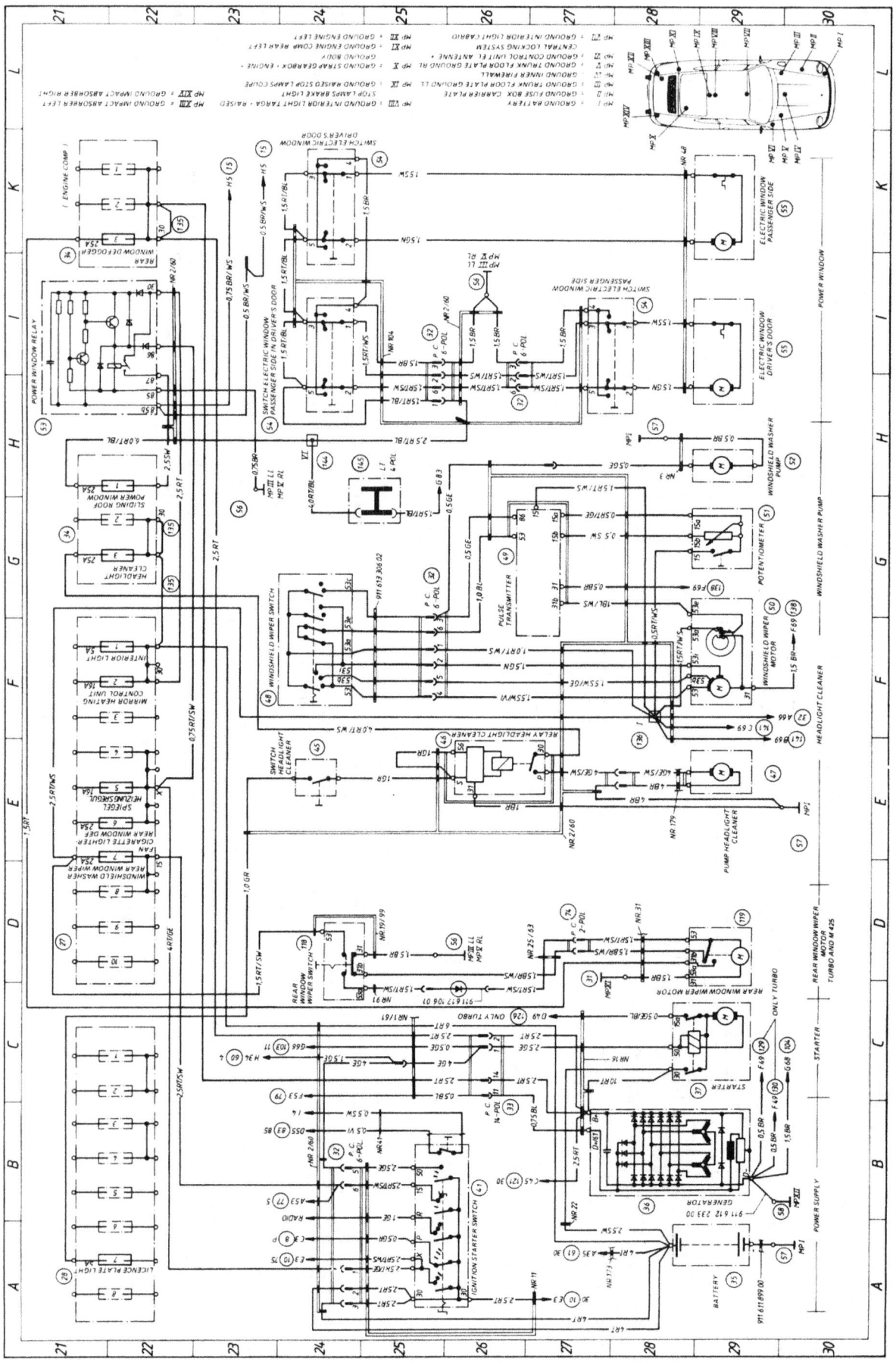

Current flow diagram for 911 Carrera, 1985 models (4 of 13)

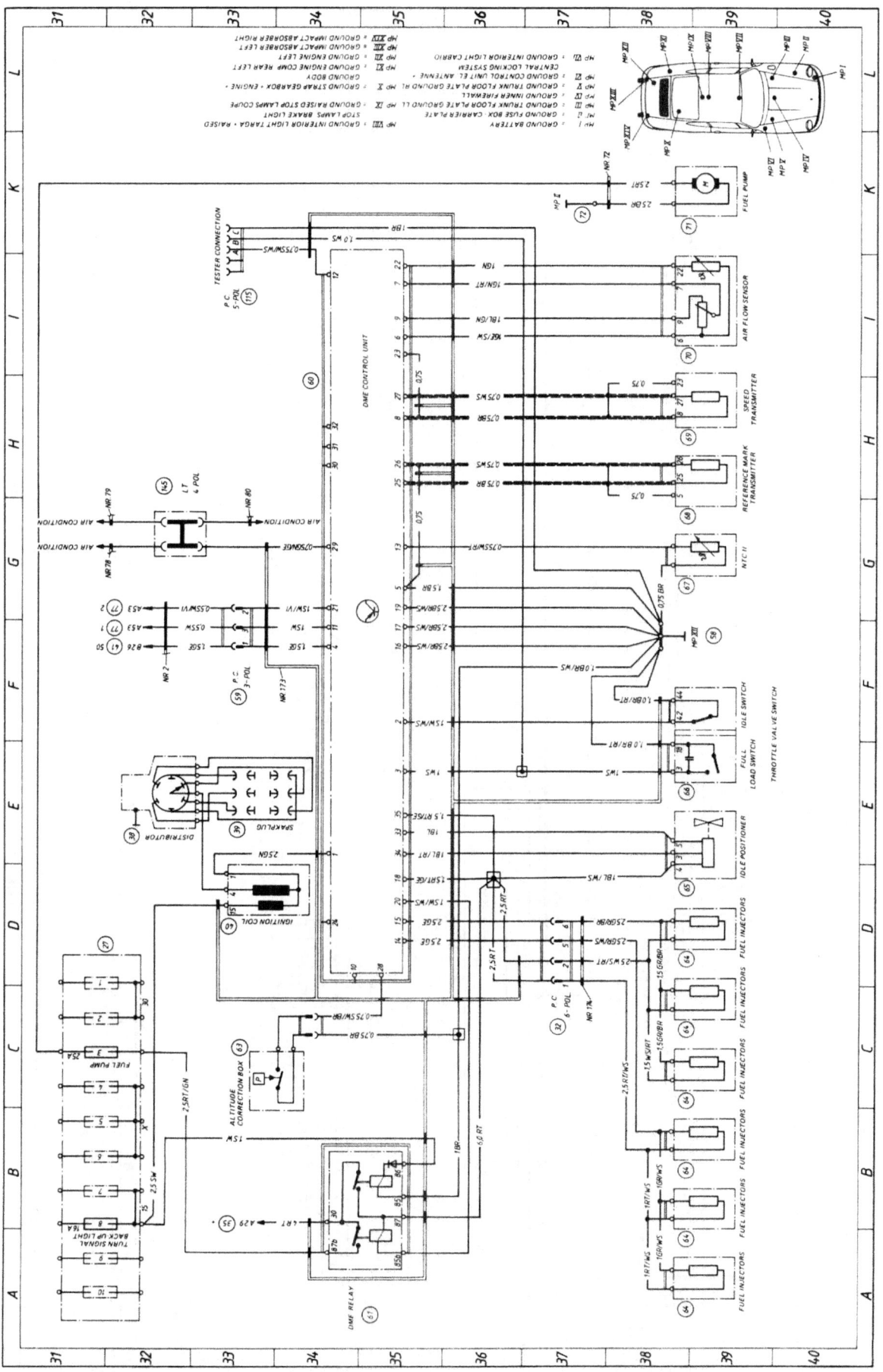

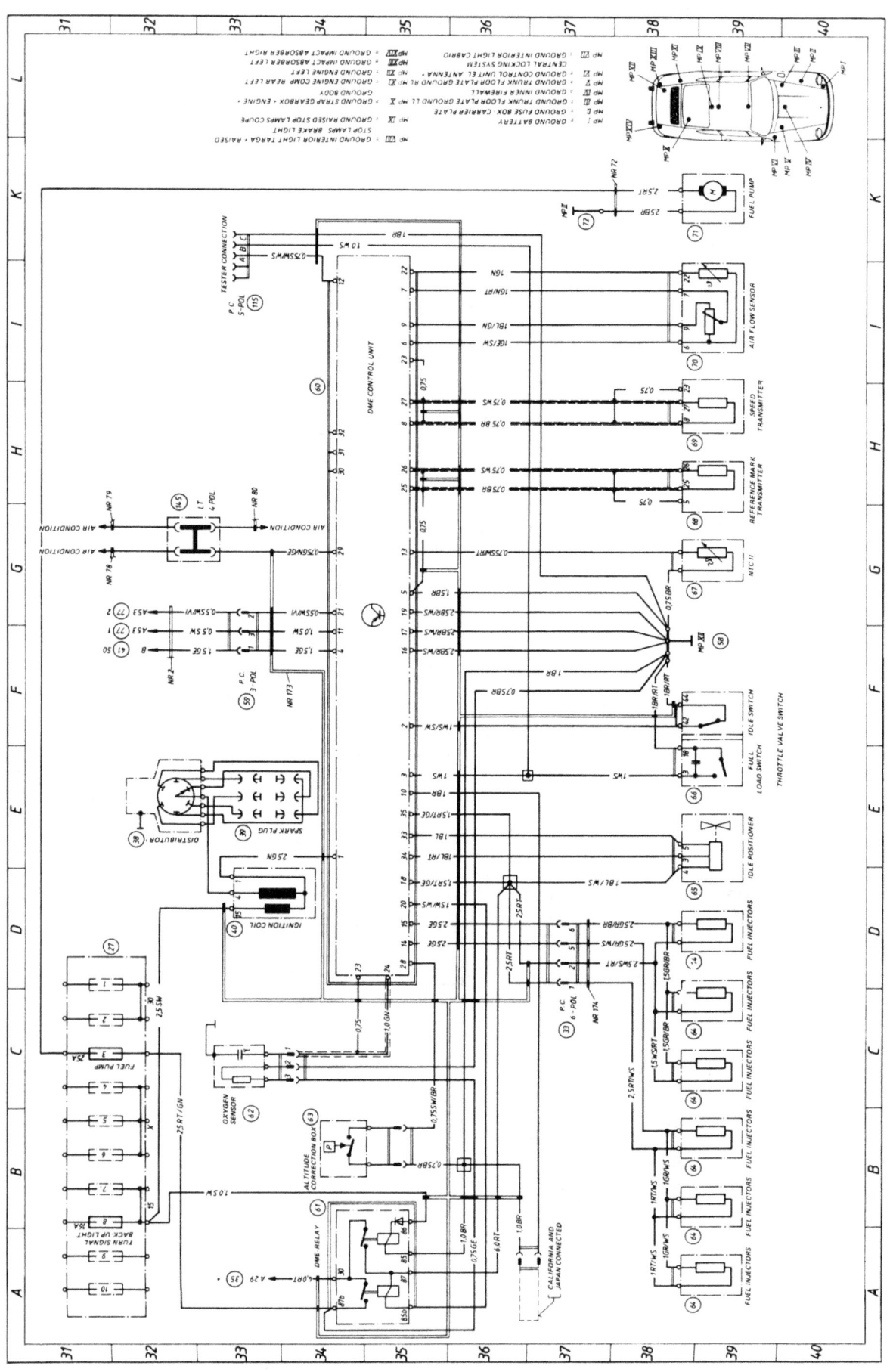

Current flow diagram for 911 Carrera, 1985 models (6 of 13)

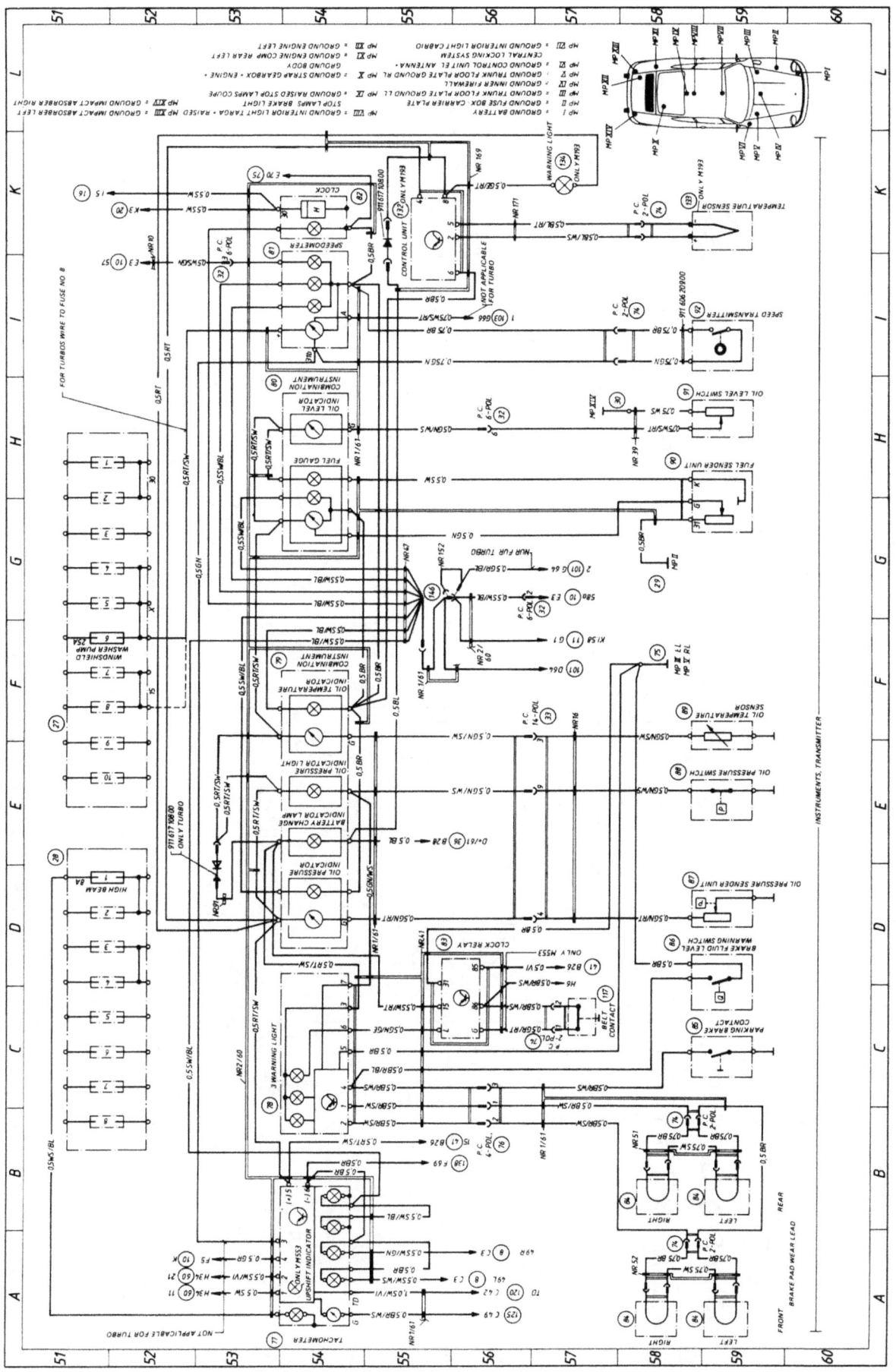

Current flow diagram for 911 Carrera, 1985 models (7 of 13)

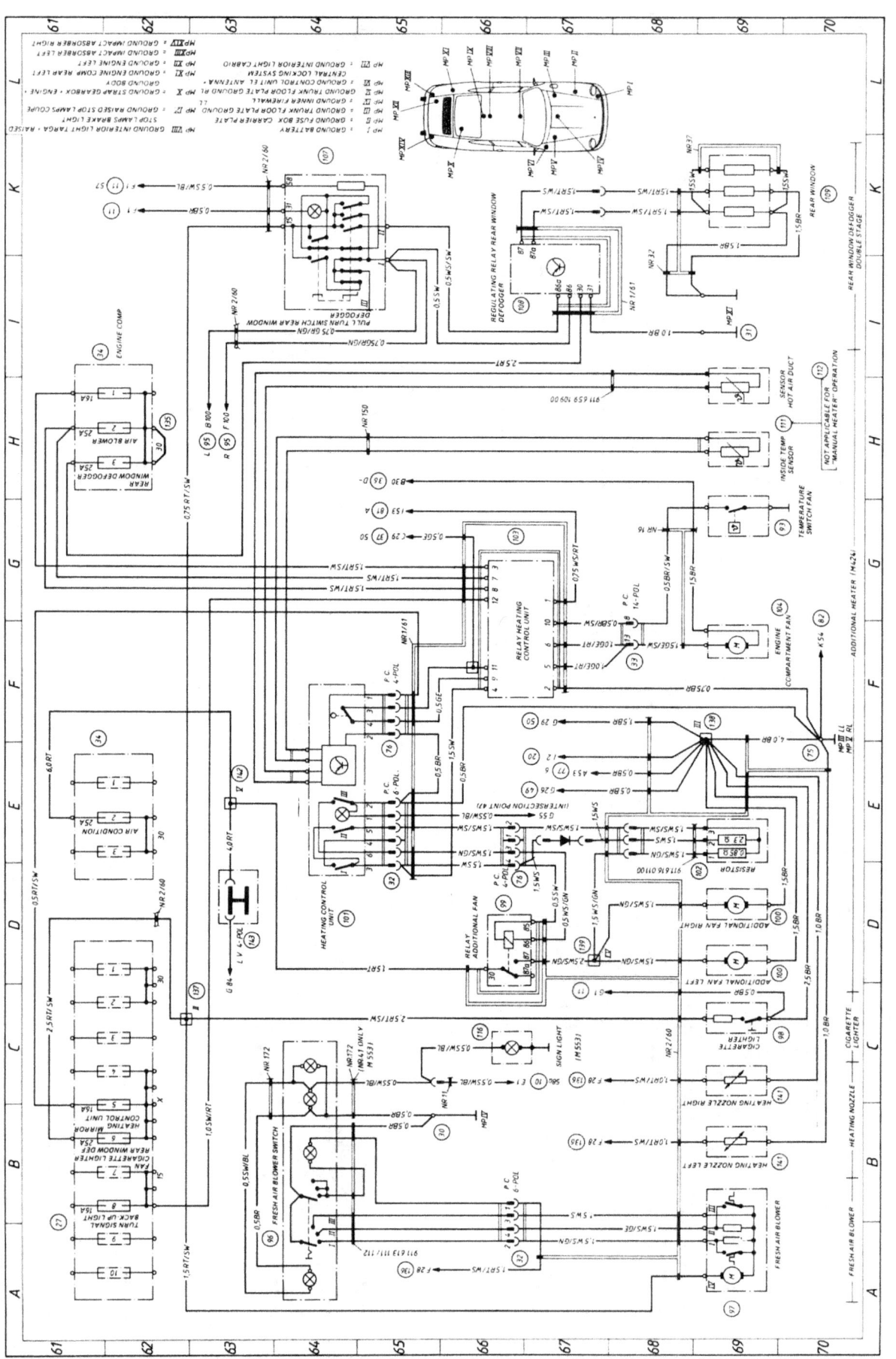

Current flow diagram for 911 Carrera, 1985 models (8 of 13)

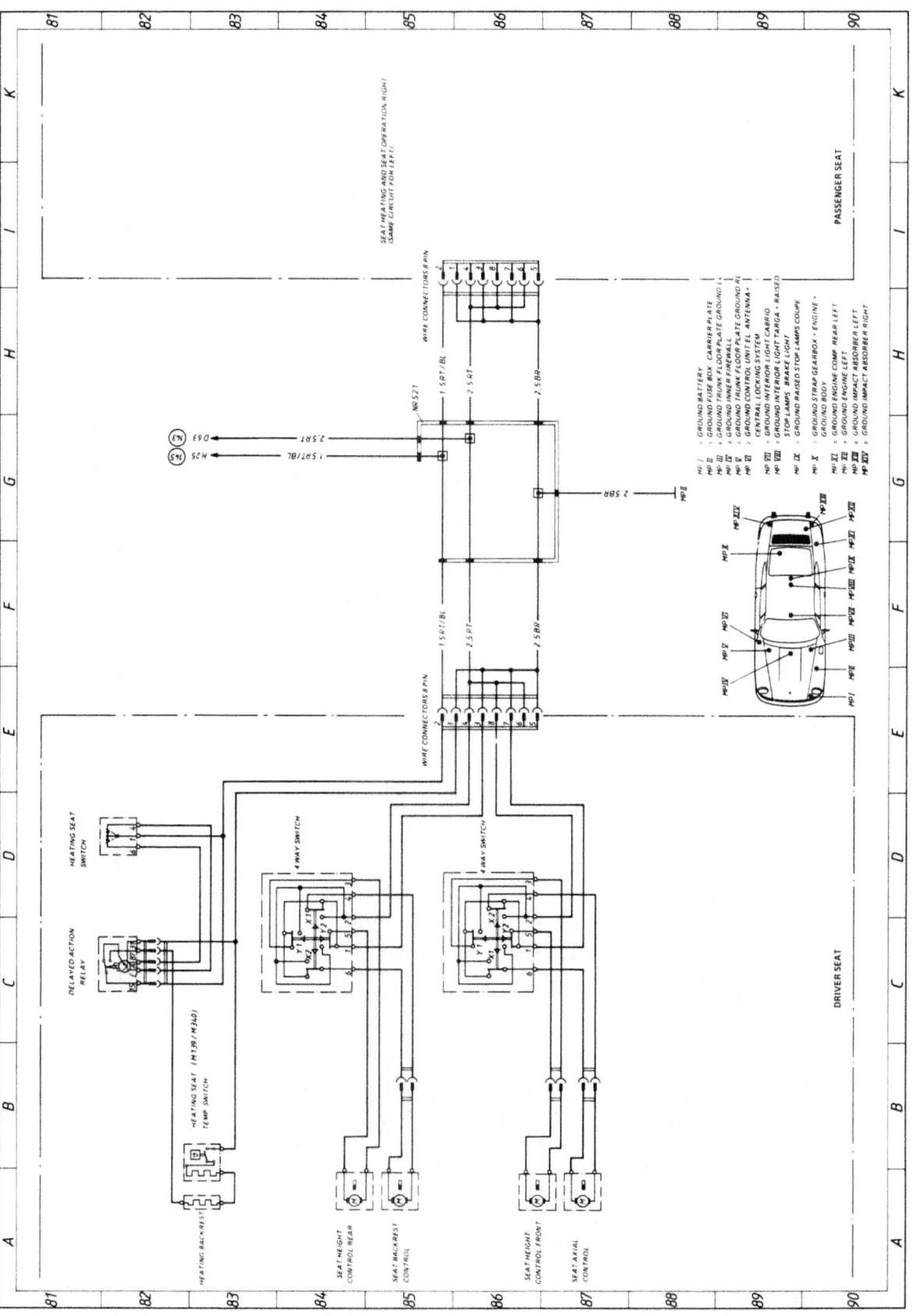

Current flow diagram for 911 Carrera, 1985 models (9 of 13)

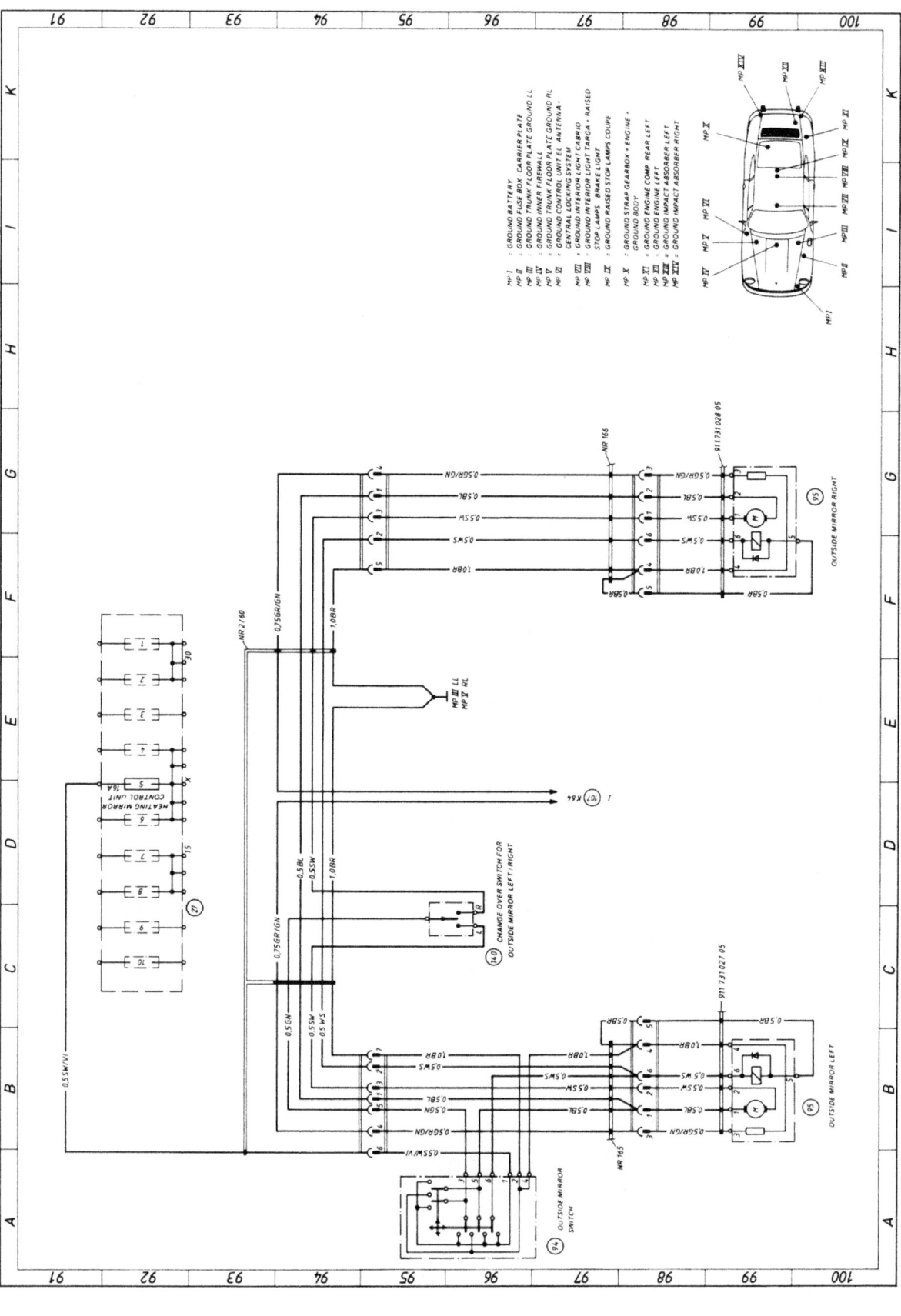

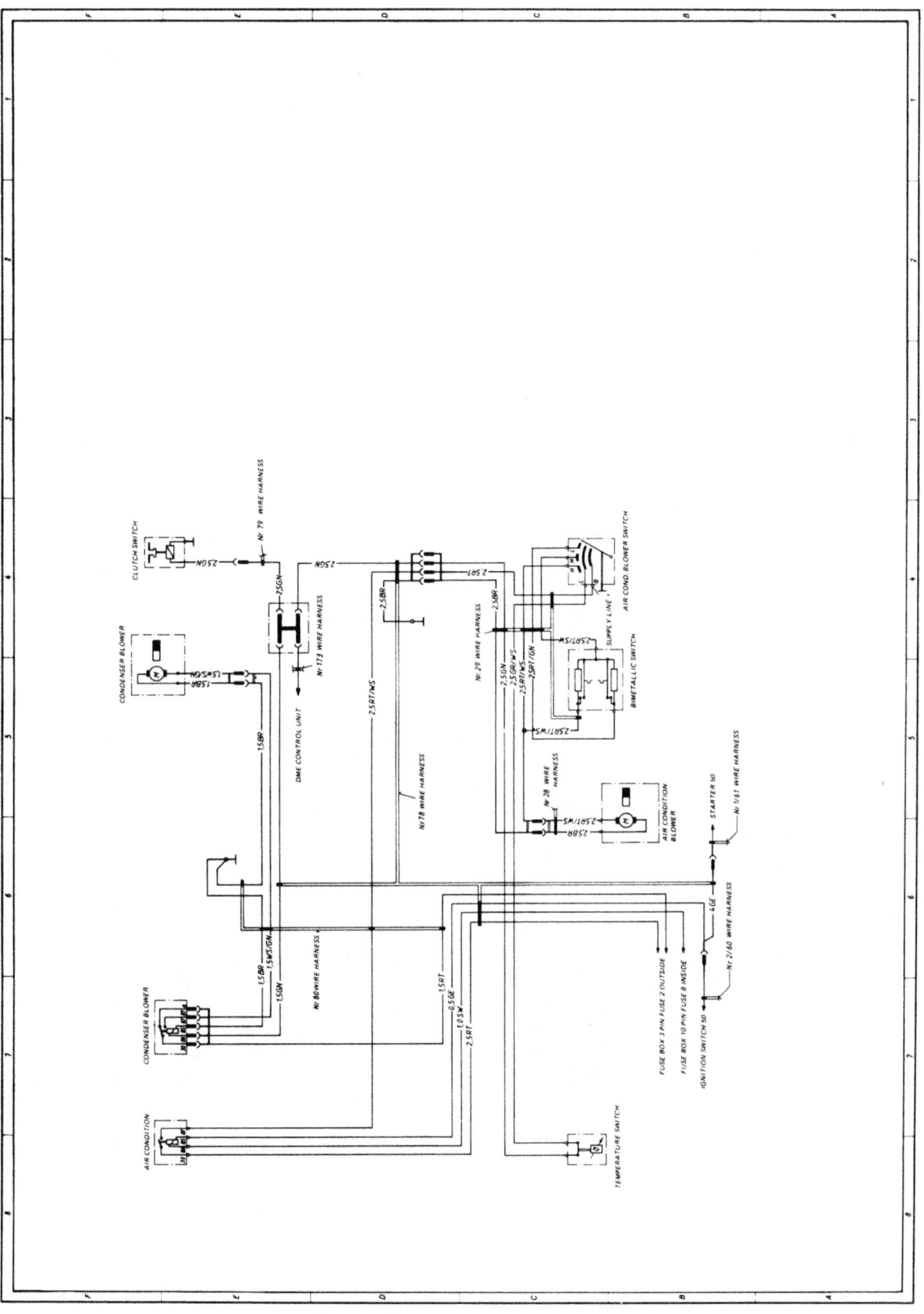

Current flow diagram for 911 Carrera, 1985 models (11 of 13)

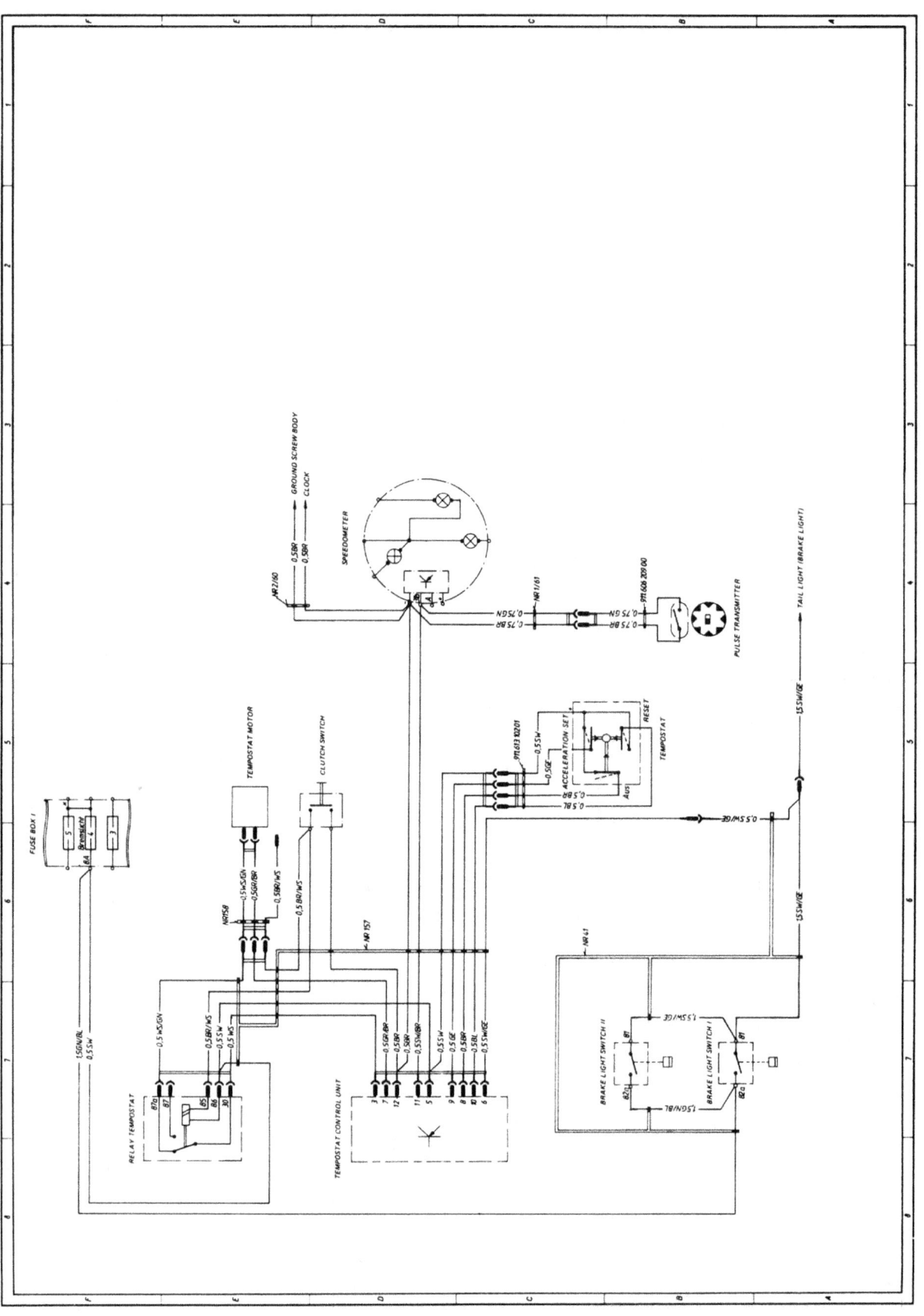

Current flow diagram for 911 Carrera, 1985 models (12 of 13)

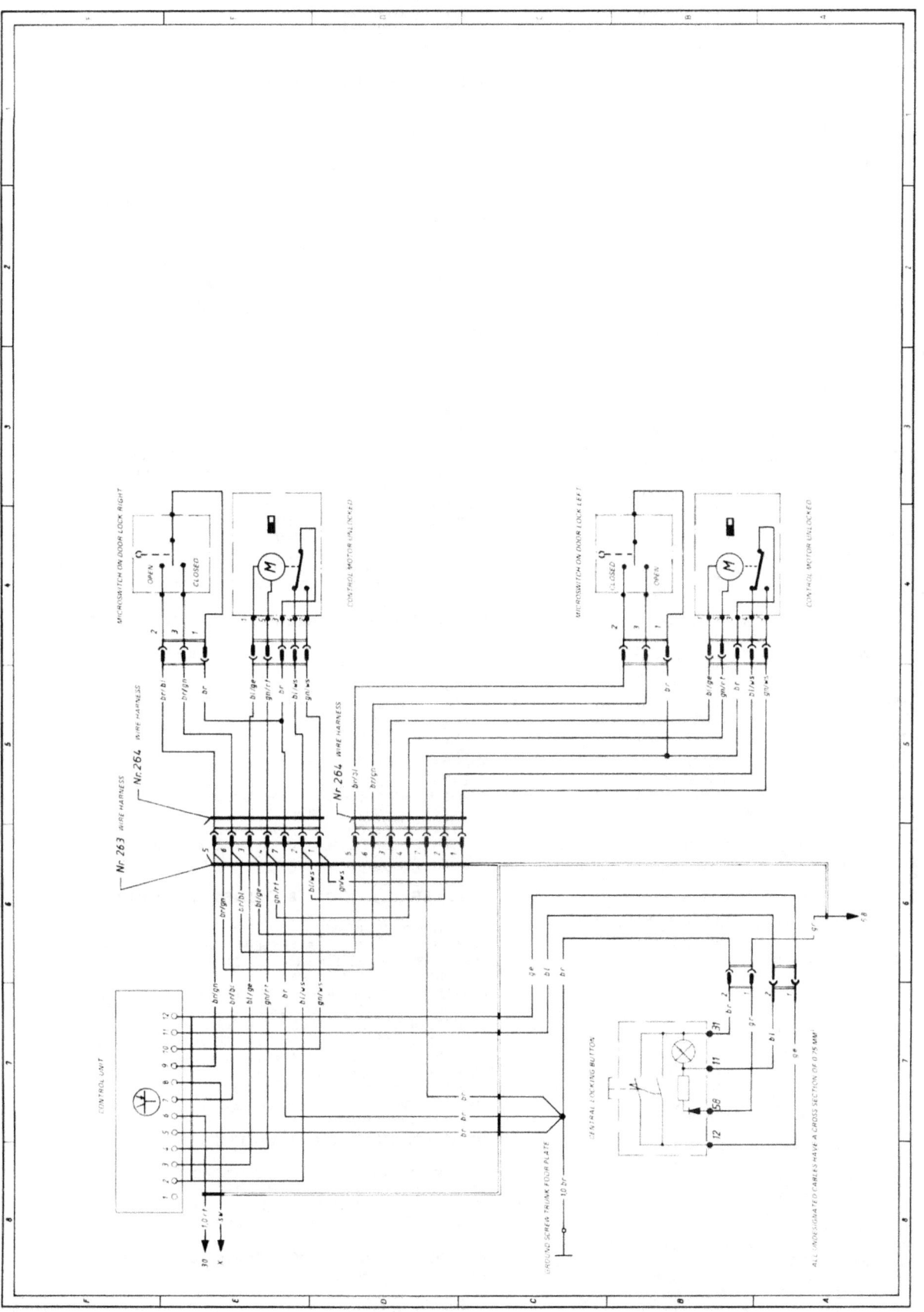

Current flow diagram for 911 Carrera, 1985 models (13 of 13)

VELOCEPRESS MANUALS - MOTORCYCLE

1930'S BRITISH MOTORCYCLE CARBS & ELEC COMPONENTS (BOOK OF)
1930'S BRITISH MOTORCYCLE ENGINES (OVERHAUL & MAINTENANCE)
1930'S BRITISH MOTORCYCLE GEARBOXES & CLUTCHES (BOOK OF)
AJS 1932-1948 SINGLES & TWINS 250cc THRU 1000cc (BOOK OF)
AJS 1945-1960 SINGLES 350cc & 500cc MODELS 16 & 18 (BOOK OF)
AJS 1955-1965 SINGLES 350cc & 500cc (BOOK OF)
ARIEL UP TO 1932 (BOOK OF)
ARIEL 1932-1939 PREWAR MODELS (BOOK OF)
ARIEL 1933-1951 (WORKSHOP MANUAL)
ARIEL 1939-1960 4 STROKE SINGLES (BOOK OF)
ARIEL 1958-1964 LEADER & ARROW (BOOK OF)
BMW R26 R27 (1956-1967) FACTORY WORKSHOP MANUAL
BMW R50 R50S R60 R69S (1955-1969) FACTORY WORKSHOP MANUAL
BRIDGESTONE 90 SERIES FACTORY WSM & PARTS CATALOGUE
BRIDGESTONE 175 SERIES FACTORY WSM & PARTS CATALOGUE
BSA BANTAM ALL MODELS FROM 1948 ONWARDS (BOOK OF)
BSA SINGLES & V-TWINS UP TO 1927 (BOOK OF)
BSA SINGLES & V-TWINS UP TO 1930 (BOOK OF)
BSA SINGLES & V-TWINS UP TO 1935 (BOOK OF)
BSA SINGLES & V-TWINS 1936-1939 (BOOK OF)
BSA OHV & SV SINGLES 250-600cc 1945-1959 (BOOK OF)
BSA OHV & SV SINGLES 250cc (ONLY) 1954-1970 (BOOK OF)
BSA OHV SINGLES 350 & 500cc 1955-1967 (BOOK OF)
BSA TWINS 1948-1962 (BOOK OF)
BSA TWINS 1962-1969 (SECOND BOOK OF)
CYCLEMOTOR (BOOK OF)
DOUGLAS 1929-1939 PREWAR ALL MODELS (BOOK OF)
DOUGLAS 1948-1957 POSTWAR ALL MODELS FACTORY SHOP MANUAL
DUCATI 160cc, 250cc & 350cc OHC MODELS FACTORY SHOP MANUAL
HONDA 50 ALL MODELS UP TO 1970 INC MONKEY & TRAIL (BOOK OF)
HONDA 90 ALL MODELS UP TO 1966 (BOOK OF)
HONDA 125-150cc TWINS C/CS/CB/CA FACTORY WORKSHOP MANUAL
HONDA 250-305 TWINS C/CS/CB FACTORY WORKSHOP MANUAL
HONDA 450 CB/CL 1965-1974 K0 TO K7 WORKSHOP MANUAL
HONDA C100 SUPER CUB FACTORY WORKSHOP MANUAL
HONDA C110 SPORT CUB 1962-1969 FACTORY WORKSHOP MANUAL
HONDA TWINS & SINGLES 50cc THRU 305cc 1960-1966 (BOOK OF)
HONDA TWINS ALL MODELS 125cc THRU 450cc UP TO 1968 (BOOK OF)
INDIAN PONYBIKE, BOY RACER & PAPOOSE ILL PARTS LIST & SALES LIT
J.A.P. ENGINES 1927-1952 & MOTORCYCLES 1934-1923 (BOOK OF)
LAMBRETTA 1947-1957 ALL 125 & 150cc MODELS (BOOK OF)
LAMBRETTA 1957-1970 LI & TV MODELS (SECOND BOOK OF)
MATCHLESS 1931-1939 ALL MODELS 250cc THRU 990cc (BOOK OF)
MATCHLESS 1945-1956 350 & 500cc SINGLES (BOOK OF)
MATCHLESS 1955-1966 350 & 500cc SINGLES (BOOK OF)
NEW IMPERIAL ALL SV & OHV FROM 1935 ONWARDS (BOOK OF)
NORTON 1932-1939 PREWAR MODELS (BOOK OF)
NORTON 1932-1947 (BOOK OF)
NORTON 1938-1956 (BOOK OF)
NORTON 1955-1963 MODELS 19, 50 & ES2 (BOOK OF)
NORTON 1955-1965 DOMINATOR TWINS (BOOK OF)
NORTON 1957-1970 TWINS FACTORY WORKSHOP MANUAL
NSU PRIMA 1956-1964 ALL MODELS (BOOK OF)
NSU QUICKLY 1953-1963 ALL MODELS (BOOK OF)
PANTHER 1932-1958 LIGHTWEIGHT MODELS 250 & 350cc (BOOK OF)
PANTHER 1938-1966 HEAVYWEIGHT MODELS 600 & 650cc (BOOK OF)
RALEIGH MOPEDS 1960-1969 (BOOK OF)
RALEIGH MOTORCYCLES 1919-1933 (BOOK OF)
ROYAL ENFIELD 1934-1946 SINGLES & V TWINS (BOOK OF)
ROYAL ENFIELD 1937-1953 SINGLES & V TWINS (BOOK OF)
ROYAL ENFIELD 1946-1962 SINGLES (BOOK OF)
ROYAL ENFIELD 1958-1966 250cc & 350cc SINGLES (SECOND BOOK OF)
ROYAL ENFIELD 736cc INTERCEPTOR FACTORY WORKSHOP MANUAL
RUDGE 1933-1939 (BOOK OF)
SUNBEAM 1928-1939 (BOOK OF)
SUNBEAM 1946-1957 S7 & S8 (BOOK OF)
SUZUKI 50cc & 80cc UP TO 1966 (BOOK OF)
SUZUKI T10 1963-1967 FACTORY WORKSHOP MANUAL
SUZUKI T20 & T200 1965-1969 FACTORY WORKSHOP MANUAL
SUZUKI TWINS 1962 ONWARDS 125-500cc WORKSHOP MANUAL
TRIUMPH 1935-1939 PREWAR MODELS (BOOK OF)
TRIUMPH 1935-1949 (BOOK OF)
TRIUMPH 1937-1951 (WORKSHOP MANUAL)
TRIUMPH 1945-1955 FACTORY WORKSHOP MANUAL
TRIUMPH 1945-1958 TWINS (BOOK OF)
TRIUMPH 1956-1969 TWINS (BOOK OF)
VELOCETTE 1925-1970 ALL SINGLES & TWINS (BOOK OF)
VESPA 1951-1961 (BOOK OF)
VESPA 1955-1963 125 & 150cc & GS MODELS (SECOND BOOK OF)
VESPA 1955-1968 GS & SS (BOOK OF)
VESPA 1963-1972 90, 125 & 150cc (THIRD BOOK OF)
VILLIERS ENGINE UP TO 1959 INC. 3 WHEELERS (BOOK OF)
VILLIERS ENGINE UP TO 1969 (BOOK OF)
VINCENT 1935-1955 (WORKSHOP MANUAL)
YAMAHA 1961-1967 YA5 & YA6 (WORKSHOP MANUAL & ILL PARTS LIST)
YAMAHA 1971-1972 JT1 & JT2 (WORKSHOP MANUAL & ILL PARTS LIST)

VELOCEPRESS TECHNICAL BOOKS – MOTORCYCLE

CATALOG OF BRITISH MOTORCYCLES (1951 MODELS)
MOTORCYCLE ENGINEERING (P.E. Irving)
SPEED AND HOW TO OBTAIN IT (Motor Cycle Magazine UK)
TUNING FOR SPEED (P.E. Irving)

VELOCEPRESS MANUALS - THREE WHEELER'S

BSA THREE WHEELER (BOOK OF)
VINTAGE MORGAN THREE WHEELER (BOOK OF)

VELOCEPRESS MANUALS - AUTOMOBILE

ALFA ROMEO GIULIA WORKSHOP MANUAL 1300 TO 2000cc 1962-1975
ALFA ROMEO GIULIA TECH MANUAL CARBURETED CARS FROM 1962
ALFA ROMEO GIULIA TECH MANUAL FUEL INJECTED CARS FROM 1969
AUSTIN-HEALEY 6-CYLINDER WORKSHOP MANUAL
AUSTIN-HEALEY SPRITE & MG MIDGET WORKSHOP MANUAL 1958-1971
BMW 600 LIMOUSINE FACTORY WORKSHOP MANUAL
BMW 600 LIMOUSINE OWNERS HAND BOOK & SERVICE MANUAL
BMW 2000 & 2002 1966-1976 WORKSHOP MANUAL
BMW ISETTA FACTORY WORKSHOP MANUAL
CORVAIR 1960-1969 WORKSHOP MANUAL
CORVETTE V8 1955-1962 WORKSHOP MANUAL
FIAT 500 FACTORY WORKSHOP MANUAL 1957-1973
FIAT 600, 600D & MULTIPLA FACTORY WORKSHOP MANUAL 1955-1969
JAGUAR E-TYPE 3.8 & 4.2 SERIES 1 & 2 WORKSHOP MANUAL
JAGUAR MK 7, 8, 9 & XK120, 140, 150 WORKSHOP MANUAL 1948-1961
METROPOLITAN FACTORY WORKSHOP MANUAL
MGA & MGB OWNERS HANDBOOK & WORKSHOP MANUAL
MG MIDGET TC, TD, TF & TF1500 WORKSHOP MANUAL
PORSCHE 356 1948-1965 WORKSHOP MANUAL
PORSCHE 911 2.0, 2.2, 2.4 LITRE 1964-1973 WORKSHOP MANUAL
PORSCHE 911 2.7, 3.0, 3.2 LITRE 1973-1989 WORKSHOP MANUAL
PORSCHE 912 WORKSHOP MANUAL
TRIUMPH TR2, TR3, TR4 1953-1965 WORKSHOP MANUAL
VOLKSWAGEN TRANSPORTER, TRUCKS & WAGONS 1950-1979 WSM
VOLVO 1944-1968 ALL MODELS WORKSHOP MANUAL

VELOCEPRESS TECHNICAL BOOKS - AUTOMOBILE

FERRARI 250/GT SERVICE AND MAINTENANCE
FERRARI GUIDE TO PERFORMANCE
FERRARI OWNER'S HANDBOOK
FERRARI TUNING TIPS & MAINTENANCE TECHNIQUES
HOW TO BUILD A FIBERGLASS CAR
HOW TO BUILD A RACING CAR
HOW TO RESTORE THE MODEL 'A' FORD
MASERATI OWNER'S HANDBOOK
OBERT'S FIAT GUIDE
PERFORMANCE TUNING THE SUNBEAM TIGER
SOUPING THE VOLKSWAGEN
SOLEX CARBURETORS (EMPHASIS ON UK & EU AUTOMOBILES)
SU CARBURETORS (EMPHASIS ON UK AUTOMOBILES)
WEBER CARBURETORS (EMPHASIS ON ALFA & FIAT)

VELOCEPRESS BOOKS & GUIDES - AUTOMOBILE

ABARTH BUYERS GUIDE
COMPLETE CATALOG OF JAPANESE MOTOR VEHICLES
FERRARI 308 SERIES BUYER'S AND OWNER'S GUIDE
FERRARI BERLINETTA LUSSO
FERRARI BROCHURES AND SALES LITERATURE 1946-1967
FERRARI BROCHURES AND SALES LITERATURE 1968-1989
FERRARI OPP, MAINTENANCE & SERVICE H/BOOKS 1948-1963
FERRARI SERIAL NUMBERS PART I - ODD NUMBERS TO 21399
FERRARI SERIAL NUMBERS PART II - EVEN NUMBERS TO 1050
FERRARI SPYDER CALIFORNIA
HENRY'S FABULOUS MODEL "A" FORD
MASERATI BROCHURES AND SALES LITERATURE

VELOCEPRESS BOOKS – RACING

CARRERA PANAMERICANA - MEXICAN ROAD RACE (BOOK OF)
DIALED IN - THE JAN OPPERMAN STORY
IF HEMINGWAY HAD WRITTEN A RACING NOVEL
VEDA ORR'S NEW REVISED HOT ROD PICTORIAL

AUTOBOOKS WORKSHOP MANUALS & BROOKLANDS ROAD TEST PORTFOLIOS

FOR A COMPLETE LISTING OF THE AUTOBOOKS & BROOKLANDS TITLES THAT WE CURRENTLY HAVE AVAILABLE, PLEASE VISIT OUR WEBSITE.

www.VelocePress.com

www.ingramcontent.com/pod-product-compliance
Lightning Source LLC
Chambersburg PA
CBHW060247240426
43673CB00047B/1889